AF412587

Hungary under the Early Árpáds, 890s to 1063

Z. J. Kosztolnyik

Though free they are not absolutely free;
for they have a master over them, the law.
Herodotus, vii:104

EAST EUROPEAN MONOGRAPHS, BOULDER
DISTRIBUTED BY COLUMBIA UNIVERSITY PRESS, NEW YORK
2002

EAST EUROPEAN MONOGRAPHS, NO. DCV

Printed in the United States of America

To my wife Penelope

Contents

Preface

The Hungarian Anonymus wrote in the introductory note of his *Gesta Ungarorurm* that he obtained the truth about past historic events from the reliable narrative of written sources and the rational interpretation of earlier chronicles. He wrote about the Magyars' ur-country, their heroic ancestors, reported on the Scythians and their land, the headmen of the seven Magyar tribes—joined by the tribe of the Kabars—, and the blood-oath they took (a common custom among other peoples, C. A. Macartney observed). Anonymus recorded that Álmos was the first ruling prince of the Magyars, a handsome man with large black eyes, of great physical build, but narrow at the hips, wise and humane, pious and benevolent, whose son, Prince Árpád, took possession of the Danube–Tisza region in the Carpathian basin, and destroyed all his enemies.

Anonymus the chronicler fused the so called "Hun-legend" with the events borrowed from early Magyar history, when he, for instance, mentioned how the whole *Magyar [nation]* (!) rejoiced when the ruling prince, Árpád (the land-taker) entered Attila's City: Óbuda (Acquincum), together with his headmen and nobles; Anonymus stressed the notion of social equality prevalent among the Magyars of the age by remarking that they feasted every day, as they ate their meals in Attila's palace: Prince, headmen, and nobles sitting together, side by side.

The anonymous monk and author wrote his piece some two hundred years after the Magyars' land-taking of the mid-Carpathian basin; consequently, he discussed late ninth century events from the view point of his own times, the late twelfth century. The non-Magyar sources of the ninth–twelfth centuries refer to Magyar historical events from a different, and not always sympathetic angle—they never provided regular discussions of historical developments in Hungary—though they show uncustomary friendliness toward King St. Stephen I. It remains a question how, and becomes a challenge, to write about Hungarian history in this period according to non-Magyar sources, and approaching it from a western Latin–Christian angle.

Writing this book, I owe a great deal to the loving patience and understanding of my wife, Penelope, and to the active cooperation of our daughters, Karen and Elizabeth Irene, who carefully read the manuscript and helped in preparing it for publication.

Z. J. Kosztolnyik
Texas A&M University

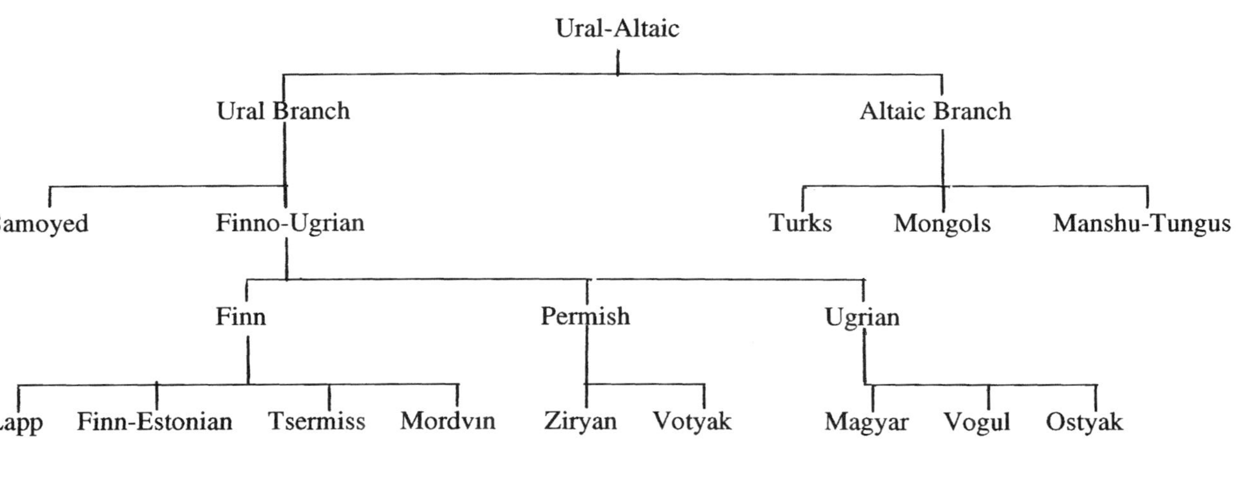

Stemma:
Family tree of the early Magyars

Stemma: The early Árpáds

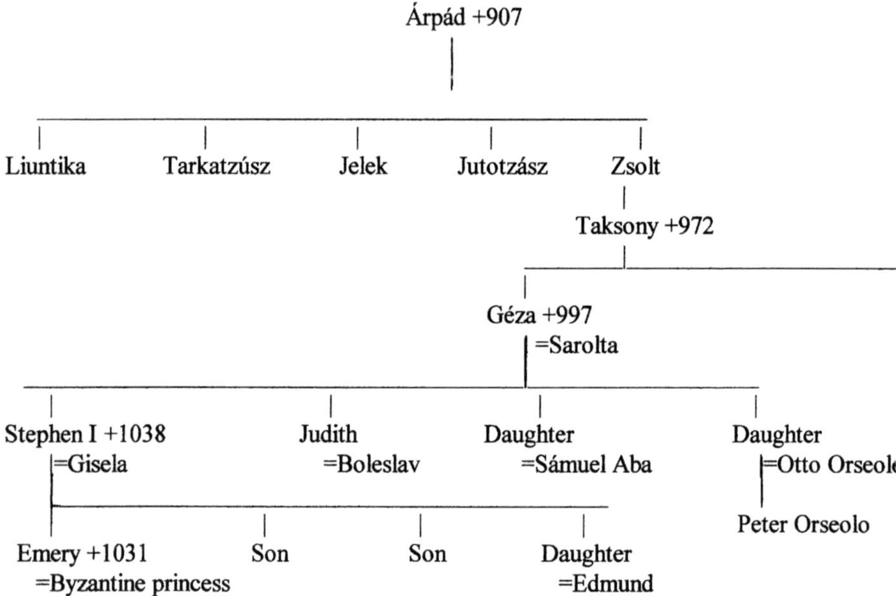

Stemma: The early Árpáds

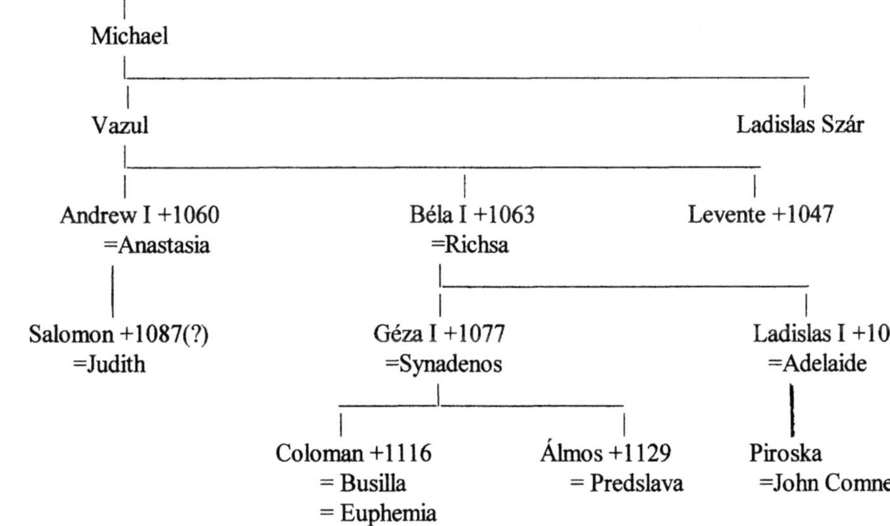

List of Abbreviations

ASS	*Acta sanctorum Bollandiana*
ÁÚO	Wenczel, *Árpádkori új okmánytár*
Bartoniek	Bartoniek, *Szent István törvényeinek XII századi kézirata*
CB	Bonn Corpus; *Corpus scriptorum Byzantinorum*, Bonn series
CD	Fejér, *Codex diplomaticus Hungariae ecclesiasticus ac civilis*
FRA	*Fontes rerum Austricarum*
Hodinka	*Orosz évkönyvek magyar vonatkozásai*
HZ	*Historische Zeitschrift*
Itk	*Irodalomtörténeti Közlemények*
Mansi, *Concilia*	Mansi, *Sacrorum conciliorum amplissima collectio*
MKSz	*Magyar Könyszemle*
MGHLL	*Monumenta Germanie historica, Legum collectio*
MGHSS	*Monumenta Germaniae historica, Scriptores*
MPH	*Monumenta Poloniae historica*
MPG	Migne, *Patrologiae cursus completus, series graeca*
MPL	Migne, *Patrologiae cursus completus, series latina*
Moravcsik, *Fontes*	Moravcsik, *Fontes Byzantini historiae Hungaricae*
RA	Szentpétery-Borsa, *Regesta diplomatica regum stirpis Arpadianae*
RHM	Endlicher, *Rerum Hungaricarum monumenta Arpadiana*
RISS	Muratori, *Rerum Italicarum scriptores*
SSrG	*Scriptores rerum Germanicarum ad ususm scholarum*
SSH	Szentpétery, *Scriptores rerum Hungaricarum*
Závodszky	Závodszky, *A Szent István, Szent László és Kálmán korabeli törvények és zsinati határozatok*

I

Magyar Beginnings

Accidit autem Dule principis Alanorum in illo
prelio inter ilos pueros duas filias comprehendi,
quarum unam Hunor, aliam Magor sibi sumpserunt
in uxorem.

Chronicon pictum, c. 5

The hypothesis that the Magyars had evolved from the fusion of Finno-Ugrian and Turkish peoples is based upon comparative linguistics—comparing the names of peoples and persons on record that would project the image of a people; and, upon the reports of medieval Hungarian chroniclers who at some length have dealt with early Magyar [Hungarian] history.[1] Simon de Keza, a late thirteenth century chronicler, for example, preserved for posterity the legend of *women capture*; Hunor [*Hun-eri*: man of sin] and Magor [=Magyar] were leaving their habitat in the swamps of the Meothian Lake when they came upon the wives of *Belar* (=Belgar[us], or Bolgar[us]) who were dancing on the meadow without their male companions, and the daughters of Dulan, prince of the Alans, among them whom Hunor and Magor had taken to wife. Chronicler Keza had argued that it was from the marriage of Hunor and Magor that the *Huns* and *Magyars* descended.[2]

The Hungarian *ur-gesta* that [may have] originated at the end of the eleventh century (it became lost), and the Hungarian Anonymus, chronicler in the late twelfth century, who most probably borrowed heavily from the *ur-gesta*; and, the anonymous author-contributor(s) of the mid-fourteenth century *Chronicon pictum* [Hungarian *Chronicle*] had entertained the idea of the Hun-Magyar blood relationship by depicting the ruling dynasty of the Árpáds (from about the mid-ninth century, to 1301) as the descendants of Attila the Hun (d. 453), thereby projecting the concept of Hun-Magyar blood ties of the

Hungarian nobility in the middle ages. "Tunc elegerunt sibi querere terram Pannonie, quam audiverant fama volante terram Athile regis esse, de cuius progenie dux Almus pater Arpad descenderat."[3]

Two thousand years before the birth of Christ, the forefathers of the Magyars were living in the family of Finno-Ugor peoples on the western slopes of the Ural mountains, in the region of the mid-Volga river and its tributaries, and maintained relations with the forefathers of the Turk[i]s[h peoples] who were located east of them. Linguistic expressions like *arany* [gold], *ezüst* [silver], *méh* [bee], *méz* [honey], *száz* [hundred] in the Magyar (Hungarian) vocabulary date back to this time and place during their migration.[4]

The Finno-Ugors branched off into two segments: the *western* Finn-Perm *ur-people*—out of whom the Finns and Estonians evolved at a later date—and the *eastern* Ugrian *ur-peoples*, such as the Ostiak, Ugor, *ur-Magyar*, who migrated from the Volga to the crest of the Urals and lived there in family clans headed by the *Úr* [Lord, clan-head]. They did not possess a political organization at this stage of their development. Judged by their vocabulary, they knew of metals [= *fém*], the decimal system, and of business concepts, such as purchase and sale. They must have come in contact with the *Altai-Turkish* Bulgarians, and they, together with them, moved to the lower region of the Kuban river. It is more than likely that the Bulgarians had conquered the [*pre-*]Magyars, had their clans organized into a tribe, and had the tribe attached to their own tribes. During this period (of centuries), the *pre-Magyars* had evolved into a horse-riding people—otherwise they could not have passed through the prairie with such ease. Words like *ló* [horse] and *nyereg* [saddle] in their vocabulary date back to this period, as they are of Ugrian origin. The pre-Magyars also learned about the everyday Bulgarian occupations in agriculture, husbandry, gardening, and, judged by their language, of ethical concepts, like *érdem* [merit], *bűn* [sin], and *gyarlóság* [wickedness].[5]

Often a leader would emerge from among the people who were joined by the tribes of other peoples; and a tribe that came to a command leadership shall rule over the other tribes—though such tribal rule may easily fall apart in a brief period of time. Tribes who had joined later would be sent by the head-tribe to fight in the forefront in time of war, and the warring effort may diminish them altogether.

About 830, the Magyars were living north of the Black Sea, on the lands named *Lebedia* between the Don and Dnieper rivers, and remained there until attacked by the Pechenegs in 889.[6] One may argue on linguistic grounds that they were members of the *Onogur Subir* Turks, as it is evident that, by this time, they had borrowed expressions like *kard* [sword], *vért* [shield], *süveg* [hat], *vám* [toll], *híd* [bridge] from the vocabulary of the Alans; the ornaments on their weapons related to Persian designs. Out of the Turkish *Onogur* [ten tribes] the Latin word *Ungari* developed depicting the Magyars, who were known as *Ungar* in German, in French *hongrois*, and *venger* in the Russian language.[7]

During the sixth through the ninth centuries, the Magyars formed a part of the Khazar segment of the Turk[ish] empire. The *kagan* [ruler] of the Khazars appointed a leader for them in time of war: he was known as the *kende* [kündü] who, together with the *gyula* [prince], ruled over them. Although the pre-Magyars went through strong ethnic changes during the ninth century, their culture and political structure remained Turk[ish].[8]

The empire of the Khazars fell apart by the mid-ninth century, and the Magyars' social-political organization came under the leadership of the Megyer[i] tribe.[9] About a century later, Emperor Constantine VII Porphyrogenitus in his work, *De administrando imperio*, preserved for posterity the names of seven Magyar tribes and tribal chiefs. On linguistic grounds, the Magyar (Megyer[i]) tribe—like the Bulgar tribe to the Bulgarians—gave a common name and dignity to the *Magyar* tribal confederation consisting of the tribes of *Kürt-Gyarmat*, *Nyék* [border; held responsible for defending the borders of the territory of the tribal confederation], *Tarján* [smith-king, to denote the dignity of viceroy], *Jenő* [confidant; advisor], *Kér* [great], *Keszi* [fragment], and of the *Kabars*—three small Khazar tribes who had joined and formed one tribe in the Magyar confederation. The Khazars had learned the Magyars' tongue, and the Magyars learned the Khazar language from them. In such a manner, the Magyars became a bilingual people during the ninth century.[10]

Because of the continued Pecheneg attacks—the Magyars' ancient enemies—a small portion (*Szavard*) of the Magyar tribal confederation fled to the Caucasus mountain region; they, eventually, formed *Greater Hungary* in Baskiria along the Volga river. In the earlier half of the 1230's, shortly before the Mongol invasion of east-central Europe, Dominican friars led by Friar Julian had come upon them.[11] The majority of the Magyar confederate tribes had emerged in *Lebedia*, a region bordered by the Don and the Dniester, on the northwestern shore of the Black Sea, during the 830's; they were leading a nomadic way of life. Under continued military threat from the east, the Magyars continued to migrate toward the west, to *Etelköz–Atelkozu*: "region between the rivers," the area that would be Bessarabia and Moldavia in modern terminology. There, because they wanted to defend their territory better, and wished to lead successful marauding campaigns against their richer neighbors, they had elected a prince, who would rule them in time of peace, and in war lead their armed forces to battle. They chose Árpád, son of Álmos, of the strong Megyeri tribe, whom they raised on their shields in accordance with Khazar custom.

The Hungarian Anonymus recorded that that when the "headmen of seven Magyar tribes" had selected their commanding leader, they swore an oath of allegiance to him, and to his descendants, and had their oath sealed with their blood in the *Blood Oath* they took. "Tunc ipsi VII principales personae conmuni et vero consilio intellexerunt, quod inceptum iter perficere non possent, nisi ducem ac preceptorem super se habeant. ...Tunc superdicti viri...more paganismo fusis propriis sanguinibus in unum vas ratum fecerunt iuramentum."[12] This loyalty oath, taken *communi consensu*, assured them, and their descendants, of their constitutional rights—bearing in mind that Anonymus had Árpád in mind when he spoke of Álmos. "Ergo libera voluntate et communi consensu VII virorum elegerunt sibi ducem ac preceptorem in filios filiorum suorum usque ad ultimam generationem Almum filium Vgek et qui de eius generatione descenderent."[13]

Viewed from today's perspective, the participants (and their peoples—the tribal chiefs took the oath *commune consensu*) became, by taking this "Blood Oath," artificial blood relatives (blood brothers), had entered into a relationship that, in principle, excluded the threat of blood feud among them. By establishing a blood-relationship they had arranged for the military defense of their common territory and possessions, and for a peaceful way to co-exist with one another, thereby laying a foundation of communal living—nationhood; statehood—among themselves.[14]

After they had taken the blood-oath, the tribe chiefs would bring their grievances before the chief-judge: the *karchas*, or *horka*, who had to find a peaceful solution to their problems. The office of the *horka* was referred to as late as in an eleventh century document.[15] In the tenth century, *Karchas* Bulcsu had earned the reputation of one who could diffuse a blood feud. The Hungarian Anonymus preserved for posterity the ancient Magyar custom by recording the Blood-Oath—though it is known that various ancient peoples had practiced it—and he explained it according to more advanced political-constitutional views of his age, the last quarter of the twelfth century.[16]

In the beginning of the 890's, when the main armed force of the Magyars invaded Great Moravia, a Bulgarian-Pecheneg united military onslaught exterminated their families left behind in Atelkozu under the protection of the home guard of old men, and the Pechenegs occupied the region.[17] In order to prevent another surprise Pecheneg attack, Árpád made a westward move with his strongly decimated people, to find a permanent home in the mid-Danubian Carpathian basin. In 896, the Magyars had at first settled down along the Tisza river, and began their marauding ventures toward the west and the southwest; at the same time, the stronger of the tribes took possession of Transdanubia for a permanent home, the area south and west of the Danube, more appropriate for military self-defense and political survival.[18]

What sort of population did the Magyars find in their new country? Slav and Turk[ish] comparative linguistics may provide an answer to the question, as, for instance, geographical names [of rivers]. The people arriving in a region last shall take over, borrow, the geographical designations from the earlier inhabitants and change them according to the rules of their own language. Through their continuous formation the geographical names bear witness to ancient peoples who may have died out a long time ago. The ferocious fury of the *barbarian* migrations destroyed even the traces of Roman

civilization in [the Roman provinces of] Pannonia leaving only life-
less ruins behind, though those ruins came back to life in the legends
with which the newcomers (or, survivors) had surrounded them. The
Huns, the various German tribes, or the Avars, were not able to establish a permanent home in the mid-Danubian region. The Bulgaro-
Turk[ish] Avars were swept aside by the armies of Charlemagne who
extended his power all over Pannonia during the 790's.[19]

After 845, the eastern segment of the Carolingian empire fell into
the sea of Slavs that had inundated Europe during the ninth century.
The Moravians were the first Slavic people to establish a lasting state,
as the greater Moravian realm of Svatopluk included the Czech
region, together with the area of the Small Carpathians, as far east as
the valley of the Garam river. There, the Byzantine Church with its
Slavic liturgy had begun to strike roots. On linguistic grounds it can
be argued that Slovaks, Quad tribes and some Illyrians were living in
the region around N[y]itra at the time of the Magyars' arrival during
the 890's.[20]

In the Rába river–Lake Balaton–Drave river geographical
triangle of Transdanubia (former Roman province of *Pannonia*), the
Pannonian Slovenes were establishing their statehood by the mid-
ninth century. They had submitted to the political predominance of the
east-Frankish court, and the Bavarian clergy began to convert them to
the Christian faith.[21] In the Magyar language, expressions related to
the Christian religion were borrowed from the Slovene vocabulary. In
northern Pannonia newcomers from Bavaria had settled down, among
them an Avar remnant around—what today would be—the area of
Győr-Sopron. In the southwest, between the Mura and Drave streams,
Old-Slovenes; in the Danube–Drave triangle Bulgaro-Turks, while
neo-Latin folks had settled south of Lake Balaton. Balkan Slavs
formed scattered settlements in the land east of the Danube and west
of the Tisza rivers, and in the *Serem* region (south of the Danube,
north of the Save rivers). East of the Tisza, and west of the low
mountain range, that formed the western geographical border of
Transylvania, Slavicised Bulgarians established settlements they
shared with Bulgaro-Turk[ish] ethnic groups. Turk[ish] folk elements
retained permanent residence in the region bordered by the Maros–
Temes–Szamos rivers.

The sound of river names provide evidence for the existence of these settlements. The (names of) Karassó and Küküllő (streams) are of Bulgaro-Turkish origin; personal names like Gyula, Gyécsa [=four], Karoldu, Sarolt[u] [= black and white weasel(s); in Hungarian: *mennyét*] that were in use in the princely family at the Hungarian court in the 990s may serve as further proof that members of the Árpád princely family also spoke Turk[ish] as a second language. It means that the Turk[ish] cultural influence continued to prevail among the Magyars who had settled down in the mid-Danubian Carpathian basin—as if to counterbalance the linguistic and cultural impact the Slavic ethnic element might have had upon them.[22]

The Bulgaro-Turk[ish] and Slavic ethnic strata among the population did not possess an organized political and military structure, a centralized government, and they did not assert strong resistance to the conquering Magyars. The Slavs lived in larger groups around the dirt-forts (*grad*) of their clan chiefs. It was only the personal rule of Svatopluk, though, that, for example, held the Moravian realm together. In 892, King Arnulf of the east-Franks had, with help from the Magyars, devastated Moravian lands; two years later, Magyar forces laid waste to Pannonia. Upon the death of Svatopluk, because of a feud among his sons, the Moravian realm fell apart, and another Magyar attack contributed to its demise. Frantisek Palacky, historian of the Czechs, had noted in the nineteenth century that the invasion and settlement of the Magyars in the Carpathian basin did have far reaching consequences for European history. The Magyars' arrival and settlement was the greatest misfortune that had befallen the Slavs. Palacky had argued that without the Magyars a great Slav empire would have developed in east-central Europe under the hegemony of Byzantium, just as the Franks had built up an empire under the aegis of Rome. The settlement of the Magyars along the Danube and Tisza rivers had separated, in fact, alienated the Slavs from each other.[23]

The conquering Magyars did not have great enough manpower to occupy all of the Carpathian basin. They took actual possession mainly of the region that would be the Hungary of today, *and* of the Danube–Tisza–Maros area, together with the territory south of the Drave river. In order to prevent, or at least minimize, the expected confrontation among tribal chiefs over territorial possessions, they left large strips of heavily wooded land, and land to be set aside for the border marches, unoccupied. Forests rich in game, waters abundant in fish, wide flood plains of rivers continued for a long period of time to cover large segments of the country.[24]

They settled down, with their servants and domestics, in already inhabited areas of the land, where the vanquished peoples would increase the numbers of their servants—who actually did the agricultural work on the fields, while their masters were engaged in war or the pleasure of hunting. The land-takers had soon achieved strong population density in the culturally advanced regions of Pannonia—despite the devastations that had been caused by the barbarian migrations. The Slavic population eventually dissolved into the Magyars; that is why so many Slavic words enriched the Hungarian vocabulary, especially terms of religious and ecclesiastical nature, expressions pertinent to state, or government functions, words dealing with industry and the industrial arts that were cultivated at a high rational level.[25]

The core of the Magyar tribe was made up of the clan of the *hadnagy*, clan chief, the family clan that had settled down on both banks of a river, at the estuary, so that it could guard the natural [military] road[s] leading through the river valley. This core was surrounded by the territories held by the other clans of the tribe. The leading Magyar [Megyeri] tribe had, for example, occupied both banks of the Danube [on the northeastern and eastern edge of Pannonia]; the other tribes took possession of the regions around it. They had the responsibility of guarding the military routes. Large segments of the area east of the Tisza and of Transylvania remained unoccupied, partly on grounds of lacking manpower, and, partly, for reasons of military security. Árpád and the tribal chiefs must have been concerned about the threat of continued invasions by their former enemies.[26]

In winter, the Magyars lived on the plain, along the rivers; at the time of early spring floods, they moved with their animals to higher ground and remained there until the fall season. In such a manner, every tribe possessed two living areas in the country. One learned from linguistics that they knew of primitive house construction, because they did borrow words depicting parts of a house from the Slavs, but they imitated Slavic house construction designs.[27]

Woman-theft—eloping with the bride—was be part of their culture; as late as the early tenth century, Magyar marriage custom involved the "purchase" of the wife [to be]—in Hungarian: *nővásár*, as the woman to be purchased was called the *bride for sale*. The Arab chronicler Mahmud Gardēzī reported on Magyar marriage customs around the year 1050 that when a man wished to marry a woman, the man had to pay, according to his wealth, one or more horses to the father of the young woman. While they were negotiating the *kalim*: the number of horses of the marriage-deal, the father of the bride had to take the father of the young man (groom): the purchaser—in Hungarian: *vevőlegény*, *vőlegény*, the *young* man who makes the purchase—to his home, and place before him furs of weasels, beavers, squirrels, martens and foxes, of which the young man shall select ten, then bind the bundle of selected furs to the back of the horse of the groom's father, who now returned to his own home. Thereupon, the groom shall send his [share of the] *kulim* [purchase price] comprising horses, money, and goods to the father of the [purchased] bride, and upon receipt of the goods, the bride shall be taken to the house of the groom. *Meny[ét]* [weasel] is a Magyar word, of which the word *menyasszony* [weasel-woman; bride] had evolved. Purchasing a wife was an Ugor custom, dating back to an age when the purchasing price had to be paid in animal furs.[28]

The widow could be forced to marry against her will by the dead husband's relative (so that the dearly purchased inheritance would not be lost in the family). This right of the brother-in-law, based on a Jewish custom, was known as the institution of the *leviratus*. It was still customary in the early eleventh century Hungary, because King Stephen tried to eliminate it through legislation.[29] (The first Hungarian laws made it clear, though, that a Magyar father did have unlimited power over his children.)

The essence of the Magyars' religion, like the religion of other Turk[ish] peoples, comprised respect for their ancestors—that is, ancestor worship. They appeased the souls of the ancestors with the fire kept constantly burning on the family hearth. They buried the dead with his, or her, utensils, with horses and weapons—so that he, or she, have everything they need at his, or her, disposal in the afterworld. They even killed the servants of a dead noble so that they continue to serve him in afterlife. They reconciled the memory of the dead by holding a wake followed by a festive meal. The spread of Christianity had altered these burial customs: the dead man's horse would not be killed, but given to the Church; the servants would not be killed either, they would be emancipated—on the condition that they, the freed souls: *torlok* [*dusnok* in Slavic, from *dusa*, meaning soul] would on a given day of the year, after the harvest, offer grain, beer and other field products to the Church for Masses to be said for their dead master.[30]

The Magyars did commercial business with money, furs, live bullocks, and, at one time, with slave trade. During their stay in *Lebedia* they used to sell their slaves at the slave markets in the harbor cities of the Black Sea.[31]

The *land-taking* by the Magyars in the Carpathian basin that had been carried out during the 890's, was not yet identical with establishing statehood in the mid-Danubian region. The Magyars retained their tribal organization. Only in time of war did they accept unified leadership among themselves.[32] The tribal chiefs conducted independent marauding ventures in order to acquire rich booty abroad. The chronicles, and oral tradition, record the names of Bulcsu, Lél and Botond, as tribal leaders of the marauding expeditions, but mention nowhere the name of the Magyar prince, Árpád's successor.[33] As a matter of fact, besides naming Árpád's youngest son, Zoltán, and the latter's son, Taksony, the chroniclers did not mention anybody else from among the members of the ruling dynasty, and only Constantine Porphyrogenitus spoke of Termacs [Termach], as a descendant of Jutacs [Jutach], son of Árpád.[34] It may thus be concluded that the marauding expeditions carried out by the Magyar tribes in the tenth century were not "national" undertakings, but simply tribal ventures, and may serve as proof of the fact that the centralized authority of the Árpád dynasty fell completely apart during the tenth century, until Prince Géza came to power in 970.[35]

The secret of the Magyars' early marauding ventures was their military strategy, entirely unknown in the west, depicted by the Byzantine emperor, Leo VI the Wise (d. 912), in his book named *Tactica*. The Magyars (the emperor referred to them as Turks), clever with handling their arrows, Leo VI wrote, stunned the enemy with their hail of arrows, then pretended to withdraw from the scene of the encounter, while constantly continuing to shoot their arrows from the backs of their horses at the enemy pursuing them. When the enemy opened up its closed ranks, the Magyars re-grouped their forces in order to renew their attack, and fought the enemy in close combat with swords and lances. They took no booty until they fully demolished the opponent. In military actions, the tribes who had joined them last had to fight in the front line [and suffer casualty in action].[36]

The other reason for their success in the marauding ventures was the total dissolution of the Carolingian empire. During the tenth century, the centralized government structure of the Carolingians fell apart, and no new government organization replaced it. The Saxons and Bavarians gained strength, but the Saxon and Bavarian tribal leaders could not, did not want to, establish one common military defense system that would have protected them all. Anarchy prevailed in Italy, where various parties were fighting each other. Nowhere did the marauding Magyar tribal chiefs face strong military resistance, while the riches and wealth of the Latin west only whetted their desire for an easy and rich booty. The west was far advanced in terms of social and economic development in the tenth century, and the raw ugly faces of the intruding Magyars, their brutality combined with the fact that they suddenly appeared, and just as unexpectedly disappeared from the area of their attack, had caused fear among the population, reported the chroniclers.[37]

In 899, after the death of King Arnulf, the Magyars had ravaged Italy: they rapidly moved to Verona and Pavia. The region promised them rich loot, their appearance was fully unexpected, and there was no one to resist them. King Berenger attempted to oppose them at Brentana, but suffered defeat at their hands; the marauders moved fast as lightning through Lombardy, laid waste the valley of the Po river down to the Moena–Reggio line, as far as Ticino. They captured and murdered Bishop Liutward of Verceli, the former arch-chancellor of Charles III, who had tried to escape before them. The invaders spent a full year in Italy before returning to the mid-Danubian lands they by that time regarded as their *home*.[38]

After they had carefully explored the region, the Magyars broke into Bavarian country in 901 (during the reign of Lewis the Child), and—to quote a Frankish chronicler—caused damage beyond human comprehension. Strong Magyar cavalry forces devastated the territory of the *Ostmark* ; as it was their custom, they appeared out of nowhere, and suddenly disappeared when a Bavarian cavalry unit arrived to clash with them. One segment of the invading force had bad luck, however; Margrave Leopold was able to hunt them down and demolish them north of the Danube. The Bavarians had erected the fort Ennsburg [near the Roman Lauriacum] to protect their territory from further sudden invasions.[39]

In 902, the Magyars devastated Carinthia, then a Moravian army met and defeated them. In 903, the chronicles reported another Magyar-Bavarian military encounter. And yet, peaceful conditions prevailed and made it possible for trade and commerce to be carried on undisturbed in the *Ostmark*: the region between the Danubian (Vienna) Woods and the Bavarian border, as far north as the Moravian plateau. The merchants paid toll in coins, or in goods. In and across the valley of the Salzach and Traun rivers they traded with salt, with horses and cattle, food, wax, and other household goods as well. The peaceful political-economic situation in the region only became blurred after the collapse of Moravia, as one Moravian province became Czech land (at a time, when, one may remark, only the Moravians would have had the ability to establish a permanent Slavic state in east-Central Europe).[40]

The Magyars were marauding in Saxony in the year 906—at a time when the east-Frankish armies had to struggle with the armed troops of the Babenbergs; as if the Magyars had been "invited" to go in search of plunder in Saxon land—to prepare for another military engagement with the Bavarian forces on July 5, 907, in which the Magyar armies scored a full fledged victory over the army of Duke Liutbold of Bavaria. *It was because of this victory, that the Magyars were able to settle down permanently in Pannonia.* The river Enns became the eastern frontier of the east-Frankish realm: the common Bavarian-Hungarian border. In 918, the Magyars devastated Bremen, in 924, they invaded Pavia and burned the city's forty-four churches to the ground; they were also marauding in southern German territory, in Elsass and Lorraine, laid waste the regions around Verdun two years later, and robbed Tuscany with a heavy hand.[41]

Henry I the Hunter (918–36) purchased a nine-year truce with them, because he wanted to gain time to prepare his land for an effective military defense against, and a decisive military action with the enemy. The light Magyar cavalry units could accomplish nothing by besieging the recently erected stone forts, and stone-walled cities on east-Frankish soil, nor could they meet successfully the newly developed tactics of the east-Frankish armed forces that now would attack in a phalanx-like closed formation and would not allow themselves to be sidetracked. In 933, Henry I the Fowler denied further monetary payments to the Magyar tribal chiefs, and easily defeated the revenge seeking Magyar armies at Riad near Merseburg.[42] Their defeat was so devastating, that the Magyar tribal chiefs did not dare invade German territory until the summer of 955, when they had met firm military resistance from the armies of Otto I the Great (936-73). On the meadow of Lech near Augsburg, the new *German* armies thoroughly demolished the Magyar tribal military forces, and had their leaders, Lél and Bulcsu, captured and hanged.[43]

Fortunately for the Magyars, Otto I the Great—the German chronicler Widukind referred to him as "defensor tocius Europae"— did not pursue them further east; he only instructed the duke of Bavaria to keep a close eye on them. Otto I had restored the fort defense system in the territory of the *Ostmark* [*Ostarrichi*], and placed it under the supervision of the Babenberg family.[44]

The Hungarian Anonymus in the late twelfth, and Simon de Keza in the latter half of the thirteenth century, had argued that the marauding ventures dissipated much of the strength of the Magyars as a *nation*. Their tribal chiefs had to realize that they could not gather riches, nor could they continue living while constantly devastating neighboring regions. Indeed, Keza claimed—if his words are to be interpreted correctly—that the Magyar tribal leadership must suddenly have realized that they could not continue with their marauding life style, that their tribes had to establish unity among themselves, and set up permanent settlements in the country, so that they would lead peacefully lives there, and call it *home*.

Otherwise, their people would go under, would pass from existence among the multitude of peoples who were encircling them in their new surroundings in the Carpathian basin—like the Huns, or even the Avars, who had disappeared from the public scene many years before them. At least that is the message one may read into the remark made by Keza: "Communitas itaque Hungarorum cum suis capitaneis seu ducibus, quos pro tempore praeficere usa erat, usque tempora ducis Geichae hinc unde huic mundo spolia et pericula dinoscitur intulisse,"[45]—a remark, one may note, the compiler of the *Chronicon pictum* had shortened in the text, and even corrected the name of Prince Géza to that of Prince Taksony: "...hec et alia huiusmodi usque ad tempora Toxun ducis gessisse perhibetur."[46]

The interpretation of this passage ought not be weakened by the fact that the "R" initial on fol. 17' of the *Chronicon pictum* manuscript depicted Lél [and Bulcsu] in front of Emperor *Conrad I* (so stated in the text!), as if Lél had, with a horn in his hand, hit the emperor so hard on the head that he died. It is known from the non-Hungarian chronicles that the emperor in question was Otto I, and not Conrad I, who had Lél captured after the battle of Augsburg, 955, and had him hanged.[47]

The inhabitants in western Europe had during these centuries reached and lived according to an advanced political existence that rested on Christian foundations. Therefore, it now became the duty of the head of the Magyar tribe—who had been elected the *prince*: leader of all the Magyar tribes—to build a (diplomatic) bridge toward the (Latin) Christian west, and establish direct contact with the German ruler, Otto I, who had recently been crowned emperor. The German empire meant world power. During the times of Charlemagne (d. 814), the Frankish empire formed the basis for the expansion and growing influence of the Roman Catholic Church. Under east-Frankish—eventually German—successors of the Carolingians, however, the empire did no longer include only the Teutonic peoples; it was now the Roman Church that would hold together the peoples of the West. It was the universality of the Roman Catholic Church that provided the intellectual foundation for realizing the universal plans of the empire of the Ottos.[48]

In the 960's, Otto I the Great had sojourned in Rome to help elevate the papacy from the moral degradation it had fallen into during the earlier part of the century, and to have himself crowned emperor by the pope, whom he had placed on the throne of Saint Peter.[49]

An additional remark will be in order here. Before he had arrived in Rome, Otto I—not in person, but through a representative—promised Pope John XII that he shall restore to Saint Peter lands of the Petrine patrimony that came under his political-military control during his excursion into Italy.[50] Upon his coronation, however, after Otto I had left the City, John XII began to question the validity of the coronation he had performed; thereupon, the emperor returned to Rome, had John XII deposed, and named a layman to be made pope. The new pontiff, Leo VIII, granted in 963 *Emperor* Otto I the right to choose the pope and to invest bishops with the insignia of their spiritual offices everywhere.[51]

Consequently, the Magyar prince, Géza (970-97), had a hard choice to make. Were he, and his people, to join the western: Latin Christian community where imperial German bishops directed the spreading of the Christian faith among the population, the missionary activities of the *imperial* bishops and of their missionary clerics would lead to the expansion of the political sphere of the German empire over their country.[52]

Christianity established by German missionary priests among the Czechs and the Moravians remained for a long period of time under the spiritual jurisdiction of the German metropolitan, the Archbishop of Mainz, forcing the Czechs to acknowledge the political superiority of the empire—thereby preventing them from, and delaying development of their own ecclesiastical and political, independence.[53] Similar conditions had prevailed at the Polish royal court that cultivated political ties with the German court.[54] As it soon became evident from the missionary activities of Pilgrim, bishop of Passau (who wanted to become archbishop soon), and his clerics, the missionary work of the *imperial* Church—including that of Pilgrim of Passau—had aimed at expanding the political influence of German political circles over Pannonia.[55]

The issue Géza had to face was this: how could he join the western Latin Christian community without endangering the political freedom and independence of his people? The Christian faith had already been known to the Magyars. It took planning and cooperation from the Hungarian leader, however, to let religion strike roots among the population. In order to plan the people's political future and the religious belonging of the population, the prince, first of all, had to restore leadership to his office among his tribal chiefs, and the people. He had to break down the independent rule of the tribes (who soon were joined by Slav inhabitants in the land, later by some Pechenegs, and even by some Bulgarians), and of the armed political resistance of the tribal chiefs to his, the central power of the prince of the House of Árpád, to make it possible to have foreign-born military personnel settle down in the country.

Géza and his family had converted to the Christian faith of the Latin-rite. Géza had asked for the hand in marriage of the daughter of the Bavarian Duke Henry for his son Vajk, who had been given the name of Stephen in Christian baptism according to the Latin rite. It was the irony of history that it was the father of Duke Henry who, upon orders given by Otto I, had Lél and Bulcsu hanged after the battle at Augsburg, in 955.[56]

Notes

1. Bálint Hóman – Gyula Szekfű, *Magyar történet*, 5 vols., 6th ed. (Budapest, 1939), I, 23 ff.; Bálint Hóman, *Geschichte des ungarischen Mittelalters*, 2 vols. (Berlin, 1940–43), I, 8ff.; György Székely – Antal Bartha (eds.), *Magyarország története: előzmények és magyar történet 1242-ig* [History of Hungary: Pre-history and Hungarian history to 1242] (Budapest, 1984), 377ff.; Jenő Szűcs, *A magyar nemzeti tudat kialakulása* [Development of the Magyar ethnic consciousness] (Budapest, 1997), 185ff., 252f., nn. 121-29, and 296ff.; István Bóna, *A magyarok és Európa 9 – 10 században* [The Magyars and Europe in the ninth – tenth centuries] (Budapest, 2000), 15ff., 25ff.; idem, *A hunok és nagykirályaik* [The Huns and their great kings] (Budapest, 1993), 24ff., and 122ff., and my review of this volume in *East European Quarterly*, 30 (1997), 529f.

2. Cf. Simon de Keza, *Gesta Hungarorum*, in *Scriptores rerum Hungaricarum*, ed. Emericus Szentpétery, 2 vols. (Budapest, 1937–38), revised and expanded by Kornél Szovák and László Veszprémy (Budapest, 1999), cited hereafter as *SSH*, I, 141ff., cc. 4-5; C.A. Macartney, *The Medieval Hungarian Historians* (Cambridge, 1953), 89ff.

3. See the Hungarian Anonymus, *Gesta Hungarorum*, *SSH*, I, 33ff., c. 5, further, cc. 1, 8, 9; the "Chronicon pictum"—henceforth to be cited as the Chronicle, cc. 25-26, etc.; selections in Gyula Pauler – Sándor Szilágyi (eds.), *A magyar honfoglalás kútfői* [Historical sources of the Magyar land-taking] (Budapest, 1900), cited hereafter as *MHK*, 314ff. Hóman, *Ungarisches Mittelalter*, I, 302ff.; for a different argument, cf. János Horváth, *Árpád-kori latinnyelvű irodalmunk stílusproblémái* [Stylistic questions of the Latin language literature of the Árpád age] (Budapest, 1954), 315ff.; Gyula Kristó, "Szempontok Anonymus Gestájának megitéléséhez" [Contributions a l'évaluation la de valeur historique de la Gesta Hungarorum"], *Acta historica Szegediensis*, 66 (1979), 45ff.

4. Hóman – Szekfű, I, 49ff.; Székely – Bartha, 419ff.; Gyula Németh, *A honfoglaló magyarság kialakulása* [The formation of the Magyars as a people who had taken possession of Hungary], 2nd rev. ed., ed. Árpád Berta (Budapest, 1991), 56ff.; Sándor L. Tóth, "A magyarok *etelközi honfoglalása*" [La *conquête du pays d'Etelköz* des hongrois], *Acta historica Szegediensis*, 98 (1993), 3ff.

5. Németh, 76, 84f., 145.

6. Cf. Arnold J. Toynbee, *Constantine Porphyrogenitus and his World* (Oxford, 1973), 464ff.; C. A. Macartney, *The Magyars in the Ninth Century* (Cambridge, 1930; repr. 1968), 90ff.

7. Cf. Németh, 146ff. and 225f.; . Hóman – Szekfű, I, 65 ff., and 633f.; Székely – Bartha, 498ff.; S. L. Tóth, *Levediától a Kárpát medencéig* [From Levedia to the Carpathian basin] (Szeged, 1998), 41ff.

8. Anonymus, cc. 6 and 46, in *SSH*, I, 41,12, further, I, 95,5-8 and 95,19-28; Keza, c. 31, *ibid.*, I, 166,12-13; Mahmud Gardēzī, in Macartney, *Ninth Century*, 206; Pauler – Szilágyi, 141ff., esp. 167. For details, see Constantine VII Porphyrogenitus, *De administrando imperio*, Greek text edited by Gyula Moravcsik, English translation by R. J. H. Jenkins (Budapest, 1949; 2nd ed. Washington, 1967), cited hereafter as *DAI*, c. 38; selections also in Henrik Marczali (ed.),*Enchiridion fontium historiae Hungarorum* (Budapest, 1901), 29ff., c. 38; also in Gyula Moravcsik (ed.), *Fontes Byzantini historiae Hungaricae aevo ducem et regum ex stirpe Arpad descendentium* (Budapest, 1984), 34ff., c., 38; Toynbee, 464ff. and 599ff.; Hóman – Szekfű, I, 67ff.

9. *Ibid.*, I, 63ff.; Székely – Bartha, 528ff.

10. *DAI*, c. 40; for analytical details, see Németh, 184ff. S. L. Tóth, "A konstantinosi *Turkia* értelmezéséhez" [Interpreting the meaning of *Turkia* in the work of Constantine Porphyrogenitus], *Magyar Nyelv*, 92 (1996), 54ff.

11. Macartney, *Ninth Century*, 157f.; idem, *Hungarian Historians*, 85ff.; Z. J. Kosztolnyik, *Hungary in the Thirteenth Century* (New York, 1996), 130ff. and 146f., nn. 90-111, also 309 and 316, nn. 78-79; and a review of this book in *Századok*, 132 (1998), 261ff.; and, *English Historical Review*, 116 (2001), 935f.; Hóman – Szekfű, I, 533f.

12. *SSH*, I, 40,16-19; *DAI*, c. 40, made no mention of it.

13. Anonymus, c. 5, *SSH*, I, 40,14-21; Macartney, *Hungarian Historians*, 68.

14. Anonymus, c. 6, *SSH*, I, 40f.; "the Magyars accepted the house of Árpád as their hereditary rulers...and they took an oath to this effect before entering Hungary"— Macartney, *Hungarian Historians*, 69.

15. *DAI*, c. 40; see Hóman – Szekfű, I, 159, 161.

16. Anonymus, cc. 5 and 6; M. Gyóni, *A magyar nyelv görög feljegyzéses szórványemlékei* [Die Streudenkmäler der ungarischen Sprache in griechischen Texten] (Budapest, 1943), 43ff. and 60f.; idem, "Kalizok, kazarok, kabarok, magyarok" [The Caleese, Khazars, Kabars and the Magyars], *Magyar Nyelv*, 34 (1938), 86ff. and 159ff.; on the Khazars and Kavaras, cf. Németh, 162ff., and 216ff., respectively.

17. *DAI*, c. 37; Georgius monachus continuatus *Chronicon*, in *Theophanes Continuatus, ...Georgius monachus*, ed., I. Bekker, *CB* (Bonn, 1838), 817,20 – 819,15 and 231,1-233,10; further, 853,1 – 855,7, on the alliance with Byzantium. *Regionis abbatis Pruminsis Chronicon*, ed. Fr. Kurze, SSrG (Hannover, 1890)—written about 960— placed the Pecheneg attack anno 889. On Regino, W. Wattenbach, *Deutschlands Geschichtsquellen im Mittelalter*, 2 vols., 6th ed. (Berlin, 1893–94), I, 258ff.; Erich Wisplinghoff, "Untersuchungen zur Geschichte des Klosters Prüm an der Wende vom 9 zum 10 Jahrhundert," *Deutsches Archiv für Erforschung des Mittelalters*, 55 (2000), 439ff.

18. *DAI*, c. 40; Hóman – Szekfű, I, 102ff. Ferenc Makk, "A turulmadártól a kettős keresztig" [From the bird *Turul* to the double Cross], *Szabolcs-Szatmár-Beregi Szemle*, 31 (1996), 153ff.

19. Cf. *Einhardi Vita Caroli Magni*, ed. O. Holder-Egger, 6th ed. (Hannover, 1911; repr. 1927), c. 13; Wattenbach, I, 179ff.; see A. Kollautz's very impressive 49 page essay, "Die Awaren," *Saeculum*, 5 (1954), 129ff.; on the Avars, see also "Karl der Grosse unde der Untergang des Awarenreiches," in *Karl der Grosse: Lebenswerk und Nachleben*, ed. H. Beumann, vol. I (Düsseldorf, 1967), 717ff.; Adolph Bachmann, "Die Völker an der Donau nach Attilas Tode," *Archiv für österreichische Geschichte*, 61 (1880), 189ff.; see further, István Bóna's thorough study on the Avars, in Béla Köpeczi (ed.), *History of Transylvania* (Budapest, 1994), 90ff.; also, István Bóna, "Die Awaren: ein asiatisches Reitervolk an der mittleren Donau," in his *Die Awaren in Europa* (Frankfurt am Main–Nuremberg, 1985).

20. Francis Dvornik, *Les légendes de Constantine ét de Méthode vues de Byzance* (Prague, 1933), 212ff.; Imre H. Tóth, "Métod találkozása az 'ugor királlyal'" [Methodius meets the "King of the Ugors"], *A honfoglalás 1100 éve és a Vajdaság* [The 1100th anniversary of the Magyar land-taking] (Ujvidék, 1997), 113ff.; Károly Mesterházy, "Avarok, szlávok, magyarok a Bükk hegységben" [Remains of Avar, Slav, and Magyar settlements in the Bükk Hills], *Századok*, 130 (1996), 861ff.; Imre Boba, *Moravia's History Reconsidered* (The Hague, 1971; Hungarian translation by István Petrovics [Budapest, 1996]); for Heinrich Fichtenau's reaction to Boba's arguments, cf. his *Beiträge zur Mediävistik*,

vol. II (Stuttgart, 1977), 157f., and 167, n. 41; further, my review of the Heinrich Fichtenau volume in *Austrian History Yearbook*, 17–18 (1981–82), 354ff.

21. On this, cf. "De conversione Bogoariorum et Carantanorum libellus," *MGHSS*, XI, 4ff.; Pauler – Szilágyi, 301ff.; Wattenbach, I, 288ff.; F. X. von Funk – K. Bihlmeyer, *Kirchengeschichte*, 2 vols., 8th ed. (Paderborn, 1926–30), II, 4f., and II, 8ff.; W. Levison, "Die älteste Lebensbeschreibung Ruperts von Salzburg," *Neues Archiv*, 28 (1903), 283ff.; Hildebrand Merkl, "Eugippius, Vita s Severini. Das Leben des Heiligen Severin," in Klemen Kramer – E. K. Winter (eds.), *St. Severin – der Heilige zwischen Ost und West*, 2nd ed. (Vienna, 1981), reprint; Franz Zagiba's important 55 page study, "Die bairische Slavenmission und ihre Fortsetzung durch Konstantin (Cyrill) und Method," *Jahrbücher für Geschichte Osteuropas*, Neue Folge, 9 (1961), 1ff.

22. Antal Bartha, *Hungarian Society in the Ninth and Tenth Centuries* (Budapest, 1975), 83ff., and my review of this book in *American Historical Review*, 83 (1978), 1243f.; György Székely, "La Hongrie et Byzance aux Xe–XIIe siècles," *Acta historica Academiae Scientiarum Hungaricae*, 1967, 291ff.; Köpeczi, *Transylvania*, 110ff.; László Szegfű, "Sarolta," *Memoria saeculorum Hungariae*, vol. I (Budapest, 1974), 239ff.

23. Franz Palacky, *Geschichte von Böhmen*, vol. I, 2nd printing (Prague, 1844), 118ff. and 195ff., and compare with Hóman's rather convincing arguments—*Ungarisches Mittelalter*, I, 111ff.; see further, *DAI*, c. 41; *Annales Fuldenses sive Annales regni Francorum*, ed. G. H. Pertz – Fr. Kurze, SSrG (Hannover, 1891), anno 898 (!); it dated the death of Svatopluk anno 894, and so did Regino, a. 894. Further, see the remarks made by Otto of Freising, *Chronica sive Historia de duabus civitatibus*, rev. ed., ed. A. Hofmeister, SSrG (Hannover, 1912), vi:12, and Otto of Freising's less flattering annotations, *ibid.*, vi:10. Tóth, *Levedia*, 189ff.

24. Hóman, *Ungarisches Mittelalter*, I, 106ff.; S. L. Tóth, "Birodalmak, államok és népek a IX századi Európában" [Empires, kingdoms and peoples in Europe of the ninth century], *Életünk*, 1996/6-7, 571ff.

25. Németh, 282ff.

26. Köpeczi, *Transylvania*, 114ff. and 129ff.; Székely – Bartha, 605ff.

27. See *Ottonis et Rahewini Gesta Friderici I imperatoris*, 3rd ed., ed. G. Waitz – B de Simson, SSrG (Hannover, 1912), i:32; György Györffy, *Wirtschaft und Gesellschaft der Ungarns um die Jahrtausendwende* (Vienna–Graz–Budapest, 1983), 20ff. and 129ff.

28. Cf. Mahmud Gardēzī's report on this in Macartney, *Ninth Century*, 209; and *MHK*, 152ff., esp. 172f.; Györffy, *Wirtschaft*, 145ff.; and József Bálint, *A lármafák népe* [Life in a Székler village] (Paris, 1953), 58ff.

29. See *Leges s. Stephani regis*, in Emma Bartoniek (ed.), *Szent István törvényeinek XII századi kézirata: az admonti kódex* [The Laws of King St. Stephen in the twelfth century Admont MS], with a down-sized facsimile of Admont MS, 712, ff.119–126 (Budapest, 1935), 15ff., art. i:26; further, aa. i:7 and ii:2. Text of the laws, based on the edition by Levente Závodszky (ed.), *Szent István, Szent László és Kálmán korabeli törvények és zsinati határozatok forrásai* [Sourcebook of the laws and synodical acts enacted during the reigns of Kings St. Stephen, St. Ladislas and Coloman] (Budapest, 1904), 141ff., is also available in Györffy, *Wirtschaft*, 263ff. and 275 ff.; or [selections] in Marczali, *Enchiridion*, 69ff., 87ff., and 103ff., respectively.

30. See, for instance, the Laws of King Stephen, aa. i:13, 14, 15, 17; and aa. ii:3-4; and the resolutions of the Synod of Szabolcs, 1092, or, of the First Synod of Esztergom held in the early years of King Coloman's reign—Marczali, *Enchiridion*, 88ff. and 112f.; Hóman, *Ungarisches Mittelalter*, I, 310ff. and 318ff.; Z. J. Kosztolnyik, *From Coloman*

the Learned to Béla III (1095–1196): Hungarian Domestic Policies and their Impact upon Foreign Affairs (New York, 1987), 7ff. and 58ff.; and a review of this book in *American Historical Review*, 95 (1991).

31. György Györffy, *István király és műve* [King Stephen and his work] (Budapest, 1977), 397ff.; and my review of this book in *Austrian History Yearbook*, 17–18 (1981–82), 365ff., and of the book's version in English in the *Catholic Historical Review*, 81 (1995), 646f.

32. Cf. Leo VI the Wise, *Tactica*, *MPG*, 107, 627ff., aa. xviii:43, 46, 53; Pauler – Szilágyi, 11ff.; on Leo VI, cf. Georg Ostrogorsky, *Geschichte des byzantinischen Staates*, 2nd ed. (Munich, 1952), 204ff., and György Györffy, *A magyarok elődeiről és a honfoglalásról* [The forefathers of the Magyars and the land-taking], 2nd ed. (Budapest, 1975), 108ff.; further, see Theodora Antonopoulou's introductory remarks in her *The Homilies of Emperor Leo VI* (Leiden–Cologne, 1997), 4ff.; and my review of Antonopoulou in *Church History*, 68 (1999), 154ff.

33. Leo VI, *Tactica*, xviii:47; *DAI*, c. 40; the Hungarian Anonymus, *Gesta Hungarorum*, cc. 54-56, *SSH*, I, 108ff.; the *Chronicon pictum*, cc. 54-61, *ibid.*, I, 304ff.; on the Hungarian chroniclers, see Hóman, *Ungarisches Mittelalter*, I, 297ff.

34. *DAI*, c. 40.

35. Hóman, *Ungarisches Mittelalter*, I, 138ff.; Györffy, *István király*, 54ff.

36. Leo VI, *Tactica*, xviii:42-68; *DAI*, c. 40.

37. See, e.g., the *Annales Fuldenses, sive Annales regni Francorum orientalis*, ed. G. H. Pertz – Fridericus Kurze, SSrG (Hannover, 1891; repr. 1978), aa. 894, 895, 896, 900 [in Bavaria]; or, *Annales Altahenses maiores*, ed. W. de Giesebrecht – E. L. B. ab Oefele, SSrG (Hannover, 1891; repr. 1979), aa. 911, 943, 949, 955; Adam of Bremen, *Gesta Hammaburgensis ecclesiae pontificum*, 3rd ed. ed. Bernhard Schmeidler, SSrG (Hannover–Leipzig, 1917; repr. 1977), i:55, 58; Liutprand's "Antepodoseos," in *Liudprandi episc. Cremonensis opera*, 3rd ed., ed. J. Becker, SSrG (Hannover, 1915), i:36; Widukind of Corby, *Rerum gestarum Saxonicarum libri III*, 4th ed., ed. G. Waitz – K. A. Kehr, SSrG (Hannover, 1904; repr. 1925), i:20; i:38 [a. 933, at Riad]; ii:5, ii:14, iii:44 [at Augsburg, a. 955]; or Flodoard, "Annales," a. 924, *MGHSS*, III, 363ff., etc. Also, Robert Holtzmann, *Geschichte der sächsischen Kaiserzeit, 900–1024*, 4th ed. (Darmstadt, 1961), 84ff. and 162ff.; Karl Hampe, *Das Hochmittelalter, 900–1250*, 5th ed. (Cologne–Graz, 1963), 5ff.

38. Liutprand, "Antepodoseos," i:36; ii:1-5 and 61; Widukind, i:32; also "Benedicti monachi s. Andreae Chronicon," *MGHSS*, III, 697ff., a. 922.

39. Fulda Annals, a. 901; Widukind, i:19; Regino, a. 901; the Hungarian Anonymus, c. 53; *Chronicon pictum*, c. 58, *SSH*, I, 305f.; Karl Oberleitner's 166 page article, "Die Stadt Enns im Mittelalter. Ein Beitrag zur Geschichte der deutschen Städte," *Archiv für österriechische Geschichte*, 27 (1861), 1ff.

40. Erna Patzelt, *Österreich bis zum Ausgang der Babenbergerzeit* (Vienna, 1947), 74ff.; Alfons Dopsch, *Wirtschaftensentwicklung der Karolingerzeit*, 3rd ed., ed. Erna Patzelt, 2 vols. (Cologne–Graz, 1962), II, 186ff.; Palacky, I, 158ff.

41. Widukind, i:20; Thietmar Merseburgensis *Chronicon*, ed. I. M. Lappenberg – F. Kurze, SSrG (Hannover, 1889), i:8 [15]; "Annales Alamannici," anno 907, *MGHSS*, I, 63ff.; Adam of Bremen, *Gesta Hammaburgensis ecclesiae pontificum*, i:55; Flodoard, *Annales*, anno 924, *MGHSS*, XIII, 363ff., with full text in *MPL*, 135, 494ff.; Patzelt, *Österreich*, 77; Engelbert Mühlbacher, *Deutsche Geschichte unter den Karolingern*, 2 vols. Phaidon reprt. (Essen–Darmstadt, n.d.), II, 461ff.

42. Widukind, i:38; Flodoard, *Annales*, anno 933, *MGHSS*, XIII, 381.

43. *DAI*, c. 40; Widukind, iii:44; Thietmar, ii:4 [9-10]; the Hungarian Anonymus, c. 56; *Chronicon pictum*, c. 60; further, cf. Thomas von Bogyay, *Lechfeld: Ende und Anfang* (Munich, 1955), 46ff.; Bóna, *Magyarok*, 51ff.

44. Patzelt, *Österreich*, 91ff.; Bogyay, *Lechfeld: Ende und Anfang*, 54ff.

45. Keza, c. 42, *SSH*, I, 172,5-8; compare with Anonymus, cc. 55 and 56; and the comments by Jenő Szűcs on the development of a nomadic ethnic national identity (among the early Magyars) in his *A magyar nemzeti tudat kialakulása* [Essays on the formation of the Magyars' ethnic image] (Budapest, 1997), 296ff.; further, idem, *Az utolsó Árpádok* [The last of the Árpád kings] (Budapest, 1993), 312ff.

46. The Chronicle, c. 62, *ibid.*, I, 311,18-20.

47. Cf. Dezső Dercsényi (ed.), *Chronicon pictum: Képes Krónika*, 2 vols. (Budapest, 1963), I [facsimile], fol. 17'; in the text, c. 60—for the passage concerned, see *SSH*, I, 308,3-17.

48. As evidenced by Thietmar, iv:38 [59], the new approach taken by the Hungarian court proved to be effective—though, undoubtedly, much depended on the goodwill of the German emperor—cf. Thomas von Bogyay, *Stephanus Rex* (Munich, 1975), 14ff., and my review of this book in *Austrian History Yearbook*, 14 (1978), 209ff.; Györffy, *István király*, 82ff.; Friedrich Heer, *Europäische Geistegeschichte*, 2nd ed. (Stuttgart, 1965), 56ff.

49. Hans Kühner, *Neues Papstlexikon*, Fischer Bücherei (Frankfurt–Hamburg, 1965), 52; Györffy, *István király*, 229ff.

50. Cf. *MGHLL*, sect. IV, 1, n. 10 and 12; Walter Ullmann, *The Growth of Papal Government in the Middle Ages*, 2nd ed. (London, 1962), 232ff.; Oliver J. Thatcher – Edgar H. McNeal (eds.), *A Source Book for Medieval History* (New York–Boston, 1905), 114ff. and 118f.; Peter Partner, *The Lands of St. Peter* (Berkeley–Los Angeles, 1972), 90f.

51. See *MPL*, 134, 992ff.; Thatcher – McNeal, 18f.; Funk – Bihlmeyer, II, 41f.; or, indirectly, the arguments of J. A. Brundage on Widukind's ideas of the empire, in *Medieval Studies*, 22 (1960), 15ff.; M. Andrieu, "La carriere ecclesiastique des papes," *Revue des sciences religieuses*, 21 (1947), 109ff.; Carl Erdmann, "Das ottonische Reich als Imperim Romanum," *Deutsches Archiv*, 6 (1943), 421ff.

52. Keza, c. 42, *SSH*, I, 172,5-8; Gyula Kristó, "Géza fejedelem és István király" [The ruling prince Géza and Stephen the monarch], *Aetas*, 2000/3, 25ff.

53. Cf. Thietmar, iii:3 [anno 975], and *Annales Hildesheimenses*, ed. G. Waitz, SSrG (Hannover, 1878), anno 975; it was only in 1347 that Emperor Charles IV of the Luxemburg-Bohemian line established the Czech bishopric of Prague under the auspices of Rome. Cf. Wolfgang Eggert – Barbara Petzold, *Wir-Gefühl und Regnum Saxonum bei frühmittelalterlichen Geschichtsschreiben* (Vienna–Graz, 1948), 98ff.; Palacky, II, 238ff. and 240, n. 326.

54. Bruno Gebhardt, *Handbuch des deutschen Geschichte*, 4 vols., 8th ed., ed. Herbert Grundmann (Stuttgart, 1954, etc.), I, 180ff.; Holtzmann, 359ff.; A. F. Czajkowski, "The Congress of Gniezno in the Year 1000," *Speculum*, 24 (1949), 339ff. For a counter-argument, see Tadeusz Manteuffel, *The Formation of the Polish State*, tr. Andrew Gorski (Detroit, 1982), 56ff. and 64ff.

55. See the letter of Bishop Pilgrim of Passau, dated 974, and addressed to Pope Benedict VI—cf. Marczali, *Enchiridion*, 57ff., text based on an early twelfth century codex, MS 1051, in the Austrian Nationalbibliothek, Vienna; also, Holtzmann, 265ff. See

further the fascinating arguments, "Zu den Urkundenfälschungen Pilgrims von Passau" by Heinrich Fichtenau in his *Beiträge zur Mediävistik*, vol. II: *Urkundenforschung*, 157ff.; and my review of this work in *Austrian History Yearbook*, 17–18 (1981–82), 354ff.

56. As recognized by Thietmar, iv:38 [59]; Anonymus, c. 57; Holtzmann, 363ff. Thomas von Bogyay, *Stephanus Rex*, 23ff., provided a rather guarded interpretation; see my review in *Austrian History Yearbook*, 14 (1987), 290ff., and compare with Györffy, *István király*, 137ff.

II

Early Magyar-Byzantine Relations in the View of the Byzantine Court and of the Byzantine Chroniclers

…Geula genuit duas filias, quarum…altera vocabatur Saroltu, et Sarolt[u] fuit mater sancti regis Stephani.

Anonymus, *Gesta Ungarorum*, c. 27

In his work *Tactica*, the Byzantine emperor Leo VI the Wise referred to his contemporary Magyars, who were known to him as "Turks," as a disciplined, warlike people who lived under a single ruler who controlled them by terror and fear, under threat of strict punishment.[1] They had occasionally fought on the side of Byzantium as military allies, and were enemies of the Bulgarians. The emperor preferred the Bulgarians to the Turks, because the former had been christened in 864, therefore, the Bulgarians had already abandoned their nomadic way of life. The Turks persevered in hardships, equally tolerated hot and cold climates, though remained unreliable as political and military allies; nor did they cultivate friendly relations with other peoples. They did not honor oaths they had taken, and ignored political agreements they had made. Their military tactics included shooting volleys of arrows from the backs of running horses, but failed to prevail in hand-to-hand combat, nor were they trained for night warfare.[2]

Emperor Leo VI wrote his cited work between 904 and 912, when the Magyars had already been living in the mid-Danubian region of the Carpathian basin. Even though they were not (yet) regarded as Christians, the emperor noticed that through their dealings with Byzantium they maintained contact with the Christian faith. In their totemistic shamanic religious vocabulary the word *cross* was already known to them.[3]

The Finno-Ugrian (pre-)Magyars lived in the region north of the Caucasus Mountains and of the Lake of Meotis during the fifth century, where they came under strong Bulgarian-Turkish influence. By the early 800's, they moved to the area what would be modern-day Bessarabia, and because of the ongoing Bulgarian-Byzantine military conflicts and the Pecheneg attack directed against them, they migrated into the mid-Danubian region of the Carpathian basin, where they live today.[4]

About forty years later, Constantine VII Porphyrogenitus reported that after the Kabars—the tribe that separated from the Khazars—had united with the *Turks* [Magyars], the Turks, as allies of Emperor Leo VI, crossed the Danube, invaded the territory of, and thoroughly defeated, Symeon of Bulgaria at Mundraga, and returned to their own region. They were led by Árpád's son, Liüntika (known perhaps as Tarkacsu), whose name is recorded by Constantine in the same entry a few lines further down, listed as Árpád's first-born son).[5]

Symeon, however, made peace with the emperor of the Romans (that is, of Byzantium), and turned to the Pechenegs with the proposal that they defeat the Turks together. Indeed, when the Turks departed on a military campaign, Symeon, together with the Pechenegs, moved against the Turks, devastated their land, murdered their families, and gleefully expelled the elderly guards left behind to protect the land. After the returning Turks had found their homes destroyed and their families murdered, under the leadership of their Prince Árpád, they migrated to and occupied the country that is theirs today, the emperor wrote.[6]

The emperor described the land they had taken possession of by the name of the rivers Temes, Tutis (unknown), Maros, Kőrös, Tisza, making the remark that the river Istris, also known as the Danube, separated them from the Bulgarians. The learned scholar born in the imperial purple further stressed the fact that although the Turks were not subservient to their chief(s), they fought side by side against their common enemy in time of war, or under threat common to them all. He referred to their chief dignitaries as *gyula* and *karcha* (*kharkasz*); in their chain of command, the latter served directly under their Prince.[7]

A word of observation is in order here. The historian born-in-imperial-purple ostentatiously recorded mainly Magyar (Turk[ish]) events as related to the Khazars; for example, he described at great length the circumstances surrounding the election of their (first) prince—tendentiously, from a Khazar point of view. At the same time, he enumerated the names of the Magyar tribes, the locations of their earlier regional settlements in a manner that, again, reflects Khazar coloring. He discussed the reason for the migration of the Magyars into the Danube–Tisza area, the settling down of the tribes in their new home—simultaneously with the establishment of the Magyar political community led by the Prince, as to imply that he has indeed had authentic intelligence on the Magyars of his time period.

This writer for one feels obligated to note, though, that the "Hungarian" names of the rivers mentioned by Constantine Porphyrogenitus appear differently in the English translation of the Greek text by R. J. H. Jenkins, who wrote "settlement of Turkey," instead of using the term "Magyar conquest" or *land-taking*, of the mid-Danube region. In his transliteration of the Greek text, the rivers become Timisis, Toutis, Morisis, Krisos, and Titza. Likewise, the Hungarian tribes spoken of in the same chapter emerge in the English translation as *Kabaroi, Nekis, Megeris, Kourtougermatos, Trianos, Genach, Kari* and *Kasi*. Jenkins further translated as *gylas* and *karchas* the designations of the chief Turk [Magyar] dignitaries serving their Prince (Árpád, and his successors). Also, the sons of Árpád mentioned in the chapter by Porphyrogenitus—Tarkacsu, Jeleg, Jutosa and Zoltan—are listed, in Jenkin's interpretation, as Tarkatzous, Ielech, Ioutotzas and Zaltas.[8]

The chronicler of the *Annales Fuldenses* made no mention of the withdrawal of the Byzantine forces, nor did he make a note of any deliberation that might have been going on between the Greeks and the Bulgarians, but recorded a diplomatic act in connection with the Turk-Magyars. He had in mind the events of the year 892, when the Magyars (to whom the chronicler now referred to as *Avars*) had aided the east Frankish king Arnulf in his war effort with the Moravians. The war was renewed in the year 893: "Avari, qui dicuntur Ungari, in his temporibus ultra Danubiam...totam Pannoniam...deleverunt."[9] The chronicler added, anno 895, that the Magyars also invaded Bulgarian territory, but had suffered defeat; and made a brief remark on the importance of the Byzantine-Bulgarian contract. One may draw the conclusion that the Turk-Magyars had taken the mid-Danubian area into their possession by the year 896.[10]

The imperial author is the only one among the Byzantine chroniclers who did mention that it was the Pecheneg invasion that caused the Magyars to emigrate from their previous area of habitation—recorded by the emperor as "Etel" and "Kouzou" (in Jenkin's interpretation of the Greek text.) The imperial author, however, made no references to his source[s] of intelligence. Most probably, he obtained his intelligence data from envoys sent to the Magyars, or from Magyar visitors at the imperial court. Termacs, the great grandson of Árpád, accompanied by *Karchas* Bulcsu, had sojourned at the court, a circumstance that may explain why the emperor wrote much in detail about the Magyars.[11] One may recall that in his report on the Magyars, the emperor described mostly the area where Priscos *rhetor* had sojourned during *his* diplomatic mission to the Huns during the fifth century.[12] When he discussed earlier events, Constantine presumably followed a written outline he himself had prepared from previous imperial embassy reports, and included it into his unfinished, or at least unedited, work.[13]

The emigration of the Magyars from the region of the Caucasus to the Carpathian mountain range lasted over four hundred years. During this time, they came under the influence of the Alan-Persian language and culture, and entering the political sphere of Byzantium they experienced the Byzantine cultural-religious input, even though they did not become (Byzantine) Christians themselves. Christianity grew deep roots on the Crimea already during the 280's; in the fourth century, the Goths who lived there since the mid-third century became Christians, although Theophilos, "Episcopus Gothie," represented only the Goths from "the area around the banks of the Danube" at the Council of Nicea in 325. The Goths living along the Danube were Arian Christians.[14]

On the southern shores of the Black Sea Christianity struck roots in the 180's. In the region reaching to the Caucasus mountains, the Armenians had already become Christians. Gregory the Illuminator was their missionary Apostle.[15] In the sixth century, especially during the reign of Justinian the Great, Byzantine missionaries went everywhere. Their missionary territory reached the Caucasus, and beyond, to the northern slopes of the mountain range, the land occupied by the Alans. Gregory the Illuminator previously preached the Christian faith among them; according to a tenth century source, a monk named Euthymios was their missionary, and around 902 the Alans became Christians. They had their own bishop, ordained by the Patriarch of Byzantium.[16]

Fourth century Byzantine sources mentioned the Huns, Bulgarians, and Turkish peoples who were living on the northern shore of the Black Sea; and Saint Jerome, the Latin church father, who had earlier referred to the Huns as the wolfs of the north,[17] spoke of them later as the ones who were already learning the psalms.[18] It can be assumed that Gregory the Illuminator had also done missionary work among the Huns. Saint Jerome further mentioned that the Huns of the Caucasus had invaded Syrian territory by passing through Armenian lands in Asia Minor (about 395), which could mean that a segment of the Huns remained behind in the Caucasus, because they took no part in fording of the Volga in 376.[19]

Sozoman stated in his Ecclesiastical History that at the end of the fourth century, Byzantine bishop Theotimos was an active missionary among the Huns at the estuary of the Danube,[20] as if to support the remark made by Cosmas Indicopleustes that, besides Persia, Christian churches existed on lands held occupied by the Huns.[21]

On the northeastern shores of the Black Sea, across from Bosporus in the Crimea, it was the Bishop of Phanagoria who took care of their spiritual needs of peoples living along the Kuban river. During the fifth century, the Huns occupied the Crimean peninsula, though, by the sixth century, the city of Bosporus was once again in Byzantine hands.[22] In 552, Nestorian monks had secretly introduced silkworms from China into the Byzantine empire; they were busy missionaries among the Persians, Turkish and Mongolian peoples.[23] Nestorian monks had served as scribes of Turkish and Mongol rulers; not only had they developed a method of writing with Turkish letters, but even started the Korean script. In the twelfth century, the ruler of the *Carakita*, peoples living west of Lake Baikal, in the *Orkon* region, was a monk-king: Priester John, whose territory might have been the "Land of Prester John."[24]

The Turks became Christians by the end of the eighth century; in such a manner, the "forefathers" of the Magyars avoided religious confrontation with Nestorian missionaries. Iohannes Malalas' *Chronographia* of the sixth century may throw some light upon Byzantine Christian missionary politics, though the work only survived in an eleventh century extract.[25] In the ninth century, a certain Theophanes had, in his work also called *Chronographia*, copied data from Malalas' chronicle, and since he relied upon earlier manuscripts of the work, although not the original of the work, he preserved the Malalas report in more detail.[26] The data published by Theophanes were further copied by Ioannes Scylitzes in the eleventh century, whose work, therefore, remains secondary in value.[27]

Malalas had recorded, according to Theophanes, that during the former half of the sixth century, Huns resided in the neighborhood of the city of Bosporus [*Boon phoros*: "cattle tax"], a city founded by Herakles of Iberia; their leader named Grodas was baptized a Christian in Constantinople, and returned home to his kindred so that he, as godson and ally of Emperor Justinian, represent Byzantine interests among his people in the region of Bosporus in the Crimea. His conversion served the political purpose of enabling the Byzantine court to establish a firm foothold in Bosporus. After all, the Huns controlled the area in the Crimea between the cities of Chaerson and Bosporus. Malalas wrote that Grodas had the assignment to support the not overly strong Byzantine garrison of Bosporus were the Huns to attack the city.

Prince Grodas had taken his assignment too seriously. He began to use physical force in converting his people to the new faith; he gave orders to melt down the pagan idols. In doing this, however, he made the pagan priests angry. Members of the clergy now formed a conspiracy with Muageris, brother of Grodas, against Grodas, had the populace stirred up, and Grodas was assassinated. Muageris became the new Prince, who now issued orders to massacre the Byzantine garrison of Bosporus, and occupied the city by force. Thereupon, the Byzantine court made war on land and on sea against the Huns, who had fled the region before the approaching Byzantine forces. Bosporus and its surroundings came once again, and without any military action, under Byzantine rule.[28]

The report by Malalas seems to be confirmed by an event dated in the times of Emperor Heraclius in a writ by Patriarch Nicephorus, who died in 829, that in the early seventh century the leader of the Huns visited Constantinople with his nobles' entourage to accept Christianity; he had been baptized and returned to his home territory. The problem with the remark by Nicephorus is that he dated these events exactly a century earlier before their actual occurrence.[29]

Not so long ago, historical research concluded that the descriptive term *Magyar* derived from the name of (Prince) Muageris, by arguing that "Muageris" had to be a personal name taken from the descriptive designation of a people. It presented the hypothesis that the Huns in the Crimea were, really, the *Onogurs*, and the names of the two princes mentioned by Malalas as living in the region of the Maeotian Lake (Sea of Azov) and of the Kuban stream during the earlier half of the sixth century, actually referred to people under the rule of the *Magyar* tribe.[30]

Further developments had occurred on the northern shore of the Black Sea. According to the report of Theophanes, seemingly supported by the annotations of Patriarch Nicephorus, Phanagoria—on the eastern shore of the Meótis—and Bosporus—the eastern portion of the Crimea—came under the rule of the Khazars by the end of the seventh century. The Khazars occupied the eastern part of the Crimea and the Kuban river region, from where they expelled the Bulgarians, forcing them to leave and move toward the west to find [a new] home along the Danube. The Goths, however, who had been living in the southern mountainous part of the Crimea since the sixth century, held the fortress of Doros under their control until the eighth century. Doros, successfully defended by Bishop Iohannes of the Goths, who had organized an insurrection against Khazar rule, was conquered by the Khazars in 787.[31]

Therefore, in the second half of the eighth century, the Crimea, including Bosporus and Phanagoria, was in Khazar hands, with the exception of the area of the Byzantine bishopric of Chaeronea that belonged since the early eighth century under the jurisdiction of the Gothic-Byzantine Greek metropolitan of Doros. The bishopric performed a religious-political function in the field of regional missionary policy.[32]

The contemporary writ, *Notitiae episcoporum*, recorded that the "Bishop of the Huns" came under the jurisdiction of the metropolitan of Doros, together with the "Missionary bishop—that is, a bishop without a permanent see—of the Onogurs." He further recorded the see of a Byzantine bishop in the city of Itil, under Khazar control along the Volga river, as if to refer to the fact that during the second half of the century, the Christian religion had been spread out among the Khazars.[33] The anonymous author of the "Constantine–Cyril Legend" mentioned that when the missionary [Cyril] had visited them (in the 860's), the Ugors (Magyars) had attacked him with wild cries, but the monk, deep in prayer, paid no attention to them; and, after he had friendly spoken to them, he had peacefully departed from among them.[34]

On the other hand, the author of the "Methodius Legend" noted that when the missionary monk Methodius sojourned in the region of the Lower Danube (at its estuary?), the king of the Ugors visited him, and treated the missionary with respect. After a friendly conversation he let him go in peace. The "king" of the Ugors mentioned in the legend could have been one of the Magyar tribal leaders.[35]

Thus, it would come as a surprise (or, rather, knowing about the political-diplomatic aims of Byzantine church politics, less of a surprise), that in the late eighth or early ninth century, the Jewish religion had gained ground among the Khazars. Their leading social stratum had converted to the Jewish faith.[36] As already pointed out by Gyula Németh, the first historically known region of the *Magyars* was located in the area along the Kuban river; the *Onogurs* may have played an important role in the formation of the Magyars as a people. On these grounds, one may hypothesize that the Magyars and Onogurs were the same people, just as it might be assumed that the Onogur-Huns had become a part, as they may have played a major role in the formation, of the Magyars as a people.[37]

The concept of the Hun-Magyar family relationship referred to and explained by the Hungarian Anonymus of the late twelfth century,[38] and by Hungarian chronicler Simon de Kéza writing in the latter half of the thirteenth century, might have had its socio-historic origins here.[39] The compiler—who followed earlier data of information—of the *Chronicon pictum* (Chronicle), written and edited during the mid-fourteenth century, discussed the origins and development of the early Magyars, and confirmed the notion of the Hun-Magyar relationship; one of the chroniclers noted in the Chronicle—in accordance with the *Chronicle* of Bishop Saint Sigilbert of Antioch—that the Magyars descended from *Magor*, the son of Iaphet; Iaphet and his wife Ené had begotten Magor and Hunor, "a quo Magari et Huni sunt nominati." The compiler of the Chronicle described and referred to the arrival of the Huns in the Carpathian basin during the fourth century as the "First entry of the Magyars into Pannonia," while referring to the arrival of the Magyars in the same area during the 890's as the "Second entry of the Huns" in Pannonia: "let us see, when did they return to Pannonia." On the other hand, the author in the Russian Annals mentioned, anno 898, that the Magyars were passing by Kiev at that precise time.[40]

On these grounds, one would even assume that the bishop of the Huns who lived north of the Caucasus Mountains was be identical with the bishop of the Onogur-Magyars. During the mid-eighth century the (Onogur-)Magyars lived east of the Maeotian Lake; a century later, they were living west of the area.

The wanderings of the Magyars, the beginnings of their expansion "on the eastern end of Scythia," were narrated at some length, in a legendary manner, by the *Chronicon pictum*.[41] On a more positive side, one Byzantine source reporting on the 837 uprising in Macedonia referred to the Magyars by three different names in recording that they hurried to the aid of the Bulgarians who lived alongside the Danube at that time.[42]

Hungarian and Byzantine historical sources speak of the visits paid by two Magyar leaders to Constantinople during the mid-tenth century. During the 930's, an exchange of prisoners of war and a five-year truce followed the Magyar raids into Byzantine territory, though, according to chronicler Scylitzes—from whom Cedrenus had copied portions of his own report—the Turks (Magyars) had been ceaselessly devastating the Roman (Byzantine) lands when finally their leader, named Bulcsú, visited Byzantium to accept the Christian faith.[43]

One of the legendary figures of the anti-Byzantine Magyars campaigns was *Botond*, "a true Magyar; the least important among them," so the chronicler of the Chronicle recorded, who with his mace had cut such a big hole into the doors of the City's bronze gate that a five-year-old child could easily walk through it; Botond would throw his opponents to the ground so forcefully that they died immediately on the spot.[44]

Bulcsú was baptized; Emperor Constantine VII Porphyrogenitus was his godfather, who honored Bulcsú by naming him a "Patrician," providing him richly with gifts, and sending him back to his own people. Soon thereafter Gyula, Prince of the Turks, also visited the City, was baptized a Christian at the imperial court, was well treated, and given gifts. Upon his departure he was allowed to be accompanied by the monk *Hierotheos*, whom Patriarch Theophylact had previously ordained "Bishop of Turkia."[45]

Gyula had kept the faith, did not invade Byzantine territory again, treated the Christians well, had all Christian prisoners of war emancipated. On the other hand, Bulcsú did not keep the faith, breached the understanding he had reached with the emperor; he continued to devastate Byzantine territory. He behaved in a same manner toward the Franks, who defeated him in battle, captured and hanged him.[46]

The Russian Annals, *Provest' vremennÿkh let*, recorded, on the grounds of a later manuscript, in an added insert in the text, anno 1015 (the insert does not, really, strengthen the reliability of the Annals notorious for wrong dating of events), that two Magyar-speaking princes became Byzantine Christians, together with their peoples. Stefan, spoken of by the Russian author as "one who had done much good," might be identified with *Gyula* as recorded in the report by Scylitzes. In the Russian chronicler's opinion, the Byzantines had remained less forceful in the field of religion [than the Romans], and observed that when [missionaries] had arrived from Rome, they had been able to convert the Magyars to their own false beliefs.[47] J. B. Bury placed the arrival of the two leaders at the Byzantine court in the year 948; they had visited the City to negotiate extension of the truce they had previously reached with Byzantium, he wrote.[48]

The data provided by the Byzantine chroniclers—including Ioannes Zonaras of the twelfth century—were verified by Emperor Constantine VII Porphyrogenitus in his work, *De administrando imperio*, who mentioned that *Termacs[u]*, "our friend," the son of the deceased *Tavel[i]*, had visited the court, and was accompanied by

Bulcsu, the third ranked prince: *karcha*, of Turkia. The imperial author further noted that Árpád's first born was named Tarkacsu, whose son was Tavel[i], the father of Termacs[u].[49]

During the last decades of the tenth century, the politico-religious policies of the Byzantine court were gaining strength along the Maros river in the Carpathian basin. *Ajtony*, the all-powerful lord of the Maros region, whose territory reached from the Kőrös to the Tisza river, from there to Szörény, and from Szörény down to Vidin, maintained personal relations with Gyula. At Vidin, he submitted to Byzantine Christianity, and gained further political influence from the Byzantine court. At his headquarters in the town of Maros, he had a monastery built for Byzantine monks, and a church dedicated to John the Baptist. The monks lived in accordance with the Basilian rule.[50]

Early political success made Ajtony overconfident. He did not allow the passage across his territory of salt shipments on the Maros river. Therefore, King Stephen I of Hungary attacked his territory. Csanád, the royal steward and commander of the royal troops, defeated Ajtony, and occupied his territory. He buried the dead in the cemetery next to the monastery. The victorious Csanád did not, however, expel the Greek monks from the town of Maros; in order to fulfill the promise he had made before the battle, he had a monastery built in the honor of Saint George, and had the Byzantine monks transferred there, and gave orders that one-third of the town provide for their needs.[51]

The available source material provides no satisfactory information about the date of these events. The attack led by Csanád against Ajtony may be related to the war Emperor Basil II had fought with the Bulgarians. Ajtony was a Bulgarian ally, while King Stephen I supported Basil II.[52] A contemporary source even reported that King Stephen had treated the Bulgarian prisoners captured in the war well.[53] After an eight-month siege, the emperor captured Vidin and reached the border line of Ajtony's territory.[54] Ajtony now had no alternative but to submit to the emperor; it was *then* that he became a Byzantine Christian. Therefore, the Csanád-Ajtony military confrontation must have taken place after the Byzantine-Bulgarian war, when Ajtony, who retained full control over his territory, in 1028 prevented the shipping of salt on the Maros, and turned against King Stephen I;

it was then that the monarch had ordered military action against Ajtony, and the royal steward Csanád defeated Ajtony.[55]

In spite of the defeat suffered by Ajtony at the hand of King Stephen's forces, relations between the Hungarian court and Byzantium remained peaceful during Stephen's reign. The ties that had been formed between Gyula of Transylvania and Byzantine Bishop Hierotheos eventually began to influence the Magyar princely (later royal Hungarian), court, in that Sarolta, the daughter of Gyula, became the wife of Prince Géza; she had been baptized according to the Byzantine rite by Bishop Hierotheos. Sarolta was the mother of King Stephen. The Latin chronicler Bruno of Querfurt reported about Sarolta that "qua duce erat christianitatis coepta."[56]

A Latin (Benedictine) monk, Gerard [of Venice], became a trusted associate in the inner circle of King Stephen I, was appointed bishop of Csanád, and transferred—upon the defeat of Ajtony and with the approval of reeve Csanád—the Byzantine monks to nearby Oroszlános, and turned the church and monastery of Saint John into his episcopal church and the seat of his bishopric. The Basilian monastery in Oroszlános also became a Benedictine house in the thirteenth century.[57]

King Stephen I followed the line of a western-oriented Latin diplomacy, but the Greco-Latin variety of Byzantine cultural influence remained manifest in the realm for a longer period of time. As a matter of fact, the king had erected a Latin-rite church in Constantinople, built with the help of Byzantine craftsmen, and provided it with all necessities.[58] The Chronicle reports in a brief insert—the insert, presumably, rests on contemporary evidence, and it is not a tendentious twelfth century addition to the text—that for the construction of the church the monarch had erected in Óbuda, he relied upon Greek (Byzantine) craftsmen, artisans, and stonemasons, as if to point to the emphasis he had placed upon continued contacts with the Byzantine world during his reign.[59]

Since Byzantine Greeks were living in the country, Byzantine cultural influence made itself felt.[60] In the catalogue of books in the Benedictine abbey of Pannonhalma they had listed a *Psalterium Graecorum*; in one of the liturgical books of Hungarian origin preserved in Zagreb, the text for the "Blessing of the Font" on the feast of Epiphany was translated by the compiler of the volume from the Byzantine rite. The first known Latin translation of the writings of John of Damascus and Maximos was likewise prepared for the abbey of Pannonhalma; a monk named Cerbanus had translated it from a manuscript preserved in the abbey of Pilis.[61]

The royal founding charter drawn up in Greek for the community of nuns in Veszprémvölgy further shows Byzantine-Greek cultural influence; it came down to posterity in the official transcript issued by King Coloman the Learned in 1109.[62] The "renovatio" drafted in Latin follows the copied Greek text of the royal document explaining why it became necessary to renew the writ.[63]

The document reads that King Saint Stephen had, in accordance with the Byzantine-rite, an archiepiscopal monastery established in Veszprém in honor of the Mother of God. He had gathered there a multitude of religious women for the spiritual benefit of all Pannonia. The writ enumerated all of the donations and privileges granted to the monastic community; it authorized the community to expel everyone (servants, lay personnel) who would not want to live under its supervision.[64] The king granted jurisdiction over the monastery to the archbishop of Esztergom, instead of the regional bishop of Veszprém. It may be concluded from the text of this document that the monastery was founded for the Byzantine-born wife of Prince Emery, the heir to the Hungarian throne.[65] Next to the abbey he had established at Tihany in 1055, King Andrew I (1046–60) also founded a Byzantine-rite community near Visegrád.[66]

In 1204, Pope Innocent III complained that the Byzantine-rite monasteries in Hungary were in a spiritual decline, and, in order to prevent this, he wished to gather them into a bishopric.[67] According to the writ, dated April 20, 1221, of Pope Honorius III, the Hungarian king, Andrew II (1205–35), replaced the deceased Byzantine monks of this Pilis-Visegrád community with monks of the Latin rite.[68] The papal letter of January 29, 1218, made mention of the Basilian-rite monastery at Szávaszentdemeter.[69]

Byzantine-Magyar relations that dated back to the ninth century and the Byzantine Church transplanted into Magyar territory—the "first" bishop of the Magyar land (Turkia) had been ordained by the Byzantine patriarch—forced Prince Stephen (whose mother was a

Byzantine Christian, but his wife, Gisela, a Roman Catholic) to decide: would he submit to the political-religious policies of the Byzantine court—the Byzantine state structure at the peak of its political and cultural powers[70]—or turn to the Latin west establishing a foundation for his reign and the future of his country? It is a matter of record that Stephen turned to the West in the year 1000 by requesting a crown from Pope Sylvester II.[71]

Notes

1. See the report by Emperor Leo VI the Learned ["Leo Sapiens"], *Tactica*, xviii:60-61—text in *MPG*, 107, 672ff.; selections in Henrik Marczali (ed.), *Enchiridion fontium historiae Hungarorum* (Budapest, 1901), 14ff.; *MHK*, 11ff.; Gyula Moravcsik, "Bölcs Leó Taktikája mint magyar történelmi forrás" [The *Tactica* by Leo the Wise as a source for Hungarian history], *Századok*, 85 (1951), 334ff., French translation in *Acta historica Academiae Scientiarum Hungaricae*, 1 (1952), 161ff.; for background, see Ostrogorsky, 201ff., and 212ff.; György Györffy, *A magyarok elődeiről és a honfoglalásról* [Pre-Magyars and the Conquest of 896], 2nd ed. (Budapest, 1975), 108ff.; Edward Gibbon, *Decline and Fall of the Roman Empire*, LV:2 (Great Books, vols. 40-41, Chicago, 1952).

2. *Tactica*, xviii:44-48 and 64. The *unconverted* Magyars had fought on the side of Byzantium against the Bulgarians in the early 890's; the Bulgarians became [Byzantine] Christians in 864—A. Vaillant – M. Lascaris, "La date de la conversion des Bulgares," *Revue des études slaves*, 13 (1933), 6ff.

3. C f. Constantine Porphyrogenitus, *De administrando imperio*, ed. Gy. Moravcsik – R. J. H. Jenkins, rev. ed. (Washington, DC, 1967), cited hereafter as *DAI*, cc. 3, 8, 40, and 51; *MHK*, 110ff.; remarks by Karl Krumbacher, *Geschichte der byzantinischen Literatur*, 2nd ed. (Munich, 1897), 252ff.; C. A. Macartney, *The Magyars in the Ninth Century* (Cambridge, 1930; repr. 1968), 80ff. *Theophanes...Georgius monachus continuatus*, ed. I. Bekker, *CB* (Bonn, 1838), 763ff., esp. 817,20 – 819,15, had referred to the Magyars as "Unogurs," "Huns," and "Turks." See further Johannes Zonaras, *Epitomae historiarum*, libri xiii-xviii, ed. Th. Büttner-Wobst, *CB* (Bonn, 1897), 442ff., compare with the annotations of the Russian Annals, where in the Laurentian MS, anno 902, and in the Nikon MS, anno 903, references were made to the Magyars. Cf. Antal Hodinka (ed.), *Az orosz Évkönyvek magyar vonatkozásai* [Annotations in the Russian annals related to Hungarian history] (Budapest, 1916), 46, 48, and the pertinent remarks by the editor, *ibid.*, 17ff.; selections from Russian texts in Latin and in Hungarian translations, *MHK*, 362ff. Márta Font, *Oroszország, Ukrajna, Rusz· fejezetek a keleti szlávok történetéből* [Russia and the Ukraine: Chapters of the History of the Eastern Slavs] (Pécs, 1995), 27ff., and 107ff., and a review of the book by Daniel Bagi, in *Aetas*, 1997-2/3, 251ff.; further, cf. George Vernadsky – Michael de Ferdinándy, *Studien zur ungarischen Frühgeschichte* (Munich, 1957), 7ff., esp. 10ff. on "die Madjaren in den altrussischen Chroniken; and "die Madjaren in Kiew," *ibid.*, 26ff.; J. Deér, "A IX századi magyar történet időrendjéhez" [The chronology of Hungarian events in the ninth century], *Századok*, 79-80 (1945-46), 3ff.; K. Czeglédi, "A IX századi történelem főkérdései" [Main issues in the ninth century], *Magyar Nyelv*, 41 (1945), 33ff.

4. *DAI*, c. 40; G. Fehér, "A bolgár-törökök kapcsolatai a magyarsággal és a legújabb magyar őstörténetkutatás" [The Bulgaro-Turkish relations with the Magyars, and the state of recent Hungarian historical research], *Századok*, 69 (1935), Suppl., 513ff.; S. L. Tóth, "A honfoglalás időpontja" [Remarks on the date of the Conquest], *Acta historica Szegediensis*, 102 (1995), 3ff.

5. *DAI*, c. 40; Cf. Georgius Monachus continuatus in *Theophanes Continuatus, Ioannes Cameniata, Symeon Magister, Georgius Monachus*, ed. I. Bekker, *CB* (Bonn, 1838), 357,12 – 359,16; S. L. Tóth, "A Liuntika-rejtély [The Liutica mystery], *Magyar Nyelv*, 90 (1994) 168ff.

6. *DAI*, c. 40; Toynbee, 464ff., and 599ff.

7. *DAI*, c. 40.

8. *DAI*, c. 40; Romilly J. H. Jenkins provided a warm, human, and humane characterization of the imperial author born in purple in his *Byzantium: the Imperial Centuries, AD 610-1071* (London, 1966, repr. Toronto–London, 1987), 256ff., a book "not written for the scholar, but for the student"; Gyula Moravcsik's most impressive study, "Sagen und Legenden über Kaiser Basileios I," *Dumbarton Oaks Papers*, 15 (1961), 59ff.; see also G. Fehér, "Ungarns Gebietsgrenzen in der Mitte des X Jahrhunderts — nach dem De administrando imperio des Konstantinos Porphyrogennetos," *Ungarische Jahrbücher*, 2 (1922), 37ff.; Györffy, op. cit., 115ff.; S. L. Tóth, "Árpád *magas arkhón* ciméhez" [The *magas archon* title of Árpád], *Magyar Nyelv*, 86 (1990), 228ff.; idem, "A kabarok (javarok) a 9 századi magyar törzsszövetségben" [Place of the Kabars in the Magyar tribal framework during the ninth century], *Századok*, 118 (1984), 92ff.; idem, "A magyar fejedelmi méltóság fejlődése" [Formation of the princely dignity among the Magyars], *Acta historica Szegediensis*, 83 (1986), 3ff.

9. Cf. *Annales Fuldenses sive Annales regni Francorum orientalis*, ed. G. H. Pertz – F. Kurze, SSrG (Hannover, 1891; repr. 1978), a. 896; in *DAI*, c. 50, the "Slavs" were defeated twice; *DAI*, c. 40, mentioned only one defeat; E. Dümmler, *Geschichte des oströmischen Reiches*, 2nd ed., 3 vols. (Leipzig, 187-88), III, 443ff., and III, 451.

10. Regino, anno 894, but Svatopluk had died in that year; as recorded in *DAI*, c. 41, his sons had fought among themselves—as if to point to the conclusion that the Magyars had exploited the family feud and conquered the Danube-Tisza region. Incidentally, in the papal correspondence Svatopluk is being referred to *Sphentopulco principi*, or *Zventopolco*—cf. Potthast, nn. 3407 [2649], and 3708, or *Zvuentapu de Maravna* (!)—cf. Potthast, nn. 3267, 3368, and *Sfentopulco*—*ibid.*, n. 3319 [2540]; Ferenc Makk, "Külföldi források és a korai magyar történelem" [Non-Magyar sources dealing with early Hungarian history], *Acta historica Szegediensis*, 102 (1995), 25ff.

11. Cf., e.g., *DAI*, c. 8; Toynbee, 464ff.; also, the 76 page study by Ernst Dümmler, "Über südöstlichen Marken des fränkischen Reiches unter den Karolingern," *Archiv für österreichische Geschichte*, 10 (1853), 1ff., esp. 15ff., 52ff., and 58ff.; S. L. Tóth, "A honfoglalás időpontja," 3ff.; György Györffy – B. Zólyomi, "A Kárpát medence s Etelköz egy évezred előtt" [The Carpathian basin and the Land-Between-the-Rivers a thousand years ago], *Magyar tudomány*, 103 (1996), 899ff.

12. Cf. H. Homeyer, *Attila der Hunnenkönig von seinen Zeitgenossen dargestellt* (Berlin, 1951), 166ff.; István Bóna, *A húnok és nagykirályaik* [The Huns and their Great Kings] (Budapest, 1993), 37ff., 59f., and my review of this work in *East European Quarterly*, 30 (1996-97), 529f.; I. Bóna, "Régészetünk és a magyar honfoglalás" [The Hungarian archaeologist's view of the Magyar land-taking], *Magyar tudomány*, 103 (1996), 927ff.

13. Cf. *DAI*, c. 40; Emperor Constantine VII ostentatiously recorded mainly Magyar [Turk] events related to the Khazars—as, for instance, he depicted tendentiously the election of their prince; he enumerated the names of the Magyar tribes, regions of their previous settlements in a manner that reflected Khazar coloring. Cf. Toynbee, 498ff.

14. See the list of names of bishops attending the Synod of Nicea, 325, in J. D. Mansi (ed.), *Sacrorum conciliorum nova et amplissima collectio*, 31 vols. (Florence–Venice, 1759-98), cited hereafter as Mansi, *Concilia*, II, 692ff., esp. 696d, and the remarks by Philip Labbe, *ibid.*, II, 702b; also, F. Dölger, "Rom in der Gedankenwelt der Byzantiner," *Zeitschrift für Kirchengeschichte*, 56 (1937), 1ff., esp. 39ff. Eusebius of

Caesarea, *Historia ecclesiastica*, ed. Kirsop Lake – J. E. L. Oulton, Loeb ser. (Cambridge, MA, repr.), iii:1, remarked that the Apostle Andrew had already visited Scythia; cf. A. Harnack, *Die Mission und Ausbreitung des Christentums in der ersten drei Jahrhunderten*, 2 vols., 4th rev ed. (Leipzig, 1924), I, 108.

15. Many Armenians became Christians, *ibid.*, II, 747ff., in reference to Eusebius, ix:8; J. Markwart, "Die Entstehung der armenischen Bistümer," *Orientalia Christiana*, 27 (1932), 141ff.; on Gregory, see P. de Lagarde, "Die Akten Gregors von Armenien," *Abhandlungen der k. Gesellschaft der Wissenschaften zu Göttingen*, 35 (1888), 89ff., esp. 115f., and compare with K. Lukácsy, *A magyarok őselei hajdankori nevek, lakhely, eredeti örmény kútfők alapján* [The early ancestors of the Magyars according to ancient names, places of residence, and original Armenian sources] (Kolozsvár, 1870), 114f.

16. Cf. The letters of Nicholas Mysticus, *MPG*, 111, 9ff., esp. 40ff.; and, Harnack, II, 750, 762. Letter XX of the Patriarch is of interest, where he mentioned that Symeon, the Bulgarian khan, had re-read the old histories (and learned from them)—*MPG*, 111, 133; the Patriarch argued that Symeon had nearly succeeded in capturing Byzantium—cf. Letter V, *ibid.*, 111, 45. One is to recall that it was the Patriarch who had crowned Symeon—Georg Ostrogorsky, "Die Krönung Symeons von Bulgarien durch den Patriarchen Nikolaos Mysticos," *Actes du IVe Congrès international des études byzantines*, vol. I (Sofia, 1935), 275ff.

17. Cf. *MPL*, 22, 600 and 695—that is, epp. 60 and 77.

18. See *MPL*, 22, 870, ep. 107—or, *Jerome, Select Letters*, ed. F. A. Wright, Loeb ser. (Cambridge, MA, 1933; repr. 1991), 337ff.

19. Saint Jerome, ep. 77, c. 8, *ibid.*, 307ff.

20. See Sozomen, "Historia ecclesiastica," vii:26, *MPG*, 67, 1500; P. de Lagarde, "Die Akten Gregors von Armenien," 115f.

21. Cf. Cosmas Indicopleustes, *Christian Topography*, ed. E. O. Winstedt (Cambridge, 1909), 119, who said that, besides Persia, one could find Christian churches also on Hun territory.

22. Georg Ostrogorsky, *Geschichte*, 62.

23. R. Hennig, "Die Einführung der Seidenrapenzucht ins Byzantinerreich," *Byzantinische Zeitschrift*, 33 (1933), 295ff.

24. R. Hennig, "Das Christentum im mittelalterlichen Asien und sein Einfluss auf die Sage vom Priester Johannes," *Historische Vierteljahrschrift*, 29 (1934), 234ff.

25. See Ioannes Malalas *Chronographia*, ed. L. Dindorf, *CB* (Bonn, 1831), 431,16 - 432,12.

26. For the same segment, cf. Theophanis *Chronographia*, ed. C. de Boor, *CB*, 2 vols. (Bonn, 1883), I, 175,24 - 176,17; for the Latin translation, see *ibid.*, II, 133f.

27. Georgios Cedrenos Iohannes Scylitzae *Opera*, ed. I. Bekker, 2 vols. *CB* (Bonn, 1838-39), I, 644,13-645,6. E. M. Jeffreys, "The attitude of Byzantine chroniclers toward ancient history," *Byzantion*, 49 (1979), 192ff.

28. Cf. Theophanes, I, 175f., and II, 133f.; Gyula Moravcsik, "Muageris király [King Muageris]," *Magyar Nyelv*, 23 (1927), 258ff.; for background study, cf. Károly Kerényi, *Görög mitológia* [Greek mythology] (Budapest, 1977), 265ff., and 303ff.; this part of the book did not appear in the English version, *Greek Gods*, tr. Magda Kerényi (London, 1972); see further, Gustav Schwab, *Die schönsten Sagen des klassischen Altertums*, 30th ed., ed. Gotthold Klee (Güthersloh, 1907), 137ff.

29. See Nicephori archiepiscopi Constantinopolitani *Opuscula historica*, ed. C. de Boor (Leipzig, 1888), 12.

30. Gyula Németh, *A honfoglaló magyarság kialakulása* [Formation of the Magyars as a people before the conquest of 896] (Budapest, 1930), 165ff.; according to the revised new edition, ed. Árpád Berta (Budapest, 1991), 195f., the author(s) expressed a different opinion: there is not even a trace of mentioning Grodas and Muageris in the text. See further, *ibid.*, 146ff. Bálint Hóman – Gyula Szekfű, *Magyar történet* [Hungarian history], 5 vols., 6th ed. (Budapest, 1939), I, 50f. One ought to note that, as late as the ninth century, the Bulgarians were known as Huns; cf. "Altera Vita s. Joannici monachus," by Peter the Monk, i:5, in *Acta sanctorum Bollandiana*, 60 vols. to October XI (Paris–Rome, 1864-76), cited hereafter as *ASS*, Nov. II-1, 386.

31. Cf. "Vita Iohannis episcopis Gothiae," i:5 and ii:7; he described his bishopric, ii:8-13, and made mention of the Khazars, iv:22-28. Cf. *ASS*, Iun. V, 190ff.; see further "De s. Joanne episcopo Gothiae," *ibid.*, Iun. V, 184ff. Compare with Gyula Moravcsik, *Az onogurok történetéhez* [History of the Onogurs] (Budapest, 1930), 30f.

32. Cf. C. de Boor, "Nachträge zu den Notitiae episcopatuum," *Zeitschrift für Kirchengeschichte*, 12 (1890), 303ff., and 519ff., especially 531 and 533f.; and, 14 (1893), 573ff.; on the date of origin of this "Notice," see the discussion by H. Gelzer, "Die kirchliche Geographie Griechenlands vor dem Slaweneinbruch," *Zeitschrift für wissenschaftliche Theologie*, 35 (1892), 419ff.

33. The "Notitiae" mentioned the Khazar town of Itil (=Volga), seat of a bishop, *ibid.*, 533; Németh, 164ff.; Sozomen, "Historia ecclesiastica," vii:26, recorded the relations of Theotimus, bishop of Tomi, with the Huns—cf. *MPG*, 67, 1500.

34. The "Vita ss. Cyrilli et Methodii" version in *Archiv für Kenntniss österreichischen Geschichtsquellen*, XIII (1854), 153ff., deals mainly with Cyrill; compare with E. Dümmler – R. Miklosich, "Die Legende vom hl. Cyrillus. Vita Methodii russicoslovenice et latine," in *Denkschriften der kk. Akademie der Wissenschaften, hist. Klasse, Wien*, XIX (1870), 214ff.; *MHK*, 348ff.; Francis Dvornik, *Les légéndes de Constantin et de Méthode vues de Byzance* (Prague, 1933), 148ff.; I. Sági, "Szent Cyrill és Metód életműve a legújabb kutatások alapján" [The life work of Sts. Cyrill and Method in the light of recent research], *Vigilia*, 28 (1963), 592ff.; Péter Király, "A Konstantin és Metód legenda Magyar részletei" [Data concerning the Magyars in the Constantine and Methodius legends], *A honfoglalásról sok szemmel* [In search of the land-taking under many aspects], ed. György Györffy, 4 vols. (Budapest, 1994-1997), vol. II: *A honfoglalás írott forrásai* [The written source evidence of the land-taking], eds. László Kovács – László Veszprémy (Budapest, 1996), 113ff.; also, Péter Király, "A magyar-szláv kapcsolatok a honfoglasásig a szláv írott források tükrében" [Magyar-Slavic contacts before the land-taking in the mirror of Slavic written sources], *Magyar tudomány*, 87 (1980), 357ff.

35. The author of the *Vita Methodii*, c. 15, recorded that on the lower Danube—at the estuary?—the king of the Ugors had met and treated with great respect the missionary monk Methodius; cf. H. Brückner's argument, *Die Wahrheit über die Slawenapostel* (Tübingen, 1913), 94ff., that the term "Hungarian king" had been added by a Russian scribe to the text because Pannonia and Moravia at that time were under Hungarian rule, and R. Ratkos, "Über die Interpretation der Vita Methodius," *Byzantinoslavica*, 28 (1967), 118ff., on the title "Hungarian king," challenged by Péter Király, "A magyarok említése a Method legendában" [Mention of the Magyars in the Methodius legend], *Magyar Nyelv*, 70 (1974), 269ff., and 406ff.

The eventual conquest of Moravia by the Magyars was regarded in a thirteenth century *legend* as the to-be-expected just punishment of God because of the lawlessness and heresy that had prevailed on Moravian soil—cf. Gyula Kristó – Imre H. Tóth, "A legrégibb Naum-legenda s a magyar honfoglalás" [The oldest Naum-legend and the Magyar land-taking], *Acta historica Szegediensis*, 58 (1977), 13ff., in referring to, and printing, a Hungarian translation of the *Naum Legend*—text published in *Magnae Moraviae fontes historici II*, vol. 118 of *Opera Universitatis Brunensis* (Brno, 1967), 177-79; also, Franz Zagiba, "Zur Geschichte Kyrills und Methodius und der bayerischen Ostmission," *Jahrbücher für Geschichte Osteuropas*, 9 (1961), 1ff.

36. Regarding the Jewish faith and its impact upon the Khazars, see Németh, *Honfoglaló magyarság*, 163f.; further, the reports by Ibn Rusta and Gardēzī, in Macartney, *Ninth Century*, 197ff.; see also the record by Ibn Fozlan and el-Mas'udi, *ibid.*, 198 and 201; *MHK*, 141ff., and 197ff.; further 247ff. Observations made by Németh, 224ff., and nn., 28–32, ought to be compared with J. Mayendorff's study, "Byzantine view of Islam," *Dumbarton Oaks Papers*, 18 (1964), 115ff.; also D. M. Dunlop, *The History of the Jewish Chazars* (Princeton, 1954), 89ff.

37. Németh, 146ff, and 182ff.; Moravcsik *Onogurok*, 35f.

38. Cf. the Hungarian Anonymus, *Gesta Ungarorum*, in *MHK*, 392ff.; Scriptores *rerum Hungaricarum*, ed. Emericus Szentpétery, 2 vols. (Budapest, 1937-38), cited hereafter as *SSH*, I, 33ff., cc. 1 and 50; on Anonymus, cf. C. A. Macartney, *The Medieval Hungarian Historians* (Cambridge, 1953), 33ff.; János Horváth, *Árpádkori latinnyelvű irodalmunk stílusproblémák* [Stylistic questions of the Latin literature of the Árpád age] (Budapest, 1954), 350ff.; further, the learned arguments of Gyula Kristó, "Szempontok Anonymus Gestájának megítéléséhez" [Some comments on the importance of the work by Anonymus], *Acta historica Szegediensis*, 56 (1979), 45ff.

39. Simon de Kéza, *Gesta Ungarorum*, cc. 3-4 and 24; cf. *SSH*, I, 141ff.; Macartney, *Hungarian Historians*, 89ff., esp. 95ff.

40. The *Chronicon pictum*, referred to as the Chronicle; for text, cf. *SSH*, I, 239ff., cc. 3-4 and 26; Sigilbert mentioned, *ibid.*, I, 249,13-16; see note 6, and compare with the Hungarian Anonymus, *Gesta Ungarorum*, c. 1; see further, Regino, anno 889. On the text of the Chronicle, cf. Macartney, *Hungarian Historians*, 133ff. The author-compiler of the Russian Annals did note, anno 898, that the Magyars had passed by Kiev—cf. S. H. Cross – O. P. Sherbowitz-Wetzor (eds.), *The Russian Primary Chronicle* (Cambridge, MA, 1953), 62, and 235, n. 28; or, selections in Hodinka, *Orosz évkönyvek*, 40, 42. Further, see Font, op. cit., 13ff., or Makk, art. cit. (1995), 39f. The drawing in the Chronicle—cf. Dezső Dercsényi (ed.), *Chronicon pictum: Képes Krónika*, 2 vols. (Budapest, 1963), vol. I: facsimile, fol. 2'b—depicted Hungarian horsemen on a scout mission, as they were "spying for" the natural riches of their future homeland. The facsimile (that is, volume I), ought to be compared with Christopher de Hamel, *Medieval Craftsmen, Scribes and Illuminators* (Toronto, 1992), esp. 45ff.

41. For cc. 5–6, see *SSH*, I, 250ff.; S. L. Tóth, "Megjegyzések a honfoglalás szakaszaihoz" [Some remarks concerning the time sequence of the Magyar conquest of the Carpathian basin], *Századok*, 130 (1996), 877ff.

42. See *Georgius Monachus continuatus*, etc., ed. I. Bekker, *CB* (Bonn, 1838), 818f.; Gyula Moravcsik, "Sagen und Legenden über Kaiser Basileios I," *Dumbarton Oaks Papers*, XV (1961), 59ff., esp. 75; also, György Székely, "La Hongrie et Byzance aux Xe – XIIe siècles," *Acta historica Academiae Scientiarum Hungaricae*, 13 (1957), 291ff.; Ferenc Makk, "Les relations hungaro-byzantines aux Xe-XIIe siècles," *European intellectual trends and Hungary*, ed. Ferenc Glatz (Budapest, 1990), 11ff. [offprint].

43. For detail, cf. *Ioannis Scylitzae Synopsis historiarum*, ed. I. Thurn (Berlin–New York, 1973), 231,55-57, and 237,59-76. On Scylitzes, see Gyula Moravcsik, *A magyar történet bizánci forrásai* [Byzantine sources of Hungarian history] (Budapest, 1934), 134ff. Idem, *Byzantium and the Magyars* (Amsterdam–Budapest, 1970), 61ff., and 135f. The exchange of prisoners of war in 934 was mentioned by *Georgius Monachus continuatus*, cited *CB* ed., 855, and 913,16 – 914,5; the referred to five-year truce was also recorded by *Theophanes Continuatus*, cf. *ibid.*, 430,22 - 431,3.

44. Chronicle, c. 62, *SSH*, I, 310f.; further, Anonymus, c. 43, *ibid.*, I, 87f., and Kéza, c. 42, *ibid.*, I, 171. Henrik Marczali, "A Botond-legenda történeti kapcsolatai" [Historical meaning of the Botond Legend], *Akadémiai Értesítő*, 27 (1916), 90ff.

45. Scylitzes, ed. cit., 239,59-76. Ödön Málnási, "A kereszténység Magyarország területén a honfoglalásig," [Christianity on the territory of Hungary before the Conquest], *Katholikus Szemle*, 40 (1926), 462ff.; J. Karácsonyi, "Mi köze a görög egyháznak a magyarok megtéréséhez?" [Did the Byzantine Church play a role in the Magyars' conversion?], *ibid.*, 14 (1900), 306ff.

46. Scylitzes, ed. cit., 237,73-76; *Ioannis Zonarae Epitomae historiarum libri XIII-XVIII*, ed. Th. Büttner-Wobst, *CB* (Bonn, 1897), 484,7-19. Bulcsú's execution recorded by Anonymus, c. 55, *SSH*, I, 109ff.; by Kéza, c. 40, *ibid.*, I, 169; and, in the Chronicle, c. 60, *ibid.*, I, 308. Moravcsik, *Bizánci források*, 185ff.; Georgius Pray, *Annales veteres Hunnorum, Avarorum et Hungarorum* (Vienna, 1761), 358ff.

47. Hodinka, 52, 54, and 53, n. 2. This segment is, understandably, missing from the Cross – Sherbowitz-Wetzor edition.

48. J. B. Bury, "The Treatise De administrando imperio," *Byzantinische Zeitschrift*, 15 (1906), 517ff., esp. 561f.

49. See *DAI*, c. 40. Bulcsú held the position of "karcha." See Tóth, art. cit. (1990); Gy. Györffy, "A honfoglaló magyarság települési rendjéhez" [Settlements of the Magyars after the conquest], *Archaeológiai Értesítő*, 97 (1970), 191ff.

50. Ajtony, cited also as Ohtum, or Othum, cf. *SSH*, I, 50,1-4, where Csanád—who had Ajtony defeated in battle—will be referred to as *nepos regis*; further, *ibid.*, I, 89,11-25, and I, 90,9-10; and, compare with the "Legenda maior s. Gerardi," cc. 8 and 10, *ibid.*, II, 494ff. Géza Fehér's 164 page study, "Bulgarisch-ungarische Beziehungen in den V–XI Jahrhunderten," *Keleti Szemle*, 19 (1921), 25ff., esp. 145ff., and 152; Hóman – Szekfű, I, 178f. The time frame recorded in the Legend can be debated—cf. József Deér, *Magyar torzsszervezet és a magyar királyság külpolitikája* [Magyar tribal organization, and the foreign policy of the Hungarian court] (Kaposvár, 1928), 47.

51. Cf. Gerard's "Legenda maior," cc. 8, and 9—*SSH*, II, 490; Macartney, *Hungarian Historians*, 154ff., esp. 157f.

52. *SSH*, II, 493,13-29; K. Juhász, *A csanádi püspökség története alapításától a tatárjárásig* [History of the Csanád bishopric since its foundation to the Mongol invasion] (Makó, 1930), 38, 46; idem, *Die Stifte der Tschanader Diözese im Mittelalter* (Munster, 1927).

53. See "Fundatio ecclesiae s. Albani Namucensis," anno 1047, *MGHSS*, XV-2, 963; the Chronicle, c. 67, *SSH*, I, 317; Harry Bresslau, "Fundatio ecclesiae S. Albani Namucensis," *Neues Archiv*, 8 (1883), 592—in sharp contrast, indeed, with the attitude of the Byzantine emperor, cf. Scylitzes, 348,9 – 349,44.

54. Idem, 346,44 – 347,75; Cedrenus, 454f.; Jenkins, 325f. Gyula Kristó, *Megjegyzések az úgy nevezett 'pogánylázadások' kora történetéhez* [Some remarks to the history of the so-called 'age of pagan uprisings'] (Szeged, 1965), 5ff.

55. Gerard's "Legenda maior," c. 8, *SSH*, II, 489f.

56. See *MGHSS*, IV, 607; and, Anonymus, c. 26, *SSH*, I, 68f., or the Chronicle, cc. 30 and 63, *ibid.*, I, 290f., and I, 312,1-4.

57. Gerard's "Legenda maior," c. 8; Juhász, *Stifte*, 66.

58. See "Legenda maior s. Stephani regis," c. 11, *SSH*, II, 386; Hartvic's "Life of King St. Stephen", c. 13, *ibid.*, II, 419,26-29. Gyula Kristó, "A nagyobbik és a Hartvik-féle István-legenda szövegkapcsolatához," [Some remarks on the textual relationship between King Stephen's 'Legenda maior,' and Hartvic's 'Life of King St. Stephen'], *Acta historica Szegediensis*, 90 (1990), 43ff.; B. Leib, *Rome, Kiev et Byzance a la fin du XIe siècle* (Paris, 1924), 82.

59. If the Chronicle, c. 67, report rests on contemporary evidence—cf. *SSH*, I, 317,7-9; could, however, this sentence be a late insert? See János Horváth, *Stílus-problémák*, 341f.; György Györffy, *Krónikáink és a magyar őstörténet* [The Hungarian chronicles and early Magyar history] (Budapest, 1948), 157 and 178.

60. Chronicle, c. 53, *SSH*, I, 303,11-22.

61. Cf. *Translatio latina Ioannis Damasceni: De orthodoxa fide, I: iii, 108, saeculo XII in Hungaria confecta*, ed. R. L. Szigeti (Budapest, 1940); Ch. H. Haskins, *The Renaissance of the Twelfth Century* (Cambridge, Mass., 1927), 296; idem, *Studies in the History of Medieval Science* (Cambridge, Mass., 1927), ch. 8; Jean Leclercq, *The Love of Learning and the Desire for God* (New York, 1961), 122, and, "Origène au XIIe siècle," *Irénikon*, 24 (1951), 425ff., esp. 433ff. On John of Damascus, see also Funk – Bihlmeyer, II, 57 and 60.

62. See *Regesta regum stirpis Arpadianae critico-diplomatica*, ed. Emericus Szentpétery – Iván Borsa, 2 vols. (Budapest, 1923-87), cited hereafter as *RA*, nn. 1 and 42; Bálint Hóman, "A veszprémvölgyi 1109-i oklevél hitelessége" [Authenticity of the 1109 founding charter for the monastery in Veszprém Valley], *Turul*, 29 (1911), 123ff., and 167ff.; Géza Fehér, "A bolgár egyház kisérletei és sikerei hazánkban" [Successful attempts made by the Byzantine Church in Hungary], *Századok*, 61-62 (1927-28), 1ff.

63. Idem, "Szent István király görög oklevele" [The Greek charter issued by King St. Stephen], *ibid.*, 51 (1917), 99ff., and 225ff.; J. Darkó, "A veszprémvölgyi apácamonostor alapító leveléről" [Some remarks on the founding charter of the monastic community for religious women in Veszprém Valley], *Egyetemes Philológiai Közlöny*, 41 (1917), 257ff., and 336ff.

64. Gy. Czebe, *A veszprémvölgyi oklevél görög szövege* [The Greek text of the charter of the monastic community for women in Veszprém Valley] (Budapest, 1916); text also in Emil Jakubovich – Dezső Pais (eds.), *Ó-magyar Olvasókönyv* [An Old-Hungarian Reader] (Pécs, 1929), 14ff. It resembles a writ addressed to a private person.

65. The founder: *auctor*, came from among the members of the royal family, as it is implied by the detailed care shown in the charter for the monastic community; could the Byzantine-born wife of Prince Emery, King Stephen's son and heir to the throne, have been the founder of the community, or did the foundation honor the Princess? According to the "Vita Emerici," c. 5, *SSH*, II, 454f., the prince had to marry a royal princess, although the princess could also have been Polish!—see *ibid.*, note 1. The phrase, however, in the Latin text, "iuxta linguam auctoris monasterii," may refer to a Byzantine wife—*RA*, n. 42. According to the "Legenda Beatae Margaritae de Hungarian," c. 12, she had to be Byzantine; cf. *SSH*, II, 689. Imre Madzsar, "Szent Imre herceg legendája" [The legend of Prince St. Emery], *Századok*, 65 (1931), 34ff.

66. Cf. "Legenda maior s. Gerardi," c. 15, *SSH*, II, 503,26-29; A. Hodinka, *A munkácsi görögkatolikus püspökség története* [History of the Greek Catholic bishopric of Munkács] (Budapest, 1910), 13ff.

67. August Potthast (ed.), *Regesta pontificum Romanorum*, 2 vols. (Berlin, 1875), n. 2184, dated April 16, 1204, and addressed to [the] Bishop [Simon] of Várad; text in G. Fejér (ed.), *Codex diplomaticus Hungariae ecclesiasticus ac civilis*, 44 vols. (Budae, 1829–42), cited hereafter as *CD*, II, 429f.

68. Cf. Potthast, n. 6619; text in August Theiner (ed.), *Vetera monumenta historiam Hungariae sacram illustrantia*, 2 vols. (Romae, 1859–60), cited hereafter as *VMH*, n. 53; and, *CD*, III-1, 310f.

69. Potthast, n. 5681; *VMH*, n. 16.

70. Ostrogorsky, op. cit., 217ff.; Robert Browning, *The Byzantine Empire* (New York, 1980), 96ff.; Jenkins, *Byzantium*, 198ff., and 256ff.

71. On this, cf. Hartvic's "Vita sancti Stephani regis," cc. 9–10, *SSH*, II, 412ff.; and, the record in the Chronicle, cc. 64-66, *ibid.*, I, 312ff.; Gábor Frank, "Die Änderungen des Images Stephans des Heiligen in der Geschichtserziehung unseres Zeitalters," *Specimina nova dissertationum ex Instituto historico Universitatis de Iano Pannonio nominatae*, 4 (1988), 111ff.

III

The Question of Belonging

1. The Imperial Church and the Papal Curia

> Qui tamen (i.e., Leo papa III), postquam nullus probator criminum esse voluit, coram omni populo in basilica beati Petri apostoli evangelium portans ambonem conscendit invocatoque sanctae Trinitatis nomine iureiurando ab obiectis se criminibus purgavit.
>
> *Annales regni Francorum*, anno 800*

The Magyars, who had fled to and settled in the mid-Danubian basin during the mid-890s, took possession of the territory the Avars had left behind when they were annihilated by Charlemagne's forces during the 790s. Before the Magyars' arrival various peoples had partitioned the Avars' "inheritance." The Franks expanded their sovereignty over the former Roman province[s] of Pannonia; the Moravians predominated over the Vág [Váh] river valley in the north, as far as the estuary of the Garam stream into the Danube, while of the eastern part the Bulgarians became the new masters. Khan Omortog of Bulgaria moved westward along the Drave river to expel the Franks, masters of the Slavs who had previously settled there, from the southern parts of Pannonia; now, it was the Bulgarian *rectores* who ruled over the Slavic population. The Franks, however, forced the Bulgarians to withdraw to Sirmium. In 824, the Bulgarians not only had to pay respects to the [east-]Frankish ruler, but they became his allies—though they would expand their sway over the Great Plains (east of the Danube, and on both banks of the Tisza river) up to the line of the Mátra mountains; as allies of the Franks, however, they did not invade Moravian territory.[1]

"Greater Moravia" included the earlier settlements of the Quadi, the region between the Morava and Garam streams, and reached the northern border of the territory occupied by the Bulgarian Khan. Transylvania was also under Bulgarian control at this time; the salt mines of Transylvania provided the khan with solid source of revenue.[2]

Mountains closed off the mid-Danubian region from the north and from the east; rivers opened the way toward the west and the south, as well as along the Olt river toward the southeast. It was in this geographical area that the population had been contacted by Christian missionaries.[3] On the western border of Pannonia, Saint Rupert, the missionary of the [east-] Franks laid the foundations of Latin Christianity at the time, when Prince Theodore of Bavaria had visited Rome to gain baptism in 715. The Anglo-Saxon Boniface, "praeceptor" of the Germans, with papal approval organized the ecclesiastical administrative structure of the east-Frank territories during the 730s. The Church had earlier converted the Carantanians and the Avars to the Christian faith under the aegis of Rome.[4]

On the south-eastern border of the east-Frank territory, Pannonia also became a part of this developing ecclesiastical organization. The regional (Slavic) rulers, however, wanted to organize their church into autonomous regions. They did not particularly wish to appease the Roman See in their endeavor. That is the reason why in the European northwest Pope Gregory the Great in 597 authorized the Roman Catholic mission in Anglo-Saxon England.[5] That was why popes Gregory II and Gregory III wanted to missionize the Frankish-Bavarian territory under the headship of the Roman curia—leaving out of consideration the possibility that the strengthened papal organization would soon clash with the gradually evolving Frankish-Bavarian administrative political structure that aimed at gaining territorial predominance in the area.[6]

The Frankish court with its centralizing policy that reached back to, or even beyond Charlemagne, suspected, and not without reason, the well timed political tendencies, the religious-diplomatic activities of Rome, and it did everything possible to counteract them. That is why Duke Tassilo of Bavaria, the diplomatic champion of the Roman See, had to fail in the face of the massively aggressive ecclesiastical policies of Charlemagne.[7] According to the imaginative plan of the

Carolingian court, the Christian ruler held the role of *Vicarius Christi* in the administrative structure of the territorial ("Imperial") Church, while the bishops of the Church were royal public servants. In other words, the bishop in charge of the planned "imperial" missionary policy in Pannonia had to perform a territorial task by expanding Christianity and extending the Frank court's political might along with it in the region assigned to their care.[8]

Pepin, son of Charlemagne, who was in charge of the anti-Avar campaign of the 790s, had met with the bishops in Regensburg—the bishops were all appointees of Charlemagne—in order to discuss with them planned policy of Christianization, and the policy associated with it, in the occupied territories. They decided to set up three missionary districts, and placed the bishop of *Passau* in charge of the left bank of the Danube, in the Moravian region; the bishop of *Salzburg* had to take [religious-]spiritual control of the right bank of the Danube as far south as the Drave river, and as far east as the Rába stream (a territorial triangle bordered by the Danube, the Rába and the Drave); while the See of *Aquileia* would take care of converting the Crain (Krajna) region between the Drave and Suave rivers.[9] The Franks had previously conquered the region of Carantania; after defeating the Carantanians, Charlemagne had assigned the area south of the Drave to the care of Aquileia.[10] Charlemagne further elevated Bishop Arno of Salzburg to the position of archbishop in 798; as the first archbishop of Salzburg, Arno said Mass, preached sermons, and consecrated churches in the territories under his jurisdiction. His vicar was Theoderic, who aided the archbishop in his missionary endeavors.[11]

In the field of this missionary endeavor carried out with political undertones, the *chorepiscopi* had played an important role: these did not have their own diocesan sees, but, as "migrant bishops," remained under the jurisdiction of the [regional] archbishop, or bishop.[12] Vergilius of Salzburg (767–84) had, as late as the 770s, sent out migrant bishops with directions to consecrate the recently built churches in his ecclesiastical territory.[13] The Carantanians, however, being early converts to Christianity, were served only by presbyters for their spiritual needs. On the other hand, Archbishop Adalram of Salzburg (821–36) had ordered his episcopal vicar Otto to visit the lands of the

Carantanians.[14] The bishop of Passau had authorized migrant bishops to carry on with missionary work in the areas assigned to his see; mainly, the church of St. Peter played a major role in missionary work.[15] The clerics of St. Peter's had converted, in about 836, the Avar Khagan to the Christian faith.[16]

It is against this religious-political backdrop that one is to understand why the Czechs were paying tax to the Frankish court since the times of Charlemagne.[17] In 822, Czech and Moravian envoys presented gifts to Louis the Pious, and fourteen Czech nobles asked Louis the German for sending Christian to them in 845.[18] The Moravians lived under their Prince Moimar in the lands between the Morava and Vág streams, and requested Frankish support. East of Moimar's territory, in the region of Nitra (=Nyitra), Prince Pribina ruled. In 836, Adalram of Salzburg consecrated a church in Nitra in honor of St. Emmeram, at a time when Pribina was still a pagan.[19]

Moimar and Pribina did not maintain a good relationship with one another. When Moimar invaded the land east of the Morava, and Pribina had to flee to Ratbod, duke of the Ostmark, where he was baptized a Christian. Ratbod disliked Pribina, and Pribina, with son Kocel, visited the court of Bulgaria, where they were unwelcome and sought refuge at the court of Ratimir, the Croatian prince of Siscia (=Sziszek). Ratimir, however, had a military encounter with Moimar, lost his throne, and Pribina had no alternative, but to reach an understanding with the east-Frankish court.[20]

Louis the German donated land to Pribina in a marshy region, at Moosburg ['fort in the marsh'; later, the Magyars shall name it Mocsárvár]. Pribina thus became a vassal of the east-Frankish court. He had a church built in Moosburg, that was consecrated in the year 850 by Archbishop Liutprand of Salzburg in honor of the Blessed Mother of God.[21] He also appointed the archbishop's cleric, Dominic, who originally came from Regensburg, as his court chaplain.[22] He had two more churches erected there that were consecrated in the honor of Saint Hadrian and of St. John the Baptist.[23]

Archbishop Adalwin of Salzburg, Liutprand's successor, wished to parry Pribina's political moves by naming an archpriest as spiritual coordinator of religious matters in Pannonia (as if the archbishop had been afraid of both Pribina's political success and the increasing influence of a *chorepiscopus* in Pannonia).[24] Soon thereafter, Pannonia ceased to be missionary territory.[25] It must have been no coincidence that Kocel, Pribina's son, will now be addressed in papal letters as *Comes de Sclavis*—an expression that, according to Constantine VII Porphyrogenitus, corresponded to [the Byzantine] *archon* among the Franks.[26]

During the mid-ninth century, Pope Nicholas I was able to break down the separatist independent stand taken by the *territorial* Church that developed under Carolingian rule. During the former half of the ninth century, Rome had been unable to determine European religious politics north of the Alps, but Pope Nicholas I had changed all that. He had informed the Frankish royal courts (and, simultaneously, the Byzantine Patriarch), that the visible head of the Church resided in Rome.[27]

The first ecclesiastical-political initiative of Rome was aimed at the Dalmatian-Croatian seashore. The Roman See had the bishopric of Nin taken from the jurisdiction of Aquileia, on the grounds that Dalmatia had belonged to the *Patrimonium Petri*, over which the Frank territorial Church had no right to claim spiritual authority. In his letter, addressed to "clero et plebi Nonensis ecclesiae," the pontiff had emphasized that without papal authorization—he made no mention of a bishop—one could not establish a church (parish). The first bishop of Dalmatia might have been named Theodosius, mentioned by Pope John VIII in one of his letters of 879.[28]

Osbaldus, *chorepiscopus* for Pannonia and southern Carantania, had requested from Rome separation of his religious activities from the jurisdiction of the archbishop of Salzburg, and asked for permission to establish a bishopric that would be independent of the Salzburg *territorial* church province.[29] Simultaneously, Frankish political influence had weakened among the Moravians after Louis the German deposed Moimar and in 846 named Rastislav, Moimar's nephew, prince of Moravia. In nine years, Rastislav strengthened his political-military position in Moravia, invaded Pannonia, had Pribina murdered, and placed his people under the ecclesiastical primacy of Rome.[30]

Rastislav, however, had made too fast a political move, without giving consideration to a change in papal politics. Pope Nicholas I had been preoccupied with the marriage case of Lothair,[31] and needed to rely upon the sympathy and aid of the east-Frankish ruler who, in turn, could not have managed without the support of the papal curia. Nicholas I could not have supported Rastislav, because he had hoped that Louis the German would approve of the plan then under negotiation for the Christianization of Bulgaria. On the other hand, Rastislav supported Karlomann against Louis the German and did everything possible to get rid of Frankish predominance.[32] Rome had to assume a less than friendly attitude toward Rastislav, and the ruler of Moravia had to turn to Byzantium for sympathy and support for no other reason that this would neutralize a possibly hostile Bulgarian reaction toward him. After all, Moravia shared a common border with Bulgaria.[33]

Boris of Bulgaria likewise followed Janus-faced politics. He had made certain demands to Rome, when Louis the German had dispatched his envoy, Bishop Salomon of Constance, to negotiate with him. Now, the Byzantine court was disturbed by this turn of diplomatic events—the plan for establishing a papal-[east-]Frankish-Bulgarian (religious-political) axis, and applied military action. Boris underestimated the diplomatic skills of the Byzantine court. Because the Greeks had defeated the Arabs in 863, the *basileus*, now free of a continuous Islamic military threat, turned his arms against Bulgaria. Sensing the awkwardness of the situation, Boris had no alternative but to conclude peace with Byzantium in the hope that he would obtain an autonomous Byzantine-rite church province for Bulgaria; however, Patriarch Photius refused to cooperate.[34]

Boris now turned to the papal curia; both the Franks and the curia sent envoys to the Bulgarian court (though Rome protested the presence of the Franks in Bulgaria, and the envoys had to return home).[35] The Bulgarian khan had made no headway with the Roman See, as he failed to obtain an autonomous Latin ecclesiastical administration for his country.[36] Exploiting Rome's newly developed diplomatic blunder, Patriarch Ignatius now approached Boris with the proposal for setting up a Byzantine church province with ten suffragan bishops on Bulgarian soil.[37]

Patriarch Ignatius had displayed the same diplomatic chess game approach toward the ruler of Moravia. Rastislav had dreamed about establishing a separate bishopric, even an archbishopric, for Moravia, but Ignatius only sent two missionary brothers to help him. Cyril and Methodius performed the liturgy in the Slavic tongue and in the interest of spreading the Slavic liturgy, they developed the Glagolitic script (*glagol*: verb), so that they could translate sacred Scripture [passages] into Slavic. Rastislav was taken by surprise: he received more than he had bargained for; and, when he suffered defeat at the hands of the east-Franks, he canceled the Byzantine mission and, again, approached the papal curia. By undertaking this step, he embarrassed the Byzantine missionary brothers.[38]

Cyril and Methodius visited Rome and took the relics that were found at Chaerson of Saint Clement with them.[39] By dispatching Cyril and Methodius to the curia, however, Rastislav unwittingly played into the hands of the Roman See. The curia unexpectedly had an opportunity to establish a church province in Pannonia that would have included the Dalmatian seashore and Moravia, with its seat at Nitra. In such a manner Svatopluk, Rastislav's co-ruler, would also have participated in the plans of the Roman See.[40]

Cyril and Methodius had entered the service of the Latin Church: they said the Latin liturgy in the Slavic tongue. It was no coincidence, though, that they visit to Rome coincided with the fall from (political: imperial) grace of Patriarch Photius who, according to Anastasius Bibliothecarius, was a loyal friend, "amicus fortissimus," of Cyril. The record has it that Pope Hadrian II now permitted the use of the Slavic tongue in the Roman liturgy, on condition that the Creed and the Gospel passage for the day must be at first recited in Latin.[41]

The attitude of the Moravian ruler Rastislav had made Adalwin the archbishop of Salzburg angry, on the grounds that Salzburg had already claimed Pannonia as a Frank (territorial) church province. Rastislav (and Kocel) wanted to establish Slavic bishoprics under the headship of Roman See within the (planned) Pannonian–Moravian–Dalmatian church province. Methodius was ordained bishop in Rome, so that he would take control of the new church province and make certain that Rastislav supported the curia.[42] Methodius has stated his position at the 869–70 church synod gathered in Byzantium that debated in detail the Bulgarian question; he insisted on his right to the episcopal see of Sirmium (Mitrovica on Bulgarian territory), on the grounds that it was the see of the former archbishop of Sirmium. Until the onslaught by the Avar, Frank, and Bulgarian conquerors, Methodius had argued, the jurisdiction of the archbishop of Sirmium had extended over the whole of Pannonia.[43]

Methodius was a bishop of the Roman rite, whose ecclesiastical jurisdiction extended over *peoples*—as Pope John VIII explained it in the letter, he sent to Methodius, where he addressed him as "legatus ad gentes" —who performed the Latin liturgy in Slavic. At this time, the western portion of the Drave-Save river region belonged to the Franks; the eastern portion came under Bulgarian administration; there, Rome had the town *Singidinum* (Belgrade) elevated to a bishop's see in 878 (as if to underline the idea that the curia would not recognize the validity of Byzantine appointments in this particular segment of Bulgaria).[44] The town of Mursa (Eszék) in the western segment of the region was an important ancient Roman road junction, and the Frankish court was very much interested in retaining it.[45] The Pannonian-Croatian territory remained under the political supremacy of Kocel.[46]

The Bulgaro-Byzantine Church still would not soften its resistance. Methodius could not occupy his see at Sirmium: "et si eum ceperit, vitam habiturus non est."[47] It made his position even more difficult that Salzburg intervened in the controversy on the grounds, the archbishop claimed, that, in order to punish Pope Gregory III, the emperor, Leo III, had Illyricum detached from the canonical jurisdiction of the Roman patriarch in the year 732. Salzburg ignored the reasoning of Methodius that he was a papal legate and the ordained bishop of Sirmium; his ecclesiastical territory did not belong to the spiritual jurisdiction of Salzburg, because it belonged to Saint Peter. By referring to the decrees of the 813 and 868 synods held in Mainz, the archbishop of Salzburg had Methodius imprisoned; though in Rome he pretended to be ignorant about Methodius' whereabouts.[48]

It was the curia's turn to find an answer to the argument. Pope John VIII had reasoned that Pannonia had formed a part of *Illyricum* under the late imperial Roman administration, and it was only on account of warring activities and of confusion caused by the migrations, that the Roman See had not established a bishopric there. But that did not mean cessation of Rome's ecclesiastical jurisdiction over the area. In accordance with Roman law, a legal claim would expire only after the passage of one hundred years; it had only been for seventy-five years that Salzburg claimed the territory.[49] In reality, indeed, the *territorial* church, as administered from the Frankish court, had fought a judicial battle with a carefully phrased disciplined demand, based on clear legal reasoning, presented by the papal curia.[50]

A word of explanation is in order here concerning the diplomatic background of the issue. In the late 860s, Louis the German and Charles the Bald clashed over dividing Lorraine, when Louis II, the son of Lothair I, who inherited Lombardy, demanded also the inheritance of his deceased elder brother, Lothair II. Louis II was the neighbor of the papal patrimony, and the Roman See understandably supported him against his two royal relatives.[51] On condition that he would receive Lorraine, Louis II had been willing to acknowledge the interests of Karlomann, son of Louis the German.[52] It is evident from the papal writ addressed to Karlomann that, in theory at least, Rome had gained the upper hand in this game of diplomatic chess: Louis the German had recognized the claim of the Roman See to exercise ecclesiastical jurisdiction over the area.[53] Although forbidden to say Mass in Slavic,[54] Methodius now could transfer his residence to Moravia.[55]

In such a manner, Archbishop Theotmar of Salzburg was able to reach a compromise with the papal curia: he would retain the Pannonian territory under his jurisdiction, but under the auspices of Rome. In the region north of the Danube, Regensburg would remain active in the missionary field; in the Rába–Danube–Drave triangle, Passau would predominate a somewhat expanded missionary scene that included the Moravians, as far as the Garam river. Passau would, however, curtail the missionary activities of the *territorial* church.[56]

Svatopluk, now an ally of Karlomann, playing his game of Moravian domestic politics, however, turned against Rastislav, and in the resulting war the east Franks occupied Rastislav's territory; as a matter of fact, the Franks even coveted the area held by Svatopluk. Under these circumstances Passau—in defiance of the curia—considered establishing a territorial church province in the region, but Svatopluk took quick evasive military action. He turned on and defeated the Franks in battle in 871, and dismissed the Frankish missionary clergy from his territory.[57] Archbishop Theodore of Salzburg pretended to be outraged, and bitterly complained to the Holy See: he insisted on his claim to the whole of Moravia, as his field of (religious and political) missionary activity—under the auspices of the Roman curia.[58]

In the 874 Treaty of Forchheim, Svatopluk had submitted, as a vassal, to the east Frankish court;[59] however, out of sheer despair, he had turned to Rome again. He had informed the curia that, although the Frank clergy have done good missionary work in his country, he would have preferred the Roman See to establish a functioning administrative ecclesiastical structure in his country.[60]

And yet, Methodius with his overly stubborn attitude had caused the Moravian court to withdraw its support from him;[61] he would not listen to Pope John VIII who had to point out to him that if Svatopluk wanted the Mass to be said in Latin, Methodius had to honor the ruler's request.[62] Evidently, Methodius failed to comply with the wish of the prince. Indeed, an 880 papal writ addressed to Methodius—who had been summoned to Rome to defend himself against charges of heresy—spoke of him as *archiepiscopus pro fide*, a diplomatic alias for a missionary bishop without a permanent see.[63] Now, the bishop of Passau wanted to exploit the peaceful conditions that had prevailed between Svatopluk and the east Franks from 874 and 882, in order to fulfill his influence among the Moravians. Pope John VIII, however, took immediate counteraction; he decided to ignore the Moravian request for the removal of Methodius from his office, confirmed Methodius in his spiritual dignity, but obligated him to ordain a bishop for Nitra in the person of Wiching. The record has it that Wiching had already regarded himself as the successor of Methodius.[64]

In 877, Patriarch Ignatius had died in Byzantium, and the patriarchate was, once again, held by Photius, whom the Roman See had earlier excommunicated. Photius now requested that the curia recognize him as the Patriarch. He had been aware of the fact that, at this time, the Arabs posed a serious threat to the papal patrimony and that the Byzantine court had promised to send a naval unit to defend the patrimony from Islamic attack. Pope John VIII had to make a compromise; he officially recognized Photius as Patriarch—regardless whether Photius would surrender *de facto* jurisdiction he held over the Church in Bulgaria.[65]

The Roman Pontiff must have held a higher diplomatic goal before his eyes. He knew that Methodius was a friend of Photius, and it was through Methodius that the curia wished to reach an understanding with the Patriarch over Bulgaria; the curia wanted the court of the Patriarch to recognize the archbishopric of Sirmium—that included Moravia and Pannonia—as being under the jurisdiction of the Roman See. In the realization of this papal goal, John, a presbyter (and an acquaintance of Cyril and Methodius), had played a role. In the spring of 879, John visited Rome (taking with him the letter Svatopluk wrote to Pope John VIII complaining about Methodius); he made his journey through Croatian–Dalmatian territory, where serious religious-political changes were taking place. In 878, *Zdeslav* took possession of the Croatian throne with Byzantine support, and placed himself, and his country, under the jurisdiction of the Byzantine court. Within a few months, however, and with the help of John presbyter—and of the clergy of Nin—*Branimir* gained control of Croatia (879–92); Branimir turned to Rome for recognition as the (Christian) ruler of that land. It is known from a papal letter addressed to Branimir that John presbyter traveled, as papal envoy, through Croatia to ascertain that the cities in Dalmatia and the Bulgarians recognize Rome's jurisdiction in matters of religion.[66]

It is known from the sources that Methodius did go to Byzantium. The *Vita Methodii* remarked that Methodius went there because the emperor wished to see him, and making use of the opportunity, Methodius persuaded the emperor of the need for, and correctness of, the Slavic liturgy; but the *Vita* said nothing about Methodius' travel to, or through, Bulgaria.[67] In view of the fact that the Methodius Legend described a meeting [that may have taken place] between Methodius and the Magyars (who at that time resided at the lower estuary of the Danube), it may be that Methodius only visited Byzantium and that he traveled by sea. In other words, while John presbyter visited the Bulgarians, Methodius visited with the Greeks on official business. In Rome, they looked upon Methodius as the Byzantine-Greek who moved on familiar grounds in the surroundings of the Patriarch.[68]

The game of diplomatic chess played by the papal curia had not been successful. Pope John VIII died in 882, Methodius in 885, and the Bulgarian question disappeared from the diplomatic scene. In Moravia, Wiching, ordained bishop of Nitra, vehemently opposed the public activities of Gorazd, a faithful Methodius disciple.[69] Nor was Gorazd aided by the latest directive of Rome forbidding the use of Slavic in the liturgy—except in homilies on Scripture. Methodius's disciples had to flee the area to find refuge in Bulgaria and on the Dalmatian seacoast.[70]

One may summarize that the Slavic script—and Slavic church language—remained the accomplishments of Cyril and Methodius. Did the Slavs realize what treasure their missionary Apostles had left them? Cyril and Methodius, although Byzantine-Greeks, were *humanists*; they wanted the Slavs to retain their Slavic identity.

The Cyril and Methodius legends were written to prove that the Slavs had expected establishment of a national church from the usage of the Slavic liturgy; and yet, language seem to have played a secondary role in the realization of such an idea. The rulers of Nin, for instance, did not demand the usage of Slav liturgy. Boris (Bogoris) of Bulgaria expected from the papal curia and from the Byzantine Patriarch establishment of an autonomous ecclesiastical province (or, patriarchate) for his country. Only the Cyril and Methodius *vitae* emphasized the pint of view that both Rastislav and Kocel looked upon the religious-political use of the Slav liturgy as their life goal, when, in fact, both rulers had fought for establishing an autonomous church region in their countries.[71]

Upon the arrival of the Magyars during the 890s, what would be called the ecclesiastical administrative structure in the mid-Danubian region had collapsed. In the western portion of the region, in the former Roman province of Pannonia, and further up north, among the Moravians, Moosburg became the seat of a Roman deanery. Rome further established a bishopric in the Slavic belt of the region—to the great consternation of the east-Frankish court. Through the Croatian-Dalmatian bishop of Nin, Rome would claim the whole Slavic area for its jurisdiction, except the Carantanian territory. After 885, Gorazd, Methodius' disciple and bishop designate, after 893, Wiching, an ordained bishop—he never became archbishop of Sirmium—ceased to be listed in official writs. Archbishop Theotmar of Salzburg in his letter addressed to Pope John IX made mention of Bavarian-Moravian church contacts, and spoke of an archbishop and three bishops in the region under Hungarian occupation. The Slav Christian population had strong influence upon the arriving Magyars; numerous clerics of the declining church administrative structure were spreading the faith among the "conqueroring" Magyars, who had previous acquaintance with Christianity.[72] The nomads have always been tolerant of various religions.[73]

Under Magyar rule, Moosburg (now Zalavár), continued to play a role in the Christianization of the region; Mór (=Maurus), a Benedictine monk at Pannonhalma, and, eventually bishop of Pécs [Quinque-ecclesiae], was educated in Nitra, the former episcopal see of Wiching.[74] After the Magyar takeover during the 890s, the influence of the clan of Árpád the Conqueror had declined; other clans gained regional leadership in *Magyar land*. It was the clan of Horka, for instance, that directed marauding ventures toward Italy; Horka and Lél both pursued military action in the Latin west. In the southeast, as far as the gates of Byzantium, the clans of Gyula, Botond, also Horka, were active militarily. The clan chiefs Gyula and Bulcsú took over planning and the directive in the field of religious missionary policy. It was clan chiefs Ajtony, Horka, and Botond who represented their people's interests in Byzantine religious politics and raised the attention of the Patriarch to converting the newcomers.[75]

During the early 940s, these clan chiefs concluded a five-year peace with the Byzantine court through the efforts of Patriarch Theophanes (943–48). Before 948, Bulcsú had visited Constantinople to be baptized, and returned home with the rank of [a Byzantine] *patricius*. Gyula imitated his example; he gained the baptismal name of Stephen in Constantinople, and had the monk *Hierotheus* accompany him on his journey back home. The Byzantine court must have taken their conversion seriously because, in 956, Patriarch Theophanes had ordained Hierotheus bishop for *Turkia*. The Byzantine chronicler Cedrenos Skylitzes recorded that Gyula had remained loyal to his Christian faith but that Bulcsú did not.[76]

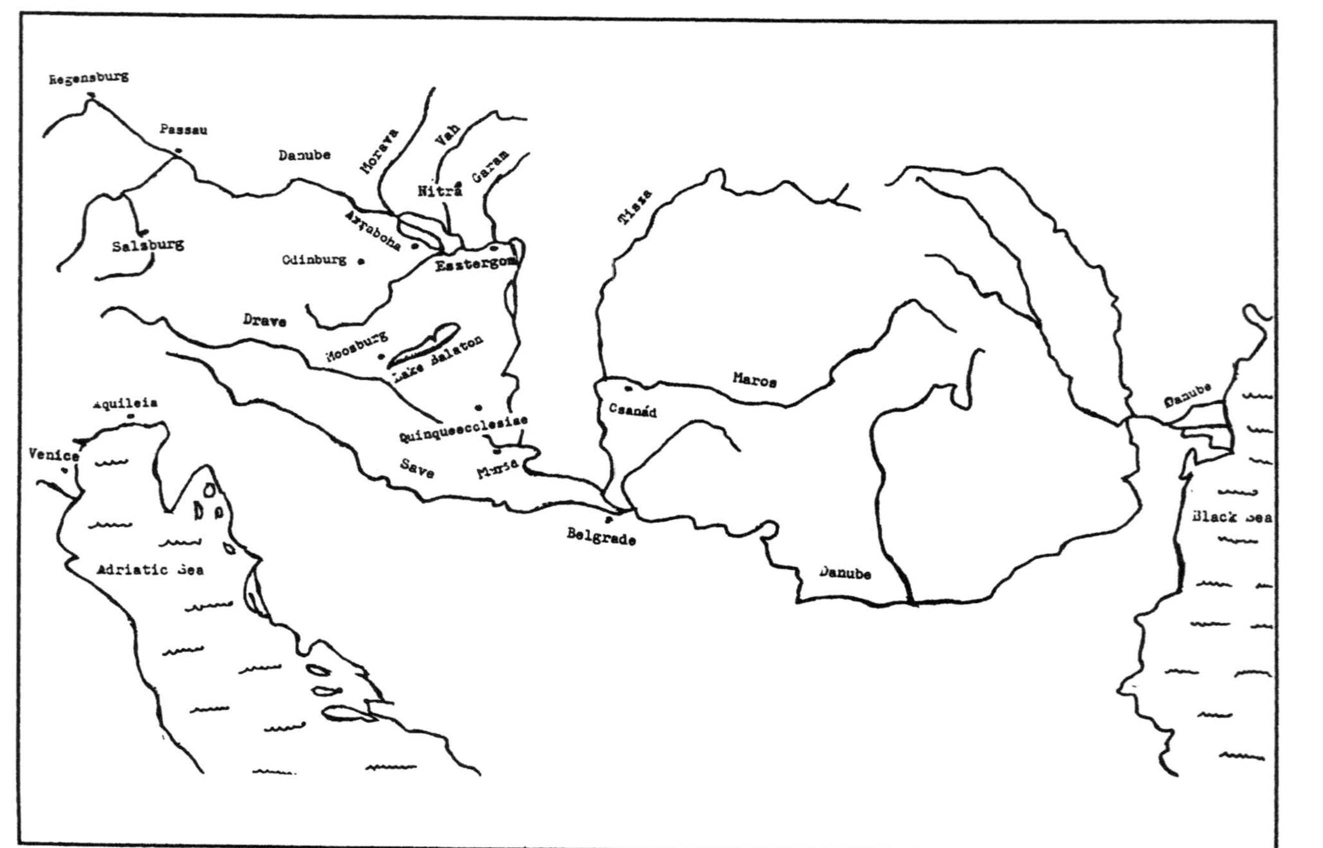

Regensburg
Passau
Danube
Morava
Vah
Garam
Nitra
Arrabona
Salzburg
Odinburg
Esztergom
Tisza
Drave
Moosburg
Lake Balaton
Maros
Aquileia
Csanád
Danube
Quinqueecclesiae
Venice
Save
Mura
Belgrade
Adriatic Sea
Danube
Black Sea

2. Unfriendly Magyar Reaction to the Missionary Politics of Pilgrim of Passau

> Factum est ergo, ut pene tota Ungarorum natio sit prona ad percipiendum fidem sanctam, sed et alie Sclavorum Provinciae ad credendum promptae, et est ibi messis multa, operarii autem pauci.
>
> *Pilgrim of Passau to Pope Benedict VI*, anno 974*

The Byzantine Church struck firm roots in the area of the lower Maros (stream) on Magyar territory, the region of clan chief Gyula. Hierotheus, bishop of the Byzantine Church, became the Magyars' first bishop. At the end of the tenth century Ajtony, lord of Marosvár, visited Bodon (Vidin) to be baptized a Byzantine Christian; at his seat in Marosvár, he had a church built in honor of Saint John the Baptist, to be occupied by Byzantine monks.[77]

Because it was the clan chiefs, and not the descendants of Árpád, who asserted leadership among the Hungarians in the mid-Danubian region during the tenth century, one may hypothesize that had Bulcsú remained loyal to his Byzantine religious affiliation, the Byzantine Church would easily have engulfed the Hungarian court politically. It was not without reason that Constantine VII Porphyrogenitus remarked that Bulcsú on his visit to Byzantium had taken Termács with him, the great-grandson of Árpád the Conqueror.[78]

Sarolta, the wife of Prince Géza, and the mother of King [Saint] Stephen I of Hungary (997–1038), was the daughter of Gyula, a Byzantine Christian, founder of the Basilian-rite monastery at Veszprém in western Hungary [Pannonia].[79] King Stephen's grandfather had been baptized Stephen [*Stephanos*] in Constantinople—and the king had a house erected for Hungarian pilgrims in Constantinople.[80]

During the latter half of the tenth century, the deep faith and revived religious spirit of the Cluniac monks penetrated Christianity in Latin Europe. The guiding principle of the abbey of Cluny and of the monastic communities that followed its directive rested on a renewal of one's soul and intellect, free election of the abbot, and protection of the monastery from the great powerful regional potentates by far away Rome. According to Odo, the great abbot of Cluny (d. 942), it had to be a monk's main concern to take part in the struggle between good and evil, to live according to the faith, and instead of disobeying God's commands to realize one's life goal with humility and asceticism. Abbot Odo stressed the need for spiritual renewal among the secular clerics also on the grounds that the clergy were the spiritual leaders of their society.[81]

In the eleventh century, Abbot Odilo of Cluny (d. 1054) was the one who, according to similar principles, guided the program of inner renewal for his monks and retained the understanding support of the German imperial court—in a sense that the inner renewal program radiating from Cluny closely supported the political-religious interests of Otto I the Great.[82]

The domestic and foreign policies of Otto I aimed at breaking down German tribal particularism, to replace it with a politically and economically united and administratively centralized state.[83] The Slavs, who settled in central and eastern Europe, had, by their conversion to Christianity, established some foundation for their political stability.[84] In the European southeast, after Emperor Basil I defeated the Bulgarians, thereby demolishing the ambitions of the Bulgarian khan, Byzantium once again emerged as a great power.[85]

The princely Magyar court at this point had to find an answer to one essential basic question: how the Magyars, living in the Carpathian basin since the 890s, could find their place—and their future—in the newly developing political-economic, religious-cultural framework of Latin Europe. After their defeat at Augsburg in 955, the Magyar leadership ended the marauding ventures toward the west.[86] In about 970, when the Byzantine court turned down the proposal of Sviatoslav of Kiev, an ally of the Magyars, that together they fight against the enemies of the empire,[87] it was the turn of Prince Géza to show determination in establishing a policy of mutual understanding toward his neighbors and, doing so, turn over a new leaf in Hungarian history.[88]

The court of the Ottos relied upon the expansion of Christianity for a specific political purpose, even if such policy sooner or later had to cause a confrontation with the Roman curia. To cite but one example, Pope John XIII handed down a decision that the jurisdiction of the newly erected *imperial* archbishopric of Magdeburg only extended over peoples of the already occupied territories, and he did it on the grounds that only the Roman See could care for the conversion of the Slavs *without* the political cooperation of the German court.[89]

At Easter, in Quedlinburg, where the envoys of Géza, too, were present,[90] negotiations were conducted regarding the administration of Slav territories, deciding, for instance, that the Czechs and the Moravians accept the spiritual jurisdiction of the archbishop of Mainz in their lands. (The archbishopric of Mainz, established in 975, held the Czechs and the Moravians under its jurisdiction until 1347, when Emperor Charles IV established the archbishopric of Prague.[91]) The information his envoys must have obtained in Quedlinburg caused the Magyar prince to make a decision: he would work toward setting up in his country an autonomous Latin-rite ecclesiastical administrative structure that would be responsible to the Roman See—a decision only his son and successor would be able to realize to a full extent. Stephen, through reliance on Rome, would obtain administrative freedom for the Church in Hungary from the to be expected attempt by the German imperial ecclesiastics to incorporate the Church in Hungary into the political framework of ecclesiastical administration in the German empire. After all, the Church in Bohemia remained for centuries under the direct jurisdiction of the archbishop of Mainz, the Primate of Germany.[92]

In bringing about a centralized Magyar government that could tolerate no contradiction by another party; by beginning a policy of Christianization in accordance with the Latin-rite among the people, Sarolta, daughter of Gyula of Transylvania, and the wife of Géza, had played an important role. Sarolta was a strong-willed and determined woman, who drank and rode a horse like a man, who would even order her husband around, a German chronicler recorded.[93] The ruling couple's policy of administrative centralization rested on the support and cooperation of the Magyar tribe [clan], and of the tribe [clan] of Gyula of Transylvania—tribes that did not take part in the earlier marauding ventures in the west and/or in the continental southeast. In the judgement of Géza and Sarolta, a ruling team of prince and princess, the political-cultural destiny of their people had to be formulated according to the standards of the Latin west—in spite of the fact that Sarolta had been a baptized Byzantine Christian—and they made this decision at a time, when Byzantium represented, in fact, offered, a far more advanced culture than the west.[94]

Simultaneously, Géza and Sarolta had to face a rather politically motivated religious-personal attempt by Pilgrim, the bishop of Passau, who wanted to expand the Christian faith in the whole of the mid-Danubian area, in the former Roman province[s] of Pannonia.[95] Although it was St. Wolfgang, a Benedictine of Einsiedeln, who with true missionary zeal free of personal political ambition initiated the spread of the Christian faith in the region, the bishop of Passau cleverly voided Wolfgang's initiative.[96] As Arnold, another Benedictine monk of the abbey of St. Emmeram in Regensburg who spent six weeks in Pannonia reported, Wolfgang had to accept the bishopric of Regensburg upon orders of the Frankish court, though Wolfgang kept on wondering why did he have to so unexpectedly depart from Pannonia? The archbishop of Salzburg, a politician in his own right, who officially named Wolfgang bishop of Regensburg, cleverly rendered Wolfgang's chaste spirituality and idealism as qualifications for the appointment.[97]

And yet, the key to the answer lies somewhere else. Reliable sources report that the German court, including the hierarchy, planned a political-religious expansion toward east central Europe that included Pannonia. For example, the erection of the archbishopric of Magdeburg in 967 served the purpose of realizing the political-religious expansionist missionary policy of the Ottonian court.[98] In the case of Pannonia, it would have been under the hypothetical direction of the (*an Arch*)bishop of Passau—in this instance, *Bishop* Pilgrim of Passau—who would have been called upon to direct missionary activities of the bishop of Regensburg—in this instance, Bishop Wolfgang—among the recently arrived Magyars in Pannonia, with the purpose in mind that they serve the political goals of the imperial court.[99] The envoys sent by Géza to Quedlinburg—did the Magyar prince send them, or did they have to attend because of an invitation received from the Saxon court?—may have played a key role in making it clear before the Magyar ruler that the religious intentions of the imperial advisors regarding [the Magyars in]

Pannonia were mainly political. When Otto II sent an envoy, Bruno of Verdun, to the Magyar prince, the emperor had to instruct the bishop of Passau to ensure the envoy's safe arrival at the Hungarian border.[100]

Pilgrim reported to Pope Benedict VI that Bruno not only reached his destination, but concluded an agreement with the Magyar prince, that said that Bishop Pilgrim would be taking charge of Christianization of the region recently occupied by the Magyars. It must have been characteristic of Pilgrim's overconfident and arrogant attitude that he dared to refer to Bede the Venerable's History of the English Church and People to compare his planned missionary activities in Pannonia with those of Augustine's of Canterbury among the Anglo-Saxons in the early seventh century.[101] Although it remains a historic fact that Prince Géza and son Vajk—who received the name of Stephen in baptism—and brother Michael, were christened by the priests of Pilgrim (the patron saint of the Passau bishopric was St. Stephen the First Martyr), the bishop made the extraordinary claim that he had baptized some five thousand Magyar nobles [noble families?], and stated that all the Magyars had accepted Christianity.[102] The record has it that Gyula of Transylvania, the great uncle of Vajk (now baptized Stephen), had also been baptized Stephen—at the *Byzantine* court.[103]

The conversion of Géza further assured religious freedom among the non-Magyar prisoners of war, and/or the Slav population of the land. The conversion of both Géza and Sarolta to the Latin-rite had been carried out with the firm conviction that others would follow the ruling couple's personal example.

The actual historic political reality was very different. Emperor Otto II was preoccupied with domestic troubles; Henry of Bavaria revolted against the emperor, and the duke received support from the Magyars. Bishop Pilgrim, the emperor's loyal adherent, now turned against him.[104] The warring effort gradually subsided, Henry of Bavaria made peace with the emperor's court, and Bishop Pilgrim had to pay a price for his treacherous behavior toward the emperor. Because his missionary endeavor among the Magyars, too, remained unsuccessful, Pilgrim had to withdraw from public life. The coin, though, may have had another side to it: Archbishop Frederick of

Salzburg would hardly have been in favor of Pilgrim's politically oriented missionary goals, on the obvious grounds that the archbishop was not at all pleased with the idea of another *archbishopric* being established in his neighborhood; on this issue the Roman curia fully agreed with the Salzburg metropolitan.[105] Pilgrim may have made two miscalculations: for the sake of political gain, he turned against his former patron and supporter, the German emperor; and, he failed previously to consult with the archbishop of Salzburg about the missionarization of Christianization of *Pannonia*.

In the Hungarian court, they must have known about the hostility, and its peaceful ending, between Emperor Otto II and Duke Henry of Bavaria; they may even been aware of the strained relationship between the archbishop of Salzburg and the bishop of Passau, and of the overheated personal ambitions of Pilgrim; after all, it was Wolfgang who had begun the Christian missionary work in Pannonia during the last decades of the tenth century.[106]

Géza soon realized Pilgrim's true political intentions—and blamed the German court circles for it. He remained in contact with the Byzantine court; his wife had been a baptized Christian of the Byzantine rite. The Magyar ruler knew that without higher—the imperial court's—authorization an archbishop, or a bishop, could not have been in a position to plan and *enforce* the conversion of a people to the Christian religion, especially since Pilgrim had personal ambitions to become archbishop himself. It would not have been in the Byzantine Church, and Géza was aware that it was unlikely to occur in the Latin west. One may reach this conclusion from an unguarded—or, perhaps, purposefully made—remark by the Magyar prince that he regarded himself as a lord powerful enough to serve two gods simultaneously. As Géza had displayed some hesitancy in carrying out his resolution to convert his people to the Roman Christian faith, he may have had second thoughts about approaching the Latin west, instead of Byzantium. The chronicler's derogatory remark that the Magyar prince "cum christianus efficeretur, ad corroborandam hanc fidem contra reluctantes subditos servit et antiquum facinus zelo Dei exestuans abluit," may serve as proof of a change in policy.[107]

The prince regarded the politically oriented activities of Salzburg and Passau with growing concern and suspicion, and his conversion (was it sincere; or, was it politically motivated?) to Latin Christianity did not alter his world of inner thought. He and his wife wisely knew that for the sake of dynastic survival—after all, his domestic political opposition was centered about the Maros region in the southeast of his country, where the Byzantine Church retained a stronghold until the late eleventh century—he had to follow a *Latin* Christian course. A remark made by another chronicler points in that direction; "inmo uxor eius, quae totum regnum manu tenuit, virum et quae erant viri ipsa regebat."[108] That may have been the reason why he had arranged for the marriage of his [their] son—Vajk, baptized Stephen—to the Roman Catholic Gisela, daughter of Duke Henry the Quarrelsome of Bavaria. It would be the responsibility of his son, and eventual heir, to establish the institutions and culture of Latin Christianity in the country, among his people. It would be through the efforts of Gisela that the ecclesiastical religious reform spirit of Cluny penetrate Hungarian royal court circles that, in turn, assure the spread of the Roman Catholic faith among the realm's population.[109]

It was [Saint] Adalbert, the bishop of Prague, a relative of the German ruling dynasty and of the Bavarian princely family (he later died a martyr among the pagan Prussians), who may have played an important role in establishing firm foundations for Roman Christianity in Hungary. As the bishop of Prague, he made little progress influencing the manner of living among his Czech faithful, or the personal lives of his clergy. By nature, he was more inclined toward leading the life of a monk, or that of a missionary working among the pagans, and paid scant attention to church canons, regulations, ecclesiastical formalities.[110] As member of the German and Bavarian ruling families, he was a political appointee to the Prague bishopric. The bishop, who had a vocation for the life of a monk, but had been assigned to head a bishopric, decided to follow his monkish-missionary instinct by visiting the monastery of Saints Alexius and Boniface in Rome, and stopped en-route in Esztergom, at the court of the Hungarian ruling prince. He may have visited there out of curiosity; a scion of aristocratic families, he knew of the court of the Magyar prince, about his personal-political interest in the Latin-Christian mission in his country.[111]

This topic poses several questions. First of all, according to the frequently incorrect geographical descriptions provided by the Moor of Ceuta, Edrisi [or, Idrīsī, d. 1166], and by the so easily to be misinterpreted data of Albericus, a monk of the monastery Trium Fontium [d. 1255], there had developed a mistaken concept of the geographical expansion of the boundaries of the Prague bishopric, and of the extent of the area[s] taken over by the Magyars in the mid-Danubian region during the late ninth century. According to their data, the Czech Premysl family had, after the defeat of the Magyar armies at Augsburg in 955, occupied the area north of the Danube that included the upper Tisza river basin, a region that upon the incorporation of the area of the Moravia into the Prague bishopric came under the spiritual jurisdiction of the bishop of Prague. According to Idrīsī, Esztergom also came under the jurisdiction of Prague as the southern Christian religious and cultural center of the bishopric.[112] Thus Adalbert in visiting Esztergom actually sojourned to a location under his spiritual jurisdiction. The Magyars regained the area north of the Danube in 1008, when Prince Géza, in alliance with Emperor Henry II, used force to take it away from the Polish ruler Boleslav.[113]

One may add here that unlike other locations in the Danubian area, as, for instance, in Veszprém, Zalavár, Pécs, where archaeological excavations unearthed rich early, pre-tenth century Christian remains, no such archaeological evidence had been unearthed in Esztergom; or, one is to consider the geographical factor that Esztergom is located on the right hand bank, that is *south*, of the Danube river, are factors that rather weaken Idrīsī's statement.[114]

It is further evident from the *vitae* of King [Saint] Stephen that Esztergom had been the seat of prince Géza's government already during the 970s, and that King Stephen was born in Esztergom. Archaeological excavations uncovered foundations, dated to the *tenth* century, of a Christian church dedicated to St. Stephen the First Martyr, as if to point to the fact that missionaries from Passau had already frequented Géza's court, since Saint Stephen the First Martyr was the patron saint of the church in Passau, and Vajk, Prince Géza's son and heir, received his baptismal name *Stephen* from St. Stephen the First Martyr. Adalbert visited the seat of Géza's government during his sojourn[s] to Esztergom, and one may conclude from the wording of Stephen's *vitae* that it may have been during one of his visits that he had confirmed Stephen, and become the spiritual guide of the young prince.[115]

It is more than unlikely, however, that Adalbert carried out much missionary work in Esztergom, or in the country, during his visits. Missionary work was continued by the monks who accompanied him, who restored and built upon the ruins of the missionary activities left by the clerics of Pilgrim of Passau.[116] The Magyar ruling prince sought help from Adalbert in establishing the Roman Catholic Church in the country, from the relative of German and Bavarian princely families and bishop of the Czechs, who fled from his episcopal see in Prague because of the persevered immoral behavior of his "hard headed and stone hearted" Czechs. He went to Rome to sojourn in the monastery of Saints Alexius and Boniface (a community that, incidentally, did not follow the Cluniac spiritual revival movement).[117] The Czechs had him recalled, Adalbert returned with twelve monks, not to Prague, but to Brevnov, to establish the first Benedictine monastic community on Czech soil. His confrere, the Benedictine Anastasius, became the abbot of the new monastery.[118]

It must have been during his second visit to Rome in 990 that Adalbert visited Prince Géza in Esztergom, where he was received with great joy at the court, Bruno of Querfurt reports. Ast[e]ric, Adalbert's [episcopal] court chaplain, accompanied him to Esztergom, and monks Anastasius and Radla sojourned in the country during the 990s.[119]

Bruno of Querfurt noted that although Adalbert left only a slight imprint of Christianity upon the Magyars during his brief stay in Esztergom, the time he spent there was sufficient to influence the mind and soul of the young Vajk—now, baptized *Stephen*—and upon Stephen's generation. Stephen was born and raised in a Christian environment, was prepared, "regali nutrio educatu," to rule his country when called upon.[120]

The available source material does not actually record meetings between Stephen and Adalbert; however, one may conclude from the correspondence of Adalbert with Emperor Otto III, and from the record of discussions they may have had in Mainz and in Rome, that the Czech bishop and the young heir to the Hungarian throne talked with each other.[121] Adalbert certainly admonished Stephen not to be too self-confident because of his high office, to fear God, and to despise earthly goods. Adalbert called Stephen's attention to, what he regarded as a fact, that although Emperor Otto III excelled over other secular rulers in the dignity of his office, political supremacy he did not assert over them, grounds for Stephen the future king to ponder, were he want to develop an independent policy within the political framework of Latin Christendom.[122]

It is very likely that in his conversations with the emperor, Adalbert discussed the Latin-oriented Christian politics of the Hungarian court. It must have been the result of such a conversation that would support the remark by Thietmar of Merseburg, that it was "Imperatoris predicti—i.e., Otto III—gratia et hortatu," that Stephen "gener Heinrici, ducis Bawariorum, Waic in regno suimet episcoples cathedras faciens coronam et benedictionem accepit" from Pope Sylvester II. The imperial chronicler made it quite clear that it was because of that policy that Stephen set up, or was in a process of establishing, episcopal sees, *in regno suimet episcopales cathedras faciens*, that the emperor gave his approval for the papal recognition of Stephen as the ruling monarch of his country.[123]

Upon the bloodbath at Libice, after the thugs of Boleslav of Bohemia mercifully spared the life of Abbot Radla, Radla fled to Hungary, while Adalbert disobeyed the directive of the archbishop of Mainz to take up residency at his episcopal see in Prague, and departed for Polish territory. He even asked Sarolta, wife of Prince Géza, to persuade Radla to follow him to Poland, and wrote Radla instructing him to *escape* from the Magyar court and join him in Poland.[124]

Radla held a different opinion, however. He regarded Adalbert's behavior as irresponsible, *ardua scandentem*. It was not for the first time, he said, that he had to part company with Adalbert.[125] During his visit to King Stephen's court, Bruno of Querfurt met with Radla in 1003. Some of the monks of Brevnov joined Adalbert in his newly established abbey in Meserlitz, now headed by Abbot Ast[e]ric, while other monks found a new home in the abbey of Pannonhalma in Hungary.[126]

Adalbert died a martyr's death at the hands of pagan Prussians on April 23, 997, near what is now Danzig.[127] The monks of Meserlitz led by their abbot Ast[e]ric fled to Hungary, where they pursued their missionary work and educational-cultural activities.[128]

The marriage of Stephen and Gisela took place upon the death of Duke Henry of Bavaria, when Stephen's father, Prince Géza, had still been alive, and Henry—later emperor Henry II—was the one who gave away the bride at the wedding.[129] The missionary Wolfgang, later bishop of Regensburg and a friend of the Bavarian ducal family, was the mentor-educator of the princely children: Henry (later Emperor Henry II), and Gisela (now the wife of Stephen).[130] Queen Gisela's mother, also named Gisela, was born in Burgundy; thus, the argument could be made that it was through King Stephen and Queen Gisela that the reformed spirituality of Cluny, through the influence of the Roman curia made a lasting impact upon Hungary at the very beginning of its Christianization of the country.[131]

One needs to bear in mind at this point that Ajtony, ruler of the Maros region, was a Byzantine Christian, and so was Sarolta, King Stephen's mother; they could have easily become political tools in the hands of Bishop Hierotheus, the representative of Byzantine political-religious politics in the region.[132]

The overheated plans of the Byzantine court had only limited success. Sarolta's husband, Géza, out of political consideration turned to the Latin West; their son Vajk, baptized Stephen in the Latin Church—for whom his father had sought a wife of western up-bringing: Gisela of Bavaria—decided to join the western Latin Christian political community. As the Russian chronicler correctly remarked, this time Rome had carried the upper hand—though, as it is evident from the Hungarian record, Byzantine religion and politics continued to play a significant role in the realm of the Árpáds for many more decades to come.[133]

King Stephen continued the work his father had begun. It is on record that it was King Stephen who had established the *Latin* Christian Hungarian kingdom, and laid the foundation of Hungarian statehood that endured more than a thousand years.[134]

Notes

1. The Imperial Church and the Papal Curia

* Cf. *Annales regni Francorum*, ed G. H. Pertz and F. Kurze, SSrG (Hannover, 1895; repr. 1950), 112, anno 800.

1. The regional Bulgarian officials were known as *rectores*; however, the Bulgarians were unable to retain their hold on the region between the Drave and Save rivers, except Sirmium, and, in 824 they paid their respects to the Frankish court—cf. *ibid.*, annorum 818, 824, 826; Ernst Dümmler, *Geschichte des ostfränkischen Reiches*, 2nd ed., 3 vols. (Leipzig, 1887-88; repr. Hildesheim, 1960), I, 36ff.; József Deér, *A magyar törzsszövetség és patrimonális királyság külpolitikája* [Foreign policy of the Hungarian clan organization and of the patrimonial kingdom] (Pécs, 1928), 10ff.; Fr. von Šišić, *Geschichte der Kroaten*, I (Zagreb, 1917), 66ff.; S. L. Tóth, "A honfoglalás időpontja" [The approximate date of the Hungarian conquest], *Acta historica Szegediensis*, 102 (1995), 3ff.

2. The Hungarian Anonymus, *Gesta Ungarorum*, in Emericus Szentpétery (ed.), *Scriptores rerum Hungaricarum*, 2 vols. (Budapest, 1937-38), cited hereafter as *SSH*, I, 44ff., cc. 9, 11, 12, 14; on Nitra [=Nyitra], *ibid.*, cc. 33, 35, and cc. 44-46.

3. Cf. Bálint Hóman – Gyula Szekfű, *Magyar történet* [Hungarian History], 6th ed., 5 vols. (Budapest, 1939; repr. 1990), I, 79ff.; Bálint Hóman, *Geschichte des ungarischen Mittelalters*, 2 vols. (Berlin, 1940-43), I, 89ff.

4. Cf. "De conversione Bogoariorum et Carantanorum libellus," c. 5, in *Monumenta Germaniae historica, Scriptores*, ed. G. H. Pertz, 30 vols. (Hannover, 1854, etc.), cited hereafter as *MGHSS*, XI, 4ff.; the M. Kos edition (Laibach, 1936), remained inaccessible to me. On the missionary activities of Rupert, see F. X. von Funk – K. Bihlmeyer, *Kirchengeschichte*, 8th rev. ed., 2 vols. (Paderborn, 1926-30), II, 4f., and, on the background, *ibid.*, II, 8ff.; also Friedrich Prinz, *Frühes Mönchtum im Frankreich: Kultur und Gesellschaft in Gallien, den Rheinlanden und Bayern am Beispiel der monastischen Entwicklung* (Munich-Vienna, 1965), 394ff.; H. v. Schubert, *Geschichte der christlichen Kirche im Frühmittelalter* (1921), 304f.; see also E. Caspar, *Geschichte des Papsttums*, 2 vols. (Tübingen, 1933–35); his *Papsttum unter fränkischer Herrschaft* (Darmstadt, 1956), would have been the third volume of this opus. W. Levison, "Die älteste Lebensbeschreibung Ruperts von Salzburg," *Neues Archiv*, 28 (1903), 283ff.; A. Brackmann, "Die Anfänge der Slawenmission und die Renovatio imperii des Jahres 800," *Sitzungsberichte der Preussischen Akademie der Wissenschaften*, phil.-hist. Klasse, 13-9 (Berlin, 1931); Franz Dölger, "Die Familie der Könige im Mittelalter," *HJb*, 60 (1940), 397ff.

5. On the Anglo-Saxon mission of Pope Gregory the Great, see his letters, *Gregorii I papae Registrum epistolarum*, ed. Paul Ewald – Ludo M. Hartmann, 2 vols. (Hannover, 1897-99), cited hereafter as *MG Epp*, I, 228ff.; his writ addressed to Emperor Maurice in 593, *ibid.*, I, 220ff.; Ph. Jaffé (ed.), *Regesta pontificum Romanorum*, 2 vols. (Leipzig, 1885; repr. Graz, 1956), n. 1266; Funk – Bihlmeyer, II, 27ff.; see further, Venerabilis Baedae *Historia ecclesiastica genti Anglorum*, ed. C. Plummer, 2 vols. (Oxford, 1896), i:23-27 [- to, 31]; F. Homer Dudden, *Gregory the Great, His Place in History and Thought*, 2 vols. (London, 1905; repr. 1967), II, 105ff.; *Pope Gregory as a jurist and an organizer*, *ibid.*, II, 292. Ferdinand Gregorovius, *History of the City of Rome in the*

Middle Ages, tr. Ann Hamilton, 8 vols. (London, 1899), II, 29ff., provided a character study of the great pontiff, and discussed the historical background of his activities.

6. For the correspondence of popes Gregory II and Gregory III, cf. Jaffé, nn. 153, 2157, 2159-62, 2164, 2239, 2245-47, 2249, 2251, etc.; further, Helmut Michels, "Zur Echtheit der Briefe Papst Gregors II an Kaiser Leo III," *Zeitschrift für Kirchengeschichte*, 99 (1988), 376ff.

7. On matters related to Tassilo, see the *Annales regni Francorum*, a. 787; and the "Annales qui dicuntur Einhardi," a. 787, *ibid.*; Caspar, *Geschichte des Papsttums*, II, 504ff., and 676ff.; Peter Schwenk, "Frühes Christentum in Baiern: Bemerkungen zur christlichen Kulturkontinuität von der Antike zum Frühmittelalter," *Zeitschrift für bayerische Landesgeschichte*, 59 (1996), 15ff.

8. Discussed by P. v. Váczy, *Die erste Epoche des ungarischen Königtums* (Pécs, 1935), 64; F. Kampers, "Rex et sacerdos," *HJb*, 45 (1925), 496ff. Karl Hengst, "Karl der Grosse und Papst Leo III, 799, in Paderborn," *Theologie und Glaube*, 90 (2000), 20ff.

9. The three missionary districts were determined at the 803 Synod of Regensburg, cf. "Conversio," cc. 6-7; and *Concilia aevi Karolini*, ed. Albert Werminghaft, 2 vols. (Hannover, 1906-08).

10. "Conversio," c. 6, *MGHSS*, XI, 9; in 750, Caranthania had been separated by the east Franks from Avar territory—*ibid.*, c. 10; Dümmler, I, 35; H. Pirchegger, "Karantanen und Unterpannonen zur Karolingerzeit," *Mitteilungen des Institutes für österreichische Geschichtsforschung*, 33 (1912), 272ff.; Funk – Bihlmeyer, II, 141; K. Mesterházy, "Avarok, szlávok, magyarok a Bükk hegységben" [Remains of Avar, Slav, and Magyar settlements in the hills of Bükk], *Századok*, 130 (1996), 861ff.

11. Salzburg became an archbishopric in 798, and Pope Leo III sent the *pallium* to Arno, first archbishop of Salzburg, cf. Jaffé, nn. 2496(!) and 2498; also, "Annales Iuvavenses maiores," anno 798—cf. *MGHSS*, I, 87; "Conversio," c. 8.

12. *Ibid.*, c. 9.

13. "Conversio", cc. 5 and 7.

14. Archbishop Adalram of Salzburg authorized the cleric Otto to act as episcopal vicar for the Carantanians in Pannonia—"Conversio," c. 9.

15. "Annales Iuvavenses, supplementum" a. 805, *MGHSS*, III, 122; "Annales Emmerammi Ratisponensis," a. 805, *ibid.*, I, 93.

16. The Avars' khagan became a Christian in 805—cf. *Annales regni Francorum*, a. 805.

17. Their envoys, together with the Moravians, brought gifts for Louis the German—cf. *ibid.*, aa. 815 and 822.

18. *Annales Fuldenses sive Annales regni Francorum orientalis*, ed. G. H. Pertz – F. Kurze, SSrG (Hannover, 1891; repr. 1978), 845; Dümmler, I, 284ff. Wolfgang Eggert, *Das ostfränkisch-deutsche Reich in der Auffassung seiner Zeitgenossen* (Vienna-Graz, 1973), 15ff., esp. 49ff.

19. "Conversio," cc. 10-11.

20. *Annales Fuldenses*, a. 871.

21. "Conversio," c. 10 -11; Šišić, I, 67f. It was also during the pontificate of Archbishop Liutprand, "temporibus Liuprammi," that a church—or churches—in Pécs, "ad Quinque basilicas" (hence: *Quinqueecclesiae*) had been dedicated; cf. "Conversio," c. 11, loc. cit.; also, *MHK*, 311.

22. Cf. *MG Necrologium Germanicarum*, II, 28, 66, 19.

23. "Conversio," cc. 11-13.

24. *Ibid.*, c. 12.

25. See *Epistolae Karolini aevi*, ed. Ernst Dümmler – Ernst Perels (Hannover, 1925), cited hereafter as *MG Epp*, VI, 660f., n. 142. Funk – Bihlmeyer, II, 34ff.

26. Cf. *Epistolae Karolini aevi*, ed. Erich Caspar – Gerhard Laehr (Hannover, 1928), cited hereafter as *MG Epp*, VII, 282 and 283; Constantine VII Porphyrogenitus, *De administrando imperio*, ed. Gyula Moravcsik, English translation R. J. H. Jenkins, rev. ed. (Washington, DC, 1967), cited hereafter as *DAI*, c. 30, on the "archon"; further, cf. Šišić, I, 96ff.

27. The letters of Pope Nicholas I, in Jaffé, nn. 2682, 2684, 2691-92, 2713, 2721, 2730, 2758, 2766, 2791 and 2796; *MG Epp*, VI, 659: "Ecclesia id est," addressed to "cleri et plebi Nonensis ecclesiae,"—Jaffé, n. 2851—mentioned no bishop, but emphasized the fact that no church province might be established without papal authorization; Šišić, 61f. See further Karl F. Morrison, *Tradition and Authority in the Western Church, 300-1140* (Princeton, 1969), 155ff.

28. Theodosius, bishop of Nin—see the writ by Pope John VIII, anno 879, in Jaffé, n. 3255; *MG Epp*, VII, 153; also, F. Rački (ed.), *Documenta historica Croatiae*, in *Mon. Slav. merid*, vii, nn. 2 and 12; Francis Dvornik, *Les légendes de Constantin et de Méthode vues de Byzance*, Byzantinoslavica, Suppl. I (Prague, 1933; rev. ed. Hattiesburg, Mississippi, 1969), 264f.

29. According to a papal writ, cf. Jaffé, n. 2765 (Nicholas I, in 864); *MG Epp*, VI, 660f.; Jaffé, n. 2854, and "Conversio," c. 15; Dümmler, II, 175; Morrison, 213ff.

30. Cf. *Vita s. Methodii, archiepiscopi Pannoniensis*, ed. Fr. Miklosich (Vienna, 1870), c. 5, refers to a letter of Pope Nicholas I, see *MG Epp*, VI, 99, n. 599; according to the Cyril legend, the Moravians were, by this time, Christians, cf. E. Dümmler – Fr. Miklosich, *Die Legende vom Heiligen Cyrillus*, cited hereafter as *Vita Constantini*, c. 14, *Denkschriften der Akademie der Wissenschaften, Wien*, phil.-hist. Kl., XIX (Vienna, 1870), 242; *MHK*, 352f., and 356ff. Hildegard Schaeder, "Geschichte und Legende im Werk der Slawenmissionare Konstantin und Method," *HZ*, 152 (1935), 229ff. The author, following *Vita Constantini*, c. 8, discussed the poor impression created before the Chazars by the Jewish-Arab-Latin religious conflict; and, based on *Vita Methodii*, c. 5, analyzed the religious-political contradictions between Rome, Byzantium and the Germans that had created a bad impression upon the Moravians and the Kievans; the latter decided to turn to, and accept baptism in, the Byzantine Church (p. 245f.). Dvornik, *Les légendes*, 349ff., published his French translation of the legends; the legends complement each other—Schaeder, 235.

31. See *Annales Fuldenses*, aa. 846 and 855; and "Annales Bertini," aa. 846 and 855; Dümmler, I, 298, and 388ff. Rastislav had turned to Rome—cf. *Vita Methodii*, c. 8; Dvornik, 156, though one is to realize that it was at this time that Pope Nicholas I had to intervene in the marriage troubles of Lothair II—cf. H. von Schubert, *Geschichte der christlichen Kirche im Frühmittelalter*, 2 vols. (Tübingen, 1927), I, 421f.; R. E. Sullivan, "The papacy and missionary activity in the early middle ages," *Medieval Studies*, 17 (1955), 46ff.

32. Mentioned in a papal writ, Jaffé, n. 2847; *MG Epp*, VI, 293; Dümmler, II, 85f.; Dvornik, 156.

33. Karlomann, the opponent of Louis the German, sought the support of Rastislav—*Annales Fuldenses*, a. 863; Jaffé, nn. 2748-51, and the papal writ, *MG Epp*, VI, 293; Böhmer – Mühlbacher (eds.), *Regesta imperii*, I, (1908), nn. 1148a, and 1450c and e. Mainly, the activities of Cyril and Methodius were dealt with in the *Vita Methodii*,

c. 5, that spoke of a three year sojourn, while the *Vita Constantini*, c. 15, of forty months, in Moravia.

34. Cf. *MG Epp*, VI, 82, n. 438; the envoy of Louis the German was Bishop Salomon of Constance—*ibid.*, VI, 59, n. 293; Schubert, 423ff. The Byzantine victory over the Arabs and its ecclesio-political consequences were discussed by Dvornik, 187ff.; Robert Browning, *The Byzantine Empire* (New York, 1980), 60f.; Bogoris failed to receive an autonomous ecclesiastical province, as it is evident from Photius' letter to the Khan of Bulgaria, in J. P. Migne (ed.), *Patrologiae cursus completus, series graeca*, 166 vols. (Paris, 1857-66), cited hereafter as *MPG*, 102, 628f.; also, R. E. Sullivan, "Khan Boris and the conversion of Bulgaria," *Studies in Medieval and Renaissance History*, 3 (1966), 53ff.

35. Hincmar, "Annales," a. 864, *MGHSS*, I, 465.

36. Nor was he given an independent Roman church province; not even a bishop was assigned to his territory!—"Vita Nicolai papae," *MPL*, 119, 766.

37. Patriarch Ignatius received Bogoris with joy; Bo[go]ris was now assigned a Bulgarian archiepiscopal province, with ten suffragans—cf. Schubert, 517f.

38. In 867, Pope Nicholas I had summoned the missionary brothers to Rome, cf. Jaffé, n. 2888. The missionary brothers went to Rome—Jaffé, n. 2888; the activities of Cyril and Methodius, and the *Glagolitic* script were recorded by Pope John VIII—*MG Epp*, VII, 223, esp. 255; also, "Conversio," c. 12, and *Vita Constantini*, c. 16; Schubert, 519f.; Dvornik, 166ff.; I. Sági, "Szent Cyrill és Metód életműve a legújabb kutatások alapján" [The life work of saints Cyril and Methodius in the light of recent research], *Vigilia*, 28 (1963), 592ff.

39. Jaffé, n. 2924; *Vita Constantini*, cc. 15-17; *Vita Methodii*, cc. 6, 8; Erna Patzelt, *Österreich bis zum Ausgang der Babenbergerzeit* (Vienna, 1947), 74ff.

40. The letter of Pope John VIII, *MG Epp*, VII, 222ff.; Cyril died on February 14, 869; cf. *Vita Methodii*, c. 8.

41. Cf. Jaffé, n. 2924; *Vita Methodii*, c. 8; Patriarch Photius's career came to an abrupt end by the end of 867; Anastasius Bibliothecarius spoke of him as a loyal friend of Cyril—cf. J. D. Mansi, *Sacrorum conciliorum nova et amplissima collectio*, 31 vols. (Florence–Venice, 1759-98), cited hereafter as *Concilia*, xvi, 6a—he was a former professor of Cyril, as pointed out in the *Vita Constantini*, c. 4. In the Slavic liturgy, the Creed and the Gospel had to be recited in Latin at first—cf. *Vita Methodii*, c. 8; also, V. Jagic, "Zur Entstehungsgeschichte der kirchenslawischen Sprache," *Denkschriften der Akademie der Wissenschaften, Wien*, phil.-hist. Kl., 47 (1902), 19ff.

42. Jaffé, n. 2924; a papal writ dated 879—*MG Epp*, VII, 160, 200; Jaffé, n. 3268; L. Duchesne (ed.), *Liber pontificalis*, 3 vols. (Paris, 1886, etc., repr. 1957), II, 182ff., on the church synod of 869-70; one may consult the article by Imre Boba, "Szent Metód és Szventopolk kapcsolata Sirmiummal és Szlavóniával" [The relationship St. Methodius and Sventopolk had maintained with Sirmium and Slavonia], *Essays in Church History in Hungary*, 7 (1995), 5ff. One must point out, though, that in Jenkin's English version of the Greek text of the *DAI*, c. 41, "Sventopolk" appears as Sphendoplokos, while in Marczali's Hungarian translation (cf. Marczali, *Enchiridion*, 52), he is still "Spendoplokos."

43. Methodius had also spoken at the synod, Jaffé, n. 3267; Dümmler, II, 262. Methodius' [new] church district (bishopric) anchored at Sirmium (Mitrovica)—a Roman bishop's see until 582—also included Bulgarian territories. See Ch. A. Frazee, "The

Balkans between Rome and Constantinople in the early middle ages,"_Balkan Studies_, 34 (1993), 213ff.

44. Sirmium was an important town—*DAI*, c. 40; Singidunum (Belgrade), a bishop's see in 878—*ibid.*, c. 40.

45. Cf. "Conversio," c. 10; further, "Annales Rudberti Salisburgenis," *MGHSS*, IX, 770; "Auctarium Garstense," a. 838, *ibid.*, IX, 565; Dümmler, II, 363f.; Mursa [=Eszék] was since ancient times, an important road junction.

46. Šišić, I, 68ff.; C. Jirecek, *Geschichte der Serben*, 2 vols. (Gotha, 1911-18), I, 194; Georg Ostrogorsky, *Geschichte des byzantinischen Staates*, 2nd rev. ed. (Munich, 1952), 76f., and 98.

47. Methodius served as Rome's spokesman in Slavic matters: "et si eum ceperit, vitam habiturus non est," that is, as the ordained bishop of Sirmium! Cf. *Vita Methodii*, c. 13, though, he could not occupy his see—writ dated Nov. 10, 871, by Pope Adrian II, in Jaffé, nn. 2943-44; *MG Epp*, VI, 760, 762, and the remarks made by John VIII in this context, *ibid.*, VII, 277, 294f., 296, etc.; Jaffé, nn. 2962, 2976; Dvornik, 248f. According to John VIII, the new church province also included the Moravians and the Serbs, *MG Epp*, VII, 282, a. 873; Methodius had been assigned peoples, not territory, wrote the pontiff—cf. *ibid.*, VII, 286; *Vita Methodii*, c. 8.

48. This is why the "Conversio" was written, c. 14; Methodius had been held captive by the archbishop of Salzburg, *Vita Methodii*, cc. 9-10; Salzburg kept referring to the resolutions of the synods of Mainz, 813, and of Mainz 868—Mansi, *Concilia*, XIV, 71, and XV, 879. Methodius' response, that the area concerned had belonged to St. Peter, not Salzburg, *Vita Methodii*, c. 9, was supported by papal correspondence, see—*MG Epp*, VII, 284ff., esp. 286,30; Dümmler, II, 377, and n. 1; further, see B. Bretholz, "Über das 9. Capitel der pannonischen Legende des hl. Methodius," *MIÖG*, 16 (1895), 342ff.

49. *Ibid.*, VII, 282, 283ff.; Dümmler, II, 380f.

50. Pope John VIII based his arguments upon the line of reasoning by Pope Nicholas I.

51. *MG Epp*, VII, 276, 297 (fragments 6 and 41).

52. *Ibid.*, VII, 295, 152-54; Dümmler, II, 339ff.

53. In principle, Rome had carried the day—see the papal writ addressed to Karlomann, *MG Epp*, VII, 281 (fragment 16).

54. The papal curia forbade Methodius to say Mass in the Slavic tongue in vain, "quia aliter doceat, coram sede apostolica se credere et verbis et litteris professus sit," Jaffé, n. 2978; Methodius remained disobedient, as it is evident from a papal letter, *ibid.*, VII, 161, n. 202.

55. Cf. *MG Epp*, VII, 222, n. 255.

56. Theotmar received the *pallium* as archbishop of Salzburg, *ibid.*, VII, 57f, nn. 54 and 65.; also, Hubert Mordek, "Kirchenrechtliche Autoritäten im Mittelalter," in *Recht und Schrift im Mittelalter*, ed. Peter Classen, vol. 23 of *Vorträge und Forschungen* (Sigmaringen, 1977), 237ff., on Canon law being formulated to please royal power and prerogatives.

57. Hincmar "Annales", a. 871, *MGHSS* I, 492; "Annales Xantenses," *ibid.*, II, 234; *Vita Methodii*, c. 10; Dümmler, II, 294f., and 318f.

58. As recorded in the writ, anno 900, by Theotmar to Pope John IX; cf. Marczali, *Enchiridion*, 20ff.; *MHK*, 323ff.

59. Cf. the letter by Pope John VIII to Svatopluk, dated in 879, *MG Epp*, VII, 160,15-16; further, *ibid.*, VII, 222, 223,1-6.

60. Cf. August Potthast (ed.), *Regesta pontificum Romanorum*, 2 vols. (Berlin, 1875), n. 25252; also, nn. 25256 and 25257.

61. *Vita Methodii*, c. 11; Dvornik, 263ff.

62. As late as 873, John VIII still permitted the use of Slavic in the Mass—cf. *MG Epp*, VII, 224.

63. On Zobor Hill in Nitra, across of the church dedicated to St. Emmeram, a monastery was built in honor of St. Hypolitus. In view of the fact that the church in Sankt Pölten was named after St. Hypolitus, and Sankt Pölten came under the jurisdiction of the bishop of Passau, erection of the monastery would have meant that the bishop of Passau had tried to realize his claim over the region around Nitra. Cf. *MG Epp*, VII, nn. 184, 190-92, 196, 206, 295; Šišić, I, 98ff.; Bernard Hamilton, "The Monastery of S. Alessio and the religious and intellectual renaissance in tenth-century Rome," *Studies in Medieval and Renaissance History*, 2 (1965), 265ff.

64. *MG Epp*, VII, 222ff.

65. *Ibid.*, VII, 245, 259; and, related to this, see *ibid.*, VII, 207, 208, and 209. On the background, cf. I. Hergenröther, *Photius, Patriarch von Byzanz*, 2nd ed., (1867; repr. New York, n.d.), 291ff.

66. Dvornik, 255ff.

67. *Vita Methodii*, cc. 12-13.

68. *Ibid.*, c. 16.

69. *MG Epp*, VII, 243, 244, 276.

70. *Vita Methodii*, c. 17; Dümmler, III, 253ff.; G. Friedrich (ed.), *Codex diplomaticus et epistolaris regni Bohemiae*, vol. I, in two parts (Prague, 1904), I-1, 22ff., nn. 26 and 27; Dvornik, 312ff.; Sándor Tóth, "Megjegyzések a honfoglalás szakaszaihoz" [Some remarks on the various phases of the Hungarian conquest of the mid-Danubian region], *Századok*, 130 (1996), 877ff.; Senga Toru, "Morávia bukása és a honfoglaló magyarok" [The fall of Moravia and the conquering Magyars], *Századok*, 117 (1983), 307ff.

71. Franz Zagiba, *Die altbayerische Kirchenprovinz und die hll. Slawenlehrer Cyrill und Method* (Salzburg, 1963); Erna Patzelt, "Die Mission Cyrills und Methods in verfassungsgeschichtlicher Schau," *Studi medievali*, 3rd ser., 5 (1964), 241ff.; Bernard Hamilton, "The city of Rome and the eastern churches in the tenth century," *Orientalia Christiana periodica*, 27 (1961), 5ff.

72. In reference to the bishopric of Nitra, see the writ of John VIII—Jaffé, n. 3332 (false!), and nn. 3319 and 3344; Laehr, *Neues Archiv*, 47 (1928), 164ff. The entering Magyars had made an end to the church province in Moravia: on this, Archbishop Theotmar's letter, in Marczali, *Enchiridion*, 24f.; *M H K*, 323ff. Dusan Třeštik, "Grossmähren, Passau und die Ungarn um das Jahr 900; zu den neuen Zweifelen an der Authentizität des Briefes der bayerischen Bischöfe an Papst Johann IX aus dem Jahr 900," *Byzantinoslavica*, 59 (1998), 137ff; and, Luděk Galuška, "Christianity in Great Moravia and its center in Uherské Hradiště–Sady," *Byzatnioturcica*, 59 (1998), 161ff.

73. *Vita Methodii*, c. 16.

74. Mór [Maurus], later bishop of Pécs, who, together with Archbishop Benedict [of Esztergom], bishops Clement and Nicholas, had signed King Andrew I's founding charter for the abbey of Tihany, 1055; cf. *Regesta regum stirpis Arpadianae critico-diplomatica*, ed. Emericus Szentpétery – Ivan Borsa, 2 vols. (Budapest, 1923-87), cited hereafter as *RA*, n. 12; and the 1057 royal writ addressed to the bishop and his bishopric (only the first half of the writ can be regarded as authentic), *RA*, n. 14—who grew up in

Nitra, as evidenced by the "Legenda Zoerardi," cc. 1, 3, 4, cf. *SSH*, II, 347ff. The bishopric of Pécs, headed by Bishop Bonipert, was founded in 1009 by King Stephen in the presence of the papal legate, Bishop Azo, cf. *RA*, n. 5.

75. On the settlement and landed interests of the Magyar clans, see the detailed report by the Hungarian Anonymus, *Gesta Ungarorum*, *SSH*, I, 33ff., esp. cc. 12, 14, 20, 25, 33-35, etc.; *MHK*, 392ff.; also, the map in Hóman – Szekfű, I, 144; Sándor Tóth, "Az első fejedelem: Árpád, vagy Álmos?" [Who was the first elected Magyar prince?—was it Álmos, or was it Árpád?], *Acta historica Szegediensis*, 103 (1996), 31ff.

76. Cf. Ioannes Zonaras, *Epitomae historiarum*, libri XIII-XVIII, ed. Th. Büttner-Wobst, CB (Bonn, 1897), xvi:21; Ioannis Skylitzae *Synopsis historiarum*, ed. I. Thurn (Berlin,-New York, 1973), 237, 59-76. Bulcsú's visit to Constantinople was mentioned in *DAI*, c. 40.

2. *Unfriendly Magyar Reaction to the Missionary Politics of Pilgrim of Passau*

* Cf. Marczali, *Enchiridion*, 21ff.; on Pope Benedict VI (973–74), see Hans Kühner, *Neues Papstlexicon*, Fischer Bücherei repr. (Frankfurt-am-Main–Hamburg, 1965), 53.

77. Pilgrim's letter, Marczali, *Enchiridion*, 57ff.; Henrich Fichtenau's reaction, in his *Das Urkundenwesen in Österreich vom 8 bis zum frühen 13 Jahrhundert* (Vienna–Graz, 1971), 166ff. For background, see "Vita Gerardi [episcopi Chanadiensis]" (Gerard, bishop of Csanád), c. 10, in *SSH*, II, 494ff.; on the "Vita," see Macartney, *The Medieval Hungarian Historians* (Cambridge, 1953), 154ff.; on Bishop Gerard, see Kosztolnyik, *Five Kings*, 46ff., and 161ff.

78. *DAI*, c. 40; Bulcsú was accompanied by Termács, Árpád's great-grandson, cf. *ibid.*

79. See "Chronicon Posoniense," c. 44, *SSH*, II, 305, n. 1; comments by Macartney, 142f.; Bálint Hóman, *A szent László-kori Gesta Hungarorum és XII-XIII századi leszármazói* [The "Gesta Hungarorum" of the times of Ladislas I, and its continuators in the 12th and 13th centuries] (Budapest, 1925), 88ff. On the parents of Stephen, see the observations made by R. F. Kaindl, "Studien zu den ungarischen Geschichtsquellen, I-II," *AföG*, 81 (1894), 323ff., who had also referred to the Hungaro-Polish Chronicle—in *Monumenta Poloniae historica*, ed. A. Bielowski, 6 vols. (Lvov–Cracow, 1864-93; repr. Warsaw, 1960-61), I, 494f., and 502. I could not gain access to the edition prepared by Béla Karácsonyi (*Chronica Hungaro-Polonica, Pars* I, *textus cum varietate lectionum*), *Acta historica Szegediensis*, 26 (1969).

The Greek founding charter—cf. *RA*, n. 1, text by Gy. Czebe (ed.), *A veszprém-völgyi oklevél görög szövege* [The Greek text of the charter of Veszprémvölgy], vol. 24/3 of *Értekezések a történelemtudományok köréből* [Studies in History] (Budapest, 1916), 15f., and 17f.; E. Jakubovich – D. Pais (eds.), *Ó-magyar Olvasókönyv* [Old Hungarian Reader] (Pécs, 1929), 14ff.; A. Balogh, "A veszprémvölgyi görög monostor alapítása: a legrégibb magyarországi oklevél [The foundation charter of the Veszprémvölgy monastery, the oldest extant document in Hungary], *Regnum: Egyháztörténeti Évkönyv*, 6 (1944-46), 21ff.

80. See Hartvic, "Vita s.Stephani regis Hungariae," c. 13, *SSH*, II, 419,26-29; King Stephen's "Vita maior," c. 11, *ibid.*, II, 386,26-28; György Györffy, *István király és műve*

[King Stephen and his work] (Budapest, 1977), 77ff., and my review of the book in *Austrian History Yearbook*, 17–18 (1981–82), 356ff.

81. Funk – Bihlmeyer, II, 88f.; Max Heimbucher, *Die Orden und Kongregationen der katholischen Kirche*, 3rd ed., 2 vols. (Paderborn, 1933-34), I, 183ff. For the founding charter of Cluny, cf. A. Bruel, *Receil des charters de l'abbaye de Cluny* (Paris, 1876); Martin Bouquet (ed.), *Recueil des historiens des Gaules et de la France*, IX (Paris, 1879), 709ff. Abbot Odo (*ob.* 942) wrote the *Collationum libri III* to explain his obligations as abbot—cf. the "Bibliotheca Cluniacensis" collection in J. P. Migne (ed.), *Patrologiae cursus completus, series latina*, 217 vols. (Paris, 1844-55), cited hereafter as *MPL*, 133, 517ff., esp. ii:36,6, iii:18, iii: 24, iii:30, iii:32, iii:47; E. Sackur, *Die Cluniazenser*, 2 vols. (Halle, 1892), I, 71ff., and 99ff.; A. Hessel, "Odo von Cluni und das französische Kultur-problem im frühen Mittelalter," *HZ*, 128 (1923), 1ff., esp. 18.

82. Abbot Odilo (*ob.* 1054) earlier enjoyed the patronage of Empress Adelheid; cf. "Ex epitaphio et miraculis Odilonis abbatis Cluniacensis," *MGHSS*, XV, 813ff.; Iotsald, "Life of Abbot Odilo," i:6, *ibid.*, XV, 812ff. [selections]; *MPL*, 142, 897ff.; also, Herbert Paulhart (ed.), *Odilonis Cluniacensis abbatis Epitaphium domine Adelheide auguste: Die Lebensbeschreibung der Kaiserin Adelheid von Abt Odilo von Cluny*, in *MIÖG*, suppl. vol. 22-2 (Graz–Cologne, 1962), 27ff. As directed by the imperial court, there existed a coalition between religion and political interests; cf. G. Schnürer, *Kirche und Kultur im Mittelalter*, 3 vols., 2nd ed. (Paderborn, 1927-28), II, 119f.; Jaffé, n. 3690: papal consent to the previous establishment (by the German court!) of the archbishopric of Magdeburg.

83. On Otto I the Great, see Widukind of Corby, *Res gestae Saxonicae*, 5th ed., ed. P. Hirsch – H. E. Lohmann, SSrG (Hannover, 1935), aa. 955 and 973; Hader Keller, "Grundlagen ottonischen Königsherrschaft," in *Reich und Kirche vor dem Investitur-streit: Gerd Tellenbach zum achtzigsten Geburtstag*, ed. Karl Schmid (Sigmaringen, 1985), 17ff.; Wolfgang Eggert – Barbara Petzold, *Wir-Gefühl und Regnum Saxonum bei frühmittelalterlichen Geschichtsschreiben* (Vienna-Graz, 1948), 98ff.; Peter Váczy, *A középkor története* [History of the Middle Ages], vol. II. of Bálint Hóman (ed.), *Egyetemes történet* [Universal History], 4 vols. (Budapest, 1936-38), 330ff., and 344ff.; Karl Hampe, *Das Hochmittelalter*, 5th ed. (Cologne–Graz, 1963), 28f., and 49.

84. Cf. Lamperti *Annales*, in *Lamperti opera*, ed. O. Holder-Egger, SSrG (Hannover–Leipzig, 1894), a. 973; *Annales Altahenses maiores*, ed. E. L. B. ab Oefele, SSrG, 2nd ed. (Hannover, 1891; repr. 1976), a. 973; also, Thietmar, ii:20; on the arch-bishopric of Mainz, see the *Annales Hildesheimenses*, ed. G. Waitz, SSrG (Hannover, 1878).

85. Cf. Georgius monachus *Continuatio*, in *Theophanes Continuatus*, etc., ed. I. Bekker, CB (Bonn, 1838), 763ff., 817,20 – 819,15; or, in Leo Grammaticus, *Geographia*, ed. I. Bekker, CB (Bonn, 1842), 231,1 – 233,10; likewise, the letters of Nicolaus Mysticus, *MPG*, 111, 149ff., epistola 23.

86. On this, see Widukind, iii:44-49 [51]—an insert only?—cf. Eggert – Pätzold, 82, note 454. Simon de Keza, "Gesta Ungarorum," c. 40, *SSH*, I, 144ff.; "Chronicon pictum," c. 36, *ibid.*, I, 239ff.; on Keza, and the Chronicle, see C. A. Macartney, *Hungarian Historians*, 89ff., and 133ff. Ch. R. Bowlus argued that the water-soaked terrain, and the undisciplined greed of Magyar troops led to their defeat in 955—cf. his "Die Reitervölker des frühen Mittelalters im Osten des Abendlandes," *Ungarn-Jahrbuch*, 22 (1995-96), 1ff. See further, Thomas v. Bogyay, *Lechfeld, Ende und Anfang* (Munich, 1955), 25ff., and 54ff.; for referring to data in *MGHSS*, IV, 401, cf. K. L. Leyser, *Medieval Germany* (London, 1982), 43ff.; István Bóna, *A magyarok és Európa a 9–10*

században [The Magyars' arrival and the European background in the ninth-tenth centuries] (Budapest, 2000), 51ff.

87. Cf. Ioannis Scylitzes, 288,15-22; 289,48 – 291,4. The Magyars (Turks he called them) held the Greeks at bay—*DAI*, c. 4.

88. József Deér, *A magyar törzsszövetség és patrimonális királyság külpolitikája* [Foreign policy of the associated Magyar clans and of the patrimonial Hungarian kingdom] (Kaposvár, 1928), 30, 35.

89. Cf. Jaffé, n. 3710, and n. 3690.

90. Thietmar, ii:20; Widukind, iii:75; Lampert, *Annales*, in *Lamperti opera*, ed. O. Holder-Egger, SSrG (Hannover-Leipzig, 1894), a. 973; "Annales Magdeburgenses" a. 973, *MGHSS*, VI, 153; H. F. Schmid, "Otto I und der Osten," *MIÖG*, suppl. vol. 22-1 (Graz–Cologne, 1962), 70ff.; Bóna, cited as above, n. 10, 72ff.

91. Cf. Thietmar, iii:2; A. Brackmann, "Die Ostpolitik Ottos des Grossen," *HZ*, 134 (1926), 242ff.; Othmar Hageneder, "Weltherrschaft im Mittelalter," *MÖIG*, 93 (1985), 257ff.; on Emperor Charles IV, cf. Franz Palacky, *Geschichte von Böhmen*, II-2, 3rd printing (Prague, 1874), 238ff., and 240, note 326.

92. Cf. Bede Jarrett, *The Emperor Charles IV* (New York, 1935), 69ff., esp. 78; Hartvic, cc. 4 and 9; Bálint Hóman, *Stephan der Heilige: die Gründung des ungarischen Staates*, tr. N. von Roosz (Breslau, 1941), 76ff.

93. Thietmar, iii:3, who had referred to Sarolta as "Beleknegini." Sarolta tolerated no contradiction, and clearly saw her religio-political objectives—cf. Bruno of Querfurt, *Vita Adalberti*, c. 23, *MGHSS*, IV, 596ff.; "Chronicon Posoniense," c. 44, *SSH*, II, 35. (On the *Chronicon Posoniense*, cf. Macartney, *Hungarian Historians*, 142f.) Bruno of Querfurt was a relative of the emperor, held position of imperial chaplain under Otto III, and entered the Sts. Alexius and Boniface monastery in Rome—cf. Peter Damian, "Vita s. Romualdi," c. 27, in *MPL*, 144, 977; he was ordained *episcopus in partibus*, and died a martyr among the pagans in Eastern Europe. Cf. H. G. Voigt, *Brun von Querfurt, Mönch, Eremit, Erzbischof der Heiden und Märtyrer* (Stuttgart, 1907).

94. See Scylitzes, CB, 237,59-76; on Byzantine culture, Ostrogorsky, 238ff., and 284ff.; A. A. Vasiliev, *History of the Byzantine Empire* (Madison Wisconsin, 1952), 301ff.; Robert Browning, *The Byzantine Empire* (New York, 1980), 96ff.

95. See Marczali, *Enchiridion*, 57ff.

96. Othlo of St. Emmeram, "Vita s. Wolfkangi episcopi," cc. 13-14, and 30, in *MGHSS*, IV, 525ff.; "Rythmus de s. Wolfgango," (Mondsee MS), *AAS*, Nov. II-1, 583ff. For some background data, see Arnold of Emmeram, "Liber II de memoria beti Emmerami et eius cultorum," *MGHSS*, IV, 557ff. Lajos Csóka, "Cluny szellemű volt-e a magyar egyház a XI században?" [Did the Church in Hungary have a Cluniac orientation in the eleventh century?], *Regnum: egyháztörténeti Évkönyv 1942-43* [Regnum: Annals of Church History] (Budapest, 1943), 141ff.

97. Annotations in "Arnoldi libri de s. Emmerammi," ii:1, *MGHSS*, IV, 546ff.; Othlo von Emmeram, "Vita sancti Wolfkangi episcopi," *ibid.*, IV, 527ff.; "Rythmus de s. Wolfkango," based on a Mondsee MS, ASS, Nov. II-1, 583ff., and compare to István Jákli, "A magyarokhoz küldetett" ["He who had been sent among the Magyars"] (Pannonhalma, 1992), 67ff.; Gabriel Adriányi, "Der Eintritt Ungarns in die christlich-abendländische Völkergemeinschaft," *Ungarn-Jahrbuch*, 6 (1974-75), 24ff.; Bóna, *Magyarok*, 72 and 77.

98. Widukind kept silent on Magdeburg, cf. Eggert – Pätzold, 87, note 490; Othlo, c. 14; E. Donnert's interesting study, "Studien zur Slawenkunde des deutschen

Frühmittelalters vom 7 bis zum beginnenden 11 Jahrhundert," *Jahrbuch für Geschichte der UdSSR und der volksdemokratischen Länder Europas*, 8 (1964), 289ff.

99. Thietmar, ii:20; *Annales Hildesheimenses*, anno 973; Cosmas of Prague, "Chronica Boemorum," i:25, in *MGHSS*, IX, 1ff.; R. F. Kaindl's study, "Zu Cosmas," *MIÖG*, 16 (1895), 349ff., is worth reading.

100. Cf. G. Fejér (ed.), *Codex diplomaticus Hungariae ecclesiasticus ac civilis*, 44 vols. (Budae, 1829-44), cited hereafter as *CD*, I, 257.

101. Cf. Marczali, *Enchiridion*, 57ff.; and/or, St. L. Endlicher, *Rerum Hungaricarum monumenta Arpadiana* (Sangallen, 1849; repr. Leipzig, 1931), cited hereafter as *RHM*, 131ff.; compare with Bede the Venerable's *Historia*, i:23-27, as cited above, n. 5.

102. Stephen grew up a Christian—see his "Vita minor," c. 2, *SSH*, II, 394; however, neither Wolfgang, nor Adalbert were the ones who had baptized him, as it had been wrongfully implied by Hartvic, cc. 3 and 4, and in Hartvic's main source, Stephen's "Vita maior," cc. 4-5, *ibid.*, II, 380f. Compare with Ademari *Historiae libri III*, iii:31, *MGHSS*, IV, 129,88-89. Géza, Stephen's father, might also have been baptized Stephen—as suggested by Gaufridus de Bruil, *Chronica*, *ibid.*, XXVI, 199ff., esp. 202, and n. 5.

103. Skylitzes, CB, II, 237,59-66.

104. Cf. Robert Holtzmann, 250ff.; Hóman – Szekfű, I, 168; Hóman, *Ungarisches Mittelalter*, I, 168; Bruno Gebhardt, *Handbuch der deutschen Geschichte*, 4 vols., 8th rev. ed., ed. Herbert Grundmann (Stuttgart, 1954, etc.), I, 192ff.

105. Jaffé, n. 3767 (anno 973); *CD*, I, 258f.; *MPL*, 135, 1081.

106. Cf. Othlo's "Vita s. Wolfkangi," cc. 13-14, *MGHSS*, IV, 525ff.; and, compare with *SSH*, II, 471,32-35; and, *ibid.*, II, 484,42-46.

107. Thietmar, viii:3 [ix:4]; Jenő Szűcs, "König Stephan in der Sicht der modernen ungarischen Geschichtsforschung," *Südost-Forschungen*, 31 (1972), offprint.

108. *MGHSS*, IV, 607.

109. Hartvic, "Vita s. Stephani regis Hungariae," cc. 7, 8; King Stephen's "Vita minor," c. 2, *SSH*, II, 394; F. Galla, *A cluny reform hatása Magyarországon* [Influence of the Cluniac reforms in Hungary] (Pécs, 1931), 44ff.; Csóka, art. cit., in *Regnum* (1942-43). Idem, "A magyarok s a kereszténység Géza fejedelem korában" [The Magyars and the issue of Christianity in the reign of Prince Géza], *Emlékkönyv Szent István király halálának kilencszázadik évfordulókán* [Memorial volume on the 900th anniversary of the death of King Saint Stephen], ed. Jusztinián Card. Serédi, 3 vols. (Budapest, 1938), I, 267ff.

110. Thomas Wünsch, "Der heilige Bischof—zur politischen Dimension von Heiligkeit im Mittelalter und ihrem Wandel," *Archiv für Kulturgeschichte*, 82 (2000), 261ff.; Karl Bosl, "Herzog, König und Bischof im 10 Jahrhundert," *Bohemia sacra: das Christentum in Böhmen, 973-1973*, ed. Ferdinand Seibt (Düsseldorf, 1974), 269ff.; Thomas von Bogyay, *Stephanus rex: Versuch einer Biographie* (Vienna, 1976), 10f.; my review of this book in *Austrian History Yearbook*, 14 (1978), 290ff.

111. Cf. Bruno of Querfurt, "Vita Adalberti episcopi Pragensis et martyris"—*Vita altera!*—cc. 14, 15, 16 and 23, *MGHSS*, IV, 596ff.; I was unable to gain access to the recent edition by Hedwig Karwasińska, in MPH, series nova, IV-2 (Warsaw, 1969); Iohann Canaprius, "Vita s. Adalberti episcopi Pragensis et passio," in *MPL*, 138, 859ff., has limited information on Adalbert's sojourn in Hungary, while Adalbert's *Vita* by an anonymous author, "excerpts" in *Zeitschrift für die Geschichte und Alterthumskunde Ermlands*, 7 (1881), 26ff., has nothing to report on Adalbert's visits to Hungary.

112. Cf. *Opus geographicum: Liber ad eorum delectationem qui terras peragere studeant*, ed. E. Cerulli et al., "una cum aliis," A. Bombaci et al. (Naples–Rome, 1978), Climate VII, parts two and three. Idrīsī depicted the area north of the Danube and northern historic Hungary as part of Bohemia; cf. István Elter's impressive study, "Magyarország Idrīsī földrajzi művében (1154)" [La Hongrie dans la géographie descriptive d'Idrīsī, 1154], *Acta historica Szegediensis*, 82 (1985), 53ff., and a colored map, *ed. Baġdād, 1970*, facing p. 57. On Idrisi, suffice here to refer to the remark made by H. Marczali, "...übereinander gehäuft sind dort die einzelnen Angaben. Kaum dass eine Stadt genannt wird, die man ohne harte Mühe wiedererkennen könnte; die Lage der Städte aber zur Grundlage nehmen und so den Text erklären wollen, ist überhaupt unmöglich." See his *Ungarns Geschichtsquellen*, 159; see further Ch. H. Hapgood, *Maps of the Ancient Sea Kings*, rev. ed. (New York, 1979), 181f.; on Idrisi's "World Map" [*Weltkarte des Idrisi*], ibid., 10, and consult the Map Division of the Library of Congress [map, A.D. 1150, in Arabic], six sheets. Albericus Trium Fontium, "Chronicon," *MGHSS*, XXIII, 631ff.; on Albericus, cf. Wattenbach, II, 461ff.

113. Cf. *SSH*, II, 307, 41-45.; Václav Chaloupecky, "Radla-Anastasius," *Bratislava*, 1 (1927), 210ff., though one is to recall that Moravia became already in 983, a part of the Czech diocese of Prague—cf. Harald Zimmermann (ed.), *Papstregesten, 911–1024*, vol. II-5 of *Regesta Imperii* (Vienna–Graz, 1969), n. 609. Boleslav I of Poland (d. 1025) requested, but failed to receive, papal recognition—cf. "Vita s. Romualdi," *MGHSS*, IV, 852f.; for background, cf. "Chronicon Hungarico-Polonicum," cc. 5-6, *SSH*, II, 299ff., and the comments by Macartney, *Hungarian Historians*, 173ff.

114. Albericus'—and to a certain extent—Sigibert of Gembloux's arguments, that only in 1008 had King Stephen Esztergom recovered [from Boleslav; Albericus dated King Stephen's 35 years of reign as of 1006], consequently, Gembloux wrote, the Magyars became Christians in 1010, cf. *MGHSS*, XXIII, 779, are based on hearsay. Gembloux's "Chronik...jetzt beginnt ihr Ansehen zu schwinden, ...da die Ungenauigkeit seiner Angaben nachgewiesen ist." Cf. Wattenbach, II, 160. Esztergom, for instance, became an archiepiscopal see in 1001—cf. Zimmermann, *Papstregesten*, n. 942. Related to Nitra, see the writ of Pope John VIII, in Jaffé, n.3332 [*dubiae fidei*], and letters under nn. 3319 and 3344; on Zalavár, cf. "De conversione Bogoariorum et Carantanorum," c. 11, in *MGHSS*, IX, 4ff.; *MHK*, 311. Z. J. Kosztolnyik, "Róma és a területi egyház küzdelme a közép Duna-medencében a 9 század folyamán" [The struggle between Rome and the territorial Church in the mid-Danubian basin during the ninth century], *Aetas*, 1997/2-3, 212ff. Related to Pécs, see the founding charter of its bishopric issued, in 1009, by King Stephen, in *RA*, n. 5; the name of the bishopric—"qui vocabitur Quinque-eclesiensis"—may refer to a continuous Christian past prior to the Magyars' arrival at *Sophianae*, the ancient name of the place, *MHK*, 311 (c. 11). For text, cf. Iosephus Koller, *Historia episcopatus Quinqueecclesiae*, 3 vols. (Posonii, 1782-84; vol. VII, Pesthini, 1812), I, 62.

115. On Stephen's place of birth, see his "Vita minor," c. 2, *SSH*, II, 394,11; that Adalbert had [only] *confirmed* him, is evident from Stephen's "Vita maior," c. 5, ibid., II, 380, 26-27, and 380,44-45.

116. See Pilgrim's letter to Pope Benedict VI, in Marczali, *Enchiridion*, 57ff.; Kosztolnyik, art. cit., in *Aetas*, 218f.

117. *MGHSS*, IV, 581ff., and 596ff.; H. G. Voigt, *Adalbert von Prag* (Westend-Berlin, 1898), 296; H. Spangenberg, "Die Grundung des Bistums Prag," *HJb*, 21 1900), 758ff.; Archbishop Willigis of Mainz called upon Adalbert to take charge of his episcopal

see at Prague, but Prince Boleslav had prevented him from returning there. Adalbert continued missionary work among the "pagans"—*MGHSS*, IV, 590, c. 22.

118. Instructions given by Pope John XV, dated May 31, 993, in Jaffé, n. 3849; *MPL*, 137, 847f.; Querfurti Bruno, "Vita s. Adalberti," cc. 14, 15, *MGHSS*, IV, 596ff., here 602, 603. On Bruno, the emperor's relative, *MGHSS*, IV, 574, and 578; as a monk, Bruno had assumed the name of Boniface—cf. Peter Damiani, "Vita s. Romualdi," c. 27, *MPL*, 144, 933ff., esp. 977. On the ongoing debate, see, for instance, J. Karácsonyi's arguments in *Századok*, 1892), 202f., offprint; on Radla and Astric, cf. Raimund Friedrich Kaindl, "Studien zur ungarischen Geschichtsquellen," *AföG*, 81 (1894), 326ff.; Thomas von Bogyay, "Adalbert von Prag und die Ungarn—ein problem der Quellen-Interpretation," *Ungarn-Jahrbuch*, 7 (1976), 9ff.

119. Bruno of Querfurt, cc. 16 and 21, *MGHSS*, IV, 603, 606; Hartvic, c. 4, *SSH*, II, 406f. The correspondence between Otto III and Adalbert, and their meetings in Rome and in Mainz, were mentioned by Johannes Canapario, "Vita antiquior s. Adalberti," *MGHSS*, IV, 581ff., c. 27: Stephen must not become overconfident, must have faith in God, and have only contempt for the goods of this world; there is some striking similarity here, with the "Instructions" of the Egyptian Vizier Ptah-hotep addressed to the heir of the Egyptian throne. Cf. James B. Pritchard (ed.), *The Ancient Near East: An Anthology of Texts and Pictures*, 2 vols. (Princeton, 1958), 234ff.

120. Bruno of Querfurt, c. 16; King Stephen's "Vita minor," c. 2.

121. *MGHSS*, IV, 591.

122. Cf. Knut Görich, *Otto III, Romanus Saxonicus et Italicus* (Sigmaringen, 1995), 39ff.; Karl Hampe, "Kaiser Otto III und Rom," *HZ*, 140 (1920), 513ff.

123. Thietmar, iv:38 [59]; Görich, 76ff.

124. *MGHSS*, IV, 603ff., cc. 21, 17-18, and 22-23.

125. *Ibid.*, c. 22; according to another source, it was not for the first time that Radla had left Adalbert—cf. "Vita antiqua ab Ioanne Canapario," cc. 2-3, *ibid.*, IV, 581ff.; one may add that Adalbert's sermon given in honor of St. Alexius was based on an earlier homily of Bede the Venerable—Voigt, *Adalbert*, 358ff.

126. *Ibid.*, IV, 607; also, "Chronicon Pulkawae," in Döbner, *Monumenta historica Boemiae*, III, 108. Pope John XV in one of his letters in 993 made mention of the monastery of Bresnov dedicated to saints Benedict, Boniface and Alexius, cf. *MPL*, 137, 847f., in a letter that came down to posterity in a twelfth century manuscript—cf. Jaffé, n. 3849. On the founding charter of the abbey of Pannonhalma—cf. *RA*, n. 2; text in László Erdélyi (ed.), *A pannonhalmi Szent Benedekrend története* [History of the Benedictines in Pannonhalma], 12 vols. (Pannonhalma, 1902-07), I, 589f.; comments by J. Stilting, "De sancto Stephano, primo Hungarorum rege," in *Acta sanctorum Bollandiana*, 60 vols. to Oct. XI (Paris-Rome, 1864-76), cited hereafter as ASS, Sept. I, 456ff.; Z. J. Kosztolnyik, *Five Eleventh Century Hungarian Kings, Their Policies and Their Relations with Rome* (New York, 1981), 4f.

127. See Adalbert's "Vita antiquior," cc. 26, 27, and 30, *MGHSS*, IV, 594f. Before that, Adalbert had established a monastery in Poland at Meserlitz, under the direction of Astrik [Ascherik], cf. "Passio Adalberti," *ibid.*, XV, 706ff.; also, Mirow, *ibid.*, IV, 613ff., cc. 4-5. When he heard the news about the death of Adalbert, Otto III in Rome had a monastery erected on the island in the Tiber in the honor of Adalbert, wrote Pope Leo IX, who recorded this information in one of his letters—cf. Jaffé, n. 4163; text in *MPL*, 143, 598ff., esp. 601f.; E. Male, *Rome et ses viellies églises* (Paris, 1942), 139f.; Gaudentius, brother of Adalbert, visited Rome as the envoy of Prince Boleslav during the fall of 999,

when Pope Sylvester II named Gaudentius archbishop of Gnesen; cf. Görich, 45ff., and 59f., also, 80ff.; F. Dvornik, *The Making of Central and Eastern Europe* (London, 1949), 143ff.; Dvornik further discussed the political situation in Bohemia during the 990's, see *ibid.*, 95ff.

128. King St. Stephen's "Vita maior," c. 2.

129. King St. Stephen's "Vita maior," c. 9.

130. *MGHSS*, IV, 538.

131. Cf. "Chronicon Posoniense," c. 44, *SSH*, II, 35f.

132. See Ioannis Skylitzae, *Synopsis historiarum*, ed. I. Thurn (Berlin-New York, 1973), 237,59-76; also, Ioannes Zonaras, *Epitomae historiarum*, ed. Th. Büttner-Wobst, CB (Bonn, 1897), xvi:21, and compare to *DAI*, c. 40.

133. See the "Russian Primary Chronicle," a. 1015—segment based on the Nikon MS—in Antal Hodinka, *Az orosz Évkönyvek magyar vonatkozásai* [Entries in the Russian Annals related to Hungarian history] (Budapest, 1916), 52b-54b; the segment, understandably, is missing from the Cross – Sherbowitz-Wetzor edition. See further Márta Font, *Oroszország, Ukrajna, Rusz* [Russia, the Ukraine and the Rus] (Pécs–Budapest, 1998), 34ff.

134. Hartvic, cc. 8-9, and c. 13, esp. *SSH*, II, 419,26-29; Stephen's "Vita maior," c. 11, *ibid.*, II, 386,26-28; Hóman, *König Stephan*, 105ff.; Kosztolnyik, *Five Kings*, 14ff.

IV

The Arrival of the Magyars in the Mid-Danubian Carpathian Basin

> Et primus rex Scithie fuit Magog, filius Iaphet, et gens illa a Magog rege vocata est Moger....
>
> Anonymus, *Gesta Hungarorum*, c. 1

The predecessors of the Magyars had during the ninth century settled down near the Black Sea, between the Don and Dnieper streams, in a region named Levedia.[1] East of them there lay the mighty, already declining, empire of the Khazars, while toward the west there lived Slavic tribes united into one people by a Scandinavian adventurer.[2] In 889, the Pechenegs, an Asiatic migrant people who had been expelled from their habitat near Url, broke into Levedia, forced the Magyars to leave,[3] and the Magyar tribes headed westward, crossed the Dnieper stream south of Kiev, and temporarily settled down to live in the region of the Sereth, Pruth and Dniester rivers.[4] In 895, the Pechenegs in a renewed conflict attacked them from the east and simultaneously the Bulgarians, who intended to wipe them out, invaded their land from the south.[5] It is from the "Region between the rivers" named Atelkozu [=Etelköz],[6] that the Magyars migrated toward Galicia, crossed the Carpathians through the Verecke Pass, and through other mountain passes, and penetrated the mid-Danube and Tisza region of the Carpathian basin during the mid-890's.[7]

During the course of six years, two military disasters devastated, decimated the ranks of the Magyars, and most probably frightened them, but failed to break their spirit; the nomadic Magyars, according to Ibn Rusta, they [must have] numbered about 200.000 souls,[8] remained daring and brave, prepared to face further military action. One is to remember, though, that the numerical data of medieval historical sources lack credibility.[9]

In their earlier homeland Levedia, the nomadic *Magyars* had formed seven tribes that consisted of clans, and large families; the tribe was led by the tribal *vajda*. It was the Byzantine emperor Leo VI the Wise who had named the Magyars tribal chiefs *vajda*;[10] it is known, for example, that, during the early eleventh century, Gyula, the governor in Transylvania—"gubernator partium Transylvanaraum"—had retained his power as a tribal *vajda* until King Stephen had not subdued him.[11] The tribal chiefs did not form a confederacy under a common head-chief until their predecessors had elected Árpád, son of Álmos "ducem et preceptorem."[12]

The men rode on horseback, women and children traveled in wagons; they followed their herds of horses, sheep and cattle that provided them with food, drink and clothing. They ate meat, did not eat much fish; drank milk, dressed in cured animal skin (leather); wore broad fur coats and crudely shaped shoes. When he stayed at home, the man rested in his tent, listened to heroic tales; his wife, women and slaves, did house work, though they accepted many of the freed slaves into their social ranks, and they all had fought together in battles together.[13]

They liked to go hunting, to fight wars, to break into cultivated lands seeking booty, and to capture prisoners whom they would sell as slaves to the Byzantines for money, gold, and velvet clothing.[14] When entering battle, the men wore headgear (*sisak*) and leather shirt on their bodies for protection; they carried straight, or bent, short swords, held shields (*dzsida*) in their left hand. On their shoulders they carried bows, and a supply of arrows in their quiver (*tegez*). Their war tactics consisted of covering the enemy ranks with a hail of arrows, pursue and confuse them with their *huj-huj!* battle cry, and thoroughly demolish them. If they did not succeed, they would renew their tactics, start shooting their arrows again, and pursue the enemy to the very end. They were short of stature, had brownish complexion, loved their freedom, and, the record has it, they could easily get out of control.[15]

The three tribes that had separated from the Khazars—and were united into the *tribe of the Kabars* [*insurgents*]—joined them in Levedia.[16] During their continued struggle with the Pechenegs, one group of the Magyars had separated from the main body and moved eastward, but the majority migrated toward the west, and, in time, crossed the Carpathian mountains.[17] In Levedia the seven Magyar tribes, and now the Kabars, had concluded a *blood oath* with one another, and elected a common leader, Árpád, son of Álmos, of the *Magyar* tribe. By electing a common leader they became a *nation*, and named themselves *Magyar(s)*, after Árpád's tribe.[18] According to Ibn Rusta, the seven tribes shared a common name: *Mazsgar*. (Ibn Rusta noted that, in a similar manner, one of the three Bulgarian tribes had once been known as *Bulgar*.)[19] The *blood-oath* they had taken in Levedia was mentioned by Ibn Rusta, Regino of Prüm,[20] and, following him, by Liutprand in the tenth,[21] Otto of Freising in the twelfth,[22] and by the Hungarian Anonymus at the end of the twelfth century.[23] Álmos's son Árpád, their elected leader, held the loosely organized tribes together in one socio-political body, gained control over domestic problems and tribal dissent, and established a home for his people, in the mid-Danubian–Carpathian basin during the mid-890's.[24]

Of the events discussed here the narrative by Emperor Constantine VII Porphyrogenitus, the previously cited *De administrando imperio*—hereafter to be referred to as the *DAI*—provided information, but not a clear picture of their activities.[25] The (*Türk-*)Magyars lived in Levedia, near the Khazars, the imperial author reports, who at that time were not called Turks, but were known by the name *Savartoi asphaloi*. The Pechenegs, known as *Kangars*, attacked them, divided them into two segments, one of which migrated south finding refuge in the Caucasus; they were still known by that name in the mid-tenth century, when the emperor prepared his report.

Their other segment moved west, and entered into an alliance with the Khazars. But the Pechenegs had again attacked those who had migrated to the west, and the defeated Turk-Magyars had no alternative but to migrate *further* west, and to take possession of the territory they had occupied by the time Porphyrogenitus was writing his report. In other words, the imperial author spoke in a brief description of two military defeats of the Turk-Magyars, and of two Turk-Magyar migrations westward.[26] Their first defeat would be identical with the one recorded—or, might have been reported—by Regino of Prüm, anno 888, or 889, an event that had caused their forced migration from the area west of the Don to the mid-Danubian region.[27]

It was after *Levedias* that they named the region *Levedia*—the region crossed by the Chidmas (Cinhul) stream. Levedia was located next to the land of the Khazars, a geo-political condition that may mean that the Magyars in the ninth century lived on the right bank of the Don river.[28] The attack by the Pechenegs must have occurred there, because, according to the imperial author, the Pechenegs had attacked the Magyars in a region, where they were having their habitat *now*. The *DAI* observed that the eastern border of Pecheneg territory reached to Serkel along the Don, an observation that may lead to the conclusion that Levedia could not have been located east, or south, of the Don stream. Many rivers crossed the region between the Danube and the Don—the Dnieper and the Dniester being the most important—together with smaller streams, like the Sereth and the Pruth.[29]

The name of Levedias appeared recorded in historical sources as Eleud (Előd), one of the seven tribal chiefs who, according to the Hungarian Anonymus, descended immediately from Almus (Álmos) on the family tree: "Almus pater Arpad, Eleud pater Zobolsu…,"[30] though, the chronicler Keza described him as the father of Álmos, "Arpad filius Almi filii Elad."[31] The name of the tribal leader, however, was Eleud, not Levedias, therefore, Levedia could not have been named after Eleud. Most probably, the similarly sounding names had confused the Slavic interpreter of the imperial author. "Levedia" must have sounded well in Greco-Slavic; the unusual sounding Magyar name had a less pleasant tone to it. In other words, the land *Levedia* referred to by the imperial author's Slavic interpreter had to be located on the right bank of the lower estuary of the Don stream.[32]

The question remains, though, what had happened during the intermediate years? Flodoard of Reims in his *Historia* referred to the Magyars' intrusion into Frankish Gaul in 937;[33] an entry, anno 862, in the *Annales Bertiniani* reported that the kingdom of the Danes, most probably the east Frankish lands of Louis the German, were destroyed with fire and sword by the ferocious until then unknown enemy, named Magyars.[34] The Salzburg Annals, anno 881, record a *first* battle with the Magyars at the otherwise unknown Weinia.[35] In the opinion of Emperor Constantine, the Kanagors had attacked the Turk-Magyars and forced them to flee toward the west, where the Pechenegs had lived. The region of the Pechenegs, Etelköz [*Atelkozu*, land between the rivers]—where the Turk-Magyars lived before them—was named after the streams that crossed it. Because of the Pecheneg attack, the Turk-Magyars, led by Árpád, penetrated the territory of Greater-Moravia, the imperial author reports, and found a new home in Pannonia, that is, in the mid-Danubian basin.[36] The names of the rivers that crossed Atelkozu (Etelköz), the land where the Turk-Magyars had lived before they had been forced to leave for Pannonia, were cited by the illustrious author, and they would, in modern usage, be known as the Dnieper, Bug, Dniester, Pruth and Sereth. One is tempted to note that the illustrious chronicler must not have had the same region in mind when he wrote about *Atelkozu*, that is, *Etelköz*.[37]

They must have spent several years in a region north of the estuary of the Danube, the area known as *Etelköz* [*region between the rivers*]. Although this segment of the *DAI*, c. 38, is, most probably, a later insert, one may conclude that it was from the right bank and estuary of the Don river that the Turk-Magyars had, in time, migrated toward Pannonia.[38]

The one-sided record in the *DAI* is filled in by the remark of Regino of Prüm who wrote that the Magyars had been forced to migrate westward, away from the Don, in the year 889. In this entry, Regino depicted the Magyar as a ferocious folk without self control, worse then wild beasts who previously did not even had a name. Regino may have referred to the Magyar-Pecheneg war of the early 890's, and maintained that the Pechenegs were far superior in number and military know-how to the Magyars. The latter could not fight regular battles, he wrote, would fight only on horseback, and sham-withdrawal was their favored tactic. They did not know how to besiege towns; their method of warfare was dangerously Scythian.[39] In the words of Regino, this godless people had also destroyed a major portion of the Italian kingdom—most probably referring to the Magyars' ventures in Lombardy during the months in 899–900; Regino dated 901 (or was it 899?) the Magyars' intrusion into Italy, when they had, indeed, devastated everything by fire, thievery and murder, as exemplified by the case of Bishop Liudward of Vercelli (earlier the trusted advisor of King Charles III), who tried to escape with all his treasures before them, but the Magyars found him, murdered him, and took all his treasures.[40]

A word of clarification is in order here concerning Magyar political-military events during the earlier 890's. In the learned opinion of C. A. Macartney, Emperor Constantine's *DAI*, c. 38, provided two reports on the same event, the Magyar-Pecheneg encounter; the chapter itself was not edited, as it remained a rough draft of a heap of notes, depicting the event twice, though somewhat differently.[41] First, it recorded that the Turk-Magyars lived near the region of the Khazars, in Levedia, the land they had named after their first known leader, a land crossed by the Chidmas (Cinhul) stream. They were known as *Savartoi asphaloi,* organized into seven hordes (tribes), with Levedias was their leader. They were closely associated with the Khazars. The Khazar khan had waited until the Magyar hordes had separated from his people, then he had summoned Levedias to his presence with the idea that, in recognition of the valuable military assistance they had provided for him, he, the khan, would give Levedias a Khazar woman for wife, of whom he could expect a son to be born. But Levedias could have no children.[42]

In the second report, the imperial author recorded that Levedias, on the grounds that he was unworthy of such an honor, had politely turned down the marriage offer the Khan had made to him, and recommended a younger person instead. Soon thereafter war broke out between the Turk-Magyars and the Pechenegs [previously known as Kaggars]; the Magyars had been defeated, and the Pechenegs expelled them from the area.[43]

The imperial chronicler did not elaborate about the plans of the Khazar Khan; he did not say whether it remained unsuccessful because of the—accidental, or purposefully well timed?—intervention of the Pechenegs, who had neutralized the khan's move on the board of a diplomatic game of chess. Nor did the *DAI*, c. 38, time schedule of the event provide any help in determining the dates of the Magyar-Khazar association, nor did it set a date for the Magyars' westward migration. The 830's could have been the time of the Khazar-Magyar alliance, and of "family-oriented" Khazar diplomacy with Levedias.[44] The imperial author did say, though, that three Khazar clans, forming one [Khazar] tribe, joined ranks with the departing Magyars in their association with the (seven) Magyar tribes.[45]

A note of observation on the geography of the area is in order here. South of the Carpathians, Slavic tribes were living on marshlands cultivating primitive [methods of] agriculture; they based their social framework upon the greater family [of several generations] that formed the *ethnic clan* among them. Every Slavic tribe constructed an earth fort—*grad*—and centered around it. They made a good appearance as a people, being tall, with brownish-blond hair, not overly proud, and yet possessing self-dignity. They obeyed their superiors. The Slavs living within the Carpathian mountain range in Pannonia were very similar to the Slovenes settled west of them.

Transylvania: *Erdőelje*, was separated by a mountain chain from the Great Plain that spread out southward on both banks of the Tisza river; the Szamos, Kraszna, Berettyó, and Maros streams broke through these low mountains. The western portion of the region, *Tiszasíkság*: plain east of the Tisza river, formed a flood basin, mostly unfit for human habitation, though Bihar land—located centrally in the region—seems to have had formidable Slavic settlements.[46]

South, and southeast of the origins of the Tisza river, in the area *beyond the forest*, before the year 1000, a particular province had been formed out of an urban population of the land, who derived their living from the salt mines in the area, as well as from the gold mines that provided the basis for their economy. A network of roads serving military and commercial needs crossed the region; the Roman military highway went from Zilah via Kolozsvár and Gyulafehérvár, southward to the Maros river. The region had been a part of Dacia conquered by Emperor Trajan, though its civilization had been swept away by the storm of the barbarian migrations; the Romans withdrew, the towns turned into ruins, its neglected mines ceased operation. Salt, however, remained a necessary commodity in the age, and for that reason mining for salt continued, and so did, although under far more primitive conditions, mining for gold. The headquarters of Docebal located south of the Maros river became a ruin; the area inhabited by the Széklers today, must have then been sheer wilderness.[47]

The region between the Danube and the Tisza rivers had a higher elevation, was not a flood-plain, but the Romans never took possession of it. Slavic tribes lived there in the ninth century; among them, the Bulgarians became the neighbors of the Franks, and by having penetrated the area they prevented salt shipments of Transylvania from reaching Moravia in the northwest.[48]

In the judgment of Emperor Constantine, Moravia was at that time a great power; it included the Morava region, the land ruled by Svatopluk that spread further east, down to the Danube.[49] In Roman times, the Quadi and Markomans lived in the area; there, Nitra became an episcopal see in the ninth century, and the region was protected by many forts.[50] Further south, Pannonia formed a Roman province [or two] for centuries.[51] The northern half of Pannonia was wilderness, its southern segment mere marshland; a wide range of forest on the Bakony Hills formed the dividing line. The area between the Drave and Save rivers was also a wilderness of ancient forests; the banks of the Drave were covered with trees. West of Lake Balaton, the Slavic prince, Pribina, had developed Moorsburg [Fort Mud; fort in the marsh], that served as his headquarters, into an ecclesiastical center, very much like the location Siscia [Sziszek], whose Slavic prince was a vassal of the east-Franks.[52] Christianity had found its way into the villages of the region. The Slavs in the area did not welcome the Magyars' arrival, nor did they resist the forceful Magyar occupation of the land.[53]

The family feud among Svatopluk's sons described by the imperial author had made it easier for the Magyars to take the territory, and to settle down in the mid-Danubian region.[54] At first, it was Arnulf, the east-Frankish prince, who had called upon the Magyars for military aid against the Moravians.[55] There, however, on a second occasion, the sons of Svatopluk could not, recorded Emperor Constantine, prevent the Magyars from entering what was then considered as the eastern *Mark* in Pannonia, at the time under Moravian rule.[56] Regino of Prüm also referred to, anno 894, the death of Svatopluk, and to the fact that Svatopluk's sons fighting among each other could not resist the Magyars' arrival; his remark that they had destroyed everything may apply to the fall of the Moravian principality in the year 902.[57] Within five years, the Magyars had occupied the mid-Danubian lands reaching westward to the Lake Fertő on the border of Noricum, and to the Carpathian Mountains in the east and southeast—a frontier that had remained the country's natural border until 1918. The Szerém region—land south of the Carpathians and north of the Danube—remained in Bulgarian hands.[58]

The newly arrived Turk-Magyars divided the occupied territory according to tribal claims; the majority of the Slavic population had stayed. The Magyars' attitude toward them depended upon the behavior they displayed toward their new masters. Some became slaves, many remained poor folk, but all paid taxes, that is, they—as tax payers—had to have held *freemen* status in the new Magyar (Hungarian) society, as equal social partners of the conquerors in the emerging new social-political order.[59]

Emperor Constantine evidently had been informed that the Magyars took possession of territory what would correspond to Transdanubia today, and of the regions beyond the Danube, and further east of the Tisza river, with all the inhabitants thereof; Magyar settlements developed as far south as the Save stream. Their new country was rich in food supplies, such as wild meat animals, bison in Transylvania, bears in the mountains.[60] Fishing was easy, assuring them rich catches of fish; in fact, the term *tanya*, Hungarian for *hamlet*, originally meant a "place to fish." The Turk-Magyar land-taking, *conquest*—C. A. Macartney referred to it with the German term: *Landnahme*[61]—must have been completed by 900, because, in that year, they already devastated the east-Frankish military frontier in the west, and invaded Italy, *but returned to their own country*: "redierunt, unde venerant, ad sua in Pannoniam," the chronicler of the Fulda Annals recorded.[62]

In the spring of 900, Archbishop Theotmar of Salzburg wrote a letter to Pope John IX to report about and to condemn the doubtful work of Slav missionaries among the Magyars in Pannonia, who had marauded in Italy. And yet, the archbishop expressed willingness to cooperate with the Slav missionaries, despite the fact that the missionaries had tried to curtail the archbishop's jurisdiction in their area of activity, for the sake of their own selfish religious-political interest.[63]

The referred to Fulda Annals recorded, year by year, the "notorious" marauding invasions of the Magyars in the Latin west. In 892, they devastate Moravia in alliance with (the east-Frankish) King Arnulf; in 894, the Avars who are named Magyars (the annalist's own interpretation) were marauding the Danube region murdering men and old women, taking young women captive to satisfy their own sexual desires, devastating all of Pannonia. He is pleased to record that, in the following year, when they were invading Bulgaria, the Bulgarians mercilessly defeated them. And the Bulgarians thoroughly defeated

the Magyars again, when the latter, in alliance with the Byzantine emperor, engaged them in a military skirmish.[64]

In an entry for the year 900, the annalist most probably referring
to events of 899, recorded the Italian campaigns of the Magyars
accusing them of causing horrible damage and murdering all bishops.
King Berengar tried to stop them, but lost the engagement; the
Magyars left the region the way they came and returned to Pannonia.
(This is the sentence, cited above, that may be interpreted that the
Magyars had [by this time] already settled down in Pannonia.[65])

But the Magyars would not rest. They devastated Bavarian lands
destroying everything in their way; and yet, they now received their
punishment. Margrave Leopold of Bavaria, accompanied by the
bishop of Passau, followed them, and when they began to destroy the
region north of the Danube, he (and the bishop) surprised and "nobly"
defeated them. Still, the Magyars' losses must not have been too
heavy because the annalist, anno 901, briefly reports, they broke into
southern Caranthanian lands.[66]

In a discussion, or argument about the Magyar marauding
ventures in the Latin west during the first half of the tenth century it
would be worthwhile to concentrate on the remarks by Widukind of
Corbey who, in four entries before the Magyars' defeat at Augsburg,
had dealt with the havoc caused by the Magyar invasions.[67] Thus, he
mentioned, anno 906, that the Magyar contingent fighting in alliance
with the Slavs had caused much devastation in Saxony, where they
invaded twice; another Magyar unit caused awful damage in
Dalmatia.[68] In 924, they again devastated Saxony, and devastated it so
thoroughly that, politically and economically speaking, Saxony, its
administrative structure, nearly collapsed. But the east-Frankish
king's (Henry I) army captured one of the Magyar leaders; to redeem
him, the Magyars agreed to a nine year truce with the Franks.[69]
During that time the king (Henry I) had sufficiently built up his armed
force of veterans to face the enemy in open confrontation. When the
Magyar envoys arrived to collect their annual gifts (tribute?) from the
king, the king refused. Thereupon the Magyars invaded Saxon lands
again in early 933, but the king resisted them, and the Magyars
realizing that they were facing heavily arm[or]ed German cavalry

units, took to flight leaving their camp and captured booty behind. The king's men were able to free all the prisoners.[70]

About five years later (in 938?), the Magyars again marauded Saxon soil, Widukind complains; some of their units went as far as Strasbourg, but the town people realized that the invaders were tired, so they met the enemy before the town walls and defeated them, killing and capturing many of them; those who escaped were captured and killed by the inhabitants of other towns. One Magyar army unit was entrapped near Dromling (Wolfsburg), and destroyed, its leader captured but released on ransom. Afterwards, the Magyars left Saxony alone for the next thirty years.[71]

In other words, the Magyars retained their militant attitude toward neighboring territories for about another half a century; every year, they invaded Bulgaria, Byzantium, and the region around Thessalonika.[72] In the west, they penetrated lands as far as the Rhine valley, devastated locations as far as north as Bremen. In west-Frank territories, they devastated Aquitaine and Burgundy, nor did they spare the Po valley in Lombardy.[73] They moved on their horses like lightning, brought their own food supplies with them on wagons, erected temporary wagon forts, then spread out, surveyed, then robbed the particular area. Their tactics included causing fear among the regional population by burning down houses and churches, killing people, and by capturing men and women to sell them as slaves on the Byzantine market.[74]

Charlemagne's kingdom was by that time a memory of the past, Byzantium faced problems of its own; the unthwarted intruding Magyars were met by no serious organized resistance. Their raids were only ended by the emerging unified east-Frankish state; as mentioned above by quoting Widukind, in 933, Henry the Hunter had met and defeated them at Riad near Merseburg;[75] twelve years later, at Augsburg, Otto I the Great demolished their intruding forces in 955.[76] Widukind reports that in early July, 955, Otto I had met with Hungarian envoys in Saxony; the envoys came to pay him their respects, but, at the same time, to observe his domestic political and military situation. The German monarch dismissed them with some gifts of no value, when he received news from his brother, the duke of Bavaria, that the Magyars had invaded the borderlands and did heavy fighting.

Thereupon, Otto I began to make war preparations: his Saxon-Bavarian troops set up camp at Augsburg, where his brother-in-law, Conrad the Red of Lorraine, arrived with his heavy cavalry; from their scouts both the invaders and the invaded knew that they were close to each other. On the day of the battle, the troops took a loyalty oath to the king, and under their standards moved into battle, a total of eight legions. The first three legions were Bavarian, led by the officers of Henry of Bavaria. (The duke was ill; he had died soon after.) The fourth legion consisted of Franconians led by Duke Conrad; the fifth legion drew a protective shield around the king and the royal standard that depicted an angel; Swabians made up the sixth and seventh legions, led by their duke Burchard. The eighth legion consisted of thousand selected Czech knights, who had good weapons, but bad luck in the field; they were to guard the baggage and the goods, and to form the rear guard.[77] Otto I, or rather, one of his military leaders, Henry of Bavaria, the father of Henry the Wrangler, had two of the Magyar clan chiefs, Lehel and Bulcsú, publicly hanged after the battle of Augsburg.[78]

The Magyar leadership must have realized by this time that their behavior would only cause resentment and continued hostility toward them. After 955, they did not invade the west anymore, and, by the late 960's, they had also kept their distance from Byzantium.[79] They began to think in terms of military defense of their own country and of their families. They had erected fortified military defense zones (in Hungarian: *gyepü*) on their borders, with openings (*gyepü-kapu*), to make entry into their land possible. In the western region, near Lake Fertő, the old Roman military road served such a purpose, or the old fort near Moson on the Lajta stream; north of the Danube, Fort Nitra controlled the commercial-military road from Moravia toward the south.[80]

They had ceased to live like nomads. The Magyar population began to grow slowly, but their chattel in goods and animal stock increased greatly, and they had to find a way to settle down on farms and to live from agriculture, despite the fact that it was not the Magyars, but the Magyars' servants—they knew a good deal about agriculture—who cultivated their fields. Bulgarian and Greek migrants wanting to reside among them were given horses and agricultural tasks. Magyar words, such as *búza, kalász, sarló, arat, őröl* [that is, wheat, ear-of-wheat; sickle, to grind, to masticate] were very old, and now they began to add new terms to their vocabulary, such as *gabona, rozs, szalma, iga, járom, borona, osztag, petrence* [that is, corn, rye, straw, yoke, harness, harrow, hay-stack, rake], borrowed from their subordinated, and gradually emancipated, Slav peoples. Living by agriculture meant permanent settlements; it meant to be tied to the land, to a home—no matter how poor, or simple, that home would be.[81]

Their living quarters must have at first been of very low quality; their wooden buildings must have been mere shacks, stone buildings they had but few, though, in the Magyar (Hungarian) vocabulary, every part of a house had a name, as for instance, *pince, konyha, grádics* [that is, cellar, kitchen, steps], all of Slavic origin.[82] They would not want, however, to live among four walls all year long, and weather permitting, they lived under tents during the summer—as witnessed by the objectively critical chronicler Otto of Freising of the twelfth century.[83] Their settlements were erected near, or, at places occupied by Slavic settlers, assuming the name of the place; in case of a new settlement, they named it after a leader from among them-selves.[84]

Land property was not in private hands, and the record shows that inconsistencies frequently led to misunderstanding over mis-interpretation of property borders; the leaders who claimed the land were powerful and rich, able to acquire "chattel" in goods and live stock more easily, enabling them to move up the social ladder. The poor had to carry their own burden, could barely cultivate the field segments allotted to their use. Personal intelligence, the individual use of (military, or mere physical) force, and developing social contacts created a new aristocracy, whose members were not identical with the social stratum of the earlier nobles.[85]

The relationship between the tribes, and their clans, grew weaker; during the tenth century the tribal order fell apart—except in Transyl-vania, where one tribe (under its tribal head, the *vajda*) was able to maintain control of its territory until 1003.[86] The prestige of the tribal chiefs had further declined, and the Prince, the successor of Árpád, became a mere "first among the equals." The prince had to assert leadership to retain his powers, though Árpád was both Lord and the military leader of his people,[87] but his successors, as, for example, his son, Zulta [Zsolt], and grandson Taksony, were not.[88] Taksony, son of Zulta, held no command over the whole body of the Magyar armed forces.[89]

The Magyars who now occupied the country had their own religion, though were not overly religious people. They had no interest in abstract religious thought. They believed in God as the Supreme Being, but had only vague concepts about the supernatural deity. The *sámáns* [druids] performed religious sacrifices in nature, at a tree, at a well, near a river site, and believed in given ethical principles that had to prevail within their society's pattern.[90]

In marriage, they lived in monogamy; the husband could kill his wife caught in adultery; if the wife became a widow and had no children, she could marry the next of kin.[91] The husband could keep a mistress, but would not abandon his wife! Actually, he could not leave her. The wives legally married to their husbands were of a fiery nature, who knew their obligations *and their rights*.[92] The Magyars buried their dead. It was an early Magyar burial custom to lay the free [fighting] man into the grave with his faithful dog.[93]

The Magyar political-military leadership of the mid-tenth century had to consider forthcoming political, social and ethical-religious changes in its people's political-social structure. The Germans in the west were a powerhouse. The record has it that Prince Géza had sensed, in fact, he knew of the possible threat presented by the powerful and expanding political German neighbor in the Latin west—and took diplomatic action; "...in omnes large proveniens, quia nullum spernit, sed 'omnes homines vult salvos fieri et ad agnitionem veritatis venire,' ad Ungaros usque, quos Christianorum flagellum quodam fuisse constat, diffusum est."[94]

He, and his son, Vajk, the later King Stephen, clearly saw, however, the possible threat of political and religious German influence to their people's interests, and had made a powerful diplomatic countermove. The Prince reasoned that Magyar soil had to remain in Magyar hands, under Magyar leaders control. The princely family, young and vigorous, was also able to judge the political situation realistically. The dynasty, and the country, could not afford remaining an enemy of the German imperial court. Géza of the Árpáds had to find the peaceful means to approach the German neighbor, and to accept the religion of the Latin west.

Sarolta, the wife of Géza and the mother of Stephen, was the daughter of Gyula of Transylvania; she was a Byzantine-rite Christian, and possessed a forceful, manly personality, who would even dominate her husband.[95] It is to be pointed out, though, that, on the other hand, a Polish chronicler reported that it was Jesse, sister of Mieszko, who became the wife of the Magyar Prince Géza,[96] while Thietmar of Merseburg had referred to the mother of Stephen, and to Stephen's Polish uncle, Boleslaw, without, however, recording anything about family blood ties between Stephen and the son of Mieszko.[97]

Sarolta must have realized that Byzantium was further away from the borders of the country of her husband, than the German territories, next door neighbors within easy reach through the Danube valley. It was in accordance with her views that Géza had sent delegates to Quedlinburg to greet, and to establish diplomatic relationship with, the crowned German emperor. The "XII primates Ungarorum" Géza dispatched to Quedlinburg were members of the high nobility, as if to emphasize the point of view that the Magyar court had taken the occasion seriously by sending twelve noblemen as delegates—and not mere princely envoys[98]—dispatched with instructions to explain the purpose of their mission: (1) establishing contact with the emperor's court, and (2) requesting missionaries to spread the (Latin-rite) Christian faith among his people. "Ea siquidem tempestate, qua gens prefate Dei ecclesiam depopulabatur, erat in ea princeps quidam quartus ab illo, qui ingressionis Hungarorum in Pannoniam dux primus fuit, nomine Geysa, veluti potentialiter agens in suos, misericors autem et liberalis...et precipue in Christianos...."[99] The record has it that, in order to belong to the Latin west, one also had to keep a political-diplomatic balance with the west, wherefore, the court of Géza had to turn to Rome: "quod etiam ipsa mundi totius metropolis Roma, cum monarchia dignitatis imperatorie Christi fidei colla submittens vanitatum erroribus renunciavit."[100]

The road of religious-political approach of Prince Géza's court toward the Latin west thus became clear. Unfortunately, the bishop of Passau made use of the opportunity to claim, as a missionary region, the Pannonian territories conquered by the Magyars. It is a curious twist of history, though, that Magyar (Hungarian) expressions corresponding to *Christian* terms, such as *püspök, pogány, bérmálás, pap, szerzetes*, that is, "bishop," "pagan," "confirmation," "priest," "monk," etc., are all of Slavic, that is, of Sloven, and *not* of German origin.[101]

The conversion of the Magyars to western Latin Christianity became a historic fact. Johannes Enenkel spoke tersely about the conversion of the Magyars, "Ungari Christiani fiunt," in his entry made anno 826 (!—it has to be a late addition), though the Olaf's saga Tryggvssonar also made mention of the Magyars' conversion to Christianity;[102] Ellenhardus Argentinensis—judged by his name, a chronicler from Augsburg—placed their conversion in the days of (Emperor) Henry II,[103] while an Italian writer, without rendering his reasons as to why, dated it earlier, in the times of (Emperor) Otto II.[104] A Polish source leaning toward the extreme, made Cyril and Methodius directly responsible for the conversion of Prince Géza: "...Yesse dux Ungarorum [the father of King Stephen] per Cirilum [sic] et Methudium [sic] fuit in fide cathecisatus."[105] As it has been pointed out above, the Polish chroniclers stressed the role of the Polish Adelheid (Atleyde!) had played—besides the Bavarian-born Gisela—in the conversion of the Magyars to Christianity, and that on the grounds that *Atleyde* had already been *a* Christian, *before* her marriage to [Prince Géza]; she was well versed in the teachings of her faith, and led her pagan husband on the path toward the Christian religion.[106] Other Polish authors had expressed different, sometimes confusing, opinions.

A Polish chronicler would not leave the Polish ruling family out of the picture: the author of the Silesian Annals recorded that, next to Gisela, it was the Polish *Adelheid*—Prince Géza's second [Polish] wife?—who played an important role in the conversion of the Hungarians.[107] The Roczik Krasinekich reported that it was (after all) Bishop Adalbert who had instructed (the Magyar) Prince Géza in the Christian faith.[108] On the other hand, the non-Polish Gauredus de Bruil wrote that "Rex [sic!] Ungarie Gonzalco [sic!] a Brunone baptizatus dictus est Stephanus, qui genuit Stephanum." The report not only made it clear that it was Bruno of Querfurt who had baptized Géza, but that Géza had [also] been baptized *Stephen*—a newsworthy remark that occurred in several non-Hungarian historical sources, as, for instance, in the Chronicle of Ademar Cabannensis, who noted that it was Bruno [of Querfurt] who baptized Géza, the father of the later King Stephen, on the feast day of Stephen the First Martyr (on December 26—hence the baptismal name *Stephen*). "S. Brunus regem [sic!] Ungrie baptizavit, qui vocabatur Gouz, et mutato nomine in baptismo Stephanum vocavit."[109] Ademar made the additional remark that the emperor, Otto III, himself had agreed to be the godfather, and presented the neophyte with a lance—the symbol of the ruler's secular power.[110]

The conversion of Géza had not been sincere, opinionated Thietmar of Merseburg. Although he firmly opposed those who had threatened the expansion of the Christian faith in the country, the Prince regarded himself as a man powerful [rich] enough to sacrifice to two gods [did he mean paying lip-service to two religions?], Thietmar wrote; "...Deo omnipotenti variisque deorum inclusionibus immolatus, ...divitem se ad haec facienda satis potentem affirmavit."[111]

The remark made by Thietmar—the [imperial] bishop-chronicler made no distinction between German political goals and the geographical designations of a country in his age—must have served a political-diplomatic purpose, because an Italian chronicler, for instance, only spoke of Pannonia when he referred to the conversion of the Magyars to Christianity during the reign of Emperor Henry II (who "totam Pannoniam per sororem suam Christianam fecit"); now, in eleventh century geographical terminology, *Pannonia* designated the whole country under Magyar rule at that time.[112]

Ademar further drew a distinction between *white* Magyars, "in Ungariam, que dicitur Alba Ungaria," and *black* Magyars, "Ungare Nigre, ...velut Etiopes."[113] Did he daringly wish to distinguish between (baptized) *Christian* and (non-baptized) *pagan* Magyars? After all, were the Monophysite Ethiopians orthodox Christians? It may very well be that some medieval chroniclers simply left the possibility out of consideration that not every Magyar, who had actively taken a part in the *land-taking* of the mid-Danubian Carpathian basin, had become a Christian—a probability that became evident from the word usage by the Hungarian chroniclers, who distinguished between *white*, that is, Catholic Christian, and *brown* (in Hungarian *szár*, meaning *bald*, or, someone "blackened" by the Sun), that is, un-baptized *pagan*, with *black soul*, that is, land-taking Magyars. The author of this segment of the Chronicle, c. 88, characterized King Andrew I as *white* and *Catholic*—"ipse quidem rex Albus Andreas et Catholicus est vocatus,"—as in c. 96, he spoke of Béla I, Andrew I's the younger brother and successor, as someone bald and brown (who had the black soul of a pagan, or of a fallen-away, Catholic)—"Hic enim Bela erat calvus et in colore brunus"—*brunus* meaning *szög* (in Hungarian, that is, *fuscus* = dark brown, black), as someone *blackened* by the Sun—and this might have mattered greatly that Béla had to war with Salomon, the anointed and crowned monarch of the land.[114]

The chronicler's statement is supported by a remark of the chronicler Simon de Keza who wrote that "post hunc [that is, King Andrew I, the elder brother and predecessor of Béla I] regnavit Benyn Bela, quo regnante Hungari fidem derelinquunt, anno in fide aberrantes, ut nec pagani, nec catholici viderentur."[115] If by referring to Béla as *Benyn* [benignus?] the chronicler meant a ruler who was *too kind* (or, too weak!) to enforce the country's Christianization against the will of the majority of the inhabitants, then he must have depicted a situation where the pagan leaders of the land, subdued under the reign of Andrew I, had fought back quite effectively to halt, or to delay, the country's Christianization process—a circumstance that may explain why Béla I had died (had to die?) such a sudden death on a collapsing throne in the year 1063. "In regali allodio, corruente solio confractus corpore irremediabiliter cepit egrotare."[116]

Could it have been a coincidence that the non-Hungarian monk Albericus had referred to Béla I as *pugil*, alias *fistfighter*, a hard man to get along with?[117] As it shall be argued in a chapter below, there is another view of the unexpected death of the monarch. The collapsing throne was not, it could not have been sheer coincidence, but a carefully prepared political-dynastic murder; the death of the monarch opened the way for the return of Salomon, the protégé of the German court, to the Hungarian throne.

Various contemporary historical evidence may point to direct imperial German influence upon the political background that surrounded the conversion of the Magyars stressing the role Queen Gisela (may have) played, next to her husband, in the conversion of the people. The Magyars, "hactenus idolatrie dedita...," became

Christians "per Gislam sororem imperatoris," recorded one, though the chronicler could not resist making the statement that the Magyars had been converted because Gisela had persuaded her husband that he, and his people, accept Christian baptism.[118]

Herimannus Augiensis noted in his Chronicle that the German court looked upon the marriage of Gisela to Stephen of Hungary as a (political-diplomatic) contract that made Gisela responsible for the conversion of the Magyars; "Gisela Stephano regi Ungariorurm, cum se ad fidem Christi converteret, quasi vere iuxta nomen suum fidei obses in coniugium data."[119] The anonymous "Chronica minora auctore Minorita Erphordensis" wanted to know that several Bavarian nobles had accompanied Gisela to the Hungarian court (also remained there), and, before the wedding, had knighted Stephen (who was "statura pusillus, corde magnus"), so that he be a guardian of peace and of the Christian faith among his people.[120]

The Italian chroniclers, of course, would not leave Bishop Adalbert out of the picture, stressing the role the bishop of Prague—seeking solace in the monastery in Rome—and the Bavarian-born Hungarian Queen had played in the conversion of the Magyars to Christianity.[121]

The Czech, and other Polish, historical sources seemed to have agreed with this point of view, regardless whether the Czech bishop, for example, knew the Magyars' language, or not; whether he spoke to them through an interpreter; or, whether he spent long enough time in the country to be able to prepare both Stephen *and his people* for the sacrament of the Latin-rite of baptism. As it had been argued above, the Czech bishop did not convert all of the Magyars, but only a (very small) portion of the Magyar population.[122]

The bishop undoubtedly must have had discussions with the Magyar Prince, and with members of his immediate family, who were already familiar with the Catholic faith from previous encounters with other missionaries visiting the country. Bishop Adalbert had, before his arrival at the Magyar court, dispatched missionaries to Magyar land, as he was concerned about the expansion of the Catholic faith among the Magyars.[123] One cannot, however, accept at face value the statement made in the *Catalogue of the Archbishops of Gnesen* that said that Adalbert had visited Hungary with the approval of the

Roman pontiff, and remained there to convert (until he converted) the whole country.[124]

There are chroniclers, of course, whose imagination knew no boundaries, as, for instance, the one who wrote that Adalbert of Prague had not only stayed in Hungary, but was buried there, and it was from *there*—from Pannonia—that the emperor, Otto III, had the bishop's *dexter*—right arm—sent, as a relic, to Rome.[125]

Notes

1. Cf. *DAI*, c. 38; Macartney, *Ninth Century*, 90ff.; G. Fehér, "Ungarns Gebietsgrenzen in der Mitte des zehnten Jahrhunderts," *Ungarische Jahrbücher*, 2 (1922), 37ff.; *voivode*: they lived under the leadership of one ruler, their *voivode*, *woyvoda*; cf. Leo VI the Wise, *Tactica*, xviii:46, in *MPG*, 672ff.; or, in Gyula Pauler – Sándor Szilágyi (eds.), *A magyar honfoglalás kútfői* [Collection of historical sources dealing with the Magyars' land-taking of 896] (Budapest, 1900), 11ff.; also, Moravcsik, *Fontes Byzantini*, 14ff. On Constantine VII (selections of his work also in Pauler – Szilágyi, 110ff.), see also N. G. Wilson, *Scholars of Byzantium*, rev. ed. (Cambridge, MA, 1996), 140ff.; Emperor Leo VI the Learned (d. 912) must not be confused with Leo the Philosopher (790–869)—cf. *ibid.*, 79ff.; further, S. L. Tóth, "A magyarok *etelközi honfoglalása*" [The Magyars in Atelkozu], *Acta historica Szegediensis*, 98 (1993), 3ff.

2. See Macartney, *Ninth Century*, 5f.; for [his] English translations of Magyar-related sections of Arabic sources, as, for instance, the early tenth century Omar Ibn Rusta (Abu 'Ali Ahmad), *Book of precious jewels* (St. Petersburg, 1889), the mid-eleventh century Mahmud Gardēzī (Abu Sa'id 'Ab al-Hajj ad Dahhak), *Chronicle* (St. Petersburg, 1897), and of 'Abd al-Aziz al-Bekri (Abu 'Ubaid 'Abdallah), *Book of kingdoms and roads* (Journal Asiatique, 1849), a Spanish Arab, who died in 1092, see *ibid.*, 206ff. See further the Russian record, S. H. Cross – O. P. Sherbowitz-Wetzor (eds.), *The Russian Primary Chronicle* [Laurentian text] (Cambridge, MA, 1930, rev. 1953), aa. 860-62 [aa. 6368-6370], and 6ff.; Hodinka, 36a, a. 862, and, *ibid.*, 22ff.; or, selections in Pauler – Szilágyi, 362ff.; Martha Font (ed.), *Magyarok a Kijevi Évkönyvben* [Mention of the Magyars in the Kiev Annals] (Szeged, 1996), 40ff. See also, Heinrich Kunstmann, *Die Slaven: ihr Name, ihre Wanderung nach Europa und die Anfänge der russischen Geschichte in historisch-onomastischer Sicht* (Stuttgart, 1996), 241ff.; V. Thomsen, *Der Ursprung des russischen Staates* (Gotha, 1879), 59, and passim; Werner Schenk, *Geschichte Russlands* (Munich, 1977), 23, and 24ff.; Arnold Toynbee, *Constantine Porphyrogenitus and his World* (Oxford, 1973), 464ff.; Ferenc Makk, "Külföldi források s a korai magyar történelem" [Some remarks on the non-Magyar historical sources of early Magyar history], *Acta historica Szegediensis*, 102 (1995), 25ff.

3. *DAI*, c. 37; the Turks (Magyars) were afraid of the Pechenegs, c. 3, did not dare to attack them—c. 8. Further, Hincmar of Reims, a. 852; and the "Annales Sangallenis maiores," anno 863, *MGHSS*, I, 77; Dümmler, III, 507ff., and 507. nn. 2, 3.

4. *DAI*, c. 38; Cross – Sherbowitz-Wetzor, *Russian Chronicle*, a. 898 (a. 6406), and 235, n. 28. Anonymus, "Gesta," c. 7, *SSH*, I, 41f.

5. *DAI*, c. 38; Macartney, *Ninth Century*, 98ff.; Pauler – Szilágyi, 355ff. One is to know about the Bulgarians that, in the ninth century, they were tax-paying subjects of Byzantium; a segment of their people had remained behind in the mid-Volga region. Cf. Theophanes, *Geographia*, ed. C. de Boor, 2 vols. (Leipzig, 1883-85), I, 544, 546; see further, Ostrogorsky, 205f. and A. A. Vasiliev, *History of the Byzantine Empire* (Madison, WI, 1952), 281f.; S. L. Tóth, "Az etelközi magyar–besenyő háború" [The Magyar-Pecheneg war in Atelkozu], *Századok*, 122 (1988), 541ff.

6. *DAI*, c. 40; Macartney, *Ninth Century*, 94f.; Antal Bartha, *Hungarian society in the 9th and 10th centuries* (Budapest, 1975), 83ff., and my review of this work in *American Historical Review*, 83 (1978), 1243f.; S. L. Tóth, *Levediától a Kárpát medencéig* [From Levedia to the Carpathian basin] (Szeged, 1998), 41ff.

7. *DAI*, c. 41; Anonymus, "Gesta," c. 12, *SSH*, I, 50ff.; Toynbee, 464ff.; S. L. Tóth, "A honfoglalás időpontja" [The date of the Magyar land-taking in the Carpathian basin], *Acta historica Szegediensis*, 102 (1995), 3ff.

8. *MHK*, 152ff.; DAI, c. 40, and compare with Leo VI the Wise, "Tactica," xviii:46; Toynbee, 466.

9. See Macartney, *Ninth Century*, 206f.; J. Marquart, *Osteuropäische und ost-asiatische Streifzüge* (Leipzig, 1903; repr. Darmstadt, 1961), xxxi, and 26. Ibn Rusta mentioned ten thousand horsemen, which may suggest a population of 110 to 160 thousand souls. (Medieval reports on numbers can be misleading; e.g., on the defeat of Béla IV by the Tartars in 1241, the Austrian chroniclers spoke of 80 to 100 thousand, even 300 thousand dead left behind on the battlefield [!]—*MGHSS*, IX, 559, 640, 655, etc.; according to the compiler of the "Continuatio Vindobonesis," the dukes of Brabant and Flanders commanded an army of 1.2 million [!] men on the move against Aachen and Cologne in 1278—cf. *ibid.*, IX, 711.)

10. The people live under the rule of one who rules over them by terror; cf. Leo VI, "Tactica," xviii:46; [in the selective edition *MHK*, 33ff;, and in Marczali, *Enchiridion*, 15, it is recorded under c. xviii:45]; *DAI*, c. 38; Gy. Györffy, *A magyarok elődeiről és a honfoglalásról* [The ancestors of the Magyars and their taking of the land] (Budapest, 1985), passim.

11. "...gubernator partium Transilvanarum," *Chronicon Monacense*, c. 29, *SSH*, II, 66f.; the Chronicle [*Chronicon pictum*], c. 65: "gubernaculum totius Ultra Silvarum regni possidebat," *ibid.*, I, 314, and under c. 30, "Gyula capitaneus, dux magnus et potens," *ibid.*, I, 290; Keza, "Gesta," c. 43, spoke of "Iula, avunculus [that is, of King Stephen] de Septem Castris," *ibid.*, I, 172. In Anonymus, "Gesta," c. 27, Gyula appeared as "capitaneus," [one of the seven tribal chiefs], *ibid.*, I, 69.

12. That is, prior to the election of Árpád as their leader; cf. Anonymus, "Gesta," c. 5, *ibid.*, I, 39f., esp. 40,6-12; Ibn Rusta, in *MHK*, 163ff. S. L. Tóth, "Az etelközi magyar fejedelemválasztás" [Election of the (first) Magyar Prince in Atelkozu], *Studia varia* (Szeged, 1998), 141ff.; idem, "Az első fejedelem: Árpád, vagy Álmos?" [The identity of the first Magyar Prince], *Acta historica Szegediensis*, 103 (1996), 31ff.

13. See Cross – Sherbowitz-Wetzor, 53; Hodinka, 32b; Anonymus, c. 57, *SSH*, I, 113ff.; further, *ibid.*, I, 35,6-15; c. 14, *ibid.*, I, 53f.; c. 50, *ibid.*, I, 101,15-19; also, cc. 24, and 25-27, *ibid.* I, 65,19; and, I, 87,9-10; Anonymus referred to his sources, see *ibid.*, I, 87,7-11; Z. J. Kosztolnyik, "A view of history in the writings of Gerhoch of Reichersberg and the medieval Hungarian chroniclers," *Die ungarische Sprache und Kultur im Donauraum: Vorlesungen des II International Kongresses für Hungarologie, Wien, 1986* (Vienna–Budapest, 1989), 513ff.; Dümmler, II, 445ff., provided a summarized listing of some (not very flattering) information; see further, Györffy, *István király*, 25ff.; Hóman, *Ungarisches Mittelalter*, I, 57ff.

Important is Gyula Kristó's 58 page study, "A honfoglaló magyarok életmódjáról" [Some remarks on the living conditions of the Magyars at the time of the Conquest], *Századok*, 129 (1995), 3ff.; Cyrill Horváth, *A régi magyar irodalom története* [History of early Hungarian literature] (Budapest, 1899), 5ff.; János Horváth, *A magyar irodalmi műveltség kezdetei* [Beginnings of Hungarian literary culture], 2nd ed. (Budapest, 1944), 5ff., and Pintér, I, 46, and 172ff. See also the "Life of Bishop Gerard of Csanád," in *SSH*, II, 471ff., esp. 475; II, 497f., and note on 498; László Szegfű, "Kortörténeti problemák Gellért püspök Deliberatiójában és legendáiban" [Contemporary issues mentioned in Gerard of Csanád's *Deliberatio*, and in his *vitae*], *Acta historica Szegediensis*, 83 (1986),

11ff.; on Gerard, see Kosztolnyik, *Five Kings*, 36ff., and 157f., nn. 9-24. Előd Nemerkényi, "Fictive audience. The second person singular in the *Deliberatio* of Bishop Gerard of Csanád," in Gerard Jaritz and Michael Richter (eds.), *Oral History of the Middle Ages: The Spoken Word in Context* (Krems–Budapest, 2001), 39ff.

14. *DAI*, cc. 4, 13, 14; Keza, cc. 95–96, *SSH*, I, 192f.; Scylitzes, CB, II, 222, 228, 231, 237. Leo VI, *Tactica*, xiv:42; and, xviii:48-51; Otto of Freising, *Chronicon*, vi:10; the *huj-huj* Magyar battle-cry was recorded by Liutprand, "Antapodosis," ii:30, in *Liudprandi episcopi Cremonensis Opera*, ed. J. Becker, SSrG, 3rd ed. (Hannover, 1915), 1ff.; for his "Historia Ottonis," see *ibid.*, 159ff.; for his "Legatio," see *ibid.*, 176ff.; László Vajda, "A népvándorlások kédéséhez" [Some remarks on the migration of peoples], *Századok*, 129 (1995),107ff.; Kristó, art cit., *ibid.*, 129 1995), 118ff.

15. Leo VI, *Tactica*, xviii:45-46, and 61.

16. *DAI*, cc. 39-40. S. L. Tóth, "Kabarok és fekete magyarok" [The Kavars and the Black Magyars], *Acta historica Szegediensis*, 84 (1987), 23ff.

17. *DAI*, c. 38; Macartney, *Ninth Century*, 86ff., and 102ff.

18. *DAI*, c. 38. According to Ibn Rusta, the Magyars' chief-king was known as *Kendeh*, but the man directly in charge of them was known as the *dsila*; *MHK*, 167.

19. Macartney, *Ninth Century*, 192.

20. Cf. Regino of Prüm [Reginonis abbatis Prumensis] *Chronicon*, ed. Fr. Kurze, SSrG (Hannover, 1890), anno 889. On Regino, see Eggert – Pätzold, 74ff.; W. Eggert, *Das ostfränkisch-deutsche Reich in der Auffassung seiner Zeitgenossen* (Berlin, 1973), 208f.; M. Lintzel, "Zur Chronik Reginos von Prüm," in his *Ausgewählte Schriften*, II (Berlin, 1961), 299ff.

21. Liutprand, "Antapodosis," i:13.

22. Otto of Freising, *Gesta*, i:32; his *Chronica*, vi:10, and vi:14. Kristó, art. cit., 1995, 33ff.

23. Anonymus, c. 5, *SSH*, I, 40,18-21; c. 6, *ibid.*, I, 40f.

24. *DAI*, c. 40; Anonymus, cc. 14, 46, 47, 50, 57, *SSH*, I, 53f., 93ff., 99ff., and 113ff.; S. L. Tóth, "A magyar fejedelmi méltóság öröklődése" [La succession de la dignité princière hongroise], *Acta historica Szegediensis*, 83 (1986), 3ff.

25. *DAI*, cc. 37-41; Toynbee, 599ff.

26. *DAI*, c. 38; Toynbee, 466f.

27. Regino of Prüm, annorum 888 and 889. H. Löwe, "Regino von Prüm und das historische Weltbild der Karolingerzeit," in his *Von Cassidor zu Dante: ausgewählte Aufsätze zur Geschichtsschreibung und politischen Ideenwelt des Mittelalters* (Berlin–New York, 1973), 149ff.; Eggert, *Ostfränkisch-deutsches Reich*, 155ff.

28. *DAI*, c. 38; Tóth, *Levediától*, 41ff.; idem, "Levedi és Árpád személyisége" [Personal identities of Levedi and Árpád], *Acta historica Szegediensis*, 107 (1998), 11ff.

29. *DAI*, cc. 37-38; Toynbee, 466f.

30. Anonymus, cc. 6 and 20 (*SSH*, I, 61ff.).

31. Keza, "Gesta," c. 27.

32. *DAI*, c. 38; Macartney, *Ninth Century*, 90ff., and 100f.; J. Deér, "A IX századi magyar történet időrendjéhez" [On the chronology of Magyar historical events during the ninth century], *Századok*, 79-80 (1945-46), 3ff.

33. Flodoard, "Historia Remensis ecclesiae," ii:13, anno 837, *MGHSS*, XIII, 409ff.; Mühlbacher, II, 131f.

34. *Annales Bertiniani*, ed. G. Waitz, SSrG (Hannover, 1883), anno 862.

35. "Annales Iuvavenses," anno 881, *MGHSS*, XXX-2, 732ff., and 732, n. 4; it also recorded, anno 912 (or, 913?), that Arnulf of Bavaria defeated the Magyars at the river Inn; further, under anno 942, that Berthold of Bavaria had defeated (and killed) them (all) at Trungowe (near Wels—cf. Károly Szabó, *A vezérek kora* [Age of the princes] [Pest, 1869], 221); István Bóna, *A magyarok és Európa a 9–10 században* [The Magyars and Europe in the ninth–tenth centuries] (Budapest, 2000), 48ff.

36. *DAI*, cc. 40, 41; on the election of Árpád, *ibid.*, c. 40; Macartney, *Ninth Century*, 177ff.; Toynbee, 467f.

37. *DAI*, c. 38; G. Fehér, "Ungarns Gebietsgrenzen in der Mitte des zehnten Jahrhunderts nach dem De administrando imperio des Konstantinos Porphyrogennetos," *Ungarische Jahrbücher*, 2 (1922), 37ff.

37. Cf. Macartney, *Ninth Century*, 98ff.; K. Krumbacher, *Geschichte der byzantinischen Literatur*, 2nd ed. (Munich, 1897), 252ff.

38. See Regino, anno 889; Johannes, priest of Venice, Chronicon Venetum," *MGHSS*, VII, 4ff., esp. 22—in connection with the election of Peter Tribuno as the doge of Venice, when the Magyars had invaded Italy, and King Berengar could not stop them; also, Dümmler, III, 438ff.

39. Cf. György Györffy, "A besenyők európai honfoglalásának kérdéséhez" [Some comments on the European settlement of the Pechenegs], *Történelmi Szemle*, 14 (1971), 281ff.

40. Regino, anno 901 (*recte*: 889?); Dümmler, III, 507ff., and 507, nn. 2 and 3; on Liutward of Vercelli, *Erzkaplan* of Charles III, see *ibid.*, III, 109f., and III, 528f.

41. 37. Cf. J. B. Bury, "The Ceremonial Book of Constantine Porphyrogenitus," *English Historical Review*, 22 (1907), 209ff., and 417ff.; Warren Treadgold, *A History of the Byzantine State and Society* (Stanford, 1997), 564f.

42. *DAI*, c. 38.

43. Macartney, *Ninth Century*, 139f.; K. Czeglédi, "A IX századi magyar történelem fökérdései" [The main questions regarding ninth century Hungarian historical events], *Magyar Nyelv*, 41 (1945), 33ff.; S. L. Tóth, "Az etelközi magyar–besenyő háború," 541ff.

44. Cf. Gyula Németh, *A honfoglaló magyarság kialakulása* [The ethnic formation of the land-taking Magyars], 2nd rev., ed. Árpád Berta (Budapest, 1991), 218ff., 226f., and 228ff.; M. Gyóni, "Kalizok, kazárok, kabarok, magyarok" [Some remarks on the Kaleez, Chazars, Kabaroi, and Magyars], *Magyar Nyelv*, 34 (1938), 86ff., and 159ff.; Tóth, op. cit., 29ff.

45. *DAI*, c. 39; Bartha, *Hungarian society*, 47ff.; S. L. Tóth, "A kabarok (kavarok) a 9 századi magyar törzsszövetségben" [The Kabars in the Magyar tribal structure of the ninth century], *Századok*, 118 (1984), 92ff.

46. *MHK*, 174ff.; Anonymus, "Gesta," cc. 19, 20, 24, and 51; Chronicle, *SSH*, I, 281,17; Toynbee, 619ff. See further, Dvornik, *Les légendes*, 148ff., and 157f.; Hóman, *Ungarisches Mittelalter*, I, 85f., and 87f.; Kristó, *Arpaden Dynastie*, 39ff.

47. Important is István Bóna's essay, in Béla Köpeczi et al. (eds.), *Erdély története* [History of Transylvania], 3 vols. (Budapest, 1986), I, 46ff., and 107ff.; my review of the three volume-set, in *Austrian History Yearbook*, 22 (1991), 170ff. "Present-day Romanians claim to be the descendants of the Latin-speaking colonists planted in Dacia [Transylvania] in the first century AD. There is no evidence for the survival of these colonies in the ten centuries between the overthrow of the Roman province in AD 270 and the first mention of Vlachs [Romance speakers] in Romania in AD 1230. ...A more

plausible origin for the Romanians lies in the Latin-speaking population south of the Danube, where Roman institutions struck deeper roots and survived much longer. ...The Vlachs only moved into present-day Romania in the thirteenth century, when the nomads' grip on the region began to slacken;" cf. Colin McEvedy, *The New Penguin Atlas of Medieval History* (New York, 1992), 4, n. 1.

48. See Anonymus, "Gesta," cc. 11, 14, 38; Hóman, *Ungarisches Mittelalter*, I, 89f.

49. *DAI*, c. 41; Ch. R. Bowlus, *Franks, Moravians and Magyars, 788–907* (Philadelphia, 1995), 46ff., and 235ff.; idem, "Die Reitervölker der frühen Mittelalters im Osten des Abendlandes," *Ungarn-Jahrbuch*, 22 (1995-96), 1ff.

50. On N[y]itra, cf. "Conversio," c. 11, *MGHSS*, XI, 12; further, Cosmas of Prague, "Chronica Bohemorum," *ibid.*, IX, 64,13-14; Anonymus, "Gesta," cc. 35, 37; Keza, "Gesta," c. 44; for the papal writ of John VIII—cf. Jaffé, n. 3332 (falsification!), also, nn. 3319, 3344; Dvornik, *Les légendes*, 222, and 261.

51. Cf. Theodor Mommsen, *Das Weltreich der Cäsaren*, Phaidon reprint (Vienna, 1955), 190ff.; idem, *History of Rome*, trans. W. P. Dickinson, 4 vols. (New York, 1894), III, 202ff.; Hóman, 90f.; György Székely – Antal Bartha (eds.), *Magyarország története a legrégibb időktől 1242-ig* [History of Hungary since ancient times to 1242] (Budapest, 1984), 199ff.

52. Cf. Hóman, *Ungarisches Mittelalter*, I, 92f., and 94; Dvornik, *Les légendes*, 212ff.; V. Vavrinek, "Die Christianisierung und Kirchenorganisation Grossmährens," *Historica*, 7 (1963), 5ff.; Franz Zagiba, "Zur Geschichte Kyrills und Methods und der bayerischen Ostmission," *Jahrbücher für Geschichte Osteuropas*, 9 (1961), 1ff., a very important, fifty-six page scholarly article; also, see idem, "Bayerische Slawenmission und ihre Fortsetzung durch Kyrill und Method," *ibid.*, 9 (1961), 247ff.; Székely – Bartha, 346ff.

53. "Conversio," c. 11, *MHK*, 311. See the Hungarian Chronicle [*Chronicon pictum*], *SSH*, I, 239ff., cc. 25 and 54; they were not received with open arms, "invitis gentibus memoratis," *ibid.*, I, 286,20.

54. *DAI*, c. 41; Chronicle, cc. 23 and 28; Palacky, *Böhmen*, I, 118f., and 195ff.; Gyula Kristó, "A legrégibb Naum-legenda és a magyar honfoglalás" [The oldest Naum-legend and the Magyar land-taking], *Acta historica Szegediensis*, 58 (1977), 13ff.

55. Cf. *Annales Fuldenses*, a. 892.

56. *DAI*, c. 41; S. L. Tóth, "A honfoglalás szakaszai" [Chronological phases of the Magyar land-taking of 896], in *Honfoglalási emléknapok* [Commemoration of the Conquest of 896], ed. Sabbas Jancsák et al. (Szeged, 1996), 8ff.

57. Regino, *Chronicon*, probably referring to events of 899-900; compare with the remarks by John the Deacon (court chaplain of Doge Peter Orseolo of Venice), "Chronicon Venetum," *MGHSS*, VII, 4ff., esp. 22.

58. Anonymus, "Gesta," c. 40, 41; the Chronicle, cc. 26 and 54; S. L. Tóth, "Megjegyzések a honfoglalás szakaszaihoz" [Some comments on the chronology of the Magyar land-taking], *Századok*, 130 (1996), 877ff.

59. Hóman, I, 106f.; Székely – Bartha, 605ff., and 634ff.; Kristó, *Arpaden Dynastie*, 15ff.

60. *DAI*, c. 40; Székely – Bartha, 577ff.

61. Cf. Macartney, *Ninth Century*, 177ff.; Hóman, *Ungarisches Mittelalter*, I, 102f., had used the same expression.

62. *Annales Fuldenses*, a. 900; Németh, 235ff.; Tóth, *Levediától*, 189ff.

63. On background, cf. "Annales Bertiniani," a. 862, *MGHSS*, I, 423ff.; also, *MHK*, 301 (text based on Cod. 6448 of the Royal Library in Brussels). On the marauding Magyars, Engelbert Mühlbacher, *Deutsche Geschichte unter den Karolingern*, 2 vols., Phaidon repr. (Essen, n.d.), II, 457ff.; Gyula Kristó, *Az Árpád-kor háborúi* [Wars of the Árpád age] (Budapest, 1986), 21ff.; Holtzmann, *Sächsische Kaiserzeit*, 84ff. For the text of the letter, see Marczali, *Enchiridion*, 21ff., and/or *MHK*, 323ff.

64. *Annales Fuldenses*, aa. 892, 894; also, selections only, *MHK*, 316ff.

65. *Annales Fuldenses*, a. 900; Gina Fasoli, *Le incursioni ungare in Europe nel secolo X* (Florence, 1945), 96f.; A. F. Gombos' 84 page article, "A honfoglaló magyarok itáliai kalandozásai" [The Magyars' marauding ventures in Italy], *Hadtörténelmi Szemle*, 28 (1927), 429ff.; Bóna, *Magyarok és Európa*, 43ff.

66. *Annales Fuldenses*, aa. 900 and 901.

67. Widukindi Corbeiensis *Rerum gestarum Saxonicarum libri III*, 5th ed., ed. G. Waitz – K. A. Kehr (Hannover, 1935), cc. i:20, 32, 38, and ii:14; Wattenbach, I, 328ff.

68. Widukind, i:20 (a. 906).

69. "Annales Iuvavenses maximi," *MGHSS*, XXX-2, a. 933, and Widukind, i:32.

70. Widukind, i:38.

71. *Ibid.*, ii:14.

72. Discussed at some length by the Chronicle, cc. 55-62, *SSH*, I, 304ff.; Hóman, I, 116ff.; Székely – Bartha, 651ff.

73. Cf. Chronicle, c. 61, *SSH*, I, 308ff.

74. *Ibid.*, c. 62; Richard Szántó, "Spanyolországi források a kalandozó magyarok 924 évi hadjáratáról" [Spanish sources on the Magyars' marauding venture in the year 924], *Acta historica Szegediensis*, 103 (1996), 43ff.

75. In the *Annales Altahenses maiores*, ed. W. de Giesebrecht – Edmund L. B. ab Oefele, SSrG (Hannover 1891, repr. 1979), anno *943*, the entry reads: "Praelium cum Ungariis in Weles, et occisi sunt a Bawaris," and see note 3, on page 8. See also Robert Holtzmann, *Geschichte der sächsischen Kaiserzeit, 900–1024* (Munich, 1941; repr. Darmstadt, 1961), 84ff.; Hóman, I, 123f.; Székely – Bartha, 680ff.

76. Cf. Widukindi Corbicensis *Rerum gestarum Saxonicarum libri III*, iii:44 and 46 (anno 955); Thietmari Merseburgensis episcopi *Chronicon*, ed. I. M. Lappenberg – F. Kurze, SSrG (Hannover, 1889), ii:4 [9-10] (anno 955); on background, see also Folcuin, "Gesta abbatum Lobbiensium," c. 25, *MGHSS*, IV, 54ff.; Holtzmann, 162ff.; for the Magyar viewpoint, cf. Keza, c. 40; Thomas von Bogyay, *Lechfeld: Ende und Anfang* (Munich, 1955), 25ff. and 54ff.; further, Bowlus, in *Ungarn-Jahrbuch*, 22 (1995-96).

77. Widukind, iii:44, and 46; Gerhard, priest of Augsburg, "Vita s. Udalrici," c. 12, *MGHSS*, IV, 384ff.

78. Widukind, iii:48; Anonymus, c. 55 (*SSH*, I, 109ff.).

79. Cf. Chronicle, c. 62; Keza, c. 42 (*SSH*, I, 171f.); see Hóman, I, 134ff., for the political background of those raids, and, for his comments on Bulcsú, *ibid.*, I, 146f., and compare with Bogyay, *Lechfeld*, 37ff.

80. Hóman, I, 138ff.; Székely – Bartha, 702ff. A spurious royal writ (anno 1006?) did refer to Fort N[y]itra—*RA*, n. 4.

81. Hóman, I, 151; Németh, 132ff., and 137ff. On Volga-Bulgars living in the town of Pest, see Anonymus, c. 57, *SSH*, I, 114f., and the Chronicle, c. 83. (For King Béla IV's town charter for Pest, see *RA*, n. 781; text in *RHM*, 466f.).

82. Németh, 285ff.; Székely – Bartha, 634ff.

83. Otto of Freising, *Gesta*, i:32; *Chronicon*, vii:13; Z. J. Kosztolnyik, *Hungary in the Thirteenth Century* (New York, 1996), 333f.; idem, "Early Hungarian towns, and town life, in the record of western chronicles," *Specimina nova Universitatis Quinque-ecclesiae de Iano Pannonino nominatae*, 11 (1995), 251ff.

84. See Gyula Kristó, *Szempontok korai helyneveink történeti tipológiájához* [Some remarks on the historical development of geographic local names in Hungary] (Szeged, 1976), 7ff., and 15ff.; Kosztolnyik, *Thirteenth Century*, 318ff., and 328, n. 21. Odo de Deogilo, *De profectione Ludovici VII in orientem*, ed. V. G. Berry [Latin-English] (New York, 1948), 30.

85. See, e.g., King Stephen's Laws, aa. i:1, i:16, i:18, i:20; ii:6, 7—Marczali, *Enchiridion*, 69ff.; Székely – Bartha, 717ff., and 795ff.

86. *SSH*, I, 314; *Annales Altahenses maiores*, a. 1003; Chronicle, c.65.

87. Chronicle, c. 28.

88. Chronicle, c. 26.

89. Chronicle, cc. 54-55.

90. Györffy, 67ff.; Hóman – Szekfű, I, 110ff.; Hóman, *Ungarisches Mittelalter*, I, 79ff.; Cyrill Horváth, 15ff.; Tíbor Klaniczay (ed.), *A magyar irodalom története* [History of Hungarian literature], vol. 1 (Budapest, 1964), 24ff.

91. King Stephen's Laws, aa. i:15, and i:26; cf. Levente Závodszky (ed.), *A szent István, szent László és Kálmán korabeli törvények és zsinati határozatok forrásai* [Sources of the laws of St. Stephen, St. Ladislas and Coloman and of synodical acts of the period] (Budapest, 1904), 141ff.; or, in Marczali, *Enchiridion*, 69ff.

92. *Ibid.*, a. i:28.

93. Hóman – Szekfű, I, 108f.; Hóman, *Ungarisches Mittelalter*, I, 77ff.

94. Cf. Hartvic, "Vita s. Stephani regis," c. 1, *SSH*, II, 402,14-17, and insert on p. 402**.

95. Spoken of by Bruno of Querfurt, cf. *MGHSS*, IV, 602; also, by the author of the "Vita s. Wolfkangi," *ibid.*, IV, 530; Anonymus, c. 27, and the Chronicle, cc. 15 and 35, referred to her as the daughter of the prince of Transylvania, while a Polish source, regarded her as Adelheid, the sister of Mieszko; cf. *Monumenta Poloniae historica*, ed. A. Bielowski, 6 vols. (Lvov–Cracow, 1864-93; repr. Warsaw, 1960-61), cited hereafter as *MPH*, I, 495ff.

96. Cf. "Chronica principum Poloniae," *ibid.*, I, 438, 669, and 700.

97. Thietmar, *Chronicon*, iv:38. See R. F. Kaindl's study, "Studien zu den ungarischen Geschichtsquellen," *Archiv für österreichische Geschichte*, 82 (1896), 859, and 84 (1898), 523, referring to the remarks concerning Sarolta by Anonymus and by Keza, as confusing nonsense.

98. "Illuc venere legati Graecorum Beneventorum cum muneribus, XII primates Ungarorum, Bulgariorum duo"—cf. *Annales Altahenses maiores*, anno 973; Thietmar, ii:20; *Lamperti monachi Hersfeldensis opera*, ed. Oswaldus Holder-Egger, SSrG (Hannover–Leipzig, 1894; repr. Hannover, 1984), anno 973; also, "Annales Magdeburgenses," anno 973, in *MGHSS*, XVI, 153.

99. That is, King Stephen's father, Géza, who would be looked upon as "severus quidem et crudelis,"—Hartvic, "Vita S. Stephani regis," c. 2, *SSH*, II, 403f., and compare with Stephen's "Vita minor," c. 2, *ibid.*, II, 394; Hóman, *Ungarisches Mittelalter*, I, 154ff.

100. *SSH*, II, 378,11-13.

101. Györffy, *István király*, 364ff.; Klaniczay, 46ff.; Jenő Pintér, *A magyar irodalom történetének kézikönyve* [Handbook of the historical development of Hungarian literature], 2 vols. (Budapest, 1929-30), I, 42ff.; idem, *Irodalomtörténet*, I, 108ff.; Elemér Mályusz, *Egyházi társadalom a középkori Magyarországon* [Status of the clergy in medieval Hungary] (Budapest, 1971), 13ff., and my review of this book in *Austrian History Yearbook*, 14 (1978), 288ff.

102. "Ungari Christiani fiunt," recorded the "Annales Weingartenses Welfici"—Iohannes Enenkel, "Von den Königen," anno 826 (!), MGH ling. vern., III, 540; "Olaf's saga Tryggvasonar," c. 76, *MGHSS*, XXIX, 392f.; also, "Saga of Óláf Tryggvason," in Snorri Sturluson, *Heimskringla: History of the Kings of Norway*, trans., with introduction by Lee M. Hollander (Austin, TX, 1991), 144ff.

103. Ellenhardus Argentenensis "Chronicon," *MGHSS*, XVII, 120.

104. Gervasius Ricobaldus Ferrariensis "Istoria imperiale," *RISS*, IX, 319.

105. Cf. *MPH*, III, 128.

106. "Annales Kamenzenses," anno 1161 [!], *MGHSS*, XIX, 581; Adalbert had baptized *King* Stephen (!), the emperor's brother-in-law, with the approval of the Pope!—*ibid.*, 582. Bruno, who was learned in Scripture, "a Leone papa in Ungariam praedicando fidem mittitur"—cf. "Gesta archiepiscoporum Magdeburgensium," c. 14, anno 992, *MGHSS*, XIV, 391. It ought to be noted, though, that Pope Leo VIII reigned from 963 to 965, while Leo IX, from 1049 to 1054—see Angelo Mercati, "The New List of the Popes," *Medieval Studies*, 9 (1947), 71ff., a corrected reprint of the article in *Annuario Pontifico* for the year 1947. See further, the "Chronica principum Poloniae," *MPH*, III, 438.

107. "Annales Silesiaci compilati," c. 3, *MGHSS*, XIX, 537; "Chronicon mixtum [Hungarico-Polonicum]," c. 4, *SSH*, II, 299ff.; or, *MPH*, I, 498.

108. *Ibid.*, III, 128; also, "Catalogus archiepiscoporum Gnesenensium," *ibid.*, III, 391.

109. See "Chronicon," i:65, *MGHSS*, XXVI, 202.

110. Ademar Cabannensis Chronicon, c. 31, *MGHSS*, IV, 130. On the German Holy Lance, see A. Bühler, "Die hl. Lanze: ein ikonographischer Beitrag zur Geschichte der deutschen Kleinodien," *Das Münster*, 16 (1963), 85ff. Bóna, *Magaryok és Európa*, 82ff.

111. Thietmar, Chronicon, viii:3 [ix:4]. Péter Váczy, *A magyar történelem korai századaiból* [Scenes from the early centuries of Hungarian history] (Budapest, 1994), 77ff., commenting on Thietmar's remarks about the coronation of Hungarian rulers.

112. Cabannensis' remark, in *MGHSS*, IV, 130.

113. *Ibid.* See further, Hóman – Szekfű, I, 178 and 199; Sándor Tóth, "A fehér s fekete magyarok kérdéséhez" [The meaning of the terms *white* and *black* Magyars], *Acta historica Szegediensis*, 75 (1983), 3ff., esp. 7f. A certain Bishop Baldricus of Leodiens had prayed for the conversion of all Magyars—cf. "Historia monasterii s. Laurentii Leodiensis," in E. Martene – U. Durand (eds.), *Veterum scriptorum et monumentorum collectio*, 9 vols. (repr. New York, 1968), IV, 1046.

114. Cf. Chronicle, c. 88, *SSH*, I, 344,23-24, and, c. 96, *ibid.*, I, 360,23-24.

115. Cf. Keza, c. 59, *ibid.*, I, 180.

116. *Ibid.*, I, 360,16-18.

117. Cf. *MGHSS*, XXIII, 793, 795, 798.

118. See the "Chronicon mixtum," *MPH*, I, 498; Adam of Bremen's remark in his *Gesta Hammaburgensis ecclesiae pontificum*, ed. B. Schmeidler, 3rd ed. SSrG

(Hannover, 1917), ii:43, made anno 1010(!); "...per Gislam, sororem imperatoris," *MGHSS*, VI, 354.

119. *Ibid.*, V, 117.

120. See the "Chronica minora auctore Minorita Erphordensis," *ibid.*, XXIV, 183.

121. Dandalo, "Chronicon Venetum," ix:1,46, *RISS*, XII, 233; Albericus Trium Fontium, *anno* 1010, *MGHSS*, XXIII, 779; further, Henricus de Heimburg, "Cronica Boemorum," *ibid.*, XVII, 712.

122. Cf. *ibid.*, XXII, 465; "Insignus signifer Christi, praesul Adalbertus, retibus fidei cepit Pannoniam,"—cf. Cosmas of Prague, "Chronica Bohemorum," i:31, *ibid.*, IX, 54.

123. Cf. "Annales Polonorum I," anno 982 (!), *ibid.*, XIX, 616 and 617; also, Ptolomaeus Lucensis "Historia Ecclesiastica," xvii:26, *RISS*, XI, 1043. The author of "Vita s. Bogomuli," c. 1, remarked that Adalbert was concerned about the spread of the Catholic faith among the Poles and among the Magyars, see *ASS*, Iunii II, 337.

124. See "De s. Adalberto Pragensis episcopo," *MGHSS*, XV-2, 1180. For the Catalogue, cf. *MPH*, III, 391f.

125. *MGHSS*, IV, 613; Görich, 125f., and 247ff.

V

King Stephen's Christian Kingdom

1. The Country's First Catholic Monarch

> ...cum episcopis et primatibus Ungarie statutum
> a se decretum manifestum facit, in quo scilicet
> uniuscuisque contrarium dictavit antidotum.
>
> *Vita maior s. Stephani regis*, c. 9.

Géza became a Christian in about 974.[1] He was baptized *Stefanu*, while his brother received the baptismal name of Michael. Géza promised to convert his people to Christianity, and to demolish pagan religious cults. His conversion, however, remained more of a dogmatic nature; he did not convert to Latin Christianity out of ethical consideration, but for the reason of political survival of his dynastic policy. "Geiza, qui et credulus in Ihesum...misericors autem et liberalis in alienos et precipue in christianos, ...credidit ipse cum familiaribus suis et baptizatus est, omnes ditioni sue subditos... mancipaturum."[2] He believed in God, in the Holy Trinity; he knew of the commandments, though the question remains, did he obey them? He was rather inclined to sacrifice to *pagan idols, to honor the ancients*—"ritu paganismi licet obvolutus"—than to practice mind control, or to show compassion toward the enemy, as proscribed by the code of Christian behavior.[3] On the other hand, he insisted that every Christian who entered his country be received warmly and granted protection of the law, if to make certain that the Christian faith did forge solid roots in Hungarian soil.[4]

The family descent and inheritance of King Stephen became a favored topic for western chroniclers. They wanted to know who his ancestors were. The chronicler of the thirteenth century—cited frequently above—had assumed that Stephen was the seventh ruling prince of the Magyars, "a primo duce Almo septimus,"[5] while the fourteenth century Polish source—whose author, too, has frequently been referred to above—recorded Stephen's direct descent from Attila, arguing that the Huns and the Magyars were one and the same people. When Attila had made his military move against the City of Rome (in the year 452), the chronicler said, he had a lively dream about the earthly *arrival* (birth) and glorification of Stephen.[6] Stephen's father, Prince Géza, was even better known to the chroniclers, though they recorded his name differently—as, for instance, *Geiza sive Geyza*[7]—who, to quote Bruno of Querfurt, was an unprincipled, passive, weak person,[8] while Thietmar of Merseburg insisted that he was a strong, determined man, overbearing and forceful, and had appeared out of the dark clouds of the unknown.[9] The remark by a Bavarian chronicler may complete the picture, who wrote that the daughter-in-law of Géza, the wife of son Stephen, was Bavarian, and because of her Stephen not only had to assume a strictly correct attitude toward the guests visiting in his country, but also act with loving care toward non-Magyar Christians who were seeking settlement in the land. Stephen simultaneously had to seek the emperor's friendship, to reach an understanding with him.[10]

On the other hand, the German and Polish sources seem to disagree on the identity of Prince Géza's wife. In the Polish sources, Adelheid, the daughter of Micislav I of Poland, appears as the wife of Géza—consequently, as the mother of King Stephen—a deeply religious woman who led her husband toward the faith of salvation.[11] The German Thietmar in a similar manner described the princely wife of Géza with Slavic characteristics, and named her *Belekngini*—a term he interpreted as *pulchra domina*. She was of a merry nature, he wrote, with the strong manners of a man, who drank heavily, and on one occasion even had killed a man in sudden anger.[12] She held her husband under control, and the reins of his government, Bruno of Querfurt recorded: "totem regnum manu tenuit, virum et quae erant viri ipsa regebat;" therefore (the chronicler used the word "but"), the Christianization process they had begun together in the country remained rootless and shallow; "cum paganismo polluta religio...et trepidus christianismus."[13]

It appears to this writer that, despite the Slavic terminology Thietmar seemed to have characterized Sarolta, daughter of Gyula of Transylvania, as a German amazon the more so because, according to another Polish chronicler, *Adelheid* could have been the *second* wife of Prince Géza.[14] It is likely that the bishop of Merseburg had relied too heavily on Polish for information, thereby confusing Sarolta, the *first* wife of the prince, with the Magyar prince's second wife, the Polish Adelheid. There are several German chroniclers who refer to Gyula of Transylvania as the uncle of King Stephen, mentioning that Géza had two sons.[15]

Paganism had to take second ranking in the Magyar princely court and in the tribal court circles. Still, paganism survived, in fact, flourished, among the inhabitants of the land, and so did the cult of evil spirits. As late as 992, when Adalbert, bishop of the Czechs, visited the Hungarian court in Esztergom, he noticed that Christianity remained a soft, less strictly observed religious issue in the country, strongly fused with popular "pagan," non-Christian, features.[16] Adalbert preached the Gospel with great enthusiasm to his own people, but was unwilling to compromise Christian teaching because of the wild, brutal personal behavior of his Czechs. He had met with tremendous difficulties ["living hell"] while carrying out his missionary work, and grew disillusioned about—one may say, disgusted with—the wild behavior and unpleasant personal habits widely spread among his people. The bishop of Prague since 983, Adalbert literally had fled the country of the Czechs in order to find physical, spiritual and mental rest in a monastery at Rome. When he was ordered to reassume his episcopal duties in Prague, he could subject neither himself nor his office to the physical threats and mental pressure from the Czechs—so the record has it—and once again left his episcopal see.[17]

Vajk, son of Prince Géza and his wife Sarolta, who took the baptismal name of Stephen the First Martyr—the patron saint of the cathedral of Passau[18]—received a Christian education at home.[19] *Prince* Stephen may have been small in stature, very serious as a person, who—the record has it—never laughed. Blessed with high intelligence, brainy Stephen combined his mental capabilities with an understanding, humane attitude; he felt prepared for the task to guide his people[s] on the road of western Latin Christianity.[20] He must have met Bishop Adalbert in Esztergom, but unlike the Czech ecclesiastic, the Magyar prince was a realist, a statesman blessed with a persistent view of heaven, who clearly saw his earthly life-goal: to be able to observe and to identify with people of all social strata, even with those at the lower "muddy" level in his country's population. He had laid out before him certain political-diplomatic and religious-cultural objectives he knew he would be able to reach and make effective. Wild were his people, whom he understood how to control firmly—and yet not too harshly—in order to assure that, in time, the hard-headed pagan Magyars become believing Christians.[21]

Polish chroniclers discussing the birth of King Stephen argued that Stephen's mother was the Polish Adelheid; "Adilheid genuit Stephanum regem Hungariae,"[22] they emphasized the existence of a Hungaro-Polish royal family tie, as if to reason that the mother of the first Christian Hungarian monarch, and of the first Hungarian saint, was a Polish princess. One may, of course, contend that by marrying a Polish princess as his (second) wife, if such a family relationship had existed at all, the widower Prince Géza had successfully pursued a dynastic diplomacy based on marriage that cemented friendly ties between the ruling families of two new Christian kingdoms in cast central Europe.[23]

The Polish chronicle report on the circumstances under which Pope Sylvester II had a royal diadem sent to the Hungarian court reveal a similar tendency. It is the Polish sources that record in detail how the Hungarian prince Stephen obtained the royal diadem that, originally, had been prepared for the Polish prince Boleslav; "...exinde regio insignari voluit atque in perpetuum dignitate vel regni ipso futuris saeculis gaudere."[24] It is to be noted, though, that in the Polish record the name of Pope Leo VIII [d. 965!] replaced that of Pope Sylvester II,[25] or, that the chronicler used the name of Pope Benedict VII [d. 983!] instead.[26] Although a record correctly named Boleslav Chobry [d. 1025] instead of Micislav,[27] the "Chronica principum Poloniae," on the other hand, spoke of a Micislas II [d. 1034!] as a political force in the background,[28] while another *Polish* source knew nothing about the existence of Archbishop Lambert of Cracow.[29] Nor did the Polish chroniclers record that the Magyar

Stephen, by receiving a crown from Rome, had not only gained diplomatic recognition from the Roman See, but obtained authorization to establish, and organize, the Roman Catholic ecclesiastical administration in his realm.[30]

The pious legend—that Adelheid expecting her child had a dream where Stephen the First Martyr had appeared to her and informed her that she would bear a son who would accomplish great deeds—is of Polish origin.[31] Western sources enriched the legend by recording that Stephen had been baptized in Esztergom,[32] on the feast of Stephen the First Martyr, the day after Christmas, and that was why he was given the baptismal name of Stephen.[33] Thietmar, however, who closely observed and commented on Hungarian events tied in with the interest of the German imperial court, still kept referring to Stephen by his "pagan" name; he called him *Waic*.[34]

Because of the fusion of legends with historical facts, the circumstances surrounding the baptism of Stephen remain obscure. The observation made by various chroniclers that during Bishop Adalbert of Prague's visit to Pannonia during the reign of Emperor Otto II, he who had baptized the Magyars' first *king-to-be*, must be based upon the record of visits the Czech ecclesiastic paid to Hungary.[35] Albericus, on the other hand, reported, *anno* 1010 (!), that it was Adalbert who had baptized *King* (*regem*) Stephen.[36] A later remark, recorded *anno* 1161 (!), that it was Saint Adalbert who in the days of Henry II had baptized the German emperor's Hungarian brother-in-law,[37] is of little significance, on the grounds that another chronicler named Bruno of Querfurt as the bishop who had christened Géza's son, Stephen, upon instructions given by Prince Géza.[38]

Numerous sources chronologically fuse the baptism *and* marriage of (King) Stephen into one event, and date both events to the days of the German Otto III and Henry II.[39] In a similar manner, the chronicler Albericus spoke, *anno* 1010, of the Hungarian queen Gisela as the sister of Emperor Henry II, though in his annotations to the year 1041 he referred to her as the sister of King Peter Orseolo—King Stephen's successor on the throne.[40]

There are other western reports that indicate that several Bavarian nobles accompanied Gisela on her journey to Hungary, and settled in the realm permanently. It was these noble lords who, at the wedding of Gisela to Stephen, had conferred Christian knighthood on Stephen—thereby to assure his acceptance in their Latin-German social circle of ruling families, so that "rex Ungarorum statura pusillus, corde magnus," may become a worthy guardian of the Christian faith and peace in the land.[41] The German imperial and aristocratic circles evidently looked upon the marriage of the Hungarian ruler with the Bavarian princess as a contract, in which Gisela had appeared as a guarantor; "Gisela Stephano regi Ungariorum, cum se ad fidem Christi converteret, quasi vere iuxta nomen suum fidei obses in coniugium data," recorded Herimannus Augiensis in his chronicle.[42]

It is quite evident from the wording of Hartvic, who followed the text of Stephen's *Vita minor* in his report, that it was with the consent of "his people"—the land-taking nobility—that Prince Géza designated son Stephen as his successor in government.[43] Géza had made certain that the descendants of the land-taking Magyar social stratum supported his son Stephen in his government of the country,[44] and chose the Bavarian-born Gisela as wife for him from the region where, *he knew*, his people wreaked bloody disturbance and havoc a few decades earlier.[45]

Gisela's father was Henry of Bavaria; her brother was Henry—later the emperor, Henry II; their grandfather had frequently fought with the Magyar intruders and, as a matter of record, it was he who had one of the marauding leaders, Bulcsú, hanged after the battle at Lechfeld (Augsburg) in 955.[46] (Henry the Quarrelsome had also taken a stand against Otto I in domestic German politics, though, following his father's advice, remained loyal to the German monarch and displayed a Christian behavior all his life.[47]) Gisela had a strong Christian family background; another brother, Bruno, became bishop, and a sister, Brigitta, abbess in Regensburg. The saintly Wolfgang had been the tutor of both Henry and Gisela and had foretold Gisela that a *royal* future awaited her.[48]

It is an irony of fate that in spite of the great interest displayed by western chroniclers toward the beginnings, and the development, of the Catholic Church in Hungary, there is not one western biographer who would recorded the life of King Stephen.[49] Evidently, nobody in the Latin west had been interested in piecing together a continuous narrative of at least the main events of his reign—as, for instance, conditions surrounding his establishment of a Christian kingdom, or of the ecclesiastical administration in his land; even "back at home" Bishop Hartvic, who had authored a *Vita s. Stephani regis* based on information gathered from earlier written data, provided a rather sketchy report on the activities of the saintly monarch.[50] The sporadic references by western chroniclers to the formation of the Latin Church in the Hungarian realm remained of no lasting value; therefore, the conversion of the Magyars in the early eleventh century, and the establishment of their Christian kingdom, received a kind of different, heavily locally-colored, parochial treatment at the pens of serious Latin authors.[51]

Stephen and Gisela were prepared to fulfill leading roles in society; both of them had been brought up rationally, believing in the Catholic tradition, and made it their life-goal to bring peace and unity to *their* people[s]; they planned to realize this goal by developing the ecclesiastical administration in the[ir] country. Stephen and Gisela both understood that the church administration, even if it worked hand-in-hand with the secular one, had to have its own sphere of public activity. The chief goal of their policy was establishing Christianity on firm religious and legal, political, and economic foundations—and that within the framework of the Christian realm.[52]

Several chroniclers date the christening of the Magyars (as a people) at the time of the marriage of Stephen and Gisela. King Stephen had earnestly begun with dedication and a strong hand the conversion of his people[s] to the Catholic faith: "Rex sacramenta suscepit baptismatis per eum omnis populs sibi subiectus."[53] The chronicler of Trium Fontium went as far as to note that "rex Stephanus sua praedicatione Ungaros convertit."[54] The record has it that even the late contemporaries of the monarch would visualize an inner change in the soul of the Magyar people in that they, who used to be a curse upon the peoples of the Latin west before their conversion, had now become Christian.[55] It must have been the reason why the author—for example, of the *Vita* of Emperor Henry II, written during the mid-twelfth century—depicted King Stephen as an Apostle,[56] and why Pope Innocent III in his writ of September 15, 1204, addressed to King Emery of Hungary, stated that King Stephen, by the grace of God, had made his country belong to the Catholic faith.[57]

The German sources characterized the confrontation between the Hungarian monarch and Gyula of Transylvania as a religious conflict by recording that [it was] Stephen [indeed who] had converted Transylvania to Latin Christianity[58] (the note in the *Sächsische Weltchronik* that King Stephen had even converted the Poles to the Catholic faith is, though well meant, not correct).[59] The German chroniclers credited the emperor, Henry II, for the conversion of the Magyars as well. The fact that it was the German monarch himself who gave his own sister in marriage to the Hungarian ruler must have pressured Stephen to accept Christianity for his people.[60] Otto of Freising in the twelfth century drafted his observation more gently: the emperor gave his sister in marriage to Stephen in order to enable him, and his people, to accept the Christian religion[61]—an imperial religious-political goal that had actually been realized: as chronicler Ekkehard recorded in an entry under the year 1001, the Magyar ruler had married, "in coniugium expetivit," the sister of both Emperor Henry and Bishop Bruno.[62]

The deacon of Bamberg, and a biographer of Henry II, made a similar statement: the Emperor gave the hand of his sister in marriage to [Magyar Prince] Stephen, in order to convert his people to Christianity,[63] while another author looked upon the development of events differently: the emperor, Henry II, had through his sister converted all of Pannonia, "totam Pannoniam per sororem suam Christianam fecit."[64] One is to assume that *Pannonia*—an expression used by this author—meant not only Transdanubia, but all territory under Magyar control.[65] The Holy See placed great emphasis upon the cooperation of the German imperial court in the conversion of the Magyars. In his writ of March 14, 1146, issued on the occasion of the canonization of Henry II, Pope Eugene III declared that it was the emperor who, together with King Stephen, had converted all of the Hungarian realm.[66]

The record has it that Queen Gisela also played, next to the Hungarian monarch and the German emperor, an important role in the conversion of the Hungarians. By the grace of God "gens Ungarie ad fidem convertit super Gislam"—the emperor's sister, and wife of the Magyar king.[67] There are chroniclers who, citing sources, stress the merits of Gisela, the German emperor's sister, who was able to convince her royal husband of the need for converting his pagan Magyars to the Christian faith.[68] An Italian's remark that the conversion of the Magyars was mainly due to Adalbert and Gisela[69] does not weaken the role played by King Stephen in the process of conversion because, as a Czech chronicler reported, next to Stephen, Gisela, and Henry II, Adalbert too shared in the missionary role of converting the Magyars to Christianity.[70] A Polish chronicler went even further in saying that the conversion of the Magyars was the *common* enterprise of both Gisela and Adelheid—in the Polish point of view, Prince Géza's second, Polish, wife.[71]

The Bavarian-born Gisela, whose brother in time became emperor, had indeed contributed to the expansion and establishment of the Christian faith and of western Latin culture in Magyar-land.[72] She came from a deeply religious family. Saint Wolfgang, bishop of Regensburg, had been responsible for her, and for her brother's, religious upbringing. The remark by the German chronicler that she "multum iuvit ad plenam conversionem Ungariae," was not over-stated,[73] and several historical sources depicted Gisela, her brother the emperor, and Adalbert, the bishop of Prague, as the ones who had played important roles in spreading the Catholic faith in the land.[74] The Italian Andrea Dandalo frankly stated that Gisela and Adalbert had convinced King Stephen of the need for accepting the righteousness of the Catholic cause.[75]

The missionary activity of Adalbert in Magyar-land was depicted by various chroniclers, though according to the testimony of his own biographers, the Czech bishop had been in transit—fleeing from the Czechs in Prague—when he paid a brief visit to the court of the Hungarian ruler in Esztergom, and had only limited opportunity to personally observe and familiarize himself with the situation of the Church in Hungary.[76] And yet, some chroniclers regard him as the missionary who had converted the Magyars to Catholicism. A Polish chronicler, for example, noted that Adalbert visited Hungary with *papal approval*, and converted the *whole country*,[77] as Adalbert went to Pannonia to convert and to baptize the Hungarian king with *all* of his people.[78] This chronicler, though, seems to have forgotten the essential question of language ability; how many interpreters did the bishop of Prague have at his disposal who knew the language of the Magyars, and how long had they needed for the conversion of the *entire* Magyar-land—without even speaking their language?[79]

According to the record, one may assume that Adalbert was concerned about strengthening the Catholic faith among the Magyars, and among the Poles, because he could not missionarize the whole country by himself, but had access to only a portion of the population,[80] even though he received help from his co-workers, whom he had sent (there) before him.[81]

Western (German) historical sources place heavy emphasis upon the role Emperor Henry II held in establishing a firm foundation for Christianity in Magyar-land, since the emperor had his sister marry the Hungarian ruler with the intent that their marriage would assure the latter's conversion (regardless of the fact that, as recorded by the emperor's biographer, Gisela had already married a *Christian* Stephen—"qui non prius tamen quam fidem suscepit."[82] Besides the Germans, numerous Polish and Italian chroniclers agree with this interpretation; the latter report that the Magyars had already been converted to Christianity.[83] The rather ambitious author of the "Life of Saint Romuald" even argued that the saint had to prod the emperor to give his sister's hand in marriage to the Hungarian prince.[84] It would be of some interest, though, to comment on the geographical definition by the chroniclers of Magyar-land. An Italian source, for instance, spoke of Pannonia in recording that Emperor Henry II "totam Pannoniam per sororem suam Christianam fecit," bearing in mind that in the then contemporary usage *Pannonia* meant all of the land under Magyar control.[85]

In sum, there are chroniclers who place less emphasis on the idea of a direct German role in the Christianization of Magyar-land; instead, they argue that, next to King Stephen, Queen Gisela held a hand in the conversion of the Magyars to Christianity. The Magyars, "hactenus idolatrie dedita"—wrote one of these chroniclers—became Christians "per Gislam sororem imperatoris," because it was she who persuaded her husband that he, and his people, accept Christianity.[86] The author of the Silesian Annals could not omit the role [that may have been] played by the Polish royal family in the record: besides Gisela, the Polish-born Adelheid (Prince Géza's second wife) had a role in the Magyars' conversion to the Catholic faith, he wrote. On the other hand, the Italians could not leave Adalbert out of the historic picture of the Magyars' conversion to Christianity.[87]

The Czech and Polish chroniclers seem to agree with this point of view. Although their argument that Adalbert only converted a portion of the Magyar people—not the whole country—has credibility, they fail to realize that the bishop of Prague did not know Magyar, nor did he spend a long period of time on Hungarian soil. As remarked by a Polish source, Adalbert had sent missionaries before him to Hungary in order to prepare the population there for his arrival. Such a remark—modified by the chronicler—could have been based on a note found in Adalbert's *Vita*, still, it remains a hypothesis like the above mentioned remark that Adalbert was buried in Magyar soil, and it was from there that Emperor Otto III had his *dexter* sent to Rome—pure fabrication.[88]

The western chroniclers reported nowhere, nor did they emphasize the fact, so characteristically referred to by Hartvic (who based his information on Stephen's *Vita minor*), "ipsosque secundum ecclesiasticam doctrinam instituens, iugum et legem discipline subpositis cervicibus adhibuit, omnesque in munditas malorum prorsus destruxit"—even though some scholars question the reliability of Hartvic's report[89]—that Stephen, the ruling prince, and Stephen the anointed monarch, wanted to avoid, and during his reign actually avoided, dependence upon the Roman Church in temporal politics, although he remained steadfastly loyal to the teaching of the Church. King Stephen needed the cooperation of churchmen in both spiritual and secular matters, because in his age it was the bishops and learned monks who had formed the intelligentsia of a country, and who—in sharp contrast with the descendants of the land-taking nobility who knew only of military matters—pursued intellectual interests.

Besides the remarks by Hartvic, there are ideas expressed in the *Admonitiones*: a royal mirror, inspired by King Stephen for the instruction of his son and future heir[s] to the throne, that throw some light on the mind of the monarch;[90] and one may also find some references in the *Deliberatio*, the work by Bishop Gerard of Csanád, King Stephen's trusted co-worker, who on a given occasion remarked, "Istiusmodi thesauurum no potuit habere darius rex, no xerses [sic], non arthaxerses [sic], ...non alexander macedo,"[91] or, noted on another occasion how "infelix terra, que inter deum et hominem discordiam operatur."[92]

King Stephen did not separate Church and kingship in the land, but he did separate religion from politics—in sharp contrast with western, German, and southeastern, Byzantine, policies where the Church, members of the clergy, and religion as such, served serious political interests. In the realm of King Stephen, the king's office would not become dependent on the Church. Stephen may have obtained a crown from Pope Sylvester II because of the intercession and good willed consent of the German emperor, and he requested— because he had retained for himself the right that Rome allow him to select members of his country's hierarchy, who were also his administrative and political advisors—to confirm them in their ecclesiastical positions. The monarch's churchman, his advisor, indeed, possessed *two bodies*: as an ecclesiastic, he was held responsible for caring for the spiritual needs of the faithful and fulfilling his church administrative duties; as the king's loyal man, he fulfilled the role of an advisor standing by the monarch both in season and out of season. The entry in King Stephen's *Admonitiones* where he warned his heir[s] to the throne that the Church in the land, and members of the Royal Council—individuals who were in public service—to be given public respect and appreciation, refers to this mental disposition of the monarch. The king wanted his churchmen, and secular advisors, to pay constant attention to the interests of the kingdom, and to serve both Church and country faithfully in their spiritual and temporal statutes.[93]

The Hungarian monarch enacted legislation on his own: "nos quoque dei nutu notram guernantes monarchiam, ...decretali meditatione nostre statuimus genti,[94] decrevimus nostra regali potentia, ...ut gens huius monarchiae...remota et quieta maneat, secundum decretum regalis concilii penitus interdictum est,"[95] as if to refer to the Preface of the *Institutes* (within the *Corpus Iuris Civilis*) of Justinian the Great (527–65): "Imperatoriam maiestatem non solum armis decoratam, sed etiam legibus oportet esse armatam, ut utrumque tempus et belorum et pacis recte possit gubernari."[96]

The King legislated with the consent of his royal council, "consensimus igitur petitioni totius senatus,"[97] and ordered that every goods- or landholder in the realm be free to handle his possessions as he saw fit; when the goods- or landholder died, his wife, sons and daughters, and, as a matter of fact, his relatives, could inherit the goods, or could donate them to the Church, without anyone questioning their decisions before *their* death.[98] The King and Queen owned the land; they looked upon every inhabitant of the kingdom as friends and brothers, who were allowed, by law, to inherit, and to increase their chattel and the size of their landed goods.[99]

The monarch would make certain demands in order to maintain his personal dignity, as the King's decrees guaranteed the inviolable right of private property for anyone who had them.[100] In other words, a *private sector* had developed in the emerging social order out of donations: land-grants, made by the monarch from the royal domain. One who held land, or owned it, was lord and master over his estate;[101] the landless elements were the slaves,[102] while *free men* in society served the king's public interest with their weapons and physical strength.[103] If, and when, the poor[er] social element could join the rich[er] one, and remain loyal to it in good and bad times, the poor would obtain from the rich the usufruct of their landholdings.[104]

King Stephen rewarded and supported the services of *his* retainers out of the royal domain; he permitted others to aid their own armed retainers. The social stratum, whose members' status-quo rested on military service they owed the monarch—and on land-grants they held from the monarch—actually enabled the king to appoint trusted officials to represent him everywhere, and to aid him in the government of the realm.[105] In establishing his country-wide administration, King Stephen followed the west-Frankish examples. He, for example, drew territories together into one administrative unit, placed the regional unit under one administrative head—the reeve, or *comes* [title and position being a mixture of tribal chief, the Frank count, and the Slavic *span*]—who in time became the powerful royal reeve—*ispán*—in the centralized public administration of the land.[106] The reeve/*comes*, in lieu of payment received a land-grant out of the royal domain, though he had to share the income with the king. This is how the *royal county* (*district*—bearing a strong resemblance to the

Slav *mazda*, meaning border), that is, a territory within its [own] borders under the supervision of the reeve's (that is, *ispán's*) regional fort, developed into a public administrative unit in Árpádian Hungary.[107]

2. The Monarch Asserts Leadership

> Stephanus…favore principum et plebis in regni
> solium laudabiliter provectus ardentiori animo
> veritatis cepit propogator existere…
>
> Stephen's *Vita minor*, c. 2.

The non-Hungarian chroniclers had determined that the Hungarian monarch, King Stephen, could assert a strong leadership role when the situation required it.[108] For example, they stated that the King did resort to the use of arms against those who dared to revolt against—who refused to become a part of—the new political order of his realm.[109] With his army, he attacked and defeated Gyula, the stubborn *voivode* of Transylvania, and imprisoned him.[110] The German chronicler Thietmar mentioned a certain Procui who, and whose wife, had to flee the country from the wrath of the king,[111] while other German and Polish chroniclers recorded that King Stephen gave orders for the blinding Vazúl, son of his uncle Mihály [Michael], and had Vazúl's three sons, Andrew, Béla, and Levente, expelled from the country.[112]

One of the sisters of Stephen—named Gisela in one of the sources—married Otto Orseolo, Doge of Venice, whose son Peter Orseolo succeeded King Stephen on the Hungarian throne in 1038.[113] Another sister, Judith, was married to the Polish Lord Boleslav (later, Boleslav I, "Boleslaus cognomento Chrobri vel Acer"), who died in 1025. The record has it that the Polish monarch had four wives. Judith was his second wife; they were married in 984, "accepit Iudith filiam Iestae ducis Hungarorum in coniugem," and they had a son named Micislaus.[114] Thietmar noted that the son was named *Besprim*, who for a time period lived in the court of King Stephen, after Boleslav had Judith expelled from his court, "similiter expellens eam." (The term *similiter* used by the chronicler may imply that the Polish king had done it *again*—sending his wife away—bearing in mind that Boleslav at that time was an unbaptized pagan.)[115]

King Stephen had to defend his country against the attacks by Emperor Conrad II, and forced the guilty German ruler to conclude peace with him.[116] He successfully fought against the Polish Boleslav Chrobry, a great supporter of the nobles who conspired against the Hungarian court. The Polish prince was playing politics, and Stephen reacted firmly: a decisive military action against the Polish ruler enabled him to make peace on his own terms, though, afterwards, he was even willing to support Boleslav with auxiliary troops in the latter's campaign against Kiev.[117]

After he suppressed the uprising of Gyula of Transylvania, and stood his ground against the ambitions of the German court; after he made an end to the situation that his political opponents could find political exile and support at the Polish court, King Stephen now had the opportunity to warn, even to threaten, the unruly peoples on the Balkans,[118] and send military aid to the Byzantine emperor against the emperor's enemies.[119] The military aid provided for the Byzantine court was appreciated. In order to express his thanks for the military support he had received, Emperor Basil II presented King Stephen with a small piece of the relic of the true Cross. Stephen's son, Prince Imre, donated a fragment of this relic to the Polish Holy Cross monastery. A western source recorded, anno 1043, that King Samuel Aba (1041–44) donated the fragment of this relic to Emperor Henry III, but the German monarch gave the piece to Margrave Adalbert of Austria.[120]

There are several non-Hungarian chroniclers who wrote about Prince Imre (Emery), "vir sanctus nomine Hemericus [sic!]," King Stephen's only son,[121] whom his father had carefully prepared for succession to the throne,[122] for whom the father had even chosen a wife, according to Polish sources a Polish,[123] but according to the thirteenth-century *Vita* of Blessed [now, Saint] Margaret of Hungary, a Byzantine princess.[124] The Greek text of the royal founding charter of the monastic community for religious women in Veszprém confirms the correctness of the assertion made in the Margaret legend.[125] And yet, it is the Polish chronicles that throw more light on Prince Imre; for instance, they record that he led a chaste married life, and that miracles occurred at his grave site.[126]

King Stephen went into battle with Koppány at Veszprém, under the standard of Saint Martin.[127] Now, it is known about Martin that when he ate his meal, he sat next to his slave—in an age when the slave was regarded as an object, not as a person;[128] the young Hungarian monarch must have been determined to imitate the example of the Pannonian saint when he formulated his own policy, his personal attitude toward serfs and slaves in his realm.[129] From Stephen's Christian point of view, men were regarded as equals within the existing framework of society;[130] though, from a practical realistic point of view, the monarch had to realize that the *land-taking* Magyar social stratum remained an influential ruling minority in the country; consequently, he made it certain that the *land-takers* submitted to the principle of equality of persons in the emerging social framework of the realm, even if ecclesiastical law *temporarily* recognized the existence of slavery within that society.[131] Lord and servant, master and slave, were all members of the Christian *body politic* in the ecclesiastical *commonwealth*, whose laws and guidelines not only controlled the use of naked force, but guided society itself.[132]

Serfdom and slavery did prevail in the early eleventh century,[133] but the young Hungarian monarch worked hard to accomplish a change in the public outlook; he renounced, and enabled others to renounce (political, social, physical) power over their fellow men.[134] The spread of Christian teaching would eventually cause a revolution among the slaves; they wanted to free themselves from the unwelcome social and professional yoke they had been forced to carry.[135] Nor did the young monarch want a slave to be at the mercy of his master's household. He decreed that a slave must also receive land allotment[s] for his labor, land he had to cultivate for his master, but an allotment of land that enabled him to live from it; the King made it certain that besides their many obligations, slaves possessed [basic] human rights. The monarch had caused the question of *this is mine, that is yours* to be an issue in his legislative acts. "Nec pro ullis [sic!] (ullius?) causa reatus detrimentum bonorum suorum [sui] patiatur quis, nisi consiliatus mortem regis aut traditionem regni fuerit vel in aliam fugerit provinciam."[136] The monarch decreed that a former slave previously emancipated by his master, should retain his freedom. He gave his loyal slaves land to cultivate for their own benefit, and placed them under the supervision of the regional royal reeve (of a fort district), or, directly under the directive of the Palatine at the royal court.[137]

A word of explanation is in order here. The institution of slavery, actually, was against *natural* law [*ius naturale*], though, as Iraeneus at the University of Bologna explained, even the servant possessed *facultas naturale*, though he could only exercise it with the consent of his master.[138] His master could not, however, treat a servant badly, could not physically beat him, nor punish him without reason.[139] The Synod of Mainz, 847, pronounced excommunication on anyone who willingly, or unintentionally, had killed his servant, or slave.[140]

Abbot Smaragdus had argued that one had to treat one's servant, or slave, as if he (or, she) were one's own brother (or, sister), or one's own immortal soul. Let a ruler set [all] servants, or slaves, free.[141] Therefore, a slave [or, servant] could be ordained a priest with the permission of his lord, but the lord could not reclaim his [former] slave, servant, who had already been ordained to the priesthood—who had already been handed over to the bishop.[142] In a similar manner, if a slave, or servant, sought refuge [freedom] in a monastic community, and his lord located him in that community within a period of three years, the lord must prove that the servant belonged to him, "dicens eum servum suum esse," who had fled to the monastery because he wanted to escape work in the fields, "ad culturam agrorurm effugeret," or had committed a crime, "propert furta," the servant had to be returned to his lord—on condition that the lord promise under oath that he would not punish the returned slave.[143] And yet, Azo, professor of laws at the University of Bologna in the early thirteenth century, maintained that a slave did not possess *persona*, "quia quantum ad ius civile servus pro murtuo habetur."[144]

It is more than likely that King Stephen's advisors followed the guidelines of a Jonas of Orleans, who, to quote from a letter of Pope Gregory the Great (d. 604), "namque omnes homines natura equales sumus," argued that human nature remained the same regardless how rich, or well learned, the individual had been, had become.[145] The Lord creates everyone equally, but there are (shall be) some inclined to follow evil.[146] The argument of Hincmar of Reims that clerics ought to know canon law, could as well be applied to the court advisors of King Stephen, as they were well versed in the articles of Church Law.[147]

It is known from contemporary sources that the Hungarian king had surrounded himself by trustworthy co-workers. He, indeed, had great need for reliable co-workers—advisors he could trust—because, as recorded by the non-Magyar sources, his people really were impatient and intolerant among themselves and toward outsiders.[148] For that reason, the king maintained a positive attitude toward the neighboring peoples—even toward those who (may have) disliked him; "gubernabat et pacem servabat cum Bohemis, Polonorum infest-issimus inimicis,"[149] remarks confirmed by a Kievan writer who wrote that the Hungarian king held the role of peacemaker among enemies.[150] In King Stephen's kingdom, peace had to prevail (the chronicler, Ortilo de Lilienfeld, used past tense, "pax aurea floruit"), on account of the friendly relations the Hungarian monarch main-tained with his neighbors.[151] When Duke Henry of Bavaria insur-rected against his brother, Emperor Conrad II, and fled to the court of Stephen, the Hungarian monarch did not politically exploit the unexpected situation; he entertained the duke as his house guest, but on Friday he had a meat dish placed on the table before him, to let the surprised prince know that it was a graver sin to revolt against his crowned brother, than to eat meat on Friday.[152]

The majority of the clergy active in missionary work in the country was at this time mostly of Slavic, Italian, or German origin. The letter by Fulbert of Chartres, dated about 1009, and addressed to Bishop Bonipert of Pécs, provides information on the development of church conditions in Hungary at this time.[153] In his efforts to lay the foundations for the Christian religion and Hungarian kingship [state-hood], Gerard of Venice—who, afterwards, became the first bishop of Csanád—distinguished himself among the king's close co-workers. Two of Gerard's *Vitae* bear witness to his religious-missionary, and political-advisory activities in Hungary,[154] and so does Gerard's major work on a theological theme, *De deliberatione supra hymnum trium puerorum*, that not only throws light on his religious-political ideas and activities in the realm, but places the development of the king's ecclesiastical politics in a new prospective.[155] The abbot of the Scottish abbey in Vienna remarked about Gerard that he came from Venice, and Hungary's first king had made him bishop.[156]

There were two *legendae* written about Bishop Gerard, and the relationship of the two "lives" is subject to debate. According to one school of thought, his *Vita maior* was written down at first, while the *Vita minor*, a brief[er] composition, was only a revised outline of the former—to serve a liturgical purpose. The other school of thought insists, though, that the *Vita minor* was written down at first, with the *Vita maior* drafted during the 1300s, as its author had to rely and expand on events recorded in the *Vita minor*. It is possible that the rough draft of what became known as the *Vita maior* was written at first, as it was abbreviated in form of a sermon.[157]

Besides Bishop Gerard of Csanád, the German-born Benedictine monk Astric (Aseric), who, previously, had been the associate of Bishop Adalbert of Prague, and, afterwards, became the abbot of Pécsvárad, and, at a later date, as *Archbishop of the Magyars*, played an important part in formulating Hungarian foreign policy—in realizing the king's ideas as how to establish firm foundations for the ecclesiastical administration in the country.[158] Next to the information provided in the Hungarian chronicles, church records, numerous non-Magyar chroniclers dealt with Astric, who on the document that recorded the event[s] of the 1007 Synod of Frankfurt, signed his name as Anastasius, Archbishop of the Magyars: *Anastasius Ungarorurm archiepiscopus interfui et subscripsi.*[159] Therefore, it is no small wonder, indeed, that the author of the "Annales Boiorum," with well intentioned logic and justification, identified Anastasius with Astric, "Aschericus qui et Anastasius," as if to point out the fact that the "Archbishop of the Hungarians" had in everyday official capacity referred to himself as *Anastasius* (in Hungarian, *Anasztáz*).

Did the monk Aventinus, author of the "Annales Boiorum," commit an error? That seems to be improbable, and it may be even more improbable that in that age, when official writs were already held in high esteem, someone would later have inserted—"signed in"—the name of Anastasius (instead of Astric), as the Hungarians' archbishop. Most probably, the written usage of the name Astric(us), in Latin, or its German pronunciation, caused the non-Magyar chronicler to fuse the two names into one, *Aschericus qui est Anastasius*, in order to prevent a misunderstanding, or to assign to the Hungarian archbishop a mistaken identity.[160]

Bishop Hartvic also identified Astric with Anastasius, *Ascricum presulem, qui alio nomine Anastasius dictus est*, whom [King] Stephen, according to Hartvic, did name [Arch]bishop of Kalocsa: *Cognoscens vero prudens dux predicti Asscrici* [sic!] *religionem, pontificalis ipsum dignitatis infula decoratum electione canonica sublimavit et ei Colocensis episcopatus dignitatem obtulit.*[161]

The *Vita minor* of Bishop Gerard confirmed Hartvic's record: Astric-Anastasius was the abbot of Pécsvárad at the time Gerard arrived in Hungary: "...*accidit dominum Anastasium Waradiensem abbatem* [italics mine] illis diebus Quinqueecclesiae pervenire," who visited with Bishop Maurus of Pécs.[162] Certain Polish sources remembered him as "Astricus presul Strigoniensis,"[163] or as Adstricus,[164] even as Affricus.[165] A monk from the abbey of Melk spelled his name as Astricius.[166]

Among King Stephen's clerical co-workers who were also known abroad, was Bonipert, the first bishop of Pécs—the addressee of a letter from Bishop Fulbert of Chartres—who exemplified *foreign* contacts members of the Hungarian hierarchy maintained with the Latin west. Bonipert sent his cleric, Hilduin, to Chartres with the request to borrow for his cathedral school at Pécs a copy of Priscian's Grammar from the bishop of Chartres.[167] Both, the Venetian-born Gerard, and Bonipert, were, in a given sense, educators *and* theologians who amidst their missionary work carried on with their scholarly religious studies during the former half of the eleventh century.[168]

The monk Astric-Anastasius, abbot of Pécsvárad, later archbishop,[169] fulfilled an important role in laying the foundation for King Stephen's foreign diplomacy, when he obtained from the hands of the Roman Pontiff the royal diadem for his Prince, thereby to gain *diplomatic recognition* of Stephen as the first Catholic king of Hungary.[170]

In order to establish Latin Christian kingship and the ecclesiastical administration in the country, the Hungarian ruler had to ascertain that he, the elected prince of his people, was publicly recognized—given *diplomatic recognition*—as the anointed and crowned ruler of his realm. He sent the foreign-born Benedictine

Astric-Anastasius, who had been trained in the Latin west, as his envoy to Rome,

first, to inform the Holy See about conditions in the land;

second, to request from Pope Sylvester II recognition of the See of Esztergom as the seat of the ecclesiastical administrative structure in the kingdom, and the pontiff's personal blessing for members of the Hungarian hierarchy;

last, to obtain papal-*imperial* approval of Hungary as a Latin-Christian kingdom.

The latter point is of great importance because it is evident from the record that the Roman pontiff acted with the previous consent of the emperor, Otto III, in sending a royal diadem to the Hungarian ruler.[171]

About eleven years later, on May 6, 1012, Astric, as the "Magyars' archbishop," participated in the consecration of St. Peter's church in Bamberg, when he actually consecrated a side altar in honor of three *Confessors* [*of the faith*]: "...altare ante criptam consecravit *Aschericus Ungarorum archiepiscous* in honorem sanctorum confessorum Hylarii, Remegii, Vadasti" [italics mine], as recorded in the official document and by a contemporary chronicler.[172]

Presul Astric-Anastasius (the expression *presul* applied by Bishop Hartvic), played a key role at the very beginning of Hungarian *multi-national* diplomacy (if the term is applicable in that age), as evidenced by numerous non-Magyar historical sources—even though they all spelled his name differently. He undoubtedly became known because he had obtained from the Holy See the *royal* recognition of his prince.

The Polish chroniclers were especially enthused about him, most probably because of the simultaneous two requests—so the Polish chroniclers argued—for royal crowns by the *Polish and* Hungarian ruling princes from Rome, when, the Polish record has it, the crown requested by, and prepared for, the Polish prince had actually been sent to the Magyar Prince, thanks to the diplomatic cleverness of *Adstricus*, alias *Affricus* (!); and, according to the testimony of the Magyar chroniclers, Stephen had, indeed, been crowned with the diadem diplomatically obtained by Astric-Anastasius from Pope Sylvester II.[173]

An explanatory remark would be in order here. King Stephen's *Vita minor*, c. 2, made no mention of such "diplomatic" activity, as its author recorded nothing about the Magyar prince's receiving a crown from the Roman See. The anonymous author of the *Vita* merely noted that, upon the death of his father, Stephen had been elected by the headmen and by the people; "post cuius obitum Stephanus adhuc puer favore principum et plebis in regni solium laudabiliter provectus," and began his reign.[174] Although Hartvic repeated the statement (he wrote *adolescens* instead of *puer*),[175] by borrowing from Stephen's *Vita maior*, c. 5, he argued that it was Stephen's father, Prince Géza, who had summoned the headmen of the land before his death to discuss succession, and, *with their consent*, named his son, Stephen, to succeed him as the ruling prince, and asked those present to take an oath on this. The passage is worth quoting: "…convocatis pater suus Ungarie primatibus et cum ordine sequenti, *per communis consilium colloquii* [italics mine] filium suum Stephanum post se regnaturum populo *prefecit*, et ad hoc corroborandum a singulis sacramentum exegit."[176]

The author of Stephen's *Vita minor*, and Hartvic (both were ecclesiastics) attempted to trace the beginnings of Catholic Magyar kingship to divine providence, the grace of God—*vox populi, vox Dei!*—because they had serious doubts about ascribing the origins of Hungarian kingship solely to German imperial favor, and papal good will. One is to recall that the author of King Stephen's *Vita minor* lived during the reign of Ladislas I (1077–95), and Hartvic was active in the reign of Coloman the Learned (1095–1116), to remember that both Hungarian monarchs conducted their domestic affairs and diplomatic decisions independently of foreign influence.[177]

Details on the request made for the crown—and the *legend* of the Crown—were recorded by Polish chroniclers who wrote that the Polish prince, Miciklas I [Meske; Meschko] dispatched Archbishop Lambert of Cracow to Rome with the petition that Pope Sylvester II provide him with a royal crown. The Roman pontiff was willing to fulfill the request of the prince, and ordered a crown to be constructed and handed to the Polish envoy.[178]

Simultaneously, Bishop *Affricus*, the envoy of the Hungarian prince also arrived in Rome, the Polish chronicler wrote, "Stephanus dux Ungarorum misit Affricum episcopum pro corona etiam sibit potenda," to inform the pontiff that the Catholic faith had struck deep roots in Hungary, "quod Ungaria fidem catholicam recepit," as Prince Stephen himself had been baptized by Bishop Adalbert [of Prague].[179] The pontiff heard the news joyfully, the chronicler reported, because he has had a vision during the previous night, when an angel had warned him—"Papa vero monitus visione angelica nocturnali"—that he hand over the royal circlet, that had been prepared for the Polish prince, to the delegate of the Magyar ruler, Stephen. The pontiff, indeed, sent the crown to the Hungarian prince, thereby granting him, and his successors, royal power and dignity; "exinde regio titulo voluit atque in perpetuum ea dignitate vel regni ipso futuris seculis gaudere."[180]

The legendary material—because it is legendary—underwent various versions as the century wore on. Some chroniclers replaced the name of Pope Sylvester II with that of Leo VIII,[181] or with Benedict VII;[182] Prince Miciklas appeared in the record as Boleslav Chrobry (corresponding to reality, as Boleslav had died the first Polish Catholic monarch in 1025).[183] (Another chronicler, though, wrote in Miciklas II, who died in 1034.[184]) There is at least one Polish chronicler who knew nothing about Archbishop Lambert of Cracow as the envoy sent to Rome to request a royal crown for the Polish prince,[185] while Peter Damian around 1040 confirmed the validity of the *legend* about the request the Polish court had made to the Roman curia. As Damian noted, through efforts of the monks of Saint Romuald who went as missionaries to Poland, Boleslav attempted to receive a crown from Rome, but a political counter-move on part of the German court prevented him from achieving his objective. "Busclavus volens coronam sui regni ex Romana auctoritate suscepere, …Imperator autem Henricus Busclavi consilium non ignorans, undique vias custodiri praeceperat, ut, si Busclavus Romam nuncios mittet, in eius manibus devenirent."[186]

Before he became archbishop, Astric-Anastasius was the abbot of the abbey of Pécsvárad, a Benedictine community, established in the honor of the Mother of God, and of Saint Benedict [of Nursia], not too far from Pécs (Sopiana; Quinqueecclesiae). The monarch placed 200 men of horse (knights?) at the service of the abbey to protect it in case of an insurrection, and twelve men out of the 200 were to accompany the abbot whenever he had to visit the royal court.[187] The monks were expected to carry on with missionary work, and preach through interpreters; one may wonder, though, how effective such an effort: preaching in a foreign language, could have been among the population?[188]

It had to be under these conditions that the monarch had to think seriously of the necessity of establishing a functioning ecclesiastical administration in the land. He had plans for setting up twelve bishoprics, headed by the archbishop of *Esztergom* as the Hungarian Primate, with another archbishopric later to be established at *Kalocsa*.[189] (Kalocsa means *muddy [place]* in Slavic.[190])

Hartvic chose his words carefully, when he recorded that Abbot Astric-Anastasius was sent by *Prince* Stephen to Rome to *inform* the Holy See about political conditions in Hungary, and request *recognition* of the see of Esztergom as the seat of the church administrative structure in the land, accompanied by a papal blessing for members of the Hungarian hierarchy, thereby to *acknowledge* Hungary as a Catholic kingdom.[191] Hartvic mentioned no imperial favor, or papal benevolence. Hartvic' tone was most respectful, but cautious. He made it clear to his royal master, King Coloman, that the foundations of Hungarian kingship rested on the will and consent of the Magyar people.[192]

Astric-Anastasius actually went to Rome in the fall of 1000, at a time, when Emperor Otto III visited Boleslav of Poland, the son of Miesko.[193] Boleslav was still a pagan, with barbarian manners, who knew of the Christian faith and its commandments, and expected his people to observe them, but he personally ignored them.[194] He was a feudal vassal of the imperial court, and as an imperial vassal he received the visiting German monarch in Gnesen.[195] Adalbert [of Prague] was buried in Gnesen; it was in Gnesen that Boleslav began to organize the Polish church hierarchy. It was the bishop of Posen, under the spiritual jurisdiction of the archbishop of Magdeburg, who had been in charge of the administration of the Church in Poland before that. By appointing Gaudentius (Radim), the half-brother of Adalbert, archbishop of Gnesen, Boleslav made certain that the Church on Polish soil had a direct line of communication with the Roman curia. It is worth noticing that the German contemporaries of Otto III disliked the idea that their emperor dealt on personal terms, as an "associate," with Boleslav *the Slav*, whom the German nobles only regarded as an "ally" of the imperial court.[196]

In Rome, Pope Sylvester II—Gerbert of Aurillac of Frankish descent—earlier the archbishop of Ravenna, sixty years old, headed the affairs of the Church.[197] He was a wise man of his age, a philosopher and a mathematician, whose understanding of world affairs rested on the knowledge he had learned from the ancients. He knew his Virgil, Horace and Cicero; had the means to realize ideas that, in the long run, would support the interests of the Church. He had been active at the court of Otto II as the tutor to the future Otto III, and he became a friend and an advisor of the young emperor.[198]

Sylvester II had been elected to the papal office at a critical time. The *fin-de-siècle* was filled with visions of the approaching end of the world, though the concept of the year 1000 remained chronologically undetermined. The year 1000 might have fallen, according to today's calendar, between the feast of the Annunciation (March 25th), 999, and the end of the month of March, 1000;[199] Abbot Abbon (Abbo) of Fleury (d. 1004)[200] did not hesitate to announce that the end (of the world) would come when the Feast of the Annunciation and Good Friday fell on the same day—a coincidence that had actually occurred in 992.[201]

It is evident from Hartvic's text, and from papal correspondence, that the Roman Pontiff was pleased to receive the personal envoy of the Hungarian ruler; Prince Stephen regarded the Roman pontiff as the highest authority in both spiritual and secular matters in Latin Christendom. The record has it that Pope Sylvester II fulfilled the request of *Prince* Stephen in that he sent him a royal diadem, and empowered him to act, according to *his own judgment*, in ecclesiastical matters of his kingdom.[202] The Pontiff permitted Stephen to have the Apostolic double cross to be carried in front of him at all official functions, on the grounds that the Hungarian ruler had, indeed, done the Apostles' work in Christianizing and developing an administrative structure for the Church in his realm. The Roman pontiff was only "Apostolic," Astric had so been told by the Pontiff, Hartvic wrote, but Stephen a real Apostle; "ego sum apostolicus, ille vero...Christi apostolus," a statement supported by the testimony of domestic, and non-domestic chroniclers.[203]

The mission of Astric-Anastasius had been successful. On Christmas day, 1001, the first day of the new year, Stephen—who had earlier been duly elected to succeed his father as the ruling prince—was anointed with holy oil, and crowned with the circlet sent to him from Rome; "...presulibus cum clero, comitibus cum populo laudes congruas adclamantibus, ...unctione crismali perunctus, diademate regalis...rex...feliciter coronatur."[204]

Numerous members of the "old guard," descendants of the *landtakers* of the 890s, opposed King Stephen's new, Christian-political, orientation toward the Latin west. Changes initiated by Prince Géza deeply hurt the pride and interests of the leading members of the declining former social elite. It had to come about that a military insurrection broke out in Transdanubia—territory south and west of the Danube—headed by a regional tribal chief named *Koppány*, son of Szerind, possibly a blood relative of King Stephen.[205] The people of Koppány lived on the land of Somogy, a region south of Lake Balaton and north of the river Drave; to the north, Somogy bordered on lands of the king's domain, directly controlled by the Árpáds. The geographical center of the insurgents' attack was Veszprém, the former Roman Cimbrina north of Lake Balaton, where Svatopluk's father had once a fort constructed, where Prince Géza liked to visit—and visit he did when he went hunting—where King Stephen liked to sojourn.[206]

At Veszprém, the insurgent forces ferociously attacked King Stephen in person, and, by challenging the monarch, they turned against Christianity, the king's Latin Christian political program itself. The monarch was stunned by the sudden act of military violence, but reacted quickly. Trusting in God, self-confident, saying a prayer for the intercession of Saint George, the great military saint of Gaul, and of saint Martin, the famous son of Pannonia (a former soldier himself), the king took defensive action. Two German knights, Hunt and Paznan, girded Stephen with a sword to prepare him for battle, and supported him with their troops.[207] The fortified town of Veszprém now under siege bravely resisted the insurgents until the arrival of Stephen's forces. Another German knight named Vencelin commanded the king's army in battle, where Magyar fought stubbornly against Magyar. Stephen's forces carried the day, Koppány died in the engagement, his military might fully disintegrated.[208]

In order to set a dreadful example in that still barbaric age, the king had the body of the insurgent cut into four pieces and ordered the body pieces to be publicly displayed: nailed on the town gates of Esztergom, Veszprém, Győr, and even as far as in Transylvania [*Erdelw*], the latter to warn Gyula who still held tribal control of the region.[209] Out of the captured booty Stephen kept nothing for himself, but donated the Somogy region to Saint Martin, to the new Benedictine monastery of Pannonhalma at that time under construction. The nobles of his court circle, however, lively protested the king's donating a whole region—county—to a monastic community, even one named after St. Martin; to them, it appeared to be too large an endowment to be made. Stephen altered his decision and ordered, instead, that the people of Somogy pay an annual tithe that included offering a male offspring of every family as an oblate to the abbey. Offering a male child could also have been regarded as ransom for a family's emancipation from serfdom, or slavery, in the Somogy region.[210]

Stephen also ordered that ten villages build one (parish) church, and named worthy clerics to head bishoprics and parishes.[211] In order to express his gratitude for his victory over his opponent[s], the king had a church erected in Rome in the honor of St. Stephen the First Martyr, had a monastery built, and provided for a community of monks, in Jerusalem, and a beautifully decorated church, "ecclesia mirifici operis," and well provided for, to be constructed in Constantinople.[212]

The anonymous author of Stephen's *Vita minor* noted that in a dream Stephen had been warned about the impending invasion by the Pechenegs in Transylvania, and the king issued orders to the *hadnagy* [reeve; the official in charge] of the region to be ready for a defensive military counterattack against the intruder.[213] And, when the king had found out that certain disloyal royal servants had murdered, or wounded, and plundered the bodies of some sixty Pecheneg nobles who, by due process of the law, were seeking refuge at Stephen's court, he had those faithless servants hanged two by two along country roads.[214]

Toward the end of his reign political and personal opposition to Stephen grew so strong that some members of the nobility—the chronicler spoke of four—had planned to murder the king in his bed. When one of those nobles with a naked sword in his hand had entered the king's bedchamber at night, but let his sword drop to the ground, the noise awakened the king, and the assailant, trembling with fear, begged the king for forgiveness. Stephen did not punish him who had confessed his evil intention, but gave orders to seek out the conspirators, whom he had blinded, had their hands cut off, so that people learn to respect their lord[s], the record has it.[215] Besides the chronicle report, Stephen's later legislative acts bear witness to this assassination attempt made at his life.[216]

King Stephen I died in 1038. He was buried in the church he had built in the honor of the Blessed Mother of God at Székesfehérvár.[217] During the reign of Ladislas I the Saint (1077–95), in the year 1083, he had been canonized a saint.[218]

An additional remark would be in order here. As late as the fourteenth century, numerous chroniclers recorded details on the request of Stephen for a royal crown from Rome, the crown itself, and on the coronation insignia (*insignia regalia*), such as, the "Coronation cloak of King Stephen" (it was actually a *pluviale*, tradition has it, the handiwork of Queen Gisela), on the orb, the sceptre and on the lance. The chroniclers also recorded that, in the early 1300's, Otto, duke of Bavaria, during his visit to Bohemia, forced Venceslaus, king of Bohemia, to hand over to him the Hungarian royal insignia: *corona, tunica s. Stephani regis, diademate et sceptro,* despite the opposition of Albert, king of Rome, and Rudolf, duke of Austria (alias Albert of Austria, German emperor, 1208–1308; and, Rudolf, the first Habsburg on the German throne, 1273–91), who had warned him against undertaking such a move.[219]

The Austrian chronicler, Thomas of Ebendorfer, also referred to the Hungarian crown, "et alia insignia regalia cum tunica s. Stephani."[220] One eleventh century writer spoke of the *royal lance* given by the papal legate as a gift to the new Hungarian monarch, but captured in battle by a (the) king's opponent[s], and returned to Rome.[221] Ademar Cabanensis suggested that it was Otto III who had donated the (a) lance to the Magyar prince Géza (Stephen's father), that is, before the year 997.[222]

Sigibert Gemblacensis (Gembloux) wrote, and the *Annales Leodienses* recorded, that after Emperor Henry III had defeated the Hungarian king Aba in battle in 1044, he had the lance captured,[223] and sent back to Rome.[224] The latter statement was confirmed by Pope Gregory VII himself in his latter of October 28, 1074, addressed to King Salomon of Hungary.[225] And yet, later writers, including the author of the "Austrian Rhymed Chronicle,"[226] and as late as the "Annales Mechovienses," anno 1304, cited the lance as part of the Hungarian *insignia regali.*[227]

Notes

1. The Country's First Catholic Monarch

1. Géza, too, had been baptized *Stephen*; cf. "Vita maior s. Stephani regis," c. 2, *SSH*, II, 379, note 4; Hóman – Szekfű, I, 64f.; see also Gaufridius de Bruil, "Chronicon," *MGHSS*, XXVI, 202, while a twelfth century source, "Annales s. Disiboldi," *MGHSS*, XVII, 27, spoke of Geysa as Wardiz (!). The name Waic must have remained in common use—see a 1245 writ about a "Martinus banu filius Waic"—*CD*, IV-1, 386.

2. Cf. King Stephen's "Vita maior," c. 2, *SSH*, II, 379,1-6; Hartvic's Life of King Stephen, *ibid.*, II, 403,4-12.

3. *Ibid.*, II, 379,8-13, and Hartvic, *ibid.*, II, 403f.

4. As it is evident from the remarks of the "Vita maior," c. 3, *ibid.*, II, 379.

5. The son of Yeche, "a primo duce Almo septimus;" cf. Albericus Trium Fontium (d. 1252), "Chronicon," anno 1041, *MGHSS*, XXIII, 786. Gyula Kristó, "Mikor lett fejedelem Géza?" [When was Géza elected *Ruling* Prince of the Magyars?], *Acta historica Szegediensis*, 102 (1995), 11ff.; further, S. L. Tóth, "A magyar fejedelem méltóság öröklődése" [Inheriting the dignity of the Hungarian *ruling* prince], *Acta historica Szegediensis*, 83 (1986), 3ff.; idem, "Megjegyzések a magyar honfoglalás szakaszaihoz" [Some comments on the periods of the Hungarian conquest], *Századok*, 130 (1996), 877ff.

6. Cf. "Chronicon Hungarorum mixtum et Polonorum," c. 3, in *MPH*, I, 496ff., and in *SSH*, II, 299ff.; Macartney, *Hungarian Historians*, 173ff.; Attila in Italy, cf. Bóna, *Hunok*, 90ff.

7. "Geiza sive Geyza"—see Andreas Dandalo, "Chronicon Venetum," ix:1,46; ix:2,1, *RISS*, XII, 233, 235; and, "Catalogus archiepiscoporum Gnesenensium," *MPH*, III, 392; further, cf. Thietmar, viii:3.

8. See "Vita Adalberti," c. 23, *MGHSS*, IV, 607. This writer could not gain access to the more recent additions by Hedwig Karwasińka, *S. Adalberti Pragensis episcopi et martyris vita altera auctore Brunone Querfurtensi, MPH* ser. nova, IV-2 (Warsaw, 1962), and *S. Adalberti Pragensis episcopi et martyris vita prior, MPH* ser. Nova, IV-1 (Warsaw, 1962).

9. Thietmar, viii:3 [ix:4].

10. See Aventinus, "Annales Boiorum," in Cisnerus, *Aventini Annales Boiorum, libri VII* (Basel, 1580), 393 and 402.

11. Cf. "Annales Cisterciensium in Heinrichow," a. 971, *MGHSS*, XIX, 544; "Annales Kamenzenses," *ibid.*, XIX, 581; the "Chronicon mixtum," c. 3, *MPH*, I, 498; also "Chronica principum Poloniae," c. 8., *ibid.*, III, 438.

12. "...pulchra domina, id est, Beleknegini...," Thietmar, viii:3; Szegfű, art. cit., *Memoria saeculorum*, I, 239ff., esp. 243 ff.

13. They had Christianity established in Hungary, "qua duce erat christianitas coepta," but it remained a "religio cum paganismo polluta," recorded Bruno of Querfurt, "Vita Adalberti," c. 23, *MGHSS*, IV, 607.

14. Adelheid was the second wife of Géza—cf. "Genelogiae regum Polonum," in I. Pistorius, *Polonicae historiae corpus*, 3 vols, (Basileae, 1582 etc.), III, 148.

15. See *Annales Altahenses maiores*, a. 1003; *Annales Hildesheimenses*, anno 1003; Annalista Saxo, "Chronicon," a. 1003, *MGHSS*, VI, 652; "Auctarium Ekkehardi Altahense," anno 1003, *ibid.*, XVII, 363.

16. "Vita Adalberti," cc. 8, 18 and 19, *MGHSS*, IV, 581ff.; Karl Uhlirz, *Jahrbücher des Deutschen Reiches unter Otto II und Otto III*, 2 vols. (Leipzig, 1902–04), I, 187ff.

17. Cf. Brunonis, "Vita Adalberti," cc. 15, 16, *ibid.*, IV, 596f.; also, "Miracula s. Adalberti," c. 3, on Adalbert's visit to Esztergom, "ubi sedes erit principalis tocius monarchiae," *ibid.*, IV, 613ff., and compare with Cosmas of Prague, *ibid.*, IX, 54. Did Hartvic write his "Life of King [St.] Stephen" under Czech influence?—cf. Wattenbach, II, 195.

18. Cf. Thietmar, iv:38; on wife Sarolta, see the brief sketch by János Melıch, "Sarolt," *Magyar Nyelv*, 20 (1922), 110ff.; László Szegfű, "Sarolta," *Memoria saeculorum Hungariacae*, I, 239ff., offprint.

19. Cf. Stephen's "Vita minor," c. 2, *SSH*, II, 394,8-11.

20. See Stephen's "Vita maior," c. 9, *ibid.*, II, 384f.; Stephen was really of small stature—"statura pusillus, corde magnus," cf. "Legenda Minorita," *MGHSS*, XXIV, 183; for a study of his personal character, see his "Admonitiones," preface, *SSH*, II, 619ff.

21. Stephen's "Vita maior," cc. 10 and 12, *ibid.*, II, 385f., and II, 387,7-19. On relations between the Ottonian court and Cluny, see the study by Ernst Sackur, *Die Cluniacenser in ihrer kirchlichen und allgemeingeschichtlichen Wirksamkeit bis zur Mitte des elften Jahrhunderts*, 2 vols. (Halle a. d. Saale, 1894; repr. Tübingen, 1971), II, 449ff.; Alois Dempf, *Sacrum imperium*, 4th ed. (Munich–Vienna, 1973), 172ff.

22. "Adelheid genui Stephanum, regem Ungariae," wrote the unknown scribe of the "Annales Cistercienses in Heinrichow," anno 975, *MGHSS*, XIX, 544; see also "Annales Kamenzenses," anno 975, *ibid.*, XIX, 581; "Chronica principum Poloniae," c. 8, *MPH*, III, 438.

23. *Ibid.*

24. "…exinde regio titulo insignari voluit atque in perpetuum dignitate vel regni ipso futuris saeculis gaudere," cd. "Zdarzenia godne pamięci," *ibid.*, III, 299; further, "Annales a primo christiano duce Meschone Polonorum," a. 1001, *ibid.*, II, 829; "Annales s. Crucis Polonici," *MGHSS*, XIX, 678; "Annales Polonorum I et III," *ibid.*, XIX, 618 and 619; "Annales Silesıaci compilati," a. 1000, *ibid.*, XIX, 537; "Catalogi episcoporum Cracoviensium, IV," *MPH*, III, 332; Rocznik entered it under the year 965 (!), *ibid.*, III, 60f.

25. Cf. *MGHSS*, IV, 392. On Leo VIII, see Kühner, 53.

26. On this, see Martin, prior of Melk, "Nota de corona regni Hungariae," in Pez, *Thesaurus anecdotorum*, vi-3, 232. On Benedict VII, cf. Kühner, 53.

27. In "Annales Polonorum IV," a. 1000, *MGHSS*, XIX, 619.

28. Cf. the "Chronica principum Poloniae," c. 10, *MPH*, III, 445.

29. See "Vita s. Stanislai maior," ii:27, *ibid.*, IV, 392.

30. See Hartvic, c. 9, *SSH*, II, 412f.

31. Cf. *MPH*, III, 128.

32. Wrote Abbot Martin of the monastery Vienensis Scotorum, in H. Pez (ed.), *Scriptores rerum Austricarum*, 3 vols. (Regensburg, 1721–45), cited hereafter as *SSRA*, II, 667.

33. Hartvic, c. 3, *SSH*, II, 406; Ademar Cabanensis "Chronicon," c. 31, *MGHSS*, IV, 130.

34. Thietmar, iv:38 [iv:59].

35. Martinus Oppaviensis "Chronicon" recorded that Adalbert visited Pannonia during the reign of Otto II to baptize the first king of the Magyars (!)—cf. *MGHSS*, XXII, 465; "Annales Polonorum," a. 982 (!), *ibid.*, XIX, 616.

36. Cf. *ibid.*, XXIII, 779; see further *MPH*, II, 828f. For the Hungarian point of view, see Hartvic, c. 3, and Keza, c. 76, *SSH*, I, 188,6-12. Gyula Kristó, "I. István és családja árpádkori történetírásunkban" [King Stephen I and his family history in the record of the Árpád age], *Acta historica Szegediensis*, 40 (1972), 51ff.

37. The "Annales Kamazenses," anno 1161 (!) recorded that during the days of Emperor Henry [II] Saint Adalbert had, with the consent of the Roman pontiff, baptized the Hungarian king Stephen, the emperor's brother-in-law—cf. *MGHSS*, XIX, 582.

38. According to Ademar Cabanensis, c. 31, it was Bruno of Querfurt who, upon the request of his father, did baptize Stephen—*ibid.*, IV, 130.

39. Stephen's baptism and marriage were recorded together, as having had taken place during the times of Otto III and Henry II—see "Historia fundationis coenobii Mellicensis," in Pez, *SSRA*, I, 196, in the year of 991, *ibid.*, I, 761; also, *MGHSS*, IV, 130 (Ademar); the year of 1001 is rendered in *MGHSS*, VI, 192; and it is the year 1002 in Annalista Saxo, *MGHSS*, VI, 650.

40. Albericus, under the year 1010, referred to [the Hungarian] Queen Gisela as the sister of Henry II, but in his entry under 1041, he described King Peter (Orseolo) as her brother—*MGHSS*, XXIII, 786.

41. Cf. Keza, c. 78, *SSH*, I, 189,1-2; further, "Chronica minor Minoritae Erphordensis," in *Monumenta Erphesfurtensia saec. XII, XIII, XIV*, ed. Oswaldus Holder-Egger, SSrG (Hannover–Leipzig, 1899), 486ff., esp. 614f.

42. Explained it in an entry, anno 995 (!)—cf. *MGHSS*, V, 117

43. Cf. Hartvic, c. 5, *SSH*, II, 407; Stephen's "Vita minor," c. 2, *ibid.*, II, 394.

44. Cf. Stephen's "Vita maior," c. 5, *SSH*, II, 381,5-10.

45. *Ibid.*, II, 384,16-20 (c. 9); and *ibid.*, II, 378,16-24 (c. 1), and compare to Rudolf Lüttich, *Ungarnzüge in Europa im 10 Jahrhundert* (Berlin, 1910), passim; on the Italian campaigns, Gina Fasoli, *Le incursioni ungare in Europa nel secolo X* (Florence, 1945), passim; further, her essay, "Unni, avari e ungari nelle fonti occidentali e nelle storia dei paesi d'occidente," *Popoli della steppe: Unni, Avari, Ungari* (Spoleto, 1988), 32ff.

46. Widukind, iii:46, anno 955; Thietmar, ii:4, anno 955; "Lamperti Annales," in *Lamperti opera*, anno 955; "Annales Weissenburgenses," anno 955, *ibid.*, 9ff.; Heinrich Büttner, "Die Ungarn, das Reich und Europa bis zur Lechfeldschlact des Jahres 955," *Zeitschrift für bayerische Landesgeschichte*, 19 (1956), 433ff.

47. See Holtzmann, 152ff. and 175ff.; Joachim Wollasch, "Der Einfluss des Mönchtums aufs Reich und Kirche vor dem Investiturstreit," *Reich und Kirche vor dem Investiturstreit*, ed., Karl Schmid (Sigmaringen, 1985), 35ff.

48. See "Vita Wolfgangi," *MGHSS*, IV, 525ff., c. 30; Jákli, 107ff. and 127ff.

49. In a tersely recorded statement, in retrospect of events of the past, "Ungari Christiani fiunt," cf. "Annales Weingartenses Welfici," *MGHSS*, XVII, 308ff.; and yet, as Wattenbach, II, 393, noted, only its entries "von 1167 an sind gleichzeitig."

50. Cf. Horváth, *Árpádkori irodalmunk*, 149ff.; Macartney, *Hungarian Historians*, 165ff.

51. See, for instance, the "Vita Romualdi fundatoris Camaldulensium," cc. 28-29, *MGHSS*, IV, 852f.

52. Cf. *SSH*, II, 384,20 – 385,6, and references to his legislation, *ibid.*, II, 384,7-15, and Hartvic, c. 10, *ibid.*, II, 415,1-6; see further, Endre Tóth, "István és Gizella munkássága" [The accomplishments of Stephen and Gisela], *Századok*, 131 (1997), 3ff.

53. Cf. Martinus Gallus (d. 1113), "Chronicon," i:18, *MGHSS*, IX, 437; Bonitho, bishop of Sutri, "Liber ad amicum," *MPL*, 150, 816. Bernoldus s. Blasii, "Chronicon," a. 1038, *MGHSS*, V, 425.

54. Albericus Trium Fontium, "Chronicon," a. 1010, *ibid.*, XXIII, 779.

55. Friedrich Heer, *Geistesgeschichte*, 77ff.

56. "Vita Heinrici II" (composed about 1146), i:29-30, *MGHSS*, IV, 810.

57. Pope Innocent III to King Emery of Hungary, Sept. 15, 1204, in Potthast, n. 2282; *CD*, II, 432f., and Katona, IV, 714ff.; Kosztolnyik, *Thirteenth Century*, 13 and 23, n. 131.

58. King Stephen had even converted Transylvania to Latin Christianity under the auspices of Rome—see *Annales Altahenses maiores*, anno 1003; Ademar Cabanensis "Chronicon," c. 33, *MGHSS*, IV, 131; Annalista Saxo, anno 1003, *ibid.*, IV, 652.

59. Cf. "Sächsische Weltchronik," c. 104, in MGH ling. vern., II, 167; Martinus Fuldensis Chronicon, anno 1012, in Ekkehardus, *Corpus*, I, 1679.

60. Emperor Henry II gave his elder sister in marriage to Stephen, and made him convert, together with his people, to the Catholic faith; cf. "Auctarium Garstense," anno 1009, *MGHSS*, IX, 657; the "Admont Annals," anno 1000, *ibid.*, IX, 574; also, Paulus Langius Cygnaeus, "Chronicon Citizense," anno 1013, in I. Pistorius – B. G. Struvius, *Rerum Germanicarum scriptores*, 3 vols., rev. 3rd ed. (Ratisbonae, 1731), I, 1136; Martinus Abbas Viennae, "Senatorium," *SSRA*, II, 669.

61. Otto of Freising, *Chronica*, vi:27; "Kaiserchronik," MGH SS ling. vernac. I–1, 373; see also "Annales Reichersbergenses," anno 1004, *MGHSS*, XVII, 445; Godefridus Viterbiensis "Pantheon," xiii:32, *ibid.*, XXII, 240; "Chronicon Salisburgense," anno 1009, *ibid.*, IX, 772; Anonymi Leobiensis "Chronicon," anno 991 (!), *SSRA*, I, 761; "Historia fundationis ceonobii Mellicensis," *ibid.*, I, 296; "Chronica principum Poloniae," c. viii—cf. *MPH*, II, 438; or even Giovanni Villani, "Historie Florentine," iv:4, *RISS*, XIII, 99. (On Villani, see, for instance, John Larner, *Italy in the Age of Dante and Petrarch* [London–New York, 1980], 10f.)

62. See "Ekkehardus Uraugiensis Chronicon," anno 1001, *MGHSS*, VI, 192; Annalista Saxo, anno 1002, *ibid.*, VI, 650.

63. Reported Adalbert, deacon at the Bamberg cathedral, in his "Vita Heinrici II imperatoris," i:29-30, *ibid.*, IV, 810.

64. Henry II, "totam Pannoniam per sororem suam Christianam fecit," *ibid.*, X, 137; see also *RISS*, XXII–2, 23.

65. As it is evident from the Hungarian Anonymus, c. 12, *SSH*, I, 50f.

66. On account of Emperor Henry's canonization, Pope Eugene III in his letter of March 14, 1146, addressed to Engelbert, bishop of Bamberg—cf. *MPL*, 140, 183.

67. See Adam Bremensis *Gesta Hammaburgensis pontificum*, ed. B. Schmeidler, SSrG, 3rd ed. (Hannover, 1917), ii:43, anno 1010. Further, Jacobus de Voragine, xi:13, *RISS*, IX, 29.

68. "Historia monasterii s. Laurentii Leodiensis," Martene – Durand, IV, 1046; also, "Gest abbatum Trudonensium," anno 1010, *MGHSS*, X, 383.

69. The Magyars "hactenus idolatriae dedita" became Christians "per Giselam sororem imperatoris," who was married to the Hungarian monarch, whom she had persuaded to have his people convert to the faith—cf. Sigibertus Gemblacensis

"Chronographia," anno 1010, *ibid.*, VI, 354. Dandalo, "Chronicon Venetum," ix:1,46, insisted that it was Adalbert *and* Gisela together who had carried out the work of conversion, *RISS*, XII, 233.

70. Heinricus de Hainburg, "Cronica Boemorum," *MGHSS*, XVII, 172.

71. The noble work of both women, Gisela and Adelheid—see "Annales Silesiaci compilati," *ibid.*, XIX, 537.

72. Queen Gisela had, indeed, contributed to the conversion of the Magyars—"Hungari fidem recipiunt ger Gilam" [sic]; cf. the Carthusian Wernerus Rolevinck Larensis, in Martene – Durand, V, 97.

73. "…multum iuvit ad plenam conversionem Ungarie," in Fasciculus temporum, Pistorius – Struvius, *Rerum Germanicarum scriptores*, II, 537.

74. Heinricus de Hainburg, "Cronica Boemorum," *MGHSS*, XVII, 172.

75. "Chronicon Venetum," ix:1,46, *RISS*, XII, 233.

76. "Insignus signifer Christi, presul Adalbertus, retibus fidei cepit Pannoniam," cf. Cosmas Pragensis, "Chronica Bohemorum," i:31, *ibid.*, 54; Franz Palacky, *Geschichte von Böhmen*, vol. I, 2nd ed. (Prague, 1844), 195ff. and 225ff.

77. See "Zdarzenia godne pamięci," *MPH*, I, 299; "Catalogus archiepiscoporum Gnesenensium," *ibid.*, III, 391f.; Annalista Saxo, anno 996, *MGHSS*, VI, 641.

78. See Ptolomaeus Lucensis, "Historia eccelsiastica," xvii:26, *RISS*, XI, 1043.

79. On this, see the published doctoral dissertation of István Legeza, "Szent Adalbert missziós szerepe a magyar történelemben" [The role of Christian missionary played by St. Adalbert in the background of Hungarian history], Péter Pázmány Theological Academy, Budapest, 1952, reprinted in *Kelet–közép–Európa szentje: Adalbert (Vojtech–Wojciech-Béla)*, ed. Ádám Somorjai (Budapest, 1994), 117ff.

80. "Vita s. Bogumili," c. 1, *ASS*, Iunii II, 337; also, *MGHSS*, XXII, 465; "Annales Polonorum, I – IV," anno 982 (!), *ibid.*, XIX, 616 and 617. Adalbert did establish a monastic community at Brevnov—the founding charter, dated May 31, 993, was signed by Pope John XV, cf. Thomas von Bogyay, "Brevnov und die Ungarnmission," *Tausend Jahre Benediktiner in den Klöstern Brevnon, Braunau und Rohr*, ed. J. Hoffmann (St. Ottlien, 1993), 137ff.; Tadeusz Manteuffel, *The Formation of the Polish State*, trans. Andrew Gorski (Detroit, 1982), 58ff.

81. Cf. Bruno of Querfurt, "Vita s. Adalbertı," c. 16, *MGHSS*, IV, 603, also mentioning the name of Anastasius – Ascheric [Astric] as that of one and the same person; see further, "De s. Adalberto Pragensis episcopo," *ibid.*, XV–2, 1180, and compare, *ibid.*, IV, 613. "Annales Posonienses," anno 997, *SSH*, I, 125; H. G. Voigt, *Adalbert von Prag: ein Beitrag zur Geschichte der Kirche und des Mönchtums im zehnten Jahrhundert* (Westend Berlin, 1898). The Zagreb MS, MR 89: a *benedictionale* prepared before 1083, referred to the Church in Esztergom as *domus s. Adalberti*; cf. Dragutin Kniewald, *Zagrebački liturgijski kodeksi xi–xiv stoljeća* (Zagreb, 1940), 12ff.; Polycarp Radó, *Index codicum manu scriptorum liturgicorum regni Hungariae* (Budapest, 1941), 54, entry 269.

82. Cf. *MGHSS*, IX, 657, and X, 137.

83. *Ibid.*, XIX, 549 and 581; *MPH*, III, 438.

84. *MGHSS*, IV, 852f.

85. *RISS*, XIII, 99 and XXII–2, 23; Hóman, *Ungarisches Mittelalter*, I, 160ff.

86. See "Annales Wirziburgenses," anno 1037, *MGHSS*, II, 243; further, the "Chronicon Wirziburgense," anno 1038, *ibid.*, Vi, 30; Bernoldus sancti Blasii "Chronicon," anno 1038, *ibid.*, V, 425 and 348f.; Leo Marsicanus, "Chronica," *ibid.*, VII, 674; Rodolphus Glaber regarded the inner changes that had occurred in the Hungarian

realm as the result of their conversion, see his "Historia Francorum," *ibid.*, VII, 59, 62; Bishop Bonito of Sutri remarked, in his "Liber ad amicum," that "Stephanus Ungarorum rex sacramenta suscepit baptismatis et per eum omnis populus sibi subiectus," *MPL*, 150, 816. See also *Annalaes Marbacenses*, anno 1039; Martinus Gallus spoke of King Stephen as the one who with loving care, but a firm hand, directed the process of conversion, cf. his "Chronicon," i:18, *MGHSS*, IX, 437; the author of the "Vita Heinrici II," i:29-30, in the 1140's referred to King Stephen as a royal Apostle; cf. *ibid.*, IV, 810—an idea also expressed by Pope Innocent III in his letter, dated September 15, 1204, to King Emery of Hungary; by the grace of God, it was King Stephen who had made Hungary a member of the Catholic faith—Potthast, n. 2282; *CD*, II, 432f.; Katona, IV, 714ff.

87. Heinricus de Heimburg, "Cronica Boemorum," *MGHSS*, XVII, 712.

88. Villani, as cited above, iv:4, *RISS*, XIII, 99—and in a sense that his remarks pertinent to eleventh century Hungary, though well meant, are unreliable; Villani is a first rate *renaissance Italian* historian. Cf. Denys Hay and John Law, *Italy in the Age of the Renaissance, 1380–1530* (London–New York, 1989), 293.

89. See his "Life of King St. Stephen," c. 8, *SSH*, II, 411,24-28—segment based upon Stephen's *Vita minor*, c. 2; Legeza, art. cit., in Somorjai, *Adalbert*, 122ff. and 182, nn. 124-25; Macartney, *Hungarian Historians*, 165ff.

90. Cf. "Libellus," aa. iii-iv, *SSH*, II, 619ff.

91. *Deliberatio supra canticum trium puerorum*, Munich Staatsbibliothek, MS 6211, f. 44',26 – 45,3; on the MS, cf. Kosztolnyik, *Five Kings*, 46f.; idem, "The role of Gerard of Csanád in preserving the Church in Hungary," *Cithara: Essays in the Judaeo-Christian Tradition*, 15–2 (1976), 20ff. A new edition of the text was recently published by László Szegfű and Béla Karácsonyi (eds.), *Deliberatio Gerardi Moresanae aecclesiae episcopi svpra Hymnum trium pverorum* (Szeged, 1999), 176, 178; [and another edition in preparation by Balázs Déri in Budapest].

92. "Infelix terra, que inter deum et hominem discordiam operatur;" Munich MS 6211, f. 64,25-26; Szegfű – Karácsonyi, 254; Kosztolnyik, *Five Kings*, 161f., nn. 1-6.

93. "Libellus," a. vii, *SSH*, II, 625f.

94. Cf. King Stephen's Laws, preface, and art. i:6, i:18, and i:20, all in Emma Bartoniek (ed.), *Szent István törvényeinek XII századi kézirata: az admonti kódex* [The twelfth century manuscript of the Laws of King St. Stephen: the Admont codex, with reduced facsimile of the Admont MS 712, ff. 112-26, now as *Cod. Lat. Medii aevi* in the Széchenyi National Library, Budapest] (Budapest, 1935), Latin text, 15ff.; Hungarian translation, 43ff.; notes, 63ff.; for text, see also Marczali, *Enchiridion*, 69ff.; Závodszky, 141ff. On the laws, cf. Hóman, *Ungarisches Mittelalter*, I, 226ff.; Györffy, *István király*, 268ff.; Kosztolnyik, *Five Kings*, 110ff.

95. Laws, a. i:26; compare with "Lex Baiuwariorum," xv:7, *MGHLL*, III, 319.

96. Cf. *Justinian's Institutes*, ed. Paul Krueger, with introduction by Peter Birks and Grant McLeod (Ithaca, NY, 1987), 32, and i:1,1; "Iuris prudentia est divinarum atque humanarum rerum notitia, isti atque iniusti scientia." Wilhelm Schubart, *Justinian und Theodora* (Munich, 1943), 75ff. and 80f.; Tony Honoré, *Tribonian* (Ithaca, NY, 1978), 187ff.; John Moorhead, *Justinian* (London–New York, 1994), 32ff.

97. King Stephen's Laws, aa. i:15, "secundum decretum regalis senatus" (and compare with "Edictus Rothari," c. 200, *MGHLL*, IV, 49); art. i:30, "ut genus utriusque sexus certa lege et absque iniuriis maneat et vigeat, in hoc regale decretum statutum est" (and, compare with "Decretum Vermeriense, about anno 760, *MGH Legum sectio* II: Capitularia regum Francorum, 2 vols. [Hannover, 1883–87], I, 41); and, in art. i:34,

"...secundum decretum senatus statuimus" (and, compare to "Capitulatio de partibus Saxoniae, about 775–90, c. 23, *ibid.*, I, 69); for King Stephen's Laws, cf. Bartoniek, 15ff. or Marczali, *Enchiridion*, 69ff. On Rothair's edict, see Katherine Fischer-Drew, *The Lombard Laws* (Philadelphia, 1973), 39ff.

98. King Stephen's Laws, aa. i:7 and i:35—in a sense that *invasio domorum*, invading one's home, had breached public, that is, the King's peace, and the monarch would have to take action, "volumus, ut firma pax et unanimitas sit inter maiores et minors;" likewise, o the freedom of slaves, where and when a fair price had to be paid in the interest of public peace, "Rex autem ex sua parte tertia tribuat comiti," *ibid.*, aa. ii:5 and 8. Compare to Justinian's *Institutes*, 1:3 and 15, and with Stephen's Laws, art. i:21 and with "Pappini regis Capitula," annorum 754, 755, cap. vii, in *MGH Legum sectio* II, I, 32.

99. On legislation and the laws, see Hóman, *Ungarisches Mittelalter*, I, 226ff.; Györffy, 265ff.; Székely – Bartha, 799ff.; Kosztolnyık, *Five Kings*, 110ff.; Richard Szántó, "A királyi hatalom isteni eredete a nyugati politikai gondolkodásban az 5–8 században" [Divine origin of royal power in western political thought of the fifth through the eighth centuries], *Aetas* (Szeged, 1997/2–3), 137ff., an impressive study; Gábor Hamza, "Die Gesetzgebung Stephan des Heiligen und Europa," *Ungarische Jahrbücher*, 22 (1995–96), 27ff. One may further consult notes of the debate by Miklós Takács and László Révész over the book by Gyula Kristó, *A magyar állam születése* [Birth of the Hungarian state], in *Századok*, 131 (1997), 168ff. and 215ff.

100. *Ibid.*, a. i:7 (and compare to "Capitularia missorum," anno 829, cap. 1, *MGH Leg. sect.* II–II, 9).

101. "Ita sunt sub defensione regis, sicut proprie sue hereditatıs," King Stephen's Laws, a. i:1, aa. i:26 (!), i:32, and a. ii:2; compare to "Lex Baiuwariorum," xv:7, *MGHLL*, III, 319 and with "Capitula Baiuwariorum," anno 810, cap. 3, *MGH Leg. sect.* II–I, 158. Stephen's a. ii:2 ought to be compared with the "Edictus Rothari," cap. 1, *MGHLL*, IV, 13. Further, Györffy, *István király*, 268ff.

102. King Stephen's Laws, a.i:14c [idem aliud], and see Council of Ancyra of 314, cap. 22, Mansi, *Concilia*, II, 527; further, Stephen's Laws, aa. 18, 20, 21; and a. ii:5-6 and Council of Mainz, 847, cap. 9, *MGH Leg. sect.* II–II, 178, or Mansi, XIV, 905. For Stephen's law, aa. i:20-21, see *Codex Iustinianus*, IV:20,7, and "Capitularia legi Salicae addita," of 819 (or shortly thereafter), cap. 2, *MGH Leg. sect.* II–I, 292; Justinian's *Institutes*, i:8; Székely – Bartha, 802ff.; Manlio Bellomo, *The Common Legal Past of Europe, 1000–1800*, trans. Lydia G. Cochrane (Washington, DC, 1995).

103. King Stephen's Laws, aa. i:16, 17, 23, 35; ii:2: "Consensimus igitur petitioni totius senatus, ut unusquisque propriorum simul et donorum regis dominetur..."—cf. Marczali, *Enchiridion*, 69ff.

104. Laws, aa. i:6 and 7; and a. i:23: "Volumus, ut unusquisque senior suum habeat militem..." and compare with MGH leg. sect. II, I, 282 (anno 818, c. 6), and II, 9 (anno 829, c. 1).

105. King Stephen's Laws, aa. i:1, 7; ii:2.

106. Laws, aa. i:2, 8, 9, 15, 22; a. i:16, emphasized the need for public peace: "Ut pax firma et incontaminata per omnia maneat tam inter maiores natu, quam inter minores;" and compare with "Leges Burgundionum," cap. 37, *MGHLL*, III, 547, and with Stephen's Laws, art. i:20 that, again, reached back to the Justınian Code, iv:20,7. Gyula Kristó, *A vármegyék kialakulása Magyarországon* [Development of the counties and the county-system in Hungary] (Budapest, 1988), 21ff.; compare with Elizabeth M. Hallam,

Capetian France, 987–1328 (London–New York, 1980), 13ff. and 78ff., and with J. M. Wallace-Hadrill, *The Frankish Church* (Oxford, 1983), 181ff. For a more "humane" perspective, see Adolf Waas, *Der Mensch im deutschen Mittelalter* (Graz– Cologne, 1964), 152ff.; on conditions in England, see Paul Vinogradoff, *English Society in the Eleventh Century* (Oxford, 1908; repr. 1968), 219ff.

107. Hóman – Szekfű, I, 208ff. and 229ff.; Gyorffy, 211ff.; Antal Bartha, *Hungarian Society in the 9th and 10th Centuries* (Budapest, 1975), 83ff., and my review of this book in the *American Historical Review*, 83 (1978), 1243f.

2. The Monarch Asserts Leadership

108. "Bene rexit Vngaricam gentem, celerem satis et vehementem;" cf. "Chronica aulae regiae," *Fontes rerum Bohemicarum*, IV, 12.

109. "…tam vir, quam timore et amore," Ademar Cabannesis "Chronicon," c. 33, *MGHSS*, IV, 131; Martinus Gallus, "Chronica Polonorum," i:18, *ibid.*, IX, 437.

110. *Annales Altahenses maiores*, anno 1003; Annalista Saxo, anno 1003, *MGHSS*, VI, 652; "Auctarium Ekkehardi Altahense," anno 1003, *ibid.*, XVII, 363; *Annales Hildesheimenses*, anno 1003; Kristó, in *Századok*, 1988, 6ff.

111. Thietmar, viii:3 [ix:4].

112. Matthias de Michowia, "Chronica Polonorum," iii:11, in Pistorius, II, 28; *Annales Altahenses maiores*, anno 1041.

113. Wipo, "Gesta Chuonradi II Imperatoris," in *Wiponis Opera*, 3rd ed., ed. Harry Bresslau, SSrG (Hannover, 1915), c. 38; Dandalo, ix:2,1 in *RISS*, 235; Andreas Naugerus, "Storia della repubblica Veneziana," a. 1010, *RISS*, XXIII, 958; named Gisela by Ortilo de Lilienfeld, "Nostulae anecdotae priores," anno 1039, in Hanthaler, 108— though, Hanthaler's is a notoriously unreliable piece of work, cf. Lhotsky, *Quellenkunde*, 199.

114. Judith, wife of Lord Boleslav of Poland, in "Geneologiae," Pistorius, III, 148f.; "Boleslaus, cognomento Chrobri vel Acer," the first Polish monarch (died in 1025), who had four wives; Judith was his second wife—she bore him a son named Micislaus. He had married her in 984, "accepit Iudith filiam Iestae ducis Hungarorum in coniugem," recorded Mattias de Michowia, ii:1, in Pistorius, II, 20.

115. Besprim, who for a short duration had been living in King Stephen's court, was the son of Judith and Boleslav, noted Thietmar, iv:37 [c. 58], mentioning that Boleslav had *also* sent Judith away, "similiter expellens eam."

116. Cf. Wipo, "Gesta Chuonradi II imperatoris," in *Wiponis Opera*, 3rd ed., ed. Harry Bresslau, SSrG (Hannover, 1915), c. 26 [anno 1030].

117. Cf. Thietmar, viii:3, "Annales Cistercienses in Heinrichow," anno 1025, *MGHSS*, XIX, 544; "Annales Kamazenses," anno 1025, *ibid.*, XIX, 581; Martha Font, "Magyarok a 'Poveszti vremennih let'ben" [References made to the Magyars in the Russian Chronicle], *In memoriam Barta Gábor*, ed. István Lengvári (Pécs, 1996), 39ff.; idem, *Oroszország*, 41ff.

118. Thietmar, viii:16 [ix:31-32]; Dandalo, ix:1,46, *RISS*, XII, 233f.

119. "Fundatio," *MGHSS*, XV-2, 963f.

120. Cf. Matthias de Michowia, "Chronicon Polonorum," ii:7, in Pistorius, II, 24; Rocznik, *MPH*, III, 61; Ortilo de Lilienfeld, "Notulae anecdotae priores," anno 1042, in Hanthaler, 109f.

121. "...filium habuit unicum virum sanctum nomine Hemericum," Albericus, anno 1041, *MGHSS*, XXII, 768,

122. Dandalo, ix:1,46, in *RISS*, XII, 233f.

123. For the Polish point of view, cf. "Annales sancti Crucis Polinici," *MGHSS*, XIX, 678; also *MPH*, II, 61 and 300; and "Chronica Iohannis de Gwerche archidiaconi Goriciensis," in *Monumenta spectantia historiam Slavorum meridionalium*, ed. South Slavic Academy of Sciences, 43 vols. (Zagreb, 1868–1918), cited hereafter as *MHSM*, VII, 471ff.

124. Cf. "Vita s. Emerici ducis," c. 5, *SSH*, II, 454f., and supported by the statement: "...beati Henrici filii eiusdem sancti Stephani regis sanctissimam virginitatem, qui cum haberet sponsam nobilissimam, utpote filiam imperatoris Romanorum...," in "Quaedam legenda beatae Magaritae de Ungaria Ordinis Praedicatorum," c. 12; cf. Cornelius Böle (ed.), *Árpádházi Boldog Margit szenttéavatási ugye és a legősibb Margit-legenda* [The Canonization process of Margaret of the House of Árpád, and the ancient Margaret Legend], Proceedings of the Saint Stephen Academy, sect. phil. and theol., vol. III (Budapest, 1937), 17ff.; or *SSH*, II, 685ff.

125. See King Stephen's "Typicon Vespremiense"—its 1009 *renovatio*, issued by King Coloman the Learned (d. 116), in Gyula Czebe (ed.), *A veszprémvölgyi oklevél görög szövege* [The Greek text of the Veszprémvölgy Charter] (Budapest, 1916), 15f.; also Emil Jakubovich – Dezső Pais (eds.), *Ó-magyar olvasókönyv* [Old-Hungarian Reader] (Pécs, 1929), 15f.

126. See Martinus Oppaviensis, "Chronicon pontificum," *MGHSS*, XXII, 433; Ptolomaeus Lucensis "Historia," *RISS*, XI, 1055; Gervasius Ricobaldus Ferraiensis "Historia pontificum et compilatio chronologica, et Istoria imperiale," *ibid.*, IX, 173, 241, 325. On his death, the *Annales Hildesheimenses*, ed. G. Waitz, SSrG (Hannover, 1878), anno 1031.

127. *SSH*, I, 313,7-8.

128. Cf. Sulpicius Severus, "Life of St. Martin," in F. R. Hoare (ed.),*The Western Fathers* (London–New York, 1954), 3ff., editor's introduction; and text by Severus, *ibid.*, 10ff. Further, cf. H. O. Taylor, *The Medieval Mind*, 2 vols., 4th ed. (London, 1925), I, 52 and 86.

129. It may be evident from King Stephen's Laws, as, for instance, from a. i:14b, that the murderer, instead of being executed, had to do penance, "et penitentiam, quod dictum est, agat." Also, King Stephen's Laws, aa. i:18, i:22b, and ii:5.

130. *Ibid.*, a. i:13.

131. "Ut firma pax et incontaminata per omnia maneat tam inter maiores natu, quam inter minores...," *ibid.*, a. i:16; "ut gens huius monarchiae ab omni incursu et accusatione servorum et ancillarum remota et quieta maneat...," *ibid.*, a. i:20.

132. *Ibid.*, i:1, 2; further, "ut nemo eorum, qui libero consentur nomine cuiquam quid iniurie facere audeat...," a. i:29; also, aa. i:33-34. Marc Bloch, *Feudal Society*, trans. L. A. Manyon (Chicago, 1961), 72ff.; compare with Jacques Maritain, *The Living Thought of Saint Paul* (New York, 1941), 52ff.

133. As late as the year 1000, Emperor Otto III forbade the unfree classes to attempt to liberate themselves (!)—cf. W. Altmann – E. Bernheim, *Ausgewählte Urkunden zur Erläuterung der Verfassungsgeschichte Deutschlands im Mittelalter* (Berlin, 1904), n. 61, though, in 1050, Henry III had, for instance, freed a female serf (slave?)—cf. Harry Bresslau, *Diplomata centum regum et imperatorum Germaniae* (Hannover–Berlin, 1879), 49; on the ecclesiastical view of slavery, see Funk – Bihlmeyer, II, 92f.

134. King Stephen's Laws, aa. i:9, 13 (!), 27, 28a-b, 35; ii:3, 6, 8, 10-11, 20 [art. ii:14 in the Admont MS], and a. ii:16 [article *not* in the Admont MS].

135. Laws, aa. i:20-22; ii:4 and 21 [a. ii:15 in the Admont MS].

136. Laws, aa. ii:2—"ut unusquisque propriorum simul et donorum regis dominetur…"—ii:7: "…si quis liberorum…venundatus furtum conmiserit, legibus servorum subiaceat."

137. King Stephen's Laws, aa. i:16, 35; ii:2 and 16 [art. ii:16 not in the Admont MS]: "si quis servus curti regali vel civitati praeficitur, testimonium eius inter comites recipiatur." In the Marczali, *Enchiridion*, 79, version the text reads *seniorum* instead of *servorum*.

138. "Libertas v. naturalis, …" in Irnerius, "Glosses on Digest, vet.," ed. Enrico Besta, *L'opera d'Irnerio: contributo alla storia del diritto italiano*, 2 vols. (Turin, 1896), Digest, i:5,4; James A. Brundage, *Medieval Canon Law* (London–New York, 1995), 44ff.; "servitus autem est iuris gentium constitutio"—Irnerius, "Glosses on Digest. vet.," in F. C. von Savigny, *Geschichte des römischen Rechts im Mittelalter*, 2nd ed., 7 vols. (Berlin, 1834–51), IV, ch. xxvii, n. 49; also, Master Hugolinus, "Summa on the three Digest," i:5, in Azo, *Opera* (Basel, 1583). Gaines Post, *Studies in Medieval Legal Thought* (Princeton, 1964), 450ff. On medieval jurisprudence, cf. Charles H. Haskins, *The Renaissance of the Twelfth Century* (Cambridge, 1927), 193ff.

139. Cf. Jonas of Orleans, "De institutione laicali," ii:22: a slave ought not be treated savagely—*MPL*, 106, 121ff.; *Justinian's Institutes*, ed. Paul Krueger; intr. by Peter Birks and Grant McLeod (Ithaca, NY, 1987), i:8: "de his qui sui vel alieni iuris sunt." Azo, *Summa Codicis*, i:12 (Pavia, 1566; repr. Turin, 1966). M. Tullius Cicero, *De republica*, ed. F. W. Müller (Teubner ed.), i:25,39; iii:22; St. Augustine (Aurelius Augustinus), *De civitate Dei*, ed. B. Dombart – A. Kalb, 5th ed., ed. J. Divjak, Teubner ed. (Stuttgart, 1931; repr. 1981), xix:15.

140. Synod of Mainz, 847, in *MGH Leg. sectio* II–II, n. 248, a. 22.

141. Smaragdus abbas, "De via regia," cc. 1 and 30, and compare with his "Vita Benedicti abbatis Aniensis," *MGHSS*, XV–1, 200ff., and 199, n. 1.

142. Synod of Frankfurt, 794, in *MGH Leg. sect.* II, *const.* I, nn. 28, 112, 114, 138, 173, 252.

143. *Novellae*, of Justinian's *Corpus Iuris civilis*, ed. P. Krueger – Th. Momsen – R. Schoell, 3 vols. (Berlin, 1895–99), III, c. cxxiii:17; Wilhelm Schubart, *Justinian und Theodora* (Munich, 1943), 126ff. and 144ff.

144. Azo, *Comments on Digest*, lib. xvii; idem, *Summa Codicis*, i:3,14; and i:3,16. Post, *Studies*, 450ff.

145. Jonas of Orleans, "De institutione laicali," ii:22, quoting from Pope Gregory the Great, "Moralia," xxi:15, and St. Paul, Colossians, 4:1. In a similar manner, Hincmar of Reims, "De regis persona," c. 3, *MPL*, 125, 833ff., and *Opus* lv:14, *ibid.*, 126, 323f. Further, the master's thesis of one of my former students, Sammy Mac McClure, "The Pontificate of Pope Gregory I the Great," unpublished Master's thesis, Texas A&M University Library, 1998.

146. Agobard of Lyons, in MGH Epp. V: *Epistolae Karolini aevi*, ed. Erich Caspar – Gerhard Laehr, et al. (Hannover, 1912–28), epistolae iv and vi. "Quia quantum ad ius illud [civile] servus pro mortuo habetur;" Azo, *Summa Codicis*, iv:36 and ix:14, and compare with Azo, *Summa Institutionum* (Basel, 1563), i:8. General principle of the (Roman and Canon) law is expressed in the maxim: "Sic utere tuo ut alienum non laedas" [Make such use of your own as not to harm another's], that implies private ownership; cf.

Ch. H. McIlwain, *The Growth of Political Thought in the West* (New York, 1932), 161. In accordance with the earlier directives, King Stephen's advisors, too, were trained in law, "quoniam lex consensu populi et constitutione regis fit;" cf. *Edictum Pistense*, anno 864, in *MGH Leg. sectio* II–II, 273; also II–1, nn. 92-95, 97-98.

147. Hincmar von Reims, *De ordine palatii*, rev. ed., ed. Thomas Gross – Rudolf Schieffer, SSrG (Hannover, 1980), c. iii.

148. Herimann Augiensis Chronicon, anno 1038, *MGHSS*, V, 123. "Bene vexit Ungaricam gentem, celerem satis et vehementem," the "Chronicon aulae regiae," i:6, reported, cf. *Fontes rerum Bohemicarum*, IV, 12.

149. Cf. "Chronicon principum Poloniae," c. 11, *MPH*, II, 446.

150. See entry in the Russian Primary Chronicle, Nikon MS, anno 998, in Hodinka, 52b, and the entry in the Voskresens MS, anno 996, *ibid.*, 72a.

151. Ortilo de Lilienfeld, a. 1019, in Hanthaler, 106, though, on Ortilo and Hanthaler see Alfons Lhotsky's remark, who quoted Joseph Chmel on Ortilo's record in the Hanthaler edition: "…ein Schüler der Diplomatik wird das angebliche Autograph als einen, und zwar plumpen, Betrug erkennen," Chmel characterized Ortilo's work— *Sitzungsberichte der kaiserlichen Akademie der Wissenschaft, Wien*, 5 (1850), in fact saying that Ortilo's work was not reliable; cf. Lhotsky, *Quellenkunde*, 199.

152. "…servire in fratrem et hodie carnes assumere eque tibi licitum est;" see the "Annales Palidenses," *MGHSS*, XVI, 67f.; also, the entry in "Historia imperatorum," anno 1025—Menckenius, *SS rerum Germanicarum*, III, 85f.; see further, "Sächsische Weltchronik," c. 168, in *MGHS SS ling. vern.*, II, 170.

153. Cf. "Epistola Fulberti episcopi Carnotensis ad Bonipertum Quinque-eclesiensium praesulem," in *MPL*, 141, 189f.; J. Holub, "Bonipertus," *Janus Pannonius Múzeum Évkönyve, 1959* (Pécs, 1960), 97ff. On Priscian, mentioned in the letter, see R. W. Hunt, *Medieval and Renaissance Studies*, vol. I (London, 1943), 194ff.; E. R. Curtius, *European Literature and the Latin Middle Ages*, trans. W. R. Trask (Princeton, 1953), 42ff. and 43, n. 22; also, László Mezey, *Deákság és Európa* [The Latin classics and Europe] (Budapest, 1979), 105ff.

154. His "Vita minor" and his "Vita maior," in *SSH*, II, 471ff.; Macartney, *Hungarian Historians*, 152ff. and 154ff.; F. Bánfi, "Vita di s. Gerardo da Venezia nel codice 1622 della Biblioteca Universitaria di Padova," *Benedictina*, 2 (1948), 262ff., with edited text, *ibid.*, 288-330; Horváth, *Árpádkori irodalmunk*, 158ff.; Tibor Klaniczay, *A magyar irodalom története 1600-ig*, vol. I (Budapest, 1964), 60ff., very Marxist, places the term: *saints*, between quotation marks. Z. J. Kosztolnyik, "The importance of Gerard of Csanád as the first author in Hungary," *Traditio*, 25 (1969), 376ff.; idem, *Five Kings*, 23ff.; László Szegfű, "La missione politica ed ideologica di san Gerardo in Ungheria," *Venezia e Ungheria nel rinascimento*, ed. Leo S. Olschki (Florence, 1973), 23ff.

155. See the Munich Staatsbibliothek late eleventh century MS, 6211; recent edition of the opus, *Deliberatio Gerardae Moresanae aecclesiae episcopi Svpra hymnum triunm pverorum*, eds. L. Szegfű – B. Karácsonyi (Szeged, 1999), 2-665, to be cited hereafter as *Deliberatio Gerardi*; Kosztolnyik, *Five Kings*, 46ff. and 161ff., nn. 6, 17, 20; László Szegfű, "Kortörténeti problémák Gellért csanádi püspök Deliberatiojában és legendáiban" [Some of the then contemporary issues depicted in the *Deliberatio* and in the *vitae* of Gerard of Csanád], *Acta historica Szegediensis*, 83 (1986), 11ff.; idem, "Szent Gellért családjáról" [The family descent of St. Gerard], *ibid.*, 75 (1983), 11ff.

156. Cf. Pez, *SS rer. Austricarum*, II, 664. King Stephen did not want Gerard to remain an obscure monk; he summoned him to the active life, made him bishop, and ordered him to preach to his people; see Gerard's "Vita minor," c. 3, in *SSH*, II, 473,2-4.

157. The "Vita minor" did appear at first—cf. Kosztolnyik, *Five Kings*, 35f., and Csóka, 263ff.

158. Cf. Hartvic, c. 9, *SSH*, II, 412ff.; St. Katona, *Historia critica regum Hungariae stirpis Arpadianae*, 7 vols. (Pestini, 1779–82),I, 194f.; Fejér, *CD*, III–2, 120f.; D. Fuxhoffer – M. Czinár, *Monasteriologiae regni Hungariae*, 2 vols. (Vienna– Esztergom, 1869), I, 180f.; Imre Szentpétery, *Szent István király pécsváradi és pécsi alapítólevele* [King St. Stephen's founding charters for Pécs and Pécsvárad] (Budapest, 1918), 11ff. and 22, although the Pécsvárad charter is a falsified document based on King Stephen's writs issued for (the abbey of) Pannonhalma and for (the bishopric of) Pécs—on this, cf. *RA*, nn. 2, 5 *and* n. 6.

159. "Anastasius Ungarorum archiepiscopus interfui et subscripsi;" cf. *MGH* Leg., sect. IV, const. I, 59ff.; *MGH Dipl. regum et imperatorum Germaniae*, vol. III: Heinrici II et Arduini diplomata, ed. Harry Bresslau – Hermann Bloch (Hannover, 1900–03), 169ff.; *MGHSS*, XVII, 635f., based on a fourteenth century manuscript, with an entry made in the fifteenth century—cf. *ibid.*, XVII, 636, n. 8; further, *ibid.*, IV, 795f.

160. Cf. Aventinus, "Annales Boiorum," in Cisneros, *Aventini Annales*, 403; *Annales Hildesheimenses*, anno 1012; "Reichersberg Annals," *MGHSS*, XVII, 636, and IV, 756; Györffy, *István király*, 141.

161. Hartvic, c. 8, *SSH*, II, 412,2-5.

162. Gerard's "Vita maior," c. 4, *ibid.*, I, 485,25-32.

163. *MPH*, I, 500 and 503; also, *ibid.*, III, 129; further, the "Chronica principum Poloniae," c. 10, *ibid.*, III, 445.

164. "Annales Kamazenses," anno 1000, *MGHSS*, XIX, 581.

165. "Annales Cracovienses," *ibid.*, XIX, 586; the "Annales Polonorum I," anno 1001, and "Annales Polonorum IV," *ibid.*, XIX, 618, 619; or, the "Catalogue of the Bishops of Cracow," in *MPH*, III, 332.

166. See Martinus de Sengign Mellicensis, "Nota de corona regni Hungariae," in Pez, *Thesaurus anecdotarum nova*, VI–3, 232.

167. Bishop Bonipert, addressee of a letter from Fulbert of Chartres—cf. *MPL*, 141, 189f.; Kosztolnyik, art. cit. in *Traditio*, 1969, n. 7—was the first bishop of Pécs, see *RA*, n. 5. On Priscian, cf. Taylor, *The Medieval Mind*, II, 150ff.

168. See Gerard's "Vita minor," c. 4, *SSH*, II, 474,17-20.

169. Péter von Váczy, *Die erste Epoche des ungarischen Königtums* (Pécs, 1935), 64ff.; Kosztolnyik, *Five Kings*, 9 and 132, n. 51.

170. "Regio etiam dignaretur ipsum diademate roborare, *ut eo fultus honore cepta per dei gratiam posset solidius stabilire*" [italics mine], cf. Hartvic, c. 9, *SSH*, II, 412f.

171. Thietmar, iv:38 [59]; Péter Váczy, "Merseburgi Thietmar a magyar király- koronázásról" [Remarks by Thietmar of Merseburg about the Hungarian royal corona- tion], *Történelmi Szemle*, 28 (1985), 68ff.; Bogyay, *Stephanus Rex*, 23ff.; János Karácsonyi, *Szent István király* [King St. Stephen] (Budapest, 1904), 17ff. Important, straight to the point observations by Bóna, *A magyarok*, 88ff.; also Éva Kovács – Zsuzsa Lovag (eds.), *Die ungarischen Krönungsinsignien*, rev. ed. (Budapest, 1988), 18ff.

172. *MGHSS*, IV, 756; also, XVII, 636.

173. Ph. Jaffé (ed.), *Bibliotheca rerum Germanicarum*, 6 vols. (Berlin, 1865; repr. Darmstadt, 1964), V, 479ff., esp. 481; also, in *MGHSS*, XVII, 635f., and note 8 on p. 636

(in a reference to *ibid.*, IV, 604), on *Ashericus* who consecrated the side altar, though both versions were based on a fifteenth century manuscript, *ibid.*, XVII, 636, n. 8. On the consecration of the Bamberg *ecclesia maiore*, referred to in a strictly German context, see also Thietmar, vi:40; Arnold, "De s. Emmaramo," *ibid.*, IV, 547,44-45, mentioned Anastasius "qui et Astricus," n. 3.

174. Stephen's "Vita minor," c. 2, *SSH*, II, 394,24-26.

175. *Ibid.*, II, 407,19-22.

176. *Ibid.*, II, 407,3-13.

177. As it is evident from his letter to the Abbot of Montecassino, dated ca. 1090, St. Ladislas I of Hungary (d. 1095) had to stress his independence of the Holy See in secular politics; for text of the letter, cf. Vilmos Fraknói, *Magyarország egyházi és politikai összeköttetései a római Szentszékkel* [Hungarian ecclesiastical and political relations with the Holy See], 3 vols. (Budapest, 1901–03), I, 403f.; Kosztolnyik, *Five Kings*, 100f.,—an independence Frederick I Barbarossa had to assert at Besançon, in 1157—see *Ottonois et Rahewini Gesta Friderici*, iii:11.

178. "Annales s. Crucis Polonici," *MGHSS*, XIX, 678; "Annales Kamazenses," anno 1000, *ibid.*, XIX, 581. Josef Karpat's 123 page essay, "Corona regni Hungariae im Zeitalter der Árpáden," in *Corona regni*, ed. Manfred Hellmann (Darmstadt, 1961), 225ff.

179. A Polish remark about *Steffaust* saying "Affricus exinde regio titulo insignari voluit atque in perpetuum ea dignitate vel regni ipso futuris seculis gaudere," *MPH*, III, 299. Also, *ibid.*, II, 829 and III, 332.

180. "Annales Silesiaci compilati," anno 1000, *MGHSS*, XIX, 537, and Rocznik, anno 965 (sic!), *MPH*, III, 60f.

181. In the "Lives of the Archbishops of Cracow," ii:27, *MPH*, IV, 392—though Pope Leo VIII had died in 965; see Angelo Mercati, "The New List of the Popes," *Medieval Studies*, 9 (1947), 71ff., a reprint, with corrections, from the *Annuario Pontifico* for 1947; R. L. Poole, "The Names and Number of Medieval Popes," in his *Studies in Chronology and History*, ed. A. L. Poole (Oxford, 1934; repr. 1969), 156ff.; Hans Kühner, "Leo VIII," in his *Neues Papstlexikon* (Zurich, 1956), 53.

182. See Martin, Prior of Melk, "Nota de corona regni Hungariae," Pez, *Thesaurus*, VI-3, 232. Benedict VII died in 983!—Mercati, loc. cit.

183. "Annales Polonorum IV," anno 1000, *MGHSS*, XIX, 619.

184. See the "Chronica principum Poloniae," *MPH*, III, 445.

185. The "Vita s. Stanislai maior," ii:27, *ibid.*, IV, 392.

186. Cf. his "Vita Romualdi fundatoris Camaldulensium," cc. 28-29, *MGHSS*, IV, 852f.

187. Cf. *CD*, III–2, 120ff.: Katona, *Historia critica*, I, 194; Imre Szentpétery, *Szent István király pécsváradi és pécsi alapítólevele*, 11ff.; Josephus Koller, *Historia episcopatus Quinqueecclesiarum*, 3 vols. (Posonii, 1782–84), II, 270ff. It is a falsified document—see *RA*, n. 6, and arguments by Harry Bresslau, *Handbuch der Urkunden-lehre*, 2 vols., 2nd ed. (Berlin, 1912–31), I, 71.

188. See "Vita minor s. Gerardi episcopi Csanadiensis," c. 6, *SSH*, II, 471ff.; Bishop Gerard's "Vita maior," c. 9 (*ibid.*, II, 494,10-14); Kosztolnyik, *Five Kings*, 23ff., esp. 25 and 147, nn. 18-20. R. F. Kaindl's 58 page "Studien, xiii," *AföG*, 91 (1902), 1ff.; J. Melich, *A honfoglaláskori Magyarország* [Hungary at the time of the land-taking] (Budapest, 1925).

189. Astric, Asheric, Anastasius, etc.—cf. King Stephen's "Vita maior," c. 9; Hartvic, c. 9, *SSH*, II, 412f.; Hóman, *Ungarisches Mittelalter*, I, 185ff. and 189ff.; Györffy, 141ff.; Váczy, *Erste Epoche*, 50ff. To make a comparison, one may consult the *Bereg Agreement*, anno 1233, signed by King Andrew II in front of the papal envoy—cf. *RA*, n. 500; text in *VHM*, I, 116ff., nn. 195-198, or in *RHM*, 436ff.; Kosztolnyik, *Thirteenth Century*, 110f. and 118, nn. 60-66.

190. Hóman – Szekfű, I, 643f.

191. *SSH*, II, 412f.

192. Hartvic's introductory remarks, *ibid.*, II, 402,11-18.

193. "Chronicon Hungarico-Polonicum," c. 6, *SSH*, II, 309f.; additional remarks by Hartvic, c. 9, *SSH*, II, 413f. Further, Robert Holtzmann, *Geschichte der sàchsischen Kaiserzeit, 900–1024*, 4th rev. ed. (Darmstadt, 1961), 359ff.

194. "Chronicon Hungarico–Polonicum," cc. 6-7, *ibid.*, II, 299ff.; Bogyay, *Stephanus Rex*, 23ff.

195. See A. F. Czajkowski, "The Congress of Gneizno in the year 1000," *Speculum*, 23 (1949), 352ff.; Oscar Halecki, "Poland and Christendom," *The Annual B. K. Smith History Lecture*, University of St. Thomas (Houston, 1964), 9ff.; Manteuffel, 56ff. and 64ff.

196. See Holtzmann, 359ff.

197. Cf. Philippe Wolff, *The Awakening of Europe* (New York, 1968; reissued 1985), 113ff. and 172ff. H. P. Lattin (ed.), *The Letters of Gerbert with his Papal Privileges as Sylvester II* (New York, 1961), 3ff., and a papal writ of April 18, 999, *ibid.*, 305ff.; Mathilde Uhlirz, *Untersuchungen über Inhalt und Datierung der Briefe Gerberts von Aurillaci* (Göttingen, 1957); Karl Uhlirz, *Jahrbücher*, I, 146ff.; Funk – Bihlmeyer, II, 43; on the cultural background, see also Bloch, *Feudal Society*, 72ff.

198. *Ibid.*, 79ff.; Wolff, 179ff.; P. E. Schramm, "Briefe Ottos III und Gerbert," *Archiv für Urkundenforschung*, 9 (1926), 87ff.

199. Cf. A. von Brandt, *Werkzeug des Historikers*, 2nd ed. (Stuttgart, 1960), 38ff., for his comments on both the *stilus Pisanus* and the *mox Gallicus*.

200. Abbon, Abbot of Fleury, *Apologeticus*, in *MPL*, 139, col. 472; on Abbot Abbon, see Wolff, 117 and 154f.; Gordon Lef, *Medieval Thought* (Baltimore, MD, 1958), 90, called him Abbo. Further, the essay in *Revue Bénédictine*, 52 (1935)–reprint.

201. As it actually did happen in the year 992—cf. *MPL*, 139, 472. Wolfram Brandes, "Liudprand von Cremona (Legatio, cc. 39–41) und eine bisher unbeachtete west-östliche Korrespondenz über die Bedeutung des Jahres 1000 AD," *BZ*, 93 (2000), 435ff.

202. As evidenced by the Preface of King Stephen's Laws, cf. Bartoniek, 15; Hartvic, c. 9, *SSH*, II, 413; the bull attributed to Pope Sylvester II, cf. *MPL*, 139, 274ff., is a falsification; see S. Heinlein, "Neure Forschungen zur Sylvesterbulle," *Ungarische Rundschau*, 2 (1913), 912ff.; Kosztolnyik, *Five Kings*, 51 and 164, nn. 33 and 35; also, Georgius Györffy (ed.), *Diplomata Hungariae antiquissima*, vol. I: 1000–1131 (Budapest, 1992).

203. *SSH*, II, 414,9-18; also, Thietmar, iv:38; Annalista Saxo, "Chronicon regum Francorum," *MGHSS*, VI, 542ff., anno 999 (!); Petrus Ransanus, *Epithoma rerum Hungararum*, ed. Peter Kulcsár (Budapest, 1977), 102f., index IX; and my review of the work in the *Austrian History Yearbook*, 17–18 (1981–82), 361f.

204. *Ibid.*, II, 414,19-22; Hóman, *Ungarisches Mittelalter*, I, 185ff.; Endre Tóth – Károly Szelényi, *A magyar Szent Korona. Királyok és koronázások* [The Hungarian Holy

Crown: Kings and Coronations] (Budapest, 1999), 30; József Gerics, *Egyház, állam és gondolkodás Magyarországon a középkorban* [The Church, the realm, and political thought in medieval Hungary] (Budapest, 1995), 51ff.

205. "Cupan filius Calvi Zyrind," *SSH*, I, 313,1 (Chronicle, c. 64).

206. *Ibid.*, I, 313,6-12; István Bóna, *Az Árpádok korai várai* [The early forts of the Árpád age], 2nd rev. ed. (Debrecen, 1998), 49ff.

207. "Totius exercitus sui principem et ductorem Vencilinum hospite Alamanum genere prefecit," *ibid.*, I, 313,12-14.

208. *Ibid.*, I, 313,15-18.

209. *Ibid.*, I, 313f.; Keza spoke of Stephen's *avunculus*, *ibid.*, I, 172,15; and compare with *DAI*, c. 40. Further, with Stephen's "Vita minor," c. 3, *SSH*, II, 395,8-13.

210. *Ibid.*, I, 314,2-5; see further the Founding Charter of Pannonhalma Abbey, in László Erdélyi (ed.), *A pannonhalmi Szent Benedekrend története* [History of the Benedictines of Pannonhalma], 12 vols. (Budapest, 1907–12), I, 589f., with facsimile, *ibid.*, I, 56. The document is an interpolation—cf. *RA*, n. 2; Hóman – Szekfű, I, 177f. Recently, there appeared a detailed study to commemorate the thousand years of the abbey—cf. *Mons sacer, 996–1996, Pannonhalma 1000 éve*, ed. Imre Takács, 3 vols. (Pannonhalma, 1996); and László Veszprémy, "A pannonhalmi bencés apátság könyvei a 11 század végi összeírás alapján" [Library holdings of the Benedictine abbey of Pannonhalma according to the late eleventh century catalogue], *ibid.*, 327ff. Further, Ádám Somorjai, "Bencés monostorok Magyarországon a X – XVI századokban" [Benedictine monasteries in Hungary during the tenth – sixteenth centuries], *Regnum: Essays in Church History in Hungary*, 8 (1996), 9ff.; Joseph Pál – Ádám Somorjai (eds.), *Mille anni di storia dell'Arciabbazia di Pannonhalma* (Rome–Pannonhalma, 1997), 27ff. and 39ff.; Kosztolnyik, *Five Kings*, 5 and 129, n. 18.

211. King Stephen's Laws, art. ii:1, in reference to a. 9; Stephen's "Vita minor," c. 4, *SSH*, II, 396,12-16.

212. Hartvic, c. 13, *SSH*, II, 414,15-29.

213. "...perge, ait, adire, festina properare et mea tollens mandata, dic tribuno plebis in ulterioribus moranti...," *ibid.*, II, 397,8-23.

214. Stephen's "Vita minor," c. 6, *ibid.*, II, 398f.

215. "Ut autem reliquis essent in exemplum, et discerent dominos summo honore venerari"—*ibid.*, II, 399,23-25.

216. Cf. King Stephen's Laws, a. ii:17, though not in the Admont manuscript; Bartoniek, 41, listed it as c. 51; see Marczali, *Enchiridion*, 79.

217. King Stephen's "Vita minor," c. 8, *ibid.*, II, 399f.; compare with the record by Hartvic, c. 23, *ibid.*, II, 431f.

218. Cf. King Stephen's "Vita minor," c. 8, *ibid.*, II, 400,9-14; also Hartvic, *ibid.*, II, 433,8-11; "Vita s. Ladislai," c. 6, *ibid.*, II, 520f.; Wipo, "Gesta Conradi II Imperatoris," c. 38; "Bernoldi Chronicon," anno 1083, *MGHSS*, V, 483f.; Hóman, *Ungarisches Mittelalter*, I, 292ff.; Kosztolnyik, *Five Kings*, 99f. and 191, n. 89.

219. See "Continuato annalium s. Rudberti Salisburgensis," anno 1305, *MGHSS*, IX, 817; Gerics, *Egyház, állam és gondolkodás*, 43ff.; Kovács – Lovag, *Krönungsinsignien*, 59ff., 94ff.

220. Thomas Ebendorfer referred to the Hungarian crown "et alia insignia regalia cum tunica s. Stephani," in his *Chronica Austriae*, ed. Alphons Lhotsky (Berlin–Zurich, 1967), lib. iii; on Ebendorfer, see Lhotsky, *Quellenkunde*, 119ff., 317ff., and 336ff.

221. One eleventh century writer reported that the *royal lance*, given as a gift by the papal legate to the (new) Hungarian monarch, had been captured by his opponents in battle, and had been returned to Rome; cf. Bonitho of Sutri, "Liber ad amicum," lib. iv, *MPL*, 150, 816f., who erroneously related the event to the reign of Conrad II, while the battle he referred to took place in 1041—see *Annales Altahenses maiores*, anno 1041, and p. 25, note 1.

222. Ademar Cabanensis suggested that it may have been Otto III who gave the lance to the Magyar prince Géza—that is, before 997! Cf. *MGHSS*, IV, 130. J. Gerics — Erzsébet Ladányi, "A birodalmi szent lándzsa és Szent István lándzsája" [The imperial Holy Lance and King St. Stephen's Lance], in *Unger Mátyás Emlékkönyv* [The Matthias Unger memorial volume] (Budapest, 1991), 7ff.

223. Sigibert Gemblacensis (Gembloux) wrote that Henry III had King Aba defeated in battle, and the lance captured—cf. *ibid.*, VI, 358; on the battle, cf. *Annales Altahenses maiores*, anno 1044, and p. 35, note 2; p. 36, note 2. Incidentally, according to Sigibert Gemblacensis, the battle took place anno 1043.

224. Henry III had the lance returned to papal Rome, the "Annales Leodienses" reported, *MGHSS*, IV, 19; J. Gerics – E. Ladányi, "A Szentszék és a magyar állam a 11 században" [The Holy See and the Hungarian realm in the eleventh century], *Magyarország és a Szentszék kapcsolatainak ezer éve* [A Thousand years of Hungarian relations with the Holy See], ed. István Zombori (Budapest, 1996), 9ff.

225. Compare with Arnolphus, "Rerum sui temporis libri V," iii:6, cf. *MGHSS*, VII, 18, a statement confirmed in a writ, dated October 28, 1074, by Pope Gregory VII; see Caspar, *Regesten*, ii:13.

226. Ottokar von Steier's "Österreichische Rheimchronik," MGH ling. vern. V–1, lines 41224, 41236, 41318, 83408-24, 85283, 86498, 87135, 87338, 87499, 87550.

227. The "Annales Mechovienses," anno 1304, made mention of the lance, referring to it as part of the Hungarian *insignia regali*—cf. *MGHSS*, XIX, 668.

VI

The King as Lawgiver

1. The Background: The Three Vitae *of King Stephen*

> Hunc secundum ecclesiasticam doctrinam instituens, iugum et legem disciplene subpositis cervicibus adhibuit, omnesque inmunditias malorum prorsus destruxit.
>
> *Vita minor*, c. 2

The lifework of King Stephen was discussed in his *Vita minor*, whose anonymous author presented the activities of the great ruler briefly and truthfully, with raw realism presenting a picture of the king who had served the interests of his people[s], and of his country well.[1] The value of this work was further enhanced by the fact that the author was a stylist, a master of prose composition.[2] He wrote about reality, life as he saw it, as he conscientiously demarcated his writing from the already available, and considered reliable, *Vita maior* of King Stephen.[3] He also relied upon the testimony of still living witnesses, and on folklore, to provide a realistic report on the person and reign of the ruler. In his narrative there appeared the figure of a determined, firm-handed monarch who would, and actually had effectively administered justice among his people.[4]

The reader may find out from the briefer narrative, the "Vita minor," that King Stephen was born in Esztergom, received a thorough education, and his father was [a] *king* (rather, the ruling prince).[5] On the other hand, the mid-fourteenth century compiler of the *Chronicon pictum*—he based his information upon the late thirteenth century record by Simon de Keza—regarded *Prince* Géza as *king* because he recorded the reign of King Géza I (1074–77) as that of King Géza II as he characterized Prince Géza (d. 997) as a pagan, became a Christian converting his people to the faith in the only true God.[6]

Upon the death of his father, the headmen and common folk of the country elevated son Stephen, still minor [*adhuc puer*], to the throne. The anonymous author of the *Vita minor* made no mention of Stephen's royal anointment and coronation, nor did he refer to the role of the higher clergy may have played in elevating him to the throne, but asserted that King Stephen had laid the burden of law and order upon the shoulders of his people only recently reborn in the waters of baptism.[7]

The author narrates at some length the savage punishment meted out to the rebel Vászoly and his conspirators.[8] Vászoly was the nephew of Stephen, who had Vászoly blinded, and his conspirators' hands cut off in punishment for the role they had played in the uprising against the emerging Christian social and political order in the kingdom.[9] In view of the fact that King Coloman the Learned (1095–1116) had also blinded his brother Álmos—who in 1109 had attempted to take the throne from him[10]—one may assume that the anonymous writer of the "Vita minor" wrote his piece during the reign of King Coloman, though before Bishop Hartvic had composed his "Vita s. Stephani regis" on the grounds that Hartvic dedicating his work to "His Lord, the most excellent King Coloman," fused material he took from the *Vita minor* with data derived from the *Vita maior*.[11] King Coloman died in 1116.[12]

The fact that two lives of King [by then Saint] Stephen were written during the reign of Coloman points to the conclusion that the wording of King Stephen's "Vita minor" sharply contrasts with the idea that had already emerged in royal and high ecclesiastic court circles under Coloman's reign of Stephen the monarch who had already been canonized by the Church in the year of 1083.[13] With forceful strokes of the pen Bishop Hartvic attempted in the best manner he could to place a firm foundation under an idealized depiction of King Saint Stephen.

Citing an example will be in order here: the author of the *Vita minor* in the seventh paragraph described at some length the savage punishment meted out to the insurgent Vászoly and his associates; Hartvic, on the other hand, left out details, simply ignored the essential part of the report.[14] The unknown author of King Stephen's *Vita maior* also changed the image of a firm handed and forceful monarch into a mild and bloodless ascetic ruler.[15] He had several times referred to the dark background of the age only to present the figure of the monarch in a brighter light.[16]

The author of the *Vita maior* sought to soften the raw imprint of political reality that surrounded Stephen during his reign. The memory of the 1061 pagan uprising led by a certain Vata must have been quite alive in public consciousness, as it provided the anonymous author with information on the *dark* socio-political background of the pagan [*recte*: non-Christian] Magyars he kept referring to in his narrative. King Stephen's *Vita maior* is, really, a running commentary on domestic politics in the realm during the late 1070s, when it might have been written.[17]

Pope Gregory VII during his power struggle with the German Henry IV had found an ally in Ladislas I of Hungary (1077–95);[18] in return, Ladislas I requested, and obtained, permission from Rome for the canonization of his early Árpádian predecessors, together with Gerard the martyred bishop of Csanád—that the bodies of those who had planted the seed of Christian religion in Pannonia may be elevated—thereby to strengthen his own domestic position.[19]

Bishop Hartvic, King Stephen's chronicler-biographer of non-Hungarian birth, displayed a good writing style in his work, and altered little of the narrative of his sources, thereby preserving their authenticity.[20] By obeying higher orders, he undoubtedly displayed a given political tendency to support the diplomatic position taken by his king, the learned Coloman—Coloman earlier had been a bishop— toward the Roman See,[21] and to clarify and strengthen the position Coloman's uncle and predecessor, Ladislas I, held toward Rome. Hartvic had to prove the point that contrary to a previous under- standing the Hungarian court had reached with the Holy See in the diplomatic field, in ecclesiastical matters it would act independently of the papal curia.[22]

The display of such diplomatic maneuvering on part of the Hungarian kings must have been due to a political necessity, partly because Ladislas I had taken up a position on the side of Pope Gregory VII in the struggle between the papacy and the German empire;[23] and, partly on grounds that King Coloman had previously been ordained a bishop, "horas canonicas ut episcopus absolvebat," creating the impression in the papal curia that the Hungarian king would blindly follow the diplomatic maneuvers of the papal court, as if granting Rome a free hand to intervene any time in Hungarian domestic and foreign policy.[24] The letters Gregory VII addressed to the Hungarian (and Czech) rulers define such a papal point of view.[25]

Bishop Hartvic's *Vita* " of King St. Stephen" was really the answer by the court circles of the most excellent (King) Coloman, "rex precellentissimus," to emphasize that Coloman did not share the papal point of view. As the episcopal author following information available to him explained in an original insert made in his work, the first Hungarian king had obtained from Pope Sylvester II full authorization to direct, in accordance with his own judgment, the affairs of the Church in Hungary.[26] Hartvic made it quite clear that King Stephen had issued legislation after he had been elected, anointed and crowned king,[27] like the anonymous author of Stephen's *Vita maior*, who argued that Stephen had enacted his laws *after* he had been elevated to kingship.[28]

One ought to consider the fact further that, according to Hartvic, Astric had been dispatched as an envoy to Rome *after* Stephen had established ten bishoprics in his country, and named the archbishop of Esztergom the *Primate* of the (Hungarian) hierarchy.[29] Furthermore, it was Stephen's intention to name Abbot Astric *archbishop* of the—to be established—church province of Kalocsa. (Actually, it must have been the *intention* of King Stephen to name Astric-Anastasius archbishop; Hartvic overstated his case. He wrote that Astric was already [an] archbishop when sent to Rome.[30])

The twofold entry Hartvic recorded in his *Vita* of King St. Stephen, first that Rome approve of the ecclesiastical administration (Prince) Stephen had set up in the country; last, the papal assertion that while the Roman Pontiff himself was only *Apostolic*, but that the Hungarian ruler was a true *Apostle*,[31] in a diplomatic manner firmly refuted by the political claim raised by Pope Gregory VII that the Roman pontiff, as the spiritual-feudal overlord of Hungarian kings, could intervene at will in the ecclesiastical and secular diplomatic affairs of the country, regardless of the approval, or disapproval by the Hungarian monarch.[32]

Stephen's *Vita maior* recorded the event differently. It was during the lifetime of his father, (Prince) Géza, that Stephen, by the consent of the higher clergy and of the common people, ascended to the throne.[33] After he, "the most Christian ruler," had established ten bishoprics in the land, he had, with the consent of Rome, set up the archiepiscopal see of Esztergom and named Astric archbishop.[34] He had also built an abbey in the honor of St. Martin at the sacred mount, *Mons Sacer*, of Pannonhalma, made arrangements for its maintenance *similar* to the bishoprics, "decimationibus fecit episcopatibus."[35] It was (only) in the fifth year after his father's death that Stephen received from Rome a *Letter of Apostolic Blessing*, "benedictionis apostolice litteris allatis," while the higher clergy and priests, the district reeves and people, had him elected by acclamation, had anointed him with holy oil, and crowned him. It is clear from this passage and noteworthy that the anonymous author of the *Vita maior* made clearly no mention of Rome, of the papal origin of the (Hungarian) crown.[36]

Interestingly, and in contrast with Hartvic, neither did the King's *Vita minor* make any mention of the crown, though the anonymous author spoke of Stephen's elevation to the throne. He recorded that Stephen—at that time, still a child, *adhuc puer*—came to the throne by the grace (that is, good will) of the headmen of the land and its people.[37] Thereafter the king instructed his people according to the doctrine of the Church, and had laws enacted to abolish the filth of all evil. In other words, the writer of the *Vita minor* did not speak of any ecclesiastical and political commitment the new king could have had made to the Roman See, though in recording Stephen's legislative activity he emphasized that the ruler enacted a "Church-oriented," that is, *Christian* code of laws for his country.[38]

There is another, seemingly insignificant factor that may deserve consideration. Hartvic, and, presumably, the author of the *Vita minor*, had composed their works after King Henry I of England and Archbishop Anselm of Canterbury in 1106 had agreed to the Concordat with Rome, in which the Norman monarch renounced his claim to intervene in the ecclesiastical affairs in England (*Ecclesia*

Anglicana),[39] and *before* the completion of negotiations that by 1122 led to the signing of the Concordat of Worms, in which the German monarch renounced his demand for interfering in the inner ecclesiastical business of the empire—as, for example, to nominate bishops, or clergy for church prebends—but expected the bishop-elect, or abbot-elect, to take an oath of loyalty to the imperial court before ordination, or to receive spiritual investment with their office from it.[40]

The learned King Coloman—the former bishop himself, hence named the "Book-lover"—behaved respectfully toward the Roman curia, but reserved the right for himself to direct the domestic and diplomatic business of his country according to his own judgement. The argument presented by Hartvic that the Roman pontiff had a cross sent to Stephen to emphasize that he had been an Apostle to his people[s]; and, the wording of the introduction to King Coloman's laws in which Coloman stated that he decided to renew the laws of King Saint Stephen, support such a point of view.[41] King Stephen had made it clear in the first twelve articles of his law code, and in various entries of his Admonitions addressed to his son, Prince Emery (d. 1031), and his heir[s] on the throne that it was the Hungarian monarch's privilege that he rely on his own judgment in ecclesiastical matters.[42]

2. Royal Legislative Acts

> E t quoniam unaquequc gens propriis utitur
> legibus, idcirco nos quoque Dei nutu nostram
> gubernantes monarchiam, ...decretali meditatione
> nostre statuimus genti, quemadmodum honestam
> et inoffensam ducerent vitam.
>
> *Leges sancti Stephani regis*, Preface

Prince Stephen, son and heir of Ruling Prince Géza, had to make a decision between the Byzantine East and the Latin West. Because of his upbringing at home, and because of the advice he received from his trusted advisors, he realized that the western Latin empire that had so unexpectedly developed from the territories under Charlemagne's rule,[43] and came into being with papal sanctions: the blessing of heaven, and revived under the aegis of the German court of Otto I the Great,[44] literally guaranteed—within the cultural framework of Latin Christendom—the survival of the Magyar kingdom that had been established with papal blessing, with the crown sent by Pope Sylvester II (and, with the consent of the emperor, Otto III).[45]

The Greek-Byzantine empire in the southeast for quite some time failed to fulfill its role in securing the survival of a newly established realm—let alone the fact that it always failed to recognize its very existence; a possible joining the southeastern Byzantine power circle would not have led to the acknowledged independence of Magyar domestic and foreign policies, or the economic-cultural independence of the land; on the contrary, it could only have led to the incorporation of the newly formed kingdom into the political-cultural, and religious-economic framework of Byzantium.[46] As a good example of Byzantine policy a century later, one may cite the intention of Manuel I Comnenus of Byzantium (1143–80), who in his first edicts issued as emperor announced expansion of the borders of the empire that would have included the territory of Hungary.[47]

Joining forces with Byzantium, belonging to the Greek Orthodox faith, would have only guaranteed a brief survival of an independent Hungarian kingdom because, as King Stephen's court had noticed, the gradual decline of the empire would have weakened the Magyars case and would have led to a fast disappearance of King Stephen's country, as it would have been quickly swept away from the stage of history.

Upon his succession to power, King Stephen had—in accordance with established royal custom, "antiquos ac modernos imitantes augustos"—summoned his spiritual and temporal headmen to enact legislation with him. Because of his personality and Christian family upbringing, Stephen enacted laws only after he had listened to the advice and opinion of learned and experienced men, "consensimus igitur petitioni totius senatus," whose constituency he had clarified in article VII of his *Libellus: Admonitiones* (addressed to his son and future heirs to the throne).[48]

The monarch was convinced that it was members of the Royal Council: *regum consilium,* who alone represented, and recognized, the country's common needs and problems, or possible failures, in public policy, and it was they who could find ways to deal with them. Any law that had been acted upon by the king and his headmen would have also to be approved by the people;[49] it must have been for this reason that he had reminded his heir[s] to the throne that "cum iuvenibus et minus sapientibus nolis consiliari, aut de illus consilium querere...; ...qui cm sapientibus graditur sapientum erit amicus."[50] The royal *Senate*—another synonym applied to the Royal Council in his Laws— consisted of men the King would trust because they respected and *represented* the wishes of their people, and paid attention to the interests and expressed needs of the whole country.[51]

The aim of the whole royal legislative process was—according to the testimony of Hartvic's report, and the text of the enacted articles— to provide ethical and judicial guidelines for the country's multi-ethnic and multi-cultural population (*nam unius lingue uniusque moris regnum inbecille et fragile est!*), in order to help determine their future, and to outline, by written legal decrees, how they ought to lead honorable lives, live in peace with one another: "Statuimus genti, que-madmodum honestam et inoffensam ducerent vitam."[52] The monarch made it certain that the laws covered both spiritual and secular values, and provided proper punishment for those who had challenged [the king's] public peace.[53]

King Stephen enacted decrees against family feud and domestic in-fighting; he ordered anyone who dared to draw his sword in public be punished by the sword.[54] Were a district royal reeve, and/or individuals encouraged by the reeve, to invade a private home and devastate home property, the master of the home who had resisted the invaders and killed any of them in self defense, could not be punished. It was the purpose of the king's legislation to secure peace and order in the land by emphasizing that a country-wide unity be formed among all strata of the population, so that all inhabitants of the country become one. "In hospitibus et adventitiis viris tanta inest utilitas, ut digne sexto in hoc regalis dignitatis possit haberi."[55]

In order to maintain public order and domestic peace, it was essential in the monarch's point of view to determine the value and amount of *blood-money* [*wergeld*] to be paid for compensation in case of murder, as murder was looked upon as disturbance of the king's peace, and the assailant—"sciat se secundum nostri senatus decretum"—to be punished accordingly. The law would not tolerate family blood feud.[56]

Accidental or intentional homicide had to be compensated for by payment of a given sum of money, and members of the family had to make peace with each other. The law took into consideration the murderer's social standing, his wealth, and determined the amount and method of payment; it called for the provision that the relatives of the murdered wife would receive their share in compensation.[57]

The law punished "sin" (in a spiritual, political-religious sense), be it murder, rape, grand larceny, without any regard of the individual's social standing, on the grounds that public "sins" of murder, rape, grand larceny, etc., undermined the structure of society. The king could rely upon the support of the Church in this respect; after deciding, for instance, on the amount of a monetary fine to be paid to the victim's relatives, "blood-money:" *agdíj*, payable in gold coin, *pensa*, one pensa being worth thirty *denars*,[58] churchmen could call for additional spiritual penance to be performed by the accused found guilty of the committed sinful crime (such as, murder, rape), and the Church would order that the convicted public "sinner" (rapist, murderer) did penance by fasting for a period of ten to twelve years.[59]

Were one to kill someone out of anger, or out of sheer malice, he had to pay blood-money, one hundred and ten gold coins, an amount that increased when paid in denars.[60] Out of this amount, fifty gold coins were collected by the royal court, fifty went to the victim's family, and ten designated as court fee, to the judge for handling the case. The condemned murderer further had to perform penance in accordance with ecclesiastical canons. Were one to kill anyone incidentally, he paid only twelve gold coins and did church penance.[61] Were one, as, for instance, a royal reeve with a hardened soul: "comes obduratus corde neglectusque anima," to kill his wife, he was obligated to pay fifty bullocks to the wife's family, and fast in accordance with church law. Were a knight [*miles*], or a well to do person [alicuius vir ubertatis], to commit such a crime, he would have to pay ten bullocks, and do church penance.[62]

Gold coins, their usage in circulation, must still have been a rarity even at that social level, where a wife-murder took place. Evidently, a member of the higher social stratum committing such a crime had to be fined by a payment of ten bullocks, and performing church penance, as if murder of one's wife among members of the higher social strata would have been tolerated more, and leniently punished.[63] Were, however, the royal reeve to send his men to invade someone's property without actually participating in it himself, he would still have to make compensation with a payment of one hundred bullocks to the victim's family.[64] The question remains, of course, whether payment of hundred bullocks had covered the expenses of the destroyed home and property; or, did people in the country live at such economic poverty level that payment of one hundred bullocks would have compensated the victim, and his family, for damages.[65]

A similar question would arise when a free man (man on horseback, a knight) attacked the court (household) of a fellow free man (a knight), and paid compensation with ten bullocks for his evil deed on grounds clearly stated: "Volumus, ut firma pax et unanimitas sit inter maiores et minores."[66] The law required that when a common person invaded another person's hut, "si vulgaris quidem alterius sui similis mansinculas invaserit," in this instance: *casulam*, he had to make compensation for his misdeed with the payment of only five bullocks.[67]

The use of the term *casula* (*házikó* in Hungarian) in the text of the law decree may imply a rather primitive agricultural surrounding consisting of simple frame structures, because it is known from the twelfth century report of Otto of Freising that, as late as in the mid-1100's, many serious buildings were, as yet, not constructed in the country.[68] Such a point of view might, however, be contradicted by a clause made in King Stephen's decree that stated that if anyone had someone else's building set on fire, "alterius edificia igne cremaverit," had to rebuild it, restore the destroyed goods, and pay additional compensation of sixteen bullocks to the injured party. The Latin term *edificia* for *épület* (in Hungarian) in the legal text, would not have to refer to a "building" built of stone, or of wood, but simply a frame structure, and it is more then likely that this decree had been enacted to ensure the reconstruction of someone's purposefully destroyed wealthy hamlet.[69]

Cursing, taking false oaths, or, worse still, breaking the oath one had taken, must have been such widely spread bad Hungarian social habits at that time, that they had to be curbed by articles of law meting out strict punishment. Were a socially important person to swear in public, or to breach the oath he had taken, the law would punish him by forcing him to pay—to the king's court—a fine of fifty bullocks, or to have his hand cut off. Were a common person to swear in public, or to breach his oath, he could redeem himself with a payment of twelve bullocks.[70] On the other hand, were a free man to kill a slave, he would not have to pay blood-money, but would have to replace the slave whom he had taken with another slave, or compensate the master of the [former] slave with the purchase price of a slave, and be still subject to church punishment.[71]

The freeman was to preserve his personal integrity and freedom; however, were the freeman to have illicit relations with the daughter of his slave, or with a female slave of another freeman, he would receive corporal punishment; were he to continue with the relationship, he would be given corporal punishment again, and would have his hair shaved off, as sign of public humiliation; (at that time, it was customary for men to wear their hair long). Were the freeman to persist in continuing the relationship with the unfree woman, he would either have to became a slave himself, or pay to redeem his personal free status; "si autem tertio, sit servus pariter cum ancilla, aut redimet se."[72] On the other hand, were a slave to have illicit relations with a female slave of a freeman, he would receive corporal punishment and would have his head shaved.[73]

The rather crude mentality of the age is exemplified by the idea expressed in the decree that, were the female slave with whom a fellow slave had had a relationship to conceive a child and to die at childbirth, the female slave's master would have to seek compensation by obtaining another female slave.[74] The guilty male slave, however, who had made the unfortunate woman pregnant, would have to be sold, and the sale price divided between the slave's master and the master of the deceased female slave.[75] Following a similar trend of thought, were a freeman to marry the female slave of another person with the consent of the female slave's master, the freeman would have to lose his freedom and become himself a slave, in accordance with the decree passed by the King's Council.[76]

The purpose of legislation concerning slaves must have served maintaining the relationship between master and the slaves within the social structure, even though the law permitted the emancipation of slaves.[77] However, the law heavily punished the person who dared free slaves without the knowledge of their masters. Such an "emancipator," if found guilty, had to pay a fee of fifty bullocks for punishment, of which forty bullocks were to go the royal court, and ten bullocks were to be received in compensation by the emancipated person's former master. Were a poor person to be the "emancipator," he would have to pay only twelve bullocks, of which ten bullocks went to the royal court.[78]

The idea of the slave population not to be awarded emancipation, was an important socio-political demand in the early eleventh century.[79] "Quot servi erint, totidem mancipia solvat, ex quibus due partes regi, teria seniori servorum."[80] The king's law, on the other hand, protected the free man, "libertatis vite cusum ducere, secundum regale decretum statutum est," as if to make certain that a more powerful person would not enslave a poorer one, on the grounds that freedom that had assured a poor individual's—his, or her—standing in society would be regarded as the natural personal right of *man*.[81]

The self-sufficient territorial-agricultural economic units that formed a part of the king's domain, or were in the hands of the landholder nobles, defined the social features of Magyar [Hungarian] society in the eleventh–early twelfth centuries. Their roots dated back to an earlier period. The small landholders, "the poor," were pushed back, rather, were pressured downward on the social scale in the days of King Stephen; those who did not have any servants, or slaves, and had to cultivate their own lands, had sooner or later to become servants of others. The sword and the plow could not be handled by the same pair of hands. The servile folks also included a good many Magyars, descendants of the land-takers in 896; the seemingly ancient law of "democratic social equality" remained a myth in Hungarian society.

The individual who had accidentally killed, or physically harmed someone—because the individual, whom he had beaten, or unwittingly killed, had previously struck him down—would be punished by a payment of ten bullocks.[82] The Hungarian court followed Frankish legal customs when ordering that rebellious slaves must be made to accept the social order (and their status in society) by the use of force, if needed. The law stated that a slave could not give testimony in court of law against his/her master, or mistress. The monarch evidently wanted to make certain in such a manner that his country's people(s) remained free from false accusations of domestics and slaves, or of irresponsible trouble makers.[83]

A large segment of the Hungarian society consisted of slaves until the late twelfth, or the early thirteenth century. The slave and his family were simple objects in the eyes of the[ir] lord, who had dealt with them as if they were like any chattel the lord had possessed. A male and female slave could be sold and bought just like any object at trade in the market, distributed among the heirs in case the land had to be divided upon the death of the landholder.[84] The slave who fled from his master had to be returned to the landholder's household, just as if he and/or she were pieces of stolen property.[85] There were slave markets held in the realm as late as the thirteenth century.[86]

The laws of King Stephen contain strict legislation concerning the social and legal status of the non-free social stratum in the realm. The pious monarch who had his people converted to Christianity provided legal protection to the masters of the slaves and assured them of their ownership of their [agricultural and industrial] workforce.[87]

Even as late as the late eleventh century, King Ladislas I (1077–95) had placed the slave on the level of animal workforce: cows and oxen, and King Stephen had to punish anyone who dared to free somebody else's slave from their slavery.[88] King Stephen also downgraded the free man who had married a slave girl—most probably on the grounds that the individual who owned the slave woman also owned her offspring, and the master of the slave woman would be robbed of both the slave girl and her offspring, were she to gain emancipation by marrying a free man.[89]

King Stephen's laws—and, to a certain extent, the laws of King Ladislas—correspond to the spirit and institutions of the age. The Church accepted slavery in that time period, and the Hungarian monarchs identified themselves with the then ecclesiastically condoned legal arguments on the status of slaves. Although according to Christian doctrine everyone was to be considered a child of God, equally capable of obtaining spiritual redemption, and by nature every one was entitled to his, or her, freedom,[90] the origins of slavery were rooted in *sin*, as it was sin that had ruined the nature of man and caused social distinctions to develop.[91]

It is because of *sin* that a portion of mankind was unfit to be naturally free, and mandated the legally imposed judicial discipline that was unnecessary when man lived in his natural state. Although the Church had attempted to ease the burden of the slave, and protected his right to live, as it protected the slave from physical abuse by his master, ecclesiastical authorities also upheld the lord's right to own his slaves, and supported legal measures against emancipating them. The Church itself, the monasteries, owned slaves in the eleventh–early twelfth centuries.[92]

Synodical decrees forbade bishops and abbots to free slaves from their condition; Canon Law strongly condemned anyone who dared to encourage a slave to flee from his master, and punished the escaped slave by placing him under excommunication. The cleric who had left the Church and slave who had fled from his lord remained excommunicated—until they returned to their fold.[93]

In the case of slavery, King Stephen had followed the usage of his times: as the Church forbade the emancipation of slaves without their lords' consent, and some churchmen were actually slave-holders (they needed manpower to perform agricultural tasks in the field), the first Hungarian monarch also had assured his landholder (spiritual and secular) lords of the possession of slaves as their private property.[94] Thus it came about that if a freeman were to marry a slave girl, he would lose his freedom—on the grounds that were a slave girl to gain emancipation by marrying a freeman, her lord would not only lose her, but also her offspring who, by law, belonged to him like the ribs of a slaughtered or dead cow. On the other hand, in Hungarian law, the monarch protected the *freed man* who had gained personal emancipation from the hands of his lord.[95]

The *blood-money* mentioned in King Stephen's laws represented, in case of a murder, the social distinction between the free and the non-free, and the nobles. That is why the murdered member of a royal reeve's family had to be compensated for by a payment of fifty bullocks, while the member of the family of a freeman who performed military service for the king received only ten bullocks, and the common freeman only five bullocks. A murdered slave's family received none; however, his lord had to be compensated for *his* loss of manpower.[96]

In the early eleventh century the agricultural economy of the country went through profound stages. As it may be indicated by the usage of money in King Stephen's day, a monetary economy—based on coins minted in imitation of the money in circulation by his Bavarian father-in-law—began to replace the nomadic way of life by agriculture and husbandry, and the realm joined the economic mainstream of Latin Europe. King Stephen's money came into and remained in circulation as far north as Gothland in northern Europe.[97]

The articles of Stephen's Laws concerning orphans, single women, or widows reflect a Christian disposition. The law forbade theft of women; a captured woman had to be returned to her parents (an article of law that may imply that *women-theft* involved mostly young women of high[er] social standing or women, the social status of whose families had left them unprotected in society). The law determined that a man accused and found guilty of such a crime must pay, according to his social status, a fine of ten, or of five, bullocks to the family of the victim.[98]

On the other hand, the law punished theft by women. Were a woman-thief caught in the act of thievery, her husband could redeem her; however, on a third occasion, she would have to be sold into slavery;[99] and yet, *female-thievery: traffic in women*, could also have meant an escape route from a perhaps unhappy, or unsuccessful marriage.[100] It is of interest to know that in early eleventh century Hungary married women of higher social standing, evidently, were involved in thievery of women, as if one could speak of an aspect of organized crime: unauthorized trade in female slaves, and the king's court had to take firm legal action to make an end to it.[101]

Were a husband to leave his wife, she remained his *possession*; the law forbade that anyone would force her to marry (again) against her will. Were, however, the abandoned woman to wish to marry again, she could be allowed to take her clothing from her (previous) husband's house—though she had to leave all of her (other) belongings behind—and be free to marry somebody else. If the (former) husband, who had heard about the (planned) new marriage of his wife, would want to return to his abandoned home, he could not marry again without the local bishop's permission. This article of law leads to the conclusion that an episcopal investigation had to determine whether the man's previous marriage was valid, and whether he could get married again.[102]

King Stephen's laws paid special attention to the defense of orphans and widows. The king had ordered that if a widow wished to stay unmarried in order to remain with her children and provide for their upbringing, she could remain a widow, and not to be forced into another marriage. However, were she to marry again on her own free will, she would not be allowed to take anything from the children's inheritance with her. The childless widow would, on the other hand, retain her husband's inheritance, which would, upon her death, be inherited by the husband's relatives; if there were no relatives, the inheritance would revert to the monarch.[103]

The Royal Council had further issued orders concerning women witches, known as *strigae*, "*si qua striga inventa fuerit*," because they ate human flesh, to state that they did not exist. This article of the law is worth quoting: such a female "ducatur ad ecclesiam et commendetur sacerdoti ad ieiunandum fidemque docendam."[104] It reminds one of a very similar law provision by King Coloman the Learned of Hungary in the early twelfth century.[105]

Were someone to come upon a woman who had the reputation of a *striga*, the indicted woman would have to go before an ecclesiastical court of law to be instructed to improve her ways of living. Were she not to alter her ways, were she not to repent, the church court would condemn her to do public penance, and order to have a sign with the keys of the church to be placed upon her forehead and her chest. Were a third occasion to occur, the ecclesiastical court would have to hand her over to a secular judge, who would either sentence her—or disqualify the victim as mentally unbalanced, unfit to stand trial, and permit her relatives—so deeply hurt in their dignity by the scandalized behavior of the accused woman—to take action at their will [by taking her home, and keeping her out of public sight]. King Stephen's courts of law had to take into consideration the mental instability of anyone indicted of witchcraft.[106]

King Stephen's laws did, indeed, determine for his people how to lead decent and unperturbed lives, and besides divine commands, the population of his realm was also subject to secular laws, so that the good were enriched and guided by divine laws, while earthly laws punished those found guilty; "ut quantum boni in hi[is] divinis amplianatur, tantum rei [mali] in istis multentur."[107]

3. Non-Magyar Historical Sources on the Establishment of Christianity in Hungary

Nothing more could serve as proof of the popularity of the saintly monarch, and the importance of events occurring in Hungary during the former half of the century, than the fact that various western chroniclers had felt encouraged to deal with the reign of King Stephen and with the development of Hungarian kingship. Those contemporary authors could not emphasize enough how the monarch displayed a humane attitude toward his defeated enemies, how he did not exploit his military victories by taking booty from his subjugated enemies. Thietmar, the imperial German bishop, recorded how the Lord of Heaven aided King Stephen in solving family problems that had been caused by misunderstandings among his relatives. It was due to his intercession, for instance, that Emperor Henry II ended his family feud with his brother Bruno.[108]

Stephen maintained friendly relations with the influential Abbot Odilo of Cluny,[109] and, as *rex christianissimus*, opened his country before the pilgrims en route to the Holy Land, and provided for them during their sojourn in his country. He had done this with a political-diplomatic objective; he let it be known that his realm had become Christian, and its leaders wanted, through their support of "international" pilgrimages to Jerusalem, to join the bloodstream of the Latin west.[110]

He did, however, take a firm stand against the German emperor, Conrad II—a new dynasty on the imperial throne—who had abused the humane hospitality extended by the Magyar royal court to western (German) pilgrims passing through the land by sending, disguised as pilgrims, diplomatic messengers to the Byzantine court. King Stephen did not allow the false imperial envoys, who had entered the realm without his permission, to continue their journey to their destination. It may be regarded as a sign of special respect toward the Hungarian king that Wipo, chaplain of Emperor Conrad II and his biographer, to acknowledge that the Hungarian ruler, "rex iniuste iniuriatus," had taken the correct countermeasures toward the German court.[111]

In a similar manner, it ought to be regarded as a sign of special trust in the court of King Stephen that princes Edmund and Eduard, offspring of Edward the Confessor, the last Anglo-Saxon king, had sought, and obtained, political asylum at the court of King Stephen; as a matter of fact, one of them even married a daughter of the Hungarian monarch (or, though this is unlikely, a young Hungarian noble woman).[112]

It must have been common knowledge among his contemporaries that King Stephen possessed a personality worthy of love and respect, that he behaved with consideration toward visitors and strangers, and displayed an understanding appreciation of his co-workers in spreading the Catholic faith—qualities that assured him of an international reputation and *de facto* acknowledgment that his people and his country had, indeed, become full-fledged members of the western Latin Christian community. Thousands of pilgrims en route to Jerusalem passed through the kingdom; numerous leading ecclesiastical and secular personalities of the west visited the Hungarian court; as discussed above, Wolfgang, friend and confidant of the German ruling dynasty, later bishop of Regensburg had, for example, visited the court of Prince Géza.[113] Bruno of Verdun,[114] Bruno of Querfurt,[115] Adalbert of Prague sojourned in the court circles of King Stephen.[116] Vladimir of Kiev (*rex Russorum!*) maintained contact with him.[117]

The monk Romuald, founder of the Camaldolians, had attempted to do missionary work in Hungary, though this plan did not materialize.[118] Bishop Bruno, brother of Emperor, Henry II (both of whom King Stephen had persuaded to make peace with another), spent some time at King Stephen's court,[119] as did Archbishop Poppo (*archiepiscopus Treveriensis*) in the year 1027.[120] In 1031, Henry of Bavaria, the son of Emperor Henry II had visited the Hungarian monarch;[121] in 1035, Abbot Eberwinus (abbas s. Martini Treveriensis) and Abbot Richard of Verdun sojourned in the Hungarian court.[122] The visit by the latter was followed by a visitation of twenty-four (viginti quatuor) canons of Verdun in 1047.[123] Their visitation most probably had a purpose: to bring spiritual solace to the Hungarian court that had slowly been recovering from the pagan uprising that devastated the country in the 1040's.[124] The canons' visit to, and stay in Hungary took place during the reign of Stephen's successor, King Andrew I (1046–60).[125]

In the eyes of "strangers," the personality, behavior, and achievements of King Stephen increasingly commanded respect, as may be perceived from their characterizations of him: *rex religiosus, rex egregius, rex pie memoriae, rex bone memoriae, Deo devotus.* Sigfridus de Balnhusin had referred to him as "the most Christian king" in virtue and in deed.[126]

Simultaneously, the non-Magyar folklore tradition displayed an understanding attitude toward Hungarian historic events of this age, expressing, in fact, a deeper sympathy toward Magyar history *before* the succession of King Stephen. The non-Magyar cycles of historic legends depicted the marauding ventures—to which the legends attached little or no military significance—of the pre-Christian Magyars (*Hungari adhuc pagani*), as acts of *pagan* ignorance, for which their less enlightened leaders bore responsibility, "propter debilitatem principum, qui tunc imperabant."[127] In a similar manner had another chronicler excused the invasion by Conrad II of Hungarian territory with the remark that it had happened "ante conversionem," before the Magyar's conversion to Christianity.[128]

One may continue with the enumeration of such data. An early twelfth century record stated that the mother of the saintly Eberhard, margrave of Nellenburg, was the daughter of the Hungarian king Stephen; she had led her husband to the path of virtue, that is, their marriage had not been consummated.[129] The author of a writ, written after the canonization of King St. Stephen in 1083, who dealt with the life of the former margrave of Thuringia (who became an anchorite, known as Saint Gunther, a Czech-Bavarian hermit), could not emphasize enough that his saint was a blood-relative of King Stephen, "ipsius venerabilis viri cognati," and it was after his visit to King Stephen's court that Gunther decided to become a hermit.[130] The same author recorded a similar narrative about the life of Bishop Godehard of Hildesheim.[131] The author of the legend about St. Alban, on the other hand, went so far as to insist that his saint was a son of King Stephen, "fabulosus martyr...fabulosi filii regis Hungariae, monachi autem apud Maguntiam."[132]

3. Non-Magyar Sources on the Establishment of Christianity

The great Portuguese poet, Vaz de Camões (d. 1580), in the segment of his heroic epic, *Os Lusiadas*, depicting the Hungarian bloodties of the Portuguese royal family, wrote (following the chronicle of Duarte Galvas) that the first king of Portugal was the second son, named Emery, of a "famous Hungarian king."[133] Of course, Vaz de Camões could have been referring to King Emery of Hungary (d. 1204), who had been married to an Aragonese princess.[134]

Numerous non-Hungarian chroniclers wrote about Prince Imre (Emery), King Stephen's son, "vir sanctus nomine Henricus," whom his father had prepared for the role of governing the kingdom. His father had even selected a bride for him who, according to Polish sources, was a Polish princess,[135] while in the record of Byzantine sources, she was a Byzantine princess. The latter view may be supported by the terminology in the Greek text of the founding charter of the monastery for women at Veszprém,[136] even though the Polish chroniclers dealt with Imre more at length; they depicted the circumstances surrounding his unexpected death, and emphasized that the prince led a chaste life as a married man.[137]

The non-Magyar chroniclers had shown far less interest in the gradually evolving life of the country, and next to mentioning in general terms the development of the realm's ecclesiastical organization, they hardly spoke of anything else. The establishment of the bishoprics in Hungary did awaken their interest, however. They reported that King Stephen founded ten bishoprics and an archbishopric in Esztergom; he richly provided for their maintenance, and in his laws he called for the payment of the tithe in order to make certain that his clerics could fully devote themselves to their spiritual work.[138] Abbot Martin of Vienna mentioned by name the established bishoprics and added that the monarch further founded monasteries, one of them especially for the honor of St. Martin.[139] He had provided for the construction of many (parish) churches, of which two were especially beautiful: the one, dedicated to the honor of the Blessed Mother of God in Székesfehérvár, and the other in Esztergom built in the honor of (St.) Adalbert; "...aedificavit atque dotavit ecclesiam sanctae Mariae in Alba; ...maiorem ecclesiam Strigonii in honorem s. Adalberti instituit."[140]

The chief provider for the terrestrial needs of the Church in Hungary was Gisela, King Stephen's queen. It was she who ensured the availability of utensils needed for religious services and wove, decorated, and mended with her own hands the liturgical vestments, "vestes sacras suis manibus nebat, texebat, sarciebat."[141]

It is only the annotations in the non-Magyar sources that provide the whole picture of the tremendous work King Stephen had done in establishing and expanding the field of ecclesiastical life in his realm. He had to find non-Magyar helpers to aid him in forming conditions for the development of public and religious life in the country. Papal letters reveal that the Hungarian king did have good relations with the Roman curia; papal correspondence mentions, for instance, that Queen Gisela had a liturgical (Mass) vestment made for Pope John XIX that was inherited by Pope Leo IX.[142] King Stephen remained in contact with the doge's court in Venice,[143] with the abbots of Monte-cassino and Cluny, and with Chartres;[144] further written evidence points to relations with Luttich, the monasteries of Saint Gall and Fulda.[145]

Several German chroniclers of various, though reliable value, speak of the activities of King Stephen in Hungarian church matters; his contacts with the Czech, Polish and Russian (Kievan) courts were referred to by Czech, Polish and Kievan sources. The non-Magyar chronicle entries mention briefly the king's *foreign* contacts, as, for example, building of a church next to St. Peter's in Rome.[146]

The final years of the reign of King Stephen received relatively little publicity in the record of the non-Magyar chroniclers. The latter (it would be strange, indeed, to speak of "foreign" chroniclers at a time when in their works they discussed events that must have been "foreign" to their world) mention that Stephen designated Peter Orseolo of Venice, the son of one of his sisters whom he had adopted as his son, to succeed him on the throne upon his death.[147] On the other hand, the author of the *Annales Altahénses maiores* did emphasize that the son of Prince Géza's brother who, as an heir to the throne, had opposed the king's order and revolted against it, but King Stephen tolerated no opposition, had ordered him to be blinded, and had ordered his sons, Andrew, Béla and Levente, exiled from the realm.[148]

This eminent chronicler, who had reliable sources of information at his disposal, was referring to the 1034 conspiracy against King Stephen, directly referred to by article ii:17 (c. 51): *De conspiratione regis et regni*, of King Stephen's Laws; "si quis in regem aut in regnum conspiravit, refugium nullum habest ad ecclesiam,... anatemizatur et omnium fidelium commune privetur."[149] The disobedient blinded relative was a pagan, and on account of this, the author of the "Hagensche Chronik" remarked that it was the pagans who had murdered King Stephen.[150]

The cited conspiracy against the monarch must have had deep roots because the trend of anti-monarch conspiracies did continue during the reign of Peter Orseolo. Peter, who was not of direct royalty, nor of Magyar (Árpád) descent, was successfully opposed by one of King Stephen's brothers-in-law, named Aba Sámuel (Samuel Aba), "qui erat unus ex ipsis, de magnis principibus," supported by numerous members of the high nobility, who evidently did not realize that, through their support of Aba's cause they might have started a civil war in the country.[151]

Upon the occurrence and oppression of the conspiracy organized by Vazul (King Stephen's cousin, the son of Michael, the king's uncle, the brother of Prince Géza), Stephen became less convinced that the succession of the throne could be arranged in a peaceful manner because shortly before his death he had the great nobles of his realm summoned to his presence and made them take an oath that they acknowledged the rights of Queen Gisela *and* of Peter Orseolo, the heir-designate, to the throne and to inherit the treasure that had been assigned to them. It is known from well-informed German sources that Peter breached his oath and robbed the widowed queen of all of her possessions. Upon such a most undignified treatment, the queen left the realm. Henry III took her to Passau where she became the abbess of the Niederburg monastery for women. Queen Gisela died there in May, 1095, and an epitaph was erected for her in the monastic church of Niederburg.[152]

Some of the non-Magyar chroniclers spoke lovingly of the Queen. They characterized her with remarks like "bonae memoriae femina;" "sanctae vitae mulier;" "femina prudentissima."[153] One of them expressed a contrary opinion. Albericus of "Trium Fontium" (he died about 1250) noted, based on information derived from Hungarian sources, that during her life the Queen caused much trouble in her husband's country; "…ut dicunt Ungari, multas malitias in terra illa fecit," and, for that reason, the Magyars assassinated her upon the death of her husband.[154]

It is surprising that many non-Magyar sources correctly placed the date of King Stephen's death in the year 1038. Some of them even noted the day of his death: he had died on the feast of Assumption (August 15), 1038, "in die Assumptionis Sanctae Mariae", they claimed to know.[155] There are others, of course, who cited different dates. A Polish source quoted the year 1039, with the remark that his earthly departure left behind a real (political) void.[156] His country's peace and happiness had died with him, noted Ortilo of Lilienfeld under *anno* 1039.[157] He was buried in Székesfehérvár, the Polish chroniclers, and Martin, abbot of the Irish-Scots in Vienna, reported, as did the scribe of the "Kaiserchronik."[158]

The day of King Stephen's death served as a cross-reference date for certain political and diplomatic events. Daniel, bishop of Prague, paid an official visit to the court of Géza II of Hungary (1141–61) on the feast-day of King Stephen [did he mean the day of his earthly departure, August 15th?].[159] Béla III of Hungary and Casimir II of Poland concluded their agreement *iuxta instituta s. Stephani regis et s. Adalberi* in the year 1193.[160] Adelheid, wife of the Czech prince Sobieslav I, the daughter of Prince Álmos (the younger brother of Coloman the Learned, d. 1116), and her husband celebrated the feast of King Stephen on Hungarian soil.[161]

Polish and Czech chroniclers agree in their reports that the saintly king had performed many miracles already in his lifetime,[162] while the Italian and western chronicles note that numerous miracles had occurred at his burial.[163] The sick child placed under his protection had miraculously regained his strength, and later many other miracles would be accredited to his intercession.[164] Western and Polish sources report that his people had constantly visited his grave, and so did Boleslav III, king of Poland.[165]

The glory of miracles serve as testament to his merits. Among the western sources, Bernold of the abbey of St. Blasius, as well as Adam of Bremen, mentioned his canonization.[166] The *Annales Mechovienses* further mentioned his right hand, the "Holy Dexter," that had remained intact, as did Bishop Augustine of Lucerin in his annotations called *Exhortatio*.[167]

Domestic and foreign sources bear witness that his *Vitae* were much in circulation both at home and abroad.[168]

Notes

1. The Background: The Three Vitae of King Stephen

1. *SSH*, II, 393ff.; Pintér, I, 163ff.; Tibor Klaniczay (ed.), *A magyar irodalom története 1600-ig* [History of Hungarian literature prior to 1660], vol. I. (Budapest, 1964), 60ff.; L. J. Csóka, *A latin nyelvű történeti irodalom kialakulása Magyarországon a XI–XIV században* [Development of Latin-language historical literature in Hungary during the 11th–14th centuries] (Budapest, 1967), 119ff.; Györffy, *István király*, 59, 81, 92, 93, etc., passim.

2. János Horváth, *Stílusproblémák*, 143ff.

3. "...tamen hec breviora legite," *SSH*, II, 393f.; Hóman – Szekfű, I, 293.

4. *SSH*, II, 393,17–30 (c. 1), and 394,28 – 395,7 (c. 2).

5. *Ibid.*, II, 394,11-12.

6. "...pater eius *rex quidem*, sed primum gentilis fuit," *ibid.*, II, 394,13; in the "Zagreb Chronicle," c. 13, King Géza II [1141–62] will appear as *Geycha rex tertius*, cf. *ibid.*, I, 210; on the *Zagreb Chronicle*, see Macartney, *Hungarian Historians*, 109f. On Géza II, see his record in the Chronicle, cc. 164-68, *SSH*, I, 453ff.; Kosztolnyik, *From Coloman*, 112ff.

7. *SSH*, II, 394,13-17, and 394,24-26.

8. *Ibid.*, II, 399, c. 7. On Vászoly, see Hóman – Szekfű, I, 234ff. and 293.

9. *SSH*, II, 399,23-26.

10. Chronicle, c. 150, *ibid.*, I, 429f., and I, 430,10-15.

11. Horváth 149ff.; Hóman – Szekfű, I, 320ff.

12. Chronicle, c. 152, though dated it anno 1114—*SSH*, I, 430,16-18, and note 6; in the Zagreb Chronicle, c. 10, *ibid.*, I, 210; Coloman had died in February, 1116, according to a document issued by King Stephen II in 1124, "anno nono regni mei"—see *RA*, n. 51; Kosztolnyik, *From Coloman*, 70.

13. Cf. Bernoldi Constantiensis "Chronicon," anno 1083, *MGHSS*, V, 438f.; Hartvic, c. 24, *SSH*, II, 433,5-11; Kosztolnyik, *Five Kings*, 94 and 97. On Hartvic, see also Zoltán I. Tóth, *A Hartvik-legenda kritikájához* [An essay on the Hartvic Life of King St. Stephen] (Budapest, 1942), 114ff.

14. Compare "Vita minor," c. 7, with Hartvic, c. 21, *SSH*, II, 399 and II, 430, respectively.

15. "Erat vir iste fidelis, in omnibus actibus suis Deo perfecte deditus," c. 10, *SSH*, II, 385,17-18; Csóka, 105ff.; Pintér, I, 165ff.; Horváth, *Árpádkori irodalom*, 136ff.

16. Cf. "Vita maior," cc. 2 and 6; and compare with Hóman – Szekfű, I, 287ff.

17. See the "Vita maior," cc. 1-2, and c. 15, *SSH*, II, 337ff., 386f., and 390ff., respectively; Csóka, 398ff.

18. On this, Elemér Varjú, *Legendae sancti Stephani regis: Szent István király legendái* [The legends of King Saint Stephen] (Budapest, 1928), 86ff., on Hartvic, *ibid.*, 94ff.; Kosztolnyik, *Five Kings*, 94—though King Ladislas I later established firm[er] relations with the German court, *ibid.*, 101; further, see *RA*, n. 24; also, *MGHSS*, VI, 364.

19. For details, see the Chronicle, c. 82, *SSH*, I, 338,11-24; Bishop Gerard's "Vita maior," c. 15, *ibid.*, II, 501f.; on the latter, cf. Macartney, *Hungarian Historians*, 154ff.; Z. J. Kosztolnyik, "The Negative Results of the Enforced Missionary Policy of King Stephen I of Hungary: The Uprising of 1046," *Catholic Historical Review*, 59 (1973-74),

569ff.; idem, *Five Kings*, 66f. and 70; in the early 1060's, Vata's son, or grandson, led a (pagan) uprising (against the ruling dynasty), see Hóman – Szekfű, I, 272f.; on the events of 1046, *ibid.*, I, 253ff.

20. Hartvic, c. 1, *SSH*, II, 401; Csóka, 154ff. and 405f.; the literary classic, Cyrill Horváth, *A régi magyar irodalom története* [The history of early Hungarian literature] (Budapest, 1899), 19f. and 23; Hóman – Szekfű, I, 297ff. and 331f.

21. The Chronicle, c. 152, *SSH*, I, 432,27; I, 433,1-2; "(qui) fuit episcopus Waradiensis," says the "Zagreb Chronicle," c. 10, *ibid.*, II, 209,16–17, though Ladislas I wanted him to become the bishop of Eger—see Chronicle, c. 140, *ibid.*, I, 419,6-12.

22. See the letter of Ladislas I addressed to the Abbot of Montecassino—text in Vilmos Fraknói, *Magyarország egyházi és politikai összeköttetései a római Szentszékkel* [Hungary and the Holy See], 3 vols. (Budapest, 1901-03), I, 401ff.; Kosztolnyik, *Five Kings*, 101, 106, 107; on Coloman, idem, *From Coloman*, 68f.

23. Bernoldi "Chronicon," anno 1087, *MGHSS*, V, 446; the Chronicle, *SSH*, I, 432,27-29; "...quam fecit rex Hungariae ad mandatum papae," in E. Martene – U. Durand (eds.), *Thesaurus novus anecdotorum*, 5 vols. (repr. New York, 1968), IV, 127f.; Palacky, *Geschichte*, I, 298ff.; Gebhardt, I, 255ff. and 261f.; Alois Dempf, *Sacrum imperium: Geschichts- und Staatsphilosophie des Mittelalters und der politischen Renaissance* (Munich–Berlin, 1929), 176ff.; Kosztolnyik, *Five Kings*, 100 and 101.

24. "...horas canonicas ut episcopus absolvebat," *SSH*, I, 433,1-2; Kosztolnyik, *From Coloman*, 58ff. and 63f.

25. Cf. Erich Caspar (ed.), *Das Register Gregors VII. MGH Epp., sel. II*, 2 vols. (Berlin, 1920–23, repr. 1990), n. ii:13 (Oct. 28, 1074), and compare with the papal writ to Vratislav of Bohemia, *ibid.*, n. ii:7 (Sept. 22, 1074); on relations between Pope Gregory VII and Rudolf of Swabia, see *ibid.*, n. i:19 (Sept. 1, 1073).

26. That the Holy Father may give his blessing to the ecclesiastical organization he, Stephen, already had established in his country—cf. *SSH*, II, 412,10-13; on Stephen's Laws, see, for instance, aa. i:2, 8-9, 13; and a. ii:1—Bartoniek, 19ff.

27. *SSH*, II, 414,2-12.

28. *Ibid.*, II, 394,24-395,7 (c. 2).

29. Hartvic, c. 8, *ibid.*, II, 411f.

30. *Ibid.*, II, 412,2-5; ... *cum corona et cruce* (!), *ibid.*, II, 412,6 – 413,2; and II, 414,9-13.

31. Hartvic, c. 9, *ibid.*, II, 412,9-14.

32. Caspar, *Register Gregors VII*, n. ii:13, Oct. 28, 1074.

33. "Vita maior," c. 5, *ibid.*, II, 380f., and II, 381,7-10.

34. "Vita maior," c. 8, *ibid.*, II, 383,6-14.

35. *Ibid.*, II, 383f.

36. *Ibid.*, II, 384,3-7 (c. 9). Endre Tóth, *Magyar koronázási jelvények* [The Hungarian coronation insignia] (Budapest, 1995), 18; Éva Kovács – Zsuzsa Lovag, *Die ungarischen Krönungsinsignien*, rev. ed. (Budapest, 1980), 17ff.

37. *Ibid.*, II, 394,24-26 (c. 2).

38. *Ibid.*, II, 395,5-7.

39. Kosztolnyik, *From Coloman*, 64; Anselm of Canterbury was a "Gregorian" church reformer—cf. F. Cantor, *Church, Kingship and Lay Investiture in England, 1089–1135* (Princeton, 1958), 202f.; Z. N. Booke, *The English Church and the Papacy* (Cambridge, 1931; repr. 1989), 147ff. and 164ff. On the compromise, see Frank Barlow,

The English Church 1066–1154 (London, 1979), 289ff.; R. W. Southern, *Saint Anselm* (Cambridge, 1990), 277ff., esp. 289ff., and 330ff.

40. *MGH Legum sectio* IV, *const.* I, nn. 107 and 108; Jaffé, n. 6986; and *MGH Legum sectio* IV, *const.* I, 575ff.; Kosztolnyik, *From Coloman*, 45f.; Gebhardt, I, 278ff.; Th. von Sickel – Harry Bresslau, "Die kaiserliche Ausfertigung des Wormser Konkordats," *MIÖG*, 6 (1885), offprint.

41. Text in Marczali, *Enchiridion*, 104ff., esp. 105.; Kosztolnyik, *From Coloman*, 41ff.

42. For King Stephen's Laws, see Lederer, *Szent István törvényei*, aa. i:1-13; Závodszky, 141ff.; also, Marczali, *Enchiridion*, 69ff.; on *Admonitiones*: the "Admonitions" [De institutione morum ad Emericum ducem], see *SSH*, II, 619ff., aa. i-iii, and a. ix; Závodszky, 131ff.; also, Marczali, *Enchiridion*, 63ff.; J. Horváth, *Árpádkori irodalmunk*, 116ff. The author of the "Vita beati Heinrici filii eiusdem"—or "Vita s. Emerici confessoris filii s. Stephani regis"—in *SSH*, II, 449ff., written about 1108, 1109, cf. Horváth, 153ff.; Macartney, *Hungarian Historians*, 170f., stressed the idea of celibate life, and the passage shows a remarkable similarity with the "Sermon to the clergy" by the Archpoet: "Lingua balbus, hebes ingenio...necessitas est, non presumptio"—recorded in the *Carmina Burana* collection; cf. *Carmina Burana: Vagantenlieder aus der lateinischen Dichtung des 12 und 13 Jahrhunderts*, Latin text by Max Manitius; introduction, with German translation, by Robert Ulich (Jena, 1927), 116ff., esp. the stanza "Puniamus virtute vicium, cuius caret fine supplicium; terreat nos ignis incendium, fetor, fletus et stridor dentium," *ibid.*, 120.

2. Royal Legislative Acts

43. Though unintentionally!—cf. Einhardi, *Vita Caroli Magni*, ed. O. Holder-Egger, SSrG (Hannover, 1911), c. 28; Thomas Hodgkin, *Italy and her Invaders*, 8 vols. (New York, 1880–89, reissued 1967), VIII, 194ff. and 203ff.; Heinrich Fichtenau, *The Carolingian Empire*, tr. Peter Munz (Oxford, 1957), 47ff.; Heinrich Fichtenau, *Beiträge zur Mediävistik*, 2 vols. (1977), II, 100ff., and my review of this volume in *Austrian History Yearbook*, 17–18 (1981–82), 354ff.; Gebhardt, I, 138ff.

44. Cf. "Continuatio Regionis," annorum 962, 963, *MGHSS*, I, 625; *MGH Leg. sect.* IV, *const.* 1, nn. 10 and 12 (anno 962; Otto I and Pope John XII). Thietmar, ii:20 (30-31), commenting on the greatness of Otto I the Great; also, Heer, 56ff. and 59f.; further, Fritz Kern, *Gottesgnadentum und Widerstandsrecht im frühen Mittelalter*, 5th ed. [a repr. of the 2nd ed., 1954] (Darmstadt, 1970), 6ff. and 46ff.; Karl Hampe, *Das Hochmittelalter*, 5th ed. (Cologne–Graz, 1963), 20ff.; Holtzmann, 175ff. and 190ff.; Gebhardt, I, 183ff.

45. According to Thietmar, iv:38 (59); Hartvic, c. 10; Thomas v. Bogyay, *Stephanus Rex* (Vienna–Munich, 1975), 23ff., and my review of this volume in *Austrian History Yearbook*, 14 (1978), 290ff.; Györffy, *István király*, 137ff. and 148ff.; Bóna, *Magyarok és Európa*, 88ff. Henry III was still claiming similar rights in 1047—cf. Watterich, *Vitae Pontificum Romanorum (ab saec. IX usque ad saec. XIII)*, 2 vols. (Leipzig, 1862), I, 73ff.

46. Ostrogorsky, 228ff. and 238ff.; Jenkins, 30ff.; Robert Browning, *The Byzantine Empire* (New York, 1980), 77ff. and 90ff.

47. Kosztolnyik, *From Coloman*, 181ff., and for references, *ibid.*, 195, nn. 15-17, and 20.

48. See King Stephen's *Libellus*: "Admonitions," c. 7, *SSH*, II, 619ff., or, Závodszky, 131ff.; and compare with his Laws, preface, aa. i:15, 20, 30-31, or a. ii:2; further, *SSH*, II, 415,1-4, or the "Vita maior," c. 9, *ibid.*, II, 384,7-15; Hóman, *Ungarisches Mittelalter*, I, 225f.; Kosztolnyik, *Five Kings*, 15f.

49. "...et quoniam unaqueque gens propriis utitur legibus, ...decretali meditationis nostrae statuimus genti,"—cf. Laws, preface; further, Admonitions, a. 7.

50. *SSH*, II, 415,2-3.

51. "Secundum decretum Senatus," Laws, a. i:15; also, a. ii:2; Admonitions, c. 7.

52. *Ibid.*, c. 6; Hartvic, c. 10; and "...decrevimus, in sequentibus subnotavimus lineis" ; King Stephen's Laws, preface.

53. Laws, aa. i:1-13, aa. i:14-15, 27, 32, 35, and aa. ii:1, 18 (latter article not in the Admont MS—cf. Bartoniek, 41f.)—all to serve ecclesiastical interest.

54. Laws, a. i:16.

55. Laws, a. i:35.

56. Laws, aa. i:14, 15, and ii:5.

57. Laws, aa. i:14a-c, 15, 35, and a. ii:4.

58. Laws, aa. i:1, 2, 5, 7, 13; Hóman – Szekfü, I, 214ff.; Hóman, *Ungarisches Mittelalter*, I, 212ff., 221f., and 225f.; Peter Spufford, *Money and its Use in Medieval Europe* (Cambridge, 1988), 40ff., 80f., and 101ff.

59. King Stephen's Laws, aa. i:14a-c, and 15.

60. King Stephen's golden *pensa* was worth 30 *denars* [*denarii*]—cf. Laws, aa. i:14a-b; "blood money": fine, for murder, was set at the payment of 110 bullocks—meaning that one bullock was worth one *pensa*; also, a. ii:4; according to a. i:32, 16 bullocks were worth 40 *solidii*—therefore, one bullock had to be priced at 30 *dénár[s]*, worth *one pensa*. On Charlemagne's *solidus*, being worth 12 *denarii*, see Alfons Dopsch, *Die Wirtschaftsentwicklung der Karolingerzeit*, 2 vols., 3rd ed., ed. Erna Patzelt (Cologne–Graz, 1962), II, 289ff.; Erna Patzelt, *Die Karolingische Renaissance*, 2nd ed. (Graz, 1965), 142ff. In 1247, King Béla IV's *márka [mark]* were worth eight *pensae*—cf. *ÁUO*, VII, 266; one *pensa* was worth 30 *dénár[s] [denars]*, consequently, one *márka* [mark] worth *240 dénárs*. See also Spufford, 101ff.

61. King Stephen's Laws, aa. i:14a *and* b, 22, and a. ii:4.

62. "Si autem miles vel alicuius vir ubertatis eandem culpam inciderit...," *ibid.*, a. i:15b.

63. See King St. Stephen's "Admonitiones," a. 4, *SSH*, II, 623f.

64. King Stephen's Laws, a. i:35.

65. It seems to have been a Hungarian reality even in the twelfth century—cf. Otto of Freising, *Gesta*, i:32. For a comparison with conditions in the Latin West, see Waas, 176ff.

66. For reasons clearly stated: "Volumus, ut firma pax et unanimitas sit inter maiores et minores," —cf. King Stephen's Laws, a. i:35.

67. "Si vulgarius quidem alterius sui...invaserit," —*ibid.*

68. "...mansincula[s]...,"—cf. *ibid.*, and compare with the pointed remarks of the twelfth century eyewitness, Otto of Freising, *Gesta*, i:32.

69. King Stephen's Laws, a. i:32.

70. *Ibid.*, a. i:17.

71. *Ibid.*, a. i:14d.

72. Cf. King Stephen's Laws, a. i:28a.

73. *Ibid.*, a. i:28b.

74. *Ibid.*, a. i:28a.

75. *Ibid.*, a. i:28b.

76. *Ibid.*, a. i:29.

77. *Ibid.*, a. i:18.

78. *Ibid.*, a. i:21.

79. *Ibid.*, a. i:22.

80. "…statutum a se manifestum facit, in quo scilicet uniuscuiusque culpe contrarium dictavit antidotum…;" Hartvic, c. 10, *SSH*, II, 415,3-6; for the whole context, see II, 415,6-12.

81. King Stephen's Laws, a. i:23.

82. *Ibid.*, aa. i:18, 20—compare with "Capitulare Francium," anno 779, *MGH Leg. sectio* II–1, n. 20, and with Capitularies of the years 805, 807, 811, see *ibid.*, I, nn. 44, 49, and 73.

83. King Stephen's Laws, aa. i:18, 22b, ii:5.

84. *Ibid.*, a. i:25.

85. See the "Laws for the Cumans," Law I, a. iii, and Law II, aa. 4, 9-10, 12, issued by Ladislas IV "the Cuman" (1272–90) - text in *RHM*, 554ff. and 559ff.; or, Marczali, *Enchiridion*, 175ff. and 178ff.; for background, cf. Károly Szabó, *Kun László* [Ladislas the Cuman] (Budapest, 1886; repr. 1988), 71ff.; Jenő Szűcs, *Az utolsó Árpádok* [The last kings of the House of Árpád] (Budapest, 1993), 301ff., and Kosztolnyik, *Thirteenth Century*, 276ff. and 293ff.

86. King Stephen's Laws, aa. i:14c, 18, 20, 21; aa. ii:3, 4, 5.

87. Cf. Law II of Ladislas I, a.2; Law III, aa. 13 and 21, in Marczali, *Enchiridion*, 93ff. and 97ff.; for background, Kosztolnyik, *From Coloman*, 2 and 4f.; Max Büdinger, *Ein Buch ungarischer Geschichte, 1058–1100* (Leipzig, 1866), 86ff.; A. Huber, "Über die älteste ungarische Verfassung," *MIÖG*, 6 (1885), 385ff.

88. King Stephen's Laws, aa. i:21, ii:5.

89. *Ibid.*, a. i:29.

90. "In rein kirchlicher Beziehung bestand der Klassenunterschied überhaupt nicht. Der Sklave wird also Bruder im Herrn betrachtet und genoss dieselben Gnadenmittel wie der Herr." Cf. Funk – Bihlmeyer, *Kirchengeschichte*, I, 266. Regino, appendix, i:14; Burchard, iii:192; Ivo, Panormia, ii:73, 75. Gratian, Decretum, C. xvii, Q. 4, c. 9.

91. Human behavior will crudely interact: "Raub und Rachsucht, Grausamkeit und rohe Sinnlichkeit, Völlerei und Trunksucht, begünstigt durch die vielen Kriege und politische Wirren, ein weites Feld." Funk – Bihlmeyer, II, 92. Indirectly, E. Mayer, "Der Ursprung der germanischen Gottesurteile," *Historische Vierteljahrschrift*, 20 (1920–21), 289ff.

92. "Die Sklaverei bestand auch im Mittelalter noch vielfach fort. Doch milderte sich das Los der Sklaven bei den geänderten wirtschatflichen Verhältnissen weiter; aus vielen Sklaven und Halbfreien wurden jetzt Hörige und Leibeigene, deren Schutz sich die Kirche besonders angelegen sein liess." Funk – Bihlmeyer, II, 92; see also some "Treuga Dei" decrees of the mid-eleventh century, in *MGH Leg. sect.* IV-1, nn. 419, 421, 422; Martin Bouquet (ed.), *Recueil des historiens des Gaules et de la France*, vol. XI (Paris, 1876), 510f., concerning the Peace and the Truce of God.

93. Cf. Jean Gaudemet, *L'église dans l'empire romain (IVe – Ve siècles)*, 2nd ed. (Paris, 1989), 515ff. and 563ff. For an interpretation of medieval Canon law, see Stephen

Kuttner, *History of Ideas and Doctrines of Canon Law in the Middle Ages* (London, 1992), 1ff.—a 16 page lecture.

94. King Stephen's Laws, aa. i:18, 21, 25, and aa. ii:4-5.

95. *Ibid.*, aa. i:29, *and* i:22b, in that order.

96. *Ibid.*, aa. i:14a and 15.

97. Spufford, 80f.

98. King Stephen's Laws, a. i:27.

99. *Ibid.*, a. i:31 and ii:7.

100. *Ibid.*, a. i:30.

101. The monarch had to take the matter seriously, "...decrevimus puellam parentibus reddi," implying that he had ordered this on his own authority, and with the full consent of the Council—cf. *ibid.*, i:27.

102. On grounds, or, in the interest, of the maintenance of public order, "ut genus utriusque sexus certa lege et absque iniuriis maneat et vigeat," it was the King who had issued the order, "in hoc regale decretum statutum est," —*ibid.*, a. i:30.

103. *Ibid.*, a. i:21a-b.

104. *Ibid.*, aa. i:33 and 34.

105. Compare with art. 54, especially with art. 57 of the resolutions of the Synod of Tarcal during King Coloman the Learned's reign [1095–1116]—for text, cf. Marczali, *Enchiridion*, 104ff.; Kosztolnyik, *From Coloman the Learned*, 50 and 52, and 56, nn. 89-90; Hóman, *Ungarisches Mittelalter*, I, 202; G. J. Simmons, *The Witchcraft World* (New York, 1974), 59ff.

106. King Stephen's Laws, a. i:34; D. Kurze, "Häresie und Minderheit ım Mittelalter, *HZ*, 229 (1979), 529ff.; on *Hexenwahn*, cf. Funk – Bilhmeyer, II, 361. Joseph Gerics, *Egyház, állam és gondolkodás Magyarországon a középkorban* [Church, state (kingdom?) and the manner of thinking in medieval Hungary] (Budapest, 1995), 51ff. and 88ff. In the sixteenth century, Hungary, too, had its share of [popular] witch-trials; cf. Hóman – Szekfü, III, 532ff.

107. King Stephen's Laws, Preface, in Bartoniek, *Szent István törvényei*, 15; Marczali, *Enchiridion*, 69; T. N. Bisson, "Princely nobility in an age of ambitions (c. 1050–1150)," in Anne J. Duggan (ed.), *Nobles and Nobility in Medieval Europe*, (Woodbridge, Suffolk–Rochester, NY, 2000), 101ff.

3. *Non-Magyar Historical Sources on the Establishment of Christianity in Hungary*

108. Cf. Thietmar, vi:2-3; "Epistola Brunonis ad Henricum II, anno 1006," in *MPH*, I, 224. Adalbold of Utrecht (d. 1026) recorded that it was upon Stephen's intercession that Emperor Henry II forgave his brother Bruno—cf. "Vita Heinrici II," cc. 31-32, *MGHSS*, IV, 691. Further, on Stephen's attitude toward prisoners of war, see Thietmar, viii:3 [ix:4]; Stephen had even saved (preserved?) the relics of the church of St. George—cf. "Fundatio ecclesiae s. Albani Namucensis" (dated 1064!), *MGHSS*, XV, 963f.

109. See "Vita Odilonis," i:6 [c. 7], *MPL*, 142, 902.

110. Cf. Rodolphus Glaber (d. 1050), "Francorum historia," iii:1, *MGHSS*, VII, 62.

111. For details, see Wipo's "Gesta Chuonradi II," cc. 22 and 26, in *Wiponis Opera*, 3rd ed., ed. H. Bresslau, SSrG (Hannover, 1915), 41f., and 44f. "Unde meritis

beati viri manifestatum est hoc, ut omnes qui eum invadere vellent, 'Deum qui protector eius est' timerent"—reference to Ps. 17:19, see "Chronicon Hungarico-Polonicum," c. 8, *SSH*, II, 313,17-19.

112. On this, see Aelfredus Anglus, "Geneologia regum Anglorum," *MPL*, 195, cols. 715, and 733; the *Anglo-Saxon Chronicle*, eds. Dorothy Whitelock – David C. Douglas – Susie I. Tucker (New Brunswick, NJ, 1961), anno 1057, MS. "D;" the Florence MS added a note as to why Edward returned to England: "for the king—that is, Edward the Confessor—had determined to make him heir to the kingdom after him," see *ibid.*, 133, n. 6. Margaret, Edward Aetheling's daughter and sister to Christina and Edgar—born to King Stephen's daughter; or, if not (which is unlikely), to a Hungarian noble woman—married, tradition has it, though sources do not bear it out, a widower, King Malcolm III of Scotland. Cf. her "Vita" in *ASS*, Iunii II, 328, and W. Forbes-Leith, *Life of St. Margaret of Scotland by Turgot of St. Andrews*, 3rd ed. (Edinburgh, 1896), 19ff. See also William of Malmesbury, "De rebus gestarum regum Anglorum," ii:180, *MPL*, 179, col. 1157; and Ordericus Vitalis, "Historia ecclesiastica," i:28, *ibid.*, 187, col. 95; or the "Vita Margarithae Scotiae reginae," in *ASS*, Iunii III, 686. For comments on the authors, see Antonia Gransden, *Historical Writing in England, c. 550 to c. 1307* (Ithaca, NY, 1974), 29ff., 166ff., and 151f., in that order.

113. Othlonis "Vita Wolfgangi," c. 13, *MGHSS*, IV, 530f.; Rudolphus Glaber, "Francorum historia," iii:1, *ibid.*, VII, 62.

114. Bruno Verdensis—cf. J. Mabillon, *Acta sanctorum s. Ordini Benedicti*, V, 501f.; and the letters of Emperor Otto I the Great, in *MGH Diplomata regum et imperatorum Germaniae*, ed. Theodor Sickel et al., 10 vols. (Hannover, 1879, etc.), I, 586f.

115. Bruno of Querfurt, his letter to Henry II, dated 1006, in *ÁUO*, I, 15ff.; also, Ademar Cabanensis "Chronicon," *MGHSS*, IV, 130; "Gesta archiepiscoporum Magdeburgensium," *ibid.*, XIV, 391; further, *ibid.*, XV-2, 726; Gaufredus de Bruti, "Chronicon," i:65, *ibid.*, XXVI, 202.

116. Cf. "Vita Adalberti," anno 1004, *ibid.*, IV, 596ff.; Adam Somorjai (ed.), *Kelet–Közép–Európa szentje: Adalbert (Vojtech–Wojciech–Béla)* [A Saint of East-Central Europe: Adalbert] Florence-Budapest, 1994), 7ff.

117. If authentic, the letter, "Epistola Iohannis Smerae ad Wladimirum regis Russorum," anno 990 (?), in *MPL*, 151, col. 1407, would be quite revealing. The author's full name is Iohannes Smere Polovecius, the personal physician [medicus] of Prince Vladimir; cf. Martha Font, *Oroszország, Ukrajna, Rusz: fejezetek a keleti szlávok korai történetéből* [Russia, Ukraine, Rus: Chapters of the History of the Eastern Slavs] (Pécs, 1995), 13ff.

118. See Peter Damian's "Vita Romualdi fundator ordinis Camaldulensium," cc. 28–29, *MGHSS*, IV, 853; and Romuald's Life by Jerome the Hermit, in *ASS*, Febr. II, 134.

119. See Bishop Adalbold's "Vita Heinrici II," cc. 31-32, *MGHSS*, IV, 691; and Annalista Saxo, "Chronicon," anno 1004, *ibid.*, VI, 653.

120. "Historia fundationis coenobii Mellicensis," in H. Pez (ed.), *Scriptores rerum Austricarum*, 3 vols. (Regensburg, 1721–45), cited hereafter as *SSRA*, I, 296; and "Vita Colomanni martyris in Austria," *MGHSS*, IV, 678.

121. *Annales Altahenses maiores*, anno 1033; Ademar Cabanensis, c. 65, *MGHSS*, IV, 145f.; *Könisberger Weltchronik*, ed. W. Giesebrecht, 2nd ed. (Braunschweig, 1877), vol. II, 668ff., anno 1268[!].

122. Hugo Flavicensis "Chronicon," ii:23, *MGHSS*, VIII, 392; and the remarks by Abbot Eberwinus s. Martini Treverensis, in his "Vita s. Symeonis eremitae," *ibid.*, VIII, 210.

123. Bishop Riccardus, Abbot Hugo – Iotsald[us Sylviniacensis], "Vita Odilonis," ii:12, *MPL*, 142, col. 924; on the twenty-four canons from Verdun, see "Gesta episcoporum Virdunensium," *MGHSS*, X, 486.

124. On the uprising, see Kosztolnyik, *Five Kings*, 68ff., and *idem*, "The Negative Results of the Enforced Missionary Policy of King Stephen I of Hungary: The Uprising of 1046," *Catholic Historical Review*, 59 (1973–74), 569ff.; Sándor Tóth, "Levente és András" [Levente and Andrew], *Acta historica Szegediensis*, 82 (1985), 31ff.

125. *Annales Altahenses maiores*, anno 1046; Hóman, *Ungarisches Mittelalter*, I, 256ff.; Kosztolnyik, *Five Kings*, 72ff.

126. Cf. *Annales Altahenses maiores*, anno 1041; Ekkehardus Uraugiensis "Chronicon," anno 1038, *MGHSS*, VI, 195; Hugo Flaviniacensis "Chronicon," ii:16, *ibid.*, VIII, 392; Bernoldus s. Blasii "Chronicon," anno 1083, *ibid.*, V, 439; "Annales Mellicenses," anno 1038, *ibid.*, IX, 12; Adalbert of Babenberg, "Vita Henrici II," i:29-30, called him a religious king, "Deo devotus"—*ibid.*, IV, 810. The most Christian monarch, *claris* in his deeds and virtues he had been, wrote Sigfridus de Balnhusin, "Historia," c. 140, *ibid.*, XXV, 695; see further, "Corpus chronicorum Bononiensium II," anno 1024, in Muratori, *RISS*, XVII-1, 455.

127. Cf. "Notitia de bello, quod erat inter Henricum I et Hungaros, anno 933," *Forschungen zur deutschen Geschichte*, 15 (1875), 652; "Legenda ss. Marini et Aniani vetusta," *MGHSS*, XV-2, 1070; also, Ordericus Vitalis, vii:1, *MPL*, 188, col. 510. István Bóna, *A magyarok és Európa a 9–10 században* [The Magyars and Europe during the ninth and tenth centuries] (Budapest, 2000), 36ff.

128. The German chronicler's "defense" of the anti-Hungarian military action by Conrad II, in "Chronicon imperatorum Augustanum," anno 1030, *MGHSS*, XIII, 263; "Gesta abbatum Trudonensium, cont. III," i:2, c. 10, *ibid.*, X, 382; and Ptolemaeus Lucensis "Historia ecclesiastica," xvi:35, and xvii:2, in Muratori, *RISS*, XI, 1026, and 1031.

129. See "Vita s. Eberhardi ex comite Nelleburgensi," c. 1, *ASS*, Apr. I, 667.

130. *...de landgravis Thuringiae factus monachus*, who died about 1045—cf. "Vita b. Guntheri eremitae," by Wolfher, cc. 4–5, *MGHSS*, XI, 27.

131. Also by Wolfher, "Vita Godehardi," bishop of Hildesheim, c. 9, *ibid.*, XI, 202, and in *Acta sanctorum Ungariae* ex Bollandi et al., ...excerpta, 2 vols. (Tyrnaviae, 1743-44), II, 73ff., in the appendix.

132. Cf. *ASS*, Iunii V, 82.

133. Cf. Luiz [Luys] Vaz de Camões, *Os Lusiadas* (Lisboa, 1626), carm. iii, str. 23-25; Hungarian translation by Gyula Greguss, *Camoens Luzidája*, 2nd ed. (Budapest, 1874), 100f.; the Penguin English translation by W. C. Atkinson, *The Lusiads*, canto iii (London, 1952), 81f.

134. Kosztolnyik, *Thirteenth Century*, 28f., and 35, nn. 48-49.

135. See "Annales s. Crucis Polonici," *MGHSS*, XIX, 678; *MPH*, III, 61, and *ibid.*, III, 300; "Chronica Iohannis de Gwerche archidiaconi Goriciensis," *MHSM*, VII, 471ff.

136. Cf. Gyula Moravcsik (ed.), *Fontes Byzantini historiae Hungaricae aevo ducum et regum ex stirpe Árpád descendentium: Az Árpád-kori magyar történet bizánci forrásai* (Budapest, 1984), 80f.; Bálint Hóman, "Szent István görög oklevele" [King St.

Stephen's Greek-language document], *Századok*, 51 (1917), 99ff., and 225ff.; and the Life of Blessed [now Saint] Margaret of Hungary, c. 12, *SSH*, II, 689.

137. Cf. Martinus Oppaviensis "Chronicon pontificum," *MGHSS*, XXII, 433; on his "martyr" death—*Annales Hildesheimenses*, ed. G. Waitz, SSrG (Hannover, 1878; repr. 1947), anno 1031.

138. Thietmar, iv:38 [59]; Herimann Augiensis "Chronicon," anno 1038, *MGHSS*, V, 123; "Catalogus archiepiscoporum et episcoporum Laureacensis et Pataviensis ecclesiarum," in A. Rauch (ed.), *Rerum Austricarum Scriptores*, 3 vols. (Vienna, 1793–1794), cited hereafter as *RASS*, II, 473f.

139. Abbot Martin of Vienna named ten bishoprics and two more that established, he had assumed, by King Ladislas I. They were the dioceses [in Latin] Strigoniensis, Colocensis, Waradiensis, Albensis, Alba regalis, Quinqueecclesiensis, Nitriensis, Tzanadiensis, Iauriensis, Variensis, Zagrebiensis, Agriensis; cf. Pez, *SSRA*, II, 667; also, "Exhortatio b. Augustini Lucerini," cc. 19–42, in *ASS*, Aug. I, 297.

140. Cf. Albertus Trium Fontium, "Chronicon," anno 1006, *MGHSS*, XXIII, 779; also, "Gesta pontificum Leodiensium," ii:71, *ibid.*, XXV, 69; Andreas Dandalo, "Chronicon Venetum," xi:1,46, in Muratori, *RISS*, XII, 233.

141. Fraknói, *Magyarország és a Szentszék*, I, 359, n. 39; Aventinus, "Annales Boiorum," in Cisneros, *Aventini Annales*, 403; Lhotsky, *Quellenkunde*, 173.

142. "S. Ungarorum R et Gisla, dilecta sibi coniunx, mittunt haec munera domno apostolico Iohannis..."—cf. *Neues Archiv der Gesellschaft für ältere deutsche Geschichte*, 7 (1882), 220f.; compare with entry in "Libellus de antiqua s. Petri apostoli basilica in Vaticano," iv:114, *ASS*, Iun. VII, suppl. 72*.

143. Abbot Martin, in *SSRA*, II, 664; Dandalo, ix:2,1, *RISS*, XII, 235.

144. Leo Marsicanus, "Chronica monasterii Casinensis," ii:65, *MGHSS*, VII, 674; also, "Vita Odilonis," i:6 [7], *MPL*, 142, col. 924; further, "Epistola Fulberti ad Bonipertum episcopum," *ibid.*, 141, col. 189f.

145. "Fundatio ecclesiae s. Albani Namucensis," *MGHSS*, XV-2, 963f.; "Annales necrologici Fuldenses, a. 1038, *ibid.*, XIII, 212; "Libri et anniversariorum, et necrologium monasterii S. Galli," *MGH* Necr. I, 466.

146. Thietmar, iv:38 [59]; Annalista Saxo, anno 999, *MGHSS*, VI, 644; Hartvic, c. 9.

147. Matthias de Michowia, "Chronica Polonorum," ii:11, anno 1041, Ioannes Pistorius (ed.), *Polonicae historiae corpus*, 3 vols. (Basileae, 1582), cited hereafter as Pistorius, II, 28.

148. *Annales Altahenses maiores*, anno 1033, 1034—though his reference to Prince Emery's canonization (the deceased son of King Stephen), was premature—cf. *ibid.*, 19, n. 5.

149. King Stephen's Laws, a. ii:17—though not in the Admont MS!—Bartoniek, 41; Marczali, *Enchiridion*, 79, and n. 57.

150. "Hagensche Chronik," ii:202, in *MGHSS*, ling. vernac. VI-2, 87.

151. *Annales Altahenses maiores*, anno 1041; Albericus Trium Fontium, "Chronica," anno 1041, *MGHSS*, XXIII, 786.

152. Schritovinus, Rauch, *RASS*, II, 474; "Collactanea historica," in *Monumenta Boic*, XVI, 550f.; "Acta Giselae," *Acta sanctorum Ungariae*, II, 45ff., appendix.

153. Cf. Herimann Augiensis "Chronicon," anno 995 (!), *MGHSS*, V, 117f.; "Chronicon Leodiense breve," anno 1024, *ibid.*, XVI, 682; Ekkehardi "Chronicon," anno 1001 (!), *ibid.*, VI, 192; "Gesta ponitificum Leodensium," ii:71, *ibid.*, XXV, 69.

154. Wrote Albericus in his "Chronicon," anno 1006; he noted that he had based his information on a *Hungarian* source, see *ibid.*, XXIII, 779.

155. *Annales Altahenses maiores*, anno 1038, though the *Annales Marbacenses*, place it anno 1039, and so does the "Annales Cistercensium in Heinrichow," *MGHSS*, XIX, 544; the "Annales necrologici Fuldenses," quote the year 1038, cf. *ibid.*, XIII, 212, and so did Herimann Augiensis in his "Chronicon," anno 1038, *ibid.*, V, 123, and Bernoldus monachus s. Blasii, "Chronicon," *ibid.*, V, 425. Further, Ekkehardus Uraugiensis "Chronicon," *ibid.*, VI, 195; "Annales Mellicenses," *ibid.*, IX, 498; "Chronicon Salisburgense," *ibid.*, IX, 772. One source quoted the year 1043 as the time of his earthly death—cf. *ibid.*, XVI, 202.

156. The "Annales Cracowienses," *ibid.*, XIX, 587.

157. His "Notulae anecdotae..." edited by Chrysostomus Hanthaler (Krems, 1742), 108, though Hanthaler's work is, as noted above, unreliable. See Michael Tangl, "Die Fälschungen des Chrysostomus Hanthaler," *MIÖG*, 19 (1898), 1ff.; Lhotsky, *Quellenkunde*, 199f.

158. "Kaiserchronik," anno 1147, *MGH ling. vern.*, I, 376f.

159. Vincent of Prague, "Annales Bohemorum," anno 1158, *MGHSS*, XVII, 667.

160. Bishop Vincentius Kadlubek of Cracow, "Chronica Polonorum," iv:18, *MPH*, II, 420f.; on King Béla III, cf. Kosztolnyik, *From Coloman*, 200ff.

161. Canon of Wishegrad, "Continuatio Chronicae Cosmae Pragensis," anno 1137, *MGHSS*, IX, 143; and Iohannes de Marignola, "Chronica," *Fontes rerum Bohemorum*, III, 560.

162. Cosmas of Prague, "Chronica Bohemorum," anno 1008, *MGHSS*, IX, 64; "Annalium Polonorum fragmenta," *MPH*, VI, 678.

163. Andreas Dandalo, "Chronicon Venetum," i:46, *RISS*, XII, 234; "Historia monasterii Leodiensis," Martene – Durand, IV, 1046. Further, the Parsch Annals, *MGHSS*, XVI, 601.

164. "Chronicon mixtum," *MPH*, I, 510; "Annales Argentinenses maiores," lib. X, *MGHSS*, XVII, 154; Albertus Milioli, "Liber e temporibus," c. 144, *ibid.*, XXXI, 358; *RISS*, IX, 323.

165. "Miracula Guntherii eremitae," *ASS*, Oct. IV, 1074; Martinus Gallus, "Chronica Polonorum," iii:25, *MGHSS*, IX, 476; Matthias de Michowia, "Chronica Polonorum," iii:12, in the Polish source collection by Pistorius, II, 54. Further, see entry by Johann Dlugoss, "Excerpta..." under the year 1130, in *MPH*, IV, 11.

166. Bernoldus s. Blasii "Chronicon," anno 1083, *MGHSS*, V, 439; Adam of Bremen, *Gesta Hammaburgensis ecclesiae ponitificum*, ed. B. Schmeidler, SSrG, 3rd ed. (Hannover, 1917), ii:43.

167. On the Holy Dexter, see the remarks made by Bishop Augustine of Lucerne [episcopus Lucerini], in his "Exhortatio," cc. 19-42, in *ASS*, Aug. I, 297.

168. "Vita b. Margarithae," by Peter Ranzano, ii:11, in *ASS*, Ian. III, 523; and "Vita Stanislai Cracoviensis episcopi," *MPH*, IV, 392.

VII

Law and the King

1. The Influence of Canon Law on Hungarian Laws in the Eleventh Century

> Stephanus...statutum a se decretum mani-
> festum fecit.
>
> Hartvic, *Vita s. Stephani regis*, c.10

It was not the intention of King Saint Stephen of Hungary to codify the whole body of Hungarian customary laws, but rather to identify and deal satisfactorily with legal questions related to the new public order he had established that could not otherwise be clarified by Hungarian *consuetudines*. King Stephen I (977–1038) followed western examples in enacting legislation upon advice he had received from his counselors. In his legislative process, counselors—especially high churchmen advising him in church matters—played and important role; therefore, several of his legislators provided information on the public-legal status of the Church and ecclesiastics and ecclesiastic properties.

A definite west-Frankish and German influence can be discerned in the two books of the Laws of the monarch that had been preserved in the twelfth century Admont codex, MS 712, in Austria, and in many of his political-institutional innovations. Nevertheless, King Stephen also considered Hungarian customary law. For instance, the ancient Magyar blood-money system, and given elements of ancient property laws (which, incidentally, could not be identified with German, or Slavic legal customs). He did not introduce new western-Latin law in his acts of legislation, nor did he want to substitute or replace established "pagan" Magyar customary law. His legislative replace established "pagan" Magyar customary law. His legislative acts were mainly ecclesiastical directives that also partly protected his person and royal properties, partly secured domestic peace. King Stephen had legislated for his people, *nostrae statuimus genti*; his laws were royal acts of legislation.

King Stephen's laws ordered proper legal relations between royal officials and people, and related to the non-Hungarian ethnic folk stratum, whose members maintained a special private legal relationship with the monarch. Citations that illustrate this point include article i:22, which guaranteed personal freedom and security, and articles i:6-7, which regulated property rights, or further enactments dealing with the common good, and included the private personnel on the royal domain. This is clear from articles i:23-24 (that, again, were not borrowed from foreign sources), and was extended over servants (or, slaves) of the free stratum of the population.

The first clause of King Stephen's Laws determining the status of ecclesiastical properties in the realm, may be cited as an example of western-Latin influence upon his legislation. Article i:1 is nearly identical with art. 6 of the 847 synod of Mainz, and shows great similarity with entries ii:89, and ii:407 of the collection comprising official royal and imperial writs, and known as Benedictus Levita (pseudonym!). In Hungary, *royal* legislative acts guaranteed the untouchable judicial status of ecclesiastical property, buildings and libraries, as it is evident from art. ii:1 of Stephen's Laws. It is important to know about Benedictus Levita that the collection served common ecclesiastical interests: "sanctae Dei ecclesiae servorumque eius atque totius Christiani populi," defended church lands, and regarded every donation that had been made to the Church as gifts given to God: "Domino indubitanter consecrantur, et ad ius pertinent sacerdotum."

Art. i:2 of king Stephen's Laws which defined the authority of Hungarian bishops in ecclesiastical matters, and in matters of their co-operation with secular lords, is identical with art. 7 of the 847 Synod of Mainz. It is also similar in content to a letter attributed to Pope Evaristus preserved in the Pseudo-Isidor collection, which said that it was the bishops and priests who were the leaders of the Christian community. "Sacerdotes vice Christi legatione feunguntur." Likewise, art. i:3 of King Stephen's Laws, that determined who could bring charges against a bishop, or an ecclesiastic, may remind one of entries

23, and 72-74 of the "Càpitula Angilramni," a letter of 785 by Pope Adrian's writ shows some similarity with entries 2, and 4-5 of a writ by Pope Sylvester I, also preserved in Pseudo-Isidor, and with a decree of a likely nature of the 868 Synod of Worms. Archbishop Hincmar of Reims' *De presbiteris ciminabis*, entries 21 and 24, reflected an identical concept.

King Stephen's Laws, art. i:4-5, whether a lay person could bear witness against a clergyman—functions of the clergy—are reminiscent of entry nine of a second letter attributed to Pope Evaristus, and of decree iii:462 in the Benedictus Levita collection. Stephen's art. i:4 must have been influenced by the 888 Synod of Mainz, c. 12. By comparing texts, it can be concluded that Stephen's articles i:3-4 imitated the style of composition of Pseudo-Isidor.

On the other hand, it may cause some problems that in the mid-fifteen century "Thuróczy codex," printed by St. L. Endlicher, and Henrik Marczali, and in the sixteenth century "Ilosvay codex," printed by J. P. Migne, Stephen's articles i:3-4 correspond to *one* decree (art. i:3); furthermore, instead of the division in two books (libri), and the numbering of articles as preserved in the Admont codex, Migne, in accordance with the Ilosvay codex, printed one book of laws in fifty-five articles.

To cite some examples, the text of Stephen's art. i:14, dealing with murder and murderers, in Ilosvay – Migne corresponds to articles i:16 *and* 13, and leaves out a middle entry, what would happen to the murderer of a servant, recorded as art. i:14 in the Admont manuscript. Furthermore, the Ilosvay – Migne text completely disregards art. i:16 (in the Admont codex) which forbade drawing of a sword by anyone during a confrontation (over a personal matter); it further omits art. i:21 of Admont, which determined what would happen if someone emancipated another person's servant(s) from slavery, albeit with good intentions but limited foresight.

In the twelfth century Admont codex that preserved the text of King Stephen's Laws—or, its transcript that could also be regarded as a detailed outline—Book Two of the laws consisted of fifteen articles. On the other hand, the text editions of 1849 [1931] (*RHM*), 1901 (Marczali), and 1904 (Zàvodszky), that were further based upon the Thuróczy codex; and, the printed Ilosvay – Migne text, provide six additional articles placed between articles ii:13 and ii:14 of the

Admont text. With the additional of the six articles the second book grew to a total of twenty-one articles in the published editions.

The contents and stylistic composition of articles i:1-5, 6, 7, 8, 9, 10, 11, 12 (13) of King Stephen's Laws follow the resolutions of the Bavarian laws, *Lex Baiuwariorum*. Stephen's art. ii:6 (Migne, cc. 39-40), and art. ii:17 (Migne, c. 41), dealing with servants and freemen who had turned into thieves, may be traced back to art. ix of the Bavarian laws; and, the last article of Stephen's Laws, ii:21 (in Admont, art. ii:15; in Ilosvay – Migne, c. 55), which said that in cases of robbery a condemned thief cannot serve as a witness in a court trial, also reflects art. ix of the Bavarian law.

Art. i:10 (Migne, c. 11) encourage the keeping of Ember Days, and corresponds to c. 4 of Charlemagne's Capitulary of Paderbrunn; art. i:17 (Migne, c. 15) deals with the breaching of one's oath, mirrors c. 10 of the "Capitulare Francium." Art. i:26, on protecting widows and orphans, and art. i:27, on capturing young women, together with art. i:31, on the capture of married women (Ilosvay – Migne, cc. 24-25, and 29), once again, are reminiscent of art. of the Bavarian Laws. King Stephen's art. i:32, on setting fire on purpose, and the one who did it, may be referred to art. x of the Bavarian Laws. The scriptural quote, "Omnes unanimes estote," in art. i:35 (Ilosvay – Migne, c. 33), on the guarantee of domestic peace, that mirrors art. xi of the Bavarian laws, corresponds, in part, to 1 Peter, 3:8, and, to a lesser extent, to Paul's Letter to the Philippians, 2:2, though, as if the compiler-scribe of the Hungarian laws had not been quoting from the Vulgate.

King Stephen's art. ii:1 (Ilosvay – Migne, c. 34), which dealt with church tithe, and donations for the Church, could be related to c. 15 of Charlemagne's Paderbrunn Capitulary of 785. Art. ii:2, which dealt with the inheritance of royal land grants, making a distinction between private lands and those of the royal domain, and determining who would inherit them, corresponds to articles i:6 and 7 as cited above; those enactments clarified contemporary proprietorial and inheritance rights, and defined the very nature of a royal land-grant. "Consensimus, …ut unusquisque dominetur propriorum similiter et donorum regis, dum vivit, excepto quod ad episcopatum pertinenter comitatum."

In other words, in Hungary of the early eleventh century, various free landholdings had existed: a) the perpetual and undivided free holdings of the *gentes*; b) the royal land grants that involved military obligations on part of the grantee, and would be inherited only by the direct file: male line; c) purchased land that, according to art. i:16, was regarded as private land. Simultaneously, art. i:7, cited above, stressed the undisturbed nature of the king's private domain; it stated that while the king gave full property rights of ownership to the grantee, who was the king's subject, the latter recognized the possessory rights of the monarch over (his) domain. It calls for attention that art. ii:2 had been enacted by King Stephen with the consensus of the whole Senate, *petitioni totius senatus*, without directly imitating any "foreign" example.

The conclusion of art. ii:2 which warned that anyone who threatened the life of the monarch, or committed treason toward the realm, deserved capital punishment, must have been a later addition made during the tumultuous times following the death of the great monarch. The law, which Hartvic noted in his "Life of King St. Stephen," punished conspiracy against the king exclusively by blinding. The addition prescribing the death penalty may be further extended by art. ii:17 (not in the Admont manuscript; only the Thuróczy and Ilosvay codices carry it, the latter as c. 51), that discussed conspiracy against the king and the realm. However, art. ii:17 only stated that the conspirator seeking refuge in a church must not find it there, and must be excommunicated, and it is similar to c. 5 of the 847 Synod of Mainz. (Of the added provisions, art. ii:18 [Ilosvay – Migne, c. 52], concerning the church tithe, referred to the 785 Paderbrunn Capitulary, c. 17.)

Articles ii:6 and 7 (Ilosvay – Migne, cc. 39-40, and c. 41) of the Hungarian laws discussing theft committed by freemen and servants, are reminiscent of art. ix of the Bavarian laws, while the last clause in the Hungarian code, art. ii:21 (in the Admont MS, art. ii:15; in Ilosvay – Migne, c. 55), regarding the condemned thief who could testify in a case before a court of law, further points to art. ix of the Bavarian law code.

The anonymous compiler of King Stephen's Laws also relied upon the canon law collection known as *Decretum* by Bishop Burchard of Worms, once widely received on German soil. For example, the concept of Burchard stating the king's judicial jurisdiction rested on divine right—*Decretum*, vii:44—in criminal cases created a lasting influence upon the laws of the first Hungarian monarch. As it was the obligation of the state to control evil, punish the bad, and support the just (*ibid.*, xv:38-43; xvi:25-29), subordinate worldly powers to divine law (*ibid.*, i:2, 10; xv:8, 10); the question of emancipation of slaves (*ibid.*, iii:189), in accordance with Regino of Prüm's "Collection" of ecclesiastical directives, entry i:367; only a freed servant (or, slave) could be ordained to the priesthood (Burchard, ii:21), again following Regino of Prüm, entry i:391; furthermore, Burchard's thesis, *Decretum*, i:42, that decrees arrived at ecclesiastical synods had to have papal sanction to gain validity. This influence is evident from articles i:1-2, i:6-7 and ii:17 upon the laws of the first Christian Hungarian monarch.

Burchard's impact upon the Laws of King Stephen is even more remarkable, because in his *Decretum*, art. i:3, Burchard merely treated the Roman See as "Primae sedis episcopatus," while Stephen's law books did not mention the Roman Pontiff. Furthermore, Burchard's other entries influenced the laws of the Hungarian king. This is shown in art. i:84-86, where he emphasized the importance of episcopal juris- diction; articles i:133, and i:141-44, where he explained that only God can pass judgement over bishops, therefore, a layman could not bear testimony against a bishop, art. i:167; and art. xvi:7-8, which deter- mined who could testify against a clergyman. In a similar manner, Burchard's concept of the Church, art. iii:1, and that a church could be built with the (local) bishops' permission, art. iii:6; or, ecclesiastical property cannot be wasted, art. ii:9, and Mass only be said at a proper location, art. iii:36-38, had another impact upon Hungarian legislation, as witnessed by King Stephen's laws, articles i:1-2, 3-4, and ii:2.

Numerous decrees of Burchard's *Decretum*, as, for instance, art. xi:2 on the role of bishops; art. xv defining a bishop's spiritual authority; the directives given for Lent, and how to punish those who did not observe Lent, art. xiii:7, 8, and 10; further, false testimony given in a court of law, art. xvi:12, 16-18, or art. xvii:8-9, had also exerted influence in King Stephen's legislation.

The bloody pagan uprisings following King Stephen's death led to the intervention the German Henry III had so unwillingly under- taken in Hungary (the German monarch even went as far as to give "Bavarian" laws to the Hungarians in 1044). Following his corona- tion, King Andrew I of the House of Árpád (1046–60) recognized anew that validity of King Stephen's Laws. "Precepit itaque universe genti sue, ut…et in omnibus secundum legem illam viverent, quam sanctus rex Stephanus eos docuerat," recorded the chronicler of the *Chronicon pictum*. Probably, the text of the "Ecclesiastical Constitution" printed by J. P. Migne, who had copied it from J. D. Mansi, who in turn followed Carolus Péterffy's collection, attributed to King Andrew I, was based on this sentence of the chronicler, on the grounds that there is no trace of the "Constitution" in the Royal Register. It must have been a clever seventeenth century forgery.

The sentence taken from the chronicle was based upon reliable sources of information, and may prove that King Stephen's Laws had taken root in royal court circles of the late 1040's. On the other hand, it is evident from articles 2 and 21 of the *Third* law code attributed to King Ladislas I (1077–95)—though, probably referring to the political turmoil of the 1060's—that King Stephen's Laws could only be enforced by draconic measures. It is evident from the laws that King Stephen had in fact eliminated the traditional tribal order in domestic politics, as if to emphasize his idea that only the monarch had room to maneuver around for administrative powers.

Stephen's laws completely ignored the inherited power structure formerly held by the tribal chiefs; in the *new* order every free Magyar came under the jurisdiction of the king, who had replaced the former tribal organizations with a new cadre of royal officials such the royal *comes, comites*, in a centralized administration. In art. i:21 he drew a distinction between the *maiores natu* and the *maiores dignitatu*, just as in art. i:21, he spoke of *dives* and *pauper*, or drew the line between *liber* and *servus* (art. i:14, 22, 28-29), and officially set the amount of "blood money" in court cases accordingly (art. i:14). This arrangement for a unified royal government extended over all phases of public life and lasted until the end of the century, under Coloman the Learned, when the king's subjects asked for an active role in the exercise of governmental powers.

Besides the two books of laws the monarch also left behind Admonitions for his son and heir. "Libellum de instituitione morum conposuit," remarked Hartvic, King Stephen's biographer, neatly borrowing a sentence from King Stephen's *Vita maior*. The book(let) of *Admonitiones* in ten articles is a mirror for royalty that, in its concept and composition, shows great similarity with the letter the little known Latin monk Cathulfus wrote to Charlemagne warning him to both fear and love God because he stood before his subjects as the vicar of God. (The second place was held by the bishop, who represented Christ.) The same concept was also expressed by Archbishop Hincmar of Reims, who wrote that the earthly ruler was, "vice sua," representing the Almighty.

The introduction of the Admonitions warned the heir of the throne to remember that he was ruling by the grace of God. He must direct his mind in accordance with divine command, unless he wanted to meet the fate of King Salomon of the Old Testament. The heir must adhere to the Christian faith, confess the divine Creed without fear, and defend the Church, whose dignity he must not diminish. The order of bishops was the glory of the king's throne; if his bishops supported him, he had nothing to fear. Were he forced to reprimand was not effective, a redressing was necessary. He also needed the support and loyalty of the princes, barons, reeves, knights and nobles, so he must treat them as he were to treat his father or sons. He must treat them well, never degrade them to servant status. He must be peaceful, and an honest judge. He must not become a tyrant. He must accept foreigners settling down among his people, because they can serve him and the country well. Weak is the kingdom where only one language and one set of customs were to prevail; "nam unius lingue uniusque moris regnum fragile et ibecille est."

Without the royal council, the monarch can neither govern nor defend his country's interests from its enemies. Only with the support of the Council can he stand up to his domestic opponents, and establish towns. Therefore, he must not choose irrational greedy individuals as his counselors, rather noblemen and elders worthy of trust and respect. Let the youth excel in the art of arms, and the elders in the king's council. The ruler had to follow the ancients' example, and to pay attention to the warning of his fathers. One could not govern Latins by Greek laws, nor Greeks by Roman custom. Consequently, the heir ought to imitate his father's habits, and earn his people's loving trust. The ninth and tenth articles of the Admonitions encouraged the royal heir to pray earnestly to God and to preserve in developing Christian virtues.

King Stephen's Admonitions are reminiscent of the writings of Jonas of Orleans, the books of similar nature by Hincmar of Reims, and especially of the manual written by Dhouda, the wife of Bernard of Septmania, the treasurer of Louis the Pious, had addressed to her son who, at the time of her writing, had been held a political prisoner. This *Liber manualis* is a lasting document of parental love and worry, in which the mother, herself in dire need, encouraged her child (who, at the time the book was written, was still the expectant heir of the family wealth), to love his fellow men.

The individual who had actually authored the Admonitions undoubtedly knew the literature of his age including the work by Bishop Jonas of Orleans, *De institutione regia*, which contained the resolutions of the 829 Synod of Paris, without attaching an ideological annotations to them. The book by Jonas was the first work of political nature written in western Latin Europe. It was to the author's merit that he had accurately determined the outlook and political views of the Christian society. He had separated the king's sphere of action from the functions of a priest: it was the clergy that had formed the concept of Christian society, therefore, the question could not even be raised whether secular power could claim control over ecclesiastics, or over church goods. According to Jonas, the synodical acts had determined the unity of society of his age—"quod universalis sancta Dei ecclesia *unum corpus* eiusque caput Christus est"—according to Saint Paul's Letter to the Romans, 12, 4.

The same concept prevailed in the first three articles of King Stephen's Admonitions, as if the author, recording the ideas of the king, had addressed himself to a Hungarian intelligentsia, wanting to shape and organize its social structure. As in his laws and Admonitions, the monarch stressed the role of the hierarchy in administrative politics, but omitting any mention of the Roman See. The Hungarian court and Hungarian intelligentsia (consisting of both clergy and laymen in the 1030's) were aware of the plight of the papacy at that time, when no Sylvester II sat on the throne of Saint Peter, and the court tried hard to differentiate itself from the political leadership that prevailed in Rome.

A similar situation had existed in the ninth century; that was why Archbishop of Hincmar of Reims and Bishop Jonas of Orleans placed such an emphasis upon the role bishops had to play in the formation of a European community that rested on the foundation laid by Charlemagne. In this society, Hincmar wrote, the law was not written for the honest people, but for criminals, and when a ruler breached the law, he was condemned (on the grounds that he, by breaking the law, became a tyrant). According to the Archbishop of Reims, knowledge of the law had to be well spread throughout society; the king and the clergy must legislate together to lay the judicial foundation that formed the base of the social fabric that governed the lives and the future of the inhabitants of the region.

Abbot Smaragdus' opinion that the ruler must not tolerate slavery is also reflected in King Stephen's Admonitions. The impact of Sedulius Scotus' idea that the conscientious ruler would invite elderly and wise individuals into his council, and would not undertake any action without them (while the weak and unworthy ruler would only consider the temporary benefits), may clearly be evident from the seventh decree of the Admonitions. Likewise, Sedulius' argument that the monarch govern his people rationally, and place his trust in God, and not in himself, nor in the strength of his armed forces when facing his enemy, helped determine the sixth decree of the Admonitions. The monarch must remember that he held his commission from God; the servant of the Almighty was he, who ruled equally over both clerics and lay people.

At the end of the century, in the days of King Ladislas I (1077–95), firm royal iron will was still needed to enforce the laws. The compiler of this segment of the *Chronicon pictum*, c. 131, cited contemporary sources, and rendered a brief report of the legislative activity of the king. The so-called second law book of King Ladislas was probably enacted during the 1070's, or in the early 1080's, because it dealt with lawless domestic turmoil that had endangered one's personal freedom, or private property, handed down the death penalty to the thief who stole anything priced higher that the value of a chicken; it punished the border reeve who had allowed forbidden chattel, as, for example, horses, or other taxable goods to be taken abroad without a written permit, toll-free. Were a cleric to be accused of theft, or of a (any) crime, the bishop's court would handle the case. Small wonder that the decrees of King Ladislas' *second book* of laws were enacted by the secular lords of the realm, not in the king's presence. But the monarch himself has held a legislative church synod at Szabolcs in 1092: "In citivate Szabolch sancta synodus habita est, praesidente Christianissimo Ungarorum rege Ladislao," where bishops, abbots and nobles (*iobagiones*) had met with the monarch, and their resolutions had been approved by the people. It meant that the assembly (mixed synod) served both religious and secular interests. The expressed purpose of the synod was to expand the laws of King *Saint* Stephen, and to apply them anew. (It was during the reign of King Ladislas that King Stephen I had been canonized in the year 1083.)

The Synod of Szabolcs formulating ecclesiastical themes, cited the reform spirit of Pope Gregory VII, with the aid of the "Collection of Seventy-Four Titles" of Canon law that had been prepared in Rome in about 1050, under the pontificate of Leo IX. (Although this "Collection" may be looked upon as a kind of introduction to Burchard's Decretals, its tone of firm support of papal prerogatives almost downgrades the by then almost four decade old Burchardian collection.) Since celibacy had not, as yet, struck roots among the Hungarian clergy, the synod had ordered that a clergyman could be married once, but only to a virgin, and could not marry for a second time.

King Ladislas' legislative acts at Szabolcs—known as Ladislas I's First Book of Laws, *Decretum* I—aimed at centralization in church business, royal administrative matters, the countrywide administration of justice, and of the economy. The Ishmaelites had to be baptized (art. 9); a Jew was not allowed to marry a Christian woman, nor could he employ a Christian maid (art. 10); it dealt gently with persons who still had been following pagan religious customs (art. 22). In art. 41, that redefined the payment of church tithe, the synod made it clear that wool and linen production flourished in the country. At the same time, the legislators could not avoid references to earlier western legislative examples. Thus, Szabolcs, art. 6, again reminds one of the 847 Synod of Mainz, c. 8, and 11 actually refer to c. 12 of the 1078 Synod in Rome; Szabolcs, art. 10, is in harmony with Meaux, 845, entry 72, just as Szabolcs, articles 17-18, and 16 in a like manner correspond to cc. 50 and 73 of the 845 Synod of Meaux.

Szabolcs, articles 2 and 4, lean upon the resolutions of the 1090 Synod held at Amalfi. In ecclesiastical matters, Szabolcs, articles 1-2, and 5 emphasized the rights and privileges, spheres of activity for bishops and abbots; the jurisdictions of the latter were redefined by the mid-eleventh century "Collection of Seventy-Four Titles" that, facing the reality of the age, proscribed a unified, centralized ecclesiastic administration under aegis of the Roman pontiff. The Roman See was able to assert centralized church policy during the pontificate of Leo IX.

On the other hand, the Hungarian king had no need for papal centralization efforts in church matters of his country during the last decade of the century. In view of the then contemporary politics, Pope Urban II did not possess the necessary political base for forcefully asserting his position in the early 1090's. The First Crusade had only been announced in 1095. As King Ladislas himself wrote to the Abbot of Montecassino, he had to pursue politics contrary to papal intent and interests in his secular diplomacy. His diplomatic moves did not prevent him from supporting church and clerical reforms, however. He had expected that the spiritually renewed, and intellectually prepared Hungarian clergy would also become a pillar of royal support. Without strong papal leadership, the Church in Hungary needed a firm royal hand to guide it, especially when it became clear that Ladislas I would inherit the Croatian throne. Pope Urban II, not being sufficiently aware of Hungarian inner politics, underestimated the king's domestic situation and demand that Ladislas I become, as Croatian king, a papal vassal. Understandably, Ladislas held a different point of view, and did not comply with the papal demand.

In taking a diplomatic anti-Urban II stand Ladislas did not want to lose the support of the Hungarian clergy, especially the confidence and trust of the hierarchy; therefore, in almost direct contradiction to the articles of the "Collection of Seventy-Four Titles," the King had ordered that, in his county, any ecclesiastical initiative begin with the monarch—or bear his seal of approval, as evidenced by the decrees of Szabolcs, articles 1-2. By taking such a stand, King Ladislas I was able to ascertain that the laws of King Saint Stephen, and the institution of an independent kingship had struck deep roots in the Hungarian public consciousness at the end of the eleventh century.

The impact of Burchard of Worms' *Decretum*, or, rather, of the "Collection of Seventy-Four Titles" from the mid-eleventh century upon the legislation of King Ladislas, and the influence upon— sometimes with almost the exact identical wording of earlier western Latin church decrees—Hungarian laws did not only prove that in Hungary of the eleventh century Latin church laws had exercised a lasting impact, but also that the kingdom of King Saint Stephen had really become an active member of western Latin Christendom.

As Pope Urban II had admonished Ladislas' nephew and successor, Coloman the Learned of Hungary (1095–1116)—a former bishop himself who, by his own admission, "prefati regis sancti memoriae, Stephani lege, textum recensuit"—his Serenity ought to remember the faith of Saint Stephen, who was the first of his dynasty to accept the religious beliefs of the Church of Rome; "reminiscat serenitas tua religiosi principis Stephani, qui generis tui primus a sancta Romana Ecclesia fidei religionem suscepit."

Notes

The literature of the historical background of the period was discussed by Domonkos Kosári (ed.), *Bevezetés a magyar történelem irodalmába* [An introduction to Hungarian historical bibliography], 3 vols. (Budapest, 1951–58), vol. III; C. A. Macartney, *The Medieval Hungarian Historians* (Cambridge, 1953); György Györffy, *István király és műve* [King Stephen and his work] (Budapest, 1977) 549-70; Henrik Marczali, *Ungarns Geschichtsquellen im Zeitalter der Arpáden* (Berlin, 1882); Bálint Hóman – Gyula Szekfű, *Magyar történet* [Hungarian history] 5 vols. 6th ed. (Budapest 1939; repr. 1990), I, 225f.; Bálint Hóman, *Geschichte des ungarischen Mittelalters*, 2 vols. (Berlin, 1940–43) I, 225f., and the bibliographical essay in Z. J. Kosztolnyik, *Five Eleventh Century Hungarian Kings: Their Policies and Their Relations with Rome* (New York, 1981) 197ff.

The origins of the laws of king St. Stephen were debated, and a critical text of the laws provided by Levente Závodszky (ed.), *A szent István, szent László és Kálmán korabeli törvények és zsinati határozatok forrásai* [De fontibus legum et decretorum synodalium e temporibus sancti Stephani, sancti Ladislai et Colomanni oriundorum] (Budapest, 1904), still the most reliable edition, with the exception of the *Libellus*, royal Admonitions, edited by Joseph Balogh in *Scriptores rerum Hungaticarum,* ed. Emericus Szentpétery, 2 vols. (Budapest, 1937–8; rev. repr., 1999), cited hereafter as *SSH*, II, 619ff. (Christopher Dawson reviewed this collection of sources: the *SSH*, in his essay, "The Hungarian Middle Ages," *Hungarian Quarterly,* 5 [Budapest–New York, 1939], 585ff.) (Bishop) Hartvic, the author of "Vita s. Stephani regis," c. 10, referred to King Stephen's legislation: "statutum a se decretum manifestum fecit," *SSH*, II, 415,3-4; Hartvic followed the information of the "Vita maior s. Stephani regis," c. 9, ibid., II, 384,9-10. György Györffy, *Wirtschaft und Geschichte der Ungarn um die Jahrtausend-wende* (Budapest, 1983), 251ff., also provided a text of eleventh century Hungarian laws; however, he seems to have followed the Závodszky edition. Important and still useful is the source collection, based upon available manuscripts, by St. L. Endlicher (ed.), *Rerum Hungaricarum monumenta Arpadina* (Sangallen, 1849; repr. Leipzig, 1931), cited hereafter as *RHM*, 299ff., or the Henrik Marczali collection of sources, not always based on manuscripts, *Enchiridion fontium historiae Hungarorum* (Budapest 1901), 62ff., 67ff. [selected], and 87ff. [selected].

Emma Bartoniek (ed.), *Szent Isván törvényeinek XII századi kézirata, az Admonti kódex* [The XIIth century Admont codex of King St. Stephen's Laws] (Budapest, 1935), published a reduced facsimile of the Admont MS 712, ff. 119-26, with the Latin text based on the manuscript, *ibid.,* 15ff.; and its Hungarian translation, *ibid.,* 43ff., with brief annotations, *ibid.,* 63ff. These source collections should be compared with the texts of the "Leges s. Stephani regis," and his "Admonitiones," printed in P. J. Migne (ed.), *Patrologiae cursus completus, series latina,* 221 vols. (Paris, 1844–55), cited hereafter as *MPL*, 151, 1243ff., and 1235ff., respectively.

The other two manuscripts of the Laws of King St. Stephen were preserved in the mid-fifteenth century Thuróczy codex (Nationalbibliothek, Vienna, MS 3662, ff. 98-105'; now, Széchenyi National Library, Budapest, Clmae 407, ff. 75-79'), and in the sixteenth century Ilosvay codex, Széchenyi Library, Fol. lat. 4023. Cf. Bartoniek, 9ff., and 69, n. 38; and Kosztolnyik, *Five Kings,* 110ff.

1. The Influence of Canon Law on Hungarian Laws

King St. Stephen's legislative activity was studied and analyzed, among others, by Jakob v. Sawicki, "Zur Textkritik und Entstehungsgeschichte der Gesetze König Stefans des Heiligen," *Ungarische Jahrbücher*, 9 (1929), 395ff.; Felix Schiller, "Das erste ungarische Gesetzbuch und das deutsche Recht," *Festschrift Heinrich Brunner* (Weimar, 1910), 379ff.; Remig Békefi, "Szent István király Intelmei" [The Admonitions of King St. Stephen], *Századok*, 35 (1901) 922ff.; Imre Madzsar, "Szent István törvényei és a Lex Baiuvariorum" [King St. Stephen's Laws and the "Lex Baiuvariorum"] repr. from *Történelmi Szemle*, (1921), 48ff. See also Hóman – Szekfű, I, 226ff.; Hóman, *Ungarisches Mittelalter*, I, 226ff.; Bálint Hóman, *König Stephan I der Heilige: die Gründung des ungarischen Staates*, trans. Hildegard v. Roosz (Bresslau, 1941,) 157ff.; Györffy, *István király*, 265ff.

Western Latin influence upon Hungarian legislative authorship may be discerned in the writ the monk Cathvulf [Cathaulf] had addressed to Charlemagne, where he reasoned that the Christian ruler was the image of God, just as the bishop was the image of Christ, cf. MGH Epp IV, 502ff., "Variorum scriptae," n. 7; important is the writ "Vita regia" Smaragdus of St. Mihiel addressed to Louis the Pious, c. xviii, in which he suggested that the monarch end slavery, cf. *MPL*, 102, 933ff., esp. 967a. The intellectual co-author(s) of King Stephen must also have been impressed by Jonas of Orleans' remarks, made in his *De institutione regia* (about 834), cf. *MPL*, 106, 279ff., esp. cc. vii and viii.

Sedulius Scotus' essay, *De rectoribus Christianis* (about 854), had influenced the Admonitions. Scotus explained that a wise ruler would only invite wise men to his Council—cf. S. Hellmann (ed.), *Sedulius Scotus* (Munich, 1906) 19ff., esp. 38,16-18, and encouraged the monarch to control himself, to assert authority over his wife and children, and govern his people with common sense, *ibid.*, 34,2-4; Scotus warned the ruler that he must trust God more, then himself, when facing enemies, *ibid.*, cc. 14 and 17, on the grounds that he had to look upon himself as God's humble servant, and not as lord over his fellow men, *ibid.*, 22,14-22 and 86,5-10.

The composition and contents of the "Liber manualis" by Lady Dhouda, the wife of the Treasurer of Louis the Pious, addressed to her imprisoned son, had truly penetrated the spirit of the Admonitions; cf. *Manuel pour mon fils*, ed. P. Riché, vol. 225 of *Sources Chrétiennes* (Paris, 1975), 84ff. and 328ff.; on Dhouda, cf. Peter Dronke, *Women writers of the middle ages* (Cambridge, 1984), 36ff.

Among the writings of Archbishop Hincmar of Reims, his *De ordine palatti* emerges as the intellectual-spiritual "source" of King Stephen's legislation. The archbishop followed the work by Adelhard of Corbie, "De ordine palatii," in his opus. Archbishop Hincmar emphasized that clerics had to know the canons of the Church, as well as seculars (those in government service) had to be familiar with Roman law; law governed the lives of the inhabitants of a region. He quoted Saint Augustine by saying that an individual may assert his opinion before the enactment of the law, but the law must be adhered to by jurists, and guide judges in handing down a sentence. Cf. MGH *Legum. sectio II–2*: "Capitularia," ed. Alfred Boretius – Victor Kruse (Hannover, 1890), n. 520, c. viii. According to the law the king must be obeyed—*ibid.*, n. 272 (Edictum Pistense)—on the grounds that a valid agreement had existed between ruler and subjects, *ibid.*, n. 262, cc. x and xii. Simultaneously, remarks made by Archbishop Hincmar, "De fide Carolo rege servanda," cc. 33-34, *ibid.*; and in his "De regis persona et regio ministrando," addressed to Charles the Bald, cf. *MPL*, 125, 833ff., called for attention. For background, see "Hincmari Remensis Annales, 861–82," *Monumenta Germaniae historica, Scriptores*, ed. G. H. Perzt, 30 vols. (Hannover, 1854, etc.), cited hereafter as

MGHSS, I, 455ff., anno 872. The Archbishop of Reims had also expressed his own opinion concerning sinful clerics—cf. "De presbiteris criminalibus," especially c. 21, in *MPL*, 125, cols. 1103 and 1104.

Conspiracy against the king was condemned by the 847 Synod of Mainz, see MGH *Legum sectio II*–2, 173ff.; and J. D. Mansi (ed.), *Sacrorum conciliorum nova et amplissima collectio*, 53 vols. (repr. Graz, 1960–61), cited hereafter as Mansi, *Concilia*, XIV, 899ff., where reference is being made to the decrees of the 813 Synod of Mainz, *ibid.*, XIV, 61ff. For the text of the "Lex Baiuwariorum" that had such an impact upon King Stephen's laws, see the columns of *Monumenta Germaniae historica, Leges*, ed. G. H. Pertz, 5 vols. (Hannover, 1835; repr. 1965), cited hereafter as *MGHLL*, III, 257ff.

Fulgentius of Ruspe emphasized that it was the Roman Pontiff who held the highest authority in the Church, but in the secular sphere of Christianity it was the Emperor who held the highest forum—*MPL*, 65, 647d. Regino of Prüm, "Libri duo de synodalibus causis et disciplinis ecclesiasticis," made the statement that anyone who had organized a conspiracy against the monarch had to be placed under anathema: excommunication of the Church—cf. *MPL*, 132, 185ff., ii:301, xii:21, xv:23 and 26. (The F. G. A. Wasserschleben edition of Regino's work remained inaccessible to me.) The "Capitula Angilramni"—presumably a letter Pope Hadrian I had, in 785, addressed to Archbishop Angilram of Mainz—and the Capitularies attributed to Benedictus Levita were discussed in detail by P. Fournier – G. le Bras, *Histoire des collections canoniques*, 2 vols. (Paris, 1931–32), I, 127ff. On this, see also Horst Fuhrmann, *Einfluss und Vorbereitung der pseudoisidorischen Falschungen von ihren Aufrichtung bis in die neuere Zeit*, vol. xxiv of the *Schriften der Monumenta Germaniae historica*, in 3 vols. (Stuttgart, 1972–74), I, 191ff. See further, Walter Ullmann, *The Growth of Papal Government in the Middle Ages*, 2nd ed. (London, 1962), 179f.

Only a church court of law could review complaints filed against a bishop, cf. the 836 Synod of Mainz—MGH Concilia, III, 718. The text of the Capitularies of Charlemagne is available in MGHLL, I, 256ff., esp. 271ff.; also in Mansi, *Concilia*, 17B, 698ff. The "Capitularia" attributed to Benedictus Levita, and edited by Abbot Ansegis, were only published in Mansi, *Concilia*, 17B, 801ff., as "Libri v–vii, Collecti a Benedicta Levita." The epistle "Pseudo-Evaristus" was published by Paul Hinschius (ed.), *Decretales Pseudo-Isidorianae et capitula Angilramni* (Leipzig, 1863; repr. Aalen, 1963) 87ff., esp. Epistola, ii:4 and 9. Likewise, directives in the collection stated that accusations made against a bishop were only to be investigated by a church court of law—cf. *ibid.*, 757ff., cc. 1 and 3. On Pseudo-Isidor—"man sieht aber, dass das Papsttum als der Hort des kirchlichen Rechtes galt"—see the valuable brief study by Wilhelm Neuss, *Das Problem des Mittelalters* (Kohmar im Elsass, n.d. [1941]), 90, 94ff., esp. 95; also, Ullmann, 180ff. and 184ff. For the resolutions of the 845 Synod of Meaux, cf. Mansi, *Concilia*, XIV, 836, 845; the articles of Mainz, 888, *ibid.*, XVIII, 67. The cited entry of the 1078 Synod of Rome, *ibid.*, XX, 510, while the quoted resolution of the 1090 Synod of Amalfi was printed *ibid.*, XX, 724. Ullmann, 180ff. and 184ff.

The annotation in the *Chronicon pictum* on King Andrew I of Hungary: "ut deposito ritu paganismo...ad veram fidem Christi reverterentur, in omnibus secundum legem illam viverent, quam sanctus rex Stephanus eos docuerat," is from *SSH*, I, 344,3-6. The text of Andrew I's cited "Constitutio ecclesiastica," most probably based on this remark of the chronicler, was printed in *MPL*, 151, 1257f., following Mansi, *Concilia*, XIX, 631f. On King Andrew, see Hóman, *Ungarisches Mittelalter*, I, 258f.; Kosztolnyik, *Five Kings*, 73ff.

Anselm of Luca, *Collectio canonum una cum collectione minore*, ed. Friedrich Thaner, 2 vols. (Vienna, 1906–15; one vol. repr. Aalen 1965), published only the text of the first eleven books. The text of Burchard of Worms' *Decretorum libri XX* in 1785 chapters, still in the *MPL*, 140, 557ff., edition. For related details, see 0. Meyer, 'Überlieferung und Verbereitung des Dekretums des Bischofs Burchard von Worms," *Zeitschrift der Savigny Stiftung für Rechtsgeschichte*, kan. Abt. 24 (1935), 144ff.; Fournier – le Bras, I, 364ff.; and, P. Fournier, "Le Décret de Burchard de Worms," *Revue d'histoire ecclésiastique*, 12 (1911), 468ff., who explained that it was a popular work that remained in use for more than half a century; it was a textbook of church law. Also, Ullmann, 359f., on "juristic theology," and on Burchard, 374f.

According to Burchard, synodical enactments were only valid if they received papal sanction. In case of any doubt, one had to turn to Rome; a bishop could appeal to the Roman See, which was the *cardo*: hinge, threshold, on which everything turns. The Roman Pontiff governed the Church, Burchard explained, though he otherwise made no mention of the Pope; he rather stressed the role played by the bishops; as he saw it, the bishops yielded spiritual authority under papal supervision, although Rome seldom relied upon its supervisory role. And yet, papal *auctoritas* meant that the Pope was the highest forum for making a decision. On these grounds, he reasoned, no secular ruler would dare intervene in ecclesiastical matters, *ibid.*, 473; Ullmann, 374ff.

Therefore, to Burchard, *Decretum*, i:3: Rome remained "prima sedis episcopatuum." A bishop, he argued, could only be ordained by three other bishops, i:27, i:164. He dwelled more on bishops, in art. i:84-86, and said that only God could pass judgment over a bishop, i:133, 141-44. No secular layman may bring forth accusations against a bishop, i:167; and, he attempted to determine who could bear testimony against a bishop (in court of law), art. xvi:7, 8, 11; related to this, art. xvi:12, 16-18, on deciding the fate of one who gave false testimony against a bishop. He cited legislation on the Church, art. iii:1, 6, and on episcopal primacy, art. xi:2.; art. iii:9, on church property. Divine liturgy could only be held, Mass could only be said at a proper location, iii:56-58. He declared cases of criminal justice, vii:44; of fasting—who would fast and when, xiii:7, 8, 10. Burchard argued that it was the obligation of the king to ascertain peace and support justice—cf. art. xv:38-43, xvi:45-49. For Burchard's views of "fractio" (alias judicial customs in general), see art. xvii:8, 9, 16-18.

The edition of "Seventy-Four Titles" of the 1050's were edited by John Gilchrist (ed.), *Diversorum patrum sententiarum siue Collectio in LXXIV titulos digesta*, vol. I *of Monumenta Iuris Canonici, Corpus collectionum* (Vatican City, 1973). The significance of the Collection was debated by P. Fournier, *Le premier manuel canonique de la réforme di XIe siècle*, vol. 14 of *Mélanges d'archéologie et d'histoire* (Rome, 1894), 147ff.

On King Saint Ladislas I, cf. Hóman, *Ungarisches Mittelalter* I, 292ff.; Kosztolnyik, *Five Kings*, 92ff.; László Mezey (ed.), *Athleta patriae: tanulmányok Szent László történetéhez* [Studies on King Saint Ladislas] (Budapest, 1980); and my review of this volume in *Catholic Historical Review*, 68 (1982), 130f. On the background of the Synod of Szabolcs, cf. Hóman, *Ungarisches Mittelalter*, I, 310ff.; Kosztolnyik, *Five Kings*, 105ff.; C. J. von Hefele, *Conziliengeschichte* 6 vols., 2nd rev. ed. (Freiburg i. Br., 1973–90), V, 204ff. The text of the synodical resolutions had, once again, been preserved in the Thuróczy codex, ff. 85-88', and in the Ilosvay codex, ff. 20'-22. Published in *RHM*, 325ff.; Mansi, *Concilia*, XX, 758ff.; also in Györffy, *Wirtschaft*, 110ff. King Ladislas' "Decretum III" may be dated, by its content, in the 1060's; however, in accordance with its art. 17, that referred to the laws of King *Saint* Stephen (art. ii-17), it could be dated in, or after 1083, on the grounds that it was "anno 1083" that King Stephen's canonization was recorded by Bernardi Constantiensis *Chronicon*—cf. *MGHSS*; V, 438f.; Kosztolnyik, *Five Kings*, 94.

King Ladislas I himself had referred to his political-diplomatic misunderstanding with Pope Urban II in his letter addressed to the Abbot of Montecassino—for text, cf. Vilmos Fraknói, *Magyarország és a Szentszék* [Hungary and the Holy See], 3 vols. (Budapest, 1901–03), I, 403f., and the related writs by popes Urban II and Paschal II addressed to King Coloman the Learned of Hungary, in *MPL*, 151, col. 481b; and 163, col. 198.

The works by Ivo of Chartres, his *Decretum*, consisting of seventeen parts, and the text of his *Panormia*, divided in eight books, are still used in *MPL*, 161, 59ff. and 161, 1045ff., edition. P. Fournier, *Les collections canoniques attribuées Yves de Charters* vol. 57 of *Bibl. de l'école des Chartres* (Paris, 1896), 645ff. H. Wasserschleben, *Beiträge zur Geschichte der vorgratianischen Kirchenrechtsquellen* (Leipzig, 1839), 52ff., explained that Ivo of Chartres had also relied upon the "Tripartitum" collection when putting his work together.

From a Hungarian point of view, one may note that Ivo's remark, "Reges a recte agendo vocati sunt: ideoque recte faciendo regis nomen obtinetur, peccando omittitur," *Decretum* xvi:39, and *Panormia* viii:59, might be applicable to reign and accomplishments of Coloman the Learned of Hungary, the former bishop who became king (1095–1116). On Coloman, see Hóman, *Ungarisches Mittelalter*, I, 363ff.; Z. J. Kosztolnyik, *From Coloman the Learned to Béla III (1095–1196): Hungarian Foreign Policies and Their Impact Upon Foreign Affairs* (New York, 1987), 19ff.; R. Sprandel, *Ivo von Chartres und seine Stellung in der Kirchengeschichte* (Stuttgart, 1962), 64ff. The law, Ivo of Chartres wrote, would not be contrary to nature, as it served the just cause, and the interests of the commonwealth, because it represented the customs of the country; cf. *Decretum*, iv:168. Any anti-royal act, conspiracy, or treason, will have to be punished by ecclesiastical excommunication—cf. *Decretum*, xii:78 (like Burchard, *Decretum*, xv:22, 23). By referring to the writ of Pope Anastasius II, Ivo of Chartres rationalized that the king was commissioned by God to become his vicar and rule on this earth in his name—see *Decretum*, xvi:16. Following in the footsteps of Saint Augustine, Ivo of Chartres had argued, *Decretum*, v:7, that one had to obey worldly power, even if it was a pagan ruler who held that power.

2. The Influence of Canon Law on Royal Legislation and the Education of Churchmen in Hungary during the XII–XIII Centuries

> Ut episcopi nullum amplius ad subdiaconus gradum ordinent, nisi in praesentia episcopi ante altare sedis Deo promittat nunquam se habiturum uxorem neque concubinam: et si tunc eam habuerit, mox ei abrenunciet.
>
> *Synod II of Esztergom*, aa. 9-10.*

The kings of the House of Árpád (1001–1301) in their legislative enactments followed, next to Magyar customary laws, western Latin ecclesiastical examples reaching back to the Carolingian age, though they always applied western precedents to specific Magyar religious and temporal needs and conditions when enacting legislation. During the early twelfth century, the Hungarian royal court and royal judges handed down judicial decisions in accordance with the traditional customary law of the land. The gradual improvement of the realm's economic-financial conditions in international and domestic trade and commerce by mid- and later half of the century brought forth changes in the function of law courts always headed by the king's justice, or the regional reeve, and by the bishop at the county seats, and in the conduct of public business throughout the reign of Béla III (1172–96).[1]

In Hungary of this period, the increase and importance of, and reliance upon, written documents had much to do with the gradual improvement in the educational standards and intellectual growth of members of the higher and the lower regular and secular clergy through the training of the more learned segment of the clergymen in both Roman and Canon law. The laws enacted by Kings Ladislas I (1077–95),[2] and Coloman the Learned (1095–1116)[3] bear witness to the spread and use of written documents in public life and in business. According to the legislation issued by King Coloman, for example, the custom of funding a loan agreement between a Christian and a Jew on *cartula sigillata* had become accepted usage among merchants and men of business in the land.[4]

In order to deal with the impact of western Latin canon law upon the development of Hungarian laws in the twelfth–thirteenth centuries, one has to reach back to the last decades of the previous century. King Ladislas I—who had been canonized a saint in the late twelfth century, during the reign of Béla III[5]—had expanded his laws according to the legislative acts of his great predecessor, King Stephen I (997–1038; canonized in 1083).[6] Coloman the Learned (1095–1116), the nephew and successor of Ladislas I, himself a former bishop, "qui ab Hungaris Cunues [the *book-lover*] Calman apellatur, eo quod libros habebat, in quibus horas canonicas ut episcopus persolvebat," versed in Canon Law, who had to become king, had, through legislative innovations and synodical enactments held during his reign, further supplemented the laws of his predecessors.[7]

Opposition among members of the nobility to the legislative innovations of the learned King Coloman must have been quite firm countrywide, in that the dissenters deemed it as unnecessary to adhere to the entries of the Synod held at Tarcal, presumably in the year 1106. Why could one not to adhere to the resolutions of previous royal legislative acts, they inquired; at least, it is how the cleric Albericus, compiler of the articles of the Synod of Tarcal, had so recorded it in his prefatory remarks of the synodical record.[8] During his reign, King Saint Stephen I had to apply firm disciplinary action to make his people, averse to *foreign* religions, accept Latin Christianity. About a century later, King Coloman would only lighten the severity of religious laws, because the Christian faith had by then struck deeper roots among the population; it was not necessary to deter the people by laws on religion.[9]

The monarch was determined to face his opponents, because he had set a goal before him, and he was resolved to reach that goal. As it is evident from the preface to his legislative acts at the Synod of Tarcal, it was he who had summoned the headmen of his realm; it was he who had asked for the consensus of his *whole* Senate to examine the laws of King St. Stephen, in order to approve of them, and further, when necessary, to expand them. Coloman did this with the full cooperation and consent of all the headmen, with his clerical advisors versed in the law of the Latin Church, and of the royal Council (the text reads *Senate*: "regni principibus congregatis, tocius senatus consultu"), so that he may, even if it meant to take as a guide western canonical legislative examples, secure the position of the Church, members of all social strata, and assure the maintenance of law and order in the kingdom.[10]

King Coloman continued to base the laws he had made upon ethnic *Magyar* legislative foundations: laws that had been enacted before him; in fact, he must have had those laws laid out in front of him, as they were already available to him. However, out of political consideration—because Ladislas I, his uncle and predecessor on the throne, had been a diplomatic foreign policy opponent of the Roman See—Coloman paid less attention to many of the laws of his predecessor.[11] And yet, in his legislative acts Coloman had modified the strict, almost intolerant tone of King St. Stephen's ecclesiastical legislation.[12]

Coloman's laws of *Tarcal*, compiled by the cleric Albericus, came down to posterity in eighty-four articles—to which one may add the seven articles of Coloman's *Laws for the Jews*, enacted separately.[13] Coloman in his resolutions mentioned the Church at first, confirmed the rights and privileges granted to it by King St. Stephen, recognized the legal status of all ecclesiastical land holdings—including those of the monastic communities—and informed members of the clergy that he expected them to behave with dignity in public, or in private, to be worthy of their religious vocation. Were a cleric from abroad to arrive in the realm, he had to have a letter of recommendation from his bishop with him.[14] He acknowledged that the clergy held *privilegium fori*;[15] in a manner similar to article six of the 794 Synod of Frankfurt, he ordered that in a legal case against the chaplain of a bishop, or against the chaplain of a royal reeve, only the regional bishop, or archbishop, may issue summons for the chaplain to appear before an ecclesiastical court.[16]

Following a Carolingian capitulary, *Admonitio generalis*, anno 789, art. 28, Coloman likewise decreed that a secular person [layman] could not intervene in church judicial matters. The king rationalized that in a lawsuit between a clergyman and a lay person, or between a layman and a cleric, the layman could always be heard by a secular judge, while the cleric could remain under his bishop's jurisdiction, as it had been resolved in art. 30 of the Synod of Frankfurt, 794.[17]

At the Tarcal synod—and following canon ten of the Synod in Rome, 1059—King Coloman decreed that a secular judge dare not issue summons to a cleric citing him to appear before his *secular* court. The monarch further insisted that a judge be fair in his handing down of a sentence, any sentence. Were a judge to be unfair in his judgments, he would have to be cited, with a sealed writ, to appear before the royal court, or, if necessary, cited without a sealed writ to present himself before the synod of bishops—a resolution quite similar to chapter one of the *Edictum Theodorici*. Coloman's directive to hold episcopal synods twice a year, in the spring and in the fall, in his realm, too was based upon decrees dating back to the Carolingians.[18]

In Hungary, the Church had received the tithe since the age of King St. Stephen (see Stephen's *Leges*, ii:18); Coloman decreed that tolls collected from the great volume of trade generated by Jewish merchants—who had, since then, entered the realm in large numbers—be taxed for church tithe, in a spirit of similar resolution reached by Charlemagne in his *Capitula de partibus Saxoniae*, c. 16.[19]

In Hungary, parish clergy, monastic abbots, and high[er] officials had to pay the tithe levied on their lands. Following other Carolingian examples, as, e.g., *Capitularia missorum*, anno 803, can. 21; and, the *Liber Papiensis legum Karoli Magni*, art. 138, King Coloman ordered that in court-of-law proceedings a witness must make his confession before appearing in front of the court; were he to bear false witness, they mark him by burning a cross on his forehead.[20] One may mention here, in a purely secular economics sense, that Coloman's decree, Tarcal, art. 42, that commanded the individual who had, without royal permission, retained a homeless servant (who may have fled from his master) in his own household, to be punished by a payment of 55 *pensa*, is reminiscent of an article in the *Justinian Code*, c. iv:6,1.[21]

The Hungarian monarch punished theft, Tarcal, art. 54, by following in the footsteps of King St. Stephen (Stephen's *Leges*, ii:6-7), Ladislas I (Ladislas' *Leges*, ii:1), and in accordance with canon seven of the *Poenitentiale Merseburgense*, by declaring that were one to have stolen a four-legged animal, one had committed a major theft.[22]

Witches have always caused problems for legislators, but Coloman, the bishop who had to become king, in accepting his predecessors' previous resolutions concerning witchcraft (Stephen, i:33-34; Ladislas, i:34), looked upon the issue from a higher religious-philosophical point of view. He brought forth legislation by borrowing from Carolingian capitularies—*Capitula de partibus Saxoniae,* annorum 775–79, can. Six—and from the laws of Rothar of Lombardy, the *Edictus Rotharii*, can. 376, that said that "nullatenus est credendum, nec possibile est," for the sake of argument that one could only speak of *striga*: woman, or man, who was, had been, *possessed* by the devil.[23] In fact, the monarch had declared, Tarcal, art. 57, that *striga* did not exist, "de strigis vero, que non sunt, ne ulla questio fiat."[24]

Furthermore, in accepting western synodical resolutions—as, for example, of the Synod of Pavia, 850, can. 23; or, can. 25 of the Synod of Tricina, 850—King Coloman decreed, art. 60, that *maleficii*, women who would cause one to be, or to act, insane, were, in order to prevent personal revenge, to be punished by the ecclesiastical courts-of-law, on the grounds that the sin [attitude] of the *maleficii* not only hurt the [personality of the] individual, but breached the peace of the entire kingdom. Those who practiced lechery, art. 61, were to be dealt with by an ecclesiastical court, as prescribed earlier by can. 19 of the Council of Ancyra, anno 314.[25]

Coloman emphasized that the Church was independent of secular powers, in that neither the regional royal reeve, nor a member of the service nobility, had the power to exercise predominance over a clergyman, see Tarcal, art. 65. The king, though accepting the priest's first marriage as valid (as did King Ladislas, art. i:1), decreed, Tarcal, art. 67, that a priest must abstain from marrying a widow, or a divorced woman, or a woman left by her husband. Borrowing from can. 13 of the Council of Melfi, 1090, and from can. 10 of the 1102 Synod of London: "ut vestes clericorum sint unius coloris et calcea-menta ordinata," the Hungarian monarch demanded, Tarcal, art. 70, that a clergyman shall not, as he must not, dress like a layman. "Nullus, qui in clero estimatur, vestibus utatur laicalibus."[26]

A word of explanation is in order here. King Coloman's articles at Tarcal, enacted "regni princibus congregatis, tocius senatus consultu," and placed in writing [edited?] by the cleric Albericus (who himself had to admit that he did not know the Magyar language well, "verumtamen tu domine, qui in huius populi lingue gener minus me promptum consideras, ...tua queso solita in me benivolencia et supervacua reseces et inperfecta suppleas, errata corrigas...") , were concerned with the reorganization of public administrative matters and finances of the realm, with the development of a legal system based on the professional function of courts-of-law; they had to do with issues of inheritance, and with one's military obligations in the home defense.[27]

The king struggled with problems of ecclesiastical discipline and, by imitating western canonical examples, attempted to strengthen it; "...legalem textum recensuit, ...auxit, non tam, quasi fundator, sed superedificator," and, he made all of his resolutions applicable to, and to be obeyed by, every inhabitant of his realm, regardless of their social stratum, including slaves. "Non enim sine causa rex gladium portat, dei enim minister est, vindex in iram eius, qui malum agit": the king wore the sword and regarded himself as God's *minister*. Nobody could separate two powers operating in the realm, "ille loricam fidei populum induerat, iste terrene ambicionis superfluenta cingulo iusticie precingebat; ille gladio spiritus verbi Dei perterruit, iste galea salutis decoravit"[28]—a revealing Gelasian concept of the two authorities probably taken from Ivo of Chartres' *Decretum*, as, for instance, iv:187 ("Imperiali judicio non possunt ecclesiastica iura dissolvi"); or, iv:190 (*quod convenit regem legibus divinis subjacere*), as if the whole text of the resolutions of Tarcal had carried the mark, and, possibly, influence, of Ivo of Chartres's collection of, and commentary on, church laws.[29]

The question, though, remains: did King Coloman, the former bishop who had to become king, attempt to unite spiritual authority with temporal power in his own hands, as if to follow in Ivo's footsteps, *Decretum*, v:378: "Duo sunt quippe, imperator Auguste, quibus principaliter mundus hic regitur: auctoritas videlicet sacra [sacrata] pontificum, et regalis potestas."[30] Coloman enacted legislation to punish evil, "Dei enim minister est vindex in iram, eius qui malum agit" (Tarcal, Preface), possibly in the spirit of Ivo's *Decretum*, x:96:

"Rex debet furta cohibere, adulteria punire, impios de terra perdere, parricidas et perjurantes non sinere vivere, filios suos non sinere agere;"[31] to protect the Church, "Placuit regi et omnium concilio, ut dotis cuiuslibet possessiones monasteriis seu ecclesiis a beato Stephano rege diposite inconvulse remaneant et cetera" (Tarcal, art. 1)—as if following in the footsteps of Ivo's *Decretum*, x:99: "Quod reges Christiani defendere debent matrem ecclesiam," that is, "quia pertinet hoc ad reges saeculi Christianos, ut temporibus suis pacatam velint matrem suma ecclesiam."[32] He was fully aware that either as king, or as man, it was God he served. "Non enim sine causa rex gladium portat, Dei enim minister est, vindex in iram eius, qui malum [male?] agit, nam principes non sunt timori boni operis, sed mali." (Tarcal, Preface—as if to compare with Ivo's argument, "quod rex aliter servit Deo, ut homo, aliter, ut rex," that is, "aliter enim servit quia homo est, aliter quia etiam rex est"—*Decretum*, x:121).[33]

The Hungarian monarch decreed, art. 77, that no slave—native or of non-Magyar birth—be allowed to be sold "abroad," that is, outside the confines of the country, and Coloman did this in the spirit, and within the context, of the Anglo-Saxon King Aethelred's Ecclesiastical Resolutions dated about 1012. "Et prohibemus ne quis extra patriam vendatur; si quis hoc praesumat, sit praeter benedictionem Dei et omnium sanctorum et praeter omnem christianitatem, nisi poeniteat, et emendet, sicut episcopus suus edocebit."[34]

Although the trustworthiness of the text that preserved the articles of the Tarcal synod may be undermined by the statement made by Albericus himself that he did not know Hungarian well enough to understand everything that was discussed at the council—a remark that makes it clear that the legislative debate in the sessions must have been carried on in the Magyar language; members of the hierarchy knew Latin, but the Magyar nobles hardly knew the language sufficiently to conduct legislation in it. It's reliability may further be weakened by the fact that the text of the resolutions only came down to posterity in a fifteenth century manuscript. And yet, the letter by Pope Urban II addressed to King Coloman is proof of the legal minded intellectual attitude and spiritual readiness of the Hungarian monarch to further the legalistic administrative achievements of his reign, to assure canonical protection for churchmen and church property in the land. "Ut causae clericorum uel ecclesiasticorum rerum canonice finiantur."[35]

Until the late eleventh century, ecclesiastical legislation remained inseparable from the ecclesiastical one in Hungary; however, the gradual development of the realm's church administration called for separate canonical enactments at church synods. The decrees of the First Synod of Esztergom, presided over by Archbishop Lawrence (d. 1104) during King Coloman's reign, besides matters of clerical discipline, dealt with marriage, separation, adultery, theft of [trade in] young women, cases considered to be under the jurisdiction of canon law. The synod, as yet, recognized a priest's first marriage (art. 31), except the marriage of bishops (art. 11); curtailed the bishop's right to own private wealth (art. 12), and made the abbots of monastic communities subordinate to episcopal jurisdiction (art. 36).[36]

In order to strengthen clerical discipline, the synod ordered cathedral canons to speak in Latin among themselves (art. 5), and forbade the ordination of unlearned individuals to the priesthood (art. 6); it gently attempted to extirpate paganism in the realm (art. 7), and forbade priests to charge fees for administering baptisms and conducting funerals (art. 43). The synod strictly punished clerics who committed theft, frequented taverns, or became drunk in public (articles 57, 58, 61). It left the king's powers unaltered: "Imprimis interpellandus est rex."[37]

The sources of some of the enactments of this synod may be sought after in the resolutions of the 1095 Synod of Piacenza, and in the canons of the Synod of Poitiers, 1100—as, for example, evidenced by articles 18 ("nullus habeatur [haberetur?] in clero, qui non est adtitulatus alicui ecclesie"), and 23 ("quicunque ad titulum ordinatus est, vel cum professione susceptus, non privetur ordine vel honore, nisi super certis criminibus iudicio canonico") of the First Synod of Esztergom as being similar to can. 15 of the Synod of Piacenza, 1095 ("decernimus, ut sine titulo facta ordinatio írrita habeatur, et in qua quislibet titulatus est, in ea perpetuo perseveret"). Or, art. 36 of the First Synod of Esztergom ("Abbates mitram, sancidalia, rothecas, nolam ad capellam vel cetera episcopalia insignia non habeant, neque baptizent, neque penitenciam dent, neque ad populum sermonem faciant"), showing similarity in content with canons 38 and 11 of the Synod of Poitiers, 1100 ("Ut nullus abbatum utatur cirothecis, sandaliis, annulo, nisi quibus fuerit per privilegium presbyterorum;" and, "ut nullus monachorum parochiale ministerium presbyterorum, id est baptizare, praedicare, poenitentiam dare praesumat.")[38]

Western influence—as, for instance, cap. two of the *Capitularia*, ca. 800–810 of King Pepin of Italy—becomes even more evident in article one of the First Synod of Esztergom announcing that only *canons* of the cathedral chapters may act as *judges*, handle judicial cases at ecclesiastical forums. Article two of the First Synod of Esztergom that called upon the pastor [parish priest] of larger [parish] churches that he in his Sunday sermons explain the Lesson and Gospel passages for the day to his assembled flock, together with the Apostolic Creed, and yet, warned the priest of a smaller parish to explain only the meaning of the Lord's Prayer to his faithful, shows identity with the twenty-two entries in the *Capitularia a sacerdotibus proposita*, anno 802, and with the *Capitula de presbyteris admondendis*, article three. On the other hand, art. three of the First Synod of Esztergom that during the Easter, Pentecost, and Christmas season(s) the faithful must go to confession and receive the Eucharist, while clerics go to confession before every major holy-day, resembles closely can. 50 of the Synod of Tours, 813.[39]

The articles of the First Synod of Esztergom were preoccupied with clerical discipline, marriage court-of-law cases, broken marriages [husbands leaving their wives; wives deserting their husbands], trade in [young] woman (for prostitution; or, slavery abroad)—that is, with legal cases that came under ecclesiastical jurisdiction. The synod still recognized a priest's first marriage as valid, art. 31, except the marriage of bishops, art. 11—decrees that show some similarity with can. 48 of the 692 Synod of Trullo.[40] In order to safeguard the secular interest of the Church, the synod restricted the bishop's right of disposal over his private property, art. 12 (inspired, as it may be, by a letter, anno 494, from Gelasius, bishop of Rome, addressed "ad episcopos per Lucaniam"), and decreed that monastic abbots must remain under the jurisdiction of the regional bishop, art. 36, a decree comparable with canons 38 and 11 of Poitiers, 1100, as cited above.[41]

The First Synod of Esztergom, article five, that forbade clerics to converse in Hungarian, as it obligated canons in cathedral churches to use Latin in their conversation with one another, provides evidence of the educational and social strengthening of the clerical strand in

Hungary, as their schooling standards had improved a good deal by the early twelve century. The same conclusion may be drawn from article six, that ordered that an uneducated individual must not be ordained to the priesthood: "ut ydiote presbiteri non ordinentur; qui vero ordinati sunt, discant aut deponantur." It is a resolution that reminds one of the 769 capitulary of Charlemagne, c. 16, "...quia ignorantes legem Dei eam aliis annuntiare et predicare non possunt;" and, of the Letter by the bishops of Gaul addressed to King Louis the Pious in 829: "quod summopere studendum est, ut...docti...ad sacerdotium provehantur."[42]

The firming of *clerical discipline* in the Church is evidenced by articles 42–44, and 49 and 61, of the First Synod of Esztergom that forbade the priest to charge fees for baptism and funerals, and strictly punished the priest a) for being a thief (!); b) for frequenting taverns, and c) for appearing drunk in public. These decrees were very similar to a writ by Hincmar of Reims, addressed to his clerics, c. 15; and, to the capitulary of 803, c. 16. Aelfric's Canons for Bishop Wulfin, can. 29; and, c. 46 of the Synod of Mainz, 813, may also have, together with the *Poenitentiale Egberti*, articles xi:1 and 5, influenced the enactment of Coloman's resolutions.[43] The decree of the First Synod of Esztergom (art. 22) ordering that a cleric—be he a priest, or even a bishop—could not say Mass in a church without the pastor's permission, "contra voluntatem presbyteri ecclesiae," seems to follow a Carolingian *capitula ecclesiastica* of about 810–13.[44] The synod's resolution that a bishop, or an abbot, must not behave like a tyrant (art. 24), was based on the *Capitulare missorum generale* of the year 802.[45]

The strengthening of *public order* in the land is evident from art. 7 of the First Synod of Esztergom, that ordered only slight punishment for those who still adhered to pagan religious cults in the country; interestingly, though, this resolution could have been based on the 769 capitulary by Charlemagne, art. 6. Furthermore, the enactments of the First Synod of Esztergom present a striking similarity with numerous resolutions recorded by Ivo of Chartres in his *Panormia*.[46] Thus, for instance, King Coloman in the preface of his enactments frequently referred to the Magyar (Hungarian) legislative tradition (customary law), the laws of King St. Stephen, as if to turn to it as the source of his legislative activities.

Ivo of Chartres in his *Panormia*, and in his *Decretum*, among others refers to the letter by Pope Leo IV, where the pontiff laid down guidelines that in preparing legislation, next to the resolutions of ecclesiastical synods, one also has to take into consideration the directives of other pontiffs, and of the fathers of the Church.[47] Ivo had emphasized that an ecclesiastical gathering meeting without the summons of the Holy See was not, could not be considered to be, as an official church synod—just as in Hungary it is the monarch who summoned church synods and legislative sessions, and enacted legislation, with the consent of his whole Senate, and of the headmen of the kingdom. "At christianissimus rex noster Colombanus…regni principibus congregatis, tocius senatus consultu, prefati regis sanctae memoriae Stephani legalem textum recensuit, de quo si rem consideres nichil commuinuit, sed auxit."[48]

Coloman's idea (of legislation) related to the legislative activities of King St. Stephen; "nam quis ambigat a sancto patre nostro Stephano, uiro quippe apostolico, legem populo nostro datam,"[49] including strict punishment sought for probable conspirators against king and country, that originally rested on the reasoning of Regino of Prüm's "De synodalibus causis," and on Burchard's *Decretum*, xv:22-23,[50] and was borrowed by Ivo of Chartres in a sense that the monarch was the vicar of God.[51]

Reading between the lines of canons 52, 53, and 65 of the First Synod of Esztergom, they openly state that Canon law has [spiritual] jurisdiction over every Christian, as it had been explained by Ivo of Chartres in his *Decretum*, iv:72 and xvi:10, assuming, of course, that any legislative activity only served a useful purpose if it identified with the legal customs known to the legislators and served the interests of those for whom it had been prepared.[52]

Many of the resolutions of the First Synod of Esztergom would, however, be altered by the participants in the *Second* Synod of Esztergom (*Synodus altera*), held during King Coloman's reign. For example, while it was the king who had been called upon to enforce the decrees of the First Synod of Esztergom, this *synodus altera* placed priority in enforcing its resolution upon papal prerogative, and resolved, with the approval of the Roman curia, that daily prayers be recited for king and country—very much like that as ordered by can. 66 of the Second Synod of Chalons, 813.[53] Its decrees also enforced clerical celibacy in the realm; the bishop may only ordain to the priesthood the person who had taken the vow of chastity, art. nine, and decreed, art. ten, that the married priest, could not say Mass. These enactments, in turn, reflect the influence of the 1089 synod of Melfi, canons 2 and 3, and of can. 13 of the Synod of Rome, 1099.[54] The Hungarian decree related to clerical celibacy, however, could not, and had not been enforced in the land, as it is evident from articles 1, 9, 17, 18 of King Béla IV's *Decree of 1267*, and from canons 9–10 of the 1279 Synod of *Buda* held during the reign of Ladislas IV.[55]

The synod publicized loyalty to the monarch; it excommunicated the one who dared to conspire against the king (art. two—compare to the Second synod of Chalons, 813, can. 66). One is to remember that, at this time, King Coloman, and his brother, Álmos, were involved in a constitutional and political struggle over the throne.[56] The synod further resolved that one's marriage could not be dissolved (articles four to seven; compare with Theodorus, *Penitentiale*, tit. xii), as it could only have been performed in a church, before the priest, and other witnesses (art. 16), a decree very much phased like can. 22 of the Synod of London, 1102.[57]

A word of observation is in order here. The cited ecclesiastical canons based upon the texts of western *Latin* canonical enactments and providing interpretations applicable to compatible *Hungarian* conditions can clearly be traced back to articles cited in the *Decretum* of Burchard of Worms. To cite but a few examples, one may look at Burchard, art. i:4-5 (based upon the decrees of Popes Anacletus and Leo);[58] Burchard's entries i:155, i:159, and i:171; or, art. ii:39 (that followed the contents of Pope Adrian's resolutions);[59] further, Burchard's art. ii:40-41, and ii:43-47, and paragraphs ii:108-28, ii:129-31, or ii:139-42 (that included resolutions reached at earlier church synods).[60] One may also refer to Burchard's lengthy entry, iii:50, and entry iii:62, that repeated the contents of a writ by Pope Vergilius;[61] or, Burchard's art. iv:84, that followed the resolutions of an earlier church synod dealing with Jews, or art. iv:91, that reflected Pope Gregory the Great's opinion of the Jews, etc.[62] Therefore, one may draw the rather daring thought that the judicial advisors of the Hungarian kings who had put together the texts, thereby determining the contents, of the first law collections in Hungary—collections that came down to posterity only in fragments—were aware of, had been trained in, Bishop Burchard's *Decretum.* Consequently, one may argue that the *Decretum* did have a strong influence upon the enactment of Hungarian laws during the eleventh through the early twelfth centuries.[63]

The influence of Roman Canon law can be discerned from the ecclesiastical and secular enactments of Hungarian kings in the twelfth–thirteenth centuries, as, for instance, from the attitude of Béla III (1172–96) toward non-Christians,[64] from various articles of the 1222 *Golden Bull* issued by Andrew II (1205–35), as, for instance, aa. 5, 12, 20-21—rather, from its revised text published in 1231,[65] as, for example, aa. 2, 12, 17, 24-25, conclusion—further, from the 1267 Law of Béla IV (1235–70), bearing in mind that the latter royal *decretum* was the third version of the Bull of 1222.[66] One may further trace the impact of church laws in Béla IV's Law for the Jews, that had been issued in the year 1251,[67] as exemplified by aa. 1-2, 8-12, 24, 26, and in the *Constitutiones* promulgated with the cooperation of the hierarchy and high nobility by the last Árpád king, Andrew III, in the year 1298, as, for example, aa. 7, 20, 26-28.[68]

The royal judges of the age handled court cases, held court of law proceedings in accordance with unwritten *Magyar* (Hungarian) customary law. Such a reliance upon unwritten law was, however, largely replaced by new Hungarian laws and court proceedings prepared by the young Hungarian clerics who, trained in church schools of the realm and at western universities in Bologna and Paris, and who had, because of personal secular interest, for years delayed their ordination to the priesthood, had filled ecclesiastical or secular positions of trust at the royal court, or at the courts of the nobility.

It was under Ladislas I, and Coloman the Learned that the usage of issuing writs to begin a court of law process; or, to appear before a court, had spread in the country. As pointed out above, the Synod of Tarcal under Coloman's reign, for example, decreed in articles 74–75, that in a business deal between a Christian and a Jew the *carta sigillata* signed by both parties served as witness to the worthiness of the transaction between them—and this usage became a part of the everyday judicial process. Under the growing impact of Roman and Canon law during the twelfth century, the art of drafting legal briefs and diplomas had been introduced in some of the monasteries and parishes of the country, though the drafted writs had to be authenticated by the king's *notarius* granting them royal approval.

There existed in Hungary a stratum of ecclesiastical and secular officials versed in Canon law, whose education and activities would be evident as early as 1055, in the founding charter of Tihany abbey, issued by Andrew I (1046–60), even if the wording in the document of *doctores, philosophii, patresque nostri quam plurimi* would not, as yet, have been applicable to the cultural conditions in the country at that time; the text may have been copied from a western sample document.[69] The existence and activities of this social group can, however, be determined from a twelfth century schoolbook in Esztergom, from royal writs of 1146, and from a 1181 royal decree that verified the claim of a certain, otherwise unknown, Lady Froa.[70]

Walter Mapes met the cleric Lukács—later archbishop of Esztergom; a staunch defender of Hungarian church privileges against the king, and from the pope—at the lectures of Girardus Pella in Paris during the 1150s; "...vidi Parisius Lucam Hungarum in schola magistri Girardi Puellae, virum honestum et bene literatum."[71] Pope Alexander III, in a letter, had addressed Archbishop Lukács as someone learned in law; "...non sicut viro mediocri aut sacras scripturas ignoranti, sed tam divinis quam humanis scripturis plenius eruditio et ecclesiae doctori."[72]

Hungarian clerics like Bethlehem (whose death was reported by Abbot Stephen of Tournai of St. Genovéva, to King Béla III of Hungary),[73] Adorján (as royal notarius, as archpriest at Buda and royal chancellor, "...hanc regie constitutionis seriem Adrianus Budensis eccl. prepositus et aulae reg. cancellarius adnotavit"),[74] and Katapan, bishop of Eger and royal chancellor ("episcopus Agriensis, aulae nostrae cancellarius"), pursued studies in church law at Paris. It was *Magister* Katapan who eventually established the official format of Hungarian royal documents.[75] Bishops Peter of Eger, and Simon of Nagyvárad were versed in (church) law.[76]

Ugolinus *de genere* Csák, canon at the cathedral of Kalocsa, who had been trained in canon law at Paris, became the archbishop of Spaleto, and both he and the Church in Spaleto recipients of a land-grant from King Béla IV in 1244;[77] Albert, archdeacon at the cathedral in Esztergom, was a *Magister* of Canon law ("...magister Albertus Strigoniensis archidiaconus, qui circa fluenta iuris prelatus alios meruit edocere"), and died in the battle with the Mongols at Mohi in 1241.[78] Damasus, professor of canon law at Bologna, was a Hungarian,[79] whose pupil, Paulus Hungarus, who "actu legens erat in iure canonico Bononie"), authored *Notabilia* dealing with canon law collections.[80]

During the thirteenth century, a law academy flourished in Hungary in the cathedral school of Veszprém; contemporary evidence that includes various royal decrees, shows that its fifteen law professors provided quality training for their students. It is ironic that the school was burned down in a warring encounter between two oligarchical families in 1276.[81]

In the 1279 Synod of Buda, the papal legate, Philip of Fermo, ordered that clerics who dealt with family wills and marriage cases in church courts of law had to have at least three years of training in canon law at a university.[82] Canon Law had influenced, and prevailed in, the enactments of the 1298 Hungarian Diet that had been summoned, and its resolutions enforced, by the last king of the House of Árpád, Andrew III.[83]

On these grounds, one can argue and explain how Roman Canon law had, indeed, prevailed in the laws of Hungarian kings, including various articles of the Golden Bull of 1222, and its variant of 1231, in the legislative acts of Béla IV, and in the 1298 legalistic resolutions (*Constitutiones*) that had been enacted by Andrew III (d. 1301), to serve as evidence of the historic fact that during the twelfth and thirteenth centuries Árpádian Hungary had been an active participant in the Latin *western* political and cultural mainstream.[84]

Notes

*) based upon a resolution of the Concilium *Bituricense,* anno 1031, c. 6.

1. For background, cf. Bálint Hóman, *Geschichte des ungarischen Mittelalters,* 2 vols. (Berlin, 1940-43), I, 173ff.; György Székely – Antal Bartha, *Magyarország története 1242-ig* [History of Hungary to 1242] (Budapest, 1984), 717ff.; Z. J. Kosztolnyik, *From Coloman the Learned to Béla III (1095-1196): Hungarian domestic policies and their influence upon foreign affairs* (New York, 1987), 41ff.; essays by István Bóna and Ivan Bertényi, in László Kósa (ed.), *A cultural history of Hungary* (Budapest, 1999), 42ff., and 64ff., respectively; Gyula Kristó, *Die Arpaden-Dynastie* (Budapest, 1993), 55ff., and 99ff.; Ferenc Makk, *The Árpáds and the Comneni: Relations between Hungary and Byzantium in the 12th century* (Budapest, 1989), passim, and my review of this book in *East European Quarterly,* 27 (1993), 553f.

2. Cf. St. L. Endlicher (ed.), *Rerum Hungaricarum monumenta Arpadiana,* 2 vols. (Sankt Gallen, 1849; one-vol. repr. Leipzig, 1931), cited hereafter as *RHM,* II, 325ff., still a reliable edition; also, Henrik Marczali (ed.), *Enchiridion fontium historiae Hungarorum* (Budapest, 1901), 67ff., 87ff., and 103ff.; see further, Kosztolnyik, 7ff., and 15, n. 68.

3. *RHM,* II, 349ff.; Marczali, 103ff.; Kosztolnyik, 46ff., and 58ff.

4. For text, see Coloman's "Laws for the Jews," a. 2, *RHM,* II, 349f.; Kosztolnyik, 48f.; analyzed by Bernard L. Kumorovitz, "Szent László vásártörvénye és Kálmán király pecsétes kartulája" [The marketing laws of St. Ladislas and King Coloman's sealed *cartula*] in *Athleta patriae,* ed. László Mezey (Budapest, 1980), 83ff., and my review in *Catholic Historical Review,* 68 (1982), 130f.

5. Kosztolnyik, 267f., and 284, nn. 2–14.

6. Cf. Bernoldi Constantiensis "Chronicon," anno 1083, in *Monumenta Germaniae historica, Scriptores,* ed. G. H. Pertz, 30 vols. in 32 (Hannover, 1854, etc.), cited hereafter as *MGHSS,* V, 438f.; Hartvic's "Vita s. Stephani regis," c. 24, *SSH,* II, 433,5–11; also, Kornél Szovák, "L'historiographie hongroise à l'époque arpadienne," *Les hongrois et l'Europe conquête et intégration,* ed. Sándor Csernus – Klára Korompay (Paris–Szeged, 1999), 375ff.; Szovák's approach reminds one of the approach taken by J. M. Wallace-Hadrill toward Fredegar and the history of the Franks, in his *The long-haired kings* (1962; repr. Toronto, 1993), 71ff.

For background chronicle material, as, for example, the Hungarian Anonymus, "Gesta Ungarorum," and the "Chronicon pictum," chronicles that refer to the legislative activities of Hungarian kings, see *SSH,* I, 13ff., and I, 217ff., respectively; one is to note though that, as Professor Péter Váczy pointed out to this writer during his October, 1964 visit to the Széchenyi National Library in Budapest, one would still prefer the previous Anonymus edition prepared by Ladislaus Juhász, *P. magister...,* *Gesta Hvngarorum* (Budapest–Leipzig, 1932), to the Anonymus text published in *SSH,* I, 13ff.

7. King Coloman "...prefati regis sanctae memoriae Stephani legalem textum recensuit;" cf. Coloman's *Decretum* of Tarcal, preface, *RHM,* II, 360; Hóman, I, 310ff.

8. Cf. *RHM,* II, 359f.

9. Compare the Law of King St. Stephen, aa. i:1-13, Marczali, 69ff., with Coloman's resolutions reached at Tarcal, aa. 3-8, 20, 24, etc., *RHM,* 361ff.; important is the edition based on the twelfth century Admont codex, MS 712, ff. 119–26, and prepared by Emma Bartoniek, of the Laws of King St. Stephen, with a reduced facsimile of the eight leaves, *Szent István törvényeinek XII századi kézirata, az admonti kódex* [The

2. The Influence of Canon Law on Royal Legislation

Admont codex: the twelfth century manuscript of the Laws of King St. Stephen]
(Budapest, 1935), 15ff., and 43ff.; also, Monica Jánosi, "Gondolatok az Admonti
kódexből hiányzó kapitulomokról" [Some thoughts concerning the missing articles in the
Admont codex], *Acta historica Szegediensis*, 82 (1985), 37ff., reference to articles
ii:14–19 of King St. Stephen's Laws not entered in the codex, but placed between aa. 13
and 14 by Marczali, 79, and, listed as alias cc. 48–53, in Bartoniek, 41f., and 69f. S.
Mester's essay, "De initiis canonici iuris culturae in Hungaria," *Studi Gregoriani*, 2
(1954), 659ff., is worth reading.

10. Cf. the Preface to the articles of Tarcal, *RHM*, II, 360.

11. Kosztolnyik, 11, and 51; *RA*, n. 31; text of the letter in Vilmos Fraknói,
Magyarország és a Szentszék [Hungary and the Holy See], 3 vols. (Budapest, 1901-03), I,
403f.; Rózsa Ignácz, "Szent László," *Vigilia*, 48 (1983), 687ff.

12. "At christianissimus rex noster...vidit adutam fiem perfecte religionis robor
accepisse, legalis vinculum catenae cogitatvit relaxare prudenter...;" preface, *RHM*, II,
359.

On medieval ecclesiastical law, see James A. Brundage, *Medieval Canon Law*
(London–New York, 1995), esp. 18ff., and 44ff.; useful is Joseph de Ghellenick's 24
column entry, "Gratien," in *Dictionnaire de théologie catholique*, VI–2 (1920), cols.
1727ff. Important is Stephen Kuttner, "Harmony from dissonance: an interpretation of
medieval canon law," actually a lecture based on original research, in his *History of ideas
and doctrines of canon law in the Middle Ages* (London, 1992), 1ff., and so is Stephen
Kuttner's classic study, "Zur Frage der theologischen Vorlagen Gratians," *Zeitschrift der
Savigny Stiftung für Rechtsgeschichte*, kan. Abt., 23 (1934), 243ff.; for background, see
Stephen Kuttner's essay, "The revival of Jurisprudence," in R. Benson – G. Constable
(eds.), *Renaissance and renewal in the twelfth century* (Cambridge, Mass., 1982), 299ff.

Alphonso M. Stickler, *Historia iuris canonici latini: historia fontium* (Turin, 1950),
is a work of basic value, and so is *Gratian: the Treatise on Laws (Decretum DD 1-20)*, tr.
by Augustine Thompson and James Gordley (Washington, DC, 1993). See further
Kenneth Pennington, "Medieval law," in *Medieval studies*, ed. James M. Powell
(Syracuse, 1992), 333ff.; and the comments by John W. Baldwin, *The scholastic culture
of the middle ages, 1000–1300* (Lexington, Mass., 1971), 59ff. I. S. Robinson, *The
Papacy, 1073–1198: Continuity and Innovation* (Cambridge, 1990), 179ff., treated Canon
law at some length. Elemér Mályusz, *Egyházi társadalom a középkori Magyarországon*
[The structure of ecclesiastical society in medieval Hungary] (Budapest, 1971), 35ff.,
depicted the educational-intellectual background of the contemporary clerical body in
Hungary of this age—cf. my review of his work in *Austrian History Yearbook*, 14 (1978),
288ff.

13. Cf. *RHM*, II, 371f.

14. See Tarcal, art. 3.

15. Tarcal, art. 5; King Stephen's laws, a. i:4.

16. Tarcal, art. 5; the resolutions of the "Concilium Francfordiense, 794," c. 30, in
MGHSS, XIII, 863ff.

17. Tarcal, art. 6; the text of the "Admonitio generalis, 789," in *MGH Legum sectio*
II–1, ed. A. Boretius (Hannover, 1883), 56. On the Carolingian cultural background, cf.
Engelbert Mühlbacher's classic, *Deutsche Geschichte unter den Karolingern*, 2 vols.
Phaidon repr. (Essen–Darmstadt, n.d.), II, 26ff., and 207f.; and, Erna Patzelt, *Die
karolingische Renaissance* (Vienna, 1924; repr. 1962), 128ff.

18. "Nullus presumat secularis iudex sigillum clerico dare," Tarcal, art. 14, and compare to c. 10 of the 1059 Synod of Rome, "Ut cuiuslibet ordinis clericos laici non iudicent;" cf. J. D. Mansi (ed.), *Sacrorum conciliorum collectio*, 31 vols. (Florence-Venice, 1759-98), XIX, 898. "Iudex iniuste causas discuciens ad curiam regis cum sigillo cogatur, sed sine sigillo ad synodum," Tarcal, a. 23, to be compared with the Theodorian Edict, c. 1: "...ut si iudex acceperit pecuniam, quatenus adversum caput innocens contra leges et iuris publici cauta iudicaret, capite puniatur," in *MGH Legum sectio* I, cited hereafter as *MGHLL*, V, 152.

19. "...decimam quoque episcopis consemus," Tarcal, a. 25, vs. "decima pars ecclesiis et sacerdotibus reddatur, c.16, "Capitularia de partibus Saxoniae," *MGHLL*, V, 40.

20. On May 1 and October 6 ("in festivitate apostolorum Philippi et Iacobi, et in octavis sancti Michaelis"), Tarcal, a. 2; and, Tarcal, a. 6, "Si clericus cum laicis causam habet," is to be compared with the Synod of Frankfurt, 794, c. 30, "Et si forte inter clericum et laicum fuerit orta altercatio," *MGH Leg. sect.* II-1, 77. For direct reference, see Tarcal, aa. 27 and 83; and, for comparison, cf. the Capitularia missorum, anno 803, c. 21, *MGH Leg. sect.* II-1, 116; further, the "Liber Papiensis legum Caroli Magni," c. 138, in *MGHLL*, IV, 512.

21. Tarcal, a. 42: "Quicumque absque regis licencia vagum tenuerit, LV pensas solvat, etc.," *RHM*, II, 365, with the Justinian Code, "Quicunque fugitivum servum in domum vel in agrum, inscio domino eius sucepit, eum cum alio pari vel viginti solidis reddat;" cf. P. Krueger – T. Mommsen – R. Schoell (eds.), *Corpus Iuris Civilis*, 3 vols. (Berlin, 1895-99), II: *Codex Iustinianus*, vi:1:4.

22. King Stephen's Laws, ii:6-7, see Marczali, 78, or *RHM*, II, 322; King Ladislas' Laws, *RHM*, II, 334f. In the Merseburg Penitential, "Si quis furtum capitale fecerit, idest quadrupedia, vel domum effuderit, aut quodlibet meliorem praesidium furaverit, V ann., et si a minoribus furaverit, III ann. poen.;" see H. Wasserschleben, *Die Bussordnungen der abendländischen Kirche* (Halle, 1851), 392.

23. *RHM*, II, 367; "...quod christianis mentibus nullatenus est credendum, nec possibile est, ut mulier hominem vivum intrinsecus possit comedere." Cf. *Edictus Rotharii*, c. 376, *MGHLL*, IV, 87, and compare to King Stephen's Laws, i:33-34, cf. Marczali, 76f.; for Ladislas' Laws, i:34, *RHM*, II, 331, respectively. On witches—*striga*—see, again, "Capitula de partibus Saxoniae," aa. 775-70, c. 6, in *MGH Leg. sect.* II-2, 68f.

24. Cf. Tarcal, a. 57.

25. Tarcal, aa. 60, 61. The text of the "Concilium Ancyranum," anno 314, can. 20, in Mansi, *Concilia*, II, 526. Can. 23 of the Synod of Pavia, 850, in *MGH Leg. sect.* II-1, 23; and, for can. 25 of the Synod of Tricina, anno 850, see Mansi, *Concilia*, XIV, 938.

26. "...scissis vestibus clericos abuti ulterius prohibemus...;" Council of Melfi, 1090, can. xiii, in Mansi, *Concilia*, XX, 724; "Ut vestes clericorum sint unius coloris et calceamenta ordinata," Synod of London, a. 1102, c. 10, *ibid.*, XX, 1151.

27. See Tarcal, preface, *RHM*, II, 358ff.; Hóman, I, 310ff.; Kosztolnyik, 48ff.

28. *RHM*, II, 360.

29. Ivo of Chartres' *Decretum*; cf. J. P. Migne, *Patrologiae cursus completus, series latina*, 217 vols. (Paris, 1844–55), cited hereafter as *MPL*, 161, 47ff.; as, e.g., iv:188, iv:190, v:5. "...ostendit enim his verbis apostolus manifeste, quoniam omnis potestas, tam apud paganos quam apud Christianos, a Deo ordinata est, sive propitio, sive

irato"—cf. Atto of Vercelli, "Expositio in epistolam Pauli ad Romanos," xiii:1, *MPL*, 134,258c.

30. Cf. *MPL*, 161, 438a, actually a quote from a letter of Pope Gelasius I to Emperor Anastasius, cf. *MPL*, 59, 42a, and the Emperor's answer—a *position paper* from the imperial court? Cf. *MPL*, 59, 61ff.

31. *MPL*, 161, 721d.

32. *Ibid.*, 161, 727ab.

33. *Ibid.*, 161, 727c.

34. "Nemo servum in gener Hungarorum, vel quemlibet in Hungaria natum...nec ancillam,...extra Hungariam vendere vel ducere audeat;" Tarcal, a. 77, as compared with King Aethelred's "Leges ecclesiasticae" of about 1012, c. 5: "Et prohibemus ne quis extra patriam vendatur...; cf. Mansi, *Concilia*, XIX, 320, as if to confirm the validity of the "Lex Alemannorum Karolina," can. 37: "Mancipia foris provincia nemo vendat, nec in paganos, nec in christianos, nisi iussio ducis fuerit"—*MGHLL*, III, 143.

35. Cf. *RHM*, II, 349ff., a.1; Pope Urban II's letter to King Coloman is logged in Ph. Jaffé, *Regesta pontificum Romanorum*, 2 vols. (Leipzig, 1885), n. 5662; text in *MPL*, 151, 480ff.

36. For the text of the resolutions of the First Synod of Esztergom, cf. *RHM*, 349ff.; quote is taken from a. 1. On the synod, see Kosztolnyik, 58ff.

37. *RHM*, II, 351.

38. "Nullus haberetur in clero, qui non est adtitulatus alicui ecclesie;" "Quicunque ad titulum ordinatus est vel cum professione susceptus, non privetur ordine vel honore..."—see Esztergom I, aa. 18, and 23, as compared with can. 15 of the 1095 *Concilium Placentinum*: "Sanctorum canonum statutis consona scientes decernimus, ut sine titulo facta ordinatio irrita habeatur, et in qua quislibet titulatus est, in ea perpetuo perseveret." Cf. Mansi, *Concilia* XX, 806.

"Abbates mitram, sancidalia, rothecas, nolam ad capellam vel cetera episcopalia insignia non habeant, neque baptizent, neque penitenciam dent, neque ad populum sermonem faciant"—Esztergom I, a. 36, as compared with canons 38 and 11 of the Synod of Poitiers, 1100: "Ut nullus abbatum utatur cirothecis, sandaliis, annulo, nisi quibus fuerit per privilegium a Romana ecclesia concessum;" and, "Ut nullus monachorum parochiale ministerium presbyterorum, id est vaptizare, praedicare, poenitentiam dare praesumat;" cf. *Concilium Pictaviense*, anno 1100, canons 38 and 16, Mansi, *Concilia*, XX, 1122f.

39. The "Pippini regis Italiae capitularie," of 800–810, c. 2, in *MGH Leg. sect.* II–1, 208f.; text of "Capitula a sacerdotibus proposita," anno 802, can. 1-22, *ibid.*, 1, 106f.; the obligation of the faithful to go to confession and to receive holy communion three times a year—was decreed at the Synod of Tours [Turonense], 813, can. 50, cf. Mansi, XIV, 81ff.; Péter Erdő, *Egyházjog* [Canon law] (Budapest, 1996), passim.

40. Resolutions of the "Concilium Trullanum," anno 692 [Quinisexta], can. 48, in Mansi, XI, 966; cf. also F. X. von Funk – Karl Bihlmeyer, *Kirchengeschichte*, 8th rev. ed., 2 vols. (Paderborn, 1926–30), I, 215f.

41. The letter by Pope Gelasius, anno 494, in Jaffé, *Regesta*, n. 636, to be compared with Mainz, 847, can. 10, in Mansi, XIV, 906. The First of Esztergom, art. 17, that "ecclesia non consecretur, si dos et terra prius non dantur," might have been based on the Synod of Worms [Concilium Wormatiense], anno 863, can. 3, that the bishop "non prius dedicet ecclesiam, nisi antea dotem basilicae et obsequium ipsius per donationem chartulae confirmatum accipiat;" cf. Mansi, XV, 689.

42. See *MGH Leg. sect.* II–2, 30, to be compared with Charlemagne's *Capitulary* I of the year 769, can. 16, in *MGH Leg. sect.* II–1, 44ff.

43. Hincmar of Reims' advice *ad presbyteros*, c. 15, Mansi, XV, 478; Capitulary of 803, c. 16, *MGH Leg. sect.* II–1, 116; Aelfric's Canons *ad Wulfinum*, can. 27, in Mansi, XIX, 701; "Poenitentiale Egberti," tit. xi:1 and xi:5, in Wasserschleben, 242. Also, Concilium Cabilonense II, anno 813, can. 40, Mansi, XIV, 102; Concilium Meldense, anno 845, can. 50, *ibid.*, XIV, 830.

44. Cf. *MGH Leg. sect.* II–1, 178, can. 9.

45. Cf. *MGH Leg. sect.*, II–1, 93, can. 11, or on the "Concilium Valentinum III," of 855, can. 14—see Mansi, XV, 10.

46. Ivo of Chartres, *Panormia*, i:11-20, in *MPL*, 161, 1045ff., esp. 1049cd-1051c.

47. Idem, ii:118, *ibid.*, 161, 1110f.; and, *Decretum*, iv:72, *ibid.*, 161, 1283f.

48. *RHM*, II, 359f.; Ivo of Chartres, *Panormia*, iv:14, and *Decretum*, iv:240, *MPL*, 161, 1181c, and 161, 316b, respectively.

49. *RHM*, II, 359, and King Stephen's Laws, a. ii:17 (though not in the Admont MS!—see Marczali, 79).

50. Cf. Burchard of Worms, *Decretum*, xv:22-23, *MPL*, 140, 900f., based on Regino of Prüm, *Libri duo de synodalibus causis et disciplinis ecclesiasticis*, ed. H. Wasserschleben (Lipsiae, 1840), ii:301.

51. Ivo's *Decretum*, xvi:16, *MPL*, 161, 904ac, and in his entry under v:7, *ibid.*, 161,324cd.

52. Ivo's *Decretum*, iv:72, and xvi:10; Gratian's *Decretum*, D, iv, *post* 3, in Ae. Friedberg (ed.), *Corpus Iuris Canonici*, 2 vols. (Leipzig, 1879-81; repr. Graz, 1959), vol. I.

53. Chalons II, anno 813, c. 66, Mansi, *Concilia*, XIV, 106; and, King Stephen's laws, ii:17, *RHM*, II, 323. On the *Second* Synod of Esztergom, held about 1112, under Coloman's reign, see Kosztolnyik, 64f., and 75, n. 86; for text, see *RHM*, II, 373f.

54. Melfi, can. 2-3 in Mansi, Concilia, XX, 723; Roman Synod of 1099, c.13, *ibid.*, XX, 963.

55. For the Decree of 1267, cf. *RA*, n. 1547; text in Marczali, 168f.; also, Z. J. Kosztolnyik, *Hungary in the Thirteenth Century* (New York, 1996), 239ff.; for the resolutions of the Synod of Buda, 1279, see *ibid.*, 272ff.; *RHM*, II, 565ff.; C. J. von Hefele, *Conziliengeschichte*, rev. ed., 6 vols. [vols. 5 and 6 edited by A. Knöpfler] (Freiburg i. Br., 1873-90), V, 190ff.; Mansi, XXIV, 269ff., carries only an incomplete and modified version; see further, Sámuel Kohn, "Az 1279-es budai zsinat összes végzései" [List of all the resolutions of the 1279 Synod of Buda], *Történelmi Tár* (Budapest, 1881), 543ff.

56. Synod of Chalons of 813, can. 66, Mansi, XIV, 106; political background in Hóman, *Ungarisches Mittelalter*, I, 376ff., and Kosztolnyik, *From Coloman*, 65ff.

57. Ecclesiastical Council of London, 1102, can. 22, Mansi, XX, 1152; *Penitentiale*, tit. xii:7, Wasserschleben, 213.

58. Cf. Burchardi Wormacensis episcopi *Decretorum libri XX*, in J. P. Migne (ed.), *Patrologiae cursus completus, series latina*, 221 vols. (Paris, 1844-55), cited hereafter as *MPL*, 140, cols. 537ff., although this version is not altogether reliable; cf. J. Pétray-Gay, "Burchard of Worms," *Dictionnaire de droit canonique*, ed. R. Naz, 7 vols. (Paris, 1935-65), II, 1141ff.; J. A. Brundage, *Medieval Canon law* (London-New York, 1995), 32ff.; on the intellectual background, cf. David Knowles, *The evolution of medieval thought*, 2nd ed. (London–New York, 1988), 160ff.

59. Cf. *MPL*, 140, cols. 550f.

2. The Influence of Canon Law on Royal Legislation

60. *Ibid.*, 140, col. 632d.

61. *Ibid.*, 140, cols. 645ff., and cols. 648f.; cols. 681f., and 686bc, respectively.

62. *Ibid.*, 140, cols. 743f. On Pope Gregory's tolerant policy toward the Jews, see F. Homes Dudden, *Gregory the Great: His place in history and thought*, 2 vols. (London, 1905; reissued New York, 1967), II, 153ff.

63. See Anselm Sabbas Szuromi, "Az első három Esztergomi Zsinat és a magyarországi egyházfegyelem a XII században" [Les trois Synodes d'Esztergom et la discipline ecclésiastique en Hongrie au XIIe siècle], *Magyar Könyvszemle*, 115 (1999), 377ff.

64. Hóman, I, 408ff.; Kosztolnyik, *From Coloman*, 218f.

65. Cf. *RA*, n. 379, and n. 479, respectively; text of both versions, in Marczali, 134ff.; also, Hóman, II, 85ff.; Kosztolnyik, *Thirteenth century*, 77ff., and 103ff.; *idem*, "Triumphs of ecclesiastical politics in the 1231 *Decretum* of Andrew II of Hungary," in F. R. Swietek – J. R. Sommerfeldt (eds.), *Studiosorum speculum: Studies in honor of Louis J. Lekai, O. Cist* (Kalamazoo, MI, 1993), 155ff.

66. Cf. *RA*, n. 1521; text in Marczali, 157ff.; Kosztolnyik, *Thirteenth century*, 225f.

67. As, for example, aa. 1-2, 8-12, 14 and 26; cf. Marczali, 191ff., selections; *RA*, n. 962; Kosztolnyik, *Thirteenth century*, 374ff.

68. Cf. for instance, aa. 7, 20, 26-28, in Marczali, *Enchiridion*, 192ff.; *RA*, 4209; *RHM*, II, 630ff.; Kosztolnyik, *Thirteenth century*, 354ff.

69. Cf. *RA*, n.12; for text, see Marczali, 81ff.; Chronicle, c. 88, *SSH*, I, 354,17-19.

70. Twelfth–thirteenth century schoolbooks in use in cathedral schools in the realm are described by Remig Békefi, *A káptalani iskolák története Magyarországon 1540-ig* [History of cathedral schools in Hungary prior to 1540] (Budapest, 1910), 239ff., and 368ff.; see also, Ferdinand Knauz (ed.), *Monumenta Ecclesiae Strigoniensis*, 2 vols. (Strigonii, 1873–74), I, 180. Royal writs in 1146, bearing testimony, in *RA*, nn. 72-76; the case of Lady Froa [Froue], when King Béla III had ordered that any legal matter to be brought to his personal attention be, at first, placed into writing, cf. *RA*, n. 130.

71. Walter Map met Lukács (later archbishop of Esztergom), as a student in Paris—see Thomas Wright (ed.), *Gualteri Mapes: De nugis curialium distinctiones quinque*, distinctio ii:7 (London, 1850), 73; Z. J. Kosztolnyik, "The Church and Béla III of Hungary (1172-96): the Role of Archbishop Lukács of Esztergom," *Church History*, 49 (1980), 375ff.

72. The letter of Pope Alexander III to Archbishop Lukács, in *MPL*, 216,50; W. Holtzmann, "Alexander III und Ungarn," *Ungarische Jahrbücher*, 6 (1926), 397ff.

73. The death of Bethlehem, a Hungarian student in Paris, was reported by Abbot Stephen of Tournai of St. Genovéva, to the King of Hungary—see *MPL*, 211, 334f., and 335f.; also, Gyula Kristó – Ferenc Makk (eds.), *III Béla emlékezete* [In memory of King Béla III] (Budapest, 1981), 105f.; Kosztolnyik, *From Coloman*, 282.

74. Adorján served as royal *notarius*, cf. *RA*, n. 140, and as archpriest at Buda and royal chancellor: "...hanc regie constitutionis seriem Adrianus Budensis eccl. prepositus et au. reg. cancellarius adnotavit," as appeared on writs logged in *RA*, nn. 139, 142-44, 146; and, as bishop of Transylvania, cf. *RA*, nn. 152, 155, 169, 172-73, 175, 183-85, 193-94. His name also appeared on a 1202 royal writ issued by King Emery—see Gusztáv Wenzel (ed.), *Árpádkori új okmánytár* [Codex diplomaticus Arpadianus continuatus], 12 vols. (Pest, 1860–72), cited hereafter as *ÁÚO*, VI, 224f., though the writ is *dubiae fidei*, cf. *RA*, n. 199.

75. Katapan, or Cathapan (name spelled differently in various documents), was bishop and royal chancellor between 1190 and 1198—see *RA*, nn. 152 through 178. Tibor Klaniczay, *A magyar irodalom története 1660-ig* [History of Hungarian literature to 1660] (Budapest, 1964), 76f.; György Bónis, *A jogtudó értelmiség a Mohács előtti Magyarországon* [Der Juristendstand in Ungarn vor 1526] (Budapest, 1971), 22f.

76. On Bishops Peter of Eger and Simon of Nagyvárad, see Vince Bunyitay, *A váradi püspökség története* [History of the bishopric of Várad], 3 vols. (Nagyvárad, 1883-84), I, 89.

77. Ugolin[us] *de genere Csák*, studied theology and canon law in Paris; upon his returning home, he became a *canonicus* at the cathedral of Kalocsa, and was, later, named archbishop of Spaleto; he, as the archbishop-elect of Spaleto, was the recipient of a land-grant from King Béla IV of Hungary for the Church in Spaleto—cf. *RA*, n. 776, dated October, 1244. See also Pál Winkler, *A kalocsai és bárcsi érseki főkáptalan története* [History of the arch-deanery of Kalocsa and Bárcs] (Kalocsa, 1935), 26.

78. The death of *Magister* Albert, Archdeacon at the cathedral of Esztergom, in the battle fought with the Mongols at Mohi, 1241, as reported in the Chronicle, c. 177, *SSH*, I, 468,1-4; Kosztolnyik, *Thirteenth century*, 158f., and 163, n.76, was also recorded by Canon Rogerius [of Várad], "Carmen miserabile super destructione regni Hungarie per Tartaros facta," c. 30, *SSH*, II, 572,17-18. On *Magister* Rogerius, archpriest of Várad, and literary author, cf. Klaniczay, 79; Kosztolnyik, *Thirteenth century*, 309.

79. On Damasus, see Stephan Kuttner, *Repertorium der Kanonistik (1140-1234)*, Studi e testi, vol. 71 (Vatican City, 1937), 175f., 327f., 393ff., 419ff., 426f., and 431f. Antonine García y García, "Glosas de Juan Teutónico, Vicente Hispano y Dámaso Húngaro a los Arbores consanguinitatis et affinitatis," *Zeitschrift für Rechtsgeschichte*, kan. Abt., 68 (1982), 153ff.; C. Lefebre, "Damasus," *Dictionnaire de droit canonique*, ed. R. Naz, 7 vols. (Paris, 1935-65), IV (1949), 1014-19; F. Liotta, *La continenza dei chierci* (Milan, 1971), 360ff.; entry, in Johann Friedrich von Schulte, *Geschichte der Quellen und Literatur des kanonischen Rechts*, 3 vols. (Stuttgart, 1875–89), I, 194ff.; and, R. Weigand, *Die bedingte Eheschliessung im kanonischen Recht*, vol. I (Munich. 1963), 362ff.

80. On his pupil, Paulus Hungarus, who "actu legens erat in iure canonico Bononie," and wrote the *Notabilia*, cf. F. Banfi, "Paolo Dalmata detto Ongaro. A proposito dei codici Borghese 261 e Pal. lat. 461 della Biblioteca Vaticana," *Archivio storico per la Dalmazia*, 27 (1939), 43ff. Kuttner, *Repertorium*, 411ff., and 432, mentioned him, and so did Liotta, 367f., and Schulte, *Quellen*, I, 196f., and 230. See also R. Chabanne, "Paulus Hungarus," in Naz, *Dictionnaire*, VII, 1270ff.; and, did P. Michaud-Quantin, *Sommes de casuistique et manuels de confession au moyen âge* (Louvain–Montreal, 1962), 24ff.

81. On the law faculty at the cathedral school in Veszprém, cf. *RA*, nn. 2741, 2747, 3109, 3272. See further, Károly Szabó, *Kún László, 1272-90* [King Ladislas IV the Cuman] (Budapest, 1886; repr. 1988), 36f.; Békefi, *Káptalani iskolák*, 160ff.; Kosztolnyik, *Thirteenth century*, 260f.

82. See Z. J. Kosztolnyik, "In the European mainstream: Hungarian churchmen and thirteenth century synods," *Catholic Historical Review*, 79 (1993), 413ff.; Samuel Kohn, "Az 1279-es budai zsinat végzései," [Resolutions of the 1279 Synod of Buda], *Történelmi Tár* (1881), 543ff.; Szabó, 86ff.

83. As, for example, its aa. 7, 20, 26-28—cf. *RA*, n. 4209. For the text of the *Constitutiones*, enacted in 1298, during the reign of Andrew III, cf. Marczali,

Enchiridion, 192ff., and *RHM*, II, 630ff.; see further, Hóman – Szekfű, I, 622ff.; and, Jenő Szűcs, *A magyar nemzeti tudat kialakulása* [Development of the ethnic concept of Magyar national consciousness] (Budapest, 1997), 334ff.; Kosztolnyik, *Thirteenth century*, 354ff.

84. For an overview of the educational and cultural background of the Hungarian regular and secular clergy during this period, cf. Bóna's essay in Kósa, *Cultural history*, 42ff.; further, Bónis, op. cit., 83ff., and Mályusz, op. cit., 35ff.; also, Jenő Szűcs, *Az utolsó Árpádok* [The last of the Árpád kings] (Budapest, 1993), 322ff., an unfortunately incomplete, but masterful study.

VIII

King Stephen's Administrative Policies

Erat enim beatus rex Stephanus literatus,
...eruditus, ...qui ipso mortuo gentem tam novellam
in fide catholica posset conservare.

Keza, *Gesta Hungarorum*, c. 44

Next to the Introduction to his legal enactments,[1] and besides the guiding principles maid clear in the Preface to his Admonitions addressed to his successors on the throne,[2] the administrative program of the great King is best be characterized by a passage in his *Vita minor*, where the anonymous author, quoting from Scripture, noted that the inhabitants of the realm who had committed wrong, and those who supported—secretly agreed with—that wrong, could expect no mercy in the eyes of the monarch, because he in every possible manner proved to be the faithful and prudent steward of God.[3] Stephen began to reason how he might lift the yoke of discipline from the shoulders of his people who were only recently reborn in the waters of baptism, when he realized that without the guidance of laws the people would return to their bad habits, and lead useless lives. Therefore, he decided to educate them in accordance of the doctrine of the Church, imposing upon them the yoke of laws and discipline, in order to successfully demolish even the specter of evil from amongst them.[4]

King Stephen's ideas of government were in full agreement with the ideas exemplified by the court of Charlemagne concerning the government of the kingdom—as interpreted, for instance, by Engelbert Mühlbacher,[5] Heinrich Fichtenau,[6] or Erna Patzelt[7]—proof that it was the learned ecclesiastics who, through the legal enactments of both great monarchs, asserted tremendous influence upon the domestic policies, and the conduct of foreign affairs of their royal masters even though the concept of "foreign policy" could not as yet

237

be applied to Charlemagne in the early ninth, or to the Hungarian King Stephen in the early years of the eleventh century.[8]

From the text of Stephen's *Vita minor*—"consult a *reliable* text on this subject," the anonymous author of this briefer one admonishes the reader[9]—one may draw the conclusion that the act of coronation did not separate the monarch from his people, did not personally isolate him, but authorized him, on the grounds of natural law, to reign over his people[s]. The anonymous author of the *Vita minor* did not even mention a [the] coronation, but only recorded that Stephen, *adhuc puer*, by the good will [applause] of the headmen and of the people, had been *laudabiliter* raised to the throne of the realm; "Stephanus adhuc puer favore principum et plebis in regni solium laudabiliter provectus...."[10] In order to strengthen the validity of his statement, the chronicler added that Stephen as a ruler abided by the rules of Scripture, and remained thoughtful in judgment—keeping the words of King Salomon in mind: "iudicium et iustitiam ante oculos proponebat iuxta illud Salamonis;"[11] and, the author of the *Vita* quoted the Book of Proverbs, 1, 5.[12]

Already in the early eleventh century, legislative acts and official writs played an important role in the realization of a ruler's political and administrative goals, in that he followed written guidelines in directing everyday affairs of his land, in laying the foundations for its development. In the ninth century, Asser, co-worker and biographer of the Anglo-Saxon king Alfred the Great, reported that his monarch took personal interest in handling the administrative and judicial questions among his people. The latter could criticize the personal attitude of royal officials, and even protested their handling legal cases in courts of law, as he paid personal attention to each complaint, because he wished everyone to appeal to him for help. King Alfred expected his servants to be literate, and apply their knowledge of the law accordingly in everyday usage.[13]

The written word served a practical and a cultural purpose, wrote Asser; to the Hungarian King St. Stephen, it meant practical application even among members of the clergy; though, as it may be evident from the theological writings of a Bishop Gerard of Csanád, or from the book list: catalogue, of Pannonhalma abbey from the 1070's, Magyar rulers of the eleventh century held the written word in high literary regard because of their interest in forming their nation's cultural destiny.[14] The Anglo-Saxon court placed emphasis on the idea that its clerics in public service knew to read and write (that is, knew of administrative guidelines and had some knowledge of the law); the Magyar king[s] could not have, as yet, very high expectations in this regard, though one may assume that at least members of the higher clergy and *hospites* who had entered and settled in the land were highly literate individuals.[15]

The laws of King Alfred also show numerous similarities with the laws of King St. Stephen, be it the prefatory notes preceding the enactments, or punishment for treason committed versus the king and/or the realm.[16] Like Alfred who had sanctioned laws approved by the Witan, King Stephen sanctioned laws with the consent of his advisory Senate.[17] In a similar manner, art. *v*:26 of the laws of the Anglo-Saxon king Ethelred [saying] that one's keeping the laws merited divine mercy, might remind one of King Stephen's laws, articles i:1-12.[18]

On the other hand, the Anglo-Saxon custom of having *gemot[s]* held at the shire, and township level, or King Canute's order that a *burh-gemot* meet three times a year, the *shire-gemot* twice a year, remained unknown in Magyar usage, at least there is no written record of it—though, according to the provisions of the Hungarian Golden Bull of 1222, the Magyar court held an annual *diet* gathering on the feast of the Assumption in mid-August every year.[19] King St. Stephen's laws remained in public use for centuries because kings Andrew I, Ladislas I the Saint, Coloman the Learned, Andrew II of the Golden Bull of 1222, Andrew III during the 1290's, later Lewis the Great in 1351, had in their legal enactments all referred to the laws of King St. Stephen.[20]

King Stephen decided to turn away from the traditional structure of the socio-political order of Magyar land. Because of his election— through the efforts of his father, Prince Géza, who had summoned the headmen of his country to recognize him, *per communis consilium*, as his successor *post se regnaturum populo prefecit*[21]—and, because of his royal anointment and coronation with the diadem he had received from Rome,[22] Stephen was able to concentrate political power into his own hands.[23]

A word of explanation would be in order here. The "Crown sent by the Angel," that is, by Rome, to the Hungarian court corresponded well to the views of Emperor Otto III. Otto III had followed the guidance of his mother, the Byzantine princess Theophano[24] regarding the development of a European *state system* under the common leadership of the German emperor and the Roman pontiff, Sylvester II, whom he had previously appointed pope.[25] The Byzantine example meant that, having accepted the political sovereignty of Byzantium, a region retained its own sovereign autonomy within the empire. Consequently, in the mind of Otto III, the European regional kingdoms besides the German empire would emerge within the framework of a Christian *communitas* as full-fledged autonomous regions of the Ottonian community.[26]

Otto III inherited the ideas of his mother, the Byzantine Theophano. The crown (circlet: *corona latina*) sent with imperial consent by the Roman pontiff to the Hungarian prince Stephen—even if only a small remnant of it forms a part of what is known today as the St. Stephen's Crown—represented a token symbol in the emperor's mind of the full fledged autonomy of the Magyars' kingdom within the Latin European commonwealth—headed by the Ottonian court.[27]

This argument remains valid even though one has to consider that Empress Theophano had died at a young age in 991, and for the next three years the then sixty-one-year-old imperial widow, Adelaide, took over the regency of the empire.[28] Adelaide's ideas were different from those of her daughter-in-law. The more narrowly educated Adelaide of Lombardic northern Italy judged political conditions differently,[29] and after 994, when the fourteen year old Otto III came of age, he—most probably after listening to the advice of his carefully selected counselors, in whom he had utmost trust—returned to the policy of his mother Theophano.[30]

Therefore, in the words of Hartvic, it was the consent of Otto III to send a crown to the Hungarian prince that made it possible for Stephen of Hungary to realize his own policies as the anointed and crowned monarch of his country, though, as the elected, anointed and crowned monarch, he already had the authority, already has held his own kingly office, for governing his realm, and its people[s]. The observation made by the author of the earlier and more reliable record: "Iugum et legem discipline subpositis cervicibus adhibuit, omnesque inmunditias malorum prorsus destruxit" (wrote the anonymous author of Stephen's *Vita minor*), was only seconded in the twelfth century by Hartvic, who noted that it was after his election, anointment, and coronation that King Stephen "cum episcopis et primatibus Hungarie *statutum a se decretum* [italics mine] manifestum fecit," thereby to lay a foundation to law and order in the land, and to manifest the political sovereignty of the realm In a similar manner, King Stephen had to insist on the independence of the Church in Hungary [*Ecclesia Hungarica*], that it be administered by its own archbishop in Esztergom, because he wished to avoid any interference in the realm's religious policies on part of the Ottonian hierarchy.[31]

After the anointment and coronation—carefully glossed over by the author of the earlier *Vita*—the King reigned and ruled over the country, and the tribal heads had disappeared from the public stage of politics—a condition gently echoed by the *Vita minor*: "...[Stephen] et intelligens gubernacula possidebit."[32] The tribal divisions in society ceased to exist, and the tribal administrators of justice were replaced by royal appointees. Stephen's legislative acts said nothing about law courts functioning at the clanish-tribal level.[33] Every free inhabitant of the land lived under the powerful rule of the King. The royal *comes*—exponent of royal power—headed the country's provincial administration at the *county* (district) level.[34]

Politicum, the idea of the state as perceived by the king, penetrated all branches of the realm's political existence. In individual cases—matters of sensitive socio-political nature—royal judges handled legal court business, and handed down sentences in cases involving free men. Royal appointees administered the affairs of the country in the name of the king, while the monarch actually possessed *patrocinium,* the royal domain, and remained firmly in control of the affairs of the country.[35]

When Coloman the Learned (1095–1116), the bishop who became king, altered in the spirit of reform the political order and the administrative organizational structure of the land he had inherited from his early predecessor, the concept of King Stephen's centralized government fell to pieces.[36] In the late 1090's, the *communitas* of the [lesser] nobility refused to remain the obedient to the royal will, as its members reached out for the exercise of political power: they wanted to guide their own political destiny.[37] During the twelfth century, there would develop the *county of the nobles' estate*, that meant the end of the administrative system of the district [*county*] that had been introduced by King Stephen.[38]

In the late 1090's, a new socio-political order began to develop in the earnest in order to assure cooperation between the King: *regnum*, and society. Family blood lines were severed as the new socio-political structure based upon noble birth and acquired wealth began to take shape.[39] The new order consisted of free men and slaves, of nobles and commoners; the sum of *wergeld*: "blood-money," determined by law remained the same for every freeman because no social distinction existed among freemen. The emerging social hierarchy would not annihilate the old nobility, but the noble families—old money, old blood—had to accept members of the new service nobility as their equals in society.[40]

In the early eleventh century, however, it was the *comes: comites* who, together with members of the high clergy, occupied the top position in society; they together were the *primates, optimates* of the land, and they claimed to belong to the same social level as members of the old nobility—a circumstance that may explain why no mention was made of *milites* in the laws of King Ladislas I (1092), and why the law code of King Stephen spoke of *milites* as a stratum that held a socially higher position than the "vulgaris" element among the social strata.[41]

It is evident from the *lex liberorum*, that the social stratum of free men remained united—in contrast with the social segment of *lex servorum*—even though servants could become, *maiores natu*, emancipated. Earlier, free men in the Magyar social structure were active members of the military (in accordance with Khazar custom, in which the king would command his richest subjects to provide for the everyday needs of the members of the king's *following*).[42] The Magyar ruler had always been surrounded by a special *following* of nobles. During the twelfth century, a special military caste of royal "followers" would develop in the country.[43]

King Stephen had developed new institutions, and established a new organization based on personal service. Social concepts like "people," or "armed forces," before him had identical meaning in the Magyar mind; after the innovations he had introduced, "people" became divided into segments of *fighters* who had to fight for, and *peasants* who had to cultivate, the land. It meant that the *liber* became poorer, because, to earn a living, he had to move onto somebody else's land, thus entering someone else's service. In the process, he lost his personal right to be an active member of military readiness [insurrection], when called upon; only the richer segment of the *liber* social stratum could exercise that privilege.[44] Free men who willingly entered the service of a landlord could redeem their general military obligations with payment of money. The professional force of *milites* directly under the supervision of the king gradually took over general military obligations and training for the military defense of the land.[45]

The *comes* remained in the changing social structure on the top of the social scale, and so did the landowner *senior* who was obligated to dispatch his *miles* [*milites*] for active duty in the king's army.[46] According to the provisions of the Golden Bull of Andrew II (in 1222), rich bishoprics, and members of the high nobility also maintained private armed forces, but their contingents formed a part of the royal army.[47] Therefore, the royal armed forces consisted of units of *milites*, and of the private armed contingents of the lords both spiritual and temporal. This arrangement was not—could not have been— feudalism, rather a revised social order essentially based upon the Khazar military system depicted by Ibn Rusta.[48]

The question must be asked at this point, who was a *miles*? On the social scale, the *miles* occupied second place after the *comes* [*maiores*]; below him, next stood the commoner—*vulgaris* (plebius; plebe). King Stephen's laws spoke of an established *comes – miles – vulgaris* social structure,[49] or of the *miles – pauper – vulgaris* social element in the realm.[50]

In King Stephen's Admonitions, *comites* were being referred to as "maiores," but *milites* were not,[51] though King Stephen's laws mention them in identical terms together: "nemo militum vel comitum."[52] On the basis of birth and family wealth, the *comes* gradually became one with the *maiores natu* [*optimates*]; the *miles regis* also became a wealthy man—as it appears from the wording of an article in the laws: "si autem miles vel alicuius vir ubertatis."[53]

The concept of *miles* [mounted knight] was not clearly defined by law, certainly not by modern standards, though various articles of the laws of King Ladislas I help to clarify the personal identity of a *maior*, a *minor*, a *comes*, and a *vulgaris*,[54] or make a comparison between a *comes* and a *miles*,[55] while King Coloman the Learned in his legislation did refer to a *comes*, a *centurio*, and a *miles*,[56] and drew a comparison between the *princeps* and the *miles*.[57] Consequently, one may argue that the *miles*, like the *comes*, was a minister in public service [that is, a civil servant], and so was the landowner, or landholder, *senior*: "comiti vel ministros," making it clear that a *miles* serving as the king's public servant [minister] would not be recognized as a nobleman,[58] "nullus comitum vel militum."[59] As a matter of fact, King Coloman had made it quite clear that the "miles" and the "minister" (royal public servant) were on the social scale beneath the *comes*, though the *miles* could not always be identified as a royal servant ["minister"].[60] King Ladislas' law confirmed the existence of social stratification in the realm,[61] just as King Stephen's law had made a distinction between the *domus*: house, of the *comes* and that of the *miles*, and the cottage: *mansiculum*, of the *vulgaris* (plebeian) element in Hungarian social structure.[62]

If the *miles* lived in the household of a landowner *senior*, the *miles* was regarded as *servus* who would not be considered a member of the military personnel of the county fort (that formed the administrative center of a district).[63] During the thirteenth century, *milites* (mounted knights), who lived under the jurisdiction of a landowner, became *iobagiones* [*iobagio*, like the German *ministerialis*], and formed an elite among the population on a *senior's* domain, under whose jurisdiction they lived, and were recognized as members of the (service) nobility; the latter lived, like the fort personnel, on the King's domain. Earlier, in the eleventh century, even later, the *miles* served as a castle guard under the command of the regional *comes*.[64] The *comes* [*comites*] headed the county (district), while the knights: *miles* [*milites*], constituted the fort personnel and performed a higher level of public service; as a matter of fact, the monarch could dispatch both the count *and* the knight, as royal envoys to foreign courts.[65] The *familiaris* [*serviens*], on the other hand, at the lower level of the social scale, lived on the *senior's* domain, and was regarded as the servant of the local *senior*—the landlord.[66]

And yet, the Hungarian *miles* and the Frank *vassus*: vassal (of the age of Charlemagne), did not possess the same social identity. King Stephen's land donations given in return for (military) service, were granted *iure perpetuo*, in permanent ownership; the benefice-system (usufruct of donated land) struck no lasting roots in Hungary.[67] King Stephen had frequently accepted someone in his court for military service in exchange for a land grant. The *miles*—in fact, the *serviens*—who received land grants in return for military service owed to the king, were not regarded as royal vassals, because the grant of land they received were given to them *iure perpetuo*, in perpetuity.[68]

One good example that can be cited in support of this observation is the founding charter of Tihany abbey issued by King Andrew I in 1055, that described the lands, economy [economic structure], and personnel given to—placed under the jurisdiction of the abbot of—the newly established monastery.[69] Another example would be a royal land grant in 1199 that made Iwachin, a *miles* in the service of King Emery (d. 1204), the *landowner* of five villages,[70] while in the year 1208 King Andrew II (d. 1235) donated land to Nicholas, reeve at Vasvár, and Iwachin [here spelled Iwchym, and by now *pristaldus*] had notarized the transaction.[71]

It is evident from articles i:16, and ii:17 (not in the Admont MS) of King Stephen's Laws that strong social distinctions existed among the *maiores natu*, and the *maiores dignitatu* of the realm, though later, in the thirteenth century, the contemporary eyewitness, Canon Rogerius, recorded that *principes*: the king's head men, had gained free entry to the royal court, and had been allowed to take their seats [*stella*] with them so that they would sit down during their consultations with the monarch.[72]

The entries in article ii:17 of King Stephen's laws that provide provisions for testimony [given in a court of law] by the *servus* who headed a district, or one of the royal manors—"curti regali vel civitati preficitur"—to the effect that his testimony had to be of the same value as the one given by, or accepted from, the *comes*, clearly meant that a *servus*, as a royal appointee, could serve as head official of a royal county [district], or of a royal manor, and be regarded as a social equal of the reeve [*comes*]—"testimonium eius inter comites recipiatur." He was to be socially accepted as a royal servant who headed the administration of a county, though in the social structure he held a lower rank than the *comes*, but occupied, as the king's *man*, the same public position as the *comes* who headed the county district. The latter provision of article ii:17 in King Stephen's Laws concerning the *servus* who had murdered his lord—"servus seniorem"—or, the *miles* who had killed his [the district] reeve—"miles suum comitem interfecerit"—clearly points to a prevalent social stratification in the country that existed between the count and the knight, the lord (senior) and the servant (a serf, or a *villein?*), and drew attention to a persistently firm social distinction among the royal subordinates and members of the nobility—between the servant and his lord, and/or the knight and the reeve—that could have led to instances of blind and bloody murder.[73]

The question may be asked, of course, what did happen when the *servus* heading a district—as the official/social equal of the county reeve—had, *obduratus corde*, murdered his wife? Like the reeve, did the servant heading a district also have to pay compensation—according to the entry in the laws enacted "secundum decretum regalis senatus"—with fifty bullocks to the murdered wife's family? The question is legitimate because it is more than unlikely that the *miles*—or, a man of wealth [*alicuius vir ubertatis*] referred to in the last entry of the article—who had committed a similar crime, had to make compensation, by decree of the Senate, with ten bullocks to the wife's relatives, *and* perform penance as required by church law, belonged to the same social category as the *servus* in the king's service.[74]

In a similar manner, article i:15 of the laws, enacted by the Senate, where a common *vulgaris* who had murdered his wife, had to pay compensation with five bullocks to the wife's relatives, and perform penance according to church law, presents clear evidence of social stratification in Hungary during the early decades of the eleventh century. This decree shows strong similarity with articles i:16 and ii:18 (not in the Admont MS) of King Stephen's Laws that referred to peace between nobles and the lesser social strata, and strictly forbade the drawing of one's sword out of anger in public.[75]

Constant royal effort to keep domestic peace is mirrored in article i:16, further in articles ii:12-13 of King Stephen's laws, that bespoke the maintenance of law and order among the *maiores natu* and the *minores cuiuscunque conditionis sint* in the country. Were anyone to draw his sword in anger with the intent to kill someone, and had actually killed someone, he would be punished with death by the same sword—*regardless* of his social status; "quod si quis posthac stimulis sue audacie tactus temptaverit, eodem iuguletur gladio."[76]

Article i:35 of the first Hungarian monarch's laws provides additional evidence for the continuous struggle the monarch had to wage in order to assure peace in the realm. "We order [*volumus*], decreed the king, that firm [lasting] peace and mutual understanding prevail among *maiores* and *minores* ["nec aliquis alium invadere audeat"], and royal reeves ascertain law and order in the land." For that reason, the royal reeve did not have the right to seek revenge for an insult shown to him—or, to his office—by invading the individual's home. Were he to break in someone's home, and be killed by the house holder—who acted in self defense—the latter would not be punished for killing the reeve who had invaded his home. Were the reeve to send his men to carry out the break-in, he would have to make compensation to the injured party with one hundred bullocks. Were, however, a knight ("miles") to attack a fellow knight's home[stead]: *curtim vel domum alterius militis*, he would be required to pay compensation with ten bullocks; were a common person ("vulgaris") to invade another common person's ramshackle house (*mansincula*), he would have to pay him only five bullocks.[77]

Not even the king's person and office was beyond the reach of an individual's blind personal anger caused by a breakdown in society during the 1030's, as exemplified by article ii:18 (c. 51, not in the Admont MS) of King Stephen's laws that said that anyone who had conspired against the king's person, or against the country—"in regem aut in regnum"—was not allowed asylum in a church; and, anyone who partook in a conspiracy, or dared to support it, must suffer ecclesiastical excommunication.[78] These articles, late additions to the laws, are in agreement with the preface and articles i:14-16, and i:35, further, with articles ii:12-13, and make it clear that the monarch had to enact legislation so that the people of his realm would lead peaceful, decent lives; "et quoniam unaqueque gens propriis utitur legibus, idcirco nos quoque...decretali meditatione nostre statuimus genti...honestam et inoffensam ducerent vitam."[79]

The royal power (*potestas*) of divine origin was the foundation of the new Catholic realm, whose king *seemed* to exercise absolute power, but, because of the divine origins of that office, his powers remained *limited*. As the ruling monarch, King Stephen had, *de iure*, no limitations in the exercise of his royal office, but, on moral grounds, the law *de facto* limited his powers; he had to put that law into effect, and royal power served as the means of achieving the establishment and upkeep of the realm, whose ruler and inhabitants abided by the law. As Anonymus of York would have noted it a century later, the monarchs were anointed and consecrated *ad sanctum altare*, "ut habeant potestatem regendi populum christianum."[80]

According to the Preface of his laws, King Stephen regarded it as his foremost priority to keep domestic peace, and to maintain justice in his kingdom, as it had been in such a manner that he had interpreted *his* royal obligations. (On the Latin part—*corona latina*—of the Hungarian Holy crown, the image of the Pantokrator is surrounded by the [two] tree[s] of life.[81]) King Stephen, like other medieval kings, had taken an oath at his coronation—the rite of royal coronation followed closely the rite of a bishop's consecration to his sacred office—promising to serve the idea of peace and justice. One may argue on linguistic grounds that in eastern Europe during the middle ages royal power was, theoretically, based upon the example of Charlemagne: monarchs looked up to Charlemagne as the ideal ruler whom they ought to imitate, because it was from the name of *Charles* the Great, for example, that the word *kral* [ruler] in Slavic, and the term *király* [king] in Hungarian, took their origin.[82]

It was in following the example set by *Charles* the Great that the Hungarian monarch claimed to have the right to make laws. King Stephen, before enacting legislation, imitated the customs of old, and of more recent, rulers, *idcirco nos quoque...antiquos et modernos imitantes augustos*, and consulted with the spiritual and secular lords who surrounded him at his court, and with members of his Senate, though, like Charlemagne, he remained the fountain head of law and justice, *decretali meditatione nostre statuimus genti*, the supreme judge in his kingdom, so that his people would *quemadmodum honestam et inoffensam ducerent vitam.*[83]

It is evident from the wording of the Chronicle that Stephen's administration stood at the ready with support of the military, to enforce the law,[84] *ut quantum boni in hi[i]s divinis ampliantur, tantum rei [mali] in isti multentur.* Therefore, maintenance of law and order rested in the hands of the monarch, though remained closely tied in with the administration, with the royal Council of loyal advisors.[85]

During the reign of King Stephen, there existed a social distinction between the *maiores natu* and the *maiores dignitatu,* though in the latter half of the eleventh and during the twelfth century, the royal headmen: *principes*, did gain free entry to the king's court and, the record has it, were allowed to sit [down on their stools: *stellae*] during their talks with the king. The *comes* [princeps] held country-wide positions, but he could at any time be transferred from one county to another, as he was not allowed to strike roots in one region.[86] Many among the *comites* were of foreign birth; they were administrative office holders who depended upon the monarch for their well being.[87] Many were higher churchmen. Lower clergy, on the social level as the *milites*, formed the group of royal chaplains, *capellani regis.*[88]

The *optimates*, and the *milites-ministri* thus formed a twofold base of the court's administrative system over the country. The *milites* served in the royal fort districts, and in border guard units; many of them performed service immediately around the king's person.[89] They did not necessarily serve as lower level administrators in that capacity, but formed the king's armed body guard; eventually *milites regis, ministri regis* became the *familia regis*, later known as stratum of courtiers: *udwarnoci*, (the King's Men): "men at the court." The *miles* could function as *prestaldus*, itinerant royal judge; or he could be sent abroad as a royal envoy whose mission, because of insecure travel conditions, would be regarded as rather dangerous.[90] If the ambassadorship would be regarded as less threatening, the king could send a *comes* as his personal envoy to the court of the emperor, or to another royal court.[91]

The administration of the realm remained a personal matter for the monarch. Imitating the principle of *ubi Papa ibi Roma*; encouraged by the example of the Frankish court, described in the thirteenth century by Jean de Joinville,[92] the seat of the country's government could be anywhere the king chose to sojourn in the realm with his ambulatory court.[93] Although it was King Stephen who had set up his court offices, and set the rules for the conduct of his policies, in accordance with the Bavarian example,[94] he still organized the offices and searched for guidelines for his policies in the Frankish model.[95] It was according to the Merovingian-Carolingian tradition that he had set up his main court offices of (1) *senescalcus* (*dapifer infertor*); (2) *pincerna* (*buticularius*); (3) *comes stabuli*; and (4) *camerarius* (*cubicularius*). In addition, there were minor positions, like those of *coquus, spatarius, scario*, maintained at the Hungarian court.[96]

The *dapifer* emerged as the head official temporarily replacing the *comitem* (*comes*) *palatii* under the Capetians. On the other hand, during the reign of Robert II the Pious (d. 1031), the Frankish contemporary of King Stephen, the *palatinus* had re-emerged as the head official at the Frankish court,[97] very much like King Stephen's *palatinus* (Palatine), *palatinus comes*, alias *comes palatii*; (it would be a *comes palatii* [Samuel] Aba [Alba] who in 1041 dethroned King Peter the Orseolo—"Alba comes palacii, deiecto Petro, regalem coronam et aulam regiam sibi usurpavit").[98]

The name of Palatine Zache appeared among the signers on Andrew I's founding charter for the abbey of Tihany in 1055.[99] In about 1064, the name of *Palatinus* Atha is recorded in the Chronicle: "Atha palatinus rogavit regem;"[100] the name of Petrus, *Comes palatinus*, is recorded on the founding charter for the abbey of Sümeg, issued by Ladislas I in 1091.[101] According to a 1075 document, after the king the Palatine held the highest office in the realm.[102]

King Andrew I (1046–60) had restored, and confirmed, the offices of *főlovászmester* (Head of the Royal Stable), and *étekhordó-mester* (Headmaster of the Royal Table) at the court. Although certain office titles known by their Latin names in the West, such as *dapifer, pincerna*, remained in use in Hungary, some office designations (known among signatories of royal writs issued during his reign), disappeared from the court of Andrew I.[103] Nor were the offices of *agaso* and *infertor* unknown at the court.[104] The Hungarian Anonymus—who projected political conditions of, and relied upon terminology in use during the late twelfth century when reporting events concerning Árpád in the ninth and tenth centuries—referred to a *magister agasonum*, "et agasonibus suis magistrum prefecit."[105] On a royal writ issued by King Emery in 1198, there appears the name of Mika, reeve of Bihar and *magister cubicolorum*.[106] The diplomas of King Stephen seemed to be modified versions of digested German documents; his money imitated the Regensburg *obolus* issued by his brother-in-law, Emperor Henry II.[107]

In the conduct of administrative matters, in regulating taxes, and setting the income of its officials, the Hungarian court followed Frankish concepts; for example, King Stephen's county reeve received one-third of the district's income—so did the Frankish *comes* under the reign of Robert II (the Pious). One has the distinct notion, though, that no permanent administrative hierarchy struck roots at King Stephen's court, nor did it strike roots at the courts of the early Árpád kings, because the monarchs relied on qualified men at the court to conduct their daily business.[108] For instance, in the already cited 1091 charter, mention is made of the sword-bearer, *spatharius*, of King Ladislas I,[109] and a royal writ in 1146 listed a man named Blacha, as *blastus regis*, alias the royal treasurer: *cubicularius*.[110]

In the neighboring kingdoms, one may take note, office holders prevailed in abundance. It was the *palatinus ispanus* [*curialis comes*] who served as head official at the Croatian court, next to the *cubicularius, pincerna regalis, comes volar* [master of the stable], *ubrusar* [*dapifer*?], *regalis curiae iudex*, while the *maior domo* headed the royal household.[111]

The head official at the Czech court was the *comes palatii*, the *castellanus*; the *dapifer, pincerna, agason(us)*, and *camerarius*, further, *cellarius* [Master of the Kitchen], *curiae venator*, and *trapezita* [Master of the Wardrobe] served under him.[112] In Poland, the *palatinus* headed the administration, with the *succamerarius* acted as a vice-administrator, who controlled the royal mint; the Master of the Table, and Master of Drinks served in their own capacities, and the *sedzian* represented the king in the administration of justice.[113]

During the latter half of the eleventh century, the *nádorispán* [Palatine] replaced King Stephen's *comes palatii* at the Hungarian court. He was in charge of all *comites* (many of whom served as royal district reeves); as *camerarius*, Chief Justice, the Palatine determined the rule of the court etiquette like the (Frankish) *maior domo*; as Chief Justice, he represented (or, substituted for) the king in judicial functions. He could pronounce a judicial sentence over a *miles* [or, *milites*], and pass judgment over cases involving county reeves.[114] He could handle judicial cases, although with his seal of office he would only summon people who lived under a district reeves' jurisdiction. For instance, a *miles* could appeal to him from the sentence handed down to him by his *comes*; in such a case, the Palatine summoned both: the "miles," and the latter's lord, most probably a "senior" (*comes*), to appear before him.[115] He could not, however, pronounce sentence over members of the high nobility—the *optimates* of the land[116]—as it is evident from the text of the additional articles inserted into the 1231, strongly modified, version of the Golden Bull of 1222 (issued by Andrew II).[117] The particular provision of the Bull of 1222 that the king commissioned the Palatine to carry out the resolutions of the Golden Bull, was completely left out of its 1231 version, because the somewhat reduced role of the executor was taken over by the Archbishop of Esztergom, Primate of the Church in Hungary.[118]

The *nádorispán* [Palatine] held the office of *iudex curiae* in the mid-eleventh century. In the already cited 1055 charter, the abbey of Tihany appeared as plain *iudex* among the signatories, "signum Cupan iudicis," not to be confused with Zache, *comes palatii*, after Nana, the Head of the royal Stable, and before Preca, the Head of the royal Table.[119]

In countrywide affairs, the Palatine would act as royal deputy, though the monarch could, in fact, name anyone royal deputy. Were the monarch to begin court proceedings in a judicial matter, and leave it to someone else to pronounce sentence in the case, the Palatine would not be allowed to intervene and bring the case to completion. Were the *nádor* [Palatine] to leave the royal court for even a brief period of time, he would have to leave his seal of office with *his* deputy. Because the King handled only important judicial matters himself, professional judges took over less significant legal cases. The monarch could also handle judicial matters that customarily went before an ecclesiastical court.[120]

In the early twelfth century, the district royal judge could not summon a *comes*, or a churchman, to appear before him; an indicted clergyman would only be cited to appear before a secular judge, if the legal process was being held within a church synod that had been canonically summoned by the local bishop.[121]

It is evident from the decrees of the Hungarian Golden Bull of 1222—its articles being based upon resolutions that had been enacted by King Saint Stephen, "instituta a sancto Stephano rege"—that the *nádor* [Palatine] inherited the jurisdiction of the former Reeve of the Royal Court. He would, as *comes curialis*—"ibi erit pro nobis, id est, praesentia regia"—represent the monarch at the royal curia. In the king's curia he had his own judgment seat, and exercised judicial jurisdiction over the realm.[122] Upon leaving the royal court, he still had the authority to act, "praesentia regia," as the King's itinerant justice in the country. He could, for example, cite individuals to appear before him, and handle their cases. On the annual law-day assembly—held on the Feast of the Assumption, in mid-August—he could judge any case, "et vice nostra causas audiat, et omnes servientes nostri, et alii, qui volunt, libere, et sine timore illuc conveniant"—with the exception of legal matters pertinent to church interest, "praeter personas ecclesiasticae, et clericos…quacumque ratione videntur ad ecclesiasticum examen pertinere."[123]

The *nádorispán* [Palatine] was obliged to lead the royal armed forces into military action in time of war. He was, as Master of the Court, in charge of court protocol. Under his supervision, county reeves administered district forts and districts, collected taxes and fees for county fairs, bridge- and border tolls, and, if needed, confiscated stolen property and chattel. On the grounds that the king's income and public revenues had as yet not been separated, the Palatine further held the administration of the royal domain under his supervision; dues, gifts for the monarch went through his hands into the treasury *(fiscus regius)*.[124]

King Stephen had no permanent court notary *(notarius)* who would have held the position of chancellor; he could call upon anyone to draft an official writ to be authenticated in the royal curia: use of the royal seal meant assertion of regal power. A document of 1093—the document is *dubiae fidei*, though it is based on an official writ of 1091—that was to determine the borders of the Pécs diocese with those of the bishopric of Kalocsa, was, for instance, drafted by the court chaplain—"hoc privilegium a Thimotheo capellanorum ultimo scriptum"—who at that time may have been the keeper of the royal seal.[125]

It is further evident from the Preface and first two articles of the Golden Bull of 1222, that King Stephen, as the supreme judge of the land, would hear and hand down decisions in legal cases during the annual law-day always held mid-August (gathering, after his death, on King Stephen's feast day, August 20th). Were the monarch not to attend this annual gathering in person, the Palatine, *Comes palatii*, personified him in his capacity as Chief Justice.[126]

The Palatine heard cases, and handed down judgment in the presence of the headmen of the realm, thereby strengthening the judicial capacity and prestige of the king's court, even though the high nobility most probably objected to identifying the royal *household* (*domus regia*—whose members may not even had lived at the court, and did not necessarily belong to the high nobility) with the King's *Council* of the higher nobility and high churchmen, the *principes*, in their role as advisors of the king.[127]

Bearing in mind the research of Heinrich Fichtenau, or of Engelbert Mühlbacher, dealing with the Carolingians, one is to conclude that King Stephen kept the Frankish example in mind when establishing an administrative framework for his Christian kingdom.[128] The early Hungarian royal court did not reach the level of efficiency achieved by Charlemagne in organizing the administrative structure for his country, but the Hungarian king had brought together an administration that functioned, and stood the test of time, for almost a century—as evidenced by the laws of Ladislas I (1077–95), and Coloman the Learned (1095–1116), or even by the decrees of Andrew II in the thirteenth century.[129]

Historical data depicts the establishment of a centralized administration of the realm by King Stephen I, together with his enactment of laws; data dealing with establishing an ecclesiastical organization in the realm can be obtained from references in the enactments by kings Andrew I (1046–60), Ladislas I, and Coloman the Learned, or the Golden Bull of Andrew II, and from a few surviving royal documents and pieces of royal correspondence with the Holy See. Remarks made by the anonymous author King Stephen's *Vita minor*, by Hartvic in his *Vita s. Stephani regis* (based upon the so called *Vita maior* of the king), and from a brief reference in the *Chronicon pictum* about the establishment of a church organization in Hungary, provide more information.[130]

The same sources of information tell us that King Stephen did not determine membership in the Council. Evidently, no *miles* became a council member, as the Council must have met in an "ad hoc" fashion each time, with different individuals present. On the other hand, the Council defined its public role as representative of the public good. When the royal court followed an ambulatory itinerary, the nobles and high clergy in the king's immediate surroundings *were* his Council.[131]

The monarch, namely, maintained an ambulatory court. Evidence in King Stephen's *Vita maior* points to Székesfehérvár as a permanent royal residence, though the dates and places of issue of various royal documents prove that the king and his court were en route most of the time. The king's household (*domus regalis*) was accompanied by the monarch's permanent coworkers, with several clerics and nobles (*comites*) following them. Any visiting high ecclesiastic, or nobleman at the court, may be asked to participate in the discussions with the king.[132]

Administrative matters, legislation, and advising the monarch on interests of public concern, were not under the responsibilities of the royal household. On the other hand, only the *maiores* were called upon to function as legislators in the royal legislative Council: it is a matter of record that King Stephen frequently enacted law "nostrorum primatum conventu," or "cum episcopis et primatibus Hungariae (statutum a se manifestum fecit)."[133] Did the *people* play a direct role in enacting laws? Going by available evidence, they most probably did not. They only listened to their king's legal enactments, acknowledging the validity of the enactments.[134]

Royal elections occurred in a similar manner. As pointed out above, with evidence based on the record in King Stephen's *Vita maior*, Prince Géza had to summon his headmen to advise him on appointing his son Vajk, baptized Stephen, as his heir, inciting them to take an oath acknowledging Stephen as the successor.[135] Upon the death of ruling Prince Géza, it was the headmen and people of the land who confirmed the election of Stephen as king: "favore principum et plebis in regni solium laudabiliter provectus...cepit propogator existere."[136] The seventh chapter of King Stephen's *Admonitiones* called for the same provision: the Council elected the king, while the people acclaimed the king-elect.[137]

The high churchmen and high nobles who were members of the Council maintained their distance: they were independent of the king, just as the *primates* predominated the public scene in the legislature. And yet, King Stephen remained the legislator in the land; his *concilium* would enact legislation as the *royal* council. The Council actually presented a proposal—one could refer to it as a bill—for legislation that would be accepted by the king who put it in a final form.[138] The situation would, however, change by the late eleventh century; for example, King Ladislas I's *sancta synodus* (held in 1092) had enacted laws on its own—"hoc decreverunt;" or, "hanc legem constituerunt"—while the king only presided over the synodical legislature. The latter was summoned by the *optimates* who used the royal plural; they legislated, "omnium iure iurando," against thievery, and only referred to the resolutions reached by the monarch and the high nobles—"regis et principum decreta."[139]

King Coloman the Learned (1095–1116) assumed the exercise of royal powers at the end of the eleventh century; during his reign, the high nobility would convene upon receiving summons from the monarch. Coloman enacted legislation "tocius senatus consultu," and yet, on his own. He alone was responsible to God for his actions. He dealt with his people's needs—with guests, too, visiting the realm— on an individual basis, in accordance with the people's laws and customs, as if following King Stephen's admonition: "In hospitibus et adventitiis viris tanta inest utillitas, ut digne sexto in loco regalis dignitatis possit haberi."[140]

Otto of Freising, chronicler, Cistercian monk and bishop, and uncle of Emperor Frederick I Barbarossa, made a note during the mid-twelfth century that the Hungarian king reserved the right for himself to order his lowest subordinate to imprison any high noble who dared to disobey the royal will.[141] But the Hungarian kings could not become absolute monarchs; were they to ignore the law of the land, they would disqualify themselves for their high office.[142]

Notes

1. Cf. Marczali, *Enchiridion*, 63ff.

2. *SSH*, II, 619f.

3. Cf. Luke, 12,42-43; St. Paul, I Corinthians, 4,20.

4. Cf. *SSH*, II, 394,31-395,7.

5. Engelbert Mühlbacher, *Deutsche Geschichte unter den Karolingern*, 2 vols., Phaidon reprint (Essen–Darmstadt, n.d.), I, 357ff.

6. Heinrich Fichtenau, *The Carolingian Empire*, trans. Peter Munz (Oxford, 1957), 104ff.; idem, *Beiträge zur Mediävistik*, vol. II (Stuttgart, 1977), 18ff. and 100ff.; my review of this volume in *Austrian History Yearbook*, 17–18 (1981–82), 354ff.

7. Erna Patzelt, *Die karolingische Renaissance* (1924), 2nd ed., with Cyrille Vogel, "La réforme culturelle sous Pépin le Bréf et sous Charlemagne" (Graz, 1965), 112ff., and a reaction to Patzelt's arguments by Paul Lehmann, *Erforschung des Mittelalters*, 5 vols. (Stuttgart, 1959), II, 109ff.; also, *ibid.*, I, 154ff. On the cultural background, see the remarks by Alfred Biese, *Deutsche Literaturgeschichte*, 3 vols., 3rd rev. ed. (Munich, 1911–18), I, 45ff.; Alfons Dopsch, *Die Wirtschaftsentwicklung der Karolingerzeit*, 3rd rev. ed., ed. Erna Patzelt (Cologne–Graz, 1962), I, 202ff. and 294ff.

8. Cf. Mühlbacher, I, 287ff.; Hóman, *Ungarisches Mittelalter*, I, 173ff.

9. "...hec breviora legite...," (c. 1) *SSH*, II, 394,1.

10. *Ibid.*, (c. 2), II, 394,24-26.

11. *Ibid.*, II, 394,29-30.

12. [Vulgate:] *Liber Proverbiorum*, 1:5.

13. Cf. *Asser's Life of King Alfred*, ed. W. H. Stevenson (Oxford, 1904), ch. 106. D. J. V. Fisher, *The Anglo-Saxon Age, c. 400 to 1042* (London, 1973), 225ff.

14. Cf. King Stephen's Laws, aa. i:1-12, Bartoniek, 18ff.; and his Admonitions, a. i, *SSH*, II, 620f., to compare them with Bishop Gerard's *Deliberatio*, Munich MS, fol. 24rv. On Gerard's *Deliberatio*, see Kosztolnyik, *Five Kings*, 46ff.; the text, based on the late eleventh century Munich State Library MS 6211, has recently been edited by Ladislas Szegfü and Béla Karácsonyi, *Deliberatio Gerardi Moresanae episcopi Svpra hymnum trium pverorum* (Szeged, 1999), Latin text with parallel Hungarian translation, cited hereafter as *Deliberatio Gerardi*, 94, and 96. On the book list of Pannonhalma abbey, see Csaba Csapodi, *A legrégibb magyar konyvtár benső rendje* [Organization of the oldest known library in Hungary] (Budapest, 1957); Géza Érszegi, "A pannonhalmi bencés apátság javainak összeírása, 1093" [The 1093 description of the goods of the Benedictine abbey of Pannonhalma], in András Vizkeleti (ed.), *Kódexek a középkori Magyarországon* [Medieval codices in Hungarian libraries], Széchényi Library series, 84 (Budapest, 1985); László Veszprémy, "A pannonhalmi bencés apátság könyvei a 11 század végi összeírás alapján" [The library holdings of the Benedictine abbey of Pannonhalma according to a late eleventh century book list], *Mons sacer, 996–1996: Pannonhalma ezer éve* [Thousand years of Pannonhalma], 3 vols. (Pannonhalma, 1996), 327ff.; also, Pál – Somorjai, *Arciabbazia di Pannonhalma*, 83ff.

15. James Campbell, "Observations on English government from the tenth to the twelfth century," in his *Essays in Anglo-Saxon History* (London, 1986), 155ff.; Horváth, *Irodalmi műveltség kezdetei*, 21ff.; C. Horváth, *Régi magyar irodalom*, 17ff.

16. Cf. F. Liebermann, *Die Gesetze der Angelsachsen*, 3 vols. (Halle, 1903–16), I, 16ff.; King St. Stephen's Laws, Preface, in Bartoniek, 15. Patrick Wormald, *"Lex scripta*

and *Verbum regis*: legislation and Germanic kingship, from Euric to Cnut," *Early Medieval Kingship*, ed. P. H. Sawyer – I. N. Wood (Leeds, 1977), 105ff., esp. 115ff., and 132f.

17. William Stubbs (ed.), *Select Charters of English Constitutional History*, 8th ed. (Oxford, 1895), 62f.; Frank Barlow, *The English Church, 1000-1066*, 2nd ed. (London–New York, 1979), 96ff. King Stephen's laws, as, e.g., aa. i:22, and ii:2; Kosztolnyik, *Five Kings*, 111ff.; in more detail, idem, *From Coloman*, 237ff., and compare to Rosamund McKitterick, *The Frankish Kingdoms under the Carolingians* (London–New York, 1983), 77ff., esp. 98ff.

18. Stubbs, *Select Charters*, 73; King Stephen's laws, aa. i:1-12. Patrick Wormald, "Aethelred the lawmaker," *Ethelred the Unready: Papers from the Millenary Conference*, ed. David Hill (Oxford, 1978), 47ff., esp. 56f. and 64f. Bryce Lyon, *A Constitutional and Legal History of Medieval England* (New York–London, 1960), 36ff.

19. Canute's *Secular Dooms*, c. 18, in Stubbs, *Select Charters*, 73f.; the Hungarian Golden Bull of 1222, and of 1231, in both, art. l, Marczali, *Enchiridion*, 134ABf.; also, in *RHM*, 412ff. and 428ff.

20. Kosztolnyik, *Thirteenth Century*, 77ff., 103f. and 240ff.

21. The "Vita minor," c. 5 *SSH*, II, 381,7-9.

22. Hartvic, cc. 9-10, *ibid.*, II, 414f. Andreas Sohn, "Bilder als Zeichen der Herrschaft. Die Silvesterkapelle in SS Quatro Coronati (Rom)," *Archivum historiae pontificiae*, 35 (1997), 7ff.

23. The "Vita minor," c. 6, *SSH*, II, 381,15-23.

24. Cf. Gunther Wolf, *Kaiserin Theophanu, Princessin aus der Fremde – des Westreiches grosse Kaiserin* (Cologne–Vienna, 1991), 59ff., (and 223ff.), and 97ff.

25. See Knut Görich, *Otto III: Romanus Saxonicus, et Italicus* (Sigmaringen, 1993), 190ff.

26. *Ibid.*, 211ff.; Ekkehard Eichhoff, *Theophanu, der König Otto III und seine Welt* (Stuttgart, 1996), 36ff.; Menno tu Braak, *Kaiser Otto III: Ideal und Praxis im frühen Mittelalter* (Amsterdam, 1928), 87ff.

27. Thietmar, iv: 38 [59]; Wolf, 134ff.; Bogyay, *Stephanus rex*, 23ff. The *opinion* related to the Hungarian Crown so daringly expressed by Pierre Riché, *The Carolingians: A Family who Forged Europe*, trans. M. I. Allen (Philadelphia, 1983), 301f., does not correspond to reality.

28. Cf. Eichhoff, 378ff.; Wolf, 79ff., on Theophano and Adelaide.

29. See Eichhoff, 407ff.

30. Cf. Görich, 233ff.; Wolf, 131ff. and 223ff.

31. The "Vita minor," c. 2, *SSH*, II, 395,6-7; Hartvic, "Vita s. Stephani regis," cc. 9 and 10, *ibid.*, 412-11-12, and II, 415,2-4, respectively.

32. The "Vita minor," c. 5; the preface of King Stephen's laws: "...decretali meditatione nostre statuimus genti, quemadmodum honestam et inoffensam ducerent vitam," cf. Marczali, *Enchiridion*, 69ff.; and King Stephen's Admonitions (*Libellus de institutione morum*), preface, *SSH*, II, 619f. Nemerkényi, art. cit., *Acta classica*, 2000, 87ff. Csóka, *Történeti irodalom*, 15ff. and 58ff.; Hartvic, "Vita Stephani regis," c. 10, *SSH*, II, 415; also Gerics, *Egyház, állam*, 51ff.; J. Gerics – E. Ladányi, "A Szentszék és a magyar állam a 11 században" [Relations between the Holy See and the Hungarian realm in the eleventh century], *Magyarország és a Szentszék kapcsolatának 1000 éve* [A thousand year relationship between Hungary and the Holy See], ed. István Zombori (Budapest, 1996), 9ff.; Csóka, 154ff.

33. Bartoniek, *Admonti kódex*, 15ff.; Marczali, *Enchiridion*, 69ff.; Závodszky, 141ff.

34. As, e.g., aa. i:2, 8, 9, 15; ii:8, 10 of King Stephen's Laws, *ibid.*; Kosztolnyik, *Five Kings*, 11f. and 21ff.

35. King Stephen's Laws, a. i:7; a. ii:8; the "Vita minor," c. 6; Váczy, *Erste Epoche*, 50ff.

36. *Ibid.*, 128ff.; King Stephen's Admonitions, art. IV, *SSH*, II, 623f.; Hóman, *Ungarisches Mittelalter*, I, 185ff.; Kosztolnyik, *From Coloman*, 21ff.

37. "Placuit regi *et omnium concilio* [italics mine], and having restored peace in the realm the king "legalis vinculum catenae cogitavit relaxare prudenter;" cf. Synod of Tarcal, a. 1, in Marczali, *Enchiridion*, 106, and 105.

38. Váczy, *Erste Epoche*, 116ff.; Hóman, I, 208ff.; T. N. Bisson, "Princely nobility in an age of ambition (c. 1050–1150)," in *Nobles and Nobility in Medieval Europe*, ed. Anne J. Duggan (Woodbridge, Suffolk–Rochester, NY, 2000), 101ff.

39. King Coloman's Laws: The Synod of Tarcal (1106), Preface, in Marczali, *Enchiridion*, 104f.; Závodszky, 181ff.; Kosztolnyik, *From Coloman*, 41ff., even though King Coloman did refer to King St. Stephen's legislation—"sancto patre nostro Stephano, uiro quippe apostolico"—*ibid.*, 54, n. 41; Hóman, I, 310ff.

40. See Ladislas *Decretum I* (1092), in *RHM*, 325ff.; Marczali, *Enchiridion*, 87ff.; Závodszky, 157ff.; Kosztolnyik, *Five Kings*, 105ff.; idem, *From Coloman*, 7ff. In King Stephen's legislation, one would, next to the *maiores natu*, find the *maiores dignitatu*—cf. King Stephen's Laws, aa. i:21, 16; or, his differentiation between *dives* and *pauper,* a. i:21, between *liber* and *servus, ibid.*, aa. i:14, 22, 28, 29; a. ii:4. The *miles* occupied a [much] higher position than the *vulgaris,* on grounds of social status and wealth—*ibid.*, aa. i:15 and i:35.

41. *Ibid.*, aa. i:15 and i:35; compare to King Ladislas' Laws, iii:2; Kosztolnyik, *Five Kings*, 96ff. and 189f., nn. 45, 65.

42. English translation—in part—of Abū 'Alī Ahmad, b. Omar Ibn Rusta, *Book of Precious Jewels*, in C. A. Macartney, *The Magyars in the Ninth Century* (Cambridge, 1930), 197ff.; *MHK*, 141ff.

43. King Coloman's Synod of Tarcal, aa. 35, 45.

44. King Ladislas I's Laws, iii:2.

45. Tarcal, aa. 35, 45, 80; or, he [they] would serve as the *miles* [*milites*] of his (their) regional lord (*senior*)—cf. *ibid.*, a. 40.

46. King Stephen has laid the burden of his armed forces on the shoulder of his *milites*—cf. Stephen's Laws, a. i:7, and on service due to him from the regional lords (*seniores*), who also sent their *milites* to serve on "active duty" in the King's army—cf. *ibid.*, aa. i:23 and 25.

47. In the early thirteenth century, only rich bishoprics and monasteries sent their (private) army units on active duty to the king's army—cf. *SSH*, II, 561,15-18; *MGHSS*, XXIX, 586,5-10; Kosztolnyik, *Thirteenth Century*, 137f. and 149, nn. 164-66.

48. See Macartney's translation of Ibn Rusta, and of a segment of an extract from a Persian chronicle by Mahmud Gardēzī—in his *Magyars in the Ninth Century*, 197f.; or, *MHK*, 150f. and 152ff.

49. King Stephen's Laws, a. i:22.

50. *Ibid.*, a. i:35.

51. The Admonitiones, a. IV; and, Laws, a. i:15.

52. "...nemo militum vel comitum," *ibid.*, a. i:27; also, Ladislas I's Laws, a. iii:2.

53. King Stephen's Laws, a. i:15.

54. Ladislas I's Laws, a. ii:5.

55. *Ibid.*, a. iii:15.

56. Synod of Tarcal, prologus; text in *RHM*, 358ff.; also, in Marczali, *Enchiridion*, 103ff.; Závodszky, 181ff. On the legislation by kings Ladislas I and Coloman, cf. Hóman, *Ungarisches Mittelalter*, I, 290ff. and 318ff.; further, Kosztolnyik, *From Coloman*, 2ff. and 12, n. 1; on Tarcal, *ibid.*, 46ff. and 54, nn. 40 - 67.

57. Cf. Synod of Tarcal, c. 65.

58. Cf. *ibid.*, c. 38: "comiti vel ministros."

59. Tarcal, a. 65: "nullus comitum vel militum."

60. *Ibid.*, cc. 9, 11 and 12.

61. King Ladislas I's Laws, a. iii:21: spoke of "comes – minister – plebius," as to confirm the existence of social stratification in the realm.

62. Cf. King Stephen's laws, art. i:35.

63. The landholder "senior" was allowed to search for the "miles" and "servus" who had escaped from his service—Stephen's Laws, a. i:25, asserting the point of view that the majority of *milites* were in the seniors' service, and were not attached to a royal district fort personnel. See, e.g., Knauz, I, 280 (anno 1231!); or, the *Regestrum de Varad*, in *RHM*, 640ff., number 194; on the "Register," see Jakubovich – Pais, 81ff., and Pintér, I, 249; Kosztolnyik, *From Coloman*, 241, and 258, n. 97.

64. See Knauz, I, 306 [anno 1234]; the Várad Register, n. 306 [anno 1231]; Kosztolnyik, *Thirteenth Century*, 80f. and 89, nn. 22-24. On the "ministeriales," cf. Aloys Meister, *Deutsche Verfassungsgeschichte*, 3rd ed. (Leipzig-Berlin, 1922), 68ff. and 127ff.

65. In the early 1090's, King Ladislas sent one of his "nostrum militem" as an envoy to the papal curia—see the letter of Ladislas I to the Abbot of Montecassino, in Emericus Szentpétery – Ivan Borsa (eds.), *Regesta regum stirpis Arpadianae critico-diplomatica*, 2 vols. Budapest, 1923–87), cited hereafter as *RA*, n.31; text in Vilmos Fraknói, *Magyarország és a Szentszék* [Hungary and the Holy See], 3 vols. (Budapest, 1901–03), I, 403f.

66. King Stephen's Laws, a. ii:17. (The sentence, "...si servus seniorem, si miles suum comitem...," may appear at the end of a. ii:16—cf. Marczali, *Enchiridion*, 79, n. 55); for background study, see Kurt-Ulrich Jäschke, "Königskanzlei und imperiales Königtum im zehnten Jahrhundert," *Historisches Jahrbuch*, 84 (1964), 288ff.

67. King Stephen's Laws, a. ii:2, or, as late as the reign of Andrew II—see *RA*, nn. 255, 263, 269, 270, 277 with text, n. 279, etc.; Marc Bloch, *Feudal Society*, trans. L. A. Manyon (Chicago, 1961), 59ff.; A. Borst, "Das Rittertum im Hochmittelalter," *Saeculum*, 10 (1959), 213ff.; Mühlbacher, I, 381ff.; Dopsch, I, 293ff.

68. King Stephen's Laws, aa. i:35, ii:2; on land granted, *iure perpetuo*, by King Géza II in the year 1156, cf. *RA*, n. 85. Text in Georgius Fejér (ed.), *Codex diplomaticus Hungariae ecclesiasticus ac civilis*, 42 vols. (Budae, 1829–44), cited hereafter as *CD*, VII–5, 119f., and in 1171, confirmed by King Stephen III; cf. *RA*, n. 117, *CD*, VII–5, 121f. See further Imre Nagy et al. (eds.), *Hazai Okmánytár* [Collection of domestic writs and documents], 8 vols. (Győr–Budapest, 1865–91), cited hereafter as *HO*, VI, 97ff.

69. Cf. *RA*, n. 12; text in Marczali, *Enchiridion*, 81ff., esp. 85.

70. See *RA*, n. 183; text in *HO*, V, 1f.

71. *RA*, n. 237, with text. On both kings, who were brothers, see Jenő Szűcs, *Az utolsó Árpádok* [The last of the Árpád kings] (Budapest, 1993), 19ff. and 50ff.; Kosztolnyik, *Thirteenth Century*, 4ff. and 38ff.

72. King Stephen's Laws, aa. i:16, and ii:17 (c. 50, not in the Admont MS)—see Marczali, *Enchiridion*, 69ff.; further, Rogerius, *Carmen*, c. 4, *SSH*, II, 554f. On Rogerius' background, see *ibid.*, II, 545ff.; Pintér, I, 530f.; Kosztolnyik, *Thirteenth Century*, 133f. and 148, nn. 136-37.

73. "…anathematizetur, et omnium fidelium communione privetur; …subiaceat damnationi." Cf. King Stephen's laws, a. ii:17, in Marczali, *Enchiridion*, 79 (c. 50, not in Admont MS—cf. Bartoniek, 41).

74. *Ibid.*, 25, art. i:15; in Marczali, *Enchiridion*, 72f.

75. *Ibid.*, art. i:15.

76. *Ibid.*, aa. i:16, 18, and a. ii:12-13.

77. *Ibid.*, a. i:35.

78. *Ibid.*, a. ii:18 (c. 51—not in Admont MS).

79. Preface to the Laws—Marczali, *Enchiridion*, 69.

80. For the Anonymus of York, cf. *MGH LdL*, III, 662ff., esp. III, 663,14-664,13. See also, Z. N. Brooke, *The English Church and the Papacy* (Cambridge, 1931), 157f.; Ph. Funk, "Der fragliche Anonymus von York," *Historisches Jahrbuch*, 55 (1935), 251ff.; P. E. Schramm, *Geschichte des englischen Königtums im Lichte der Krönung* (1937), 34f.; Kern, *Gottesgnadentum*, 72ff.

81. Wolf, 134ff.; for a picture of this enamel plate, see Eva Kovács - Zsuzsa Lovag (eds.), *Die ungarischen Krönungsinsignien* (Budapest, 1988), 45. Marczali, *Enchiridion*, 69. Compare with H. R. Loyn, *Anglo-Saxon England and the Norman Conquest*, 2nd ed. (London–New York, 1991), 239ff. and 268ff.; Ian Wood, *The Merovingian Kingdoms, 450–751* (London–New York, 1994), 152ff.; Kern, 131ff.

82. Németh, *Honfoglaló magyarság*, 37, noted that *Uvaq-Kiräy* was the name of a Chosak clan—on this, cf. H. Vámbery, *Das Türkenvolk in seinen ethnologischen und ethnographischen Beziehungen* (Leipzig, 1885), 286; also W. Radolff, *Vergleichende Grammatik der nördlichen Türksprachen*, part I: *Phonetik der nördlichen Türksprachen* (Leipzig, 1882), xlii. Kristóf Lukácsy, *A magyarok őselei, hajdonkori nevei és lakhelyei eredeti örmény kútfők alapján* [The Magyars' ur-ancestors, archaic names, and living areas according to Armenian sources] (Kolozsvár, 1870), 130ff. On Charles the Great, see Janet L. Nelson, *The Frankish World, 750–900* (London, 1996), 99ff.; Rosamond McKitterick, *The Frankish Kingdoms*, 77ff.; Patzelt, 112ff.; Mühlbacher, I, 357ff.

83. King Stephen's Laws, preface, Marczali, *Enchiridion*, 69.

84. Cf. the Chronicle, c. 69, *SSH*, I, 312f.

85. King Stephen's Laws, aa. i:15, 20, 34; ii:2; compare with Mühlbacher, I, 374ff., esp. 378f.

86. The *comes* would occupy positions at the royal court, or in the country; he would serve the king in various capacity—cf. Váczy, *Erste Epoche*, 42f.

87. As it may be evident from the list of signators on the Tihany charter, many of whom were of foreign birth; cf. *RA*, n. 12; text in Marczali, *Enchiridion*, 85.

88. "…Seraphin, Copan capellani illius, Robertus de Gozlaria spatarius eius." Cf. *RA*, n. 24; for text, see Marczali, *Enchiridion*, 101.

89. King Stephen's Laws, aa. ii:9, 17 [or, last entry, ii:16]; art. ii:16 reads in Marczali, *Enchiridion*, 79, as "senior curti regali, vel civitati praeficitur…;" in Bartoniek, c. 50 [since it is not in the Admont MS!], it reads "Si quis servorum curti regali aut civitati preficitur, testimonium eius inter comites recipiatur."

90. Cf. *RA*, n. 12.

91. Among the envoys King Ladislas sent to the papal curia, there was one of *miles* status, "...et per capellaneos meos at Sorinum nostram militem;" cf. Fraknói, *Magyarország és a Szentszék*, I, 403. In 1161, King Géza II dispatched a lowly *familiaris* as his envoy to the court of Louis VII of France—*RA*, n. 95; Katona, *Historia critica*, III, 732.

92. Cf. Jean de Joinville, *Histoire de Saint Louis*, ed. N. de Wailly (Paris, 1874), 11 and 34.

93. The government of the realm would be the personal matter for the king—*RA*, n. 24; Marczali, *Enchiridion*, 100f.; King Ladislas' Laws, ii:5, and iii:1-2, *ibid.*, 93ff. and 97ff.

94. See Szentpétery, *Magyar oklevéltan*, 36ff.; Peter Spufford, *Money and its use in medieval Europe* (Cambridge, 1988), 77ff.; Hóman, *Pénztörténet*, 189.

95. King Stephen's Laws, aa. ii:5 and 8 ("...rex autem ex sua parte terciam tribuat comiti"); and King Ladislas' Laws, aa. iii:13 and 26. Further, Wood, 140ff.; Nelson, 89ff. and 133ff.; idem, "Literacy in Carolingian Government," *The Uses of Literacy in Early Medieval Europe*, ed. Rosamond McKitterick (Cambridge, 1990), 258ff.

96. Charles Petit-Dutaillis, *The feudal monarchy in France and England, from the tenth to the thirteenth century*, trans. E. D. Hunt (London, 1936; repr. 1964), 30ff., also, 94f. and 168f.; Elizabeth M. Hallam, *Capetian France, 987–1328* (London–New York, 1980), 91ff. and 160f.; compare with Mühlbacher, I, 379ff.; Kosztolnyik, *From Coloman*, 248ff.

97. R. Schroeder, *Lehrbuch der deutschen Rechtsgeschichte*, 6th ed. (Leipzig, 1922), 147ff.; Meister, *Verfassungsgeschichte*, 110ff.; Petit-Dutaillis, 30ff., 76ff.; Hallam, 69ff., 72f., 172f.

98. Cf. "Vita maior s. Gerardi," c. 14, in *SSH*, II, 500,6-8. Keza, c. 72: "...elegerunt quemdam comitem nomine Albam," *ibid.*, I, 325,4-5.

99. Among the signators of King Andrew's charter for the abbey of Tihany—see *RA*, n. 12, and Marczali, *Enchiridion*, 85.

100. The Chronicle, c. 99: "Atha palatinus rogavit regem...;" *SSH*, I, 364,12, who held land property in Slovenia—see *CD*, I, 197f.

101. Cf. *RA*, n. 24.

102. Cf. Knauz, I, 60.

103. See *RA*, n. 12; also, the chart in Hóman – Szekfű, I, 513.

104. Váczy, *Erste Epoche*, 16f.; the names of Nana, *agaso*: head of the royal stable, and of Preca, *insertor*, appeared on the 1055 charter of the abbey of Tihany—*RA*, n. 12.

105. Cf. his "Gesta Ungarorurm," c. 44, *SSH*, I, 89,2-3. On the age of Anonymus, see Lorandus Szilágyi's brief study, "De aetate ac persona P. magistri, Anonymi Belae regis notarii," *SSH*, II, 631ff., and his article in *Századok*, 123 (1989), 273ff., scheduled for publication in 1948. See further, Gyula Kristó, "Szempontok Anonymus Gestájának megítéléséhez" [Some comments on the understanding of the Hungarian Anonymus' *Gesta Hungarorum*], *Acta historica Szegediensis*, 66 (1979), 45ff.; Kornél Szovák, "Wer war der Anonyme Notar? Zur Bestimmung des Verfassers der Gesta Ungarorum," *Ungarn Jahrbuch*, 19 (1991), 1ff.

106. Cf. *RA*, n.172; for text, *CD*, II, 344f. Further, chart in Hóman – Szekfű, I, 513. On the thirteenth century Aragonese connection of the dynasty, cf. Z. J. Kosztolnyik, "The alleged political and religious impact of the Aragonese *cortes* on the Hungarian diets of the late thirteenth century," *Cithara*, 35–1 (1995), 39ff.

107. Spufford, 80; Bálint Hóman, *A magyar királyság pénzügyei és gazdaságpolitikája Károly Róbert korában* [The monetary and economic policies of the Hungarian realm during the early fourteenth century] (Budapest, 1921), 34f.; Hóman – Szekfű, I, 512; twelfth century *falsified* royal writs mentioned Master of the royal table, Master of the royal cup [cup-bearer], and Master of the royal food supply—see *RA*, nn. 60, 71, and 123.; Kosztolnyik, *From Coloman*, 249f.

108. Hallam, 69, and 78f. King Stephen's Laws, aa. i:2b—Synod of Mainz, 847—and i:15; also a. ii:8; *RA*, n. 77 (anno 1148).

109. Even if the writ is a falsified document, see *RA*, n. 24—Marczali, *Enchiridion*, 100ff., signatures on p. 101.

110. Cf. *RA*, n. 73; *ÁUO*, I, 58f.; *Pannonhalmi Rendtörténet*, I, 598f.

111. On this, see Šišić, *Geschichte der Kroaten*, I, 401f.

112. Cf. Otto Peterka, *Rechtsgeschichte der böhmischen Länder*, vol. I (Reichenberg, 1923), 34f.; on the background, cf. Palacky, *Geschichte*, I, 225ff.

113. Cf. St. Kutrzeba, *Grundriss der polnischen Verfassungsgeschichte* (Lemberg, 1912), 19ff. Also, Tadeusz Manteuffel, *The formation of the Polish state*, trans., with an introduction by Andrew Gorski (Detroit, 1982), 85ff.

114. See, e.g., King Ladislas's Laws, iii:3; King Coloman's Synod of Tarcal, art. 36; Kosztolnyik, *From Coloman*, 4ff., 46ff. and 238ff.

115. Marczali, *Enchiridion*, 100ff.

116. See, for instance, the Bull of 1231, aa. 1, 2, 5, 17, in Marczali, *Enchiridion*, 134Bff., where the texts of the two documents—of 1222, and of 1231—are printed in parallel columns. On the Hungarian Golden Bull, cf. Ákos von Timon, *Ungarische Verfassungs- und Rechtsgeschichte*, trans. Felix Schiller, 2nd ed. (Berlin, 1904), 124ff.; Hóman – Szekfű, I, 491ff.; Kosztolnyik, *Thirteenth Century*, 77ff. and 103ff.

117. Cf. 1222, a. 31, *ibid.*, 142Af.

118. Cf. 1231, conclusion, *ibid.*, 142B; Z. J. Kosztolnyik, "Triumphs of ecclesiastical politics in the 1231 *Decretum* of Andrew II of Hungary," *Studiosorum speculum: Studies in honor of L. J. Lekai*, ed. F. R. Swietek – J. R. Sommerfeldt (Kalamazoo, MI, 1993), 155ff.

119. *RA*, n. 12; for text, cf. Marczali. *Enchiridion*, 81ff., with signatures listed on p. 85.

120. King Stephen's Laws, aa. i:1-2, in fact, aa. i:3-13, *ibid.*, 69ff., though downgraded by the conclusion of the Bull of 1231—*ibid.*, 142B.

121. Cf. King Coloman's First Synod of Esztergom, aa. 1, 23, 31-32, and 64, in *RHM*, 349ff.; Závodszky, 197ff.; in Marczali, *Enchiridion*, 112f., selections only; Kosztolnyik, *From Coloman*, 58ff., esp., 62f. In a letter of November 2, 1106, addressed to the Archbishop of Kalocsa, Pope Paschal II gave his approval to the ecclesiastical jurisdiction claimed by the Hungarian monarch—*MPL*, 163, 198f.

122. The Golden Bull of 1222, Preface, Marczali, *Enchiridion*, 134A.

123. King Stephen's Laws, aa. i:15, 35; and, aa. ii:5, 8-10, 16; to appear before the King's court [of law], one had to be issued a sealed writ—Ladislas' Laws, i:41. The Kings would act as judge in church matters—royal charter of 1091, cf. *RA*, n. 24, text in Marczali, 100f. Common folk were to appear before the Palatine, see Synod of Tarcal, a. 37; royal judges who had accepted bribes were to be punished, cf. Tarcal, a. 23. On the Palatine's jurisdiction, cf. the royal *Decreta* (Golden Bull) of 1222, aa. 8, 9; and (Golden Bull) of 1231, aa. 1, 3, 17 and 19—Marczali, *Enchiridion*, 134ABff.

124. On *fiscus regius*, see King Stephen's laws, a. i:14; in the twelfth century, the *fiscus* "sat" [functioned] in Esztergom—see Synod of Tarcal, a. 79. The Palatine controlled the royal treasury and paid the expenditures of royal envoys sent abroad, Tarcal, a. 36. Hóman, *Magyar pénzügy*, 30ff. See further the Golden Bull of 1222, aa. 8, 20, 23, 26; and, the Bull of 1231, aa. 6, 15, 16, 31 and 32.

125. Cf. *RA*, n. 27; for text, see *CD*, I, 480ff.; compare with *RA*, n. 24, with text in Marczali, *Enchiridion*, 99ff.; on the Exchequer in England under Henry I (d. 1135), cf. Petit-Dutaillis, 67f.; earlier, in the Frankish west, it was the *camerarius* who handled economic matters—see Dopsch, I, 163ff.

126. Marczali, 132ABf., c. 1.

127. As it may be concluded from King Stephen's Admonitions, a. vii, *SSH*, II, 619ff. In his own household, the Palatine could only handle cases of individuals who lived under a reeve's jurisdiction; he could not judge members of the (lesser) nobility; in the eleventh century, the Palatine was still a judge at the King's court. Cf. Ladislas' Laws, iii:2.

128. Fichtenau, *Carolingian Empire*, 104ff.; idem, *Beiträge zur Mediävistik*, II, 18ff. and 100ff.; Mühlbacher, I, 357ff.; Gebhardt, I, 104ff.; Fr. Kaufman, *Deutsche Altertumskunde*, II, 405; Nelson, 89ff. and 133ff.

129. Kosztolnyik, *Thirteenth Century*, 77ff. One may refer to an age of which the author of the *Annales Xantenses et Annales Vedastini*, ed. B. von Simson, SSrG (Hannover–Leipzig, 1909), 12ff., and Mühlbacher spoke so disparagingly: "Nirgends zeigt sich die Hilflosigkeit des mittelalterlichen Staates deutlicher als in seiner *Verwaltung*. Die Mittel, über die er verfügte, reichten nicht aus, eine strammere Organisation zu schaffen..."—cf. Mühlbacher, I, 371f.

130. The Chronicle, cc. 67, 70, *SSH*, I, 316ff. and I, 322,7-18; on King Andrew I, c. 84, cf. *ibid.*, I, 344,1-6

131. King Stephen's Admonitions, aa. iv and vii. Váczy, *Erste Epoche*, 35ff.

132. King Stephen's *Vita maior*, c. 10, *SSH*, II, 385,23-27. Stephen's Admonitions, a. iii.

133. King Stephen's Laws, Bartoniek, 18ff.

134. King Stephen's *Vita maior*, c. 9, *SSH*, II, 384,7-11; Hartvic, c. 10, *SSH*, II, 415,1-6.

135. The *Vita maior*, c. 5, *ibid.*, II, 381,7-10.

136. The *Vita minor*, c. 2, *ibid.*, II, 394,24-27. Kern, *Gottesgnadentum*, 79ff.

137. The Admonitions, art. vii.

138. As, for instance, King Stephen's Laws, art. ii:2.

139. For King Ladislas' laws, see the Synod of Szabolcs, 1092, a. 18; further, Laws, ii, aa. 5, 14-15; and Laws, iii, aa. 2, 3, 15 and 21; cf. Závodszky, 157ff.; Marczali, *Enchiridion*, 88ff.; Kosztolnyik, *From Coloman*, 7ff.; idem, *Five Kings*, 105ff.

140. King Coloman's laws, Synod of Tarcal, Preface, and aa. 37 and 46—see Marczali, *Enchiridion*, 104ff. King Stephen's Admonitions, art. vi, *SSH*, II, 624,31-32.

141. Otto of Freising, *Gesta Friderici I imperatoris*, ed. G. Waitz – B. v. Simson, SSrG, 3rd ed. (Hannover–Leipzig, 1912; repr. 1984), i:32.; Kosztolnyik, *From Coloman*, 166ff.

142. King Stephen's Admonitions, preface, and art. vii—*SSH*, II, 619,19-21 (a quote from the Book of Proverbs, 1, 8), and, *SSH*, II, 625,15-19, respectively.

IX

The Rome-Oriented Centralizing Policy of the Royal Court, and its Possible Failure, in the Light of Contemporary Sources, and the Reliability of the Historical Evidence

Infelix terra, que inter deum et hominem discordian operatur.

Gerard of Csanád, *Deliberatio*

The Chronicle briefly discussed the military encounter young King Stephen, after he received the royal crown, had with Koppány[1]—son of Szár Zyrind (*filius Calvi Zyrind*)—who already during the rule of Géza had played a leading role in public life.[2] The chronicler failed to mention the coronation in detail, similar to the author of Stephen's *Vita minor*, who omitted recording it.[3]

The anonymous author of this segment of the Chronicle stated—János Horváth had argued that the chronicler was Bishop Nicholas, chancellor of King Andrew I[4]—that the cause of the confrontation was Koppány's wish to forcefully marry Sarolta upon the death of Géza, and to murder Stephen, thereby to gain control over the whole country—to quote the chronicler: "ducatumque eius sue subdere potestati."[5]

The Chronicle also recorded the political-military encounter with Gyula of Transylvania by reporting that he had fought a famous and successful campaign against his maternal uncle named Gyula, who held the whole of Transylvania under his personal rule, a wide and very rich country, "regnum latissimum et opulentissimum," rich in immense gold mines.[6] The chronicler spoke of a kingdom beyond the forest, "tocius Ultra Siluam regni gubernandi possidebat," and stated that, frankly, the uncle did not agree with the centralizing administrative policies of King Stephen; Gyula intended instead to establish an independent, and self-sufficient, kingdom of his own.[7]

The chronicler cited political and economic reasons that caused a split among them. Although King Stephen admonished the uncle several times in the past, Gyula failed to convert to the Christian faith of the Latin-rite. In other words, Gyula insisted that, as a *pagan* ruler, *or* as a ruler who accepted Christianity according to the Byzantine-rite, and had not been crowned king, persisted in remaining aloof to the administratively centralized territory: the realm of his Roman Catholic-anointed and crowned royal nephew. The richness of the region controlled by Gyula, with its well functioning economy, "et aurum terre illius optimum est," may also have been a political stye in the eyes of King Stephen.[8]

The chronicler's assertion that Gyula had constantly, without any reason, sought to cause disturbance among the Magyars may only have been the chronicler's rendering of a diplomatic cause for King Stephen to take up arms against uncle Gyula. "Super avunculum suum cum exercitu venit." The author based his data on Hungarian sources also available in the *Annales Altahenses*, though neither the German nor the Hungarian record mentioned an actual military conflict between them. The remark in German annals, "regnum vi ad Christianism compulit," does not necessarily mean that an armed encounter took place between the monarch and his uncle. The record has it that the Hungarian king ordered Gyula taken captive, along with his wife and two sons, and the transferred to Hungary. The chronicler's remark, "he had them transferred to Hungary," had a specific meaning: he wanted to point out that, in 1003, Transylvania, at least the portion under the rule of Gyula, had been a region beyond the borders of Magyar land, whose ruler regarded it as an independent country, and looked upon himself as its prince. That is why the German annalist referred to him as *rex*, and to his country as *regnum*. The illuminator, however, depicting this scene in the Chronicle did not present Gyula as king, but drew his picture with a princely hat on his head.[9]

On the other hand, the illuminated drawing on fol. 20' in the Chronicle manuscript, presumably drawn by a fourteenth century illuminator, struck a far more belligerent tone. The drawing occupies the entire upper half of the folio mirror and depicts the crowned monarch riding on a white horse against a wooded backdrop, with the crown on his head, forcefully pointing toward the captured Gyula standing in front of him wearing a princely hat, in the process of being hand-cuffed by a royal knight. In the left field of the drawing some knights on horseback dressed in chained shirts rode away, while looking at Gyula.[10]

Chapter 66 of the Chronicle provided a report on the *third* war King Stephen fought with his personal enemies, in this instance with Kean, illuminated by a full-width drawing that occupied the upper half of fol. 21 of the Chronicle. In this drawing, the king, wearing a crown, is dressed in chain of mail decorated with the coat of arms of the Árpáds: the double cross against a red field. He is depicted standing with both feet on the body of the fallen Prince Kean (who still held a drawn arrow-bow in his right hand), to symbolize victory over his enemy. A royal footman holds the stirrup of the king's saddle and the king's shield is also decorated with the double cross emblem of the Árpáds. In the background, Magyar troops pursued armed Bulgarians, in eastern dress, fleeing on horseback. In the "P" initial under this drawing, the king is depicted in full royal regalia. On his mail shirt he wears the Árpádian coat of arms, the crown on his head surrounded by a halo of gloria; in his left he held the orb, and the sceptre in his right hand. The illumination meant that the monarch had scored a full-scale military victory over his enemies.[11]

With the treasure of booty captured from the defeated Kean, the leader of Bulgarians and Slavs, King Stephen ordered a monastery built in Óbuda in the honor of the Apostles Peter and Paul. He lavished his foundation with gifts, endowed with privileges alike to those held by the church in Rome, "simili libertate Rome ecclesie fulciendo," thereby to show his respect toward the Roman See, "in memoriam et honorem curie Romane," he had also visited, *personaliter visitarat.*[12]

Even though the statement may be a later insert in the text, from its phrasing—the Roman curia "quam (King Stephen) corpolariter visitarat"—one may arrive at the conclusion that the Hungarian monarch paid a personal visit to the eternal city during his reign, as did his contemporary, Cnut the Great of England, for example, who had visited Rome as a pilgrim in 1027.[13] Petrus Ranzanus, a chronicler of the reign of King Matthias Corvinus in the fifteenth century, noted that King Stephen must have been about thirty-three years old when he undertook his journey to Rome.[14] Pelbart of Temesvár, a learned Franciscan friar and a contemporary of Ranzanus during the reign of King Matthias, made a reference in one of his sermons to the Roman visit of the first Hungarian monarch.[15]

The drawing on fol. 21', "b" column, in the Chronicle depicted the foundation of the monastery dedicated to the Apostles Peter and Paul in Óbuda. On rocky ground there often appears a brownish rocky backdrop in numerous illuminations—is there a psychological explanation for this?—though with some growing trees and flowers, the King and Queen symbolically hold a downsized replica of the church of the Apostles Peter and Paul. One is, of course, to remember the fact that it was a fourteenth century illuminator is commenting on an eleventh century event. According to the chronicler, construction of this church had only been completed in the late eleventh century.[16]

While analyzing King Stephen's personality, the chronicler mentioned that every three years the monarch had personally visited every church and monastery he himself had established, carefully observing the structures of the buildings. The Queen accompanied the king, and she and ladies-in-waiting mended with their own hands all ecclesiastical vestments used in those churches. Their son, Prince Emery, offered his personal purple clothing for preparing pendents for the altars.[17] The chronicler made the argument that the royal family sincerely cared for the Church, and took a personal interest in the upbringing and behavior of the clergy.

Of interest is the chronicler's brief insert in the text, which forms chapter 68. The insert addresses three cataclysmic events in about the year 1022: first, numerous fires that broke out in the country; second, a great earthquake that wracked the land on May 12; and, third, a solar eclipse that occurred on June 22. Although somewhat out of context, this brief insert may rest on information the chronicler obtained from contemporary data, in order to make it clear that his account was reliable because he examined only contemporary evidence.[18]

The chronicler presented Kean, the Bulgarian and Slavic leader, as a seasoned political opponent, with whom King Stephen, already on account of the geography of a difficult terrain, had fought serious military engagements before he finally defeated and killed him.[19] The chronicler—or a later editor of the text—made a distinction between the confrontation King Stephen had with Gyula (according to the western sources, the event took place in the year 1003), and the campaign against Kean at a later date. From the remark made by a western chronicler, one would assume that the Bulgarian-Slavic ruler Kean could be identified as the Bulgarian Tsar Symeon himself, against whom King Stephen had led a campaign as the ally of the Byzantine emperor, Basileus II; and yet, Gyula Kristó convincingly argued that it could not have been the case.

The western chronicle entry provides evidence that the Hungarian monarch had treated the Bulgarian prisoners of war he had captured during the campaign in a humane manner, even though Byzantine chroniclers made no mention at all of any Hungarian participation in the Bulgarian wars of Basileus II, wars that must have taken place in about the year 1014.[20]

The chronicler's remark that King Stephen had gained an immense treasure out of the booty captured in those battles, calls for attention, while the following statement that Stephen gave in perpetuity the territory he had now captured to his very old great-grandfather named Zoltan, actual lord of the region that came into his possession—"locavit ibi unum proavum suum nomine Zoltan"—and, for that reason, he became known as *Erdőelvi—Erdeelui*—Zoltan ("Zoltan from Beyond the Forest"), seemingly would weaken the reliability of the report,[21] on the grounds that, out of the captured treasures, King Stephen had founded the basilica at Fehérvár, "Albensem basilicam quam ipse fundaverat," most probably the basilica in *Gyulafehérvár* (Alba Julia), a church founded on occupied Transylvanian territory.

Such an assumption is in line with the statement the chronicler had made that the king had, among other things, donated two episcopal vestments to the basilica. Into the edges of each vestment, seventy-four marks worth of pure gold were woven, together with some diamonds. Upon the request of the Hungarian monarch, the record states, Pope Benedict (VIII) had been asked to grant the privilege to the priest who would be wearing those vestments, "racionalia, quorum utrumque...tante auctoritatis privilegio insignificavit," to have the right to officially anoint the king, crown him, and gird him with the sword, "legitime posset regem iniungere, coronare et gladio accingere." There is, however, no letter of this papal privilege logged in the papal Register.[22]

It was in this church that the king had ordered his uncle Gyula and his family to be baptized according to the Latin rite, even if against their will. He treated the uncle with the decency and respect as if he were his own father. Queen Gisela had the church richly endowed with donations.[23]

The reliability of King Stephen's *Vita minor* has been assured by the fact that its anonymous author was well educated, schooled in the classics, undoubtedly of non-Magyar descent, and based his narrative upon evidence provided by numerous earlier trustworthy sources and contemporary eyewitness accounts, "sicut fideli et veraci relatione tunc temporis viventium accepimus," proudly recommending that the reader read only his brief [though reliable] account, "hec breviore legite."[24]

Thus, this author was the first to refer to Esztergom as King Stephen's place of birth, to the campaign against Koppány (including the siege of Veszprém), to the invasion by the Pechenegs of Transylvania, unwittingly throwing some light upon the then prevalent territorial administration of the realm, "…tribuno plebis in ulterioribus moranti;" he further spoke of the laws of King Stephen; mentioned the legends of Zoerard and Benedict, recorded the punishment of the royal servants who attacked and robbed some sixty Pecheneg nobles who had entered the realm from Bulgaria wanting to visit and to seek refuge in the kingdom; and depicted the assassination attempt against the king (the reaction to which was mirrored in the tone and contents of art. ii:17 in King Stephen's Laws that called for stiff punishments for conspirators against the king and the country.)[25]

The natural flow of the narrative of the *Vita minor* bears witness to barbaric conditions that prevailed in the land during the 1030s, conditions that seemingly have not have changed much by the time the *vita* had been written during the last quarter of the eleventh century. On the other hand, King Stephen's *Vita maior* provided less reliable data on the life and reign of the monarch, though its author made mention of King Stephen's legislation, his *Institutes*: instructions addressed to the heir of the throne, and made good use of the information obtained from the *Annales Altahenses*, and from the *Vita* of Bishop Adalbert of Prague.[26]

Based upon the preserved material, one may argue that the King's *Vita minor* is the older, and the more reliable, historical source.

The king's *Vita maior* strongly stressed the spread of Christianity among the peoples in Hungary during the days of Prince Géza, and the references made by its author concerning the activities in the realm by the Czech Adalbert of Prague lack reality. Although his section dealing with the establishment of Pécsvárad abbey, and the remark that, besides Prince Emery, King Stephen had several sons; his treatment of the personal-political ties between the king and Peter the Orseolo from Venice, and his rendering of the approximate date of Prince Emery's death are based on reliable data, his record of Abbot Astric(us), whom he presented as the archbishop of Esztergom, is less dependable, and undermines one's confidence in the trustworthiness of the author's narrative.[27]

Simultaneously, Bishop Hartvic in his *Vita s. Stephani regis*—held in rather low opinion by Jenő Pintér[28]—mainly followed the narrative of Stephen's *Vita maior*, and even borrowed segments from Stephen's *Vita minor*, then added various original remarks to his statement. For example, he spoke (not in very reliable terms) of Abbot Astric(us) as the *substitute* metropolitan of Esztergom, though, at the same time, referred to him as the archbishop of Kalocsa. And yet, the final entries of his work, cc. 24–27, recording the nomination, by King Stephen, of Peter the Orseolo as his heir and successor to the throne, and the report on the events of circumstances that surrounded the final years of the King Stephen's reign, as, for instance, finding the relic of the Holy *Dexter*, King Stephen's right hand, remain truthful and quite reliable. Hartvic expanded the record in the *Vita maior* of the reception in Hungary of the royal Crown Pope Sylvester II had sent, and thereby confirmed the authenticity of this segment in the *Vita maior* report; Hartvic's remark at the end of c.18 were related to the royal book[let] of advice: *Admonitiones*, addressed to his heir(s) on the throne.[29]

On the other hand, the *Passio* and the *Vita (maior)* of Gerard of Venice, the bishop of Csanád are to be regarded as sources of historical information from a different point of view. Gerard's *Passio* (alias *vita minor*) must be a summarized version of a lengthy *vita* of the bishop that had been lost, where the anonymous author provided detailed material on Gerard's life and activities.[30] His record of Gerard's notorious Easter sermon (anno 1043), where the bishop used strong words in criticizing the behavior of the [then] ruling Hungarian monarch (Samuel Aba), is strikingly similar with c.75 in the Chronicle—or, to its version in the Buda Chronicle—and with the material provided by Keza, c. 48,[31] though the description of Gerard's martyrdom must be the author's original contribution.[32] The primary source that recorded the activities of Gerard in Hungary are his *Vita maior*, the bishop's, though incomplete, major opus, the *De Deliberatione supra Hymnum trium puerorum*, a theological treatise, where he made numerous remarks about the country's political and religious domestic scene from the 1020s until 1046.[33]

Gerard's *Vita* deals at length with his birth in Venice, and argues that Gerard was a monk since his childhood. Elected abbot of the monastery, he decides to go on a pilgrimage to the Holy Land, suffers shipwreck near Zara, and is persuaded by the monk named Rasina to continue his pilgrimage through Hungary.[34] Gerard and Rasina arrive at Pécs, meet Bishop Maurus of Pécs, and Abbot Anastasius (Astric[us]) of Pécsvárad, who accompany their visitor to Székesfehérvár; there, King Stephen graciously receives them. Gerard makes a good impression upon the monarch, who promises to make him bishop in a region (later to be known as) Csanád—as soon as his armed forces defeated Ajtony, lord of the region and the king's personal enemy.[35] Until then, Gerard shall be the tutor to the royal prince, the heir to the throne. Gerard leads an hermit's life in the Bakony Hills near Bél for seven years, where he performs miracles.[36] After Ajtony had been defeated in battle, and a monastery built for the Greek monks at Oroszlányos, Gerard indeed becomes the bishop of the region with his episcopal see at Csanád.[37]

Five chapters, cc. 9–13, describe the episcopate of Gerard, one whole chapter deals with his Easter (1043) sermon castigating King Aba Sámuel. Chapter 15 provides a detailed description of Gerard's martyrdom—and this segment resembles three entries, cc. 81–84, in the text of the *Chronicon Budense*, the Buda Chronicle.[38] The *Vita* provides further detail on the burial of Gerard's body, on miracles occurring at his grave, and records his canonization. An appendix, c. 28, added in the fourteenth century, concludes this reliable older *Vita* based on contemporary data.[39]

One may conclude from the *vitae* of Gerard of Csanád that Gerard was born in about 980 in Venice; while in his twenties his parents had offered him as an oblate to a Benedictine monastery in Venice; and he became *prior* of his monastic community. As prior, did he pursued studies at the school in Bologna; at the age of thirty, though elected abbot of the monastery, he decides to go on a pilgrimage to the Holy Land, beginning his journey on a ship from Zara, but suffering shipwreck on the Dalmatian coast; there he meets Rasina, abbot of the monastery at Pannonhalma, who persuades him to take up missionary work in Hungary. Bishop Maurus of Pécs [in Hungary] likes and approves of him, takes him along to the court of King Stephen, where the monarch persuades him—*persuades* him? The king would not let him depart: "non permittatis eum abire"![40]—to stay in his country with the promise that as soon as he gained [military and political] control of the region in the country then unlawfully held by (the Kabar chief) Ajtony, he shall name him missionary bishop of the area. Until then, Gerard is to tutor to the king's son, Prince Emery. After fulfilling his commission, Gerard withdraws to the wilderness of the Bakony Hills at Bél to live a hermit's life of prayer, meditation, and of writing books.[41]

As soon as the king's army defeats Ajtony, the king appoints Gerard bishop of the occupied territory now named after Csanád (the commanding reeve of the royal forces that defeated Ajtony). As bishop, Gerard tirelessly, with great enthusiasm, spreads the faith by preaching and working on the conversion of the population in the area assigned to him. He has to realize to his sorrow, however, that people would be thankless and unappreciative.

The greatest difficulty for him, besides the pagans, many of whom were politically motivated, lay with the clerics who were playing politics, and in the almost constant struggle with the *Bogomils* who were not only active in politics, but also spread heretical ideas among the faithful. He was well acquainted with the Bogomil heretics since his days in Venice, where the heresy had struck roots much earlier.[42]

The bishop had the Bogomils in mind, the *religious* sect that had developed from the fusion of *Adoptionism* with *Gnosticism* (Gnostic doctrines), spread over the Balkans during the eighth–ninth centuries, from there penetrated the lower Danube regions. Throughout the missionary activity of its members, the sect established a foothold among the early Magyars, but also in Bosnia and in the region that is known today as the Dalmatian seashore; from there, it entered Lombardy, and the region of Apulia on the Italian peninsula during the tenth–eleventh centuries.[43]

King Stephen authorized Gerard to preach the word of God everywhere in the land, and provided him with support personnel at his service day and night. The monarch had let him know that he would not allow him to continue his journey to Jerusalem; and, the record has it, Gerard became henceforth known as an *elected* (rather *appointed?*) bishop. And yet, as if the king had been worried about Gerard's secretly leaving the country (to continue his journey to Jerusalem), members of the bishop's assigned *support personnel* had been charged with keeping the missionary under constant observation, and, if necessary, preventing him from leaving the land.[44]

It must have been on these grounds that the monarch wished to keep Gerard in his sight and charged him with the tutoring of his son, Prince Emery.[45]

The bishop, on the other hand, wanted to prove himself worthy of the trust the monarch had placed in him, and, through interpreters, preached during the annual law-days held on the feast of the Assumption (August 15), a sermon on "Signum magnum…in coelo: Mulier amicta sole…et capite eius corona stellibus XII" (Apoc. 12:1). He left no scriptural reference untouched to quote from, the chronicler recorded.[46] It may not have been in vain that the learned Hungarian Franciscan theologian and preacher of the late fifteenth century, Pelbárt of Temesvár, remarked about Gerard (in his sermon on Prince [Saint] Emery) that Emery has been serving God through his mind, and self control, in following the advice he had received from his father, King (Saint) Stephen, and from his tutor, Bishop [Saint] Gerard: Emery constantly loved God with all his heart.[47]

Gerard lived as a hermit at Bél; in order to keep his mind preoccupied, he began to write [books], to meditate and to preach, the chronicler recorded. He already had preached a sermon upon his arrival in Hungary at Pécs on the scriptural quote from Ecclesiasticus, "But these were men of mercy, whose godly deed have not failed" (Eccli. 44:10); and, at Pécsvárad abbey he sermonized on a quote from Osee, "The just shall spring as the lily, and his root shall shoot forth as that of Libanus" (Os. 14:6) for the feast of the *elevation* of St. Benedict.[48]

The notorious and hotly debated eighth chapter of Gerard's *Vita maior*, (assuming, of course, that its text is the authentic original contribution by the author), allows a clear insight into the political and ecclesiastical life of the country during the 1030s, and the earlier half of the 1040s. The structure of this chapter differs from the rest of the narrative of the *Vita* in that it recites, in ballad-like style, the victory Csanád, commander of the king's forces, had scored over Ajtony.[49]

The Hungarian Anonymus spoke twice of the confrontation between Csanád and Ajtony (cc. 11 and 44), though Anonymus referred to Glad, Ajtony's ancestor, as the leader of Cumans, Bulgarians and Vlachs, a description that may reflect twelfth century conditions in the country's history.[50] The author of this segment at least of Gerard's *Vita* was able to include the report in his narrative. Ajtony himself was the last tribal head of the Kabars who, as one tribe, joined the Magyars during the ninth century, and who, as late as the 1020s, controlled an autonomous region in King Stephen's kingdom.[51]

Ajtony publicly displayed his political might and military strength. He had seven wives (or, mistresses), and had willfully ignored King Stephen, because he had utmost confidence in his trained military forces *militum et nobilium*.[52] It is curious at this point that the chronicler, either intentionally or unintentionally, made a distinction between knights and nobles in Ajtony's military forces. His rich lands provided him with the means of self-support; he had control over the royal salt transports on the Maros stream, and dared to collect toll on everything shipped on the river. He claimed to have political power and religious authority over the region from the Byzantine court, "accepit autem potestatem a Grecis," had Basilian monks settled down at his government seat at Marosvár, possessed a multitude of arms, and, as noted above, he insolently ignored the Hungarian king.[53]

Whether such openly hostile behavior shown toward the king was of political nature, or was it based on personal enmity (as tribal head of the Kabars, Ajtony could easily have regarded himself as an equal of King Stephen on the grounds that, from his point of view, the Árpád dynasty, a recent occupant of the royal throne, appeared as mere *primus inter pares* in Magyar political life) is not evident from the record. Only the remark that Ajtony was a very rich and powerful lord who could blindly trust his armed forces because it consisted of knights and nobles (terms used in the twelfth century), may point toward the conclusion that Ajtony did have, besides his territorial power that assured him of both regional and financial independence, access to Byzantine contacts, and for that reason he did not think he needed to acknowledge Stephen as his king and to submit to him. It is more than likely that the Byzantine Church supported him in formulating such an opinion of himself and of his political powers.[54]

Simultaneously, however, from the attitude displayed by Csanád—Csanád had previously been the most trusted advisor of Ajtony—one may conclude that not every *noble* was happy and had faith in Ajtony's political ability and leadership. It must have been with a sudden decision that Csanád had left Ajtony's camp seeking asylum at King Stephen's court acknowledging him as his king, because, the record has it, his enemies had him falsely accused of wrongdoing before Ajtony.[55] The charges brought against him may not have been groundless; Csanád had sought refuge at Stephen's court, and although the king had him baptized (in accordance with the Roman rite), they wanted to test Gerard's loyalty: he appointed him commander of the armed force[s] to be sent against Ajtony.[56]

It was in the regional geographic triangle that comprises the area east of the Tisza river and south of the Maros stream that Csanád had fought and lost an encounter with the armed troops of Ajtony; however, during the following night he regrouped his forces, attacked anew, and not only defeated the army of Ajtony, but killed him. He ordered the bodies of fallen *Christian* soldiers (does the specification mean that there may have been *non-Christians*, such as Moslems, fighting on Ajtony's side?) buried at the Saint John's Basilian monastery in Marosvár (at that time no other monastic community existed in the area), without, however, expelling the Basilian monks, Ajtony's protégés, from the area.[57] In giving thanks for his victory, Csanád had a monastery built in the honor of Saint George, and transferred the Basilian monks there from the monastery of Saint John's.[58]

The background of the transfer is interesting because Csanád had Ajtony's religious representatives (Byzantine monks of Marosvár, a monastery erected in the honor of Saint John), transferred to a monastic house dedicated to Saint George, a military saint highly regarded in the Latin west. In such a manner, the house in Marosvár (according to the Gerard's *Vita*, re-named Csanád), now evacuated by the Greek monks, became the official residence of Gerard, who now was able to take possession of the area assigned to his ecclesiastical jurisdiction, while King Stephen had ordered that priests and monks of other monastic communities be at the service of the bishop of Csanád, and that Bishop Gerard and his clergy be officially assigned their share of the church tithe legally due to them.[59] Ten ordained monks from the monastic communities of Pécsvárad, Zalavár, Bél and Pannonhalma, seven of whom would be preaching in the Magyar language, and/or act as interpreters, all learned men, had joined the bishop of Csanád's spiritual household.[60]

In other places the record here refers to both King Stephen and Bishop Gerard without calling them saints, for the evident reason that they had only been canonized in the year 1083, clearly indicating that the written record here relied upon contemporary intelligence.[61]

The bishop had a school—soon to be expanded—established under the supervision of Master Walter, to assure the education of future generations of clerics, as there must have been a tremendous need for educated and disciplined clergymen in his territory. The record has it that the bishop carried on with his diocesan duties— conducting baptisms, establishing new parishes, consecrating churches, visiting the faithful.[62] The people flocked to him.[63] The historian is a little skeptical of such statements in the record, as he is reminded by the words of Gerard, and by the record of his *Vita*, that most of the priest and monk missionaries active in the land did not know the people's language. Gerard himself had preached through an interpreter.[64]

Christianization remained an enforced affair, as it is further evident from the remarks made by Gerard.[65] The question remains, how effectively could clerics who did not know the language of the population—and knew much less about the Magyar frame of mind—spread the Christian religion in the land? One may assume, of course, that Gerard conversed in Latin when he spoke to the monarch, or to his fellow clerics. As the good pastor of his flock, he frequently intervened in personal matters of secular nature before the royal court. It might have been on one of those occasions after such a visit with the king, that at the end of the day Gerard, retiring for the night, heard the song of a Magyar woman working a handmill: she sang in Hungarian. From the question, he addressed to his associate, "Walthere, audis symphoniam Ungarorum qualiter sonat," it is evident that the bishop for the first time in his life had actually heard someone sing in the Magyar tongue (even though the editor of the text had expressed a different opinion on this question.)[66]

Gerard held no illusions, despite the numerous success he achieved in the secular and ecclesiastical politics of the land; he held doubts about the future, be it the political future of the country, or that of Latin-rite Christianity. He must have been aware that sermons given, teaching of religion done through interpreters, or, in the case of Magyar-speaking clerics the very lack of religious vocabulary: theological vocabulary in the Magyar vernacular coupled with the rather shallow theological training and knowledge of the young hurriedly graduated and ordained clerics, with their less than proper personal public manners, could not have contributed much to a real understanding of Christian doctrine among the population.[67] Nor could one leave out of consideration the numerous heresies (political dissenters?) Gerard had so often referred to in his writing,[68] among whom the trained, educated and well-heeled missionaries of the Byzantine Church were able to move about with self-assurance. One good example of this would be the transfer of Basilian monks from their monastic community at Marosvár to the then recently built monastic house of Saint George;[69] the easily perceivable progress the Basilian monks had made in their missionary efforts among the population, with whose efforts the barely educated, poorly prepared clergy of the Latin-rite simply could not compete.[70]

On a given occasion, after a three-day spiritual retreat, Gerard in an almost prophetic vision, and in dramatic colors, depicted before his clerics the near future awaiting Latin Christianity in the land. He complained that the country itself had broken up into regional political alliances, as if to state that King Stephen's centralized governmental policy had not been effective, and the realm as a whole began to remove itself from the discipline of the Latin-rite Christian religion. Although he used the future tense, "scindetur Ungaria et solvetur a iugo Christianitatis," Gerard had been referring to the then existing political conditions. They, he spoke, have only contempt for the work by the Latin-rite priests, refuse to accept the word of God, and he openly reveals the reason as to why: people look down upon the clerics of the Latin-rite because the monks wear colorful dresses, "monachi erunt varii coloris habitu"—an expression that, in the opinion of this writer, did not so much refer to the habit worn by monks, but to the circumstance that monks (and clergymen in general) began to dress like laymen, associate in public with individuals deemed unworthy of their company, many of them had been seeking vain glory, "vene glorie laudes humanas querent," and through their behavior, they made themselves subject of public ridicule.[71] This segment of the *Vita* closely resembles various remarks Gerard made in his written work, the *Deliberatio*,[72] and, in the view of this writer, it is very likely that the anonymous author of Gerard's *Vita (maior)* based his narrative on the written opus of Bishop Gerard.[73]

Although he previously wanted to visit Jerusalem to preach to the Moslems and Jews,[74] Gerard now constantly spread the word of God in Pannonia[75]—by the expression the author of his *Vita* meant the *whole* of the country—converting all its people to Christ.[76] He felt encouraged to preach, to teach and to write on Hungarian soil,[77] King Stephen called upon him to preach God's word to his people,[78] to serve Christ by converting the unbelievers. *Unbelievers*—did the monarch, or, rather, the chronicler keeping the record, refer to the *pagans*, or to the Bogomil *heretics*? As if political-personal fear sounded from the words of the monarch, or from the record as jotted down by the chronicler: "...sed magis pependit in arbitrio aliorum, quorum arbiter sathanas fuit, et nunc episcopatum...assume"[79]—to preach in towns, and yet, to live like a hermit in the countryside.[80]

His homilies, by their manner of composition, strongly resemble the written announcements of his contemporaries, as, for instance, of a Gerbert of Aurillac (later known as Pope Sylvester II).[81] To cite an example, in his letters Gerbert referred to his political and religious-theological opponents in Italy during the 980s,[82]—at a time when Gerbert had been quite active in secular politics—so much so that Leo, the papal legate, in his dispatch addressed to Hugh [the Great] and Robert, west-Frankish rulers, expressed deep concern that Gerbert dared to doubt the authority of the Roman See on account of the prevalent corruption in the papal curia, and the weak educational standards among the clergy.[83] Or, in his letter addressed to Abbot Gerald, written on behalf of the monastery of Bobbio, Gerbert spoke out in no uncertain terms against (some) worldly political potentates whom nobody would dare contradict, because nobody would obey the basic religious demands of the Catholic faith.[84] As if nearly half a century later Bishop Gerard, too, had raised similar complaints about the spread of heresy on (Italian and) Hungarian soil by flagellating the general moral corruption in one of his tirades (*philippics*?) on worldly affairs, making the complaint that many of his clerical—as well as a few episcopal—colleagues behaved spinelessly in front of those who held temporal power. "Pro dolor, uero nunc multi polluant in aecclesia, immo iam totum occupant orbem, et nemo est, qui talium ineptiis contradicat. O quantos sentio diaboli filios, quibus loqui non patior."[85]

Many among the clergy, Gerard wrote commenting on a quote from Ezekiel, 22,24-29, who flagellated the sins of the priests because they lived lives unworthy of their vocation,[86] thereby causing the Church to suffer, though not to suffer in vain: "In praesentiarum quidem passio et mortificatio aecclesiae datur, quo demum, unde doleat, prorsus non habeat."[87] Lack of personal character, reckless, unlimited worldly greed seemed to predominate everywhere, the bishop wrote.[88]

The king must be respected and God feared. In a reverse order, only conflict—lies and pretense—gain the upper hand. Fear of the Lord and love of this world [of political might] do not meet on equal terms. "Verum nullus rex dici potest in ueritate, nisi seruus dei ad ipse. Cor, ait, regis in manu dei.... Illi uero, qui tantum ut nomen habeant, regnant, et populum deuorent, et tributa expetant, seque magnificent et cetera, circa mundi appetitum in uanum rimorem expendant, non reges, sed subuersores sunt,...." (Gerard referred to the Book of Proverbs, 21,1, and concluded with a quote from I. Tim., 6,15.)[89] The remark by Gerbert Aurillac echoes in Gerard's sentences: let the power of prayer entreat the return of *divinitas* that it persist among men, keeping them away from the multitude of sins.[90]

In a similar manner, the homily Gerard preached at Easter (1043), in which he severely criticized King Aba for the crime he had committed,[91] would be most similar to the tone of the debate held in the presence of Emperor Otto II between Gerbert of Aurillac and Otric of Magdeburg,[92] even though the topic, the age, and the circumstances surrounding the discussions were different.[93]

In the life of Gerard, the seven years he spent as a cenobite in the Bakonybél forest prior to 1030 present an important time period, when, in order to find relief from his self-imposed solitude, he helped his fellow monks in physical work, as, for example, cutting down trees, dictated his meditations to be written down, worked alone on the manuscript of one of his works, and rejoiced when animals of the forest visited his hut.[94] When King Stephen had made him bishop, Walter and Ulrik, two monks of Bakonybél accompanied him to Csanád, to be joined by eight other monks from various monasteries.[95]

A lasting feature of Gerard's episcopal activity was the attitude he so bravely displayed toward King Samuel *Aba* by publicly confronting the monarch for the execution of numerous Magyar nobles during the Lent season, 1043, on the grounds that they dared to oppose him; and, in spite of his murderous deed, the king dared to attend church service in Csanád on Easter Sunday, 1043. On such an occasion, when the ruling monarch attended church liturgical service—pontifical High Mass on a high feast day—it would be the obligation of the regional bishop to officially welcome to the monarch at his residence, and to place the royal house-crown upon the monarch's head during, that is, at the end of, the solemn pontifical High Mass, an act Bishop Gerard refused to perform.[96] (One may recall at this point that it was Pope Leo III himself who on Christmas Day, 801, the first day of the new year, had personally placed the *ruler's crown* upon the head of Charlemagne at the end of the solemn pontifical High Mass at the Lateran in Rome, in order to express publicly his [personal] gratitude for the moral and judicial support just a few days earlier he had received from the Frankish monarch.[97])

The brave attitude displayed by the bishop of Csanád caused fear among his fellow bishops who carried out this public act instead of him, whereupon Gerard, in a strongly worded sermon preached through an interpreter, publicly reprimanded King Aba of having disgraced the holy feast through his bloody deed that deprived the Church and the bishop of the physical presence of their dear spiritual children, who were now dead. Fearlessly, he told the monarch to his face that, for a third time, the sword of revengeful uprising shall be rise against him the following year, and he will lose his throne because of it. King Aba listened to the stern words of the prelate, then left the church. He did not punish the bishop, who continued to head his bishop's see until the socio-political uprising broke out in the year 1046.[98]

The major written opus of Gerard, the *Deliberatio*—on the Canticle of the Three Children (Daniel, 3:52-90), though, one is to recall that this segment of the text in Daniel (iii:24-90) is available in the Septuagint version only, not in the Hebrew[99]—remained unedited and unfinished.[100] The text abruptly ends with the tenth verse of the scriptural segment in thirty-eight verses known as the *Canticle of Three Children*.[101] As an author, the bishop was such a preoccupied individual that he put his thoughts with feverishly tautologous speed into writing. He did not dictate his work. His opus thus heaps together the numerous heretical doctrines and mystical views of his times, in a hurried style, and in poorly drafted Latin. His own ideas present a very confused train of thought, his sentence structures are frequently obscure; the work creates the impression of an undisciplined mind hurriedly throwing chunks of writing together, and worse still, the writing itself remained unedited.[102]

Gerard complained about the general decline of public morals of the times; he was angrily concerned about various, and far too numerous, moral lapses within the church community, especially among members of the clergy. One had barely learned to recite the psalms, he wrote, and already wanted to become bishop. Simony was rampant; the clerics bought and sold church prebends, and many among the clergy publicly led immoral lives.[103]

He referred to his Magyar land as "our dear Pannonia," where numerous problems likewise had prevailed. High churchmen were afraid of taking a stand in front of secular powers—of speaking out in public—out of fear that they might disturb sensitive ears of the nobles, or of the monarch. And yet, the priest who is too concerned about his own well-being and is unwilling to speak the truth in front of temporal lords—lords who are here today but gone tomorrow—was not different from those who had adored the idols of the king of Babylon. A priest must be aware of how wrong it is to prefer (serve) earthly goods to heavenly (spiritual) ones, to tread with both feet upon the words of Christ, to serve the (realm of the) devil instead of (the kingdom of) God.[104]

How terrible these conditions are, he exclaimed, how frequently did these things occur. Scripture says that there is a great difference between honoring an earthly monarch and the fear of the Almighty.[105] They are afraid of an earthly ruler whose body shall be eaten by worms, a body rapidly decomposing upon death. The clerics seem to display far too much respect for the temporal ruler, thereby acting contrary to natural law. This is [we are living in] a century of falsehood, a mindless world, Gerard exclaimed.[106] The king who refused to serve God, who only rules and reigns because he wants to be known as a monarch burdening the people with heavy taxes, turning everything the world has to offer to his own vain glory, cannot be the rightful monarch. Such ruler a king cannot be, but only a tyrant, oppressor of his people.[107]

The comments Gerard had made on the contemporary scene in politics of his chosen and beloved country concerned Peter the Orseolo, who despite the solemn oath he had taken, had robbed the dowager Queen Gisela of all of her income, goods and chattel.[108] He had also spoken out against King Aba, because the latter in a sudden outburst of uncontrolled anger, and out of sheer personal frustration because of some nobles who failed to appreciate and support his misguided policies and appeared to prepare a military insurrection against him, had ordered the nobles to be executed, though he himself was one of them.[109]

One may sense from the words of Gerard that King Aba, exhibiting worthy royal behavior, still could have, as late as the Easter of 1043, halted the revolution of social-military nature that was being readied against him, an insurrection in whose preparation the political-religious *heretics*, who had been spreading false religious and political doctrines in the land, did play a decisive role.[110]

Upon the death of King Stephen the final years of whose reign had been made miserable by his political opponents and by religious dissenters (heretics) preaching false political-religious doctrines,[111] a socio-political upheaval broke out in the land aimed at those who were the followers of Latin-rite western Christianity religion and the way of life.[112]

The Magyar lords, those who were the former political opponents of King Stephen, had dethroned Peter the Orseolo (1038–41), nephew and successor of the great king,[113] and elevated a fellow noble, Samuel Aba of the tribe of the Kabars, to the throne (1041–44).[114] Soon after his elevation, King Aba abused his royal powers so much that the Magyar nobles—at least those who had earlier firmly supported King Stephen's western oriented Latin policies—now turned on him, challenged and defeated him in the battle at Ménfő,[115] to re-elect Peter the Orseolo as their king. King Peter (1044–46), however, turned to the German imperial court for political-social and economic-military support.[116]

The latest turn of political events caused another uproar in the realm among the social strata that began to form a political opposition in the land; the revolutionary forces were joined by the religious-political dissenters (heretics), and Bishop Gerard fell victim to their anger at the ferry-site on the Danube near Pest, where he and some of his fellow bishops were hurrying to meet with, and seek protection from, the Árpád princes who were returning from their exile abroad.[117]

The latest turn of political events caused another uproar in the realm among the social strata that began to form a political opposition in the land; the revolutionary forces were joined by the religious-political dissenters (heretics), and Bishop Gerard fell victim to their anger at the ferry-site on the Danube near Pest, where he and some of his fellow bishops were hurrying to meet with, and seek protection from, the Árpád princes who were returning from their exile abroad.[118]

Expressing their frustration, out of sheer anger the rebels pushed Bishop Gerard, who was traveling in a two-wheeled cart, from the top of the hill that later had been named after him, gashed his head on a rock at the bottom of the hill, and thrust a lance into his breast.[119] Their behavior symbolized the failure of a well-meant but ill-planned and poorly executed Latin-Christian policy of the royal court, as it would take sixty-odd more years until Latin Christianity struck deeper roots in Magyar soil.

Notes

1. Mentioning only that it had occurred after the coronation, cf. *SSH*, I, 314,12-13.

2. Chronicle, c. 64, *ibid.*, I, 312ff., 313,1-3. Prince Taksony had two sons, Géza (d. 997) and Michael; Michael (Mihály) had sons named Vazul and Ladislas Szár [bald; smooth?]—*ibid.*, c. 63, I, 311f.; Keza, c. 43, *ibid.*, I, 172. Of the three sons Vazul, two became kings, Andrew I (d. 1060), and Béla I (d. 1063).

3. Cf. King Stephen's *Vita minor*, c. 2, *SSH*, II, 394,24-31; Hartvic, c. 6, dated the revolt *before* Stephen's coronation—*ibid.*, II, 408f., and, the *Vita maior*, c. 6, *ibid.*, II, 381f.

4. Horváth, *Stílusproblémák*, 305ff.

5. *SSH*, I, 313,3-6. Koppány's intent to marry the widow of Géza may refer to the institution known as the *levirate*—cf. Deuteronomy, 25:5-6; Györffy, *István király*, 117f.

6. Chronicle, c. 65, *ibid.*, I, 314f.

7. *Ibid.*, I, 314,16-17; compare with *Annales Altahenses*, anno 1003.

8. *SSH*, I, 315,1-7.

9. *Ibid.*, I, 314,17-19. *Annales Altahenses*, a. 1003; for the drawing in the Chronicle text, cf. fol. 20', in Dercsényi, *Chronicon pictum*, I, 40.

10. *Ibid.*, I, 41, fol. 21.

11. *Ibid.*, fol. 21; for text, see *SSH*, I, 315,12-16 (c. 66).

12. See *ibid.*, I, 317,6-7 (c. 67); cc. 66–67 may have been a late addition made in the thirteenth century—see Györffy, *Krónikáink*, 157.

13. Cf. Florence of Worcester, *Chronicon ex chronicis*, ed. B. Thorpe, 2 vols. (London, 1848- 49), I, 185ff.; the *Anglo-Saxon Chronicle*, ed. Dorothy Whitelock, et al. (New Brunswick, NJ, 1961), 101, and 103, n. 5, anno 1027; F. M. Stenton, *Anglo-Saxon England*, 2nd ed. (Oxford, 1947), 401f.; P. H. Blair, *An Introduction to Anglo-Saxon England* (Cambridge, 1966), 180.

14. Cf. Ranzano [i.e., Petrus Ransanus], *Epithoma rerum Hungararum*, ed. Petrus Kulcsár (Budapest, 1977), ind. ix, 103, and my review of the volume in *Austrian History Yearbook*, 17–18 (1981–82), 361f.

15. Pelbart of Temesvár, OFM, made an indirect legendary mention of the Roman pilgrimage of King Stephen—cf. Pelbart's *Pomerium de sanctis* (Hagenau, 1499), pars aestivalis, sermo LII. On Pelbart of Temesvár, see Ince Dám, *A Szeplőtelen Fogantatás védelme Magyarországon* [Defense of the Immaculate Conception in Hungary] (Rome, 1955), 24ff.; Kosztolnyik, *Thirteenth Century*, 409ff.

16. Cf. fol. 21'b, in Dercsényi, I, 42; for text, *SSH*, I, 317,10-15 (c. 67).

17. *Ibid.*, 317,18-31; Gyula Kristó, "I. István és családja Árpád-kori történetírásunkban" [King Stephen I and his family in Árpádian historiography], *Acta historica Szegediensis*, 40 (1972), 51ff., esp. 54.

18. Titled *incidentia*—*ibid.*, I, 318.

19. "...ducem Bulgarorum et Sclavorum," *ibid.*, I, 315,12, and compare with Stephen's *Vita minor*, c. 7, and Hartvic, c. 17, according to whom "Bisseni in Transylvaniam irrupere iique ab eo devicti sunt."

20. Cf. "Fundatio Ecclesiae s. Alban Namucensis," *MGHSS*, XV-2, 962ff.; Gyula Kristó, "Keán, szent István király ellenfele" [Kean, the opponent of King St. Stephen], *Acta historica Szegediensis*, 98 (1993), 15ff.

21. "...et ideo vulgaliter sic dici solet: Erdeelui Zoltan," *SSH*, I, 316,1-2.

22. Based upon information drawn from the Chronicle, c. 66, cf. *ibid.*, I, 316,4-19, though, the papal Register did not log any writ of such nature—cf. Jaffé, *Regesta*, I, 506ff. Pope Benedict VIII reigned from 1012 to 1024—see Angelo Mercati, "The New List of the Popes," *Medieval Studies*, 9 (1947), 71ff.; R. L. Poole, *Studies in Chronology and History*, ed. A. L. Poole (Oxford, 1934; repr. 1969), 156ff.

23. Cf. *SSH*, I, 316,22-24; Kristó, art. cit. in n. 20 above.

24. *SSH*, II, 393,18-19, and II, 393f.

25. *Ibid.*, II, 394ff., as, e.g., cc. 4, 6 and 7; King Stephen's laws, a. ii:17—Závodszky, 141ff.

26. *SSH*, II, 377ff.; Marczali, *Geschichtsquellen*, 13ff., *corrected* by Macartney, *Hungarian Historians*, 161f., and 165ff.

27. See Horváth, *Stílusproblémák*, 136ff.; on Astric[us], see c. 8, and *SSH*, II, 383, n. 5.

28. Pintér, I, 204ff.

29. *SSH*, II, 401ff.; Macartney, *Hungarian Historians*, 165ff.

30. Macartney, *Hungarian Historians*, 152ff.; Marczali, *Geschichtsquellen*, 23ff.; Horváth, *Stílusproblémák*, 158ff., and 181ff.; L. Szegfű, "Szent Gellért családjáról" [The family background of St. Gerard], *Acta historica Szegediensis*, 75 (1983), 11ff.

31. Gerard's *Vita minor*, c. 5, *SSH*, II, 476; his *Vita maior*, c. 14, *ibid.*, II, 500f.; Keza, c. 49, *ibid.*, I, 175f.; Chronicle, c. 75, *ibid.*, I, 329f.; *Annales Altahenses*, aa. 1043 and 1044. Ransanus, *Epithoma*, ind. x,16-17.

32. Cf. the *Vita maior*, c. 15, *SSH*, II, 501ff.; record in the *Vita minor*, c. 6, reads like an extract, see *ibid.*, II, 478. L. Szegfű, "Gellért püspök halála" [The death of Bishop Gerard], *Acta historica Szegediensis*, 66 (1979), 19ff.

33. Kosztolnyik, *Five Kings*, 46ff.; János Karácsonyi, *Szent Gellért csanádi püspök élete és művei* [Life and work of Bishop Gerard of Csanád] (Budapest, 1887), 147ff.; Miklós Nagy, *Szent Gellért élete* [Life St. Gerard] (Budapest, 1946), 37ff.; József Gerics, "Az 1040-es évek magyar történetére vonatkozó egyes források kritikája" [Some remarks on the historical sources of Hungarian history in the 1040s], *Magyar Könyvszemle*, 98 (1982), 186ff., and 299ff.; László Szegfű, "Kortörténeti problémák Gellért püspök Deliberatiojában és legendáiban" [Contemporary questions mentioned in Bishop Gerard's *Deliberatio* and in his *vitae*], *Acta historica Szegediensis*, 83 (1986), 11ff.

34. Gerard's "Vita maior," cc. 1–3.

35. *Ibid.*, cc. 4–5.

36. *Ibid.*, cc. 5–6 and 8, and the observations by Macartney, *Hungarian Historians*, 157ff.

37. Gerard's "Vita maior," c. 9.

38. Cf. *SSH*, II, 501ff., and compare with the Chronicle, cc. 81–84, *ibid.*, I, 336ff.; Damján Varga, "Szent Gellért 'a bölcs prédikátor' martiromsága" [Martyrdom of Gerard of Csanád 'the wise preacher'], *A Szent István Akadémia Értesítője*, 29 (1944-46), 29ff.; János Horváth, "A Gellért legendák keletkezése s kora" [Some remarks on the origins of the Gerard legends], *Középkori kútfőink kritikus kérdései* [Critical questions concerning the medieval Hungarian historical sources], ed. J. Horváth and Gy. Székely (Budapest, 1974), 147ff.

39. Gerard's "Vita maior," c. 28, *ibid.*, II, 506.

40. *Ibid.*, II, 487,18-25.

41. "...edificans sibi cellam, in qua dictabat libros, quos propria manu scribebat," see *ibid.*, II, 488f., and he preached frequently, "pulpitum ascendit," *ibid.*, II, 476,22

("Vita minor," c. 5), or II, 488,12-13 ("Vita maior), c. 5); see further, László Szegfű, "Szent Gellért prédikációi" [The sermons of St. Gerard], *Acta historica Szegediensis*, 82 (1985),19ff.

42. Cf. *SSH*, II, 499,30-37; Kosztolnyik, art. cit., *Cithara* (1976).

43. The chief source on Bogomils [Friends of God] is Euthymius Zigabenus, "Panoplia dogmatica," in *MPG*, 130, 1289ff., tit. xxvii; they were Armenian Adoptionists influenced by Gnosticism, cf. F. C. Conybeare, *The Key of Truth* (Oxford, 1895), cxxx-xli; idem, *Manual of the Paulician Church in Armenia* (Oxford, 1898). On connection between Paulicians and the Albigenses, see S. R. Maitland, *Facts and Documents Illustrative of the Albigenses and Waldenses* (London, 1832). On the relationship between Paulicians and Bogomils, cf. Funk- Bihlmeyer, II, 58f.; Ostrogorsky, 216f.; A. Schmaus, "Der Neumanichaeismus auf dem Balkan," *Saeculum*, 2 (1951), 271ff.

44. The "Vita maior," c. 5, *SSH*, II, 487f. In connection with the—to be expected—defeat of Ajtony, see the analytical essay by László Szegfű, *Az Ajtony monda* [The Ajtony legend] (Szeged, 1972), 9ff.

45. *SSH*, II, 488,20-21.

46. *Ibid.*, II, 488,11-17.

47. Pelbart of Temesvár, *Pomerium de sanctis* (Hagenau, 1499), pars aestivalis, sermo xcii. On Pelbart, cf. Kosztolnyik, *Thirteenth Century*, Appendix II, 413f., and 422, n. 29; L. Hain, *Repertorium bibliographicum*, 2 vols. (Stuttgart–Tübingen, 1826-38; reprint in 4 vols., Milan, 1948), n.12550. Important is Antoine Zawart's book-length study, "The history of Franciscan preaching and Franciscan preachers," *Franciscan Studies*, old. ser. 7 (1928), 241ff., esp. 333ff.

48. The "Vita maior," c. 6, *SSH*, II, 488f.; F. Kühár, "Szent Gellért Bakonybélben" [St. Gerard's stay at Bakonybél], *Pannonhalmi Szemle*, 2 (1927), 305ff.; László Szegfű, "Szent Gellért predikációi", 19ff.

49. *SSH*, II, 489ff.; Gyula Kristó, *Megjegyzések az ún. 'pogánylázadások' kora történetéhez* [Some remarks on the age of the so called *pagan upheaval* in Hungary] (Szeged, 1965), 7ff.

50. Anonymus, cc. 11 and 44, *SSH*, I, esp. 49f., and *ibid.*, I, 90,6-11, respectively; also, *ibid.*, I, 102, a rather instructive n. 1; Szegfű, op. cit. (1972), 11f.

51. *SSH*, I, 89f., and *ibid.*, II, 489f.; Macartney, *Hungarian Historians*, 158f.; Györffy, *István király*, 164ff.; Szegfű, op. cit. (1972), 13f.

52. "...confidens in multitudine militum et nobilium;" *SSH*, II, 489,22-23.

53. "Accepit autem potestatem a Graecis et construxit...monasterium, ...constituens in eodem abbatem cum monachis Grecis, iuxta ordinem et ritum ipsorum; ...regem autem minime reputabat;" *ibid.*, II, 490,2-5, and 8-9 (c. 8).

54. Cf. János Karácsonyi, *A magyar nemzetségek a XIV század közepéig* [Magyar family clans until the mid-14th century], vol. I (Budapest, 1900), 368ff.; Peter Kulcsár, "A magyar államszervezés néhány problémája: István és Ajtony harca" [Some problems surrounding the establishment of Magyar statehood], *Acta historica Szegediensis*, 3 (1958), 13ff.; Georgios Györffy, *Geographia historica Hungariae tempore stirpis Arpadianae*, vol. I, 3rd ed. (Budapest, 1987), 836ff.

55. *SSH*, II, 490,10-15.

56. *Ibid.*, II, 490,15-31.

57. *Ibid.*, II, 490ff.; Györffy, *István király*, 166ff.

58. *Ibid.*, II, 492,25-29.

59. *Ibid.*, II, 493,25-29.

60. *Ibid.*, II, 493,13-20.

61. See King Stephen's "Vita minor," c. 8, *ibid.*, II, 400,9-24. Berthold's "Chronicon," anno 1083, *MGHSS*, VI, 438f.; Kosztolnyik, *Thirteenth Century*, 303, and 312, n. 22. János Karácsonyi, *Szent István király élete* [The life of King St. Stephen] (Budapest, 1904), 108ff.; on the circumstances surrounding the previous re-burial of Gerard's body, see his "Vita maior," c. 16, *SSH*, II, 503ff.

62. *Ibid.*, II, 495,18 - 496,4; there must have been a burning need for an educated clergy in the land. Gerard remarked in his *Deliberatio* that some clerics: "animam deuorauerunt; inopsis [sic!] et pretium acceperunt. Viduas multiplicauerunt in medio illius," and, quoting Ezekiel, 22:26-27, continued: "Sacerdotes eius contempserunt legem meam, et polluerunt sanctuaria mea. Inter sanctum et prophanum non habuerunt distantiam, et inter pollutum et mundum non intellexerunt;" *Deliberatio Gerardi*, fol. 64',3-9, and rendered a reason why: "Non astimes frater carissime minorem persecvtionem et heresem antiquitoribus hanc esse. In fide et ueritate fateor quod ui compellabantur intolerabilia mendatia in dei expendere sacerdotes." *Ibid.*, fol. 46',7-11. Although this writer for one is relying upon the Munich MS 6211, he is now referring to the recent edition of Gerard's opus—see László Szegfű and Béla Karácsonyi (eds.), *Deliberatio Gerardi Moresane aecclesiae episcopi Svpra hymnum trium pverorum* (Szeged, 1999), 2ff., Latin text with Hungarian translation, *ibid.*, 3ff., cited as *Deliberatio Gerardi.*

63. *SSH*, II, 494,4-9, and II, 495,9-17.

64. Gerard's *Vita maior*, c. 6, *ibid.*, II, 477,1-7.

65. Christianization remained an enforced affair, as evidenced by Gerard's remark: "dicant non insanie uigilias plenas habere in nocte morum ethnicorum prandia celebrantes, et usque auroram mensas predentes inlecebrossimias. Ut de his autem sic de ceteris quibus nulla in mundo est;" cf. *Deliberatio Gerardi*, fol. 79,6-11, and compare with *SSH*, II, 494,2-9. See further, László Szegfű, "Eretnekség és tirannizmus" [Heresy and tyranny], *ItK*, 71 (1968), 502ff.; Remig Békefi, *A káptalani iskolák története Magyarországon 1540-ig* [History of the development of cathedral schools in Hungary prior to 1540] (Budapest, 1910), 70ff.; Karácsonyi, *Szent Gellért*, 103f.; Kosztolnyik, *Five Kings*, 25f.

66. *SSH*, II, 497f., and the rather skeptical remark by the editor of the text, II, 498, n. 1; compare with Gerard's *Vita minor*, c. 5, *ibid.*, II, 475f.

67. *Deliberatio Gerardi*, fol. 46',4 -15, and fol. 47,8-16. "...die beratende Beredsamkeit ist ursprünglich in Volksversammlung oder Senat. Auch sie wird...Schulübung und heisst...*deliberativa*;" cf. E. R. Curtius, *Europäische Literatur und lateinisches Mittelalter*, 7th ed. (Bern–Munich, 1969), 78.

68. *Deliberatio Gerardi*, fol. 48,6-23.

69. *SSH*, II, 492,25-29.

70. *Deliberatio Gerardi*, fol. 15',12-16; also, fol. 145',20-24.

71. *SSH*, II, 499f.

72. *Deliberatio Gerardi*, fol. 146'-147.

73. Horváth, *Stílusproblémák*, 158f.; Szegfű, art. cit. (1986), 20.

74. *SSH*, II, 485,5-10.

75. *Ibid.*, II, 493f.

76. Gerard's *Vita maior*, c. 27.

77. *SSH*, II, 486,4-11.

78. *Ibid.*, II, 488,1-6.

79. As if one might sense religious-political fear from the words of the king, as noted by the chronicler: "...sed magis pependit in arbitrio aliorum, quorum arbiter sathanas fuit, et nunc episcopatum...assume;" *ibid.*, II, 493,1-2; compare with the wording of Gerard's *Vita minor*, c. 2, *ibid.*, II, 473.

80. *Ibid.*, II, 475,10-13.

81. Cf. Julien Havet (ed.), *Lettres de Gerbert* (Paris, 1889); Mathilde Uhlirz, *Untersuchungen über Inhalt und Datierung der Briefe Gerberts von Aurillac* (Göttingen, 1957), passim; Bloch, *Feudal Society*, 79ff.

82. Cf. Havet, ep. 12.

83. See the report of Abbot Leo, papal legate, addressed to the Frankish rulers, Hugh and Robert, in *MGHSS*, III, 686ff.

84. Cf. Havet, ep. 130.

85. In the *Deliberatio Gerardi*, fol. 46f.; also, *SSH*, II, 499, and, compare with Gerbert's writ, in Havet, ep. 44.

86. "Christi autem non[n]uli sacerdotam quomodo uictitent, solius uenationes et lites et rapinae et oppressiones et scurae, insolentiae uero ac cupiditates, transgressiones quoque diuini iuris et concubinarum turmae narrare sufficiunt..." *Deliberatio Gerardi*, fol. 64'-65.

87. *Deliberatio Gerardi*, fol. 65'.

88. "Totus pene mundus talibus abundat, adplauditurque in contaminatio negotio. Nullus sui nisi ad personam lucri adspicit causa. Omnis contra dem insurgit solius confidens in homine. Vt sultus, sic sapiens, ut indoctus, sic litteratus, ut pauper, sic dives, ut seruus, sic dominus. Vis audire, unde potior impietas totius mundi [?]" *Deliberatio Gerardi*, fol. 110'-111.

89. *Ibid.*, fol. 146'-47. The chronicler monk Richerius described how Gerbert had taught classics and [logical] clear speech to his students—cf. *Richeri Historiarum libri IV*, rev. ed., ed. G. Waitz, SSrG (Hannover, 1877), iii:47 and 48.

90. See Havet, ep. 167, though numbered as ep. 174, in *MPL*, 139, 248.

91. *SSH*, II, 500; and, II, 476f. Compare to *Deliberatio Gerardi*, fol. 147,3-12, commenting on Osee, 8,4, I Timothy 6, 15, and Job, 43,30.

92. Cf. Richerius, iii:55-65; F. J. Picavet, *Gerbert: un pape philosophe* (Paris, 1897), 143ff.

93. See *SSH*, I, 175f.

94. Gerard's *Vita maior*, cc. 6–7.

95. *Ibid.*, cc. 9–11.

96. *Ibid.*, c. 14, *SSH*, II, 501; compare with the report in the Chronicle, c. 75, *ibid.*, I, 329,11-14.

97. Cf. Einhardi, *Vita Caroli Magni*, 6th ed., ed. O. Holder-Egger, SSrG (Hannover, 1911, repr. 1911), c. 28. *Annales regni Francorum qui dicuntur Einhardi*, ed. G. H. Pertz and Fr. Kurze, SSrG (Hannover, 1895; repr. 1950), anno 801; Thomas Hodgin, *Charles the Great* (1897; repr. Port Washington, NY–London, 1970), 182ff.; Erna Patzelt, *Die karolingische Renaissance*, 2nd ed., with Cyrille Vogel, "La réform culturelle sous Pépin le Bréf et sous Charlemagne" (Graz, 1965), 32ff.; P. E. Schramm, "Die Anerkennung Karl des Grossen als Kaiser," *HZ*, 172 (1951), 449ff.

98. *SSH*, II, 501f.

99. On Daniel, 3:24-29, *recte* 3:[52]58 – 87 [88], available in Origen's *Septuagint* (the fifth column in his *Hexapla*); for Latin text, see *Biblia sacra iuxta Vulgatam versionem*, ed. Robert Weber et al., 4th rev. ed. (Stuttgart, 1994), 1348b – 1351a; for

comments, see J. E. Steinmueller, *A Companion to Scripture Studies*, vol. I (New York, 1941, 5th repr. 1950), 52f., and 159ff.

100. The Munich MS 6211, frequently referred to above; for latest edition, cited above, cf. Szegfű – Karácsonyi, *Deliberatio*, cited as *Deliberatio Gerardi*, 2ff., with bibliography, *ibid.*, 745ff. Further, Kosztolnyik, *Five Kings*, 46ff.; Max Manitius, *Geschichte der lateinischen Literatur des Mittelalters*, 3 vols. (Munich, 1911–31), II, 74ff.; D. G. Morin, "Un théologien ignoré du Xie siècle: l'êvêque martyr, Gerard de Csanád, O.S.B.," *Revue Bénédictine*, 27 (1910), 516ff.; József Balogh, "Szent Gellért és a 'symphonia Ungarorum'," [St. Gerard's comments on the "Symphonia Ungarorurm"], *Magyar Nyelv*, 22 (1926), 189ff., and 266ff.; Károly Redl, "Problémák Gellért püspök Deliberatiojában" [Some questions concerning Bishop Gerard's Deliberatio], *ItK*, 69 (1965), 211ff. It ought to be noted that this writer, for one, has obtained the Munich MS 6211 on microfilm, and has prepared a typescript of the whole text of the *Deliberatio* during the mid-1970s; he has submitted the typescript for publication to the Dutch publisher Brill, but Brill, remaining silent for a time period of over a year, turned the typescript down for no given reason. This writer was unable to gain access to Gabriel Silagi's edition of Bishop Gerard's opus, published in 1978.

101. Cf. the Book of Daniel, 3,58-87.

102. Pintér, I, 152ff.; Horváth, *Stílusproblémák*, 110ff.; Kosztolnyik, *Five Kings*, 48f., 53ff., and 161ff.

103. "Ubi itaque diuine intelligentie spiritus non est, et notionis omnis transcendentis scientia, ibi asinorum procul dubio spiritus regnat...;" *Deliberatio Gerardi*, fol. 77',16-18.

104. "Uae autem nobis qui contra istiusmodi imperium incitare non formidamus. Nullos tam caros *nostra pannonia* [italics mine] con [sic!] conseruerit habere ut tales;" Munich MS, fol. 33',2-5. (In the *Deliberatio Gerardi* edition, *Uea* reads *Vę...*; *incitare* reads *uictitare*; and, *conseruerit* reads *consueuit*.) Or, his comments: "Pro nephas nostri uidentes non foris clamant, sed intus murmurant, atque sine issv [sic] et interrogatu nil musitare audent, ne quidem aures offendant regales. Quomodo inquiunt displicentia loqui possumus regi?"—Munich MS, fol. 15',2-6, with an *additional* remark on the margin: "De adulatoribus non audentes ueritatem predicare assimilantur ydolatris statutam adorantes nabuchodonosor"—cf. *ibid.*, fol. 15',1-4.

105. "Verum nullus rex dici potest in ueritate nisi seruus dei et ipse. Cor ait regis in manu dei (Prov. 21,1). Nimirum serui dei qui se regit ad uirtutes et non at uitia seculi. ...Regnauerunt, sed non ex me, principes fuerunt [sic! - exstiterunt?], sed non noui illos (Osee, 8,4);" Munich MS, fol. 146'20-26, and fol. 147,1-5. Or, "...discretio autem mundorum et inmundorum in perfectissima et mundissima superreponitur libertate quam hirciliter uiuentes non ualent animaduertere," and quoting from Romans, 1:21, continued, "nil insipientibus deo preponere diabolum, carnalia spiritualibus, et regium manibus ferre pilleum, et christi uerba uentilare pedibus. Pro nefas frequenter talia uidimus," Munich MS, fol. 146',4-12.

106. "Pro dolor, uero nunc multi pollunt in aecclesia, immo iam totum occupant orbem, et nemo est qui talium ineptis contradicat. O quantos sentio diaboli filios, quibus loqui non patior," Munich MS, fol. 46,22-26, as if to refer to Gerard's *Vita maior*, in *SSH*, II, 499f. Gerard further wrote, "Vt [sic] de his nihilominus de omnibus qui audita cruce et aeuangelio et utriusque fide stabilitate in aecclesia gratulantur, magis adherent stultorvm [sic] neniis philosophorum, dictisque gentilium, quam eloquiis prophetarum et

aeuangelistarum, quibus totus mundus inradiatus est. …Multa autem dicta et quibusdam sorte incredibilia animaduertimus," Munich MS, fol. 61',2-12.

107. Gerard would argue that "Istiusmodi thesaurum non potuit habere darius rex, non xerses [sic!], non artrhaxerses [sic!], …non alexander macedo…;" Munich MS, fol. 44'26-45. In his point of view, "Uae nobis qui quotiens maguis principi obedimus quam deo, tociens statutam auream adoramus, et ad uocem tubae fistulae, et citharae, sambucae, et psalterii et simphoniae, et uniuersi generis musicorum nosmet prosternimus. Haec quidem omnia secundum hoc instrumenta diaboli sunt," Munich MS, fol. 3,7-12.

108. Gerard's idea concerning royal behavior: "Verum [sic] nullus rex dici potwst in ueritate nisi seruus dei de ipse. Cor ait regis in manu dei – 'Sicut divisiones aquarum, ita cor regis in manus Domino' (Proverbs, 21:1) – nimirum serui dei quɪ se regit ad uirtutes et non ad uitia, ad uitam aeternam, non ad infernum, ad laudem dei, non ad extollentiam seculi. Illi uero qui tantum ut nomen habeant, et populum deuorent, et tribut expectant seque mangnificent, et cetera circa mundi appetitum in uanum rumorem expendant, non reges, sed subuersores sunt, de quibus loquitur rex regum et domunus dominantium…"—Munich MS, fol. 146',20-25. On Peter Orseolo's irresponsible behavior toward the dowager Queen, see the record in the *Annales Altahenses maiores*, a. 1041, although previously, Queen Gisela supported Peter's succession to the throne— Kosztolnyik, *Five Kings*, 57. On the Altaich Annals, cf. Herbert Grundmann, *Geschichtsschreibung im Mittelalter*, 2nd rev. ed. (Göttingen, 1965), 24ff.

109. Sermon recorded in *SSH*, II, 500,19-27, and in *SSH*, II, 476,21-30; quoting from the Book of Wisdom, Gerard continued: "Haec fuit vitae humanae deceptio, quoniam aut affectui aut regi scientes homines, incommunicabile nomen lapidibus et lignis inposuerunt," Munich MS, fol. 78,15-19.

110. Gerard's *Vita maior*, c. 13, *SSH*, II, 499f.; his *Vita minor*, c. 5, *ibid.*, II, 477,15-30. "Si prophetas falsi nihilominus sunt in terra non plura quanquam sepissima plura et inmunda, illi narrare possunt qui uix psalmis auditis inn scola cathdras arripierunt episcoplaes. De cetero germania narret et pannonia non sileat," Munich MS, fol. 65,2-7; "Nimirum dixi quia filii diaboli qui potestates sunt teberarum ubique regnant et dominantur," Munich MS, fol. 46',24-26.

111. Cf. the Chronicle, c. 69, *SSH*, I, 318ff.; King Stephen's *Vita minor*, cc. 5–6, *ibid.*, II, 398f.; Hartvic, c. 21, *ibid.*, II, 430, and, e.g., Stephen's Laws, art. ii:17 (c. 51); Györffy, *István király*, 377ff.

112. "Vt de his nihilominus de omnibus qui audita cruce et aeuangelio et utriusque fide stabilitate in aecclesia gratulantur, magis adherent stultorvm [sic!] neniis philosophorum, …multa enim dicta et quibusdam sorte incredibilia animaduertimus;" Munich MS, fol. 61',2-12. "Vade [sic] danihel,—Gerard argued—quia clausa sunt signatique sermones usque ad tempus praefinitum. Eligentur et dealbabuntur, et quasi ignis probabuntur multi. Et impii agent impie neque intellegent omnes impii," followed by a quote from Daniel, 12,10; cf. Munich MS, fol. 145',20-24. "Itaque melius est mitti in fornacem quam ad uocem talium…qui societatem in christi regno non possident statuam adorare;" Munich MS, fol. 3',15-16. Kosztolnyik, *Five Kings*, 52 and 54.

113. Chronicle, c. 70, *SSH*, I, 322,18-21. Very briefly, *Annales Altahenses*, a. 1038; Wipo, c. 38. Gábor Klaniczay, "*Rex iuistus.* Le saint fondateur de la royauté chrétienne," in Sándor Csernus – Klára Korompay (eds.), *Les hongrois et l'Europe conquéte et intégration* (Paris–Szeged, 1999), 265ff.

114. Chronicle, c. 72; *Annales Altahenses*, a.1041.

115. Chronicle, cc. 75–76 (esp. *SSH*, I, 331,9-16); Gerard's *Vita maior*, c. 14; *Annales Altahenses*, a.1044.

116. Chronicle, c. 77.

117. Gerard's *Vita maior*, c. 15; Chronicle, c. 77 (*SSH*, I, 333,4-14); *Annales Altahenses*, anno 1044.

118. Gerard's *Vita maior*, c. 15, and compare to Chronicle, c. 81. Further, Kornél Szovák, "L'historiographie hongroise à l'époche Arpadienne," in *Les hongrois et l'Europe*, 375ff.; Kosztolnyik, *Five Kings*, 68ff. and 173ff.

119. "…et dum adhuc palpitaret, in pectore lancea percussus ac deinde super unum lapidem ipsum trahentes contriverunt cerebrum eius;" *ibid*, II, 502,31-33 (c. 15). László Szegfű, "Gellért püspök halála," 19ff.

X

The Monarch Who Reigned and Ruled

Stephanus...favore principum et plebis in regni solium laudabiliter provectus ardentiori animo veritatis cepit propogator existere....

Vita minor s. Stephani regis, c. 2.

The years of the 1030s were difficult times in the life of King Stephen. When the German emperor, Conrad II, invaded the country, the king, who was taken off guard by the unexpected attack, asked for the aid of heaven against the earthly enemy, and placed the realm under the protection of Mary, the Mother of God. If it pleases you, My Lady, he prayed, that the enemy devastate the land, this freshly planted seedling of the Christian faith, do not reckon it to my unreadiness, but to the resolution of their will. Were the pastor to deserve punishment, let him suffer it, but save the people, his innocent people from devastation.[1] One may conclude from this sentence that as early as the 1030s, the Magyars' country had been offered to the Mother of God; as Hartvic mentioned it, King Stephen had, indeed, presented his people, and his country, to the Mother of God for her heavenly protection.[2]

The author of King Stephen's *Vita minor* recorded earlier the eruption of the Pechenegs into Transylvania. He narrated that the monarch had a dream during his noon time nap warning him of the threat to ready himself for the defense of the region. The monarch, indeed, by sending a message *tribuno plebis in ulterioribus moranti*, ordered the Head Reeve of the "Land beyond the Forest"[3] to be prepared, to fortify his strongholds, pursue and put the enemy to flight, capture a few of them—most probably on grounds that he gather information as to why they had invaded the region.[4] At this time the Pechenegs were living in Bulgarian territory (in the vicinity of Niš).[5]

An interesting part of the report in the *Vita minor* mentions the peaceful arrival of some sixty Pecheneg noble families in Magyar land, who intended to settle down there because they wished to live their lives in orderly conditions, but the families encountered trouble. Some of King Stephen's armed servants attacked and plundered them en route. It may serve as proof of law-abiding conditions in the realm that the unfortunate Pecheneg nobles could directly approach the monarch on their knees requesting restitution and punishment of the faithless royal servants; the latter had been duly punished. King Stephen ordered the servants' commanding officer—Reeve of the regional [district] royal guards?—to take legal action and pronounce sentence in the case. The reeve had the servants hanged in groups of two along the country roads.[6]

From this brief passage of the *Vita minor* one may draw a two-fold conclusion: The royal order issued "tribuni plebis in ulterioribus moranti" had been addressed to the royal head reeve in charge of Transylvanian territory, which meant that, at this time, Transylvania came under King Stephen's centralized Magyar administration. Furthermore, that at the beginning of the eleventh century, the realm of the Magyars had been a law-abiding country; the monarch believed in administering fair justice by punishing any criminal (the accused who had been found guilty) of a criminal act.[7]

Among the sons of King Stephen only Prince Emery reached young manhood. Hartvic noted that the monarch had been ill for some years; although he regained his health, he continually experienced other family hardships. His sons had died as innocent infants, and the monarch compensated for his fatherly loss by his love toward Emery, with the understanding (Hartvic wrote: *hope*) that Emery inherit the throne. The king had ordered a booklet—*Libellus*—to be written, a political testament: policy of ten commandments, for the benefit of Emery (and future rulers on the Árpád throne), in order to prepare him (them) for the succession.[8] This booklet of *Admonitions*: mirror of royal conduct, provided guidance for the heir(s) of the throne under ten headings. The king warned the heirs:

(1) to preserve intact the Catholic faith;
(2) to support the Church and the clergy;

(3) to respect the dignity of members of the ecclesiastical hierarchy;

(4) to show favor to his headmen and members of the military [nobility];

(5) to be fair and just in his judgments;

(6) to be patient in taking the (any) initiative;

(7) to receive in his land visitors and foreigners with friendship and support;

(8) to make no important decisions without the consent of the Council;

(9) to look favorably upon the examples of his predecessors, and

(10) to exercise mercy with a prayerful spirit toward his people.[9]

A word of explanation is in order here regarding King Stephen's *Admonitiones* addressed to his son and (future) heir(s) on the throne. In spite of continued scholarly arguments, it is King Stephen who ought to be regarded as the spiritual author of the Admonitions, on the grounds that *his* ideas were committed to writing by the clerical author, who, following the custom of the time, borrowed from the treasury of western Latin writers to present their ideas in his work.[10] In this sense, one may accept as valid the statement made by the anonymous author of King Stephen's *Vita maior* that it was, indeed, the king himself who authored the work.[11] And if the controversial eighth entry (the monarch ought not undertake any initiative without the advice [and consent] of his Council)was not a late addition to the text, then one may argue that the king had firmly recommended that his heir[s] carry out his resolutions forcefully.[12]

The first entries relate to, what it would be called today, Church and state relations; that is, relations between religion and politics, suggesting that the monarch place the Church in his country under his jurisdiction, *recte*, political protection.[13] That is, the Church in Hungary of the Árpáds remained and functioned within the structural framework of the state, *in regno*, that is, *regnum*, were the term to be identical with the country, or kingdom, where many different peoples of various social strata, as, for example, *nobiles*, *milites*, and *hospites* lived together in one structured common society (article VI), and yet, where *regnum* would not be identical with the royal *aula*, or court, the focus of the administrative machinery of a centralized administration.[14]

Such an argument may be contradicted by article VII in the Admonitions, and by the wording of the *Vita maior* that kings could not reign and rule without the support of high churchmen, or without the cooperation of the high nobility; consequently, on those grounds, one may argue that the Church in Hungary had separated itself from royal tutelage.[15] One may cite an example of this from an event in the political struggle between King Emery I (1196–1204) and his brother Andrew, when the monarch relied upon physical punishment of the bishop of Vác, because the bishop had aided the rebellious Prince Andrew, and yet, did not dare pass a sentence upon the churchman; the case had to be appealed to the Roman curia instead.[16]

According to articles V and VI in the Admonitions, and the *Vita minor*, the monarch was the master of his country, who asserted unlimited powers over the people.[17] The king mercilessly punished the faithless royal guards for attacking and robbing the unsuspecting Pecheneg nobles who had been seeing protection from the king,[18] just as Stephen took military action against his uncle who had refused to comply with his centralizing Latin-Christian policy,[19] and issued orders that the body of the defeated Koppány be cut to four pieces and the pieces publicly displayed in four towns in the realm.[20]

In other words, King Stephen had ordered a royal *mirror*: a guide of royal behavior, to be written for his son and heir, and future heirs, on the throne. This kind of royal admonishing formed a special aspect of the foundation of medieval Christian theology. They provided advice for the governance of, and guidance in, subjectively speaking, the conduct of public business. The textual composition of King Stephen's Admonitions shows similarities with western royal mirror compositions, but in this instance one cannot really speak here of textual interpolation.[21] The book[let] differs from works of similar nature of the Carolingian age,[22] with the exception of the previously cited Admonitions of strongly ethical nature by Lady Dhouda, the wife of Bernhard of Septimania, the treasurer of Louis the Pious (814–40), addressed to [their] son, William.[23]

This writer, for one, is of the further opinion that the text of King Stephen's Admonitions shows great similarity with the Instructions of Ptah-hotep, vizier in ancient Egypt during the fifth dynasty,[24] or with the royal mirror-like guidelines by Pharaoh Amen-em-opet, parts of some of its sixteen entries, such as items 1–2, 4, 6–7, 9, 10–11, 17–18, 20, 21, 23, 25, 28, and 30,[25] that, in turn, had great influence upon the Book of Proverbs of the Hebrew Bible, specifically 22,17 to 24,22, and other chapters, as if to imply that the anonymous author of King Stephen's Admonitions had been a clergyman well versed in Scripture.[26] Aside from this, the opus attributed to King Stephen is an independent literary piece, even if it was written in the tone and textual style of ruler-guides known both in the Byzantine empire and in the Latin west.[27] The ruler is transferring to his heir[s] all the knowledge and experience he had gained from his predecessors and he personally during *his* reign. King Stephen's opus may be regarded as the first public manifestation of Magyar political literature that, in accordance with medieval usage, was interwoven with ethical and religious references.[28]

The addressee of the opus was Prince Emery, King Stephen's much beloved son, heir to his throne. Emery was moderate and intelligent, gentle and good natured, humble, and willing to aid the poor and those in need. King Stephen had prepared him to direct the public affairs of the realm, thus transferring the burden of government upon him. In fact, King Stephen had already sought out a wife, a princess of royal blood, for Emery.[29] But, to quote the *Annales Altahenses*, Emery soon departed from among the living,[30] according to the Hungarian chronicler, he had died a sudden death; "dux Emericus prepopera morte preventus est."[31] Of the circumstances surrounding his death, that Emery had been killed by a wild boar during a hunting accident, a non-Magyar source, the *Annales Hildesheimenses*, provided information anno 1031.[32]

From the remarks of the German chronicler, from the report of the Chronicle (especially if the author of the segment in the Chronicle was a contemporary witness, Bishop Nicholas, *Notarius*: chancellor, of King Andrew I),[33] and from the circumstance not mentioned in the Chronicle that Emery had died during a *hunting accident*, one may conclude that his death was not accidental.[34] This point of view is supported by the previous remark in the Chronicle that the whole country shed tears over the *unexpected* death of Prince Emery, and the pain caused by his death made the old king ill for a long period of time, never to recover his health.[35]

King Stephen suffered mainly because he could not find one in his family who would continue with his *Latin-Christian* policy upon his death; "qui nullus videbatur de consanguineis suis yodenus ad hoc, ut eo mortuo regnum in fide Christi conservaret."[36] Suddenly, the king had to realize that his Magyar people were more favorably inclined toward non-Christian religious rites, then toward the true faith in Christ; "pronior enim est gens Hungarica ritui paganismo inclinari, quam fide Christiane," that the ideal goal he has set before him—that the people[s] of the *whole* country *all* become Christians— had not been fulfilled during his long reign.[37]

Were one to consider, as a mitigating factor, the circumstance that the author of this segment of the Chronicle put his annotations into writing in a much later, a mid-fourteenth century re-write—in this instance, copying from the report of a contemporary source, Bishop Nicholas, the Hungarian royal chancellor in the 1040s, therefore, the author of this segment of the report discussed the events of the 1030s from a mid-fourteenth century point of view,[38] one would argue that these brief annotations recorded all the weakness, if not total failure, of a correct, but not completed, policy of a secular and ecclesiastical political leadership. After all, this wholly unrealized political direction carried the danger of a forthcoming, indeed, unproductive, political eruption, the seed of total failure of a religiously oriented political directive that could not be carried out, because it lacked a firm social base and political reality. This is especially evident from article ten of the *Admonitions*, where the monarch, King Stephen, warned his son and heir—and not his heirs—to be patient toward everyone, not just toward those who were exercising power, but toward members of the politically less important social stratum, lest history leave him, and his government, behind.[39] The text is worth quoting: "Sis quoque humilis, ut deu te altum faciat hic et in futuro. Sis vero modestus, ut [et?] ultra modum neminem punias, vel dam[p]nes. Sis mitis, ut nunquam iusticie repugnes. …sine quibus val[l]et nullus hic regnare, nec ad eternum pertingere regnum."[40]

The *Vita* of Prince Emery, who had been canonized in 1083,[41] was written by a pious monk, whose world outlook could be characterized as strictly ascetic, and what little is known of him, he has revealed himself in his writing.[42] He stated that he had (in 1108) accompanied Prince Álmos, the younger brother of King Coloman the Learned (*ob.* 1116) to Constantinople[43] (an event mentioned by Hartvic[44]), therefore, the pious author may be identified as Fulco who had served as private secretary to the prince.[45] It is known that Prince Álmos visited Constantinople for a second time seeking political refuge there after the death of King Coloman.[46]

Emery's biographer borrowed his information from oral history and from the lives of other saints.[47] Consequently, the historical value of Emeric's *Vita* is limited, while the writing style of the biographer reminds one of the literary style of the time of the Crusades; it must have been written during the reign of King Coloman, after the prince had already been canonized in 1083, as it is evident from the last entry of the work.[48] Fulco, the biographer of Emery (if Fulco can be referred to as a biographer), characterized the prince as an ascetic saint, and not as the royal prince who would soon inherit his father's throne. Emery had been a pious child, he wrote, who sang psalms, and when he with his father had visited the abbey of Pannonhalma, he greeted the monk Maurus (Mór, who later became the bishop of Pécs) with seven kisses, as a sign of special attention.[49]

A word of explanation is in order here. Maurus, monk of Pannonhalma—since 1036 bishop of Pécs[50]—wrote the Legend of the two anchorites named Zoerard and Benedict;[51] earlier, when he was still a "puer scholasticus" in Pannonhalma, Maurus heard about the two hermits, and when he became abbot, he was informed by Philip, abbot of Zobor, about the martyrdom of the hermit Benedict who had been murdered by robbers,[52] and the punishment meted out to the robbers who were hanged for their crime.[53] Maurus mentioned of the bishop's cathedral dedicated to St. Emmeram at Nyitra (and known under this name since 1111). St. Emmeram (*ob.* 652) had been a missionary bishop on Bavarian soil, and in time became the patron saint of the diocese of Regensburg.[54] The work by Maurus provides some information on the young novices in the monastic community who had to change their name when receiving the order's habit, and the education they were given in the monastery.

Fulco wrote that the prince did have a vision in the cathedral in Veszprém warning him to lead a chaste life; thereupon he lived in a chaste marriage with his wife of royal descent.[55] (It may be concluded from a remark made in *Vita sanctae Margarithae* that Emery's wife may have been a *Byzantine* princess.[56])

During his stay in Constantinople, Fulco wrote, he heard that the saintly Eusebius, bishop of Caesarea, was informed in a dream of the death of Prince Emery.[57] The evident problem with this statement is that Eusebius of Caesarea, bishop and church historian, died in 340,[58] and Prince Emery died in 1031, unless Fulco wished to express the idea that the great church historian—the "Father of Church History"—kept a heavenly record of the earthly departure date of a Hungarian prince of the eleventh century.[59] Numerous miracles had occurred at Emery's grave, Fulco reported. He mentioned the case of a great sinner, the German knight Konrad, who had to wear the chain of a papal penitent on his breast until the chain broke off from his chest as he visited a holy place. When Konrad visited Emery's grave, the chain tore apart and fell to the ground.[60]

There were three different introductory paragraphs prepared for Emery's *Vita*,[61] while the first segment of the work was based on the first chapter of King Stephen's *Vita maior*.[62] Fulco, a skilled writer, may have referred to as existing breach in the Hungarian social structure between the rich and the poor strata. For example, his remarks regarding "nemini onerosa sit pauperitas;" or, "nemo etiam divites a regno dei excludendos contendat, ...qui sine cupiditate possident divitias," may be interpreted as pertinent to the existing conflict among social strata in the realm during the early twelfth century.[63]

The actual chronicler of the Chronicle, perhaps out of sentiment, or on the grounds that he had no reliable data at his disposal, provided no details on the circumstances surrounding the death of Emery, the heir to the throne. He did not even report what the German source had already recorded, that the prince had been killed by a wild boar during a hunting accident, but psychologically analyzed instead the personal suffering endured by King Stephen. The grief over the unexpected death of Emery made the monarch gravely ill, wrote the learned bishop-historian; it took him days to recover, but the monarch did not regain his former mental-physical well being. He also suffered from foot trouble, but from mainly mental anguish, "et tristicia ac gemitibus afficiebatur," because among the relatives of his family he could not think of one who, upon his death, could preserve his country in the (Latin) Christian faith; "quia nullus videbatur de consanguinensis eius ydoneus ad hoc, ut eo mortuo regnum in fide Christi conservaret." With this sentence, the chronicler tactfully characterized the lifetime personal tragedy of King Stephen's thirty-four year reign.[64]

The old monarch's physical strength abated. Although he felt languid, he knew that he had to take action, wrote the chronicler. He commissioned Egyrot's [Egiruch's] son Buda to release Vazul, the son of King Stephen's great uncle, from imprisonment at N[y]itra (Vazul had been incarcerated by Stephen because of his irresolute manner of living, with the intent to give him the chance to redeem himself), in order to make him king before he died—"ut eum antequam morentur, regem constitueret."[65]

Then the unexpected—or, perhaps, the not so unexpected— happened: Queen Gisela entered the picture. In the Chronicle report, when the Queen heard the news, she summoned Buda—that good-for-nothing man; "iniit consilium cum Buda viro nephando"—ordering him to dispatch his son Sebos [Sebus] to the prison where Vazul had been imprisoned. It may be noteworthy that the chronicler here did not speak of the prison at N[y]itra, but of the prison where Vazul had been kept, "ad carcerem, in quo Vazul destinebatur," and added that in such a manner Sebos arrived at the prison before the king's messenger could reach it, "Sebus itaque preveniens nuncium regis."[66] In other words, Sebos, the Queen's messenger, with full knowledge of his father Buda, who was the King's messenger (*nuncio regis*), would preempt his father's mission by reaching the prison with specific orders from the Queen to blind Vazul, and to pour hot lead into his ears, then flee to Czech soil to escape punishment. According to the chronicler, the Queen made the arrangement for preempting her husband's intent of making Vazul his heir to the throne.[67]

The king's messenger—strangely, in the text the chronicler did not refer to Buda, but to a neutral, third person ("post hunc autem veniens nuncius regis")—had arrived at the N[y]itra prison only after the Queen's orders had been carried out. Now Buda had to take the blinded Vazul before the old king, who upon the sight of the wounded Vazul, broke into tears, but felt physically too weak to mete out an appropriately severe punishment to the culprits. (In this instance, the chronicler spoke of culprits, in plural, *malefactoribus*.[68]) Because of his illness, however, the king remained suspicious, and to pre-empt further political dynastic complications, he summoned before him princes Andrew, Béla and Levente, the sons of his nephew, László Szár (Ladislas the Bald; or, the Smooth One): "filii Calvi Ladislai," and warned them to leave the country immediately. The princes found refuge on Czech soil.[69]

A word of observation is in order here. Queen Gisela had instructed Sebos, son of Buda, to blind Vazul and make him deaf by pouring hot lead into his ear because she wished to avenge the earlier assassination attempt made on the life of her husband, King Stephen. It seems quite clear from the text-segment preserved in the Chronicle that the Queen did not regard as sufficiently harsh the legislative article II:17 (*De conspiratione regis et regni*), that meted out severe punishment for anyone who organized a conspiracy, or led an insurrection against the ruling monarch and the realm, even if it called for the accused to be placed under ecclesiastical anathema, and excluded him from membership in the Christian community.[70]

The question is why the Chronicle spoke of the three princes as the sons of Szár, when they actually were the sons of Vazul, and when the old king undoubtedly made a logical decision by ordering them to leave the country so that the princes, through their departure and sojourn in another country, assured the Árpáds' right of succession to the throne; "...fugerent, ut sic sibi salutem et corporum suorum servarent integritatem."[71]

These sentences in the Chronicle have the unpleasant aspect that—next to the Hungarian Anonymus and Keza[72]—there are other chroniclers who state with logic that the princes Andrew, Béla and Levente were the sons of Vazul, and not of Ladislas Szár (the Bald, or the Smooth One).[73] Ladislas (László) Szár was the son of Michael, the younger brother of Prince Géza (the father of King Stephen); therefore, the succession of Andrew, Béla, and even of Levente, would have meant the realization of the claim to the throne by the collateral Árpádian line in Magyar public life.[74]

There appears to be a strong anti-German slant in the reports of the Chronicle (because of Bishop Nicholas, a contemporary of King Andrew I?), and in the records by Keza. German imperial influence upon Hungarian politics had to be strong; that the chroniclers purposefully altered the Árpád pedigree, in order to curtail the expansion of German political interests in the country.[75] Punishment of a royal scion by blinding—so that he may not inherit the throne—occurred before, as, for instance, the Czech Ulrik had ordered the blinding of his brother;[76] and the Polish Boleslav had ordered the blinding of his *familiares*, Odilineres and Pribowoj.[77]

There must have been a reason why the mid-fourteenth century illuminator of the Chronicle text, fol. 22'a, preserved the scene for posterity of, what the somewhat faded rubric, in red, above the drawing refers to as, the burial of Prince Emery *and* of the blinding of Vazul. In the foreground of the picture two men placed the fully dressed body of the prince into a marble sarcophagus; in front of the sarcophagus, King Stephen stood holding his right hand close to his face while looking at his dead son. Queen Gisela (the picture is faded here) looked at the dead prince, though she kept an eye on the actual blinding of Vazul who is laid down on a rock, with hands tied: a soldier sitting on his legs, holding Vazul's hands down, and Sebos is putting out Vazul's eyes. In the left corner of the drawing three men arrive in traveling capes, the royal messengers, to free Vazul.[78] Under the drawing, in a "P" initial, the bedridden King Stephen urged the three princes to leave the country.[79]

One should emphasize here that Queen Gisela, the sister of Emperor Henry II, strongly supported the interest of the church of St. Michael in Veszprém and spoke for the benefit of many other churches in the realm. According to the laws of King Stephen, it was the bishop's responsibility to provide the priest and books [of liturgy] for a parish church (in a sense, perhaps, that it was the canons' obligation to prepare needed copies of the liturgical books), but liturgical vestments the king had to secure—in this instance, the Queen who, during her visit to the parish and surrounded by her ladies-in-waiting and maid servants, set up a sewing room where they made liturgical vestments for all clergy. The Byzantine sisters at Veszprémvögy may have taken part in such an assignment.[80]

The Queen's artistry produced two especially beautiful liturgical vestments [chasubles], what is known today as the *Coronation Robe* [kind of a *pluviale*], and the chasuble sent as a gift to the pope in Rome. The inscription on the Coronation Robe reads: "In the year 1031 of the incarnation of our Lord Christ, in the fourteenth *indictio*, King Stephen and Queen Gisela had this *chasuble* made for, and donated to, the church of Saint Mary in Székesfehérvár: *Casula haec data et operata est ecclesiae s. Mariae sitae in civitate Alba, anno incarnationis Christi MXXXI, indictione XIV, a Stephano rege et Gisela Regina.*[81]

This chasuble was altered and today is shaped like a tent; it is made of woven silk dyed purple, embroidered with features of Christ the Lord, of Mary, the Mother of God, surrounded by angels, prophets, apostles, and other saints. (In the row) below, the features of kings were embroidered, including King Stephen and Queen Gisela, with the picture of Prince Emery placed between them. (Emery was depicted as a ten-year-old, which may mean that it took some fourteen years to finish the embroidery on this vestment.)[82] The features of King Stephen bore reality; in fact, it was from this picture that they had patterned the perhaps most realistic statute of King Stephen for Pannonhalma abbey in 1870.[83]

There was another chasuble, the one donated by the King and Queen to the Apostolic Lord John: + *S[tephanus] Ungrorum rex et Gisla dilecta sibi conjunx, mittunt haec munera Domno apostolico Johanni.*[84] (The question remains, of course, which Pope John was the recipient? Was it John XVIII, 1003–09, during whose pontificate the German court kept its distance from Rome;[85] or, was it John XIX, 1024–32, who crowned Conrad II emperor at Easter, 1027—Conrad II, an enemy of the Hungarians.[86]) In the embroidery of this *casula* [chasuble], pheasants (or, parrots) were depicted in groups of twos and facing each other and pecking at the top of the tree beneath them. On an embroidered strip across the chasuble, Adam and Eve were also depicted, together with a lion, a deer, a dragon, and an eagle.[87] Pope Leo IX, 1049–54, donated this chasuble to the abbey of St. Arnulf at Metz. In 1770, Dom. Dieudonné studied it, measured it, and prepared a drawing of it. It was destroyed during the French revolution.[88]

Hermann of Reichenau made favorable remarks about Queen Gisela, but the unreliable Albericus [Troisfontes], who must have followed some unreliable Hungarian source, showed only blind hatred toward her; "sed illa Gisela regina, ut dicunt, multas malitias in terra illa fecit, et extremum post mortem sancti regis meritis exigentibus interfecta est."[89]

King Stephen, through his queen and brother-in-law (Emperor Henry II), maintained close relations with the Bavarian court, but in doing so he unwittingly undermined Hungaro–Polish diplomatic ties. The Polish prince, Boleslav the Brave, about 987 expelled his Magyar-born wife and their new-born son Veszprém; they found refuge at the court of Prince Géza.[90] Eventually Veszprém became the fort-reeve of the Queen in that the town, later bishopric, of Veszprém formed part of the domain of the Queen. The founding charter of Pannonhalma did not list a bishop of Veszprém, though the bishop of Veszprém signed the charters of 1009 and of 1018.[91])

Hungarian chroniclers following eleventh century sources, and the non-Hungarian chroniclers who based their information on thirteenth century data, presented a different picture of the Hungaro–Polish relationship. The latter seems to have argued that the Polish Boleslav had occupied the Carpathian region as far south as Esztergom on the Danube river, and, eastward, as far as the region of Eger and Sáros. One is to remark here that King Stephen's actual control of northern Hungary—that is, the region from the Carpathians to the Danube—was discussed at length in a 1271 writ issued by King Stephen V, and that the "Legenda Zoerardi et Benedicti" is a contemporary eleventh century written witness to the fact that King Stephen had control of the area. It formed a part of his kingdom.[92]

The political backdrop is rather provided by the German–Polish war fought between 1003 and 1018 over the possession of Saxon and Silesian, and of the Czech and Moravian territories. The German court tolerated the Polish expansionist policy as long as the rulers of Poland remained the feudal vassals of the emperor. Were the Poles to attempt to strike for freedom, the Germans would rely upon the Slavs (Czechs and Wends) who sympathized more with the German court than with the Polish prince.[93]

The Moravians came under Magyar rule in the early tenth century; by mid-century, the upper half of Moravia was under Czech rule, and by the end of the tenth century, the southern portion of Moravia was attached to the Bavarian *march*, whereupon the Moravians had asked for Polish help.[94] Internal struggle was devastating Bohemia, and the Czech throne pretender, Boleslav III, requested Polish aid; however, the Polish Boleslav had his Czech namesake blinded and took possession of Prague himself. In 1004, Henry II had the Polish prince expelled from Czech soil, then concluded peace with him. At this time, the Hungarian court was preoccupied with Gyula of Transylvania; it did not intervene in the German–Polish affair.[95]

In 1007, the German–Polish conflict broke out anew. Now Henry II sent his younger brother, Bishop Bruno, to King Stephen to ask for military aid against the Poles. The Hungarians may have provided aid in, or after, 1009; it was in 1009 that the papal legate Azo visited Hungary to determine the borders of the bishoprics to be established in the kingdom.[96] At the beginning of the 1010s, another German–Polish conflict broke out, when Vladimir of Kiev had been preparing for war against the Poles; thereupon, Boleslav the Brave concluded peace with Henry II and became the emperor's vassal.[97]

In 1015 Boleslav the Brave was involved in Czech politics again, and the emperor threatened him with military action when, by 1018, the Polish court renounced its claim to Czech territory (and to the margravate of Meissen). It was during these skirmishes that the Polish Boleslav took possession of some Magyar border forts—as, for instance, Fort Sárvár [Fort Mud]—as pointed out by Thietmar who was commenting on the events of 1018; according to Thietmar, Boleslav held a large fort (*urbs*; *civitas*) on the edge of his, and the Magyar, border region entrusting it to the care of the Hungarian king's uncle, whom King Stephen had earlier removed from office, but treated him with decency.[98]

Indeed, the Pecheneg invasion of the country recorded in King Stephen's *Vita minor* may have occurred between 1015 and 1018, at a time of the Hungaro–Polish confrontation, because Svatopluk, the brother-in-law of Boleslav the Brave (and an enemy of King Stephen) had called for Pecheneg military support. And yet, during his campaign against Kiev, the Polish prince was accompanied by some

500 Magyar horsemen. It is evident from the Kievan chronicles that during the thirty-five year rule of Vladimir *peace and love* prevailed between the Kievan prince and the Hungarian Stephen.[99] (The report in the Hungaro–Polish Chronicle on the military confrontation between the Magyars and the Poles is unreliable.[100])

The anonymous authors of both King Stephen's *Vita minor* and the *Vita maior* referred to it as a miracle that the monarch had been readied for the Pecheneg invasion. The authors must have accessed comprehensive intelligence on political events. In about 1015–1017, at the time of the Hungaro–Polish conflict, Svatopluk, Boleslav the Brave's bother-in-law, enjoyed Pecheneg support, and King Stephen, Svatopluk's enemy, could expect the Pechenegs to invade his country.[101]

King Stephen's Bulgarian–Byzantine foreign policy had to be based upon his father's diplomatic ideology toward the Byzantine court. On ideological grounds King Stephen's Latin rite clerics—clergymen advisors—regarded clergy and religion of the Byzantine rite as heretical, but were not concerned about Hungaro–Bulgarian relations on grounds that they were based on family ties. So it follows that King Stephen was ready to take a stand with Bulgarian support against the alliance between Ajtony and the Byzantine court—as he relied upon military force to defeat the other Byzantine ally, his own uncle: Gyula of Transylvania. On the grounds that he expected an attack from the Polish prince, and did not wish—or would have been able to—to fight a two-front war, King Stephen did not provide military support to the Bulgarians, even though Gabriel Radomir of Bulgaria was (may have been) married to one of King Stephen's sisters. Indeed, when Radomir drove his Hungarian-born wife away, the Hungaro–Bulgarian diplomatic-family relationship turned hostile. The wife was expecting a child with Radomir; their son was born on Hungarian soil. The son became known as Peter Deljan, who had lost his life during the insurrection he had organized and led against Byzantine rule over Bulgaria.[102]

A note of explanation is in order here. The fact that King *Samuel* Aba (1041–44) was baptized Samuel may have been due to the then existing diplomatic family ties between the Hungarian and Bulgarian courts. King Aba had been a *sororius* of King Stephen—"comes nomine Aba, sororius sancti Stephani regis," an expression in Latin that could mean a husband to one of King Stephen's sisters (brother-in-law), or a son of one of King Stephen's sisters (nephew). Aba was the latter, the son of one of Stephen's sisters, so he was the king's nephew, like Peter the Orseolo, son of the doge of Venice (married to one of Stephen's sisters), and Peter Deljan (son of the Bulgarian prince married to another of Stephen's sisters). Aba may have been born at a time when Hungarian–Bulgarian diplomatic relations were friendly, and out of respect for the relationship, he was named Samuel in Christian baptism.[103]

The republic of Venice lived its golden age under the doge Peter II the Orseolo, 991–1009, who maintained good working relations with both the German and the Byzantine imperial courts; he concluded favorable commercial and trading treaties with them. The son of Peter II, Otto, who succeeded his father as the doge of Venice, was married to one of King Stephen's sisters; and it may have been the strong commercial and military ties between Venice and Byzantium—and the brutal treatment by the Bulgarian prince of his Hungarian wife (the sister of King Stephen)—that led to the dissolution of the Hungarian–Bulgarian diplomatic family understanding during the early years of the eleventh century.[104]

The Chronicle reported that King Stephen led a military campaign against Kean the Bulgarian—Kean: khan, that is, tsar, ruler of the Bulgarians; the event, depicted in the Chronicle as *tertium bellum* of King Stephen, identified the Bulgarian leader [*dux; khan*] with the designation of his office among his people—had him killed in military action, and out of the rich treasures he had gained during the campaign, Stephen made a donation to the church in Székesfehérvár.[105]

One ought to study the miniature in the Chronicle depicting the event. In the middle of the drawing, on rocky ground, stands King Stephen on the body of the fallen Kean, in whose right hand there is a drawn bow to symbolize that he had fallen in battle. Stephen's head is surrounded by a halo. He wears a suit of armor decorated with the double cross (of the Árpáds). His shield-bearer, dressed in chain armor, is holding the king's shield decorated with the double cross, and the bridle of the king's saddled white horse. On the left of the drawing, in the wooded rocky background, Hungarian knights under a standard decorated with the Hungarian coat of arms and the double cross pursue some Bulgarian fighting rear guard action; two of the Bulgarians look at the king and at the dead body of their prince. Although the picture presents a view by a mid-fourteenth century illuminator illustrating an eleventh century historic event recorded by an eleventh century chronicler, the drawing is vivid proof of how King Stephen's military victory over the Bulgarians and Slavs was preserved in Hungarian historical tradition through the centuries.[106]

Beneath this drawing on fol. 21a of the Chronicle, in a "P" initial, the illuminator depicts the victorious king in full regalia with the crown on his head (surrounded by a halo), dressed in chain armor decorated with the double-cross coat of arms of the Árpáds, holding the *scepter* in his right hand (rod of justice: the king's right to hand down justice), in his left holding the *orb* (to maintain law and order in the land) as if to prove that, in a mid-fourteenth century point of view, the death penalty did not exist in Hungary during King Stephen's reign. A culprit—the monarch's political opponent?—received his just punishment in the battlefield.[107]

It was out of this booty that King Stephen could afford to build the church in honor of saints Peter and Paul in Óbuda, and to provide for the establishment of a chapter of, and the maintenance of a house for, canons at that church. The chronicler stressed the point of view that King Stephen gave special thanks to the Lord for his victory *over the Bulgarians a n d Slavs* by paying a visit to Rome; "curiam Romanam corpolariter visitaverat." In the drawing, the King and Queen kneel on rocky ground decorated with some flowers and trees, and are holding in heir hands a downsized replica of the church, as if making an offering to God.[108]

This statement made by the chronicler, and confirmed by Hartvic, that in Rome, "in capite mundi," King Stephen had established a house for (Hungarian) pilgrims, may provide evidence for the establishment by King Stephen of a Hospice for Hungarian pilgrims visiting Rome. The statement is seemingly supported by a letter attributed to Pope Benedict X, and dated May 8, 1058.[109] According to this writ, the Hungarian monarch had a church built in Rome in honor of Saint Stephen the first martyr, with a hospice next to it for Hungarian pilgrims visiting Rome. A *congregatio* of clerics headed by an *archipresbyter* (named Adalbert in the writ; two other clerics were referred to by initials R and P) provide service for both the church and the hospice. Hungarians visiting Rome as pilgrims, or on official business, may only reside in the hospice; were one of them to die, only a cleric of the *congregatio* must give him burial, and the goods left behind by the dead person must benefit the clerics and the hospice. The problem with this papal writ, however, is that Benedict X had not officially been elected Roman pontiff; the synod gathering at Siena in December, 1058, that elected Nicholas II pope, had Benedict X expelled from the throne of St. Peter.[110]

King Stephen may have established three more hospices for (Hungarian) pilgrims going abroad besides the one in Rome (as, for instance, in Jerusalem,[111] and in Constantinople;[112] the notion that he established a house for Hungarian pilgrims in Ravenna must rest on historical fiction[113]), though it is more then likely that he had not visited Rome in person.[114] Pilgrims going to the Holy Land who journeyed through Hungary were given friendly reception by the king; he guaranteed their safety, and paid special attention to their needs after the death of his son, Prince Emery.[115] It is known from a letter Abbot Odilo of Cluny wrote to King Stephen, that in 1026, a large group of nobles and clerics led by William of Angouleme traveled from the Frankish realm through Hungary to the Holy Land; the country was being recognized as part of the Latin west.[116]

The Chronicle reported that it was the Byzantine court that persuaded King Stephen to conduct war against the Bulgarians—Prince Emery's wife was a Byzantine princess;[117] it must have been through this Hungaro–Byzantine marriage contact that the Hungarian court could keep in check the family political alliance that existed between the German court and Byzantium[118]—and this in spite of the fact that the Byzantine chronicler Scylitzes made no mention of King Stephen in this anti-Bulgarian campaign, nor did other Greek chroniclers refer to the Hungarian king. On the other hand, the Chronicle connected the death of the Bulgarian *Kean* to the 1014–18 Bulgarian campaign of Basil II in that, before 1018, King Stephen had been preoccupied with his war against the Poles.[119]

Now it is known from the record in the *Annales Altahenses* that in 1030 Emperor Conrad II invaded Hungary—in the words of the chronicler, the emperor *hastened* to Hungary, "imperator in Ungariam cum exercitu properans"—implying that he expected to score an easy victory over a surprised opponent, and spent the feast of St. Alban (June 21), that fell on a Sunday, at the Altheim monastery. But the emperor returned from Hungary without an army (he had lost his army), without accomplishing his objective; his armed force *fame periclitabatur*: lacked the needed food supplies, and, worse still, the Magyars occupied Vienna—evidently unprepared for the Hungarian counterattack.[120]

An entry in the *Annales Hildesheimenses*, anno 1031, confirms the correctness of the statement,[121] while later Hermann of Reichenau made the additional remark that, because the emperor had for some time been an enemy of King Stephen, the emperor invaded Hungary and devastated it as far as the Rábca stream, but that he was greatly hindered in his military operations by the numerous rivers and swamps in [that part of] the land.[122]

The *Annales Altahenses*, anno 1033, remarks that Prince Henry of Bavaria (later King, and crowned German emperor, Henry III), visited Hungary, and through negotiations with Prince Emery, who shortly thereafter had died, "post non multum temporis obiit," Prince Henry concluded peace with the Hungarian monarch. The author of the Altaich Annals left out of consideration the year 1031 as the date of Prince Emery's death, a date recorded in the Hildesheim Annals.[123] According to Wipo, the biographer of Conrad II, Prince Henry of Bavaria, "adhuc puerulus," had, through the cooperation of Bishop Eigilbertus of Freising, though without the knowledge of his father, *patre nesciente*, but *iuste et sapienter agens*, sought to appease the Hungarian ruler who had so unjustly been attacked. The prince had renounced any German claim to the area east of the Fischa stream, the record says, and concluded peace with the Hungarian monarch, who [now; thus] became his friend.[124]

Reading carefully the report by Wipo, and the remarks made by the author of the Altaich Annals, this historian for one may want to ask two questions: first, was it really a *hunting accident* that had caused the death of Prince Emery? Did the heir to the Hungarian throne, on the threshold of taking over the reign of the realm, die in a mere "hunting accident"? In the text of the Altaich Annals there is an entry—logged two years later, in 1033—that says that the death of Emery occurred soon after peace had been concluded between the emperor and the Hungarian monarch. "Filius autem Stephani regis Ungarorum post non multum temporis obiit."[125]

Second, even more curious is the remark of the chronicler of Hildesheim when he spoke of Emery as a Kievan [Russian] prince, who had fallen victim of a hunting accident. "Henricus dux Ruzinorum in venatione ab apro discissus, periit flebiliter mortuus," as if to point toward the possibility that King Stephen, the father of Emery, may have received Kievan military aid to help him fight the unexpected German invasion of his land; therefore, the heir to the Hungarian throne, who evidently did have serious foreign diplomatic contacts—in this instance, through his marriage to a Byzantine princess—and thus maintained military relations with Kiev, had to be assassinated during the lifetime of his father, before he could even succeed to the throne?[126]

Would it have been possible that through an accident while hunting for wild boar, the emperor wanted to achieve the goal he could not reach through his disastrous military campaign—"rediit autem de Ungaria sine militia *et in nullo proficiens* [italics mine], inde quod exercitus fame periclitabatur"—that by putting Emery aside, in this instance, through means of a political assassination, he keep King Stephen and the people of his country living in fear, and leave the question of royal succession to the Magyar throne unsettled?

By quoting from King Stephen's *Vita maior*, Hartvic placed the ax at the root of the problem: by having murdered Emery, the imperial court had achieved its goal: to prevent the succession of a well-prepared prince of the House of Árpád to the Magyar throne, the prince who would have purposefully followed in his father's footsteps to build up and maintain a Latin-Christian kingdom on the eastern border, and yet within the framework of, the western European political and cultural mainstream.[127]

The court of Conrad II must have been aware of the fact that the sons of King Stephen had died young—as Hartvic had remarked, the king had all his hope and trust placed in Emery. Did the German court consider the possibility that were Emery not to succeed to the throne, the Orseolos of Venice would gain access to it, predominate Hungarian politics—the Orseolo, whose father the German emperor had dethroned as the doge of Venice, but whose right to succeed to the throne of King Stephen remained beyond any reasonable doubt unquestioned? At least that is the reason the Hungarian chronicler wishes the reader to accept.[128]

A similar conclusion may also be drawn from the report of the Altaich Annals, as if to point to an opening of the duel between the German imperial court and the Hungarian royal court, in which not only Peter the Orseolo, and, after him, King Samuel Aba,[129] but also King Salomon (1063–74) played a role;[130] and only during the reign of King Géza (1074–77) was it possible to restore peaceful domestic balance in the country.[131] However, by that time the royal court had to pay a high price, indeed, for reestablishing domestic tranquility in the realm, because during those past decades law and order, and public morals, had sunk to such low levels that, for instance, during the reign of King Ladislas I (1077–95), the court had to rely on the death penalty to punish someone for stealing goods worth more than the price of a chicken.[132]

What motivated the German emperor's invasion, what were the imperial court's practical/diplomatic reasons for invading and devastating a portion of King Stephen's realm? Could it have been the circumstance that—according to the report by Wipo—the Hungarian monarch did not allow Bishop Werinharius [Werner] of Strassburg [Argentinae], the emperor's envoy to Constantinople, to sojourn through Hungary, therefore the bishop had to travel through Venice to Byzantium in order to ask for the hand in marriage of the daughter of the last Greek emperor of the House of Macedon for Prince Henry, the son of Conrad II?[133]

The reason King Stephen did not permit the German bishop—and imperial envoy —to travel through Hungary was that in 1028, Conrad II engineered the political downfall of the doge of Venice, a brother-in-law of King Stephen. (Conrad II had been quite successful in carrying out such policies: previously he oppressed the insurgence of the dukes of Swabia and Carinthia, had successfully punished the Polish ruler Micislav, whose father, Boleslav had, on his own, in 1025, assumed the royal title and insignia—"to disgrace of the imperial court."[134]) One may note here that, in this respect, the chroniclers seem to confuse, or aggregate, various military activities in the field of politics, as, for instance, when they report on the occupation by Bretislav–Braescislaus, son of Ulrik the Czech, of the area bordered by the Vag, Garam and the Danube streams, even taking possession of Esztergom located south of the Danube.[135]

One ought to wonder why the German court had to pursue such an aggressive policy toward the east, toward the Poles and the Hungarians? German chroniclers, as for example a Widukind of Corby, a Thietmar of Merseburg, a Liutprand of Cremona, and other annalists frankly state their points of view—and not their opinions; that would be a different matter—that it had not been so much the court of Henry I (d. 936), but the empire of the Ottos that had asserted such aggressiveness toward its neighbors both west and east, because the court advisors were afraid, and had been acting out of fear, that the emerging realms gaining political and economic strength and, one ought to add, self-identity, in both west and east that would have influenced, even curtailed, the achievement of the political goals of the German imperial court.[136]

It was out of such fear that Otto I (the Great, 936–73) had through the establishment of family marriage ties intervened in the domestic, economic and diplomatic affairs of the west-Frankish Carolingian kingdom because he had to determine the formation of its economic-domestic policy, and direct its diplomacy during the reigns of Louis IV *d'Outre-Mer* ["From beyond the Sea"] (936–54), and his son, Lothair V (954–86). Gerberga, one sister of Otto I, was married to King Louis IV; another sister, Hedwig, became the second wife of Hugh the Great, the king-maker, whose son, Hugh Capet, ascended the throne of the Carolingians in 987. The House of Capet ruled France until 1328.[137]

It was out of fear that the Ottos took a firm stand toward the Poles, and were unwilling to reach an understanding with the Hungarians. One is to grant credibility to the assumption that it was Otto I who prevented Pope Sylvester II from sending a royal crown to Boleslav the Brave of Poland, thereby recognizing him as king, and his country as a (Christian) kingdom.[138] (The royal coronation of Boleslav had occurred only in 1023.) Even as Otto III who visited the bishopric of Gnesen in person and through his personal attendance made it certain that the Church in Poland remain directly under the spiritual jurisdiction of the Roman See (and not under the spiritual auspices of a German archbishop), lost his personal rapport with the German chroniclers; as a matter of fact, they grew angry with him, because the chroniclers were unwilling to comprehend why the emperor during his sojourn at Gnesen had treated the Polish ruler as his political equal.[139]

The deep hatred the German chroniclers displayed toward the Slavs sprang from their fear of the unknown and misunderstood Slavic peoples, an inferiority complex they had developed toward the Slavs, a complex of which the German court could not, or would only very slowly free itself.[140]

Toward the Magyars Otto I had displayed an attitude of dubious good will. It may be true that he left the Magyars alone after their bloody defeat at Augsburg in August, 955,[141] but one is to remember that after August, 955, even as late as the early 960s, Otto I and his second wife, the Burgundian Adelaide of Lombardy, were thoroughly preoccupied with the affairs of the empire and with the re-development of political relations with the Roman See, that reached a less than satisfactory solution under the pontificate of Pope John XII.[142]

Pope John XII did protest, however, the new Italian politics of Adelaide, and Otto I, who had been crowned emperor by Pope John XII, had to return to Rome to dethrone John XII, and to appoint as the new pontiff a layman, who assumed the name of Leo VIII, whom the emperor expected to follow closely German religious and political imperial interests.[143]

Conrad II might have begun the war with the Magyars because the German court had previously intervened in Venetian politics by expelling Doge Orseolo, a family relative—the brother-in-law of King Stephen—from the republic, and possibly on the grounds that Conrad II wished to request the hand of a Byzantine princess in marriage for his son, Prince Henry (the future Henry III), and for that reason, he had dispatched an envoy, whom he had disguised as a pilgrim en route to the Holy Land, to travel through Hungary to the Byzantine court.

King Stephen and his advisors must have been aware of the possible consequences of such a political-diplomatic marriage arrangement. A diplomatic-political tie based on marriage between the future German emperor and the Byzantine—that, incidentally, showed some remarkable similarity with the political game the Saxon rulers played with the west-Frankish realm in the tenth century[144]—would have placed the emerging Magyar Christian kingdom between two fires: the powers of Byzantium and of the German-Latin west, and for that reason King Stephen would not allow Bishop Wernier [Werner] of Strassburg—who presented himself as a pious pilgrim en route to Jerusalem—to continue his sojourn across Hungarian territory.

It may be characteristic of the emerging diplomatic-political crisis ending in a brief warring effort—a warring event the emperor had lost by losing his whole armed force during the campaign—that, *out of fear* (or, out of arrogant spite) it was not the emperor, but his son and heir, the young idealist Prince Henry who, together with the imperial diplomat, Bishop Luitprand of Cremona, concluded peace with King Stephen's son and heir, Prince Emery, who shortly thereafter had died mysteriously during a "hunting accident." In fact, the German biographer of Conrad II acknowledged that the emperor committed a crime by leading an unjust campaign against the Magyars, and that the emperor had suffered a righteous defeat in that campaign.[145] The question remains, though: did the campaign, which only brought humiliation to the German emperor, result in the Hungarian Prince Emery's death?[146]

The author of the *Vita maior* reported that shortly before his death, King Stephen invited members of the hierarchy and the *Christian* members of the high nobility—evidently, many high nobles remained pagans at heart, and the monarch had no confidence in them—to appear before him in order to inform them that they elect Peter the Orseolo from Venice as their king, and to warn them to remain steadfast in their Christian faith (that is, not to stray from the path of Latin Christianity). From the last sentence of the *Vita maior*, this writer for one draws the conclusion that King Stephen, on his deathbed, not only had been concerned about the question of royal succession, but also was very disturbed about the future of the country and of the future of the Church in the country. To remain steadfast in the orthodox faith, "fidem orthodoxam serváre"—that is, religion of the Church of Rome—must have meant that the Hungarian political leadership had, through a successful religious policy, avoided falling prey to Byzantium. On account of its Rome-oriented religious policy, the Hungarian leadership would not come under German influence, so that the western imperial Church could not again threaten the political outlook of the realm and endanger the security of its political future.[147]

The king's last recorded words did not display any hatred toward the Germans. The record simply said that the author, writing toward the end of the eleventh century had, from his own point of view reported on events, expressed concern about the political future of the people and of the country, formulating his own concern in words he attributed to King Stephen. Bishop Hartvic, who wrote about Stephen at a later date, used more diplomatic terms to express his worries by noting that the monarch had, before he died, placed the Church with the clergy, the realm with its people and lords under the protection of the Queen of Heaven, Mary, the Mother of God.[148]

King Stephen I was buried in the basilica he had built at Székesfehérvár in the honor of the Mother of God. The internment took place after the construction of the basilica had been completed.[149] King Stephen implanted the very roots of aesthetic good, of beauty, and of great spiritual values in the Hungarian soul.[150] He made ethical values the very foundation of his country's government, which survived some one thousand years.[151] His Magyars, his people[s], refer to him as their King, and named the feast of the Assumption, August 15, as the feast of the Queen of Heaven.

The author of the *Annales Altahenses* wrote, anno 1038, that in that year King Stephen had died, the King of the Ugors.[152]

Notes

1. Cf. King Stephen's *Vita maior*, c. 14, *SSH*, II, 390,1-7.; Hartvic, c. 16, *ibid.*, II, 423f., 424,1-11.

2. *Ibid.*, II, 431,9-13 (c. 22).

3. See King Stephen's *Vita minor*, c. 5, *ibid.*, II, 397,20-24.

4. "…plures in captivitatem ducti sunt;" cf. *Vita minor*, c. 5, *ibid.*, II, 397,21-31.

5. *Ibid.*, II, 398,5-10 (c. 6). "Paganorum crudelissimos Pezenegos," were they characterized by Bruno in his letter addressed to Emperor Henry II; for the letter, see *MPH*, I, 224.

6. The *Vita minor*, c. 6, *SSH*, II, 398f.

7. The king's messenger was sent directly "tribuno plebis in ulterioribus moranti"—*ibid.*, II, 397,22; also, Macartney, *Hungarian Historians*, 161; on the king's pronounced judgement, see *SSH*, II, 397,27-31, and compare with King Stephen's *Admonitiones*, art. v, *ibid.*, II, 619ff., or the more reliable edition in Závodszky, 131ff.

8. Hartvic, c. 19, *ibid.*, II, 427f.; Ágoston Nevelős, "Szent István, a keresztény Magyarország megtermtője" [St. Stephen, founder of the western oriented Magyar realm], in *Szent István, első nagy királyunk élete és alkotásai* [Life and accomplishments of our first Great King, Saint Stephen], ed. Bálint Hóman (Budapest, 1938), 45ff.

9. *SSH*, II, 428,5-19; and the already cited *Libellus de institutione morum*, aa. i - x, *SSH*. II, 619ff.; recorded as *De institutione morum ad Emericum ducem*, in Závodszky, 131-39. János Karácsonyi, *Szent István király élete* [Life of King St. Stephen] (Budapest, 1904), 104.

10. As, for instance, Smaragdus of St. Mihiel, *Vita regia*, for Louis the Pious (d. 840), in *MPL*, 102, 933ff.; and *Speculum*, 3 (1928), 392ff. Or, Jonas of Orleans, "De institutione regia," about the year 834, in *MPL*, 106, 279ff.; Hincmar of Reims, *De ordine palatii*, an adaptation of Adalhard of Corby's De ordine palatii, ed. Thomas Gross and Rudolf Schieffer, rev. ed., SSrG (Hannover, 1980); also, Sedulus Scotus, *De rectoribus Christianitatis*, ed. S. Hellmann (Munich, 1909), 19ff. See M. L. W. Laistner, *Thoughts and Letters in Western Europe, 500-900*, rev. ed. (London, 1957), 315ff.

11. *SSH*, II, 391,7-8; indirectly, András Bodor, "Szent Gellért Deliberatio-jának főforrása" [The main source of St. Gerard's Deliberatio], *Századok*, 77 (1943), 173ff.

12. Cf. "De institutione morum ad Emericum ducem," Závodszky, 131ff.; *SSH*, II, 619ff.

13. Preface and art. vii, *ibid.* 619ff.; Váczy, *Erste Epoche*, 61f.

14. Cf. Závodszky, 131ff., art. i and vii; the *Vita maior*, c. 15, *SSH*, II, 391,3-7. Compare to Aristotle's *Politica*, book I, in *The Basic Works of Aristotle*, ed. Richard McKeon (New York, 1941), 1127ff., that is, 1252a–1260b; Carnes Lord, "Aristotle," *History of Political Philosophy*, ed. Leo Strauss – Joseph Cropsey, 3rd ed. (Chicago-London, 1987), 118ff.; Váczy, *Erste Epoche*, 64ff.

15. During the insurrection against Peter's kingship, the bishops cooperated on their own and on equal political terms with members of the high nobility: "principes Hungarorum et milites consilio episcoporum adversus Petrum regem et sollicite querebant, si aliquem de regali progenie in regno invenire possent;" Chronicle, c. 72, *SSH*, I, 324f. Deér, *Pogány magyarság*, 161; Váczy, *Erste Epoche*, 116ff., cited a much later date.

16. See the letter, dated 1099, of King Emery I (d. 1204) to Pope Innocent III—*RA*, n. 187; text in *ÁUO*, VI, 198ff.; on background, cf. Kosztolnyik, *Thirteenth Century*, 4f., and 6.

17. Cf. Závodszky, 136f.; *SSH*, II, 395,5-27.

18. The *Vita minor*, c. 6.

19. Chronicle, c. 65. On the family pedigree,

- Géza's younger brother was Mihály (Michael);

- Mihály had two sons, Vazul and Szár László (Ladislas the *Bald*, or the *Smooth*);

- Vazul's sons were Andrew I (+1060), Béla I (+1063), and Levente (+1047);

- Ladislas the Bald (Szár László) had no offspring;

- Andrew I's son, Salomon (+1087?), was married to Judith, daughter of Emperor Henry III;

- Béla I had two sons, Géza I (+1077), and (St.) Ladislas I (+1095);

- King Géza I had two sons, Coloman the Learned (+1116), and Álmos (+1129).

See also Gyula Kristó, "Géza fejedelem és István király" [Ruling Prince Géza, and Stephen the king], *Aetas*, 2000/3, 25ff.

20. The *Vita minor*, c. 3, and the *Vita maior*, c. 6; Chronicle, c. 64 (esp. *SSH*, I, 313f.).

21. Horváth, *Stílusproblémák*, 116ff.; *SSH*, II, 619.

22. On this, cf. Laistner, 315ff. To cite but one example, see Hincmarus, *De ordine palatii*, 32ff.

23. See Lady Dhuoda, *Manuel pour mon fils*, ed. P. Riché, vol. 225 of *Sources Chrétiennes* (Paris, 1975), esp. 338ff.; Wilhelm Levison's observations on learning and scholarship in his Ford Lectures: *England and the Continent in the Eighth Century* (Oxford, 1946; repr. 1998), 132ff.

24. Cf. J. B. Pritchard (ed.), *The Ancient Near East, An Anthology of Texts and Pictures*, 2 vols. (Princeton, 1958), I, 234ff.; W. K. Simpson, et al. (eds.), *The Literature of Ancient Egypt* (New Haven–London, 1972), 159ff.

25. Such as entries 1-2, 4, 6-7, 9, 10-11, 17-18, 20, 21, 23, 25, and 28; see Pritchard, I, 237ff.; Simpson, 193ff.

26. Cf. *Liber Proverbiorum* (Book of Proverbs), in *Biblia sacra iuxta Vulgatam versionem*, ed. Roger Gryson et al., 4th ed. (Stuttgart, 1994), 958ff.

27. As, e.g., Eusebius Pamphyli, *Oratio de laudibus Constantini*, ed. I. Heikel (Leipzig, 1902), 198ff.; or, comments by Agapetus, "Expositio capitum amonitoriorum Imperatori Justianiano," in *MPG*, 86, 1164ff. Further, the remarks by Liudprand of Cremona, *Antapodosis*, i:11—cf. *Liudprandi episcopi Cremonensis opera*, 3rd ed., ed. Joseph Becker, SSrG (Hannover, 1915; repr. 1977), 9ff.

28. Cf. Hartvic, c. 19, *SSH*, II, 428,1-5; King Stephen's *Admonitiones*, Preface, *ibid.*, II, 619, further, compare to Michael Psellus, *Chronographiae*, ed. E. Rénauld, vol. I (Paris, 1926), 53f., and 117.

29. "Interea, cum ex paterna dispositione virgo nobilis, utpote orta de regali prosapia, beato Henrico desponsata esset et adducta, et sic ex utraque regali linea regia

potestas [*sic*; posteritas?] succederet in posterum...;" cf. see *Vita s. Emerici ducis*, c. 5, *SSH*, II, 454f., and annotations, *ibid.*, II, 777f.

30. "Filius autrem Stephani regis Ungarorum post non multum temporis obiit;" *Annales Altahenses*, anno 1033 (!); for the correct date, cf. *Annales Hildesheimenses*, ed. G. Waitz, SSrG (Hannover, 1878; repr. 1947), anno 1031.

31. "Cum itaque sanctissimus pater sanctissimo filio curam administrationis et gubernandi regni sollicitudinem intenderet committere, beatus dux Emericus *prepropera morte* [italics mine] preventus est;" Chronicle, c. 69, *SSH*, I, 319,16-19; Hartvic, c. 19, *ibid.*, II, 428.

32. Anno 1031, Hildesheim Annals, as cited above, n. 30.

33. "...prepropera morte preventus," *SSH*, I, 319,18-19; on Bishop Nicholas, chancellor of King Andrew I, see Horváth, *Stílusproblémák*, 305ff. *Nicolaus episcopus*: "N.[icolao], qui tunc temporis uicem procurabat notarii," who had signed the founding charter of the abbey of Tihany in 1055; cf. *RA*, n. 12; for text, see Jakubovich – Pais, 19ff., esp. 25; Marczali, *Enchiridion*, 81ff., esp. 85.

34. Cf. *Annales Hildesheimenses*, "mense Septembri," anno 1031.

35. Hartvic, c. 19, *SSH*, II, 428f., supported by the remarks in the Chronicle, c. 69, *ibid.*, I, 319,19-24.

36. *SSH*, I, 319,25-27.

37. *Ibid.*, I, 319f.; compare with Gerard's *Vita maior*, c. 15, *ibid.*, II, 501ff., *and* with the Chronicle, c. 86, report on the coronation of Andrew I, *ibid.*, I, 343f.

38. Macartney, *Hungarian Historians*, 113, and 134f.; Horváth, *Stílusproblémák*, 255ff.

39. "Paciens esto ad omnes, non tantum potentes, sed eciam potestate carentes;" see *Admonitiones*, art. x, *SSH*, II, 627; Závodszky, 139f.; further, Kosztolnyik, art. cit. (1973).

40. Závodszky, 140.

41. Cf. "Bernoldi Constantiensis Chronicon," anno 1083, *MGHSS*, V, 438; Hartvic, c. 24, *SSH*, II, 433,5-11; Life of St. Emeric, c. 7, *SSH*, II, 460,2-7; Kosztolnyik, *Five Kings*, 94 and 97; idem, *Thirteenth Century*, 303.

42. Life of St. Emeric, c. 6, *SSH*, II, 456, and *ibid.*, II, 777ff.

43. *Ibid.*, II, 456, c. 6.

44. According to László Erdélyi, *Szent Imre legendája* [St. Emeric's legend] (Budapest, 1930), 45f.

45. One may refer to the last will of Fulco *hospes*, known also as the former *clericus* of Archbishop Seraphim, and of various Hungarian bishops, benefiting the church in Pannonhalma, etc.; the will had been confirmed by Géza II in 1146—see *RA*, n. 73; text in *ÁUO*, I, 58f.

46. Prince Álmos, the son of Géza I, 1074-77, and the brother of Coloman the Learned, 1095-1116, had been blinded (by his royal brother) toward the end of Coloman's reign, and the prince, fearing for his life, fled the county seeking refuge in Byzantium—cf. Chronicle, c. 151; Johannes Cinnamus, *Epitomae rerum ab Ioanne et Alexio Comnenis gestarum*, ed. A. Meineke, *C B* (Bonn, 1836), 9,10-12, who had mistakenly referred to Álmos as one of the two the sons of Ladislas I, 1077-95; also, *Nicetae Choniatae Historiae*, ed. I. A. van Dieten (Berlin–New York, 1975), 17,39-18,66; like Cinnamus, Choniates also provides an erroneous family pedigree.

47. See, for instance, the Life of St. Emeric, preface and c. 7, *SSH*, II, 449f., and 457,1-5.

48. *Ibid.*, II, 459f.; Macartney, *Hungarian Historians*, 170f.

49. Emeric's Life, c. 2, *SSH*, II, 452.

50. "...nunc episcopus, ...tunc autem puer scholasticus"—cf. *SSH*, II, 357,18-19; the name of Maurus appears on the Tihany charter, 1055; cf. *RA*, n. 12: "signum Mauri episcopi," cf. Jakubovich – Pais, 24; Marczali, *Enchiridion*, 85.

51. See *SSH*, II, 357ff., and *ibid.*, II, 769f.; Macartney, *Hungarian Historians*, 151; Csóka, 101ff.; R. Prazak, "A Legenda sanctorum Zoerardi et Benedicti történelmi és kulturális összefüggései" [Some remarks concerning the historical and cultural relationship of the Saint Zoerard and Benedict legends], *ItK*, 84 (1980), 393ff.

52. *SSH*, II, 357,4-15; 359,20-29.

53. *Ibid.*, II, 359f.; *MPL*, 141, 969ff., esp. 975. On the bishopric of N[y]itra, cf. *RA*, n. 43; Fejér, *CD*, VII-4, 57ff.; László Fejérpataky, *Kálmán király oklevelei* [The official writs of King Coloman the Learned] (Budapest, 1892), 40ff.

54. *SSH*, II, 361, c. 4.

55. St. Emeric's Life, cc. 4-5, *ibid.* II, 454f.

56. Cf. the Life of Margaret, c. 12, *ibid.*, II, 685ff., based on the edition by Kornél Böle, *Árpádházi boldog Margit szentté avatási ügye és a legősibb latin Margit-legenda* [The canonization process of Blessed Margaret of the House of Árpád, and the oldest known Margaret legend] (Budapest, 1937), 17ff.; Tibor Klaniczay, *A magyar irodalom története 1600-ig* [History of Hungarian literature until 1600] (Budapest, 1964), 117f.

57. *Ibid.*, II, 456, c. 6.

58. Funk – Bihlmeyer, I, 269f.; Hans von Campenhausen, *Griechische Kirchenväter*, 3rd ed. (Stuttgart, 1961), 61ff.

59. As it may be evident from the remarks of the author: "Eadem quoque visio...per orationem sancti Eusebii revelata est. Et quoniam necessaria sunt miracula, ubi humana inbecillitas ad credendum est tarda...;" *SSH*, II, 456,18-21.

60. *Ibid.*, II, 457, c. 7.

61. *Ibid.*, II, 449; Csóka, 199ff.

62. The *Vita maior*, *SSH*, II, 377f.; and Hartvic, cc. 4 and 19.

63. *SSH*, II, 451,7-10.

64. *Ibid.*, I, 319,25-27; Csóka, 344ff.

65. For the whole passage, see *SSH*, I, 320,9-12.

66. *Ibid.*, I, 320,12-16.

67. *Ibid.*, I, 320,15-17; see the drawing by a fourteenth century hand depicting the blinding of Vazul, in Dercsényi, *Chronicon pictum*, I, fol. 22'a.

68. *SSH*, I, 320f.

69. *Ibid.*, I, 320,17 – 321,9. Compare with the remark by the Hungarian Anonymus: "Andreas, filius Calvi Ladizlay," c. 15, *ibid.*, I, 55,19, and with Keza, c. 44, *ibid.*, I, 173,14-15. On the other hand, the *Annales Altahenses*, anno 1041, referred to the three princes as the sons of Vazul, "whose parentage is disputed, but in any case they were first cousins once removed from St. Stephen," wrote Macartney, *Hungarian Historians*, 19, n. 2, and 124f.

70. On the grounds that the King defended the Church, while the Church protected the king. Cf. Závodszky, 155f., and compare with the Synod of Mainz, 847, c. 5, in Mansi, *Concilia*, XIV, 904; also, Marczali, *Enchiridion*, 79; Bartoniek, 41 (c. 51); Katona, *Historia pragmatica*, I, 236ff.

71. *SSH*, I, 321,6-7.

72. Chronicle, c. 69, *ibid.*, I, 321,1-6; Keza, c. 44, *ibid.*, I, 173, 14-15.

73. "Stephanus…filium fratris sui digniorem in regno, quia hoc non consensit, cecavit, et parvulos eiusdem exilio relegavit;" cf. *Annales Altahenses*, anno 1041 (!). For the *Chronicon Zagrabiense cum textu Chronici Varadiensis collatum*, cc. 1, 5, and 6, see *SSH*, I, 206,13-21; I, 208,3-4; and I, 208,9-11, respectively; on the latter, also Macartney, *Hungarian Historians*, 109ff.

74. *SSH*, I, 173,22-24, and n. 6.

75. Kosztolnyik, *Five Kings*, 142ff.

76. Cf. Thietmar, v:15; Palacky, *Geschichte*, I, 248ff.

77. Thietmar, iv:37; Palacky, *Geschichte*, I, 268ff.

78. See Dercsényi, *Chronicon pictum*, vol. I: facsimile, fol. 22'a.

79. *Ibid.*, fol. 22'a. For comparison, see Christopher de Hamel, *Medieval Craftsmen: Scribes and Illuminators* (Toronto, 1994), 45ff.

80. Cf. King Stephen's laws, art. ii:1, Závodszky, 141ff., and compare with the Saxon capitularies, *Capitulum de partibus Saxoniae*, c. 15, *MGHLL*, V, 40; for the founding charter of the monastic community of Byzantine nuns at Veszprémvölgy, cf. *RA*, n. 1—re-issued, in Latin, by Coloman the Learned in 1109, cf. *RA*, n. 42; text, in Jakubovich – Pais, 15ff.

81. See insert in József Szalay – Lajos Baróti, *A magyar nemzet története* [History of the Magyar nation] 4 vols. (Budapest, 1896), I, 134; further, G. Schreiber, "Stephan in der deutschen Sakralkultur," *Archivum Europae centro-orientalis*, 4 (1938), offprint; Éva Kovács, "Casula Sancti Stephani regis," *Acta historiae artium* (Budapest, 1958), offprint; Kovács – Lovag, *Krönungsinsignien*, 59ff.; von Bogyay, *Stephanus rex*, vi-26.

82. Prince Emery died in 1031—*Annales Altahenses*, anno 1031.

83. Cf. József Pál – Ádám Somorjai, *Mille anni storia dell'arciabbazia di Pannonhalma* (Rome–Pannonhalma, 1997), 215ff.

84. Cf. B[éla] K[övér], alias József Hampel, "Emlékek és leletek. Szent István féle casula" [Souvenirs and finds: the Saint Stephen chasuble], *Archaeologiai Értesítő*, new ser., X (1890), 332f.; and Tibor Gerevich, *Magyarország románkori emlékei* [Souvenirs of the Romanesque age in Hungary] (Budapest, 1938), 248f.

85. Pope John XVIII, 1003-09, during whose pontificate "sich das deutsche Kaisertum von Rom vernhielt;" Funk – Bihlmeyer, II, 43.

86. Pope John XIX, 1024–32, a protégé of Giovanni Crescentius, "ein wenig würdige Persönlichkeit," who crowned Conrad II emperor—see *ibid.*, II, 44; Kühner, *Papstlexikon*, 56.

87. Conrad II was an enemy of the Magyars—see Wipo's *Gesta Chounradi II Imperatoris*, c. 16, in *Wiponis Opera*, ed. Harry Bresslau, SSrG (Hannover, 1915), 44; also Katona, *Historia critica*, I, 320ff.

88. Cf. Ch. Rohault de Fleury, *La Messe études archéologiques sur les monuments*, vol. VII (Paris, 1888), 142f., and plate *DLXXVIII*—and re-drawn by both Hampel and Gerevich, see *supra*, n. 73.

89. See Hermann of Reichenau, "Chronicon," *MGHSS*, V, 117; further, *ibid.*, XXIII, 779; Katona, *Historia critica*, I, 497ff.

90. Cf. Thietmar, iv:37 [58]. On the Hungaro-Polish encounter, Thietmar, viii:3 [ix:4]; *Annales Hildesheimenses*, aa. 1031–1032. On the Polish-German background, see Holtzmann, *Sächsische Kaiserzeit*, 400ff.; Sigfried Hirsch – H. Pabst – Harry Bresslau, *Jahrbücher des Deutschen Reiches unter Heinrich II*, 3 vols. (Berlin, 1862–75; repr. 1975), II, 291ff.

91. For the signature of the bishop of Veszprém on the founding charter of the bishopric of Pécs, anno 1009, cf. *RA*, n. 5. Gy. J. Horváth, "A pécsi egyházmegye kezdetei" [Origins of the diocese of Pécs] in his *A pécsi egyházmegye smematizmusa* [Essays on the diocese of Quinqueecclesiae] (Pécs, 1981), 11ff.; László Koszta, "A kereszténység kezdetei és az egyházszervezés Magyarországon" [The beginnings of Christianity and of the ecclesiastical administration in Hungary], *Az államalapító* [The monarch—as the founder of the state], ed. Gyula Kristó (Budapest, 1988), 153ff.

92. Cf. *RA*, n. 2123, with full text; and the *Legenda Zoerardi et Benedicti, SSH*, II, 357ff. V. Chaloupecky's uncritical argument—see his *Stáre Slovensko* (Bratislava, 1923), 30—was firmly questioned, and rejected, by A. Brückner, in *Ungarische Jahrbücher*, 6 (1926), 460f.

93. Hirsch – Pabst – Bresslau, *Jahrbücher...unter Heinrich II*, II, 291ff., and III, 65ff.; Holtzmann, 409ff.

94. *Ibid.*, 402f.; Hirsch – Pabst – Bresslau, *Jahrbücher*, III, 55f.; B. Bretholz, *Geschichte Mährens*, vol. I-2 (Brno, 1895), 168f.

95. Cf. the Chronicle, c. 65, *SSH*, I, 314f.; Palacky, *Geschichte*, I, 248ff.

96. Holtzmann, 409ff.; Hirsch – Pabst – Bresslau, *Jahrbücher*, II, 262ff. Papal legate, Bishop Azo, was present, anno 1009, at the founding of the Pécs bishopric—*RA*, n. 5; text in Josephus Koller (ed.), *Historia episcopatus Quinqueecclesiarum*, 3 vols. (Posonii, 1782–84), I, 62f.

97. Hirsch – Pabst – Bresslau, *Jahrbücher*, II, 331ff., and II, 392ff.

98. Thietmar, viii:3 [ix:4]; Holtzmann, 449ff.

99. King Stephen's *Vita minor*, c. 5; Hodinka, *Orosz Évkönyvek*, 50a (anno 996!), and 52b (anno 998!); Cross – Sherbowitz-Wetzor, *Russian Primary Chronicle*, 122, and 251, n. 112; Marczali, *Geschichtsquellen*, 156f.

100. The report in the Polish-Hungarian Chronicle is less reliable—*SSH*, II, 310ff., and II, 766ff.; Macartney, *Hungarian Historians*, 173ff.

101. King Stephen's *Vita maior*, c. 13, *SSH*, II, 388f.; the *Vita minor*, c. 5, *ibid.*, II, 397; Hartvic, c. 15, *ibid.*, II, 422f.

102. Cf. Ioannes Skylitzes, *Opera*, ed. I. Bekker, *CB*, vol. II (Bonn, 1839), 409,87 – 410,3; 344,89 – 345,26; 346,44 – 347,75, and 348,9 – 349,44. Also, *Ioannes Skylitzes continuatus, ibid.*, II, 645,17-22. Further, *Addimenta Michaelis* (by Bishop Michael of Diabolis), in B. Prokić, *Die Zusätze in der Handschrift des Johannes Skylitzes, Cod. Vindabonensis, hist. graec. LXXIV: ein Beitrag zur Geschichte des sogenannten west-bulgarischen Reiches* #62 (Munich, 1906), 36. V. N. Zlatarski, "Wer war Peter Deljan?" *Annales Academiae Scientiarum Fennicae*, 27 (1932), 354ff.; and Székely – Bartha, 809ff.

103. Cf. *SSH*, I, 325,5 (Chronicle, c. 72). On the Orseolo, *ibid.*, I, 323,6-12 (Chronicle, c. 70); on Deljan, see Bishop Michael's *Addenda*, as cited *supra*, n. 91.

104. See G. L. F. Tafel – G. M Thomas (eds.), *Urkunden zur älteren Handels- und Staatsgeschichte der Republik Venedig* (Vienna, 1856; repr. Amsterdam, 1964), 17ff.; F. Šišić, *Geschichte der Kroaten* (Zagreb, 1917) 191ff.; idem, *Priručnik hrvata za kraljeva iz doma Arpadovića (1102-1301)* (Zagreb, 1944).

105. *SSH*, I, 315f. (Chronicle, c. 66); King Stephen's *Vita minor*, c. 7.

106. Dercsényi, *Chronicon pictum*, I, fol. 20'b, and upper half of the page mirror on fol. 21.

107. See "P" initial, *ibid.*, fol. 21a.

108. See *ibid.*, fol. 21'b, and, above it, the entry in red: *De edificatione templi per Sanctum Stephanum regem in veteri Buda pro canonicis.* Chronicle, c. 67, *SSH*, I, 316ff.

109. Cf. Hartvic, c. 13, *ibid.*, II, 419,19-26. For text of the papal writ, cf. Fraknó, I, 401f., based on Paul Kehr's study in *Nachrichten der königlichen Gesellschaft der Wissenschaften zu Göttingen*, phil.-hist. Kl., 1900, 146; Ferenc Monay, *A római magyar gyóntatók* [Hungarian confessors at St. Peter's] (Rome, 1956), 9f.; Györffy, *István király*, 304f.

110. Funk – Bihlmeyer, II, 98; Kühner, *Papstlexikon*, 59f.

111. Hartvic, c. 13; C. Erdmann, "Die Aufrufe Gerberts und Sergius IV für das Heilige Land," *Quellen und Forschungen aus italienischen Archiven und Bibliotheken*, 23 (1931-32), 1ff.; A. Gieysztor, "The Genesis of the Crusades: The Encyclical of Sergius IV (1009-13)," *Medievalia and humanistica*, 5 (1948), 3ff. The pilgrim Colomannus of Scottish descent wanted to visit the Holy Land in 1012, when en route to Palestine he was captured near Vienna, and on suspicion of being a Moravian spy, was tortured and hanged—cf. Thietmar, vii:76; "Vita Colomanni martyris," *MGHSS*, IV, 675ff. Sidney Painter's article, "Western Europe on the Eve of the Crusades," in Kenneth M. Setton (ed.), *The Crusades*, vol. I: *The First Hundred Years*, ed. Marshall W. Baldwin (Philadelphia, 1955), 3ff.

112. Hartvic, c. 13, *SSH*, II, 386,26-28.

113. See Hóman, *Pénztörténet*, 84ff.

114. King Stephen's *Vita maior*, c. 11, *SSH*, II, 386f.; Hartvic, c. 13; Vilmos Fraknói, "A Szent István révén Rómában alapitott magyar zarándokház" [The hospice established by King Stephen Hungarian pilgrims visiting Rome], *Katholikus Szemle*, 7 (1893), 170ff.; Györffy, *István király*, 293ff.

115. The *Vita maior*, c. 15, *SSH*, II, 391f.; Ralph Glaber, "Francorum historiae libri V," iii:1, *MGHSS*, VII, 48ff.

116. Cf. Ademar Cabannensis "Chronicon Francorum," *MGHSS*, IV, 106ff.; J. Hourlier, *Saint Odilon abbé de Cluny* (Louvain, 1964); F. J. Schmale, *Die Briefe des Abtes Bern von Reichenau* (Stuttgart, 1961), 51f.

117. In *SSH*, II, 685ff., c. 12. From the wording, *auctor monasterii*, in the Latin redaction issued by King Coloman in 1109 of the Greek text of the founding charter for Veszprémvölgy one may conclude that Emery was married to a Byzantine princess—cf. *RA*, n. 1 and 42; Jakubovich – Pais, 15f.; Dezső Pais, "Az 'auctor monasterii' a veszprémvölgyi apácák Kálmán-féle megerősitő levelében" [Use of the term *auctor monasterii* in the Latin language confirmation by King Coloman of the charter for the religious sisters in Veszprémvölgy], *Magyar Nyelv*, 36 (1940), 41f.

118. Karl Uhlirz, *Jahrbücher des Deutschen Reiches unter Otto II und Otto III* (Leipzig, 1902), 24ff., and passim.

119. Cf. Chronicle, c. 66; compare to Keza, c. 43; Hartvic, c. 17; Ostrogorsky, 248f.

120. "...et Vienni ab Ungris capiebatur," and Vienna came, for a brief duration, under Hungarian rule; see *Annales Altahenses*, anno 1030, and p. 18, note 4: "procul dubio Wien, cuius mentio antea nusquam fit." Also, Herimann Auguensis *Chronicon*, anno 1031, *MGHSS*, V, 121, and the *Kaiserchronik*, anno 1030, *MGHSS ling. vern.*, I, 375f., though it "behandelt...die alte Geschichte in durchaus sagenhafter Weise," noted Wattenbach, *Geschichtsquellen*, I, 260f. One may take note of a remark by Alphons Lhotsky concerning the Altaich Annals: "Annales Altahenses von 708 bis 1073 — man ersieht schon daraus, dass die Bezeichnung 'Annalen' hier gar nicht mehr am Platze ist,

dass es sich vielmehr schon in so früher Zeit eine Mischform, Chronik in Annalen-schema, handle." Cf. Lhotsky, *Quellenkunde*, 173.

121. Cf. *Annales Hildesheimenses*, anno 1031; King Stephen's *Vita maior*, c. 14, *SSH*, II, 389f.; Hartvic, c. 16, *ibid.*, II, 423f. The monarch rightfully summoned men to arms in order to defend the country—see Andrew II's *Golden Bull* of *1231*, art. xvi, in Marczali, *Enchiridion*, 136Bf.

122. Hermann of Reichenau (Contractus), "Chronicon," anno 1030, in *MGHSS*, V, 67ff., "war eine der liebenswürdigsten Gestalten der deutschen Kulturgeschichte. Seine Chronik...bleibt ein Muster vornehmer, ruhiger Schlichkeit..."—wrote Lhotsky, *Quellenkunde*, 171f.

123. See *Annales Altahenses*, anno 1033; *Annales Hildesheimenses*, anno 1031; see Herwig Wolfram, *Konrad II, 998–1039: Kaiser dreier Reiche* (Munich, 2000), 246ff., a very objective study by a German historian.

124. See Wipo's *Gesta Chounradi II Imperatoris*, c. 26, as cited *supra*, note 76.

125. *Annales Altahenses*, anno 1033 (!). "Bis 1032 stellen diese Annalen eine etwas dürftige Kompilation aus bekannten Quellen dar, dann aber bringen sie viel Eigenes, so dass man noch 1891 an Verfasserwechsel dachte — wohl mit Unrecht." Cf. Lhotsky, *Quellenkunde*, 173.

126. *Annales Hildesheimenses*, anno 1031. On the background of the text, see Eggert – Pätzold, 139ff.; for an interpretation, see *ibid.*, 231ff.

127. Cf. *Vita maior*, c.15, *SSH*, II, 391,16-20; and Hartvic, c. 19, *ibid.*, II, 428,19-25.

128. *SSH*, II, 322,18-23, and note 8.

129. The Chronicle, cc. 71-72, and cc. 75-78.

130. *Ibid.*, c. 91, and cc. 97-100.

131. *Ibid.*, c. 110.

132. *Ibid.*, cc. 111, etc.; *Leges Ladislai*, ii:1, in Závodszky, 166f.; Kosztolnyik, *From Coloman*, 4, and 14, nn. 37-38.

133. Wipo, ed. cit.; Stefan Weinfurter, *Herrschaft und Reich der Salier* (Sigmaringen, 1991), 33f., and 44ff. Wipo, ed. cit., c. 26, spoke of some Bavarian-Magyar confrontation along the border. On the Macedonian epoch in Byzantine history, see A. A. Vasiliev, *History of the Byzantine Empire* (Madison, Wisconsin, 1952), 300ff.; Ostrogorksy, 238ff.; Wolfram, 248ff.

134. Thietmar, viii:3 [ix:4]; *Annales Altahenses*, anno 1030. In 1018, Boleslav of Poland received armed Hungarian aid for his military move against Kiev—Thietmar, viii:16 [ix:31-32]; Hirsch – Pabst – Bresslau, *Jahrbücher*, vol. III, 89ff.

135. Cosmas of Prague, "Chronica Boemorum," i:41, *MGHSS*, IX, 64, and the remarks by von Bogyay, art. cit. (1976), 20ff. On Cosmas, cf. Wattenbach, *Geschichts-quellen*, I, 202ff., and Lhotsky's observation, *Quellenkunde*, 120, that "die Chronik des Cosmas an manirierter Künstelei solcher Art — i.e., *Indiviualität*, individuality — überquoll." See further *Chronica Boemorum*, anno 1030, in *MGHSS*, XXX-1, 38; and Annalista Saxo, anno 1030, *ibid.*, VI, 678.

136. See Liudprand of Cremona, "Liber de gestis Ottonis Magni Imperatoris," cc. iv, etc., in *Liudprandi opera: die Werke Liudprands von Cremona*, ed. Joseph Becker, 3rd ed., SSrG (Hannover, 1915; repr. 1975), 159ff. Becker characterized the work as a "Gelegenheitsschrift...verfasst...auf Anregung des Kaisers hin, dem...über sein Vorgehen in Rom viel gelegen seien musste," *ibid.*, xxi. Also, *Widukindi Corbiensis Rerum gestarum Saxonicarum libri III*, rev. ed., ed. K. A. Kehr (after G. Waitz), SSrG

(Hannover, 1904; repr. 1925), i:6, 8-9, 28-29, 41; further, *Richeri Historiarum libri IV*, rev. ed., ed. G. Waitz (after G. H. Pertz), SSrG (Hannover, 1877), 1:14, ii:18. For comments, see Holtzmann, 184ff., and 309ff.; Eggert – Pätzold, 206ff., and 231ff.

137. Cf. Richer, ii:29, ii:73, and iii:1-2; on the reliance of the German court upon Gerbert of Aurillac, later Pope Sylvester II, cf. *ibid.*, iii:43, etc. On the succession of Hugh Capet, cf. *ibid.*, iv:12, etc. Janet L. Nelson, *The Frankish World, 750–900* (London–Rio Grande, 1996), 183ff., and 199ff.; also, Elizabeth M. Hallam, *Capetian France, 987–1328* (London–New York, 1980), 13ff., and 30ff.; Karl Hampe, *Das Hoch-mittelalter*, 5th ed. (Cologne–Graz, 1963), 20ff.; Caspar Ehlers, "Die Anfänge Goslars und das Reich im elften Jahrhundert," *Deutsches Archiv für Erforschung des Mittelalters*, 53 (1997), 45ff.

138. Widukind, iii:69; Thietmar, ii:9, and ii:19; Wolf, *Theophanu*, 131ff.

139. Gerd Althoff, *Otto III* (Darmstadt, 1996), 126ff.; Görich, *Otto III*, 211ff.; Johannes Fried, *Otto III und Boleslaw Chrobroy* (Stuttgart, 1989), 65ff., and 123ff.

140. Cf. Adam Bremensis, *Gesta Hammaburgensis ecclesiae pontificum*, 3rd ed., ed. B. Schmeidlder, SSrG (Hannover, 1917), lib. IV, important for the early Baltic history; Wattenbach, *Geschichtsquellen*, II, 80ff.; Friedrich Heer, *Europäische Geistes-geschichte*, 2nd ed. (Stuttgart, 1965), 56ff.; Carl Erdmann, "Die Burgenordnung Heinrichs I," *Deutsches Archiv für Erforschung des Mittelalters*, 6 (1943), 59ff.

141. On Lechfeld, see Widukind, iii:44; "Flodoardi Annales," anno 955, *MGHSS*, III, 363ff.; Richer, iii:3-5, only recorded the Frankish background. Thomas von Bogyay, *Lechfeld: Ende und Anfang* (Munich, 1955), 16ff., and 54ff.; Karl Bosl, *Zur Geschichte der Bayern* (Darmstadt, 1965), 327ff.; Ch. R. Bowlus, "Die Reitervölker des frühen Mittelalters im Osten des Abendlandes," *Ungarn Jahrbuch*, 22 (1995-96), 1ff.; ideology discussed by J. A. Brundage, "Widukind of Corvey and the 'non-Roman' imperial idea," *Medieval Studies*, 22 (1960), 15ff.

142. Hagen Keller, "Das Kaisertum Ottos des Grossen in Verständniss seiner Zeit," in Harald Zimmermann (ed.), *Otto der Grosse* (Darmstadt, 1976), 218ff.

143. Johann Haller, *Das Papsttum: Idee und Wirklichkeit*, 3 vols. (Stuttgart, 1936, etc.), II-1, 190ff.; revised ed., in 5 vols. (Stuttgart, 1950-53; repr. 1962), II, 210ff.; F. X. Seppelt, *Geschichte der Päpste*, 5 vols. (Munich, 1954-59), II, 365ff.; Walter Ullmann, *The Growth of Papal Government in the Middle Ages* (London, 1955), 232ff. Leo VIII was a layman who "an einem Tag empfing alle Weihen;" cf. Funk – Bihlmeyer, II, 42.

144. Holtzmann, 127ff.

145. Cf. Wipo, c. 26; Franz-Reiner Erkens commented on the Hungarian campaign briefly, see his *Konrad II: Herrschaft und Reich des ersten Salierkaisers* (Regensburg, 1998), 154.

146. The *Vita maior*, c. 15, *SSH*, II, 391,16-22; Hartvic, c. 19, *ibid.*, II, 428f.

147. "…deinde monuit eos fidem orthodoxam servare;" cf. the *Vita maior*, c. 16, *SSH*, II, 392,15-22.

148. Hartvic, c. 23, see *ibid.*, II, 431,19 - 432,1.

149. *Ibid.*, II, 432,5-8.

150. King Stephen's *Admonitiones*, articles i–iii, and vii, *ibid.*, II, 619ff.; Marczali, *Enchiridion*, 63ff.; and Závodszky, 131ff.

151. King Stephen's Laws, articles i:1-13, Závodszky, 141ff.; Bartoniek, 18ff.; Marczali, *Enchiridion*, 69ff.

152. "Stephanus Ungarorum rex in die Assumptionis sanctae Mariae terminum fecit carnalis vitae," *Annales Altahenses*, anno 1038; Wipo, *Gesta Chuonradi II*, c. 38.

XI

Time of Troubles:
Peter Orseolo and Sámuel Aba

1. The Succession to King Stephen's Inheritance

> ...accersitis episcopis et primis palatii de Christi nomine gloriantibus, primum cum eis tractavit de substituendo pro se rege....
>
> *Vita maior s. Stephani regis*, c. 16

After the Lord glorified his mercy in King Stephen, the chronicler wrote, the king had planned, and was firmly determined, to put aside the pomp and glory of this world, to resign his crown—"temporalis regni dyademate deposito"—so that he would dedicate himself to the service of God and spend his time in quiet meditation. He wished to transfer the crown to his son, Prince Emery, who in the flower of his youth was eminent in practicing his Catholic faith and administering the public business, just like his father, the saintly old monarch. When, however, King Stephen began to transfer the problems of government and the burden of statecraft to his son, Prince Emery unexpectedly died—it is imperative to cite the Latin text: "cum itaque...pater...filio curam administrationis et gubernandi regni sollicitudinem intenderet committere, ...Dux Emericus proper[i]a morte preventus est."[1] The statement of the chronicler supports the argument this writer has expressed above that the *unexpected—propera morte!*—death of the prince and heir to the throne right before he would have taken over the reins of power, was not a coincidence. The German chronicler who based his information on Hungarian data, frankly stated that the heir to the Hungarian throne had been killed by a wild boar during a hunt.[2] What may be coincidental is that about thirty-five years earlier King William II

Rufus of England had also been *incidentally* killed during a royal hunting party, whereupon his younger brother, Henry, had assumed the crown: "Henricus qui tunc noviter fratri defuncto in regnum successerat," recorded Eadmer, an English chronicler.[3]

Receiving the devastating news, the health of the old Hungarian king broke down completely. As mentioned above, King Stephen could find nobody among his close relatives, within the House of Árpád, who could have continued the western oriented policy he had begun, keeping his realm within the framework of the Latin Catholic faith. It is evident from the words of the chronicler that even the notion of the need for western-oriented governmental leadership, in fact, western Christianity itself, did not strike deep roots in the Magyar public consciousness. "Pronior etenim erat gens Hungarica ritui paganismo inclinari, quam fidei Christiane."[4]

Thus it happened that King Stephen would designate Vazul, who was the only male of age among members of the Árpád family, as the sole heir of his throne, whom earlier he had to place under arrest because of the rather irresponsible manner of life Vazul had been leading. Now, he released him from prison in order to make him king. However, due to a horrible misunderstanding—or, perhaps, not so much because of a misunderstanding, but the intervention of some wicked people—Vazul had been blinded, thereby to make him ineligible for inheriting the kingship, and his three sons were sent into exile.[5]

The chronicler held Queen Gisela responsible for the blinding of Vazul, and recorded the exile of the three Árpád princes as if they had been sent abroad by King Stephen himself, thereby to assure the survival of the House of Arpad. It is noteworthy, though, that both the chronicler—and the Hungarian Anonymus—recognized the three princes, Andrew, Béla and Levente, not as the sons of Vazul, but as the offspring of Ladislas *Szár* (that is, the Bald); however, *Szár* was the son of King Stephen's uncle, Michael, the brother of Prince Géza, father to King Stephen.[6]

A word of explanation is in order here. The German chronicler's report obtained a generation later from Hungarian sources: the circle of (King) Andrew, son of Vazul, argued that Vazul had to be blinded, so that his incapacity to succeed would make room for Peter Orseolo of Venice to inherit King Stephen's throne. On the other hand, the

Hungarian chronicler who based his report on information reaching back to the late eleventh century, that is, the times of King Ladislas I, wanted to clear Vazul, grandfather of King Ladislas, of all the charges that had been brought against him, and named Queen Gisela, King Stephen's widow, as the one responsible for the horrible blinding of Vazul, and, for that reason, depicted Peter Orseolo as the son of one of King Stephen's sisters, thus a relative of Queen Gisela.[7]

On the other hand, the anonymous author of King Stephen's "Vita minor" pointed out directly the cause of Vazul's punishment: Four still pagan high nobles at the royal court observed that the monarch was seriously and lengthily ill, and decided to kill him. The knife fell from the hands of the murderer approaching the king's bed; the king awoke, forgave the noble who begged his forgiveness, but had the other conspirators blinded, and ordered their hands cut off. The term used by the chronicler, "nam ipsi adhuc in perfidia cordis errabant," may need some explanation. It meant the revival of the pagan rite-punishment for (attempted) regicide—very much like the case some seventy years later of Prince Álmos, the younger brother of King Coloman—when Álmos, the one who turned against the king, was punished by losing his eyesight and hearing.[8]

The chronicler referred to the sad role Vazul had played in the affair; he was the chief conspirator. This is pointed out by article ii:17 of King Stephen's Laws—partly following the resolutions of the Synod of Mainz, 847, art. 5—that said that the one who conspired against the king, or the county, may find no refuge in the church; and the person who knew of the conspiracy, and yet failed to report it, was to be punished in a similar manner.[9] The sentence had been carried out by the border reeve Sebos, son Buda, man (official) at the court.

Blinding the individual, or having him lose his hearing, was a punishment of that age; someone unworthy of the throne, had to be made physically unfit to be king, though he was left alive. The actual murderer who had committed regicide, or murdered a member of the royal family, received the death sentence—as it happened in 1213, in the case of the murder of Gertrude, the Queen of King Andrew II of Hungary.[10]

On account of Vazul's plans for regicide his sons, Andrew, Béla and Levente could not inherit the throne (the chronicler said it was King Stephen himself who had sent them into exile—"consuluit eis, ut...fugerent"—and they found (political) refuge on Czech soil.[11] It was under these circumstances that King Stephen chose as his successor the son of one of his sister's, Peter Orseolo from Venice, who had been living at Stephen's court since 1026, and was commander of the royal armed forces. (The husband of King Stephen's [probably] younger sister was Samuel Aba, who had no children.) Before he died, King Stephen had laid down in article vii of his *Admonitiones*, in accordance with the principle, and discussed his decision with members of his royal Council to gain their consent, and named, with the Council's approval, Peter Orseolo as his heir.[12]

The Hungarian chronicler relying on eleventh century data wanted to exonerate Vazul, the grandfather of his king, Ladislas I (1077–95), by placing the blame upon Queen Gisela and Peter Orseolo for the murder attempt made at the life of King Stephen, without mentioning a word—and if one included the remarks made by Simon de Keza, without *their* mentioning a word—about the political designs of the Franconian imperial family. Members of the earlier Saxon House looked upon political progress and domestic stability in the Hungarian realm with a token degree of benevolent good will, and supported similar goals of the Czech and Polish ruling families, and the alike attempts the Orseolos had been making in Venice.[13]

The Orseolos had established family ties with the Byzantine, Croatian and Hungarian ruling houses. Otto Orseolo (1009–26), the son of Doge Peter II Orseolo (991–1009) had married the elder sister of King Stephen; Peter Orseolo, who took over the Hungarian throne upon the death of King Stephen, was their son. The Orseolo family had hoped to achieve the position of a Grand Duke, but the death[s] of their mentors, and of Pope Benedict VIII (1012–24), cancelled their plans. The new pontiff, John XIX (1024–33) supported the political designs of Patriarch Poppo of Aquileia who claimed to have jurisdiction over the patriarchate of Grado, thereby opposing the ecclesiastical political goals of Patriarch Orso of Árado, the great-uncle of Peter Orseolo.[14]

When Conrad II of the Franconian ruling house announced that he planned to visit Venice, the Venetians expelled Otto Orseolo. (Bruno, the uncle of Conrad II, became Pope Gregory V, 996–99). Conrad II punished his great-grandfather, Conrad the Red—who had, in 955, organized a revolt against Otto I, and later led a campaign against the Polish rulers, and the Czech ruler, by removing them from their duchies; he conducted the same policy of punishment toward the Orseolos in Venice. The Venetians, however, disliked the rule of the doge Conrad II had appointed for them, while the Hungarian and Croatian monarchs "liberated" Trau and Spaleto from the rule of the new doge, an appointee and political stooge of the German court.[15]

This Hungarian and Croatian cooperation with the exiled Doge—a result of the developed political and military situation—gained the diplomatic, and possibly military, support of the Byzantine court, and greatly threatened the Italian interests of the German Franconian court; therefore, Conrad II dispatched Bishop Werner of Strasbourg with a large entourage to arrange for a firm anti-Hungarian–Venetian diplomatic relationship with Constantine VIII of Byzantium (1025–28), and to ask for the hand in marriage of the fifty-year old Byzantine Grand-duchess Zita for his ten-year old son, Henry, whom he had just named duke of Bavaria.[16]

The Hungarian court circles must have had access to very good diplomatic intelligence data, for they quickly saw through the German court's design; King Stephen could not allow the bishop of Strasbourg, dressed as a pilgrim, to journey through his land. Werner and his entourage thus had to take a longer route to travel and arrived too late in Byzantium to achieve their objective. Zita in the meanwhile had married someone else, and the Greek court had, with some delay, sent the German embassy back home with gifts.[17]

This was the reason why the vengeful Conrad II began a thoughtless and ill-conceived military campaign against Hungary in 1030, a military expedition even Wipo, his biographer, regarded as unjust. Conrad II based his claim on the fictitious reason that he regarded the Hungarian ruler, who occupied the former Carolingian territory of Pannonia without a cause, as a political upstart, an enemy who had to be punished. King Stephen's military tactics, however, ended the campaign quickly in a Hungarian victory; Stephen's forces occupied Vienna.[18]

2. The First Reign of Peter the Orseolo, 1038–1041

> Postquam autem Petrus factus est rex, omnem regie
> serenitatis benignitatem abiecit....
>
> *Chronicon pictum*, c. 71

The chronicler of the late eleventh century wished to bring alive the memory of Vazul in favorable colors for posterity; therefore, he depicted Peter Orseolo as a corrupt and bad person who, after he had completely disregarded the pious and graceful features of kingship, behaved viciously toward his people with Teutonic fury. He showed contempt for the nobles of the realm; with unsatisfiable hunger did he consume the goods of the country, together with his Germans who were screaming like wild animals, or his Italians, who babbled like finches—"cum Teutonicis beluina feritate rugientibus, et cum Latinis yrundinum garrulitate murmurantibus." He entrusted the garrisoning of the royal forts to only Germans and Italians; he boasted that he should fill all higher and middle grade public offices in the country with Germans: "...omnes principes et potestates...Teutonicos constituam."[19]

The king himself led a wasteful life, his retainers ("satelliti regis") left nobody among the inhabitants in the realm alone. The king lacked proper political insight, and was shy of diplomatic cleverness. On the other hand, he was a man with good intentions, a man brave and daring, but with an uncontrolled temper, who simply could not get along with the Magyar population in spite of the fact that he supported the monastic community of Pannonhalma, and it was he who had begun construction of the cathedral at Pécs.[20]

King Peter surrounded himself with the former advisors of King Stephen, including Stephen's relative, Samuel Aba, and Buda, a very influential man at the court. Peter conducted a strict government; for instance, he had, with papal approval, removed two bishops found unworthy of their spiritual vocation from their offices.[21] He asked dowager Queen Gisela, who was far too openhanded with her donations, to be cautious with her money, and to have a limited budget for her household on the grounds that he wished to retain in whole the domain he needed for the economic upkeep of royal dignity. The German chronicler (who received his information from Hungarian sources) recorded that, for a few years, Peter treated the dowager Queen with consideration and respect, but changed his attitude by placing her under house arrest in the royal court, taking away her possessions and money, forcing her to take an oath that she would not make future donations to anyone without obtaining previous royal consent. He humbled the aged Queen for three years in such a devious manner.[22]

In his foreign policy, King Peter maintained peaceful relations with his brother-in-law, Albert, margrave of Austria, as well as with King Stephen of Croatia (1030–58), whom he aided in conquering Zara.[23] It is ironic that the Hungarian chronicler of the late eleventh century who had deeply sympathized with Vazul, described domestic disorders in the realm, and the hatred of foreigners, as the factors that aided Vazul's son, Andrew, in gaining the throne of the Árpáds in 1046; and, for that reason, described in the darkest colors the kingship of Peter the Orseolo, disregarding the fact that the uprising that led to Andrew's succession to the throne did not begin with the people, among the Magyars who were the supporters of the sons of Vazul, but initiated from the royal court itself, from among members the circle of nobles who had turned against their heavy-handed, occasionally unjust king, the Orseolo.

Those nobles of the opposition were led by Peter's uncle, the greedy Samuel Aba, who had been overanxious to ascend the royal throne. In other words, the anti-Orseolo movement in the realm was headed by Samuel Aba, who strongly disliked Peter. Aba used, as pretext, the complaints of Queen Gisela, who turned to members of the high nobility with her grievances against the Orseolo. Samuel Aba was of Magyar descent—unlike the Orseolo; born in Venice to a Venetian father—he was older than Peter, as he was the husband of the older sister of King Peter's mother; he had earlier held a position of responsibility in King Stephen's court, and regarded himself, by birth and experience, more qualified for the kingship than his nephew, who had been born abroad.[24]

Members of the high nobility sympathetic to Queens Gisela's complaint demanded that King Peter return her what belonged to her; they threatened to withdraw their support from him, if he did not comply. The nobles also demanded that the king have Buda, regarded by many as the common enemy, a real culprit, the cause of much evil, executed. Peter procrastinated, the nobles killed Buda, and blinded his two sons. The Hungarian chronicler could not hide his own opinion; in a few lines below in the text he noted that the nobles had also beaten Sebos, who had carried out the blinding of Vazul, had Sebos' associates stoned, or beaten to death with iron bars. Terrified at such a turn of events, King Peter fled to the court of his Austrian brother-in-law, and turned, a western writer noted, upon the margrave's intercession, to Emperor Henry III for (military) help.[25]

According to the record of the Hungarian chronicler, the high nobles and *knights*—"principes Hungarorum et milites"—had, *consilio episcoporum* (this writer, for one, wonders about the meaning of the term; did the chronicler mean bishops who had been frightened, or intimidated into participation?), summoned an assembly, where they from among themselves had elected and anointed Reeve Aba, the husband of King Stephen's older sister—"sororium sancti regis Stephani"—accepting him as their king during the third year of Peter's reign; "Aba vero regali potestate sublimatus consecratus est in regem."

The new king called an assembly together, voided the laws that had been issued by his predecessor, and charged three of his loyal adherents, Visket (Wisce), Tojszlant (Toyzlau), and Peszlit (Pezli) to carry out his resolutions. The three men regarded their nation's freedom, "libertatem gentis sue," as their immediate goal, and made certain that leadership of the country was once again in the hands of the royal family, "regnum regali semini restituere." The chronicler stressed his point of view that the government of the land belonged to the House of Árpád.[26]

In 1042, King Aba sent envoys to the German court in order to express his peaceful intentions toward the empire. But Henry III gave the envoys no definite answer; whereupon King Aba ordered three army detachments to move against the German monarch. The Hungarians devastated the Hungarian–Austrian border zone, including the town of Tulna, gathered a rich booty, and were returning home when Margrave Gottfridus (Gottfried) surprised them at Pettau, and badly defeated them. The inserted remark by the chronicler (who must have worked with an earlier text), calls for attention: "Tunc enim Austria non duces, sed habebat marchiones"—meaning that the mid-fourteenth century author describing mid-eleventh century events had to rely upon eleventh century data in order to provide reliable information in this portion of the record.[27]

Now the German monarch with the consent of the high nobility of the empire, and with Czech military help, invaded Hungary, and took Peter with him on this campaign. Having learned a lesson from the mistakes made during the 1030 campaign, they avoided the Rába region. Accepting the advice of the Czech Vratislav, they moved ahead following the left hand bank of the Danube, where they occupied Pozsony, and then pursued Hungarian forces to the Garam stream. Unexpectedly, the monarch withdrew his army. During the fall season of next year, after refusing the Hungarian peace proposal (the Hungarian court accepted the German demands, but refused to acknowledge Peter as the legitimate king), Henry III invaded Hungary but, again, changed his mind and accepted the Hungarians' latest peace offer, in which Aba renounced the region beyond the Morava stream gained during the 1030 campaign, paid 400 gold forints, provided 400 fur coats in compensation, freed the prisoners of war captured in the earlier campaigns, and promised to return the goods Peter had taken from Queen Gisela. To guarantee the promises he had made, Aba further provided seven guarantors to the imperial court.

The chronicler, presumably relying on contemporary information, argued that Henry III had good reasons for accepting the terms of the treaty, on the grounds that at home, Gottfried (Godfrey) of Lorraine, son of Duke Gozilo (Gozelo) had staged a revolution against Henry III for the reason that, upon the death of his father, Gottfried could only inherit the area of upper-Lorraine, while lower-Lorraine was assigned to Gozelo, his younger brother. (It is of a later development that, in 1046, Gottfried made peace with his monarch, but failed to receive southern Lorraine; the region was inherited by Frederick of Luxemburg, brother of Duke Henry of Bavaria.)[28]

It is evident from the text of the Hungarian chronicler that the emperor had appeared on the Hungarian border with belligerent plans, but left the field without fighting a battle, and moved to Burgundy. His departure altered King Aba's position. Aba became self assured and arrogantly overconfident. He had only contempt for the country's nobility—though he himself was one of them!—and preferred the company of lesser social strata and the peasants, "habens semper cum rusticis et ignobilibus commune." He surrounded himself with men of lower birth. The deeply humiliated high nobles would not tolerate such an attitude; they conspired against him, with the intent to kill him, "ut ipsum occiderent."[29]

The Hungarian chronicler of the age comes slowly to the main point of his argument. Aba had usurped the king's office. The essential cause of the revolution organized against him was that, really, the throne belonged to Peter Orseolo. Aba's previous irresponsible behavior had caused him to lose his claim to rule. He, an important man at the court, a close advisor of King Stephen, had abused his master's trust, had broken the promise he had made to King Stephen. Aba led a revolt against the Orseolo, whom King Stephen had appointed as his successor, and the people had accepted as their monarch.[30]

In other words, Aba was an usurper. He lacked wisdom and a sense of justice, he ruled by the use of physical force and fear. He had voided all of the legislative acts of Peter, and, despite his given word, he refused to return the confiscated goods of Queen Gisela. Those nobles who dared to oppose him, he had murdered in cold blood during Lent, 1043.[31] Bishop Gerard of Csanád publicly berated him for his murderous deed—Gerard, as a bishop, had the legal right, according to the law of the Church, to speak out condemning the mass murder—and foretold him that he shall meet his death in the near future, as he had made himself unworthy of the office of a king. The noble lords who had escaped the bloodbath at Csanád, now turned to Henry III to recall the Orseolo to the throne, on grounds that Aba had lost his right to rule as their king.[32]

The German monarch invaded Hungary again with his military detachments from Noricum, Flanders, some Czech units, and with troops directly under his command, but disguised his war plans. Seemingly, he received the peace envoys of Aba, though he knew that at the same time Aba had ordered his army units to gather at Győr, close to the border. Henry III turned down Aba's peace offer, quickly approached and occupied Sopron, but the invasion came to an unexpected halt at the flooded waters of the Rábca stream. At this time, men loyal to Peter's cause led the German troops to a fording place, and Henry III met Aba's forces in battle at Ménfő near Győr. King Aba was confident of victory because he had heard—perhaps purposefully misled by false information—that the emperor had only brought a small army with him, but the situation on the field developed differently. Men who had fought on Aba's side left him during the battle, for the reason, the record has it, that Rome had excommunicated the Hungarians because they had their king Peter the Orseolo unjustly expelled from his throne.[33]

The military encounter at Ménfő was a battle heavily fought. King Aba put up heroic resistance, but lost the battle; his crown and the coronation insignia fell into the hands of the Germans. German war losses must have been heavy because the place where the battle took place remained for a long time known as *Ferlorum Payer*, that is, *verloren Bayer*, in bad Hungarian: "Westnempti," that is *Vessznémet* (down with the Germans). Aba had to flee, and fled toward the Tisza stream, but in a village, with whose inhabitants he had been very firm in the past, people recognized him, and in a cave next to the village, murdered him. In the chronicler's recollection, his body buried next to the church of the village was exhumed a few years later, and they found that his wounds were healed; they re-buried the body at Sáros abbey, the abbey he had established.[34]

On the other hand, the German source reports that Aba's family, and later Aba himself, had been captured and taken before King Peter; that the king's council sat in judgment over him, declared him a traitor, condemned him to die, and the sentence had been carried out, may be revengeful, thus less then reliable. After Ménfő, Henry III and Peter the Orseolo entered Fehérvár in triumph—"que est principalis sedes regni Hungarie"—where on August 15, 1044, members of the higher clergy, higher nobility, and the nobles publicly paid respects to Peter their king.[35]

3. The Orseolo's Second Kingship, 1044–1046

> Cesar...Petrum regem regfali corona plenarie
> restitutum...in basilica...sedere fecit et ibidem
> regem Hungarie et Hungaros regi reconciliavit.
>
> *Chronicon pictum*, c. 77

The Orseolo did not take possession for the second time of the
Hungarian throne as an independent sovereign monarch, but as a
vassal of the German court. Henry III treated him with consideration
in that it was he himself who placed the crown upon the Orseolo's
head, and strove to make peace between the Magyars and their monarch. It must be noted here that the Hungarian chronicler mentioned
King Stephen's royal insignia used at this act,[36] though, according to
a letter of Pope Gregory VII, Henry III had almost simultaneously
sent the crown [most probably used at the Orseolo's second coro-
nation], and the lance of King Aba, back to Rome.[37] Henry III, as the
Orseolo's feudal overlord, had re-confirmed the King Stephen's laws
based on Bavarian laws, so that the Hungarians may henceforth live in
accordance with their laws and customs. It may have been a
characteristic gesture by the German ruler that, upon his departure
from Hungary, Henry III entrusted the Orseolo's personal protection
to a German bodyguard.[38]

In 1045, the German ruler paid another official visit to Hungary.
He went to receive the *personal* feudal submission of King Peter the
Orseolo. And the Orseolo publicly and solemnly handed over the
kingdom to his German overlord.[39] In undertaking this fateful step
King Peter had lost for ever the trust and confidence of the people. It
may be the ironic twist of history that princes Andrew, Béla and
Levente who earlier had departed to Bohemia, had at this time, out of
sheer need, "propter paupertatis inopiam," left the Czech lands for
Poland, where they were cordially received at the court.[40]

Their departure from Bohemia had its reason, though the
Hungarian chronicler made no mention of it. The Czech court also
happened to be a feudal subordinate of the German court, and it was
hardly in a position to grant protection to the three exiled members of

the Magyar House of Árpád. In Poland, on the other hand, Béla had—on his own initiative, and instead of the ruling Polish king—fought a duel with the Duke of Pomerania who had previously questioned the right of the Polish monarch to levy a tax on his region. Béla defeated the Duke of Pomerania, and the thankful King Miscislav made him a prince of Poland, gave him the hand of his daughter in marriage, together with the whole amount of tax income due from Pomerania, and paid him all the honors due to his rank. Béla's two sons, Géza and Ladislas—later Hungarian kings, 1074–77; 1077–95—were born in Poland.[41]

King Peter the Orseolo became overconfident, committed one political mistake after another; surrounded himself with non-Hungarians, with newcomer Germans, but mostly with newcomer Italians, whose pride (and, more than likely, their ignorance of the language and of the customs of the land) caused hostile reaction among members of the Magyar nobility, and even among those early German settlers who identified themselves with the country's cause, and with the policies of the royal court. It seemed to them that Peter wanted to populate the country with foreigners. The king's irrational behavior soon led to a deterioration of public law and order in the land.

The rule and predominance of strangers in the country unified the supporters of the exiled Árpád princes; they included the men loyal to King Stephen and King Aba, and the former advisors of Peter whom he had early dismissed from his service. Thus, there developed a situation where princes Andrew and Levente, unwilling to exploit further the hospitality of the Polish court shown toward their brother Béla, visited, by traveling through the region of Ladomer, the court of their relative, Jaroslav (the Wise) of Kiev.[42] Jaroslav's sister was married to Ladislas *Szár*. Now, the loyal adherents of the Árpáds at home, named Viska, Buha and Buhna, formed a conspiracy against Peter the Orseolo, but two traitors, "quibusdam autem perfidis," named Buda and Devecser [Deuecher], reported the conspiracy to the Orseolo, who had the conspirators executed; thereupon an uprising broke out all over the country.[43]

Leaders of the uprising gathered at Csanád to decide what to do. After discussing the matter among themselves—"tunc nobiles Hungarie videntes mala gentis sue, in Chanad in unum convenerunt, consilioque habito…nuncios miserunt in Russiam…"—they decided to call upon princes Andrew and Levente in Kiev asking them to return home, promising them that they will loyally submit to them because they were the descendants of the House of Árpád. They requested only that the princes protect the realm from the wrath of the Germans, "ut eos a furore Teutonicorum defenderent." Andrew had already in Kiev accepted Byzantine-rite Christianity, and gained the hand in marriage of Anastasia, younger daughter of Jaroslav of Kiev; their daughter later became the wife of the Czech prince Vratislav.[44]

An additional note is in order here. Jaroslav's other daughter, Ann, was married to Henry I, king of the Franks (1031–60), which meant that Andrew of the House of Árpád was also related to the Capetian dynasty.[45] In other words, while the dynastic alliance of the Frankish court did establish a Paris–Kiev–Byzantium diplomatic triangle, thereby to preempt the realization of an anti-Frankish German political plan (in the tenth century Gerberga and Hedwig, the sisters of Otto I, had, by their marriages—Hedwig to Hugh the Great; Gerberga as the Queen of Louis IV *d'Outremer* of the West-Franks—greatly influenced Frankish politics and the economy[46]), now, by developing dynastic and cultural ties with the west-Frankish ruling family, Andrew I, who himself was an orthodox Christian of the Byzantine rite, had lessened diplomatic pressures from the German court against the background of this emerging Kiev–Byzantium–Paris political, diplomatic, and military triangle. In 1055, King Andrew's establishment of the abbey for Frankish monks at Tihany, which was placed under the protection of the Frankish Saint Anian,[47] may be regarded as a visible outcome of the new dynastic-cultural relationship between the Capetian and the Hungarian courts.[48]

Andrew and Levente must have been surprised by, though not unprepared for, the invitation to return home. The Hungarian record has it that they were suspicious, fearful of being entrapped, "timentes palliatas insidias," wherefore they had, secretly, *clamculo*, sent envoys to spy in the country. The report of the envoys must have been encouraging because the two brothers, supported by Kievan troops, arrived at Újvár, a fort built by King Aba, where a multitude of Hungarians, *multitudo Hungarorurm*, greeted them. It is to be feared, though that the "multitude" of people that greeted them were of anti-Christian disposition, who wanted to demolish the Christian faith, restore the old pagan religion of the ancients, worship old idols, murder all Christian clerics and destroy all Christian churches. In other words, in the region east of the Tisza river, an anti-Christian and anti-foreigner uprising had broken out in the land.[49]

In the eyes of the insurgents, the descent of the sons of Vászoly from the House of Árpád, and their, presumably, *pagan* disposition, were the deciding factors that made their invitation to re-enter the country desirable.[50] On those grounds, the princes had no alternative but to accept the insurgents' demands; otherwise, the chronicler argued, the rebels would not have fought, "aliter autem non pugnabatant pro," alongside Andrew, Béla and Levente, against Peter the Orseolo.[51] The insurgents originated from the area east of the Tisza river—not from Transdanubia, whose inhabitants were already Christians. They hated foreigners, and wanted to clear their country from foreign influence. The insurgents—the record says—expected from the homecoming princes, first, to remove King Peter and his advisors from power; second, to suspend officials who had been appointed by Peter from their positions; and, third, to restore paganism, together with the usage of the old Magyar customary law, in the land.[52]

The leader of the insurgents was Vata of the country of Békés, who had organized the revolt among the people of his district. The record has it that they murdered clergy and Christians loyal to their faith, tortured every priest of Italian descent they could find, destroyed churches, and demanded that people renounce the Christian religion and worship idols. As it is written in old books dealing with the deeds of the Magyars, the chronicler wrote—this sentence may serve as proof of the fact that the chroniclers relied upon earlier written sources in describing these events[53]—Christians were not allowed to marry into families of the clan of Vata and (son) János because they had forcefully led the people away from the faith of Christ, just as Dathan and Abrion (sons of Eliab) in the Old Testament revolted against the Lord.[54] Among these confusing circumstances, the Árpád princes allowed the pagan forces of Vata to proceed with their plan, so that, with their help, the princes could take their stand against Peter the Orseolo, who had been serving foreign interests himself.[55]

King Peter grew worried, the chronicler wrote, but displayed no fear in public. He broke camp, and crossed the Danube at Zsitvatő [estuary of the Zsitva stream], in order to reach Székesfehérvár. His opponents, however, quickly took possession of the city, where they held a gathering on the feast of the Assumption to decide whether to support the cause of the Árpád princes. They ultimately prevented Peter from entering the city. Meanwhile, Andrew and Levente, followed by a large number of supporters, were slowly making headway and reached the Pest terminal of the Danube ferry, where Bishop Gerard of Csanád and his episcopal confreres also were heading from the other, the right hand, side of the river. It was at the Buda terminal of the ferry (that is, on the right-hand bank of the river) that Vata and his associates had so dreadfully murdered the bishop with his fellow bishops—an event previously discussed above.[56]

The army of the princes must have been in the process of crossing the Danube when Vata and his men took possession of the right bank of the river; the sight of the bishops dressed in their pontifical regalia, combined with the fact that they (must have) conversed in (an) Italian (dialect) among themselves, made Vata furious. Beside Gerard, they killed Bishop Buldi; bishops Besztrik and Beneta entered a small boat to cross to the other shore and seek protection from Andrew and Levente, but the pagan insurgents on the Pest side (that is, the left bank of the river) wounded Bishop Besztrik who, three days later, also died of his wounds. Only Bishop Beneta had survived the bloodbath when Andrew, arriving at the river shore, saved his life. Szolnok, a royal reeve, members of the bishops' company, was crossing the river when the rover of the boat, threatened by the insurgents from the shore, had killed the reeve while still in the boat.[57]

The murdered high ecclesiastics, killed at the foot of the hill that today still bears Bishop Gerard's name (Gellért Hill), were the first Christian martyrs in Hungary.

King Peter observed that the Magyars all had joined the cause of Andrew and Levente, so he and his German troops, fled toward Fort Moson on the border to find refuge on German soil. Andrew's men, however, stationed on the border, had forced Peter to turn about and accept Andrew's invitation to visit Székesfehérvár, where the two of them would negotiate a settlement. But in the village of Zámor, Andrew's over-ambitious envoy wanted to place Peter under arrest and take him in shackles before Andrew. King Peter (who, after all, was the anointed and crowned monarch of the country), his queen, and members of the body guard resisted arrest, barricaded themselves in a country manor house, and offered armed resistance for three days. Within three days, the body guard had been massacred, King Peter and his Queen were arrested, the king blinded, the queen physically abused, by Andrew's men who had transported them to Székesfehérvár, where King Peter died of the wounds he had suffered during the blinding.[58]

Upon receipt of the news of Peter's miserable death, Andrew grew furious over the botched misdeed of his envoy whom, and whose associates, he had severely punished, the chronicler reported. Andrew gave Peter a royal burial at Saint Peter's cathedral in Pécs—the cathedral that had been established by King Peter himself: "quam ipse fundaverat"—as he had Peter buried with royal honors during the third year of his second reign.[59]

The (reconstructed) scene of King Peter's blinding, and of the moment when Prince Andrew received the crown from the hands of a bishop, were depicted in the "P" initial on fol. 30a of the Chronicle manuscript, under the caption "De morte Petri regis" that served as the title of the next chapter in the text (c. 85). In the drawing, there is depicted a *miles*, that is, a knight, fully armed, on rocky ground, kneeling on the body of the king laying on the ground, and putting out his eyes; next to Peter's head is a (the) royal crown fallen to the ground. The bishop may have been Beneta mentioned in the text, handing a (the) crown to Andrew.[60]

The adherents of the insurgents' party who had hoped for the restoration of previous conditions when every descendant of the late ninth century Magyar land-takers would claim equal rights, when no foreigners were allowed to live or hold land in the country, did accompany Andrew to Székesfehérvár, where they obtained reliable evidence that Peter, indeed, was dead, now disassembled their units, and returned to their homes.[61]

Afterwards, Prince Andrew encountered no further opposition, and he was, in the year 1047, crowned king at Székesfehérvár by the three bishops who had survived the previous bloodbath.[62]

The German source recorded as if all of these events had taken place in 1046. It may be that Andrew I had taken over the reins of power in the year 1046, and the recorded of the Altaich Annals following in the footsteps of his Hungarian informer recorded the year of 1046 as the actual date; however, it could also be that reckoning time in accordance with the "Christmas style," the coronation of Andrew I did take place on the first day of the new year, that is, on Christmas Day of 1047.[63]

Andrew's royal coronation was depicted in initial "P," on fol. 30'a, in the manuscript of the Chronicle; on the drawing, two bishops placed the crown—as it was his custom, the illuminator drew the crown semantically—upon the head of Andrew sitting on the throne, holding the orb in his left hand, while the third bishop, kneeling before Andrew, placed a sword into his right hand. In the background, there stood unarmed Magyars dressed in simple solemn clothing; they wore hats.[64]

It is noteworthy also that Levente, Andrew's older brother had stepped aside; actually, he had died during those days, the Hungarian chronicler reported. Levente was buried in Transdanubia, in the village Taksony, where his ancestor, named Taksony, had been buried. He had been living like a pagan; had he lived longer and taken over government of the realm, *paganism* would have gained control of the land.[65] On the other hand, both Andrew I and his younger brother Béla had been raised according to *Christian* standards as they were growing up in the Polish, and in the Kievan court of Prince Jaroslav the Wise. Both of them had been prepared for not persecuting the Christian faith, and for *not* destroying the life-work of their predecessor, King Stephen; on the contrary, they have been programmed for continuing it.[66]

The marriage of Andrew and Anastasia, daughter of Jaroslav, was truly a relationship based upon love in an age, when it was customary for ruling families through diplomatic negotiations to arrange marriage alliances among their sons and daughters, thereby to build up, or to strengthen their territorial land-holdings, or positions of political power. The first-born son of the blinded Vazul living in exile at the Kievan court fell in love with the daughter of the ruling prince, and because the prince had felt that he may find an ally in the Hungarian court struggling with the problem of dynastic succession, was pleased to give his eighteen-year old daughter in marriage to the twenty-three year old prince of the House of Árpád. Their marriage was celebrated according to the Byzantine rite in the Sophia cathedral with thirteen towers in Kiev.[67]

The 1046 uprising itself, a series of bloody atrocities, persecution of foreigners and priests, the bloodbath [the murder of Bishop Gerard] at the Buda terminal of the ferry (Kelenföld) had been the work of Vata and his associates. The insurrection led against Peter the Orseolo was only one aspect of this rebellion caused by the reign of the Orseolo, a vassal of the German court who served foreign interests, because King Stephen, Aba, and even the earlier Hungarian adherents of the Orseolo, had formed a socio-political unit with the nobles who leaned toward paganism.

It is the view of this writer that it was countrywide unhappiness with government policies that caused King Peter to be chased from his throne, just as it was countrywide joy and relief that led to the recall of Andrew, to the restoration of the Árpád dynasty to the throne. It was Viska, Buha and Buhna, members of the high nobility, who wanted to continue with the *Christian* policy of King Stephen. The three bishops who had escaped the bloodbath, together with members of the clergy were happy and pleased to accept Andrew of Árpád blood as monarch, because they knew that it was out of sheer political-military necessity that Andrew temporarily submitted to the demands of the pagan rebels; later, he would have turned, as he did turn, against the insurgents.[68]

Indeed, upon his coronation, King Andrew I issued legislation and ordered all his people (1) to cease, under the threat of death penalty, following pagan religious customs and practices he had previously approved of; (2) to return to the true faith of Christ; (3) to follow in every aspect the laws of King Stephen I (to cite but from the Chronicle: to live in accordance with the laws King Stephen had given them).[69] In other words, King Andrew revived the laws of King Stephen. He further ordered that (4) pagan idols must be destroyed, destructed church buildings rebuilt, and clergymen be held in public esteem. He strictly punished those who dared to ridicule God, religion, or the priests. He punished the murderers of clergymen, or of secular persons, in accordance with old laws, and the law codes of King Stephen.[70]

The chronicler in a brief entry, c. 87, referred to the fact that King Andrew and his brothers were (might have been) born out of wedlock, as their mother was a woman of the clan of Tatony; however, he added, this was a false story, because the three brothers were the sons of Ladislas *Szár* [the Bald], who most probably was married to a Kievan woman: "qui uxorem de Ruthenia dicitur accepisse."[71]

King Andrew's first diplomatic move consisted of clarifying his relations with the German court. The imperial German and the Hungarian royal advisors held different views of Hungaro-German politics. The emperor, Henry III (in order to keep the record straight, it is to be pointed out that Henry III was only *crowned emperor* by Pope Clement II in Rome on Christmas Day, 1047), had been seeking revenge, or at least some satisfaction based on military victory, in order to compensate Peter the Orseolo for the injustice he had suffered at the hands of the Magyar nobility, and to take Magyar land into his imperial possession.[72]

King Andrew I, on the other hand, wanted to assure freedom for his people, even if through military means were it become necessary. So it came to happen that the king—who had been called the *White*, and the *Catholic*, recorded the chronicler, a man of the court, Bishop Nicholas, the king's chancellor, someone fully aware of the political and diplomatic environment at the court; as chancellor, he had access to all the information[73]—during the first three years of his reign used armed force to subdue the Poles, the Czechs, and the Austrians, and made them pay tribute to him.

In order to strengthen his military might, King Andrew now had his younger brother, Béla, whose military reputation became well known in Poland, recalled from the Polish court; he wished to improve his country's domestic and diplomatic situation through Béla's knowledge of military strategy and field experience. He shared with him the wealth of the country, and made him the heir of his throne.[74]

He took counsel to provide in a princely fashion for the maintenance of the family and household of Béla. For that reason, he divided the country's territory in three parts, granting one-third to Béla: the northern part down to the Danube, and the northeast as far down as the Kőrös river. For himself, the monarch reserved the other two-thirds of the realm, Transdanubia, the land between the Danube and the Tisza rivers, and the Maros region in Transylvania.[75]

The king's court circle did not like the idea of partition, and the chronicler accurately predicted it in his report that much difficulty would arise from this subdivision. But King Andrew needed the military fitness and readiness of his younger brother; further, and this was important, the king required the military help arriving with Béla from Poland. In the Polish court they remembered Béla's military accomplishments. The king and his brother: the heir to the throne, lived in peace and great understanding with each other, the Hungarian chronicler reported.[76]

The return of Béla aided Andrew also on the diplomatic front: Conrad, the new duke of Lorraine, was the nephew of the wife of Béla. Andrew's father-in-law, Jaroslav the Wise, ruled Kiev. This Hungarian–Kievan connection seemed to have escaped the attention of the German monarch. One further ought to consider the fact that, at this time, the Byzantine emperor Constantin Monomachos (1042–54) had a troubled reign: external wars, domestic turbulence threatened his reign. He wanted to maintain friendly contacts with the Hungarian court; in fact, he did send a royal diadem (circlet) for Andrew, partly on grounds that Andrew did not have access to the crown sent to Hungary by Pope Sylvester II, and partly because, by sending him a diadem (circlet), the Byzantine court officially, through diplomatic means, approved of the kingship of Andrew I.[77]

During the same time, the German Franconian court had reached the peak of its power. The Norman princes in southern Italy recognized the emperor as their feudal overlord, and so did the Polish court, while during the second reign of Peter the Orseolo the Hungarians, too, belonged (in a feudal bondage) to the empire, together with the Czechs who, as the people of a German principality, belonged under the feudal jurisdiction of the German empire. The Danes and the Norwegians, even the prince of Kiev, were allies of the Germans. Henry III's wife, Agnes of Poitou, exercised a strong influence upon the economical and cultural attitude toward the west-Frankish orientation of the Franconian court.[78]

It was about at this time, during the mid-1040s, that Henry III, rather unwillingly, intervened in the turbulent politics of the papal curia. He permitted the assembly of bishops at Sutri in December, 1046, while knowing that church politics and intrigues were not under his jurisdiction,[79] and yet, after the synod was held, he named several

German bishops to the papal throne, as, for example, Clement II, who had crowned him emperor on Christmas day, 1047, the first day of the New Year.[80] Upon his return to the empire, he was greeted at home front by the uprising of Godfrey of Lorraine, to be followed closely by news of the uprising in Hungary. (One may wonder, indeed. Was the time factor between the two uprisings sheer coincidence?)[81]

The diplomatic danger of this political situation was that now it was Andrew I, the crowned Hungarian king, who sat on the throne of the German vassal, Peter the Orseolo, and the queen of Andrew was Anastasia, a daughter of Jaroslav the Wise of Kiev, while the sister of Queen Anastasia, Ann, was married to Henry I, king of the Franks, whose policies were supported by Agnes of Poitou, the wife of the emperor, Henry III.[82]

Still, it was Henry I, king of the Franks, who supported the uprising of Godfrey of Lorraine![83] As if the events in Hungary would have encouraged the Frankish ruler to support the attempt of the duke of Lorraine to secede from the empire. It may have been assumed, with good reason, at the Frankish court that events in Hungary would preoccupy the attention and military readiness of the emperor. What Henry I did not foresee was, however, the fact that the uprising in Lorraine actually aided the cause of Andrew I; for the German court, Lorraine presented a problem of high priority. On account of the events in Lorraine, Henry III could not invade, or at least, he would have to delay his revengeful attack on Hungary.[84]

It was under these circumstances that King Andrew sent envoys to the court of the Emperor in Speyer. His envoys explained to the emperor (1) that Andrew himself did not take part in the conspiracy aimed at Peter the Orseolo [the emperor's vassal]; (2) that he assumed the office of kingship because of the petition made to him by the people; (3) that upon succeeding to the throne, he had those who had conspired against the Orseolo, executed; (4) that he was willing to hand over to the emperor several of the anti-Orseolo conspirators who were still alive; (5) that he was offering payment of a yearly tribute, military aid, and expression of public respects to the emperor—were the emperor to acknowledge Andrew as king, and to maintain peaceful relations between the two countries.[85]

A word of explanation is in order here. One may, at this point, doubt the sincerity of King Andrew's political peace offer made to the imperial court. In the Slavic ruling circles where Andrew and Béla had been raised, feudal relationship of a vassal to his lord was looked upon as a *forced* social contract rather than a sincere agreement with ethical value. They viewed it as a *temporary* political relationship that could easily be altered as soon as, or as frequently as, the political conditions had changed. To cite but two examples, Boleslav the Strong of Poland, or the Czech Vratislav, whose political-military maneuvers in 1038 and 1039, King Andrew was able to study from his immediate surroundings, did behave in such a manner.[86] By sending a delegation to the emperor, King Andrew acted in the interests of peace; he and his country's people needed peace in order to restore domestic order, economic normalcy in the land, and to establish a rational foreign diplomacy. A possible German military invasion of the realm could have meant the end of the country so fatally weakened by domestic uprisings in the recent past.[87]

The German invasion was unavoidable, however. The blinding and forceful removal of Peter the Orseolo from the throne was a personal insult to Henry III; furthermore, the realm, regarded by the emperor as his feudal land, now was *free* at a time when the emperor, as feudal overlord, wished to deal with it as his personal property, and by donating it, to reward someone of his own choosing with it. That was why Andrew I offered his country as a feudal land to the emperor; it was his policy to divert the threat of war from his country, away from his people. The Hungarian monarch's voluntary feudal submission to the German court still seemed to offer a more favorable diplomatic solution of this question, than turning the country into a feudal dependency created by the emperor, dependency that would turn Hungry into German feudal land.[88]

Notes

1. Cf. Chronicle, c. 69, *SSH*, I, 318f.; J. I. Bakács, "Szent István megalapítja a keresztény magyar államot" [How King St. Stephen established the Christian Magyar state], in *Szent István élete és alkotásai* [On the life and achievements of St. Stephen], ed. Bálint Hóman (Budapest, 1938), 31ff.; János Karácsonyi, *Szent István király élete* [The life of King St. Stephen] (Budapest, 1904), 46ff.; Gyula Kristó, *A magyar állam megszületése* [The birth of the Magyar state] (Szeged, 1995), 317ff., though, one may find the use of the term: *state*, inappropriate in the early eleventh century; the word *regnum (kingdom, Königtum)* would be the correct expression to use—cf. Aloys Meister, *Deutsche Verfassungsgeschichte*, 3rd ed. (Leipzig-Berlin, 1922), 91ff.

The burial of King Stephen was "commented on" by the illuminator of the Chronicle MS, fol. 23'a, in "B" initial: two men placed the body of the king, dressed in blue, into the grave; in his right hand he [still] held the orb, and a palm stock in his left. Four bishops performed the ceremony; the Queen stood at the foot of the grave with hands folded in prayer. There were members of the nobility standing in the background.

2. *Annales Hildesheimenses*, a. 1031. The chronicler's expression, "dux Ruzinorum," might imply that King Stephen asked for military help from Kiev to fight the invaders from the west.

3. See, e.g., William of Malmesbury, *De gestis regum Anglorum libri V*, ed. W. Stubbs, 2 vols. RS. (London, 1887-89), v:393-94 (anno 1100), and, v:395 (a. 1101); Eadmer, *Historia novorum in Anglia*, ed. M. Rule, RS. (London, 1884), iii: 55 (anno 1100); on the composition of this work, see R. W. Southern, *St. Anselm and his Biographer* (Cambridge, 1963), 298ff.

4. *SSH*, I, 319f.

5. *SSH*, I, 320f.

6. *SSH*, I, 320,24 – 321,7; for a contrary opinion, cf. Keza, c. 44, *ibid.*, I, 173,9-15.

7. On the succession of Peter the Orseolo, cf. Wipo, c. 38; or, "Geneologia regum," 167ff.; see also, "Chronicon Polonicum," i:18, *MGHSS*, IX, 436; *MPL*, I, 414. Harry Bresslau, *Jahrbücher des Deutschen Reiches unter Konrad II*, 2 vols. (repr. of the 1879–84 ed., Berlin, 1967), I, 151ff., and 380ff. Further, Horváth, *Stílusproblémák*, 255ff., and 350ff.

8. King Stephen's "Vita minor," c. 7, *SSH*, II, 399.

9. King Stephen's Laws, ii:17, in Závodszky, 55f.; Marczali, *Enchiridion*, 79; for Mainz, 847, can. 5, see *MGHLL*, II, 177; or, Mansi, XIV, 904.s

10. *SSH*, II, 399,21-26; on the role of Buda—"consilium cum Buda viro nephando"—as discussed above, see *SSH*, I, 320,8-11. On the reasons for, and the actual blinding of, someone, cf. Thietmar, v:15, and iv:37; Meister, 103ff.

11. *SSH*, I, 321,2-9; Palacky, *Geschichte*, I, 268ff., for background only.

12. Chronicle, c. 70, *SSH*, I, 323,6-16, though, the Queen was behind all this, the chronicler claimed—cf. *ibid.*, I, 322,18 – 323,5; during the thirteenth century, the chronicler Albericus spoke ill of Queen Gisela: "sed illa Gisela regina, ut dicunt, multas malitias in terra illa fecit, et extremum post mortem sancti regis meritis exigentibus interfecta est." Cf. *MGHSS*, XXIII, 779; for the text of art. vii of the *Admonitiones*, see Závodszky, 138; omitted by Marczali, *Enchiridion*, 66. The figure of Peter the Orseolo dressed in armor is the subject of the illuminated "A" initial on fol. 24a: he is holding a sword in his left hand, and a [the] crown] in his right.

13. Holtzmann, 336ff., and 359ff.

14. Pope Benedict IX must have regarded King Peter as King Stephen's true successor, and as defender of the Church; on those grounds, he had excommunicated all those who dared to depose him—cf. *Annales Altahenses*, anno 1044. The policies of Popes John XIX and Benedict IX were discussed by Haller, II, 275ff., and by Funk – Bihlmeyer, II, 43f.; Kühner, 56; see also H. Kromayer, "Über die Vorgänge in Rom in 1045 und Sutri, 1046," *Historische Vierteljarhschrift*, 10 (1907), 161ff.; S. Messina, *Benedetto IX, 1032–48* (Catania, 1922), passim.

15. Dandalo, *RISS*, XII, 235, 239, 244; Bresslau, *Konrad II*, II, 261ff.

16. Cf. document in *MSHSM*, VII, 444; E. Dümmler, "Über die älteste Geschichte der Slawen in Dalmatien," *SB der Wiener Akademie der Wissenschaften*, 20, 533-430, even today regarded as a fundamental work. Thietmar, vi:2; Adeboldi "Vita Henrici," *MGHSS*, IV, 691; Wipo, cc. 9, 22, 26; Hermann Contractus, "Chronicon," a. 1030, *MGHSS*, V, 121; Bresslau, *Konrad II*, I, 234ff., and I, 234, n. 2. Walther cooperated in editing the canons for Burchard of Worms' *Decretum* of Canon law; "...domino Walterio Spirensi episcopo adiuvante...canones in unum corpus collegit;" cf. *MGHSS*, IV, 837 (c. 10).

17. Thietmar, viii:16; Cedrenus (CB), II, 438; Ostrogorsky, 255ff.

18. Wipo, c.26; King Stephen's "Vita maior," c. 14, *SSH*, II, 389f.

19. See Chronicle, c. 71, *ibid.*, I, 324,5-13.

20. Cf. Gyula Kristó, "A fekete magyarok és a pécsi püspökség alapitása" [The Black Magyars and the foundation of the Pécs bishopric], *Acta historica Szegediensis*, 82 (1985), 11ff.; one is to remember, though, that the letter by Bishop Fulbert of Chartres to Bishop Bonipert of Pécs is to be dated about 1020—for text, cf. *MPL*, 141, 189f. See also J. Holub, "Bonipertus," *Ianus Pannonius Muzeum Évkönyve, 1959* (Pécs, 1960), 97ff.

21. *Annales Altahenses*, a. 1044.

22. *Annales Altahenses*, a. 1041.

23. For a characterization of the Orseolo, cf. Chronicon, *SSH*, I, 323; see further the letters of Abbot Bern[o] of Reichenau, ed. by Ernst Strehlke, in *Archiv zur Kunde österreichischen Geschichtsquellen*, 20 (1855), 191ff.; also, Pez, *Thesaurus*, VI-1, 199ff; and F. J. Schmale, *Die Briefe des Abtes Bern von Reichenau* (Stuttgart, 1961); Dandalo, ccxliv, *RISS*, XII; Leo of Montecassino, "Chronicon," *MGHSS*, VIII, 674. It is of lesser importance, though significant, that Gaufridus de Bruli, late twelfth century, had referred to Salomon as a son of King Stephen—*MGHSS*, XXVI, 202.

24. Cf. Chronicle, c. 72, *SSH*, I, 324ff.; *Annales Altahenses*, a. 1041; for a thirteenth century view, cf. Albericus, *MGHSS*, XXIII, 787. On the background, see Wilhelm von Giesebrecht, *Geschichte der deutschen Kaiserzeit*, rev. ed., ed. Wilhelm Schild, 6 vols. (Meersburg, 1929), II, 342ff.

25. See Lamperti monachi Hersfeldensis, *Opera*, ed. Oswald Holder-Egger, SSrG (Hannover–Leipzig, 1894), a. 1041; Hermann Contractus, "Chronica," a. 1041, *MGHSS*, V, 67ff.; on Hermann, cf. Wattenbach, *Geschichtsquellen*, II, 42ff.; Hermann of Reichenau's brief and concise report, *MGHSS*, V, 117; St. Katona, *Historia critica regum Hungariae stirpis Arpadianae*, 7 vols. (Pest–Buda, 1779-82), I, 497ff.

26. Chronicon, c. 72. In the "A" letter on fol. 24'a of the Chronicle MS there is depicted King Aba dressed in chain armor holding a sword in his left, and the [a] crown in his right hand Was it sheer coincidence, or was it the point of view stressed by the illuminator that both, Peter the Orseolo and now Aba, were not wearing, but *holdings* their crown(s)?

27. Chronicon, c. 73; *Annales Altahenses*, a. 1042; Hermann Contractus, a. 1042.

28. Keza, c. 48, seems to have combined two campaigns into one, cf. *SSH*, I, 174f.; "Annales Sangallenses," a. 1043, *MGHSS*, I, 85; Aventinus, *ibid.*, III, 50. Giesebrecht, II, 360, makes, frankly, little sense. On the German political background, see Gebhardt, I, 235ff.

29. The Chronicle, cc. 74-75, repeats certain events.

30. See the Chronicle, cc. 72-73.

31. *Ibid.*, I, 325f.; Bishop Gerard's "Vita minor," c. 6, *ibid.*, II, 477,1-7; compare with *Annales Altahenses*, a. 1044.

32. *SSH*, I, 326f.; cf. Gyula Kristó's classic study, "Források kritikája és kritikus források az 1040-es évek magyar történetére vonatkozóan" I–II [Critical sources, and their critique, of Hungarian history of the 1040s], repr. from *Magyar Könyvszemle*, 160 (1984), 159ff., and 285ff.

33. *Annales Altahenses*, a. 1044, though the chronology is confusing; the excommunication is mentioned in the Chronicle, c. 76, *SSH*, I, 331f. The picture filling the whole of the mid-section of fol. 25' in the Chronicle MS commented on the battle depicted—just like in a theatrical stage set—between two mountains. On the right hand side the German ruler appeared leading his troops, Aba on the left; in the backdrop of the battle scene some Magyars wearing fur hats (members of Peter's troops?) were depicted as leaving. The Hungarian standard fell on the ground; the imperial flag decorated with the German eagle stood tall. In the right corner of the drawing the German monarch is kneeling before the altar giving thanks for the victory; in the left, King Aba reaches for his crown, but a soldier (*miles*) pierces his heart—as if to express the illuminator's opinion that a king who survived his disgraceful defeat in the battle field ought to die a disgraceful death.

34. Cf. *ibid.*, I, 331f.; *Annales Altahenses*, a. 1044; "Annales Sangallenses," *MGHSS*, I, 85.; Bernold's "Chronicle," *MGHSS*, V, 425. The assertion by Ralph Glaber that 6,000 German knights were opposed by some 200,000 (!) Magyars, is ridiculous—see *MGHSS*, VII, 70.

35. Chronicle, c. 77, *SSH*, I, 333.

36. *Ibid.*, I, 333,9-14; *Annales Altahenses*, a. 1044.

37. "Insignia regni…"—papal writ dated October 28, 1075; cf. Erich Caspar (ed.), *Das Register Gregors VII, MGH Epp. selectae*, 2 vols. (Berlin, 1920–23; repr. 1990), n. ii:13. Interesting is the remark in the Chronicle that Peter was "sacris insignibus sancti Stephani regis…more regio *decoratum*," [italics mine]—an expression *equivalent* to the coronation? Cf. *SSH*, I, 333,11-12. On the drawing of the "S" initial, fol. 27B, Peter receives a lance *not* kneeling, but *standing* before the emperor—cf. Dercsényi, I, 53. Further, see the *Annales Altahenses*, a. 1044; Bóna, 88f.

38. *Ibid.*, I, 333,14-18. It may be worth noting that the German source reads "scita Teutonica"—cf. *Annales Altahenses*, a. 1044.

39. See the Chronicle, c.78, *ibid.*, I, 334,4-6. Peter had to pay a vassal's dues to the Emperor—cf. Wibert, "Vita s. Leonis IX papae," ii:8, *MPL*, 143, 496bc; or, Hildebert, "Vita Hugonis," ii:7, *MPL*, 159, 864cd. Also, Contractus, *MGHSS*, V, 131,41-42.

40. *Annales Altahenses*, a. 1045; Chronicle, c. 78: when "tanta fames fuit in Boemia, ut tercia pars populi ineriret fame," Vazul's three sons had left the Czech court and went to Poland; cf. Cosmas of Prague, "Chronicon Bohemorum," *MGHSS*, IX, 75; further, "Chronicon Polonorum," *MGHSS*, IX, 438.

41. Cf. Chronicle, cc. 79-80, *SSH*, I, 334,15 – 335,29.

42. Chronicle, c. 80, *ibid.*, I, 336; the princes were recalled from "Ruscia"—*ibid.*, I, 337,7. For the genealogy of the Rurikids, see *infra*, n. 45. On previous contacts between Hungary and Kiev, see Z. J. Kosztolnyik, "Similarities between King St. Stephen of Hungary's Law Code and the Laws of Jaroslav the Wise of Kiev," *Hungary's Historical Legacies*, ed. D. P. Hupchick and R. W. Weisberger (New York, 2000), 45ff.

43. Chronicle, c. 81, *ibid.*, I, 336f.

44. Chronicle, c. 81, *SSH*, I, 337,4-13, and c. 88, *ibid.*, I, 345,17-21. On Jaroslav, see the Russian Primary Chronicle, ed. cit., 136ff.; Werner Scheck, *Geschichte Russlands*, (Munich, 1977), 37ff.

45. Cf. Genealogy of the Rurikids—based on N. de Baumgarten, "Généalogies et mariages occidenaux des Rurikides russes du Xe au XIIIe siècle," *Orientalia Christiana*, 9 (1927), in Cross – Sherbowitz-Wetzor, insert, following p. 298; also, Mór Wertner, *Az Árpádok családi története* [Family history of the Árpáds] (Nagybecskerek, 1892), 117. Ralph, a monastic writer, described King Henry I of the Franks as a man vigorous in arms and worthy of the kingdom he held; cf. *Rerum Gallicarum et Franciarum scriptores*, ed. M. Boquet, 23 vols. (Paris, 1738-1876), cited hereafter as *RHF*, XI, 481; also, Hallam, 72f.

46. *Richeri Historiarum libri IV*, rev. ed., ed. G. Waitz, SSrG (Hannover, 1877), lib. ii, discussed Frankish-German relations during the mid- and second half of the tenth century. According to Wattenbach, I, 412ff., "nicht die Tatsachen, nicht die Wahrheit sind ihm das wesentliche, sondern mehr noch die Form der Darstellung;" and yet, "*demungeachtet aber* [Wattenbach added] hat doch Richters Buch für uns einen hohen Wert; er ist der einziger Berichtstatter über jene hochwichtige Zeit, in welcher die Herrschaft von den Karolingern auf die Capetinger überging...." For background, cf. Gebhardt, I, 178ff.; Holtzmann, 127ff.; Hallam, 21ff.; Edith Ennen, *Frauen im Mittelalter*, 5th rev. ed. (Munich, 1994), 68.

47. Cf. RA, n. 12; for text, Marczali, *Enchiridion*, 81ff.; D. Fuxhoffer – M. Czinár (eds.), *Monasterilogiae regni Hungariae*, 2 vols. (Vienna–Esztergom, 1869), I, 166.

48. Andrew I had placed the church and monastery of Tihany under the protection of Mary the Mother of God, and of St. Anian, bishop in Gaul who had successfully defended the city of Orleans from the wrath of Attila the Hun: "...ad ecclesiam sancte Marie, sanctique aniani [sic!] episcopi et confessoris..."; King Andrew I intended the abbey church (eventually) to become his burial place, cf. Marczali, *Enchiridion*, 82. Or, Jakubovich – Pais, 19ff., who provided the text of the charter with different punctuation and spelling. Bóna, *Húnok*, 83ff., with a map of Aureliani/Orléans, p. 74.

49. Chronicle, c. 82.

50. "Tunc nobiles Hungarie videntes mala gentis sue...in uum convenerunt, consilioque habito tocus Hungarie," so that they recall Andrew and Levente from Russian soil, "quod tota Hungaria eos fideliter expecteret, et universum regnum eis, sicut regali semini libenter obsequeretur..."—cf. *SSH*, I, 337,4-11. Sándor Tóth, "Levente és András" [Andrew and Levente], *Acta historica Szegediensis*, 82 (1985), 31ff.

51. *Ibid.*, I, 337,26-27; Ferenc Makk, "Megjegyzések I. András történetéhez" [Some remarks concerning King Andrew I], *Acta historica Szegediensis*, 90 (1990), 23ff.

52. Chronicle, c. 82, *SSH*, I, 337f.; Gerard's "Vita maior," c. 15—cf. *ibid.*, II, 501f. Gyula Kristó, "Források," *Magyar Könyvszemle*, 1984.

53. *SSH*, I, 338,11-12. László Szegfű, "Vata népe" [The people—followers—of Vata], *Acta historica Szegediensis*, 67 (1980), 11ff., reprint.

54. *SSH*, I, 338,14-16; scriptural reference would be in the Book of Numbers, 16:12-14.

55. *SSH*, I, 338,19-24.

56. Cf. *SSH*, I, 339ff.; the "Vita maior" of Bishop Gerard, c. 15, *ibid.*, II, 501ff. László Szegfű, "Gellért püspök halála" [The death of Bishop Gerard], *Acta historica Szegediensis*, 66 (1979), 19ff., reprint.

57. Chronicle, cc. 83-84, *SSH*, I, 339ff.; and, Gerard's "Vita," *ibid.*, II, 501ff. The scene does remind one of the revengeful communist takeover in Hungary during the late 1940s—see, e.g., József Mindszenty, *Emlékirataim* [The Memoirs of Cardinal Mindszenty] (Toronto, 1974), 98ff.; N. F. Dreisziger (ed.), *The Hungarian Revolution Twenty Years After* (Kingston, Ontario, 1976), passim.

58. Chronicle, c. 85, *SSH*, I, 342f.; *Annales Altahenses*, a. 1046.

59. Cf. *SSH*, I, 343,11-16.

60. See Dercsényi, *Chronicon pictum*, I, fol. 30a. The "P" initial begins c. 85 of the text.

61. Andrew, now "a perturbacionibus hostium securus,..."—*ibid.*, I, 343,18.

62. Chronicle, c. 86, *ibid.*, I, 343f.

63. *Annales Altahenses*, anno 1046; on Christmas style, see Brandt, 38f., who follows Grotefend, I, 205.

64. See *supra*, n. 60.

65. Cf. *SSH*, I, 344,6-15; Andrew I's reforms, *ibid.*, I, 344,1-6; his *Constitutio ecclesiastica*—cf. Mansi, *Concilia*, XIX, 631f.; or, *MPL*, 151, 1257f., aa. 1 and 4—may be based upon this passage in the Chronicle; Kosztolnyik, *Five Kings*, 73f.

66. See Hóman, *Ungarisches Mittelalter*, I, 254ff.; Gyula Kristó, "I. István és családja árpádkori történetírásunkban" [Stephen I and his Family in the historiography of the Arpad age], *Acta historica Szegediensis*, 40 (1972), 51ff., esp. 63f.; Wertner, 114ff.; on the Kievan religious-cultural background during the years of Jaroslav the Wise, see Cross – Sherbowitz-Wetzor, 136ff.; Thietmar, 257, 258, referred to the wealth of Kiev; Adam of Bremen, *Gesta Hammaburgensis ecclesiae pontificum*, 3rd ed., ed. B. Schmeidler, SSrG (Hannover, 1917), 80, spoke of Kiev as the rival of Byzantium; Scheck, *Russland*, 37ff.

67. Cf. Chronicle, c. 81.

68. Cf. Chronicle, c. 86. The king must have tried hard to correct the realm's conditions Bishop Gerard so bitterly complained about: "Plene omni dolo et omnia fallacia filii diaboli inimice omnis iusticie, non definis subuertere ius domini rectas; ...quare hoc? Nimirum dixi quia filii diaboli qui potestates sunt tenebrarum ubique regnant et dominantur." Cf. Munich MS, fol. 15',2 – 16,1-2; and, fol. 46',24-25; or, Szegfű, *Deliberatio*, 60, 62, and 184.

69. See *supra*, n. 65; Kosztolnyik, *Five Kings*, 71.

70. See *Constitutio*, art. 4, in Mansi, XIX, 632.

71. Chronicle, c. 87.

72. *Annales Altahenses*, a. 1046; *Annales Hildesheimenses*, a. 1046; Gebhardt, I, 235; Giesebrecht, II, 403ff.

73. And yet, one may feel as if the chronicler's statement—that Andrew "tribus annis Polonos, Bohemos, Australes Hungaris suis armis fecit consensuales" (c. 88, cf. *SSH*, I, 344f.)—could be a rather inexact reference to Andrew's later military activities, in about 1051; on this, see Herimannus Contractus, *MGHSS*, V, 127, and the, perhaps less reliable, remarks in the *Annales Altahenses*, aa. 1050 and 1051. Further, the "Vita

Bernonis" of Osnabrück, whose author followed "populares fabulae cantilenae" in drafting his narrative, see *MGHSS*, XII, 63.

74. Cf. *SSH*, I, 345,1-7. On the identity of the chronicler, cf. Horváth, *Árpádkori*, 350ff.

75. The text is not very clear: after the king and Béla have agreed, *habito consilio*; or, after the monarch had consulted with the Council, *SSH*, I, 345,10-11. On the territorial subdivision, "diviserunt regnum in tres partes," see *ibid.*, I, 345,10-16.

76. *Ibid.*, I, 345,24-25; after this, Andrew had erected the abbey at Tihany, as he had married the daughter of the grand prince of Kiev—cf. *ibid.*, I, 345,17-20. On the background, see Keza, c. 57, *ibid.*, I, 178ff.

77. Ostrogorsky, 265ff.; Brown, 92f. On the Monomachos Crown, see Josef Deér, *Die hl. Krone Ungarns* (Vienna, 1966), 33ff.; Magda Oberschall Bárány, *Konstantinos Monomachos császár koronája* [The Crown of Emperor Monomachos] (Budapest, 1937), 59f., and passim; Nicolas Oikonomides, "La couronne dite de Constantin Monomaque," *Travaux et Mémoires*, 12 (1994), 241ff., whose arguments were convincingly challenged by Etele Kiss, "The state of research on the Monomachos Crown and some further thoughts," in Olenka Z. Pevny (ed.), *Perceptions of Byzantium and its Neighbors (843–1261)* Metropolitan Museum (New York, 2000), 60ff.

78. Giesebrecht, II, 376ff.; Gebhardt, I, 235ff., and 238ff.

79. *Annales Altahenses*, 1046, on the Synod of Sutri, December, 1046; also, Pius Engelbert, "Heinrich III und die Synoden von Sutri und Rom im Dezember, 1046," *Römische Quartalschrift*, 94 (1999), 228ff.; Funk – Bihlmeyer, II, 44f.; Gebhardt, I, 232f.; R. L. Poole, "Benedict IX and Gregory VI," *Proceedings of the British Academy*, 1917–18, 200ff.; Meyndt, 28

80. Cf. *Annales Altahenses*, 1047; Haller, II, 278ff.

81. *Annales Altahenses*, a. 1047; Gebhardt, I, 236f.

82. Giesebrecht, II, 307f.; Hallam, 72f., and 103ff.

83. *Annales Altahenses*, aa. 1044-45, 1046; Giesebrecht, II, 364ff.

84. *Annales Altahenses*, aa. 1046, 1049; Gebhardt, I, 236f.; E. Steindorff, *Jahrbücher des deutschen Reiches unter Heinrich III*, I, 293, n. 2.

85. Cf. Chronicle, c. 90, *SSH*, I, 347ff.; *Annales Altahenses*, a. 1052; Steindorff, *Heinrich III*, I, f.

86. Chronicle, cc. 80-81. Tadeusz Manteuffel, *The Formation of the Polish State*, tr. Andrew Gorski (Detroit, 1982), 56ff.; Edward Jenks, *Law and Politics in the Middle Ages* (New York, 1898), 7ff., and ch. 5, so different from in the western Latin frame of mind—cf. Ch. Howard McIlwain, *The Growth of Political Thought in the West* (New York, 1932), 149ff.

87. As it may be evident from the Chronicle, c. 88; Keza, c. 57.

88. Chronicle, c. 91. Viewed objectively, though with too much overconfidence, by Meyndt, 30ff.; for the Hungarian point of view, cf. Hóman, I, 263ff.; and, Székely – Bartha, 855ff.

XII

Kings Andrew I and Béla I

1. Henry III's Refusal of Andrew's Offer

> Teutonicorum rex cum magno exercitu obsedit vastrum Poson volens...Hungariam suo diminio subiugare.
>
> *Chronicon pictum*, c. 89

Had the emperor accepted the peace offer of the Hungarian monarch, he would have recognized Hungary as the perpetual feudal property of the Árpáds; after all, it was he who had handed the country over as a personal benefice to Peter the Orseolo. That was why he wanted to conquer the land by the force of arms, so that he would hand the vanquished property over as a feudal gift to King Andrew, or to someone else. For this reason alone, the emperor had to ignore the peace offer made by King Andrew.

On the domestic front, the emperor had, for a short while, been occupied with the uprising in Lorraine, but he did name Margrave Welf of Swabia as the Duke of Carinthia, with orders to keep a close eye on the defense of the southeastern border lands.[1] With his move, however, he unwittingly provided Andrew with an opportunity to get his realm's military defenses ready for encountering future (German) invasion(s) of Magyar land.

The Hungarian monarch did not remain idle. The record says that the monarch had filled vacant episcopal sees in the realm, and many positions in public administration. Bishop Benedict, who had escaped from the bloodbath of the uprising, became the archbishop of Esztergom, while the sees of Veszprém and Győr were assigned to, or retained by bishops, Clement and Nicholas, respectively.[2] In 1050, Bishop George became the archbishop of Kalocsa;[3] Maurus (Mór) had been the bishop of Pécs since 1036,[4] while Bishop Leodvin, a native of Lüttich, occupied the bishopric of Bihar.[5] According to the testimony of documents, Zach, member of the higher nobility, had been named the Palatine of the realm.[6] Vid was the royal reeve of Bács; royal reeves Martin of the clan of Ják, Ernye of the clan of Ákos, Andrew, Hetey, Gilco, Lutovic and Woitich headed the administration of the counties, while in 1055, Judge Koppány, and the Master-of-the-Horse, named Nuna, were members of the royal entourage.[7]

In the following year, the emperor invaded Hungary anew, but without any success; he was unable to follow up his earlier victories.[8] He failed to consider the fact that the Poles, for example, would aid the Hungarians; and Prince Casimir, although he openly did not challenge the emperor, had constantly harassed the Czech Brestislav, an ally of Henry III, thereby preventing the latter from displaying Czech armed forces in the support of Henry III on the war path against King Andrew.[9]

Henry III now arrived with a large army on the border, and he was logistically prepared for a longer campaign, the Hungarian chronicler reported, as he sent ships ahead on the Danube loaded with food supplies for his forces. The emperor placed his relative, *fratrem suum*, in charge of the fleet, Bishop Gebhardt (Gebarth) of Regensburg.[10] Now Andrew needed the military readiness of his brother Béla to meet the enemy head on. It was the tactic of Béla to vacate the to-be-invaded Hungarian territory by removing all inhabitants, animals, and available food supplies. The imperial army heading toward Fehérvár arrived in a desolate, burned out land, where food and even water were unavailable, and seemingly lost all contact with the supply fleet on the Danube; "et nesciebat ubi naves eius essent."[11]

During this time, Bishop Gebhardt had crossed the Lajta stream with his armed force, reached Győr, and dispatched a letter to the emperor requesting further instructions as to where their forces would meet. However, King Andrew's scouts—the record referred to them as *latrinculi regis*, had captured the bearer of the bishop's writ, and taken him before the king. The royal chancellor, Bishop Nicholas had the letter translated into Hungarian for the king, and the court now decided to draft a falsified letter, pretending it to be the emperor's reply, for the imperial commander, the bishop of Regensburg. At the Hungarian court, they drafted a letter, as if sent by the emperor, addressed to Bishop Gebhardt, and sent it to him by someone unknown, "quas per quendam hospitem ei miserunt," directing the bishop to withdraw from Magyars land quickly.[12]

Although this segment of the chronicle record may have originated from the pen of, or information derived from, Bishop and royal Chancellor Nicholas, it seems to be far too fantastic a narrative to be taken at face value. Could it have been, for instance, so easy to falsify the emperor's signature, and, presumably, to reproduce the emperor's seal on this writ that, after all, contained imperial orders to an imperial military subordinate? Or, was the surviving chronicle segment a later addition to the chronicler's text? And yet, this segment of the record bears witness to a masterful move of diplomatic chess by the Hungarian monarch and his chancellor. In the falsified letter (order; report) sent to Gebhardt, the bishop was advised that since great and dangerous affairs occurred in the empire: the emperor's enemies took possession of it, urgent circumstances forced the emperor to interrupt the campaign in Hungary, and instructed the bishop to scuttle his ships and hurry back, "festina et destructis navibus, quam cicius poteris," to Regensburg; he could find no secure haven on Hungarian soil.[13]

The German armies indeed left Hungarian soil, though previously they defeated the armed Hungarian border garrison at Kapuvár, broke through the Magyar armed forces' encirclement, and reached Hainburg on the German side of the border. The Hungarian report, naturally, recorded in overly strong terms the circumstances surrounding the Germans' troop withdrawal, while the German record, as, for example, the author of the Annals of Altaich, or Hermann of Reichenau, expressed only contempt for the Magyars' *robber-like* (though, evidently quite successful!) military tactics, and complained bitterly about the difficult terrain, impassable roads in the country (by that they must have meant the closed off exit roads on the defensive military frontier), and expressed pride over the fact that the German troops left Hungary by destroying and burning everything; and yet, the German chroniclers cannot deny the fact that it was the imperial forces that had been thoroughly defeated. (It may be a curious coincidence that in 1945, the commanding officer of the Sixth Tank

Division of the German Army used similar arguments for explaining why he had suffered defeat at the hands of the Russians, and had only six tanks left after a series of field battles.[14]) The German chroniclers could not obscure the fact that the emperor lost his campaign and Hungary ceased to exist as a feudal dependency of the German empire.[15]

Henry III made one more attempt at regaining Magyar land as his feudal realm. He turned down the peace efforts made on the behalf of King Andrew by Andrew's brother-in-law, the margrave of Austria, and, seeking revenge, he readied himself for another invasion in June, 1052. He moved toward Fort Pozsony. He wanted to defeat Andrew in an open battle, but the Pozsony garrison headed by Vojtek, Andrew, Vilongard, Oros and Martin, resisted the siege for some eight weeks, while a Hungarian frogman named Zotmund, during the quiet of a night was able to scuttle all of the German (supply) ships on the Danube anchored at Pozsony. The emperor suffered another humiliating defeat.[16]

The sinking of the emperor's fleet on the Danube at Pozsony is illustrated in the "E" initial on fol. 31b of the Chronicle; in the background of the illuminated initial there is Fort Pozsony depicted, in the foreground the emperor, standing with two of his knights in one of the boats filling with water. In another boat, two men are being depicted as struggling for their survival. Interestingly, as it is worth noting, in this initial the crown on the emperor's head was drawn exactly the same way as the crown on King Andrew's head, as if to imply that the Hungarian illuminator of the Chronicle (as well as the mid-fourteenth century author-editor of the text) regarded King Andrew I as the political and constitutional equal of the emperor—Andrew as *emperor* in his own country.[17]

Now the Hungarian monarch, obviously unprepared for another war with the emperor, but mainly for the sake of saving his people from further devastation and the hardships of war, personally requested from Pope Leo IX to meet with the emperor at Pozsony, to persuade him to withdraw his troops, and to conclude peace with the Hungarian court.[18] The pontiff, and Abbot Hugh of Cluny, had met with Henry III at Pozsony, convincing him to cease hostilities and prepare for peace negotiations with the Hungarians.[19]

One must consider the fact that at this time, Pope Leo IX held an unclear, rather hostile relationship with the Normans, the new masters of the Italian south; the Roman pontiff had to suffer a military defeat at the hands of the Normans before he could begin negotiations with them, and make them vassals of the Roman See. Until the papal-Norman question could be settled, the Roman curia needed the sympathy of the imperial court, and papal politics would not allow the German emperor to spread his forces thin in, what Pope Leo IX undoubtedly judged as, an unnecessary imperial war effort with the Hungarians. The pontiff was an experienced peace-negotiator; it was he who previously negotiated a three-year peace between the west-Frankish court and the German court of Henry III.[20]

The papal intervention had been successful; however, now it was King Andrew who decided not to keep the clause in the peace agreement concluded with the emperor, the agreement that obligated him to pay compensation to the Germans. The court of Andrew must have been aware of the uprising that had broken out in Bavaria against Henry III; already during the previous siege of Pozsony, Duke Conrad of Bavaria and Gebhardt, bishop of Regensburg, became deadly enemies, and, breaking the promise they had made to the emperor, their hostility broke into open war on Bavarian soil.[21]

Upon the departure of the pontiff and withdrawal of German troops, the court of Andrew refused to pay the amount of war compensation they had agreed upon. Simultaneously, it is known from the German record that, in 1053, Duke Conrad was defeated, his duchy taken from him, and the duke with his entourage had to find refuge at the court of King Andrew. There, he was well received because during the emperor's previous campaign, as a matter of fact, in the fall of 1052, it was Duke Conrad who persuaded the Hungarian monarch to seek peace with the emperor's court.[22]

This writer wishes to note at this point that Duke Conrad sent Count Potho as his personal envoy to King Andrew; Potho was one of those nobles whose goods had been confiscated by the emperor because the count was a friend of the Bavarian duke. Thus, Potho, too, remained at the court of Andrew, and when Andrew died in 1060, he married the widowed queen Anastasia (though it may have been true that, during the prolonged illness of her husband, the queen and Potho already maintained an intimate relationship). Eventually Potho was able to return home, and offer his ambassadorial services to the court of Henry IV.[23]

The circumstances surrounding the Hungarian-German *diplomatic* developments of 1052 and 1053 are in need of special investigation. In 1052, Duke Conrad of Bavaria played the role of peace-broker between the Hungarian and German imperial courts and accomplished that the Hungarian party would accept the following peace terms:

(1)   that the Magyars pay a larger amount of compensation to the imperial court;

(2)   that Andrew I obligate himself to provide military aid for the emperor against his domestic enemies;

(3)   that Andrew renounce the region his military forces had held beyond the Lajta stream, in favor of Henry III.

The emperor was willing to accept the peace plan; Andrew I, however, in an unexpected and stubborn manner, refused the terms. As he understood the issue, Andrew was convinced that through the cooperation of Duke Conrad and Béla, Andrew's brother and heir to his throne, a Bavarian-Hungarian military alliance could be established—an alliance that would protect him from further imperial military intrusion. It is the opinion of this writer that Duke Conrad had only accepted his role as an intermediary between the two parties because he wished to ascend from his dukedom immediately to the imperial throne—just as Henry II of the House of Saxony had ascended (1003–24), and as did Conrad's contemporary, Emperor Henry III (1039–56). Duke Conrad had established a Bavarian-Hungarian military understanding, worked hard on the realization of his plans to reach out for the imperial crown, and he would not tolerate militarily the threat of a less than reliable political ally, or an enemy, from the east.[24]

Duke Conrad's far too daring dynastic plans ran into political obstacles. The duke's Bavarian and Hungarian troops began marauding Carinthia and the eastern Austrian border zone. Thereupon the emperor took counteraction; he replaced Conrad by appointing his own three-year old son, Prince Henry (later Henry IV), and Henry's two-year old brother also named Conrad, as holders of the duchy of Bavaria, and temporarily entrusted the region's actual government to

Gebhardt, bishop of Regensburg. The emperor had some of his enemies, whom he regarded as traitors, executed; Duke Conrad's game of diplomatic chess proved to be a costly failure. The duke died in Hungary in 1055. The emperor himself died in October, 1056.[25]

With the death of Emperor Henry III, the whole political and diplomatic situation of the Hungarian court changed, and King Andrew I exerted considerable effort to establish peaceful contacts with the court circles of the new German monarch—*recte*—and with the dowager empress, Agnes, and Archbishop Hatto of Mainz, who actually were governing the empire.[26] In the re-constructing of Hungarian foreign policy, it was significant that, in 1055, Vratislav of Moravia fled to the Hungarian court in order to escape the wrath of his brother, Spitinev II of Bohemia; Vratislav met and married Princess Adelhaid, the daughter of Andrew I and Anastasia, returned to Moravia, and upon the death of his brother, was successor to the throne of Bohemia. Thus, Andrew I expected neither military, nor diplomatic threat from the Czech court.[27]

King Andrew now initiated a dynastic marriage policy with the Germans—at a price. He asked for the hand in marriage of Judith, the ten-year old daughter of Henry III—a sister of Henry IV—for his young son, Salomon, though he thereby broke the promise he had earlier made to his brother, Prince Béla, that Béla shall succeed him to the throne. On grounds that an imperial princess could only marry a king, Andrew named Salomon as his heir to the Hungarian crown, and had Salomon crowned in the year 1057.[28] (It is a footnote to history that Salomon actually began to rule in 1063 through 1074; most probably, he died in 1087; his wife, Judith, later married Vladyslav I of Poland; she died in about 1094.[29])

The Chronicle, c. 91, presented these events with heavy Hungarian coloring; the chronicler reported that King Andrew's request for the hand of Judith in marriage for his son occurred during the lifetime of Henry III, "postquam autem cesar Herricus [sic!] cum tanto dedecore fugit in terram suam de Ungaria," and referred to Judith as Sophia by name without, however, recording the date of the marriage that actually took place next to the Morava stream, in 1058, when Salomon had already been crowned a king. In the words of the chronicler, the court would not have agreed to the marriage of the emperor's daughter to Andrew's son without the son being crowned beforehand; and yet, the chronicler said that after the marriage (ceremony) took place, the (German) emperor and the (Hungarian) monarch joyfully returned, "cum gaudio sunt reversi," to their countries.[30]

Andrew failed to take into account Béla's natural and human reaction, however. The two brothers had lived peacefully together for some nine years. The prince was Andrew's military commandant, who always carried Hungarian interests to victory. He was the associate of Andrew, and his heir to the throne; now, he had to relinquish to a five year old child his right of succession to the throne.[31] And, when during the coronation of Salomon they sang that the crowned monarch was to be the lord of his brethren, Béla became very angry. It is worthwhile to quote the words of the chronicler. It is being said, "dicunt alii, quod," Béla and his sons, Géza and Ladislas, together with the headmen of the kingdom, had agreed to the royal anointment of Salomon, but then, encouraged by the bearer of bad tidings, began to hate each other—as if to bear proof to the fact that the chronicler had several, frequently contradictory, pieces of written evidence, or of oral history in circulation at hand, when he wrote the report.[32]

The chronicler recorded that Andrew's fatherly love overcame his sense of justice, and, unworthily of a king, he broke the promise he made to his younger brother.[33] He realized, however, that when he died, his child could not rule without the support of Béla; therefore, in an undignified manner, Andrew put Béla to test. In the royal hunting lodge at Várkony, he had the [a] crown (symbol of kingship) and a sword (symbol of dukedom) placed in front of the prince, and called upon him to make a choice. And he gave orders to two of his headmen that, were the prince to chose the sword, his dukedom remained his; however, were he to reach for the crown, he was to be executed on the spot.[34]

The event at Várkony has been depicted in two scenes in the "P" initial of fol. 32'a by the illuminator of the Chronicle, though, one must observe this, the *captio* entered above the letter in red ink, "De coronatione Salamonis a patre suo Andrea rege adhuc vivente," is actually the title of the next entry beginning with the word *Postquam*. On the drawing, Andrew, wearing his [*ruler's*] crown and sitting up half-naked on a chaise longue has [a] the crown placed on the head of his son who stands behind the chaise longue already wearing the [a] crown, with two of Andrew's men standing next to him. At the foot of the couch there stands Béla. In front of the chaise longue, on the steps the [a] crown and the [a] sword are laid out. In the other scene on the right-hand side of the drawing, there, outside the entrance, stands reeve Nicholas advising the prince to reach for the sword. The curiosity of the picture is that its illuminator depicted no bishops, as if to imply that the Church had played no role in Salomon's (first) coronation, as he received no royal anointment.[35]

The prince held a logical view of the event. Salomon's succession seemed to be assured, when Andrew, in his 45th year, suffered a stroke. The illness broke him in body and soul. He suddenly grew old and very suspicious of everybody and of everything. His evil advisors told him that Salomon's reign could only be assured if Béla were completely out of the domestic picture. Simultaneously, others encouraged the prince to size hold of the reins of power, by taking advantage of the illness of Andrew, and by exploiting Salomon's situation.[36]

Béla, concerned about the possibility of further surprises left the country, and moved to his Polish father-in-law, taking his household, wife and seven children, with him, in order to return to Hungary in the fall of 1060, accompanied by his 16-year-old son, Géza, and by the auxiliary troops—the chronicler mentioned three divisions, "tribus agminibus"—Boleslav the Brave, his wife's nephew, placed at his disposal.[37] Thereupon King Andrew sent his wife, their two sons and the young bride accompanied by Tibold, a royal reeve, to Melk, Austria. Meanwhile, Agnes, the dowager empress dispatched a large armed force, headed by Wilhelm and Potho, to the aid of Andrew.[38] She also requested military aid from Bohemia, though the Czech troops would not come for the reason that they observed troop movements on the Polish side of the Czech border. Since the Poles were on the ready and they left the Czechs unsure about their plans, the Czechs chose not to enter Hungary; thereby, unintentionally, they aided Béla's cause.[39]

Andrew was confident about the large number of his mercenaries (the chronicler does not make it clear whether they were German troops, or royal mercenaries), though very few Magyars joined the king's cause. Many of them remained loyal to Salomon, but most of them sided with Béla, the chronicler said.[40] The prince accepted the fact that his brother, the king, had many seasoned foreign mercenaries at his disposal, and prepared himself for a serious battle; "elegitque magis mori in bello, quam sine pugna ab exercitu regis declinare."[41] He had preferred death in battle to withdrawal before his royal brother, now his enemy.

Béla led his forces gathered from northern Hungary, his Polish troops, and units hurrying to him from the region east of the Tisza stream—among the latter there were participants of the 1046 uprising led by Vata[42]—and took up positions along the Tisza.[43] The participation of the followers of Vata on the side of Béla can be explained by the fact that the majority of the Magyars (at least those living in the east-of-the Tisza area) feared a possible renewal of German influence, so predominant in the country in the days of Peter the Orseolo at the expense of Hungarian interests, and that on the grounds that not only had King Andrew placed his family in safety on German (Austrian) soil, but he was preparing, with the aid of German troops and foreign mercenaries, for a warring encounter against the forces of Béla.[44]

The German units in Andrew's camp started the attack. They crossed the Tisza, encountered the army of the prince, with both parties fighting hard, though Béla gained the upper hand mainly because in the heat of the battle, Magyar units in the king's army broke ranks and joined Béla's forces. The prince staged a counterattack, pursued the enemy hard, captured William, margrave of Messen, and margrave Potho, who had fought like a lion, together with Eppo, the bishop of Zeitz. The major portion of Andrew's army, "fere omnibus teutonicis," was either destroyed, or taken captive.[45] The king took to flight toward the western border. He was ill, had to travel in a wagon, but the horses ran away, the carriage overturned, and the king was trodden under; he was captured, and taken, as Béla's war prisoner, to the royal hunting lodge at Zirc where, because of negligent care, "et negligenter detentus," he died within a few days. They buried him in the abbey dedicated to Saint Anian at Tihany, a monastery he had established five years earlier.[46]

The Hungarian record has it that during the turmoil that followed the capture and death of the monarch, the Czech duke, too, had been captured, but, without the knowledge of Béla, "sine scitu ducis bele," was blinded. In order to counteract this humanly tragic diplomatic blunder, the prince immediately released from captivity the two leaders of the German troops, margraves William and Potho.[47]

Now prince Béla, called Benyn, "vocatus Benyin," moved in triumph toward Székesfehérvár, where the bishop anointed and with the royal circlet crowned him.[48] The drawing in the "D" initial, on fol. 34a of the Chronicle, illustrated the coronation of Béla. On the left-hand side of the picture, two high nobles remove the crown from the head of Salomon, and a third noble standing on the right-side of the picture, places it upon the head of Béla. In his left hand, Béla holds the orb; another [the fourth] high noble—the text reads *bishop!*—places a sword in Béla's right hand. The events, as most of the events illuminated in the Chronicle, took place on rocky ground. Thus, in the opinion of the mid-fourteenth century illuminator, Béla's coronation was strictly a secular affair, consequently—and contrary to reading of the text—no bishop was present, as if to express the illuminator's (and, perhaps, the chronicler's) secret conviction that the dethronement of Salomon and Béla's coronation had taken place without the sanction and consent of the Church.[49]

In the record of the Chronicle, the chronicler's usage of words calls for attention: "...ibique regali dyademate, iniungentibus cum episcopis, feliciter est coronatus."[50] The question remains, what did the chronicler mean by using the term: *royal diadem*, what *crown* does his text refer to? Did the chronicler have in mind the *crown* [circlet] sent by Pope Sylvester II to be used at King St. Stephen's coronation on the first (Christmas) day of the year 1001, the crown that, according to the March 17, 1075 letter of Pope Gregory VII, Emperor Henry III had returned to Rome;[51] or, was it a *ruler's crown* perhaps made, or brought from Poland, for the special occasion?[52]

A word of explanation is in order here. This writer, for one, is in favor of the idea[53] that designations such as *King* and *corona* do not coincide with the meaning of *gubernaculum* and of *iurisdictio*, in a sense that Béla did not seem to be concerned with which crown he was crowned as long as he, upon his arrival in Székesfehérvár, "ibique regali dyademate, iniungentibus cum episcopis, feliciter *est coronatus* [italics mine]," could begin his reign as the realm's legitimate monarch.[54] What mattered to him must have been the fact that the bishops had anointed and crowned him in the town where his great predecessor, King Stephen, was buried. In practical terms, the new monarch must have regarded the crown, and the entire church-oriented coronation act, as *legal fiction*.[55]

One has to bear in mind that, in the instance of the Orseolo, the Hungarian source only recorded his being made a king, "postquam autem Petrus factus est rex," without mentioning the coronation;[56] furthermore, if one is to give credit to the drawings of the mid-fourteenth century illuminator depicting mid-eleventh century events, King Peter the Orseolo dressed in body armor in the "P" initial on fol. 24a of the Chronicle manuscript, was not *wearing* a [the] crown, but was *holding* it in his left hand (while holding the sword in his right). The scene is repeated in the "A" initial on fol. 24'a, where King Samuel Aba also held a [the] crown in his left hand.[57] Likewise, on the center miniature that depicts the battle at Ménfő—the drawing fills the whole width of fol. 25' of the Chronicle manuscript—King Aba, who had lost the engagement, reaches down to the ground for his *ruler's crown* that could hardly have been, or identical with, the crown sent to King Stephen by the Roman pontiff.[58]

When Emperor Henry III, *sitting* on a throne, made Peter the Orseolo his vassal, who wore a [the] crown and *stood* erect before him, he handed Peter not a crown, but a scepter that the Orseolo grabbed with both hands. Thus, the miniature placed in letter "S" on fol. 27b of the Chronicle contradicts the text of the chronicler who wrote that on Easter Sunday, in front of Hungarians and Germans gathered together, Peter handed over his kingdom to the emperor by handing him a golden lance; "cui [i.e., Henry III, Peter] regnum Hungarie cum deaurata lancea tradidit." During this act, Peter wore a [the] *ruler's diadem* (drawn always the same manner by the illuminator) on his head.[59]

The Hungarian chronicler reported that Andrew had received a [the] royal crown, "regalem coronam est adeptus," with which [the] three bishops had crowned him; the *royal* crown, meaning royal power, may have been a royal circlet especially made for the occasion, but it could not have been the crown of the realm. It was the anointing and crowing by the three bishops that gave constitutional validity to Andrew's coronation—at least that is what may have been referred to the miniature in the letter "P" on fol. 30'a of the Chronicle.[60] One may wonder if Béla in 1060 regarded the crown as mere *legal fiction*, and only considered as important the oath he had (must have) taken during the coronation act? The chronicler's remark is unconvincing: "Tenuit autem regnum pacifice, ...et quesivit bona genti sue."[61]

Another word of explanation is in order here. One is to distinguish between the *corona visibilis* and the *corona invisibilis*. The diadem placed upon the head of the monarch is a visible: *materialis*, crown, while the invisible crown the ruler receives from God; "quod corona regalis invisibilis impondebatur a Deo, materialis vero et visibilis erat ipsa regalia infula."

In other words, it is the visible golden crown that is placed on the ruler's head, while the invisible crown is the permanent and eternal one, originating directly from God; thus, through dynastic succession, *et statim morte partis quasi continuator dominium*, encompassing the ruler's right to govern his kingdom. *The Hungarian Crown is a visible sacred relic dating back to the reign King St. Stephen, and it became the* invisible *symbol of Hungarian kingship.*[62]

The idea the illuminator wished to express, therefore, is that Béla, who claimed his right to kingship because, and since the death, of King Andrew, had no access to the King Stephen crown, nor could he claim its symbolic (invisible) strength; on those grounds, it was not the bishops, but two temporal lords who placed a [the] *ruler's crown* on his head that enabled him to rule his country.

Now, the problem with this interpretation is that the chronicler's text presents the point of view that Béla had been anointed and crowned so that he, an anointed and crowned monarch, may rule over his realm. The illuminator's miniature pointed to an exactly opposite argument; he—rather, it—emphasized that no ecclesiastical coronation had taken place, as it was two temporal lords who took the crown from the usurper Salomon, and placed it on Béla's head, without realizing, however, that the royal crown could not have been taken from Salomon because, according to the already mentioned letter of

Pope Gregory VII, the King Stephen crown had already been returned to Rome.[63]

Upon his victory over his brother, the legitimate king Andrew, Béla, who grew up in the Polish court and was aware of the Polish concept of a royal crown,[64] wanted to be anointed and crowned king by the country's bishops, so that he could occupy the Hungarian throne as the legitimate successor of his brother of the House of Árpád, and take over, as recognized legitimate king, the government of his country.[65] The crown Béla wished to receive did not necessarily have to be the circlet Pope Sylvester II had sent to Stephen of Hungary,[66] but a [the] *ruler's crown* that, in his instance, may have been a gift for this particular occasion from the Polish court, or even the diadem sent to the Hungarian court by the Byzantine emperor, Monomachos IX.[67]

In the mind of Béla, the ideas that:

a)   he be crowned by the bishops, and

b)   he be crowned in the town where King Stephen had been buried,

were the essential factors that would enable him to take over the reins of power as King Andrew's legitimate successor.[68] Béla must have been keenly aware that the crown used at the coronation was a mere means in granting him legitimacy as a ruling monarch.

The *essence* of a coronation, of being crowned a king, consisted of:

a)   the act of *anointment* by the bishops, and

b)   the *act* of coronation,

because the visible crown symbolized the invisible one, the gift from God.[69]

It is the opinion of this writer that the manuscript text illuminator simply wished to express the point of view that Béla, who had won the battle, took over the reins of kingship on the grounds of that military victory (just as William the Conqueror did after his victory over the Anglo-Saxons at Hastings in October, 1066), not from Andrew, who had lost the engagement, and not even from Andrew's son, the *child-king* Salomon.[70]

The un-Christian pagans in the midst of those who had gathered to celebrate Béla's succession to power began to murmur, however, in protest. The demanded again that King Béla outlaw the Christian religion and exterminate the clergy. Their spokesman John, son of Vata, went as far as to encourage the pagans' wizards to appease the Magyar nobles with their talks and songs. Many a wizard held public speeches depicting the Christian religion as the cause of all evil, and called for a popular uprising (against the king and Christianity).

The anointed and crowned monarch of the House of Árpád, however, firmly stood his ground. He dismissed the demands of John, the son of Vata, and did not tolerate further hate-filled outbreaks directed against the Christian faith. With some of his armed troops, he had the rebels surrounded, their lead-conspirators executed, and their wizards imprisoned. He forbade them, and their offspring, to marry Christians. He used force to scatter the multitude. The renewed threat of a pagan uprising King Béla oppressed at its roots with an iron fist.[71]

2. *The Reign of King Béla I:*
The Representative *Royal Council*

> Dux igitur Bela vocatus Benyin…venit in civitatem
> Albam, ibique regali dyademate iniungentibus eum
> episcopis feliciter est coronatus.
>
> *Chronicon pictum*, c. 94

Early in his reign, Béla strengthened the foundations of his rule. As the chronicler recorded it, the monarch from all over the country—"misit…per totam Hungariam precones"—summoned two well-spoken (i.e., wise) old men from every village to participate in his Royal Council. This statement is so important that one must quote it in Latin: "ut de singulis villis vocarentur duo seniores *facundiam habentes* [italics mine] ad regis consilium." It means that during the 1060s, King Béla I of the Árpád dynasty, born in Hungary but raised at Slav ruling courts, had at the very beginning of his reign summoned a *representative*: representing the interests of the whole realm, *duo seniores facundiam habentes ad consilium regis*, to his Council so that he could discuss all matters of public concern with them.[72]

King Béla had summoned from every village two well-spoken old men to his Royal Council—that is, he did not ask for *elected* representatives, but for men who, in their villages, held and enjoyed public trust—that, in the spirit and in accordance with the text of article VIII of King Stephen's *Admonitions*, the representatives of the whole realm, next to members of the high clergy and high nobility, discuss public business with them, and enact legislation, when needed.[73]

King Béla's experiment with representatives of the realm taking part in his council meetings in 1060, showed similarity with experiments by the royal courts in Spain. There, in the kingdom of Leon, it shall happen some twenty years later that King Alfonzo, together with members of his high clergy, nobility and, *et cum*, "electis civibus ex singulis civitatibus," in Spanish verbal usage: *held court*, "cum celebrarem curiam apud Legionem," that is, royal council meetings where, next to members of the high clergy and high nobility, the elected *representatives* of the towns also took part; "quod omnibus de regno meo, tam clericis, quam laicis, servarem mores bonos, quos a predecessoribus meis habent constitutos."[74]

Therefore, according to the record of the Hungarian chronicler, Béla at the beginning of his kingship, summoned a gathering of representative advisors so that he should debate matters of public interests with all inhabitants of the country. The chronicler's previous report on the financial reforms of Béla; the chronicler's dealing with the fact that the monarch who recently ascended the throne had, at the very first weeks of his reign, restored law and order in the land, reflect faithfully upon the domestic-economic conditions in the realm, even though this chronicle segment might have been written toward the end of the eleventh century. The monarch could accomplish fiscal reforms, restore peaceful conditions in the kingdom only with the full cooperation of the high clergy, high nobility, and of the representatives speaking on behalf of the whole population of the realm.[75]

The monarch needed such cooperation for another reason. As the chronicler reported, a strongly pagan-oriented insurrection was in the making in the land during the first days of Béla's ascent to power because not only those who had been invited (as, for instance, the two well-spoken men from every village) went to Székesfehérvár to be present at Béla's coronation, but also an uninvited multitude of peasants, servants, and the common folk (the lesser element of the social stratum), at the sight of whom Béla himself, the high clergymen, and numerous nobles were taken aback so much that they all took refuge behind the protective walls of the city.[76]

This multitude of common folk who did not seek the country's common interests demanded the restoration of paganism in the land, the murder of all the clergy (and of *clericos*, students *in minor ecclesiastical orders* pursuing studies in various schools), further, the destruction of all churches, and the demolishing of all church bells.[77] It was against them that the king needed to have a consensus. He had to be certain that the better social element of the people, the well-spoken old men from each village (community), were on his side, supportive of his western-oriented Christian policy.

After he made certain that he had the support of the Christian element in society, the monarch took action within three days; he had the mob—a rather well-organized mob of the lowest social stratum—

dispersed with armed troops. The chronicler, probably taking information from eyewitness accounts, remarked that even the king's armed men had difficulty quieting down the rebellion, as if to imply that the king's men neither liked using physical force against insurgents, nor were they trained for social-religious-political disorder. But the troops fulfilled their obligation and forcefully held down the revolution, bringing it under control. And yet, as the chronicler bitterly remarked, it was for the second time that the Christian Magyars of King Stephen's day had since then twice, at the beginning of Andrew's reign, and during the reign of Béla, turned away from Christianity.[78]

Béla I took over the government without any further difficulty. The captured German nobles, who were treated with respect at the court, were released from captivity, and the latter, men experienced in the battle field, witnessed with their own eyes the personal virtues, wisdom and behavior of the king. It may be true that, at first, in the heat of sudden anger, and irritated by the ill intent of his brother's advisors, he had used military force to realize his legal dynastic claims, but avoided further bloodshed. He did not want to disturb the country's peaceful well-being with a constitutional struggle between Andrew and himself. He might have remembered his father's opponent who, expelled by the people, returned to the country as the servant of a foreign power. The Magyar people became the chattel of foreign strangers. He did not want that. Béla I was a man of straight open character, guided by honest intentions, a real king of Árpád's stock.[79]

He ruled his country in peace, the record has it, no enemy disturbed him; he strove hard to benefit his people. He was a wise ruler, with foresight. He had money coined, large coins—*denarii*—out of silver; forty denars were worth one Byzantine gold piece. That is why in those days (the chronicler used the expression: until today, "unde et nunc") forty denars were referred to as one Byzantine gold [piece].[80] He had introduced Byzantine gold coins in the country's monetary circulation, and tolerated no price inflation. He set the price of goods at a just rate, and everyone bought goods at the prices he had set, without cheating—he based the economy on price and wage controls and yet also on the practice of *laissez faire*. He would neither allow nor tolerate merchants and money changers who made greedy profits. The chronicler made a pointed remark that profiteers' greed, and lack of government control, caused people to be miserable, to live in poverty, and a frustrated population would only undermine the structure of society.[81]

Béla I did not seek revenge and treated fairly the supporters, and the supporters' families and properties, of King Salomon. The Salomon adherents were free to return to their homes on their own, as they did, and enjoyed their rights, privileges, and lived their lives on their homesteads in peace. Many of the former Salomon supporters had joined Béla's cause. The king had also lightened the tax burden of the population, wrote off unpaid debts, and forgave unfulfilled obligations.

The chronicler's latest remark implies that, thanks to the king's financial reforms, the Hungarian national economy quickly recovered, and the royal court could allow the luxury of forgiving unpaid debts and lightening the tax burden. One may draw the conclusion from Hungarian laws of the century—it would be sufficient to cite King Stephen's Admonitions, or various articles of King Ladislas's laws at the end of the century—that a large number of non-Christian, Jewish and Moslem social element, had entered and settled down in the country, and they played a very important role in rebuilding the economy. The record has it (stated with some overzealous ethnic pride) that the realm grew rich quickly. In wealth and in glory Hungary soon overcame its neighbors; the poor became rich, and the rich glorious during King Béla's reign.[82]

This writer is convinced that the somewhat nostalgic words of the chronicler were not a late addition to the text, but actually referred to the days of Béla I, as if to express the feeling of national tragedy caused by the early and unexpected death of the monarch. What great future could have awaited the country if King Béla had a continually productive, long reign.

3. *Anastasia Flees to the German Court.*
The Burial of Béla I

> Sepultus est autem in monasterio Sancti Salvatoris,
> quod ipse construxerat in loco, quo dicitur Zuzard.
>
> *Chronicon pictum*, c. 96

The non-Hungarian sources record the flight of Anastasia, the widow of Andrew I, to, and seeking support from, the German court, where she and her entourage supported the return claim of Salomon to his father's throne. Agnes, the dowager empress (the widow of Henry III), had a location on Austrian soil assigned for the residence of Anastasia, but kept Salomon with his wife Judith, the daughter of Agnes, with her at the imperial court.[83]

At this point one may examine the domestic situation of the imperial court. The last years of Henry III's life were shadowed by the rivalry between Bishop Adalbert of Bremen (d. 1073) and Bernard, duke of eastern Saxony, a personal confrontation the emperor would have peacefully handled had he lived longer. His son, Henry IV, was born in 1050, and in 1053 the German nobles elected him, the heir of his father, king; they crowned him in 1054. In October, 1056, Henry III, barely forty years old, had died, and, once again, as in the case of Otto III, a child ascended the German throne.[84]

Unfortunately, the mother of Henry IV was unlike Theophano, nor did she have the service of competent spiritual and temporal lords who could have helped her in the government of the empire. The new archbishop of Cologne, Anno, was a self-seeking vain individual; Adalbert of Bremen was fully preoccupied with administrative details and politically oriented expansionist policies of his diocese; Sigfried of Mainz was a well-intentioned, but weak person. The temporal lords, as, for instance, Rudolf of Rheinfelden, recently named duke of Swabia, or the Swabian Berthold of Zäringen, now duke of Carinthia, were all preoccupied with promoting their own interests. Thus, for the first six years of Henry IV's reign, the government of the empire rested in the hands of a well-intentioned, but inept woman, who was unqualified for the rulership.[85]

From the Hungarian point of view, the 1058 marriage of Andrew's son, Salomon, and Judith, the daughter of Henry III, was, proved to be, a wrong move in diplomatic chess. Andrew's newly formed family ties with the German court made him less popular, even suspect, among members of the anti-German social stratum who, until then, had supported him. Now, the majority of the anti-German social stratum that had only expressed hatred toward any western contact, now suddenly threw their support to Andrew's younger brother, Béla, as if to sharpen the dividing line—as evident at the scene at the royal hunting lodge in Várkony—between the king and the prince.[86] As it has been pointed out above, in spite, or perhaps on account, of the German military aid sent to Andrew, the king lost the struggle with his brother in 1060. Béla gained the kingship, and the crowned child, Salomon, had to seek refuge on German soil. Salomon needed German aid to regain the throne, but during Béla's short reign his attempt to reclaim the throne remained unsuccessful.[87]

In her game of dynastic diplomacy, Dowager Empress Agnes had sought the advice of her lords regarding a plan to enable Salomon, her son-in-law, to gain access to his throne. Domestic difficulties in the empire had kept her preoccupied, however; a military solution of Salomon's problem was out of the question.[88] Nor did Béla forget to reckon with a possible German invasion from the west. He realized that at the German court they would not support the claims of the fiancé of the emperor's daughter—that is, Henry IV's sister—as Béla was well aware of the Hungarian and German adherents of Andrew, who had fled the realm, that they would leave no stone unturned to regain their influence in the country, and would even break up any agreement, were Empress Agnes and the Hungarian king to reach one. Further, the soldiers and adherents of Andrew who remained on German, in this instance in nearby Austrian territory, could pose serious military threat for Béla's court. They knew Magyar military tactics, strategy, were familiar with the terrain in western Hungary, as it had become obvious during the previous campaigns of Emperor Henry III, when he supported the restoration of Peter the Orseolo to the throne.[89]

Béla I attempted to negotiate a peaceful diplomatic settlement. He treated the captured German nobles with friendly respect. He convinced them of his anti-pagan Christian-oriented domestic policy, in the pursuit of which he had followed in the footsteps of King Stephen, and released them from captivity, together with Bishop Epo. The German nobles must have left the royal court with the best of impressions. William of Weimar, the margrave of Messen, had engaged Sophia, daughter of Béla and to marry; although the marriage did not take place because William unexpectedly died en route to marry Sophia, but his nephew, Ulrik of Weimar, margrave of Kraina [Crajna] and Istria, fell in love with Sophia, and married her. Upon the death of Ulrik, Sophia became the wife of Duke Magnus of Saxony. Béla gave the hand of his other daughter, Ilona (Lepa) in marriage to Demeter Zwoinimir, who later became the king of Croatia. Through such marriage alliances the Hungarian court attempted to build up a dynastic base in both the empire and on Croatian territory, thereby to put diplomatic pressure on the imperial court.[90]

The advisors of Empress Agnes did not believe the sincerity of Béla's attempt for peace. As a matter of fact, they were afraid of him. Would he break his word, as Aba did before him? Or was he as politically cunning as Andrew has been? After all, Andrew and Béla grew up in the Polish court, they were nourished in the political atmosphere of Slavic politics, and they were married to Slav women—in the case of Andrew, a grand duchess of Kiev; Béla, a Polish princess.[91]

The testimony before the imperial court of the German nobles returning from Hungarian captivity was of no avail. The court circle of Empress Agnes was concerned because of the previously experienced intrigues of Hungarian diplomacy. Archbishop Anno of Cologne, and Bishop Adalbert of Bremen who took over the government of the empire, and who were joined by Otto of Nordheim, duke of Bavaria, were preparing for war against Béla, a plan the imperial convention gathering in 1063 at Mainz, approved. Lampert of Hersfeld claimed to know that the Russian-born mother of Salomon handed a Hungarian royal relic, the *Sword of Attila* to Otto of Bavaria with the request that he provide military aid for her son struggling to recapture the Hungarian throne.[92]

Béla was still hoping and searching for a peaceful solution. He once again sent envoys to the imperial court to negotiate. The envoys were instructed to deliver the message that Béla had played no part in the previous departure of Salomon from the country. Salomon had left the realm on his own initiative, with his father's encouragement and approval; he had not been persecuted, or expelled. The *ruler's crown* had been placed upon his head amidst the joyful support of his army. Béla expressed his willingness to submit to Salomon, the crowned Hungarian monarch, but refused to acknowledge the German emperor as his feudal overlord. Let Salomon return home in peace; Béla was ready to receive him and to hand the kingdom over to him—on the condition that he, Béla, retain his princely third of the realm's territory that was legally bestowed upon him by his brother Andrew, the country's lawful king. Béla was prepared to provide counsel and military aid to Salomon. As proof of his good intentions he offered his son as hostage to Salomon.[93]

The German court opted for a military solution. The imperial armed forces under the nominal leadership of the child-king, Henry IV, actually led by Duke Otto and Bishop Adalbert. invaded Hungary.

Béla had to face the German invaders alone. He was gravely ill, and yet, he directed the country defenses in person. At this point, the Hungarian chronicler record is less clear. During the third year of his reign, the record has it, the throne had collapsed on him at the royal hunting lodge at Dömös, wounding him so badly that he could not recover.[94] Still, he gave orders to be taken to his troops; though very ill, he wished to conduct his country's defense. He was ill, suffered from pain, and made tactical errors in judgment: he expected the enemy to invade at Kapuvár, but Salomon's Hungarian scouts directed the imperial troops to cross the frontier further up north, at Fort Moson. Realizing his mistake, Béla had himself taken to Fort Moson, but arrived too late. The confused garrison at the fort—the imperial troops were led by Magyar scouts—surrendered without any resistance, and the country lay open before the invading German army. It would have taken quick reaction and sound military judgement to give orders, but the king was already dying. He was near death when he was taken to the Kanizsa [Kynisua] creek, and, as soon as he was told of the fall of Fort Moson to the enemy, he died.[95]

They buried him in the abbey he had established and dedicated to the Holy Redeemer at Szögszárd.[96] Because Béla's color was *szög* [brownish], and as he was *szár* [bald], he had named his abbey *Szögszár[d]*.[97]

When he received the news about the death of Béla, Salomon went directly to his brother-in-law, [the German child-king] Henry IV, to request help for regaining the Hungarian throne; to quote the chronicler, he had asked the German monarch to reinstate him in his kingdom, as if to imply that the Hungarian king, now Salomon the son of Andrew I, had again recognized the German king as his feudal overlord.[98] Henry IV grabbed the opportunity. In a solemn manner he took Salomon with him to Hungary; without any military action, without any difficulty, "sine difficultitate intravit Hungariam," and reached Székesfehérvár. There, the clergy, as well as the people received him with great honors: "Rex Salomon…ab omni clero et populo tocius Hungarie…susceptus est."[99]

Henry IV gave a speech before the assembled Hungarian gathering, an overstatement by the chronicler; the barely thirteen-year-old German ruler, if he spoke at all, must only have spoken for himself, as he declared peace between Salomon and his (the Magyar) people, had crowned him, and let him ascend to his father's throne. It is essential to analyze the use of words by the chronicler describing the event: "Regem autem Salomonem in paterno solio glorie coronatum cum assensu et clamacione tocius Hungarie sedere fecit."[100] Nobody could speak here of royal anointment and coronation act carried out by the members of the Hungarian hierarchy—true, the bishops have already anointed and crowned him earlier, in 1058, during the reign of Andrew I—but one could, indeed, speak of the accomplished fact that it was now the German monarch, Henry IV, who had crowned the Hungarian king, thus to force Salomon to acknowledge the German Henry IV as his feudal overlord. This historic fact is being referred to again by another remark of the chronicler who said that after the German monarch (the chronicler kept referring to Henry IV as *emperor*, though Henry IV had not been crowned emperor yet!) had done his duty, Salomon provided rich donations for him from the wealth of his land, and Henry IV returned home.[101]

The illuminated "R" initial on fol. 35a of the Chronicle depicted the scene where the German monarch (still a minor), Henry IV, brought Salomon back to Hungarian soil. On the left field of the drawing, there is depicted the basilica of Székesfehérvár, with its red roof and four towers, in the front of it, on the right, there stands the

German monarch holding a [the] crown in his right hand, and leading his brother-in-law, Salomon, with his left hand to where King Stephen had been buried; there, with the consent of his German relative, Salomon gains anew the Hungarian crown.[102]

Béla's sons—the already grownup Géza and his younger brother—were, as yet, unready to fight or to shed Magyar blood; therefore, because Géza was intelligent and circumspect, "sicut erat prudens et circumspectus," he and his brother sought refuge in Poland.[103] Upon the departure of Henry IV, however, Géza returned to Hungary, and Salomon began to fear him. He fled to Fort Moson, close to the Hungaro-German frontier, and his troops held their defense line along the Rába stream, while the Hungarian bishops began peace negotiations with Géza.[104]

The prince was willing to make peace, to renounce the crown, but he claimed the right to retain his princely territory.[105] As he did not receive a response from Salomon's court, Géza, with his Polish auxiliaries, moved to the region east of the Tisza stream, and from there he began a march toward Győr (a town close to Fort Moson).[106] He had gained control of the country, but wanted to have peace.[107] Salomon understood his position; now, he was willing to reach a compromise. Bishop Desiderius of Győr conducted the peace negotiations; he accepted Géza's proposal—that is, that Géza peacefully hand over the country to Salomon, but retain his princely share of the realm's territory, territory also his father, Andrew, earlier had. In other words, the prince renounced the throne for the sake of domestic peace, but claimed his territorial share. In the agreement signed on January 20, 1064, in Győr, the prince obtained his region, and took an oath of loyalty to King Salomon.[108] At Easter Sunday, in Pécs, Géza placed (anew) the[*ruler's*] *crown* upon Salomon's head in presence of members of the high nobility, and led him by hand to Saint Peter's basilica in Pécs.[109]

It could have been the irony of fate that during the following night fire broke out in the cathedral, in the palace next to it, and in several buildings, a terrible conflagration that destroyed everything. It was horrible to listen to the booming sound of fire and to thuds when the bells from the towers fell down. To the chronicler, the event was a bad omen, a foretaste of trouble to come, of political confrontations in the land, though he wrote that King Salomon and Prince Géza departed on friendly terms.[110] As a matter of fact, when Zwoinimir, king of Dalmatia, requested military aid from both of them against his enemy, the Caranthanians who had occupied the mountains of Dalmatia, the king and the prince together led an army to aid Zwoinimir, and successfully reclaimed the area that had been taken from him. When Atha the Palatine requested that the king and the prince appear together in public at the consecration of the abbey he had built in the honor of Saint James at Zselice [Zelyz], the monarch and the prince did attend the event—in the words of the chronicler, they fulfilled the Palatine wish, "quod et factum est."[111]

What the chronicler did not observe was the fact that, had the German imperial court pursued its expansionist eastern policy, Hungary sooner or later would have fallen prey to its interests, and would have become a dependent of the empire. It did not occur because of the great struggle between the *sacerdotium* and *imperium*, the *investiture* controversy between the papacy and the German empire, that began to take shape during the 1060s, and broke out with full force in the 1070s between Pope Gregory VII (1073–85) and Henry IV (1056–1106)—a religious-political confrontation that involved all Christendom, and essentially changed the political situation of the Hungarian kingdom.[112] One must cite here the introduction of a letter King Ladislas I of Hungary (1077–95; canonized a saint a century later[113]) wrote to the Abbot of Montecassino, where the Hungarian monarch made the argument that it was not possible for him to always promote the cause of his earthly kingdom without committing some [politically] sinful deeds, as if to refer to the fact that in the papal-imperial/religious-political controversy the Hungarian king, out of sheer political necessity, was, at times, forced to throw his support to the German side. "Quamvis peccator existam, quum cura terrene dignitatis absque grauissimis non potest promoueri criminibus, tamen tue sanctitais culmen non ignoraui." The time had come for him to clarify his past political missteps before the new Roman pontiff, Urban II.[114]

4. The Aftermath

Salomon and Géza remained, for a brief duration, on friendly terms with one another.[115] Together, they hurried to the aid of Zara on the Adriatic, to free the fort city from the rule of Dominic Contareno, doge of Venice.[116] Géza most certainly supported the financial reforms—introduced by King Béla—of Salomon and Queen Judith, with the arrangement made that money issued by the king should only be exchanged every other year.[117] Salomon and Géza undertook military action together against the Pecheneg leader from Moldavia, named Osul, in the battle of Kerlés.[118] It must have been on account of their victory that the Greek commander of the Byzantine garrison in Nándorfehérvár ordered his Pecheneg border guards to enter the *Serem* region (north of the Suave stream), and cause heavy damage, thereby to avenge the Pechenegs' defeat at Kerlés.[119] Thereupon, Salomon and Géza occupied Nándorfehérvár, though, they developed mutual distrust toward each other, the record has it, *because* of their victory.[120] And yet, during the uprising in Byzantine Macedonia in 1072—when the emperor, Michael VII the Dukas, found himself in a difficult position because of the defeat his predecessor, Romanos IV Diogenes had suffered at the hands of Seljuk Turks at Manzikert (1071)—Salomon and Géza exploited the situation and *together* marauded the region as far as Nis[h].[121]

Historical data record further personal confrontation between Salomon and the two princes, Géza and Ladislas, however. Their conflict seemed to be serious enough for the high nobles to meet at Esztergom and negotiate a peaceful solution between them, but to no avail.[122] Salomon asked for German military aid, while Ladislas (and not Géza!) received help from Moravia. In 1074, open warfare broke out between the king and the princes; Salomon's German auxiliaries defeated Géza's forces,[123] but, within a few weeks, the armies of Géza, Ladislas and Otto of Moravia thoroughly defeated Salomon's army consisting of Magyar and foreign auxiliary units at Mogyoród.[124] Salomon withdrew to the western border of the country;[125] and Géza ascended the Hungarian throne.[126]

In the fall of 1074, Henry IV sent German troops to aid Salomon's cause. The Germans moved along the left bank of the

Danube, but at Vác (King) Géza (I) met them, and made them withdraw.[127] It must have been at this point of time that, in an exchange of letters with Géza, Pope Gregory VII acknowledged Géza as Hungarian king;[128] and, out of thankfulness, the king established the abbey Garamszentbenedek. Next to Prince Ladislas, his head officials, Archbishop Nehemias of Esztergom, and Gyula the Palatine, signed the founding document.[129] The Byzantine emperor, Michael VII the Dukas, sent him a royal diadem. Whether this circlet had been used at the royal coronation of Géza I is a question one cannot determine from the available sources.[130]

The Chronicle recorded that on Christmas day, 1077—the first day of the new year—Géza confessed before Archbishop Desiderius and other high churchmen that he was guilty of having the realm taken away from the constitutionally crowned monarch (Salomon), and wished to return the crown (realm?) to him, retaining only the princely one-third of the country for himself. He sent envoys to Salomon, but, probably because of German pressure, negotiations were broken off. Géza, referred to by the chronicler as King *Magnus*, died in late April, 1077.[131]

Upon the death of the monarch, the Hungarian nobles, *universa multitudo nobilium Hungarie*, elected, *communi consensu, parili voto et consona voluntate*, the brother of Géza, Ladislas, king.[132] The chronicler emphasized that Ladislas I became king against his will, "in regem absque voluntate sua elegerunt," and, for that reason, refused to be crowned. Still, on fol. 46'b in the Chronicle MS, there is a drawing that depicts a [the] coronation of Ladislas; in the picture stands King Ladislas wearing an ermine-lined cloak, holding the sword in his right, and the orb in his left hand, while two angels place the crown, held by two bishops, on his head. The drawing seems to underline a sentence in the chronicler's text that Ladislas wished for the heavenly, and *not* an earthly crown.[133]

During the fourth year of his reign, Ladislas concluded peace with Salomon, and assured him of a royal income, though pressured by the nobles, he could not share royal powers with him. Salomon now formed a conspiracy against Ladislas, who had no alternative but to confine him to the Tower of Visegrád.[134] On the day of canonization of the first Hungarian saints (in 1083), he released Salomon, who left the country for Regensburg to visit his wife who, however, refused to receive him.[135] Now Salomon sought support among the Pechenegs in Moldavia, with whose military help he invaded the upper Tisza region in Hungary, but suffered defeat at the hands of Ladislas' armed forces.[136]

In 1087, Salomon and (an unknown adventurer, named) Cselgü marauded Byzantine territory, but were defeated at Drinanople, and Salomon killed in action.[137] His queen, and his mother, were buried at Admont abbey.[138] The record has it that in 1091, King Ladislas I established the bishopric of Zagreb in the presence of Archbishop Acha of Esztergom, and Gyula the Palatine.[139]

What the chronicler did not observe, or purposefully ignored, was the fact that, had the German imperial court pursued an expansionist eastern policy, Hungary would sooner or later fallen prey to its territorial and expansionist interests, and become a dependent—or part— of the empire. That it did not happen was due to the great struggle of political and religious between *sacerdotium* and *imperium*—the *investiture* controversy between the papacy and the German empire— that already began to develop during the 1060s, but broke out with full force in the 1070s, between Pope Gregory VII (1073–85) and Henry IV (1056–1106). It was a religious-political confrontation that involved Latin Christendom, and essentially altered the political-diplomatic situation of the Hungarian kingdom.[140]

One is to cite here the letter of King Ladislas I addressed to the abbot of Montecassino, in which the Hungarian monarch had argued that it was not possible for him to always promote the cause of his earthly kingdom without committing some [diplomatically] sinful deed, as if to refer to the papal-imperial controversy, where King Ladislas at times, out of sheer political necessity, had to throw his support to the German side.[141]

The political-diplomatic directives drawn up by the ruling *Prince* Géza, and King Saint Stephen I, not only rested on sound economic-political reasoning, but proved to be enduring diplomatic guidelines for future Hungarian kings to observe and follow. As it is evident from the letter King Ladislas I wrote to Montecassino, the kings of the House of Árpád may have occasionally departed from their line of diplomatic orientation toward the Latin West, but, bearing the whole diplomatic picture in mind, they always reverted to it,[142] the more so, because the Byzantine empire—the counterweight of the Latin Christian-German imperial diplomatic orientation in continental diplomacy—had suffered a devastating defeat at Manzikert (1071)[143] (a defeat that eventually led to the fall of the Byzantine empire during the mis-named [*recte*: mis-conceived] Fourth Crusade in 1204).[144]

The Latin-oriented diplomatic constellation of King St. Stephen and his successors of Árpád blood, especially under kings Andrew I, Béla I, Géza I, and his brother Ladislas I, made the continued survival of the country possible during the bloody inner confrontations of the eleventh century (through the likewise bloody decades of the twentieth century), just as at the end of the eleventh, and now, at the beginning of the twenty-first century, the realm of King St. Stephen still stands on the eastern edge of western Latin Europe. As the great Latin church father, Saint Augustine of Hippo, would have said, it continues to play the role assigned to it by Divine Providence.[145]

Notes

1. *SSH*, I, 350,5-13; Giesebrecht, II, 330, 332; Karl Hampe, *Deutsche Kaisergeschichte in der Zeit der Salier und Staufer*, 12th ed., ed. Friedrich Baethgen (Heidelberg, 1968), 33f.; Hóman, *Ungarisches Mittelalter*, I, 263ff.; Ferenc Makk, "Les relations hungaro-byzantines aux Xe–XIIe siècles," *European intellectual trends and Hungary: Etudes historiques hongroises 1990*, ed. Ferenc Glatz (Budapest, 1990), 11ff.; indirectly, cf. idem, "Contributions a l'histoire des relations hungaro-byzantines au XIIe siècle," *Acta antiqua Academiae Scientiarum Hungariacae*, 29 (1984), 445ff.; idem, *Magyar külpolitika (896–1196)* [Hungarian foreign relations, 896–1196] (Szeged, 1993), 57ff.; Gyula Kristó, *Die Arpaden-Dynastie* (Budapest, 1993), 88ff.

2. As judged by the signatures of founding charter of Tihany, cf. *RA*, n. 12, and Marczali, *Enchiridion*, 85.

3. Jaffé, *Regesta*, I, 375, *and* n. 3222; Widricus, "Miracula s. Gerardi," *MGHSS*, IV, 509; "Chronicon s. Benigni," *ibid.*, VII, 237.

4. Cf. "Annales Posonienses," anno 1036, *SSH*, I, 125.

5. Leodvin [or Liedvin], the first bishop of Bihar, as referred to by name, in the "Fundatio ecclesiae s. Albani Namucensis," *MGHSS*, XV-2, 963f.; Vince Bunyitay, *A váradi püspökség története* [History of the bishopric of Bihar], 3 vols. (Nagyvárad, 1883-84), II, 317ff.

6. "Zache, *comes palatii*"—*RA*, n. 12.

7. For signatures, see *ibid.*; and Marczali, *Enchiridion*, 85.

8. Cf. Chronicle, c. 89.

9. See Hermann (Contractus) of Reichenau [Herimanni Augiensis], "Chronicon," *MGHSS*, V, 123ff.; Wattenbach, *Geschichtsquellen*, II, 42ff.; R. Buchner, "Geschichtsbild und Reichsbegriff Hermanns von Reichenau," *Archiv für Kulturgeschichte*, 42 (1960), 37ff.; *Annales Altahenses*, aa. 1052-53, and compare with the Chronicle, c. 88, on Béla's Polish relatives.

10. Cf. *SSH*, I, 347ff.

11. *Ibid.*, I, 347,14-18.

12. *Ibid.*, I, 348.

13. *Ibid.*, I, 348,11-20.

14. *Ibid.*, I, 348f., and 350,13 – 351,4, and 351, note 1. Bishop Nicholas was the royal chancellor, "qui tunc temporis vicem procurabat notarii"—cf. *RA*, n. 12; Jakubovich – Pais, 25—chronicler, or provider of eye-witness oral history—see Horváth, *Árpádkori*, 350ff. On war-events in Transdanubia [i.e., Pannonia, modern western Hungary] during the month of February, 1945, cf. Peter Gosztonyi, *A magyar honvédség a második világháborúban* [The Hungarian Army in World War Two] (Rome, 1986), 354ff.

15. *Annales Altahenses*, aa. 1053 and 1054, fused warring events in different chronological order. In the German point of view, "Herzog Konrad...wurde abgesetzt, ...und flüchtete nach Ungarn. Denn dort war die Lehenshoheit des Reiches nicht lange behauptet worden." After the war events of 1053, the Duke of Bavaria started the war anew, "in denen nun der Reichseinfluss auf das Nachbarland völlig verlorenging." Cf. Hampe, *Kaisergeschichte*, 33.

16. Chronicle, c. 89.

17. Chronicle MS, fol. 31b, letter "E"; in the background, fort Pozsony built upon a rock, in the foreground, the emperor standing with two of his knights in a boat already filled with water. Incidentally, the crown of the emperor is being depicted exactly as the one worn by King Andrew. In the other already sinking boat, there are two men fighting for their survival.

18. Cf. *Annales Altahenses*, aa. 1052, 1053; *ASS*, April II, 661; Jaffé, *Regesta*, I, 375. On the Pontiff's route on Hungarian territory, see "Chronicon s. Benigni Divonensis," *MGHSS*, VII, 237, supported by Jaffé, *Regesta*, n. 4279.

19. Evidently, Pope Leo IX maintained contact with Archbishop George of Kalocsa—cf. Jaffé, *Regesta*, n. 3222. See further, Widricus, "Miracula s. Gerardi," *MGHSS*, IV, 509. On the role of diplomacy by Abbot Hugh of Cluny, see "Vita Hugonis," *ASS*, April III, 629, 635f., and 638.

20. *Annales Altahenses*, a. 1053; Funk – Bihlmeyer, II, 95ff., and references to the Lives [*vitae*] of Pope Leo IX, in Witterich, *Pontificum Romanorum vitae*, I, 93ff.; also, W. Bröcking, *Die französische Politik Leos IX*, 2 vols. (1891–99); P. Herde, "Das Papsttum und die griechische Kirche im Süditalien vom 11 bis zum 13 Jahrhundert," *Deutsches Archiv*, 26 (1970), 1ff.; Charles H. Haskins, *The Normans in European History* (Cambridge, MA, 1915; repr. New York, 1959), 202ff.; Haller, *Das Papsttum*, II, 278ff.

21. Cf. Hermann of Reichenau, "Chronicon," a. 1052, *MGHSS*, V, 131; R. Buchner, "Der Verfasser der Schwäbischen Weltchronik," *Deutsches Archiv*, 16 (1960), 389ff.; Fraknói, *Magyarország és a római Szentszék*, I, 20ff.; Hallam, 104f. Papal intervention in this matter had undoubtedly increased the prestige of Andrew's court on the European scene.

22. Hampe, 25ff.; *Annales Altahenses*, a. 1053; Wibert, "Vita Leonis IX," ii:8, *MPL*, 143, 496bc; "Chronicon Ekkehardi," *MGHSS*, XVII, 572, and 364. Also, Z. J. Kosztolnyik, "Hungaro-German relations during the mid-eleventh century *vs.* the background of the Schism of 1054," *Proceedings of the XVth Congress of the Cleveland Hungarian Association, 1975*, eds. John B. Nádas – Ferenc Somogyi (Cleveland, Ohio, 1976), 229ff.

23. One may add here that Duke Konrad sent Count Potho as an envoy to the court of King Andrew, where he remained, and upon the death of Andrew married his widow. Eventually, he returned to the empire and entered the service of Henry IV—cf. Chronicle, c. 93; Hóman – Szekfű, I, 262ff. On the background of the dynastic marriage diplomacy of the Hungarian court, see Z. J. Kosztolnyik, "The Early Magyars, and their Political and Religious Relations with Byzantium and Kiev during the Ninth and Tenth Centuries in the Record of the Chronicles," *Congressus IX Internationalis Fenno-Ugristarum, Tartu, 2000*, 8 vols. (Tartu, 2001), VIII, 323ff.

24. Hampe, 33f.

25. *Annales Altahenses*, a. 1056; *Lamperti Hersfeldensis opera*, ed. O. Holder-Egger, SSrG (Hannover–Leipzig, 1894, repr. 1984), anno 1056; Hampe, 34.

26. For the argument raised in the Chronicle, c. 91, referring to the coronation of Salomon in 1058—see *SSH*, I, 352,8-24; Gebhardt, I, 235.

27. Cosmas of Prague, *MGHSS*, IX, 76, 77, 78; Palacky, *Geschichte*, I, 268ff.; Gerold Meyer von Knonau, *Jahrbücher des deutsche Reiches unter Heinrich IV und Heinrich V*, 6 vols. (1890, etc.; repr. Berlin, 1964), I, 206ff.

28. Cf. *Annales Altahenses*, a. 1058; *Lampert*, a. 1061 (!)—referring to a previous event; Berthold, *MGHSS*, V, 271; Chronicle, c. 91. The question remains, of course, with

which crown? Since the crown received by King Stephen had been returned to Rome—see the letter, dated Oct. 28, 1074, of Pope Gregory VII, in Caspar, *Register*, ii:13—it may have been another circlet used at the coronation in 1058, perhaps the one sent by Constantine IX Monomachos to the Hungarian court. Cf. Magda Oberschall Bárány, *Konstantinos Monomachos császár koronája* (Budapest, 1937), 92ff.; Browning, *Byzantine Empire*, 93; Deér, *Hl. Krone*, 33ff.

29. On the future of King Salomon, cf. Chronicle, cc. 133-36, *SSH*, I, 407ff., and 411, n. 2; also, "Chronicon Heinrici von Mügeln," cc. 47-48, *ibid.*, II, 191ff. On Judith, cf. Keza, c. 57, *ibid.*, I, 179,5-13; and c. 61, *ibid.*, I, 181f., with I, 182, n.1; and Wertner, *Árpádok*, 133. Background in the *Annales Altahenses*, a. 1061; in *Lambert*, a. 1060; Annalista Saxo, *MGHSS*, VI, 693, 697; Cosmas, "Chronica Boemorum," ii:17, cf. *MGHSS*, IX, 78 and 79; see von Knonau, I, 205f.

30. Chronicle, c. 91, *SSH*, I, 351ff.; *Annales Altahenses*, a. 1058; von Knonau, I, 93ff.

31. "Bele duci innotuisset, quod Solomon infantulus sibi domunus constitueretur, graviter est indigmnatus;" cf. Chronicle, c. 91, *SSH*, I, 353,1-3; *Lambert*, anno 1061; the *Annales Altahenses*, a. 1060, report is rather superficial. See also Bertholdi Chronicon, a. 1060, *MGHSS*, V, 271.

32. Cf. Chronicle, c. 92, *SSH*, I, 353,5-25; Hóman, I, 302ff.

33. *SSH*, I, 352,3-12, and I, 354f.; Kosztolnyik, art. cit., 1976, 229ff., esp. 237f.

34. *SSH*, I, 354,15 – 355,25.

35. Cf. Dercsényi, *Chronicon pictum*, vol. I [facsimile], fol. 32'a, "P" initial. Also, Elemér Mályusz, *A Thuróczy Krónika forrásai* [Sources of the Thuróczy Chronicle] (Budapest, 1967), 61ff.

36. "...non posse regnare Salomonem, nisi fratre suo Bela extincto;" *SSH*, I, 353,16-19.

37. Chronicle, c. 93; *Annales Altahenses*, anno 1060; *Lambert*, anno 1061; "Chronicon Polonorum," i:22, *MGHSS*, IX, 439. See further, von Knonau, I, 191ff.

38. Cf. Chronicle, c. 93, *SSH*, I, 356f.; *Annales Altahenses*, a. 1060, seem to have stressed only one episode; *Lambert*, anno 1061, provided more detail and depth. The record in "Bertholdi Chronicon," is, once again, brief—cf. *ibid.*, V, 271; von Knonau, I, 195ff.

39. The remarks made by Cosmas may refer to this confrontation—see *MGHSS*, IX, 78; for a Polish point of view, see *MPH*, II, 292. Bertholdi Chronicon, *MGHSS*, V, 271.

40. *SSH*, I, 356f.

41. *SSH*, I, 356,24-27. Béla is being referred to as *Bela Pugil* (warrior), *Bela the Champion*—cf. Albericus, *MGHSS*, XXIII, 793, 795, 798. Keza, c. 59, named to him "Benyn Bela," cf. *SSH*, I, 180,15. In the Chronicle, c. 94, he is described as "Bela vocatus Benyn"—cf. *SSH*, I, 358,4. In a court decision, dated 1228, handed down by Dionysus the Palatine, Béla is spoken of as "Belyn condam rex Hungarie"—cf. Gusztáv Wenzel (ed.), *Árpádkori Új Okmánytár* [New document collection of the Árpád age], 12 vols. (Pest, 1860–72), VI, 457.

42. Kristó, *Árpád-kor háborúi*, 61f.; idem, art. cit., 1984; and, the thought-provoking piece by Sándor Tóth, "A fehér és fekete magyarok kérdéséhez" [The problem of *White* and *Black* Magyars], *Acta historica Szegediensis*, 75 (1983), 3ff., esp. 7f., differentiating between *Christian* and *pagan* Magyars.

43. *SSH*, I, 356f.

44. *SSH*, I, 356,16-19; *Lambert*, anno 1061 and 1062; *Annales Altahenses*, a. 1060; Berthold, *MGHSS*, V, 271.

45. *SSH*, I, 356,19-27.

46. *SSH*, I, 357,9-14; for the founding charter of the abbey at Tihany, cf. *RA*, n. 12.

47. *SSH*, I, 357,14-18

48. Chronicle, c. 94, *SSH*, I, 358,4-6.

49. Cf. Dercsényi, *Chronicon*, fol. 34a, "D" initial.

50. On depicting the scene, see *SSH*, I, 358,4-7.

51. Dated Oct. 28, 1074, Caspar, *Register*, ii:13; see *supra*, n. 28; Fraknói, I, 357, n. 12, expressed an opinion of dissent.

52. On the *ruler's crown*, or his *house crown*, see the seminal essay by P. E. Schramm, "Die Anerkennung Karls des Grossen als Kaiser," *Historische Zeitschrift*, 172 (1951), 449ff. Josef Karpat's study [published in 1937!], "Corona regni Hungariae im Zeitalter der Arpaden," *Corona regni: Studien*, ed. Manfred Hellmann (Darmstadt, 1961), 225ff., takes a different approach; it is worth reading.

53. As expressed by McIlwain, 361ff.

54. Cf. *SSH*, I, 358,5-6.

55. The idea expressed by Pope Honorius III in 1220 in his letter to Andrew II of Hungary warning the king that he "studeat revocare, quia quum teneatur et in sua coronatione iuraverit regni sui et honorem coronae illibata servare"—cf. Ae. Friedberg (ed.), *Corpus Iuris Canonici*, 2 vols. (Leipzig, 1879–81; repr. Graz, 1959), II, 373; and August Potthast, *Regesta pontificum Romanorum*, 2 vols. (Berlin, 1875), n. 6318, would be applicable, in a positive sense, and a century earlier, to the Hungarian king. The discussion by Ernst H. Kantorowicz, *The King's Two Bodies* (Princeton, 1957), 336ff., on the crown as *fiction*, is a must.

56. Cf. Chronicle, c. 71, *SSH*, I, 323,14.

57. Cf. Dercsényi, *Chronicon*, fol. 24a, "P" letter; and, on fol. 24'a, the "A" initial.

58. See *ibid.*, fol. 25', the illuminated drawing depicting the battle at Ménfő.

59. *Ibid.*, fol. 27b, the "S" initial. The quote is from *SSH*, I, 334,4-7.

60. *Ibid.*, I, 358,6-7; Dercsényi, *Chronicon*, fol. 20'a, the "P" initial; also, Kantorowicz, 355, and n. 144.

61. *SSH*, I, 358,6-7.

62. "…quod corona regalis invisibilis impondebatur a Deo, materialis vero et visibilis erat ipsa regalia infula." In today's terminology, they place the *visible* golden crown upon the head of the ruler, and yet realizing that it is the *invisible* crown that is of permanent value, derived from God through dynastic succession. Cf. Iustinian, *Institutes*, iii:1,3: "et statim morte partis quasi contiuuator dominium;" also, Iustinian's *Decretum*, xxviii:2,11, the *corona invisibilis* compassing the ruler's right to govern his kingdom.

63. See Chronicle, cc. 79, 88, and 93 – *SSH*, I, 334f., I, 344f., and I, 355, respectively.

64. …and one who had been aware of the idea óf the crown as prevalent at the Polish court—see Alexander U. Soloviev, "Corona regni: die Entwicklung der Idee des Staates in den slawischen Monarchien," (1933), in Hellmann, *Corona regni*, 156ff.

65. Upon his victory over his brother Andrew, a constitutional king, Béla wished to make certain that the bishops of the realm crown him, thus recognize him as legitimate successor of his brother of Árpád blood on the throne—cf. Chronicle, c. 94, and compare with Iustinian, *Institutes*, iii:1,3: "quod corona regalis invisibilis supra," so that as a fully

fledged ruler recognized by the Church, he may take over the government of the kingdom—*SSH*, I, 358,4-6.

66. The chronicler recording the event spoke of a diadem—"regali dyademata est coronatus," *ibid.*, a diadem that may *not* have been identical with the circlet sent by Pope Sylvester II to Stephen I of the House of Árpád; see Hartvic, cc. 9-10, *ibid.*, II, 412ff. On papal diplomacy at the end of he tenth century, see Hans-Henning Kortüm, "*Gerbertus qui et Silvester*: Papsttum um die Jahrtausendwende," *Deutsches Archiv*, 55 (1999), 29ff.

67. In other words, a *ruler's crown*, or even the circlet sent by Emperor Constantine IX Monomachos to the Hungarian court. Cf. Bárány Oberschall, 68, 77f.; depicted by Browning, 93. Robin Cormack, *Byzantine Art* (Oxford, 2000),126ff.

68. Kantorowicz, 354f.

69. *Ibid.*, 339. "…quod corona regalis invisibilis imponebatur a Deo, materialis vero et visibilis erat ipsa regalis infula;" cf. Baldus de Ubaldis, *Consilia* (Venice, 1575), vii:37,3,5.

70. See Chronicle MS, fol. 34a, scene depicted in the initial "D." The remark by the chronicler calls for attention; upon his victory, it was Béla, he wrote, still the victorious Prince, who had William and Potho, the two captured leaders of the German auxiliaries serving the cause of Andrew and of Salomon, released to freedom. "Willelmus vero et Poth duces adducti sunt ad Belam ducem, qui eos liberos abire permisit"—cf. *SSH*, I, 357,17-18. On Hastings, 1066, and William the Conqueror, see *Anglo-Saxon Chronicle*, ed. Dorothy Whitelock et al. (New Brunswick, 1961), 144f., MS "D"; the battle of Hastings took place on the festival of Pope Calixtus, October 14. See further, Stenton, *Anglo-Saxon England*, 573ff.

71. Chronicle, c. 95, see *SSH*, I, 359,22 - 360,15.

72. Cf. *SSH*, I, 359,20-22, to be compared to a later usage, as, e.g., the *Synodus prior* (First of Esztergom), held under Coloman the Learned: "villicus cum duobus senioribus." Cf. Závodszky, 199, and King Ladislas' *Leges*, i:25, *ibid.*, 162.

73. Cf. Chronicle, c. 95; King Stephen's *Admonitiones*, art. VII: De magnitudine consilii—cf. Závodszky, 138.

74. See *Cortes de los antiguos reinos de León et de Castilla*, ed. Real Academia de la Historia, 5 vols. (Madrid, 1861–1903), I, anno 1188, articles vii:7, and vii:3.

75. On fiscal reforms, cf. *SSH*, I, 358,7-26 (c. 94). Although the report may apply to the reign of Salomon and Judith, it actually refers to conditions prevalent in the land of the early 1060s; see the three *position papers* by Rabbi Jehuda-ha-Cohen (*ob.* 1070, in Mainz) on fiscal conditions in Hungary during the 1060s. Hebrew text with Hungarian translation, in Wenzel, *ÁÚO*, VI, 573ff.

76. *SSH*, I,359,24-27.

77. *Ibid.*, I, 359,29-33.

78. *Ibid.*, I, 360,12-15.

79. "Tenuit autem regnum pacifice, sine molestacione hostium, et quesivit bona genti sue;" *ibid.*, I, 358,6-7; on the other hand, Keza, c. 59, displayed a less friendly attitude toward him—*ibid.*, I, 180.

80. *Ibid.*, I, 358,22-23; Spufford, 77f., and 95.

81. "Hec est enim causa, que maxime solet populos paupertatis et inopie periculis obvolvere;" see *SSH*, I, 358,13-14. Hóman, *Pénztörténet*, 187ff.; indirectly, Ostrogorsky, 152ff.

82. Cf. Chronicle, c. 94, *SSH*, I, 359,2-13; and, 359,14-19. The king and his court did not display any anti-Jewish, or any anti-foreigner politico-economic tendencies; cf.

Samuel Kohn, *A zsidók története Magyarországon* [History of the Jews in Hungary], vol.
I. (Budapest, 1884), 53.

83. See *Annales Altahenses*, a. 1060, in referring to the marriage in 1058; also,
MGHSS, V, 271; *Lampert*, anno 1063 [!]; von Knonau, I, 95ff.

84. *Annales Altahenses*, a. 1056; Hampe, 34; Gebhardt, I, 240f.

85. Hampe, 35, and 40ff.; von Knonau, I, 13ff.; compare with Althoff, *Otto III*,
54ff.

86. Cf. Chronicle, c. 93.

87. "Hungaros...qui in regno remanserant, plurimi ad ducem Belam confluxerant;"
cf. *SSH*, I, 356,21-24.

88. *Annales Altahenses*, aa. 1060, 1061; Hampe, 40ff.; von Knonau, I, 188ff.

89. See Chronicle, c. 78, and compare with c. 93: "Nunciatum est autem Bele duci,
quod rex Andreas maximam haberet multitudinem conductorum...," with whose aid he
was prepared to do battle—*SSH*, I, 356,24-27.

90. Hóman, *Ungarisches Mittelalter*, I, 268ff.

91. *Ibid.*, I, 255; Chronicle, cc. 79, 87.

92. Cf. *Annales Altahenses*, a. 1063; von Knonau, I, 342ff.

93. Chronicle, c. 96, *SSH*, I, 360; *Lambert*, a. 1063; Székely – Bartha, 870.

94. See *SSH*, I, 360,16-18. One may note that the east-Frankish king Arnulf has had
a similar, "corruente solio," accident when, *aedifico cadente*, befallen him in the year 897
at Forchheim; cf. Dümmler, III, 437, and note 3.

95. *SSH*, I, 360,18-21; Hóman, I, 272; Székely – Bartha, 870.

96. "Sepultus est autem in monasterio Sancti Salvatoris, quod ipse construxerat in
loco, qui dicitur Zugzard"—*SSH*, I, 20-21, though [what may be known as], the founding
charter is *dubiae fidei*; cf. *RA*, n.16 (anno 1061).

97. "Hic enim Bela erat calvus et in colore brunus, propterea suum monasterium ad
suam dispositionem Zugzard appellavit;" cf. *SSH*, I, 360,23-27. Keza, c. 59, *ibid.*, I,
180,15-27.

98. Chronicle, c. 97, *ibid.*, I, 361f.

99. *Ibid.*, I, 361,15-21.

100. *Ibid.*, I, 361,23-25; von Knonau, I, 344f.

101. *SSH*, I, 361f.; also, *Annales Altahenses*, a. 1063; *Lambert*, a. 1063.

102. Cf. Dercsényi, *Chronicon*, fol. 35a, the "R" initial.

103. *SSH*, I, 361,11-13.

104. *Ibid.*, I, 362,3-12.

105. Indirectly, though forcefully, asserted by the chronicler: "et ipse ducatum,
quem pater eius prius habuerat, pacifice teneret," as if the idea came from, and the offer
was made by, Bishop Desiderius of Győr. Cf. *ibid.*, I, 362,11-12.

106. *Ibid.*, I, 362,3-6; von Knonau, I, 347ff.; on Géza's family contacts, see *ibid.*, I,
192.

107. "Geysa deposito rancore paruit;" *SSH*, I, 362,12-13.

108. *Ibid.*, I, 362,13-20.

109. *Ibid.*, I, 362,20-27.

110. Cf. Chronicle, c. 98, *ibid.*, I, 363.

111. Chronicle, c. 99, *ibid.*, I, 363f.

112. *SSH*, I, 363,28-29, and I, 365,9-10. On the investiture, see the "position paper"
of Pope Gregory VII (d. 1085), the *Dictatus papae* of some 27 brief articles, in Caspar,
Register, ii:55a; the Pope's letter to Henry IV, of Dec. 8, 1075 [or, of Jan. 8, 1076], *ibid.*,

iii:10; the report on Henry IV's *penance* at Canossa, January 1077, *ibid.*, iv:12, 12a, and Jaffé, *Registrum*, n. 5017; or, the papal prohibition of lay investiture, dated Nov. 19, 1078—Philip Jaffé, *Bibliotheca rerum Germanicarum*, 6 vols. (Berlin, 1864 etc.), II, 332. See further, Gerd Tellenbach, *Church, State and Christian Society at the Time of the Investiture Contest*, tr. R. F. Bennett (Oxford, 1959), 126ff., and 169ff.; Z. N. Brooke, "Lay Investiture and its Relation to the Conflict Empire and Papacy," *Studies in History*, ed. Lucy S. Sutherland (Oxford, 1966), 50ff.; A. J. Macdonald, *Hildebrand: A Life of Gregory VII* (London, 1932), 102ff., also 136f., and 145f.

113. Cf. "Vita s. Ladislai regis," c. 11, *SSH*, II, 525,9-12; in presence of King Béla III, and of the papal legate, Archbishop Gregory—cf. Katona, *Historia pragmatica*, I, 689ff.; idem, *Historia critica*, IV, 333f.; Fraknói, I, 34f.; Sándor Márki's long forgotten lecture notes, *Magyar középkor* [Lectures on the Hungarian middle ages] (Budapest, 1914; repr 2000), 153ff.; Kosztolnyik, *From Coloman*, 267f., and 284, nn. 5-7.

114. Cf. *RA*, n. 31; text in Fraknói, I, 403f.

115. Chronicle, c. 98.

116. *Ibid.*, c. 99; Katona, *Historia pragmatica*, I, 381f.

117. Financial reforms as described in the Chronicle, c. 94—*SSH*, I, 358f.

118. Cf. Chronicle, c. 102; the chronicler spoke of Cumans instead of Pechenegs, and spelled Kerlés as *Kyrieleis*—most probably imitating the Magyars' battle cry: *Kyrie eleison!*—cf. *SSH*, I, 17-18.

119. Chronicle, c.104, *SSH*, 369f.

120. Chronicle, cc. 105-08; the capture of the fort is depicted in the "F" initial on fol. 37'b of the Chronicle MS; the drawing also explains the reason for the misunderstanding between Salomon and the princes: Géza received only one-fourth of the booty (instead of the customary one-half)—*SSH*, I, 374,2-3, *and*, the Chronicle, c.110.

121. Chronicle, c.111. In the "P" initial of the Chronicle MS, fol. 39'b, the Greek inhabitants of Nis submitted to Salomon and Géza. On the Byzantine defeat at Manzikert, 1071, see Ostrogorsky, 274f.; Romilly Jenkins, *Byzantium: The Imperial Centuries AD 610–1071* (1966; repr. Toronto, 1987), 361ff., esp. 369ff.

122. Cf. Chronicle, c.112, esp. *SSH*, I, 378,4-8.

123. Chronicle, c.117, *ibid.*, I, 383ff.

124. On the battle of Mogyoród, see the Chronicle, c.121; on the lower half of Chronicle MS, fol. 43, there is a miniature drawn in a simple frame depicting the battle of Mogyoród. Gy. Farkas, "A mogyoródi csata" [The battle of Mogyoród], *Vigilia*, 39 (1974), 249ff.; Kosztolnyik, *Five Kings*, 83f., and 87.

125. Chronicle, c.123, *SSH*, I, 393f.

126. See Chronicle, c.124; to quote, "Tunc Geysa dux magnus *compellentibus Hungaris* [italics mine] coronam regni suscepit"—*SSH*, I, 394,12-13. Compare with the *vision* the chronicler claims both Géza and Ladislas have had *before* the military engagement at Mogyoród—cf. *SSH*, I, 388,9-20.

127. See Chronicle, cc. 126-28, though the narrative seems to reflect more the chronicler's imagination than actual facts—*ibid.*, I, 399f. See also the "P" initial on MS fol. 44a. On the negative papal reaction to Salomon's plight, see the writ Pope Gregory VII addressed to him on October 28, 1074, in Caspar, *Register*, ii:13

128. The papal answer had to be cautious: "Notum autem tibi esse credimus regnum Ungariae," on the grounds that Hungary could not depend on another country, "nisi sancte et universali matri Romane ecclesiae;" see Caspar, *Register*, ii:63 (March 25, 1075). In his letter of March 17, 1074, the pontiff encouraged Géza to confide in the

Roman See—cf. *ibid.*, i:58 (letter recorded also in *RA*, n.18). In his writ, dated April 17, 1075, Pope Gregory VII seemingly recognized the kingship of Géza—though he still addressed Géza as *dux Ungariae*—as if on a temporary basis. Cf. Caspar, *Register*, ii:70.

129. Cf. *RA*, n. 20; text in Wenzel, *ÁÚO*, XI, 21f.

130. The Byzantine emperor, Nikephorus Botaneiates (1078–81), gave the hand of Synadene, his niece, in marriage to the king of Hungary (Géza I), recorded Iohannes Skylitzes Continuatus, *Historia*, Bekker, CB, II, 743,4-7. For background, see Anna Comnena, *Alexiad*, ed. A. Reifferscheid, Teubner texts (Leipzig, 1884), iii:4. On Nikephorus, see Ostrogorsky, 277f.

131. Cf. Chronicle, c. 130, esp. *SSH*, I, 402,25 – 403,16.

132. See Chronicle, c. 131, *ibid.*, I, 403ff.

133. "...ipsum Hungari in regem absque voluntate sua elegerunt, nunquam tamen in capite suo coronam posuit, propter quod potius celestem coronam optabat, quam terrenam...;" cf. *SSH*, I, 404f., and compare with the "Vita s. Ladislai regis," c. 4, *SSH*, II, 517ff.

134. Chronicle, c.133.

135. "Ladislaus...Salamonem Ratisponam ad uxorem suam ire permisit," Bernoldi "Chronicon," *MGHSS*, V, 439; Büdinger, 73, n. 2.

136. Cf. Chronicle, c. 134.

137. See Chronicle, cc. 135-36; the chronicler said that Salomon had simply disappeared from among his men, never to return, *SSH*, I, 410f. His death was mentioned, anno 1087, by Bernoldi "Chronicon," *MGHSS*, V, 446, and by Annalista Saxo, anno 1087, *ibid.*, VI, 724. The Hungarian chronicler noted that Salomon had once been seen in Hungary during the reign of Coloman the Learned, but had disappeared from sight without a trace; that he had also visited the city of Pola on the Istrian peninsula, and was buried there. Cf. *SSH*, I, 411,17-20.

138. His wife and mother were buried at Admont—cf. *ibid.*, I, 411,21-24.

139. As referred to in a royal writ issued by Andrew II in 1217—cf. *RA*, n.323, and in an earlier diploma of King Emery, dated 1201—cf. *RA*, n. 193.

140. See, e.g., *Lampert*, aa. 1074, 1075, 1076; Hampe, 43ff.; Hóman, *Ungarisches Mittelalter*, I, 315ff.

141. Kosztolnyik, *From Coloman*, 11, and 18, n.131.

142. Cf. *RA*, n. 31, text Fraknói, I, 403f.

143. Cf. C. Cahen, "La campagne de Manzikert d'après les sources musulmanes," *Byzantion*, 9 (1934), 613ff., esp. 637f.; Jenkins, *Byzantium*, 361ff.; Ostrogorsky, 273ff.

144. On the *Fourth* Crusade, see Niketas Choniates, *Historia*, ed. I. Bekker, CB (Bonn, 1835), 712; H. Kretschmayr, *Geschichte von Venedig*, vol. I (Gotha, 1905), 280ff., esp. 289f.; also, E. Garland, "Der vierte Kreuzzug und seine Probleme," *Neue Jahrbücher für das Klassische Altertum*, 13 (1904), 505ff.; Hans Eberhard Mayer, *Geschichte der Kreuzzüge*, 3rd repr. (Stuttgart, 1973), 170ff.; Ostrogorsky, 330ff.; Donald E. Queller, *The Fourth Crusade* (Philadelphia, 1977), 9ff., and 50ff.

145. See St. Augustine's City of God, B. Dombart – A. Kaln (eds.), *Santi Avreli Avgvstini De civitate Dei libri XXII*, 2 vols., 5th ed., ed. J. Divjak (Stuttgart, 1931; rep. 1981), xiv:28, and xix:11. Further, cf. the Vulgate Bible, IV [II] Kings, chapters 18–19; Friedrich Heer, *Europäische Geistesgeschichte*, 2nd ed., (Stuttgart, 1965), 113ff.

Appendix

The Monomachos Crown, Domestic Intrigue and Diplomatic Reality Prevalent at the Hungarian Court during the Mid-Eleventh Century

> Porro dux Andreas a perturbacionibus hostium securus effectus in regia civitate Alba regalem coronam est adeptus.
>
> *Chronicon pictum*, c. 86.

Historians are still unaware of the identity of the crown that may have been used at the coronations of both Andrew I (1046–60), and Andrew's son, Salomon (in 1058). The record has it that Byzantine Emperor Constantine IX Monomachos (1042–54) did send a royal circlet, diadem, to the court of Andrew I, though the question remains, whether the enamel plates of the particular diadem unearthed at Nyitraivánka in the early 1860s really date back to the eleventh century, or were they merely clever mid-nineteenth century imitation of Byzantine craftsmanship?

The sending of the diadem, if real, whose central enamel plate depicted Emperor Monomachos, may have served a twofold purpose. First, by sending him a crown, the emperor wished to acknowledge the validity of Andrew's coronation in 1047, and simultaneously provide him with the means to have his son, Salomon, crowned king. Second, the emperor wanted to draw the fledgling Latin-Christian Hungarian kingdom into the sphere of Byzantine politics, and retain it there, thereby to resume the conduct of foreign policy toward Hungary that had been purposefully interrupted by King Stephen I who had aligned himself with the Latin west. The emperor's objectives, however, were bound to fail, as mid-eleventh century diplomacy changed drastically since the beginning of the century. The sending of the crown did not influence Magyar domestic and foreign politics.

Both Andrew I, and his brother Béla I, pursued their diplomacy according to their own judgement. The diadem sent and decorated with the picture of the emperor remained a mere expression of good will on part of another (though Byzantine-rite) Christian court toward the royal court of the Árpáds.

In the 1030s, the cousin of King Stephen (d. 1038), Prince Vazul—the son of Michael, the younger brother of Géza, the father of King Stephen—prepared a plan to assassinate the elderly sick king. The king's court ordered a blinding of the conspirator, Vazul, whose three sons were sent into exile abroad. In addition a new article was added to the recently promulgated Laws of King Stephen, art. ii:17, concerning conspiracy versus king and country. The one who organizes a conspiracy versus the realm, may find no refuge in a [the] church. Although this decree shows similarity in concept and wording with the brief entry 5 of the 847 Synod of Mainz, the wording of the Hungarian draft of the article is firmer; it not only outlaws the traitor from the community of believers, but from the Church itself.

Upon the death of King Stephen, his nephew, Peter the Orseolo, the son of one of Stephen's sisters, and the favorite of Queen Gisela, Stephen's widow (and the sister of the German emperor, Henry II), ascended the Hungarian throne in 1038 [to 1041], and in 1044 [to 1046]. His tyrannical rule encountered strong opposition, however; Peter fled the realm, and the country's headmen elected Samuel Aba, King Stephen's brother-in-law, married to King Stephen's other sister, as their king, whose kingship the German court did not recognize.

Emperor Henry III now invaded Hungary, destroyed the border fort of Pozsony, advanced on the left bank of the Danube until the Garam stream took possession of nine fortifications. Aba, the elected Hungarian king now offered peace to the emperor, who refused it, and invaded Magyar land again, but his military advance was thwarted by the marshes of the Rábca river. In the fall of 1043, he concluded peace with Aba, thereby recognizing his royal status. However, Aba's opposition on the domestic front—consisting of Orseolo sympathizers— gained strength, the king feared another conspiracy, and, during Lent of 1043, he ordered the massacre of nobles who dared to conspire against him. Thereupon the nobles who survived the massacre requested German political intervention, in fact, military aid. Henry III once again entered Hungary, and, at Ménfő, defeated the forces of

Aba, whom the Hungarians murdered during his flight east by the Tisza river. During the summer of 1044, the German emperor entered Székesfehérvár, where he restored Peter the Orseolo to his throne.

The throne of Peter rested on shaky foundations. In order to secure his reign, he called in the spring of 1045 upon Emperor Henry III to enter the realm, from whose hands he accepted the government of Hungary, as if it were an imperial fief. The oddity of the situation, as depicted by the mid-fourteenth century illuminator of the *Chronicon pictum*, was characterized by the fact that the Orseolo received the crown *standing* from an emperor *sitting* on the throne; Peter, presumably, received *the* crown that had touched the forehead of King Stephen, and not a mere *ruler's crown* (house crown), that, having made him his vassal, the emperor could, upon performing the coronation, send back to Rome. The return of the crown to the Roman See is witnessed by the testimony of the letter, dated October 28, 1074, of Pope Gregory VII; however, in that letter, the pontiff claimed, as a papal fief, the Magyar realm (of King Salomon, 1063–74, son of Andrew).

And yet, the Orseolo did not feel secure in his kingdom, in spite—or, perhaps, because—of his feudal relationship with the imperial court; he had the district forts garrisoned by German and Italian troops—to the consternation of the Hungarian nobles who, led by Boja and Bonya, formed a conspiracy against him. The Orseolo had the conspirators executed. Thereupon, in the spring of 1046, the nobles gathered at Csanád and sent envoys to Kiev to recall from their exile the Árpád princes, Andrew and Levente, to rule over the country. In early fall of 1046, the two princes entered the realm with Kievan auxiliaries, were greeted by a multitude of dissenters, led by a certain Vata from the region of Békés. They wanted to restore paganism in the land. In order to gain time, the two princes seemingly consented to their demand, thereby opening the floodgates of an anti-Christian pagan uprising all over the land. Simultaneously, an uprising broke out in the camp of the Orseolo at Zsitvatorok [estuary of the Zsitva stream]; the king wanted to move to and enter the city of Székesfehérvár, but the city gates remained shut before him. He was captured at Zámoly, and blinded.

It was Peter the Orseolo's tragedy that he, a ruler of non-Árpád blood, had been unable to comprehend that it was his sole responsibility to maintain the country's public institutions his predecessor had established. It was his personal tragedy that, in spite of the many years he had spent in the royal court, he was unable to understand the inner spiritual world of the Magyar people.

Meanwhile, at the Pest shore ferry on the Danube, the pagan insurgents murdered Gerard, the bishop of Csanád, and Szolnok, a royal reeve. At the end of September, the three bishops who escaped the bloodbath of the uprising crowned Andrew I king in Székesfehérvár.

The invitation of Andrew proved to be in the game of diplomatic chess a draw by both parties: the nobles who invited him, and by Andrew himself. During his prolonged stay in Kiev, he gained the hand in marriage of Anastasia, daughter of Jaroslav the Wise, grandprince of Kiev, and through this marriage he assured himself of the political, and possibly military, support of Kiev for the realization of his own diplomatic-family interests in the future. The other daughter of Jaroslav, Ann, was the queen of Henry I, king of the Franks, whereby the recently anointed and crowned Hungarian monarch could hope to obtain diplomatic and cultural aid from his Frankish royal brother-in-law. The founding by Andrew of the abbey of Tihany in 1055 in the honor of the Frankish saint, Anian, may serve as proof that the establishment of Franco-Hungarian cultural-political ties had been realized. One ought to note that, two years earlier, Andrew had a monastery erected for Basilian monks in Visegrád, in order to assert his appreciation of the Byzantine religious-cultural influence he had come to know during his exile in Kiev, and, perhaps, as a symbolic friendly diplomatic gesture toward Emperor Constantine Monomachos of Byzantium.

King Andrew 's first concern was to restore peace in the land, to put the pagan insurgents into their place, and to fill unoccupied ecclesiastical positions in the country with the twenty-four canons who came to Hungary after their canonry at Verdun had burned down. In the late 1040s, he provided military aid for the Croats against Venice and the Dalmatian cities, and in the early spring of 1050, he staged a counter offensive against Bishop Gebhard of Regensburg who had invaded the country's border region. When the Hungarian scouts noted that on the German side they were rebuilding the fort of Hainburg, Andrew's border guards harassed the builders and brought construction to a near standstill. To reach a peace agreement with the empire, Andrew sent envoys to Emperor Henry III, and dispatched Archbishop George of Kalocsa to Pope Leo IX, who was at that time visiting in Lorraine, with the request that his Holiness intervene in the German court on behalf of the peace offer of the Hungarian monarch.

In 1050, Prince Béla also returned to Hungarian soil with his Polish wife. His elder brother rewarded him with a princely share of the realm's territory that meant, among other things, that Béla had the right to mint money and to have autonomy in his region [duchy], within the borders of the kingdom. Béla was already known as a military strategist. In Poland, in a duel he defeated the Prussian duke, an opponent of the Polish ruler, who refused to pay feudal dues to the Polish court, and as a reward, had gained the whole amount of feudal fees the Prussian owed to the Polish royal court.

King Andrew needed the military know-how of Béla: in the summer of 1051, when the German imperial forces gathered at Passau and, led by the emperor in person, invaded the Hungarian border region and moved against Székesfehérvár. Gebhard, bishop of Regensburg, was in charge of the supply ships on the Danube carrying food for the imperial armed forces. The imperial high command had learned a lesson from past mistakes; now, it had organized supplies of food provisions for the troops before actually starting the campaign. But Andrew's men, or the scouts Béla, in a cleverly written mischievous letter, had caused the ships to return home prematurely, thereby leaving the German troops heading toward Székesfehérvár without logistical food supplies. The armies of Andrew and Béla easily encountered and defeated the confused German troops at Bodajk near the Vértes Hill (in Hungarian, Hill of [the lost] Shields).

The imperial court now planned a counteroffensive. In the following year it had besieged the fort of Pozsony for eight weeks—to no avail. The imperial naval vessels on the Danube—it is not clear from the text whether the boats were armed ships, or food supply vessels—were sunk by a clever Hungarian frogman named Zotmund, whereupon the emperor withdrew his troops. Pozsony was located on the German border, and the imperial high command could easily have provided for the needs of its armed forces by means of land transportation. Actually, the emperor was forced to withdraw his armed forces because he had to face domestic troubles; Duke Conrad of

Bavaria revolted against him. The insurgent duke fled to the court of Andrew, and, probably encouraged by Andrew and Béla, the duke's armed men harassed the Bavarian border lands from a base in Hungary.

Unfortunately, this was the last occasion when the two brothers, Andrew and Béla, peacefully cooperated with each other. In 1053, a son, and heir: Salomon, was born to Andrew, and the king had a Basilian monastery erected at Visegrad to please his Kievan-born Queen Anastasia of the Greek Orthodox faith. In view of the fact that in 1054 schism had occurred between the Latin Roman Catholic Church and the eastern Greek Orthodox Church, and, mainly from the Hungarian prospective, on grounds that Ann, Queen of the west-Frankish monarch, was the sister of Anastasia, King Andrew in 1055 decided to establish a Latin-rite monastery in Tihany. The monarch sought to have peace and balance between the religious and political interests of the two churches and, simultaneously, he wanted the Frankish court to know that his realm formed a part of western, Latin Christendom.

Peace prevailed in the land. Archbishop Benedict of Esztergom and Zach[eus] the Palatine (*comes palatini*) were the head officials of the country. In the 1050s, Sarchas, Judge of the King's Court, prepared a census of the personnel serving on the royal estates. It may have been at this time, to quote from the D and E manuscripts of the Anglo-Saxon Chronicle, that Edward, son of King Edward's brother, Edmund (called Ironside), who had been expelled to Hungary by King Cnut the Great, had married, the chronicler reports, Agatha, a daughter of the Hungarian king; to quote from the Chronicle, "won a kinswoman of the emperor for his wife," that is, a daughter of Gisela (and of King Stephen), the sister of the German emperor Henry II—but returned to England where he died shortly thereafter; "he so speedily ended his life after he came to England." The backdrop of Edward's sudden death may be provided by a remark in the less known *Florence* manuscript of the Anglo-Saxon Chronicle: "for the king—that is, Edward the Confessor—had determined to make him heir to the kingdom after him." Perhaps certain individuals at the English court distrusted the idea that a prince who had been living abroad for years and had married into a "foreign" royal family, thereby establishing a dynastic blood tie with the imperial court, be allowed to become heir of the English throne.

The innocent entry in the Florence manuscript of the Anglo-Saxon Chronicle may, however, reveal another dynastic diplomatic aspect, that is, Andrew I of Hungary (may have) had plans with the heir of the English throne, the future king of England, who had spent years in exile at the Hungarian court, married a daughter of a monarch of the House of Árpád, a daughter who in the near future could have become the Queen of England—thereby to expand his diplomatic range beyond the confines of the German empire. In such a manner, through family blood ties with the Frankish and English royal houses, to which he could reckon his family ties with the ruling house in Kiev (and the religious-political ties with Emperor Monomachos of Byzantium), King Andrew I wanted to bring about a far reaching diplomatic plan by arranging for a well founded dynastic alliance between Judith, sister of the new German monarch, Henry IV, and Salomon, son of Andrew and Anastasia of Kiev.

The dynastic marriage relationship in formation between the Árpáds and the Franconian German dynasty against the background of Árpádian diplomatic blood ties with the west-Frankish and English, and family religious ties with the eastern, Kievan and Byzantine, courts provided a firm foundation for the policies of Andrew I, and son Salomon, in a central Europe strongly oriented toward the Latin west during the 1050s.

The Hungarian chronicler—according to János Horváth, the chronicler was Bishop Nicholas, chancellor of King Andrew I, "qui tunc temporis vicem procurabat notarii," whose name appeared twice on the Tihany founding charter (he had witnessed and signed the document), who already from his high official position must have had a clear picture of the dynastic goals of the court's foreign policy—examined the case from an entirely different point of view. Family blood ties often hinder the truth, he pointed out. Also fatherly concern in the heart of Andrew, he wrote, defeated justice, in that Andrew, old and invalid, and yet, in a manner unworthy of a king, broke the promise he had made to his younger brother Béla that, upon his death, it will be Béla who shall inherit the Hungarian throne. Instead, Andrew had Salomon, his five year old, anointed and crowned king, "in regem fecit iniungi et coronari." The chronicler excused the behavior of the king by saying that he had acted out of national interest: the German court would not have consented to the marriage of Salomon without the coronation, and yet, the chronicler pointed out, the king had made a mistake. When Béla did find out what really had happened, he justly grew indignant, "graviter est indignatus," and, what was worse, became suspicious.

Andrew now met his younger brother at the royal hunting lodge at Várkony, where, without the knowledge of Béla, put his brother to a test. Did the prince accept political reality? Would he be satisfied with his princely title and landholding, and continue as the realm's military defender during the minority of the child king, Salomon; or, would he reach out for the crown, thereby voiding Andrew's diplomatic efforts with the German court? Béla, following the advice of Nicholas, reeve of the royal court: "Si vitam optas, accipe gladium," chose, out of fear, the sword, that is, the princely title. After he had made his choice, Béla immediately left the kingdom with his family. Regardless of the fact that he had acted out of fear, the prince in deciding to flee to Poland, simply refused to identify himself with, and may have decided to undermine, his brother's pro-German game of dynastic chess.

In the fall of 1060, Prince Béla took up position east of the Tisza river in Hungary with three division of Polish auxiliaries. King Andrew grew concerned, sent his family to safety in Austria, and asked for German military aid. Through this twofold act, the already very ill monarch committed a fatal mistake. He had fully weakened his position on the home front and demolished any success he could have claimed for his foreign diplomacy. The king was no match for Béla's military know-how, not to mention the fact that the majority of the Magyars sided with the prince. Béla displayed his forces in the Tisza region—a region that formed part of his princely territory, whose terrain he knew well, where he could easily provide logistics for his men, and encircled the German troops that had reached the river. King Andrew fled to Fort Moson on the realm's western border, and, severely wounded in an accident, was captured by the men of Béla; on account of unprofessional medical treatment, the captured king soon died in the royal hunting lodge at Zirc.

A word of explanation is in order here. In this writer's opinion, King Andrew I must have felt overconfident by the success of his marriage-bound diplomacy: through his wife, he held family ties with both the Kievan ruling house and the Frankish royal family. Edward, son of Edmund Ironside, who, at least according to one of the MSS of the Anglo-Saxon Chronicle, was considered the heir of the English throne, was married to Agatha, one of the daughters of King Stephen I; there seem to have emerged a plan of a Hungaro-English diplomatic understanding between the two kingdoms. Undoubtedly, there is no record of Edward's stay in Hungary—that lasted well into King Andrew's reign—by the Hungarian chroniclers. If, however, Edward Aetheling did *not* marry one of King Stephen's daughters, but (only) a Hungarian noble woman (a case more than unlikely), knowing King Stephen's warm hospitality extended to all "foreigners," the Anglo-Saxon prince, who had lived and raised a family in Hungary, still had to have active contacts with the Hungarian royal court.

King Andrew wanted to affect this somewhat complicated and (perhaps) unrealistic policy through the marriage of *his* son to the sister of the ruling German monarch, who was still a minor (later king and emperor, Henry IV). It was Andrew's personal tragedy that his overheated ambition lacked political reality: on the one hand, the imperial court advisors of the dowager empress, Agnes, through the marriage between Salomon (anointed and crowned Hungarian king) and Judith (sister of the German monarch, Henry IV), only wanted to draw the Magyar kingdom into the sphere of imperial political influence, from which it had only recently pulled away. The German-Hungarian marriage alliance would sooner or later have led to a feudal dependency of the Magyar court upon the empire. On the other hand, Andrew's diplomacy lacked domestic reality: it ignored the *pagan* opposition—based on the ancient Magyar social habits and the manner of life—whose adherents were searching for a cause to revolt, with armed force, if needed, against the "foreign" politics of their monarch.

In early December, 1060, Béla I became king. The Hungarian chronicler referred to Béla as *Benin*, the warrior, who entered Székesfehérvár in triumph, where the bishops anointed and crowned him; "regali dyademata...est coronatus," the chronicler reported, though this writer, for one, argues that the circlet used at the coronation was not the crown that touched King Stephen's forehead, but a [the] *ruler's diadem* with which the bishops, after anointing him, had crowned him. If this *ruler's diadem* happened to be the circlet sent by the Byzantine emperor Monomachos, a diadem that the Latin-rite bishops had placed on Béla's head, the new king through his coronation may have wished to assert his determination that during his reign he shall maintain good relations with the eastern *Greek* court, but also continue, and in fact realize, the Árpáds' *western*-oriented diplomacy.

The new king, first, had to deflate once and for all the still lively "pagan" revolution in the land, and Béla made some progress by acting circumspect, but at the end, he had to rely upon military force to restore domestic law and order. The chronicler's statement that the king had summoned, countrywide, two *well-spoken men* from every village to his Royal Council to aid him in decision making—"misit etiam rex...per totam Hungariam precones, ut de singulis villis vocarentur duo seniores *facundiam habentes* [italics mine] ad regis concilium"—may refer to this resolution of the monarch. The chronicler's choice of Latin terms meant that two well-spoken elders invited from every village were, "facundiam habentes," actually *representatives* of the villages in, or before, the King's Council, whose framework King Béla now expanded from the size and structure the council had earlier been determined by King Stephen.

In other words, King Béla I in the early 1060s had—together with members of the high clergy, nobility, and elected representatives of the people—enacted legislation, placed the dismal financial problems of the country in order, and realized his clearly set domestic and foreign political aims. In England, it was Henry II who, according to the resolutions of his Assize of Clarendon, 1166, through statements taken from the local *legaliores* (who knew of a certain crime, at the certain time, at a certain place) before courts of law, would conduct legal proceedings by the "Justices in the eyre." In Aragon of the 1080s, it was *rex et regina* who shall call upon the representatives of the towns to participate in the discussion of public matters, and enact legislation.

Therefore, it was through his expanded Council that Béla I successfully handled financial matters, minted money, determined prices and wages, punished black marketing, supported *laissez faire*, introduced Byzantine gold coins into circulation; his forty silver denars were worth one Byzantine gold coin. Although some historians argue that this segment of the Chronicle could be a later addition to the text that summarized fiscal reforms in the realm in the second half of the eleventh century, this writer agrees with Bálint Hóman who said that the economic-financial improvements in the realm did reach back to the days of King Béla I. The fiscal improvements "introduced" by King Salomon, for instance, would not have been possible without the fiscal initiatives undertaken by King Béla.

One cannot leave out of consideration the fact that Béla I grew up in the Polish court, where fiscal reforms had been carried out already in the first half of the century. Béla I was aware that no matter how important his domestic and diplomatic efforts were, he could not realize them without at first placing his country's economic and monetary state on a solid foundation. In the spirit of King Stephen, he did this at the beginning of his reign acting with the full cooperation of the high clergy, the nobility, and the people's *representative* spokesmen in the Royal Council.

It was also with the consent of his spiritual and temporal lords that Béla had, at the beginning of his reign, forcefully oppressed the *pagan* upheaval countrywide. This is evident from the remark of the Chronicle that it took Béla three days to take action; as soon as he had obtained the consent of his lords, and regrouped his available army units, he mastered the situation. (The monarch was aware that it was dangerous to use troops to quell domestic unrest; the experience could have backfired: "Hungaria ad Christum convertita bis ad paganismum versa est.")

During the summer of 1063, the imperial diet meeting at Mainz decided on a military campaign against Béla I in order to restore King Salomon to his, the Hungarian, throne. The king, because he wanted to gain time to delay the invasion, or to avoid it by diplomatic means, sent envoys to the German court, but Empress Agnes was unwilling (rather, her advisors were) to negotiate. Béla I spent the early fall of 1063 at his hunting lodge at Dömös to prepare for the Germans attack, when his throne collapsed under him—it depends how one reads the sentence in the Chronicle: when the house roof fell upon him. Was the accident a coincidence, or a direct sabotage organized from abroad, an attempt made upon the life of the king? He never recovered from his wounds. They had to carry him on a stretcher to fort Moson so that he could direct military operations on the border against the approaching imperial forces, but his health did not hold out. He had to be carried semi-conscious to the Kanizsa [Kynisua] Creek, where he died, "et ibi migravit e seculo."

His sons fled to Poland to return with Polish troops by the end of the year. In early 1064, at Győr, the headmen of the realm negotiated a peace between Salomon and Béla's sons, Géza, László [Ladislas], and Levente. On Easter Sunday, Prince Géza had crowned Salomon anew in the cathedral at Pécs. Thereafter, Salomon and his wife Judith had revived—one ought to say: fulfilled—the financial reforms of Béla by establishing a system of monetary exchange of new coins (only) every two years.

King Béla I had followed a very successful domestic and foreign policy based on common sense; unexpectedly, and, perhaps, too rapidly, he achieved success with his military, administrative, fiscal, and judicial policies. His triumphs came far too soon for some of his—mostly non-Magyar—adversaries who wished nothing more than Béla's failure while King Salomon was still alive. Although a collapsing building, or royal throne, had buried ruling monarchs before, judged by the overly brief report by the Hungarian Chronicle on the reign of Béla I, the dying monarch had been aware that the Franconian court would not refrain from using any Byzantine political method—including assassination—to remove him from the throne of the Árpáds.

It may be said in conclusion that the politics of both Andrew I and Béla I would be characterized by a historian as cautious. Both monarchs passed resolutions, issued directives, undertook no action without the consent of the Council of spiritual and temporal lords, as well as the well-spoken elders *representing* the people's interests. Their foreign diplomacy relied upon marriages, forming blood ties with various ruling families, in order to counterbalance any threat from the imperial Franconian, one may add, the Byzantine courts. Domestically, both had achieved positive accomplishments. Because of their accidental or premeditated personal tragedies, however, their family policies remained mere unsuccessful attempts at dynastic diplomacy.

This writer, for one, is unable to hide his opinion—partly based on a statement made by Anna Comnena who did not depict in the most favorable colors the rather clumsy *military* interference by the already dishonored Salomon in the affairs of the Byzantine Empire (she, perhaps, followed the footsteps of Michael Psellus); partly, upon a brief remark of the German emperor, Henry IV, addressed to Salomon who, out of season, praised the military aptness of the Hungarian knights to the emperor, to which the German monarch correctly answered: "si ita est, talibus militibus repugnanatibus non recuperabis regnum," the Chronicle, c. 127, reported—that the game of dynastic diplomatic chess played by both kings, Andrew I and Béla I, on a wide geographic scale, though without any deeper political foresight (as, for instance, was it really necessary for Salomon to marry Judith, Henry IV's sister?), essentially remained unsuccessful. It may be, of course, that the royal brothers, raised to manhood in Slavic princely courts, were unable to comprehend, *or* unwilling to apply the Carolingian concept that had been accepted for quite some time in the Latin west, that the king of the *regnum* through his promulgated guidelines (*capitularia*) might exercise personal diplomacy, as if to bind his kingship to his own person, without, however, embodying the concept of the *state*.

Notes

János Érdy, "Nyitra Ivánka területén 1860 1861 évben kiszántott bizánci románcok a XI századból" [Byzantine romance enamels plowed from the earth in 1860 and 1861], *Arcaeológiai közlemények*, 2 (1861), 65ff., dealt at some depth with the excavations at Nyitraivánka; so did Zoltán Kádár, "Quelques observations sur la reconstitution de la couronne de l'empereur Constantin Monomaque," *Folia archeologica*, 16 (1964), 113ff.; Magda Obershall Bárány, *Konstantinos Monomachos császár koronája* [The crown of Emperor Constantine Monomachos] (Budapest, 1937), 86ff., 92ff.; the authenticity of the enamel plates has been questioned by Nicolas Oikonomides (died recently), "La couronne dite de Constantin Monomaque," *Travaux et mémoirs*, 12 (1994), 241ff., whose views have been challenged in a masterful essay by Etele Kiss, "The state of research on he Monomachos Crown and some further thoughts," *Perceptions of Byzantium and its neighbors (843-1261)* (Metropolitan Museum, New York, 2000), 60ff. See further, Josef Deér, *Die hl. Krone Ungarns* (Vienna, 1966), 33ff.

On events in Hungary in the mid-eleventh century, the mid-fourteenth century *Chronicon pictum* [Illuminated Chronicle], based on contemporary informative evidence of the 1040s through the 1060s, provides historical source data—cf. "Chronici Hungarici compositio saeculi XIV," cc. 70 to 99, in *Scriptores rerum Hungaricarum*, ed. Emericus Szentpétery, 2 vols. (Budapest, 1937-38; rev. repr., ed. by Kornél Szovák and László Veszprémy, Budapest, 1999), cited hereafter as *SSH*, I, 321ff.; for added comments, cf. *ibid.*, II, 750ff. Dezső Dercsényi (ed.), *Chronicon pictum: Képes Krónika*, 2 vols. (Budapest, 1963), vol. I: facsimile, f. 23v to fol. 35r. For an analysis of *contemporary* evidence, see János Horváth, *Árpád-kori latinnyelvű irodalmunk stílusproblémái* [Stylistic questions in the Latin-language literature of the Árpád age] (Budapest, 1954), 305ff.

Simon de Keza, late thirteenth century, provided some observations in his "Gesta Hungarorum," cc. 45 to 60; cf. *SSH*, I, 173ff., and so did the annalistic entries in the "Annales Posonienses," as, for example, under anno 1041: "Petrus rex elicitur et Aba in regem elevatur;" or, anno 1044: "Aba rex interficitur et Petrus rex in pristinum restituitur;" anno 1047: "...et Andreas rex elevatur;" anno 1052: "Henricus imperator Pannoniam ingreditur;" and, anno 1057: "Andreas rex infirmatur et Salamonem filium suum coronavit;" anno 1060: "inter Andream et fratrem suum Bela gravie discordia oritur et rex Andreas moritur," etc., see *SSH*, I, 125. For additional remarks were in the "Chronicon Zagrabiense," cc. 3–7, cf. *ibid.*, I, 207ff. A critical analytical summary of the material is available in C. A. Macartney, *The Medieval Hungarian Historians* (Cambridge, 1953), 111ff., 133ff., 89ff., and 109f., respectively.

The Hungarian royal writs, documents, as, for example, the founding charter of Tihany abbey, 1055, were carefully logged in Emericus Szentpétery, et al. (eds.), *Regesta regum stirpis Arpadianae critico-diplomatica*, 2 vols. (Budapest, 1923–87), cited hereafter as *RA*, n. 12; text in Henrik Marczali (ed.), *Enchiridion fontium historiae Hungarorum* (Budapest, 1901), 81ff.; or, Emil Jakubovich – Dezső Pais (eds.), *Ó-magyar Olvasókönyv* [Old Hungarian reader] (Pécs, 1929), 19ff.; background information in *SSH*, I, 354,17–19. For papal documents, as, for instance, the writ, dated Oct. 28, 1074, of Pope Gregory VII addressed to King Salomon, logged under n. ii:13 in the papal Register, cf. Erich Caspar (ed.), *Das Register Gregors VII*, MGH Epp., sel. II, 2 vols. (Berlin, 1920-23), I, 145.

Among the non-Hungarian *western* Latin sources, one may refer to the *Annales Altahenses*, rev. ed., ed. E. ab Oefele, SSrG (Hannover, 1891), aa. 1041 through 1046, 1050, 1051, 1052, 1053, 1056, 1058, 1060, 1063, etc.; the *Annales Hildesheimenses*, ed. G. Waitz, SSrG (Hannover, 1878; repr. 1947), aa. 1041–1046; Herriman Contractus, "Chronicon," aa. 1038–46, *Monumenta Germaniae historica, Scriptores*, ed. G. H. Pertz, 30 vols. (Hannover, 1854, etc.), cited hereafter as *MGHSS*, V, 126, 127. Under 1047, the entry records that Henry III would not enter Hungary because of the revolt in Flanders; under 1050; another entry mentions the attempt made by armed Magyar troops to prevent, or to delay, the re-fortification of Hainburg. In 1051, Gebhardt and Brestislav invaded Magyar land north of the Danube, while the emperor entered Hungarian territory from Carinthia. In 1053, the Germans concluded peace with Andrew at Trıbur; in 1060, Andrew, a sick man, sought safety for his family at Melk. Cf. *MGHSS*, V, 127.

Lamperti Hersfeldensis Opera, ed. O. Holder-Egger, with the Weissenburg Annals, SSrG (Hannover, 1894), recorded the same event under *anno 1061*, and made mention of William of Thuringia and Bishop Eppo; William was engaged to the daughter of Béla, but had died, and it was Udalrich of Carinthia who had married her. The remark by Cosmas of Prague, "Chronicon Boemorum," that Peter the Orseolo—some ten years after he had been captured, blinded, and buried at the cathedral in Pécs, see "Chronicon pictum," c. 85, *SSH* I, 342f.—had married the widow of the Czech Brestislav, cf. *MGHSS*, IX, 78, rests upon shaky ground, indeed; cf. J. Loserth, "Kritische Studien zur ältere Geschichte Böhmens," *Mitteilungen des Institutes für österreichische Geschichtsforschung*, 5 (1884), 366ff.; or, St. Katona, *Historia critica regum Hungariae stirpis Arpadianae*, 7 vols. (Pest–Buda, 1779–81), I, 991 and 992.

The diplomacy of Pope Leo IX, is being referred to in the *Acta Sanctorum Bollandiana*, 60 vols. (Paris–Rome, 1864–76), April, II, 661; or, in Wibert's "Vita s. Leonis IX papae," in J. P. Migne (ed.), *Patrologiae cursus completus, series Latina*, 221 vols. (Paris, 1844-55), cited hereafter as *MPL*, 143, 496bc; also Hildebert, "Vita Hugonis," ii:7, in *MPL*, 159, 864cd. King Andrew I did not comply with the agreement—see Contractus, a. 1052, *MGHSS*, V, 131,36-43. Johannes Haller, *Das Papsttum: Idee und Wirklichkeit*, 2nd ed., 5 vols. (Esslingen am Neckar, 1962), II, 278ff., spoke of a *deutsches Papsttum*. On relations between Leo IX and Archbishop Gregory, see Ph. Jaffé, *Regesta pontificum Romanorum*, 2 vols. (Leipzig, 1885), n. 3222. Z. J. Kosztolnyik, "Hungaro-German contacts in the mid-eleventh century vs. the background of the Rome-Byzantium schism," *Proceedings of the XV Annual Congress of the Cleveland Hungarian Association, 1975* (Cleveland, OH, 1976), 229ff. Karl Hampe recognized that Andrew did not regard himself as vassal of the German court; "in Ungarn war dıe Lehenshoheit des Reiches nichts lange behauptet worden." Cf. his *Deutsche Kaisergeschichte in der Zeit der Salier und Staufer*, 12th ed., ed. Friedrich Baethgen (Heidelberg, 1968), 33.

The Polish source collection is available in the *Monumenta Poloniae historica*, ed. A. Bielowski, 6 vols. (Lvov–Cracow, 1864–93; repr. Warsaw, 1960–61), cited hereafter as *MPH*, I, 495ff.; this writer was unable to gain access to the more recent edition. See also *Chronica – Polonica, pars I*, ed., with an introduction by Béla Karácsonyi (Szeged, 1969); idem, "Tanulmányok a Magyar-lengyel Krónikáról" [Studien über Polnisch-Ungarische Chronik], *Acta historica Szegediensis*, 16 (1964), repr.

Of the Russian-Kievan sources, see the *Russian Primary Chronicle*, ed. Samuel Hazzard Cross and Olgerd P. Sherbowitz-Wetzor (Cambridge, Mass., 1953), 136ff.; Antal Hodinka (ed.), *Az orosz évkönyvek magyar vonatkozásai* [Hungarian-related entries in the Russian annals] (Budapest, 1916), 52ABff., provide sparse information. Omeljan Pritsak, *The Origin of Rus'*, vol. I (Cambridge, Mass., 1981), 142ff.; idem, *On the writing of history in Kievan Rus': the millennium of Christianity in Rus'-Ukraine* (Cambridge, MA, 1988), 133ff.; also, Gy. Kristó – I. H. Tóth, "Az orosz évkönyvek néhány magyar vonatkozásáról" [Some remarks on the Hungarian-related references in the Russian annals], *Acta historica Szegediensis*, 103 (1996), 21ff. The political background is discussed in George Vernadsky, *Kievan Russia* (New Haven–London, 1948; 7th printing, 1973), 79ff.; also, Martha Font, *Oroszország, Ukrajna, Rusz* [Russia, the Ukraine, and the Rus] (Pécs, 1998), 41ff., and 70ff.

Among the Byzantine sources, Anna Comnena made some pertinent remarks on the Hungarian scene in the 1040s—see her *Alexiade*, ed. B. Leib, 3 vols. (Paris, 1937-45), I, 127,17 – 128,1, partly based on a remark made in Johannes Scylitzes Continuatus, *Historiarum compendium*, ed. I. Bekker, CB, vol. II (Bonn, 1839), 645,17–22, and on Psellus, *Chronographia*, ed. E. Renauld, 2 vols. (Paris, 1926, 1928), II, 125. For background, cf. Georg Ostrogorsky, *Geschichte des byzantinischen Staates*, 2nd ed. (Munich, 1952), 260ff.; Romilly Jenkins, *Byzantium: The Imperial Centuries AD 610–1071* (1966; repr. Toronto–London, 1987), 333ff., is worth reading; so is J. M. Hussey's study, "The Byzantine Empire in the Eleventh Century: Some Different Interpretations," *Transactions of the Royal Historical Society*, 32 (1950), 71ff.; A. A. Vasiliev, *History of the Byzantine Empire* (Madison, WI, 1952), 351ff.; Z. J. Kosztolnyik, "Similarities between King St. Stephen of Hungary's Law Code and the Laws of Jaroslav the Wise of Kiev," *Hungary's Historical Legacies: Studies in Honor of S. B. Várdy*, ed. D. P. Hupchick – R. W. Weisberger (New York, 2000), 45ff.; valuable is Robert Browning's penetrating, and yet almost forgotten study, *The Byzantine Empire* (New York, 1980), 92ff. It also carries a picture of the crown of Constantine IX, "believed to have been a gift to the Hungarian court" (p. 93). On German conditions in the 1040s and 1050s, cf. Bertholdi "Chronicon," *MGHSS*, V, 271. Lampert of Hersfeld, *anno* 1060, mentioned the confrontation between Andrew and Béla. Karl Hampe, *Deutsche Kaisergeschichte in der Zeit der Salier und Staufer*, 12th ed., ed. Friedrich Baethgen (Heidelberg, 1968), 32ff.

The return to England of *atheling* Edward—who was the son of King Edward's brother, King Edmund who was called Ironside because of his valour.... King Cnut had atheling Edward banished to Hungary in order to betray him, etc., where he had married Agatha, the king's daughter—the text has "a kinswoman of the emperor," most probably because King Stephen was married to Gisela, the sister of Emperor Henry II, is discussed in *The Anglo-Saxon Chronicle*, rev. transl., ed. Dorothy Whitelock, et al. (New Brunswick, NJ, 1961), anno 1057, MS "D"; the Florence MS added a note providing the reason for Edward's return: "for the king—that is, Edward the Confessor—had determined to make him heir the kingdom after him," see *ibid.*, 133, n. 6.

Margaret, Edward Aetheling's daughter and sister to Christina and Edgar—born to King Stephen's daughter; or, if not (which is unlikely), to a Hungarian noble woman—married a widower, King Malcolm III of Scotland. Cf. her "Vita," in *Acta sanctorum*, Iunii II, 328; and, W. Forbes-Leith, *Life of St. Margaret of Scotland by Turgot of St. Andrews*, 3rd ed. (Edinburgh, 1896), 19ff.

King Béla I called upon two *well spoken* elders of every community—cf. Chronicle, c. 93, *SSH*, I, 393,1–2; on *representation* in the Spanish *cortes*, see H. Mitteis, *Der Staat des hohen Mittelalters*, 8th rev. ed. (Weimar, 1968), 416f.; for the text of the "Assize of Clarendon" (1166), issued by Henry II of England, see William Stubbs (ed.), *Select charters of English constitutional history*, 8th ed. (Oxford, 1900), 143ff. Béla I had died because of the collapsing throne (or, building), the chronicler recorded; a similar accident befell the east-Frankish king Arnulf in 897—cf. Ernst Dümmler, *Geschichte des oströmischen Reiches*, 2nd ed., 3 vols. (Leipzig, 1887–88), III, 437. See further Gerold Meyer v. Knonau, *Jahrbücher des deutschen Reiches unter Heinrich IV und Heinrich V*, 2 vols. (1890; rep. Berlin, 1964), I, 189; for his views on the battle at Ménfő, "Pforte des Reiches," see *ibid.*, I, 198ff.; and, for Knonau's comments on the death of Béla, *ibid.*, I, 344ff.

The German background in Karl Hampe, *Deutsche Kaisergeschichte in der Zeit der Salier und Staufer*, 12th rev. ed., ed. Friedrich Baethgen (Heidelberg, 1968), 33: "in Ungarn war die Lehenshoheit des Reiches nicht lange behauptet worden;" also, Bruno Gebhardt, *Handbuch der deutschen Geschichte*, 8th rev. ed., 4 vols. (Stuttgart, 1954; 6th rev. repr. 1962), I, 224ff., and 235ff., who provides a solid survey; so does Elizabeth M. Hallam, *Capetian France, 987-1328* (London–New York, 1980), 71ff., on Frankish politics and diplomacy. See further, Robert Fawtier's analytical narrative, *The Capetian kings of France* (New York, 1966), 15ff.

The Hungarian background of events has been covered in depth—and based on original research!—by Bálint Hóman, *Geschichte des ungarischen Mittelalters*, 2 vols. (Berlin, 1940–43), I, 254ff.; György Székely – Antal Bartha (eds.), *Magyarország története: előzmények és magyar történet 1242-ig* [Early history, and Hungarian history to 1242] (Budapest, 1984), 835ff., did a clever job; Gyula Kristó, *Die Arpaden-Dynastie* (Budapest, 1993), 88ff.; Z. J. Kosztolnyik, *Five Eleventh Century Hungarian Kings: Their Policies and Their Relations with Rome* (New York, 1981), 72ff., and 175ff.

On medieval central European, and Hungarian financial conditions, see Peter Spufford's excellent work, *Money and its use in Medieval Europe* (Cambridge, 1988), 80f., and 95. Ferenc Makk, "Megjegyzések I. András történetéhez" [Some remarks on the reign of Andrew I], *Acta historica Szegediensis*, 90 (1990), 23ff.; Zoltán Kordé, "A magyarországi besenyők az Árpád-korban" [The Pechenegs in Hungary during the Árpád age], *ibid.*, 90 (1999), 3ff. Ferenc Makk, "Új forrásadatok a X század végi magyar-bizánci kapcsolatok értékeléséhez" [Neue Quellenangaben zur Bewertung der ungarisch–byzantinischen Beziehungen Ende des 10 Jahrhunderts], *A nyíregyházi Jósa András Múzeum Évkönyve*, 43 (2001), 271ff.; Gyula Kristó, *Megjegyzések az ún. 'pogánylázadások' kora történetéhez* [Background of the age of the so called "pagan" uprisings in Hungary] (Szeged, 1965), 36ff., and 49ff.; idem, "Géza fejedelem és István király" [Prince Géza, the ruler, and Stephen, the king], *Aetas*, 2000-3, 25ff.

On Anna Comnena, cf. *Anna Comnéne*, ed. B. Leib, 3 vols. (Paris, 1937–45), II, 87f.; for Psellus, see Michael Psellus, *Chronographia*, ed. C. Sathas (Paris, 1874), vi:87, etc., with a background in Ostrogorsky, *Geschichte des byzantinischen Staates*, 267ff., and with an intellectual backdrop by Browning, *Byzantine Empire*, 99, 102.

Details in the Chronicle, c. 127, *SSH*, I, 399,8–16, and the Chronicle, c. 91, *ibid.*, I, 351ff.

To cite some of the Carolingian *capitularia*, see, for example, the ones concerning royal domains, and royal estates, in *MGH Legum sectio II: Capitularia regum Francorum*, 2 vols. (Hannover, 1883–97), I, 82ff., and I, 178f. August Nietschke's 29 page study, "Karolinger und Ottonen: von der karolingischer Staatlichkeit zur Königsherrschaft," *Historische Zeitschrift*, 273 (2001), 1ff., provided an ideal ideological backdrop, and so did the masterpiece by Friedrich Heer, *Europäische Geistesgeschichte*, 2nd ed. (Stuttgart, 1965), 49ff.

Bibliography

Primary Sources

'Abd al-Aziz al-Bekri (Abu 'Ubaif 'Abdullah). *Book of kingdoms and roads.* Journal Asiatique, 1849.

Acta sanctorum Bollandiana, 60 vols. to October XI. Paris–Rome, 1864–76. Cited as *ASS.*

Acta sanctorum Hungariae ex Bollandini et al...excerpta, 2 vols. Tyrnaviae 1743–44.

Adam of Bremen. *Gesta Hammaburgensis ecclesiae pontificum,* 3rd ed. Edited by Bernhard Schmeidler, SSrG. Hannover–Leipzig, 1917; rep. 1977.

Agapetus. "Expositio capitum amonitorium Imperatori Justiniano," *MPG,* 86, 1164ff.

Albericus Trium Fontium. "Chronica," *MGHSS,* XXIII.

Anglo-Saxon Chronicle. Edited by Dorothy Whitelock, David C. Douglas and Susie I. Tucker. New Brunswick, NJ, 1961.

Annales Altahenses maiores. Edited by W. de Giesebrecht and E. L. B. ab Oefele, SSrG. Hannover, 1891; repr. 1979.

Annales Bertiniani. Edited by G. Waitz, SSrG. Hannover, 1883.

Annales Fuldenses sive Annales regni Francorum orientalis. Edited by G. H. Pertz and F. Kurze, SSrG. Hannover, 1891; repr. 1978.

Annales Hildesheimenses. Edited by G. Waitz, SSrG. Hannover, 1878.

"Annales Kamenzenses," *MGHSS,* XIX, 581.

Annales regni Francorum qui dicuntur Einhardi. Edited by G. H. Pertz and Fr. Kurze, SSrG. Hannover, 1895; repr. 1950.

Annales Xantenses et Annales Vedastini. Edited by B. von Simson, SSrG. Hannover–Leipzig, 1909.

Augustinus, Aurelius. *De civitate Dei, libri XXII,* 2 vols. Edited by B. Dombart and A. Kalb; 5th ed., edited by J. Divjak. Stuttgart, 1931; repr. 1981.

Biblia sacra iuxta Vulgatam versionem, 4th ed. Edited by Robert Weber, et al. Stuttgart, 1994.

Bresslau, Harry. *Diplomata centum regum et imperatorum Germaniae.* Hannover–Berlin, 1879.

Burchard of Worms. *Decretum [Decretorum libri XX], MPL,* 140, 537ff.

Camões, Luiz [Luys] Vaz de. *Os Lusiadas* (Lisboa, 1626). Hungarian translation by Gyula Greguss, *Camoens Luzidája,* 2nd ed. (Budapest, 1874); English translation by W. C. Atkinson, *The Lusiads* (London, 1952).

Capitularia regum Francorum, 2 vols. Edited by Alfred Boretius and Victor Krause, *MGH, Leges*. Hannover, 1890–97.

Carmina Burana: Vagantenlieder aus der lateinischen Dichtung des 12 und 13 Jahrhunderts. Latin text by Max Manitius; intr. with German translation by Robert Ulich. Jena, 1927.

Choniates, Niketas. *Historia*. Edited by I. Bekker, CB. Bonn, 1835.

Chronicon pictum: Képes Krónika, 2 vols. Edited by Dezső Dercsényi. Budapest, 1963.

Cinnamus, Johannes. *Epitomae rerum ab Ioanne et Alexio Comnenis gestarum*. Edited by A. Meinecke, CB. Bonn, 1836.

Codex diplomaticus et epistolaris regni Bohemiae, vol. I. Edited by G. Friedrich. Prague, 1904.

Codex diplomaticus Hungarie ecclesiasticus ac civilis, 44 vols. Edited by G. Fejér. Budae, 1829–42. Cited as *CD*.

Concilia aevi Karolini, 2 vols. Edited by Albert Werminghaft. Hannover, 1906–08.

Contractus, Hermann. "Chronica," *MGHSS*, V, 67ff.

Corpus Iuris Canonici, 2 vols. Edited by Ae. Friedberg. Leipzig, 1879–81; repr. Graz, 1959.

Cortes de los antiguos reinos de León et de Castilla, 5 vols. Edited by Real Academia de la Historia. Madrid, 1861–1903.

Damiani, Peter. "Vita s. Romualdi," *MPL*, 144, 933ff.

Dandalo, Andreas. "Chronicon Venetum," *RISS*, XII.

De administrando imperio—Constantine VII Porphyrogenitus. Greek text edition by Gyula Moravcsik. English translation by R. J. H. Jenkins. Budapest, 1949; 2nd ed. Washington, DC 1967. Cited as *DAI*.

"De conversione Bogoariorum et Carantanorum libellus," *MGHSS*, XI, 4ff.

Deliberatio Gerardi Moresanae aecclesiae episcopi Svpra hymnum trium pverorum. Edited by Béla Karácsonyi and László Szegfű. Szeged, 1999.

Documenta historica Croatiae, vol. VII in the *Monumenta spectantia historiam Slavorum meridionalium*, 43 vols. Edited by F. Rački. Zagreb, 1868–1918.

Eadmer. *Historia novorum in Anglia*. Edited by M. Rule, RS. London, 1884.

Einhard. *Vita Caroli Magni*, 6th ed. Edited by O. Holder-Egger, SSrG. Hannover, 1911; repr. 1927.

Ellenhardus Argentensis. "Chronicon," *MGHSS*, XVII, 120.

Emmeram, Arnold. "Liber II de memoria beati Emmerami et eius cultorum," *MGHSS*, IV, 557ff.

Epistolae aevi Karolini. Edited by Ernst Dümmler and Ernst Perels. Hannover, 1925. Cited as MG Epp., vol. VI.

Eusebius of Caesarea. *Historia ecclesiastica*. Edited by Kirsop Lake and J. E. L. Oulton, Loeb ser. Cambridge, MA, 1926; repr. 1992.

Eusebius Pamphyli. *Oratio de laudibus Constantini*. Edited by I. Heikel. Leipzig, 1902.

Flodoard of Reims. "Annales," *MGHSS*, III, 363ff.

______. "Historia Remensis ecclesiae," *MGHSS*, XIII, 409ff.

Fontes Byzantini historiae Hungaricae aevo ducum et regum ex stirpe Arpad descendentium. Edited by Gyula Moravcsik. Budapest, 1984.

Fontes rerum Bohemicarum, 4 vols. Edited by J. Emler. Prague, 1873–93.

Gardezi, Mahamud (Abu Sa'id 'Ab al-Hajj ad Dahhak). *Chronicle*. St. Petersburg, 1887.

Grammaticus, Leo. *Geographia*. Edited by I. Bekker, CB. Bonn, 1842.

Gregorii I papae Registrum epistolarum, 2 vols. Edited by Paul Edwald and Ludo M. Hartmann. Hannover, 1897–99. Cited as MG Epp., vol. I.

Hazai Okmánytár [Domestic writs and documents], 8 vols. Edited by Imre Nagy, et al. Győr–Budapest, 1865–91. Cited as *HO*.

Henricus Heimberg. "Cronica Boemorum," *MGHSS*, XVII, 712.

Hincmar Reims. *De ordine palatii*, rev. ed. Edited by Thomas Gross and Rudolf Schieffer, SSrG. Hannover, 1980.

Iotsald. "Life of Abbot Odilo," *MGHSS*, XV, 812ff.; *MPL*, 142, 897ff.

Ivo of Chartres. *Decretum* (in 17 books), *MPL* 161, 47ff.

______. *Panormia* (in 8 books), *MPL*, 161, 1037ff.

Jerome [Eusebius Sophrinus Hieronymus]. *Jerome, Select letters*. Edited by F. A. Wright, Loeb ser. Cambridge, MA, 1933; repr. 1991.

Jonas of Orleans. "De institutione laicali," *MPL*, 106, 167ff.

Justinian's Corpus iuris civilis, 3 vols. Edited by P. Krueger, Th. Momsen and R. Schoell. Berlin, 1895–99.

Justinian's Institutes. Edited by Paul Krüger, with introduction by Peter Birks and Grant McLeod. Ithaca, NY, 1987.

Karwasińka, Hedwig. *S. Adalberti Pragensis episcopi et martyris Vita prior*, MPH, ser. nova, IV-1. Warsaw, 1962.

______. *S. Adalberti Pragensis episcopi et martyris Vita altera auctore Brunone Querfurtensi*, MPH, ser. nova, IV-2. Warsaw, 1962.

Katona, St. *Historia critica regum Hungariae stirpis Arpadianae*, 7 vols. Pest–Buda, 1779–82.

Koller, Iosephus. *Historia episcopatus Quinqueecclesiae*, vols. I–III. Posonii, 1782–84; vol. VII, Pesthini, 1812.

Königsberger Weltchronik, 2nd ed. Edited by W. Giesbrecht. Braunschweig, 1877.

Lampert of Hersfeld, *Opera*. Edited by Oswald Holder-Egger, SSrG. Hannover–Leipzig, 1894.

Leo VI, the Wise. *Tactica*, *MPG*, 107, 672ff.; selections in *MHK*,11ff.; in Marczali, *Enchiridion*, 12ff., and Moravcsik, *Fontes*, 14ff.

Liber pontificalis, 3 vols. Edited by L. Duchesne. Paris, 1886, etc.; repr. 1957.

Liudprandi episcopi Cremonensis opera, 3rd ed. Edited by I. Becker, SSrG. Hannover, 1915; repr. 1977.

Liutprand. "Antepodoseos," in *Liudprandi episcopi Cremoneneis opera*, 3rd ed. Edited by I. Becker, SSrG. Hannover, 1915.

Mabillon, J. *Acta sanctorum s. Ordini Benedicti*, vol. V.

Malalas, Iohannes. *Chronographia*. Edited by L. Dindorf, CB. Bonn, 1831.

Manuel pour mon fils of Lady Dhuoda. Edited by P. Riché. Vol. 225 of *Sources chrétiennes*. Paris, 1975.

Marczali, Henrik, et al. *Enchiridion historiae Hungarorum*. Budapest, 1901.

MGH Diplomata regum et imperatorum Germaniae, 10 vols. Edited by Theodor Sickel, et al. Hannover, 1879, etc.

MGH Epp. V: *Epistolae Karolini aevi*. Edited by Erich Caspar and Gerhard Laehr. Hannover, 1912–28.

Monasterilogiae regni Hungariae, 2 vols. Edited by D. Fuxhoffer and M. Czinár. Vienna–Esztergom, 1869.

Monumenta Erphordensia saec. XII, XIII, XIV. Edited by Oswaldus Holder-Egger, SSrG. Hannover, 1899.

Monumenta Germaniae historica, Scriptores, 30 vols. Edited by G. H. Pertz. Hannover, 1854, etc. Cited as *MGHSS*.

Monumenta Poloniae historica, 6 vols. Edited by A. Blielowski. Lvov–Cracow, 1864–93; repr. 1960–61. Cited as *MPH*.

Monumenta Ecclesiae Strigoniensis, 2 vols. Edited by Ferdinand Knauz. Strigonii, 1873-74.

Nichephori archiepiscopi Constantinopolitani. *Opuscula historica*. Edited by C. de Boor. Leipzig, 1888.

Odilo of Cluny. "De epitaphio et miraculis Odilonis abbatis Cluniacensis," *MGHSS*, XV, 813ff.

Odo of Cluny. "Collationum libri III," *MPL*, 133, 517ff.

Odo de Deogilo. *De profectione Ludovici VII in orientem*. Edited by V. G. Berry [Latin–English]. New York, 1948.

Omar Ibn Rusta (Abu 'Ali Ahmad). *Book of precious jewels*. St. Petersburg, 1889.

Ordericus Vitalis, "Historia ecclesiastica," *MPL*, 187.

Othlo of St. Emmeram. "Vita s. Wolfkangi episcopi," *MGHSS*, IV, 525ff.

Otto of Freising. *Chronica sive Historia de duabus civitatibus*, rev. ed. Edited by A. Hofmeister, SSrG. Hannover–Leipzig, 1912; repr. 1984.

______. *Ottonis et Rahewini Gesta Friderici I imperatoris*, 3rd ed. Edited by G. Waitz and B. de Simson, SSrG. Hannover–Leipzig, 1912; repr. 1978.

P. magister quondam Bele regis Hungarie notarius: Gesta Hungarorurm. Edited by Ladislaus Juhász. Budapest, 1932.

"Passio s. Adalberti," *MGHSS*, XV, 706ff.

Patrologiae cursus completus, series graeca, 161 vols. in 166. Edited by J. P. Migne. Paris, 1857–66. Cited as *MPG*.

Patrologiae cursus completus, series latina, 221 vols. Edited by J. P. Migne. Paris, 1844–55. Cited as *MPL*.

Pelbartus of Temesvár. *Pomerium de sanctis*. Hagenau, 1499.

Pray, Georgius. *Annales veteres Hunnorum, Avarorum et Hungarorum*. Vienna, 1761.

Pseullus, Michael. *Chronographiae*, vol. I. Edited by E. Rénauld. Paris, 1926.

Ransanus, Peter. *Epithoma rerum Hungarorum* [the last book of his *Annales temporum omnium*]. Edited by P. Kulcsár. Budapest, 1977.

Regesta pontificum Romanorum, 2 vols. Edited by Ph. Jaffé. Leipzig, 1885.

Regesta pontificum Romanorum, 2 vols. Edited by August Potthast. Berlin, 1875.

Regesta regumm stirpis Arpadianae critico-diplomatica, 2 vols. Edited by Emericus Szentpétery and Ivan Borsa, Budapest, 1923–87. Cited as *RA*.

Das Register Gregors VII, MGH Epp. selectae, 2 vols. Edited by Erich Caspar. Berlin, 1920–23; repr. 1990.

Regino of Prüm (Regionis abbatis Prumensis). *Chronicon*. Edited by Fr. Kurze, SSrG. Hannover, 1890.

______. *Libri duo de synodalibus causis et disciplinis ecclesiasticis*. Edited by H. Wasserschleben. Lipsiae, 1840.

Rerum Gallicarum et Franciarum scriptores, 23 vols. Edited by M. Bouquet. Paris, 1738–1876.

Richeri Historiarum libri IV, rev. ed. Edited bt G. Waitz, SSrG. Hannover, 1877.

Rerum Italicarum scriptores, 28 vols. Edited by L. A. Muratori. Milan, 1723–51; reprints. Cited as *RISS*.

Sacrorum conciliorum nova et amplissima collectio, 31 vols. Edited by J. D. Mansi. Florence–Venice, 1759–98. Cited as Mansi, *Concilia*.

Scriptores rerum Austricarum, 3 vols. Edited by H. Pez. Regensburg, 1721–45. Cited as *SSRA*.

Scriptores rerum Hungaricarum, 2 vols. Edited by Emericus Szentpétery. Budapest, 1937–38; rev. repr. by Kornél Szovák and László Veszprémy, 1999. Cited as *SSH*.

Scylitzae, Georgios Cedrenos Iohannes. *Opera*, 2 vols. Edited by I. Bekker, CB. Bonn, 1838–39.

Sedulus Scotus. *De rectoribus Christianitatis*. Edited by S. Hellmann. Munich, 1909.

Smaragdus. "De via regia," *MPL*, 102.

Theophanis. *Chronographia*, 2 vols. Edited by C. de Boor, CB. Bonn,1883.

Theophanus…Georgius monachus continuatus. Edited by I. Bekker, CB. Bonn, 1838.

Thesaurus novus anecdotorum, 5 vols. Edited by E. Martene and U. Durand. Repr. New York, 1968.

Thurn, I., ed. *Ioannis Scylitzae Synopsis historiarum*. Berlin–New York, 1973.

Vetera monumenta historiam Hungariae sacram illustrantia, 2 vols. Edited by August Theiner. Rome, 1859–60.

Veterum scriptorum et monumentorum collectio, 9 vols. Edited by E. Martene and U. Durand. Repr. New York, 1968.

Widukind of Corby. *Rerum gestarum Saxonicarum libri III*, 4th ed. Edited by G. Waitz and K. A. Kehr, SSrG. Hannover, 1904; repr. 1925.

______. *Res gestae Saxonicae*, 5th rev. ed. Edited by P. Hirsch and H. E. Lohmann, SSrG. Hannover, 1935.

William of Malmesbury, "De rebus gestarum regum Anglorum," *MPL*, 179.

______., *De gestis regum Anglorum libri V*, 2 vols. Edited by W. Stubbs, RS. London, 1887–89.

Wiponis opera, 3rd ed. Edited by H. Bresslau, SSrG. Hannover, 1915.

Zonaras, Johannes. *Epitomae historiarum*, libri xiii–xviii. Edited by Th. Büttner-Wobst, CB. Bonn, 1897.

Books

Altmann, W. and E. Bernheim, *Ausgewählte Urkunden zur Erläuterung der Verfassungsgeschichte Deutschlands im Mittelalter*. Berlin, 1904.

Bárány, Magda Oberschall. *Konstantinos Monomachos császár koronája* [The crown of Emperor Constantine Monomachos]. Budapest, 1937.

Bartha, Antal. *Hungarian Society in the 9th and 10th Centuries*. Budapest, 1975.

Bartoniek, Emma, ed. *Szent István törvényeinek XII századi kézirata, az admonti kódex* [The Admont Codex: The Twelfth Century MS of King St. Stephen's laws], with a reduced facsimile of Admont MS 712, ff. 119-26. Budapest, 1935.

Besta, Enrico. *L'opera d'Irnerio: contributo alla sztoria del diritto italiano*, 2 vols. Turin, 1896.

Beumann, H., ed. *Karl der Grosse: Lebenswerk und Nachleben*, vol. I. Düsseldorf, 1967.

Biese, Alfred. *Deutsche Literaturgeschichte*, 3 vols., 3rd rev. ed. Munich, 1911–1918.

Bloch, Marc. *Feudal Society*. Trans. by L. A. Manyon. Chicago, 1961.

Boba, Imre. *Moravia's History Reconsidered*. The Hague, 1971. Hungarian translation by István Petrovics, Budapest, 1996.

Bogyay, Thomas von. *Lechfeld: Ende und Anfang*. Munich, 1955.

______. *Stephanus Rex*. Munich, 1975.

Bóna, István. *A húnok és nagykirályaik* [The Huns and their Great Kings]. Budapest, 1993.

______. *A magyarok és Európa a 9 – 10 században* [The Magyars and Europe in the ninth–tenth centuries]. Budapest, 2000.

______. *Az Árpádok korai várai* [The forts of the early Árpád age], rev., expanded ed. Debrecen, 1998.

______. *Die Awaren in Europa*. Frankfurt am Main–Nuremberg, 1985.

Bónis, György. *A jogtudó értelmiség a Mohács előtti Magyarországon* [Der Juristenstand in Ungarn vor 1526]. Budapest, 1971.

Bosl, Karl. *Zur Geschichte der Bayern*. Darmstadt, 1965.

Bouquet, Martin, ed. *Recueil des historiens des Gaules et de la France*, vol. IX. Paris, 1879.

Bowlus, Ch. R. *Franks, Moravians and Magyars, 788–907*. Philadelphia, 1995.

Braak, Menno tu. *Kaiser Otto III: Ideal und Praxis im frühen Mittelalter*. Amsterdam, 1928.

Brandt, A. von. *Werkzeug des Historikers*. Urban Bücher, 2nd ed. Stuttgart, 1960.

Bröckig, W. *Die französische Politik Leos IX*, 2 vols. 1891–99.

Brooke, Z. N. *The English Church and the Papacy*. Cambridge, 1931; repr. 1989.

Browning, Robert. *The Byzantine Empire*. New York, 1980.

Bruel, A. *Recueil des charters de l' abbaye de Cluny*. Paris, 1876.

Brundage, James A. *Law, Sex, and Christian Society in Medieval Europe*. Chicago, 1987.

______. *Medieval Canon Law*. London–New York, 1995.

Büdinger, Max. *Ein Buch ungarischer Geschichte, 1058–1100*. Leipzig, 1866.

Bunyitay, Vince. *A váradi püspökség története* [History of the Bihar bishopric], 3 vols. Nagyvárad, 1883–84.

Cantor, F. N. *Church, Kingship and Lay Investiture in England, 1089–1135*. Princeton, 1958.

Caspar, E. *Geschichte des Papsttums*, 2 vols. Tübingen, 1933–35; his *Papsttum unter fränkischer Herrschaft* (Darmstadt, 1956) would have been the third volume of his opus.

Conybeare, F. C. *The Key of Truth*. Oxford, 1895.

Conybeare, F. C. *Manual of the Paulician Church in Armenia*. Oxford, 1898.

Cormack, Robin. *Byzantine Art*. Oxford, 2000.

Cross, S. H. and O. P. Sherbowitz-Wetzer, eds. *The Russian Primary Chronicle*. Cambridge, MA, 1953.

Csapodi, Csaba. *A legrégibb magyar könyvtár benső rendje* [Organization of the oldest Hungarian library]. Budapest, 1957.

Csóka, Lajos J. *A latin nyelvű történeti irodalom kialakulása Magyarországon a XI–XIV században* [Development of the Latin-language historical literature in Hungary during the eleventh through the fourteenth centuries]. Budapest, 1967.

Curtius, E. R. *European Literature and the Latin Middle Ages*. Trans. by W. R. Trask. Princeton, 1953.

Czebe, Gy. *A veszprémvölgyi oklevél görög szövege* [The Greek text of the Veszprémvölgy charter]. Budapest, 1916.

Dám, Ince. *A Szeplőtelen Fogantatás védelme Magyarországon* [Defense of the Immaculate Conception in Hungary]. Rome, 1955.

József Deér. *Die hl. Krone Ungarns*. Vienna, 1966.

_____. *A magyar törzsszövetség s patrimonális királyság külpolitikája* [The foreign policy of the Magyar clan and the organization of patrimonial kingship]. Pécs, 1928.

Delehaye, Hippolyte. *The Legends of the Saints*. Trans. by Donald Attwater, with a new Introduction by Thomas O'Loughlin. Repr. Dublin, 1998.

Dempf, Alois. *Sacrum imperium*. Munich–Berlin, 1929.

Dopsch, Alfons. *Die Wirtschaftsentwicklung der Karolingerzeit*, 2 vols., 3rd rev. ed. Edited by Erna Patzelt. Cologne–Graz, 1962.

Dudden, F. Homes. *Gregory the Great: His Place in History and Thought*, 2 vols. London, 1905; reissued New York, 1967.

Dümmler, E. and Fr. Miklosich. *Die Legende vom Heiligen Cyrillus,* in *Denkscriften der Akademie der Wissenschaften, Wien*, hist.-hist. Kl., xix. Vienna, 1870.

Dunlap, D. M. *The history of the Jewish Chazars*. Princeton, 1954.

Dvornik, F. *The Making of Central and Eastern Europe*. London, 1949.

Dvornik, Francis. *Les légéndes de Constantin et de Méthode vues de Byzance*. Prague, 1933.

Eadolff, W. *Vergleichende Grammatik der nördlichen Türksprachen*, part I: *Phonetik der nördlichen Türksprachen*. Leipzig, 1882.

Eggert, Wolfgang. *Das ostfränkisch-deutsche Reich in der Auffassung seiner Zeitgenossen*. Vienna–Graz, 1973.

Eggert, Wolfgang and Barbra Pätzold. *Wir-Gefühl und Regnum Saxonum bei frühmittelalterlichen Geschichtsschreibern*. Vienna– Graz, 1948.

Eichhoff, Ekkehard. *Theophanu, der König Otto III und seine Welt.* Stuttgart, 1996.

Erdélyi, László, ed. *A pannonhalmi Szent Benedekrend története* [History of the Benedictines at Pannonhalma], 12 vols. Pannonhalma, 1902–07.

Erdő, Péter. *Egyházjog* [Canon law]. Budapest, 1996.

______. *Egyházi alkotmányjog* [Ecclesiastical constitutional law], rev. ed. Budapest, 1996.

______. *Az egyházjog forrásai: történeti bevezetés* [The sources of Canon law: an introduction]. Budapest, 1998.

Erkens, Franz-Rener. *Konrad II: Herrschaft und Reich des ersten Salierkaisers.* Regensburg, 1998.

Fasoli, Gina. *Le incursioni ungare in Europa nel secolo X.* Florence, 1945.

Fichtenau, Heinrich. *Beiträge zur Mediävistik,* vol. II: *Urkundenforschung.* Stuttgart, 1977.

Fischer-Drew, Katherine. *The Lombard Laws.* Philadelphia, 1973.

______. *The Carolingian Empire.* Trans. by Peter Munz. Oxford, 1957.

Fleury, Ch. Rohaiult de. *La Messe études archéologiques sur les monuments,* vol. VII. Paris, 1888.

Font, Martha. *Oroszország, Ukrajna, Rusz: fejezetek a keleti szlávok történetéből* [Russia and the Ukraine: Chapters in the History of the Eastern Slavs]. Pécs, 1995.

Forbes-Leith, W. *Life of St. Margaret of Scotland by Turgot of St. Andrews,* 3rd ed. Edinburgh, 1896.

Fried, Johannes. *Otto III und Boleslaw Chrobry.* Stuttgart, 1989.

Funk, F. X. von and K. Bihlmeyer. *Kirchengeschichte,* 2 vols., 8th ed. Paderborn, 1926–30.

Galla, F. *A Cluny reform hatása Magyarországon* [Influence of the Gallican reforms in Hungary]. Pécs, 1931.

Gaudemet, Jean. *L'église dans l'empire romain (IVe–Ve siècles).* Paris, 1989.

Gebhardt, Bruno. *Handbuch der deutschen Geschichte,* 4 vols., 8th ed. Edited by Herbert Grundmann (Stuttgart, 1954 etc.), vol. I.

Gerevich, Tíbor. *Magyarország románkori emlékei* [Romanesque period souvenirs in Hungary]. Budapest, 1938.

Gerics, József. *Egyház, állam és gondolkodás Magyarországon a középkorban* [Church, realm and political thought in medieval Hungary]. Budapest, 1995.

Giesebrecht, W. von. *Geschichte der deutschen Kaiserzeit,* rev. ed. by Wilhelm Schild, 6 vols. Meersburg, 1929.

Görich, Knut. *Otto III, Romanus Saxonicus et Italicus.* Sigmaringen, 1995.

Graff, Theodor, ed. *Die Regesten des Kaiserreichs unter Heinrich II, 1002–24.* In J. F. Böhmer, ed., *Regesta imperii*, II–4. Vienna, 1971.

Gransden, Antonia. *Historical Writing in England, c. 550 to 1307.* Ithaca, NY, 1974.

Gyóni, M. *A magyar nyelvű görög feljegyzéses szórványemlékei* [Die Streudenkmäler der ungarischen Sprache in griechischen Texten]. Budapest, 1943.

Györffy, Georgios, ed. *Geographia hitorica Hungariae tempore stirpis Arpadianae*, vol. I, 3rd ed. Budapest, 1987.

Györffy, György. *István király és műve* [King Stephen and his work]. Budapest, 1977.

______. *Krónikáink és a magyar őstörténet* [Hungarian chronicles and early history of the Magyars]. Budapest, 1948.

______. *A magyarok elődeiről és a honfoglalásról* [The Magyars' forefathers and their land-taking], 2nd ed. Budapest, 1975.

______. *Wirtschaft und Gesellschaft der Ungarn um die Jahrtausendwende.* Vienna–Graz–Budapest, 1983.

Hain, L. *Repertorium bibliographicum*, 2 vols. Stuttgart–Tübingen, 1826-38; rep. in 4 vols., Milan, 1948.

Hallam, Elizabeth M. *Capetian France, 987–1328.* London–New York, 1980.

Haller, Johann. *Das Papsttum: Idee und Wirklichkeit*, 2 vols. Stuttgart, 1936–39; rev. ed., 5 vols., Munich, 1950–53; repr. 1962.

Hamel, Christopher de. *Medieval Craftsmen, Scribes and Illuminators.* Toronto, 1992.

Hampe, Karl. *Deutsche Kaisergeschichte in der Zeit der Salier und Staufer*, 12th ed. Edited by Friedrich Baethgen. Heidelberg, 1968.

______. *Das Hochmittelalter, 900–1250*, 5th ed. Cologne–Graz, 1963.

Hapgood, Ch. H. *Maps of the Ancient Sea Kings*, rev. ed. New York, 1979.

Haskins, Charles H. *The Renaissance of the 12th Century.* Cambridge, MA, 1927.

Havet, Julien, ed. *Lettres de Gerbert.* Paris, 1889.

Heer, Friedrich. *Europäische Geistesgeschichte*, 2nd ed. Stuttgart, 1965.

Hefele, C. F. von. *Conciliengeschichte*, rev. ed., 6 vols. [vols. 5 and 6 edited by A. Knöpfler]. Freiburg i. Br., 1873–90.

Heimbucher, Max. *Die Orden und Kongregationen der katholischen Kirche*, 3rd ed., 2 vols. Paderborn, 1933–34.

Hergenröther, I. *Photius, Patriarch von Byzanz*, 2nd ed. 1867; repr. New York, n.d.

Hirsch, Sigfried, H. Pabst, and Harry Bresslau. *Jahrbücher des Deutschen Reiches unter Heinriich II*, 3 vols. Berlin, 1862–75; repr. 1975.

Hodinka, Antal. *A munkácsi görögkatolikus püspökség története* [A history of the Greek Catholic diocese of Munkács]. Budapest, 1910.

______. *Az orosz évkönyvek magyar vonatkozásai* [Annotations in the Russian annals related to Hungary]. Budapest, 1916.

Holtzmann, Robert. *Geschichte der sächsischen Kaiserzeit, 900–1024*, 4th ed. Darmstadt, 1961.

Hóman, Bálint. *Geschichte des ungarischen Mittelalters*, 2 vols. Berlin, 1940–43.

______. *Magyar pénztörténet, 1000–1325* [Hungarian monetary history, 1000–1326] (Budapest, 1916).

______. *Szent István* [King St. Stephen]. Budapest, 1938; repr. Győr, 2000.

______. *A szent László-kori Gesta Hungarorum és XII – XIII századi leszármazói* [The Gesta Hungarorurm of the times of St. Ladislas I, and its continuity in the twelfth and thirteenth centuries]. Budapest, 1925.

______., ed. *A magyar történetírás új útjai* [The new ways of Hungarian historiography] (Budapest, 1931).

______., ed. *Szent Istv*án*: első nagy királyunk élete és alkotásai* [The life and accomplishments of the first great Hungarian monarch: King St. Stephen]. Budapest, 1938.

Hóman, Bálint and Gyula Szekfű. *Magyar történet* [Hungarian history], 5 vols., 6th ed. (Budapest, 1939).

Horváth, Cyrill. *A régi magyar irodalom története* [A history of early Hungarian literature]. Budapest, 1899.

Horváth, János. *Árpád-kori latinnyelvű irodalmunk stílusproblémái* [Stylistic questions concerning the Latin-language literature of the Árpád age]. Budapest, 1954.

______. *A magyar irodalmi műveltség kezdetei* [Beginnings of Hungarian literary culture], 2nd ed. Budapest, 1944.

Horváth, J. and Gy. Székely, eds. *Középkori kútfőink kritikus kérdései* [Critical questions regarding the medieval Hungarian historical sources]. Budapest, 1974.

Jákli, István. *"... a magyarokhoz küldetett"* ["…he had been sent to missionarize among the Magyars"]. Pannonhalma, 1992.

Jakubovich, Emil and Dezső Pais, eds. *Ó-magyar olvasókönyv* [Old Hungarian reader]. Pécs, 1929.

Jánosi, Monika. *Törvényalkotás a korai Árpád-korban* [Hungarian laws of the early Árpád age. Szeged, 1996.

Jenkins, Romily J. H. *Byzantium: The Imperial Centuries, AD 610–1071*. London, 1966; repr. Toronto–London, 1987.

Jirecek, C. *Geschichte der Serben*, 2 vols. Gotha, 1911–18.

Joinville, Jean de. *Histoire de Saint Louis*. Edited by N. de Wailly. Paris, 1874.

Juhász, K. *A csanádi püspökség története* [A history of the Csanád diocese, from its beginning to the Mongol invasion]. Makó, 1930.

Kantorowicz, Ernst H. *The King's Two Bodies*. Princeton, 1957.

Karácsonyi, János. *A magyar nemzetségek a XIV század közepéig* [Magyar family clans until the mid-14th century], vol. I. Budapest, 1900.

______. *Szent Gellért csanádi püspök élete és munkái* [Life and work of Bishop St. Gerard of Csanád]. Budapest, 1887.

______. *Szent István király élete* [Life of King St. Stephen]. Budapest, 1904.

Kern, Fritz *Gottesgnadentum und Widerstandsrecht im frühen Mittelalter*, 5th ed. [a reprint of the 2nd ed., 1954]. Darmstadt, 1970.

Kéry, Lotte. *Canonical Collections of the Early Middle Ages (ca. 400-1140): A Bibliographical Guide to the Manuscripts and Literature*. Washington, DC, 1999.

Klaniczay, Tíbor. *A magyar irodalom története* [A history of Hungarian literature], vol. I. Budapest, 1964.

Knonau, Gerold Meyer von. *Jahrbücher des deutschen Reiches unter Heinrich IV und Heinrich V*, 6 vols. 1890 etc.; repr. Berlin, 1964.

Kohn, Samuel. *A zsidók története Magyarországon* [History of the Jews in Hungary], vol. I. Budapest, 1884.

Köpeczi, Béla, et al., eds. *Erdély története* [A history of Transylvania], 3 vols. Budapest, 1986.

Kosztolnyik, Z. J. *Five Eleventh Century Hungarian Kings: Their Policies and their Relations with Rome*. New York, 1981.

______. *From Coloman the Learned to Béla III (1095–1196): Hungarian Domestic Policies and the Impact Upon Foreign Affairs*. New York, 1987.

______. *Hungary in the Thirteenth Century*. New York, 1996.

Kovács, Éva and Zsuzsa Lovag, eds. *Die ungarischen Krönungsinsignien*, rev. ed. Budapest, 1988.

Kovács, S. V., ed. *A magyar középkor irodalma* [The Hungarian literature of the middle ages. Budapest, 1984.

Kretschmayr, H. *Geschichte von Venedig*, vol. I. Gotha, 1905.

Kristó, Gyula. *Die Arpaden-Dynastie*. Budapest, 1993.

______. *Az Árpád-kor háborúi* [The wars of the Árpád age]. Budapest, 1986.

______. *Szempontok korai helyneveink történeti tipológiájához* [Some comments on the historic changes of the names of early Hungarian settlements]. Szeged, 1976.

______. *A vármegyék kialakulása Magyarországon* [Development of the county-system in Hungary]. Budapest, 1988.

Krumbacher, Karl. *Geschichte der byzantinischen Literatur*, 2nd ed. Munich, 1897.

Kühner, Hans. *Neues Papstlexikon*. Frankfurt–Hamburg: Fischer Bücherei, 1965.

Kunstmann, Heinrich. *Die Slaven: ihr Name, ihre Wanderung nach Europa und die Anfänge der russischen Geschichte in historisch-onomastischer Sicht.* Stuttgart, 1996.

Kutrzeba, St. *Grundriss der polnischen Verfassungsgeschichte*. Lemberg, 1912.

Kuttner, Stephan. *Gratian and the Schools of Law*. London, 1983.

______. *Repertorium der Kanonistik (1140–1234)*, vol. 71 of *Studi e testi*. Vatican City, 1937.

______. *History of Ideas and Doctrines of Canon Law in the Middle Ages*. London, 1992.

Laistner, M. L. W. *Thoughts and Letters in Western Europe, 500–900*, rev. ed. London, 1957.

Lattin, H. P., ed. *The Letters of Gerbert with his Papal Privileges as Sylvester II*. New York, 1961.

Leff, Gordon. *Medieval Thought*. Baltimore, MD: Penguin Books, 1958.

Lehmann, Paul. *Erforschung des Mittelalters*, 5 vols. Stuttgart, 1959.

Leib, B. *Rome, Kiev et Byzance a la fin du XIe siècle*. Paris, 1924.

Liebermann, F. *Die Gesetze der Angelsachsen*, 3 vols. Halle, 1903–16.

Liotta, F. *La continenza dei chierci*. Milan, 1971.

Loyn, H. R. *Anglo-Saxon England and the Norman conquest*, 2nd ed. London–New York, 1991.

Lukácsy, K. *A magyarok őselei hajdankori nevek, lakhely, eredeti örmény kútfők alapján* [The Magyars' early ancestors according to ancient names, places of residence, and original Armenian sources]. Kolozsvár, 1870.

Lüttich, Rudolf. *Ungarnzüge in Europa im 10 Jahrhundert*. Berlin, 1910.

Macartney C. A. *The Magyars in the Ninth Century*. Cambridge, 1930; repr. 1968.

______. *The Medieval Hungarian Historians*. Cambridge, 1953.

Maitland, S. R. *Facts and Documents Illustrative of the Albigenses and Waldenses*. London, 1832.

Makk, Ferenc. *Magyar külpolitika, 896–1196* [Hungarian foreign policy, 896–1196]. Szeged, 1993.

Mályusz, Elemér. *Egyházi társadalom a középkori Magyarországon* [Structure and educational background of the clerical stratum in medieval Hungary]. Budapest, 1971.

______. *A Thuróczy Krónika forrásai* [Source material of the Thuróczy Chronicle]. Budapest, 1967.

Manitius, Max. *Geschichte der lateinischen Literatur des Mittelalters*, 3 vols. Munich, 1911–31.

Marczali, Henrik. *Ungarns Geschichtsquellen im Zeitalter der Arpáden*. Berlin, 1882.

Marquart, J. *Osteuropäische und ostasiatische Streifzüge*. Leipzig, 1903; repr. Darmstadt, 1961.

Mayer, Hans Eberhard. *Geschichte der Kreuzzüge*, 3rd repr. Stuttgart, 1973.

McIlwain, Ch. Howard *The Growth of Political Thought in the West*. New York, 1932.

McKitterick, Rosamund. *The Frankish Kingdoms under the Carolingians*. London–New York, 1983.

______., ed. *The Uses of Literacy in Early Medieval Europe*. Cambridge, 1990.

Meister, Aloys. *Deutsche Verfassungsgeschichte*, 3rd ed. Leipzig–Berlin, 1922.

Mezey, L. *Deákság és Európa* [The study of Latin classics and Europe]. Budapest, 1970.

Michaud-Quantin, P. *Sommes de casuistique et manuels de confession au moyen age*. Louvain—Montreal, 1962.

Mitteis, Heinrich. *Lehnrecht und Staatsgewalt*. 1933; rep. Weimar, 1958.

______. *Der Staat des hohen Mittelalters*, 8th ed. Weimar, 1968.

Mommsen, Theodor. *Das Weltreich der Cäsaren*, Paidon repr. Vienna, 1955.

Monay, Ferenc. *A római magyar gyóntatók* [Hungarian confessors at St. Peter's]. Rome, 1956.

Moorhead, John. *Justinian*. London–New York, 1994.

Moravcsik, Gyula. *Byzantium and the Magyars*. Amsterdam–Budapest, 1970.

______. *Az onogurok történetéhez* [History of the Onogurs]. Budapest, 1930.

Morrison, Karl F. *Tradition and Authority in the Western Church, 300–1140*. Princeton, 1969.

Mühlbacher, Engelbert. *Deutsche Geschichte unter den Karolingern*, 2 vols., Phaidon repr. Essen–Darmstadt, n.d.

Nagy, Miklós. *Szent Gellért élete* [The life of St. Gerard]. Budapest, 1946.

Naz, R., ed. *Dictionnaire de droit canonique*, 7 vols. Paris, 1935–65.

Nelson, Janet L. *The Frankish World, 750–900*. London, 1996.

Németh, Gyula. *A honfoglaló magyarság kialakulása* [The formation of the land-taking Magyars into a people], rev. ed. Edited by Árpád Berta. Budapest, 1991.

Ostrogorsky, Georg. *Geschichte des byzantinischen Staates*, 2nd ed. Munich, 1952.

Pál, J. and A. Somorjai, eds. *Mille anni di storia dell'arciabbazia di Pannonhalma*. Rome–Pannonhalma, 1997.

Palacky, Franz. *Geschichte von Böhmen*, vol. I, 2nd printing, Prague, 1844; vol. II-2, 3rd printing, Prague, 1874.

Patzelt, Erna. *Die karolingische Renaissance*. Vienna, 1924; 2nd ed., Graz, 1965.

______. *Österreich bis zum Ausgang der Babenbergerzeit*. Vienna, 1947.

Pauler, Gyula and Sándor Szilágyi, eds. *A magyar honfoglalás kútfői* [The historical sources of the Magyars' land-taking]. Budapest, 1900, cited as *MHK*.

Paulhart, Herbert, ed. *Odilonis Cluniacensis abbatis Epitaphium domine Adelheide auguste: Die Lebensbeschreibung der Kaiserin Adelhaid von Abt Odilo von Cluny*, MIÖG Suppl. XXII-2. Graz–Cologne, 1962.

Peterka, Otto. *Rechtsgeschichte der böhmischen Länder*, vol. I. Reichenberg, 1923.

Petit-Dutaillis, Charles. *The feudal Monarchy in France and England, from the Tenth to the Thirteenth Century*. Trans. by E. D. Hunt. London, 1936; rep. 1964.

Picavet, F. J. *Gerbert: un pape philosophe*. Paris, 1897.

Pintér, Jenő. *Magyar irodalomtörténet* [A synthesis of Hungarian literature], 8 vols. Budapest, 1930–41.

______. *A magyar irodalom történetének kézikönyve* [A handbook of the history of Hungarian literature], 2 vols. Budapest, 1929–30.

Planitz, Hans and Karl August Eckhardt. *Deutsche Rechtsgeschichte*, rev. ed. Graz–Cologne, 1961.

Poole, R. L. *Studies in Chronology and History*. Edited by A. L. Poole. Oxford, 1934; repr. 1969.

Post, Gaines. *Studies in Medieval Legal Thought*. Princeton, 1964.

Prinz, Friedrich. *Frühes Mönchtum im Frankreich: Kultur und Gesellschaft in Gallien, den Rheinlanden und Bayern am beispiel der monastischen Entwicklung*. Munich–Vienna, 1965.

Pritsak, Omeljan. *The origins of Rus'. The millennium of Christianity in Rus'–Ukraine*. Cambridge, MA, 1988.

Queller, Donald E. *The Fourth Crusade*. Philadelphia, 1977.

Sackur, E. *Die Cluniazenser*, 2 vols. Halle, 1892.

Sackur, Ernst. *Die Cluniacenser in ihrer kirchlichen und allgemeingeschichtlichen Wirksamkeit bis zur Mitte des elften Jahrhunderts*, 2 vols. Halle a.d. Saale, 1894; repr. Tübingen, 1971.

Savigny, F. C. von. *Geschichte des römischen Rechts im Mittelalter*, 2nd ed., 7 vols. Berlin, 1834–51.

Scheck, Werner. *Geschichte Russlands*. Munich, 1975.

Schmale, F. J. *Die Briefe des Abtes Bern von Reichenau*. Stuttgart, 1961.

Schnürer, G. *Kirche und Kultur im Mittelalter*, 2nd ed., 3 vols. Paderborn, 1927–28.

Schramm, P. E. *Geschichte des englischen Königtums im Lichte der Krönung*. Weimar, 1937.

Schramm, Percy Ernst. *Herrschaftszeichen und Staatssymbolik*. Stuttgart, 1955.

Schroeder, R. *Lehrbuch der deutschen Rechtsgeschichte*, 6th ed. Leipzig, 1922.

Schubart, Wilhelm. *Justinian und Theodora*. Munich, 1943.

Schulte, Johann Friedrich von. *Geschichte der Quellen und Literatur des canonischen Rechts*, 3 vols. Stuttgart, 1875–89; repr. Graz, 1956.

Seppelt, F. X. *Geschichte der Päpste*, 5 vols. Munich, 1954–59.

Simmons, G. J. *The Witchcraft World*. New York, 1974.

Šišić, Fr. von. *Geschichte der Kroaten*, vol. I. Zagreb, 1917.

Somorjai, Ádám, ed. *Kelet–közép–Európa szentje: Adalbert (Vojtech–Wojciech–Béla)* [Adalbert, the saint of east-central Europe]. Budapest, 1994.

Southern, R. W. *St. Anselm and his Biographer*. Cambridge, 1963.

Spufford, Peter. *Money and its use in Medieval Europe*. Cambridge, 1988.

Stenton, F. M. *Anglo-Saxon England*, 2nd ed. Oxford, 1947.

Stubbs, William, ed. *Select Charters of English Constitutional History*, 8th ed. Oxford, 1895.

Swietek, F. R. and J. R. Sommerfeld, eds. *Studiosorum speculum: Studies in honor of L. J. Lekai*. Kalamazoo, MI, 1995.

Szabó, Károly. *Kun László* [Ladislas IV the Cuman]. Budapest, 1886; repr. 1988.

______. *A vezérek kora* [The age of the ruling princes]. Pest, 1869.

Székely, György and Antal Bartha, eds., *Magyarország története: előzmények és magyar történet 1242-ig* [A history of Hungary: Pre-history and Hungarian history to 1242]. Budapest, 1984.

Szentpétery, Emericus. *Szent István király pécsváradi és pécsi alapítólevele* [King Stephen's founding charter for Pécsvárad and Pécs]. Budapest, 1918.

Szűcs, Jenő. *A magyar nemzeti tudat kialakulása* [The formation of Hungarian ethnic consciousness]. Budapest, 1997.

Tafel, G. L. F. and G. M. Thomas, eds. *Urkunden zur älteren Handels- und Staatsgeschichte der Republic Venedig*. Vienna, 1856; rep. Amsterdam, 1964.

Takács, Imre, et al., eds. *Mons sacer, 996-1996: Pannonhalma 1000 éve* [A thousand years of Pannonhalma abbey], 3 vols. Pannonhalma, 1996.

Timon, Ákos von. *Ungarische Verfassungs- und Rechtsgeschichte*. Trans. by Felix Schiller, 2nd ed. Berlin, 1904.

Tóth, Endre and Károly Szelényi. *A magyar Szent Korona, királyok és koronázások* [The Hungarian Holy Crown, kings and coronations]. Budapest, 1999.

Tóth, S. L. *Levédiától a Kárpát medencéig* [From Levedia—"Land-between-the-rivers"—to the Carpathian basin]. Szeged, 1998.

Tóth-Inokai, Zoltán. *A Hartvik-legenda kritikájához* [Comments on Hartvic's Life of King Stephen]. Budapest, 1942.

Toynbee, Arnold J. *Constantine Porphyrogenitus and his World*. Oxford, 1973.

Uhlirz, Karl. *Jahrbücher des Deutschen Reiches unter Otto II und Otto III*, 2 vols. Leizpig, 1902–04.

Uhlirz, Mathilde. *Untersuchungen über Inhalt und datierung der Briefe Gerberts von Aurillac*. Göttingen, 1957.

Váczy, Peter von. *Die erste Epoche des ungarischen Königtums*. Pécs, 1935.

Vámbéry, H. *Das Türkenvolk in seinen ethnologischen und ethnographischen Beziehungen*. Leipzig, 1885.

Varjú, Elemér. *Legendae sancti Stephani regis*. Budapest, 1928.

Vernadsky, Georg and Michael de Ferdinándy. *Studien zur ungarischen Frühgeschichte*. Munich, 1957.

Vinogradoff, Paul. *English Society in the Eleventh Century*. Oxford, 1908; rep. 1968.

Voigt, H. G. *Adalbert von Prag: ein Beitrag zur Geschichte der Kirche und des Mönchtums im 10 Jahrhundert*. Westend Berlin, 1898.

______. *Bruno von Querfurt, Mönch, Eremit, Erzbischof der Heiden und Märtyrer*. Stuttgart, 1907.

Waas, Adolf. *Der Mensch im deutschen Mittelalter*. Graz–Cologne, 1964.

Wallace-Hadrill, J. M. *The Frankish Church*. Oxford, 1983.

Wattenbach, W. *Deutschlands Geschichtsquellen im Mittelalter*, 2 vols., 6th ed. Berlin, 1893–94.

Weigand, R. *Die bedingte Eheschliessung im kanonischen Recht*, vol. I. Munich, 1963.

Weinfurter, Stefan. *Herrschaft und Reich der Salier*. Sigmaringen, 1991.

Wilson, N. G. *Scholars of Byzantium*, rev. ed. Cambridge, MA, 1996.

Winkler, Pál. *A kalocsai és bárcsi érseki főkáptalan története* [History of the archiepiscopal arch-deanery at Kalocsa and Bárcs]. Kalocsa, 1935.

Wolf, Gunther. *Kaiserin Theophanu, Princessin aus der Fremde—des Westreiches grosse Kaiserin*. Cologne–Vienna, 1991.

Wolfram, Herwig. *Konrad II, 998–1039, Kaiser dreier Reiche*. Munich, 2000.

Wood, Ian. *The Merovingian kingdoms, 450–751*. London–New York, 1994.

Zagiba, Franz. *Die altbayerische Kirchenprovinz Salzburg und die hll. Slawenlehrer Cyrill und Method*. Salzburg, 1963.

Zimmermann, Harald, ed. *Papstregesten*, 911-1024, vol. II-5, of *Regesta imperii*. Vienna–Graz, 1969.

Zombori, István, ed. *Magyarország és a Szentszék kapcsolatának ezer éve* [A thousand year relationship between Hungary and the Holy See]. Budapest, 1996.

Articles

Adriányi, Gabriel. "Der Eintritt Ungarns in die christlich-abendländische Völkergemeinschaft," *Ungarn-Jahrbuch*, 6 (1974–75): 24ff.

Andrieu, M. "La carrière ecclésiastique des papes," *Revue des sciences religieuses*, 21 (1947): 109ff.

Bachmann, Adolph. "Die Völker an der Donau nach Attilas Tode," *Archiv für österreichische Geschichte*, 61 (1880): 189ff.

Bacon, Peter K. "Critical Appraisal of Byzantine Military Strategy, 400–1000." Unpublished Master's thesis, Texas A & M University Library, 1998.

Balogh, A. "A veszprémvölgyi görög monostor alapítása: a legrégibb magyarországi oklevél" [The founding charter of the Veszprémvölgy monastery, the oldest extant document in Hungary], *Regnum: Egyháztörténeti Évkönyv*, 6 (1944–46): 21ff.

Balogh, J. "Szent Gellért és a 'symphonia Ungarorum'" [St. Gerard comments on the 'symphonia Ungarorum'], *Magyar Nyelv*, 22 (1926): 189ff. and 266ff.

Balogh, József. "A magyar királyság kialakulásának világpolitikai háttere" [The political background of the establishment of the Christian Hungarian kingdom], *Századok*, 66 (1932): 152ff.

______. "The Political Testament of St. Stephen, King of Hungary," *Hungarian Quarterly*, 4 (1938): 389ff.

______. "*Ratio* és *mos*: a római jog 'megujulásának' nyomai a szentistváni Intelmekben" [Traces of renewed interest in Roman law in King St. Stephen's *Admonitiones*], *Philológiai Közlöny*, 67 (1943): 273ff.

______. "Rex a rege regendo," *Speculum*, 3 (1928): 580ff.

Banfi, F. "Paolo Dalmata detto Ongaro. A proposito dei codici Borghese 261 e Pal. lat. 461 della Biblioteca Vaticana," *Archivio storico per la Dalmazia*, 27 (1939): 43ff.

______. "Vita di s. Gerardo da Venezia nel codice 1622 della Biblioteca Universitaria di Padova," *Benedictina*, 2 (1948): 262ff.

Bertram, M. "Some additions to the 'Repertorium der Kanonistik'," *Bulletin of Medieval Canon Law*, 4 (1974): 11, 13.

Blumenthal, Uta-Renata. "History and tradition in eleventh-century Rome," *Catholic Historical Review*, 79 (1993): 185ff.

Bodor, András. "Szent Gellért Deliberatio-jának főforrása" [The main source of St. Gerard's Deliberatio], *Századok*, 77 (1943): 173ff.

Bogyay, Thomas von. "Adalbert von Prag und die Ungarn—ein Problem der Quellen-Interpretation," *Ungarn-Jahrbuch*, 7 (1976): 9ff.

______. "Brevnov und die Ungarnmission," in J. Hoffmann (ed.), *Tausend Jahre Benediktiner in den Klöstern Brevnov, Braunau und Rohr* (St. Ottlien, 1993): 137ff.

______. "Die Kirchenorte der Conversion Bagoariorum et Carantanorum. Methoden und Möglichkeiten ihrer Lokalisierung," *Südostforschungen*, 19 (1960): 52ff.

______. "Mosapurc und Zalavár: eine Auswertung der archaeologischen Funde und der schriftlichen Quellen," *Südostforschungen*, 14 (1955): 349ff.

Bóna, István. "Die Archäologie in Ungarn und die ungarische Landnahme," *Acta archaeologica Academiae Scientiarum Hungaricae*, 49 (1997); 345ff.

______. "Régészetünk és a magyar honfoglalás" [The Hungarian archaeologist's view of the Magyar land-taking], *Magyar Tudomány*, 103 [n.s. 41] (1996): 927ff.

Bónis, György. "Szent István törvényének önállósága" [The originality of King St. Stephen's Laws], *Századok*, 72 (1938): 433ff.

Boor, C. de. "Nachträge zu den Notitiae episcopatuum," *Zeitschrift für Kirchengeschichte*, 12 (1890): 303ff. and 519ff.; and, 14 (1893): 573ff.

Borst, A. "Das Rittertum im Hochmittelalter," *Saeculum*, 10 (1959): 213ff.

Bosl, Karl. "Herzog, König und Bischof im 10 Jahrhundert," in Ferdinand Seibt (ed.), *Bohemia sacra: das Christentum in Böhmen, 973–1973* (Düsseldorf, 1974): 269ff.

Bowlus, Ch. R. "Die Reitervölker der frühen Mittelalters im Osten des Abdenlandes," *Ungarn- Jahrbuch*, 22 (1995–96): 1ff.

Brackmann, A. "Die Anfange der Slawenmission und die Renovatio imperii des Jahres 800," *SB der Preussischen Akademie der Wissenschaften*, phil.-hist. Kl., xiii–9 (1931).

Brandes, Wolfram. "Liudprand von Cremona (Legatio, cap. 39-41) und eine bisher unbeachtete west-östliche Korrespondenz über die Bedeutung des Jahres 1000 AD," *BZ*, 93 (2000): 435ff.

Bresslau, Harry. "Fundatio ecclesiae S. Albani Namucensis," *Neues Archiv*, 8 (1883): 592.

Brundage, J. A. "Widkind of Corvey and the 'non-Roman' imperial idea," *Medieval Studies*, 22 (1960): 15ff.

Bury, J. B. "The Ceremonial Book of Constantine Porphyrogenitus," *English Historical Review*, 22 (1907): 209ff. and 417ff.

______. "The treatise De administrando imperio," *BZ*, 15 (1906): 517ff.

Büttner, Heinrich. "Die Ungarn, das Reich und Europa bis zur Lechsfeldschlacht des Jahres 955," *Zeitschrift für bayerische Landesgeschichte*, 19 (1956): 433ff.

Cahen, C. "La campagne de Manzikert d'après les sources musulmanes," *Byzantion*, 9 (1934): 613ff.

Campbell, James. "Observations on English Government from the Tenth to the Twelfth Century," in his *Essays in Anglo-Saxon History* (London, 1986): 155ff.

Chabanne, R. "Paulus Hungarus," in *Dictionnaire de droit canonique*, ed. R. Naz, 7 vols. (Paris, 1935–65): VII: 1270ff.

Chaloupecky, Václav. "Radla-Anastasius," *Bratislava*, 1 (1927): 210ff.

Csóka, Lajos J. "Cluny szellemű volt-e amagyar egyház a XI században?" [Did the Church in Hungary have a Cluniac orientation in the eleventh century?], *Regnum: Egyháztörténeti Évkönyv, 1942–43*: 141ff.

Czajkowski, A. F. "The Congress of Gniezno in the Year 1000," *Speculum*, 24 (1949): 339ff. and 352ff.

Czeglédi, K. "A IX századi történelem fő kérdései" [The main questions of ninth century history], *Magyar Nyelv*, 41 (1945): 33ff.

Darkó, J. "A veszprémvölgyi apácamonostor alapító leveléről" [Remarks on the founding charter of the monastic community for women in Veszprémvölgy], *Egyetemes Philológiai Közlöny*, 41 (1917): 257ff. and 336ff.

Dawson, Christopher. "The City of God," in M. C. D'Arcy (ed.), *St. Augustine* (New York, 1957): 43ff.

Deér, József. "III Ottó császár és Magyarország az újabb történetírásban" [Relations between Emperor Otto III and Hungary in the light of recent historical research], *Századok*, 78 (1944): 1ff.

_____. "A IX századi magyar történet időrendjéhez" [Some remarks on the time-sequence of ninth century Magyar history], *Századok*, 79-80 (1945–46): 3ff.

Deutinger, Roman. "Zur Entstehung der Marbacher Annalen," *Deutsches Archiv*, 56 (2000): 505ff.

Dölger, Franz. "Die Famile der Könige im Mittelalter," *HJb*, 28 (1903): 283ff.

_____. "Rom in der Gedankenwelt der Byzantiner," *Zeitschrift für Kirchengeschichte*, 56 (1937): 1ff.

Domanovszky, Sándor. "Anonymus és a II Géza korabeli Gesta" [A possible impact upon the Hungarian Anonymus by the 'Gesta' dated to the reign of Géza II, 1141–62] *Századok*, 67 (1933): 38ff. and 163ff.

Dümmler, E. "Über die älteste Geschichte der Slawen in Dalmatien," *SB der Wiener Akademie der Wissenschaften*, 20: 533ff.

Eggers, Martin. "Beiträge zur Stammesbildung und Landnahme der Ungarn," *Ungarische Jahrbücher*, 23 (1997): 1ff.

Ehlers, Caspar. "Die Anfänge Goslars und das Reich im elften Jahrhundert," *Deutsches Archiv*, 53 (1997): 45ff.

Elter, I. "Magyarország Idīrīs földrajzi művében (1154)" [La Hongrie dans la geographie descriptive d'Idīrīs, 1154], *Acta historica Szegediensis*, 82 (1985): 53ff., with a colored map, *ed. Baġdād, 1970*, facing p. 57.

Engelbert, Pius, O.S.B. "Heinrich III und die Synoden von Sutri und Rom im Dezember 1046," *Römische Quartalschrift*, 94 (1999): 228ff.

_____. "Prágai szent Adalbert—püspökideál, politika és szerzetesség" [St. Adalbert of Prague—an episcopal ideal, politics and the monastic life], *Mons sacer*, I: 25ff.

Erdmann, C. "Die Aufrufe Gerberts und Sergius IV für das Heilige Land," *Quellen und Forschungen aus italienischen Archiven und Bibliotheken*, 23 (1931–32): 1ff.

_____. "Die Burgenordnung Heinrichs I," *Deutsches Archiv*, 6 (1943): 59ff.

Erdmann, Carl. "Das ottonische Reich als Imperium Romanum," *Deutsches Archiv*, 6 (1943): 421ff.

Erkens, Franz-Reiner. "Das Niederkirchenwesen im Bistum Passau (11-13 Jahrhundert," *MIÖG*, 102 (1994): 53ff.

Érszegi, Géza. "A pannonhalmi bencés apátság javainak összeírása, 1093" [The 1093 census of the goods of Pannonhalma abbey], in András Vízkeleti (ed.), *Kódexek a középkori Magyarországon* [Codices in medieval Hungarian libraries] (Budapest, 1985).

_____. "Szent István pannonhalmi oklevele" [King St. Stephen's Charter for Pannonhalma], *Mons sacer*, I: 47ff.

Farkas, Gy. "A mogyoródi csata" [The engagement at Mogyoród], *Vigilia*, 39 (1974): 249ff.

Fasoli, Gina. "Unni, avari e ungari nelle fonti occidentali e nelle storia dei paesi d'occidente," *Popoli della steppe: Unni, Avari, Ungari* (Spoleto, 1988): 32ff.

Fehér, G. "Ungarns Gebietsgrenzen in der Mitte des X Jahrhunderts – nach dem De administrando imperio des Konstantinos Porphyrogenitus," *Ungarische Jahrbücher*, 2 (1922): 37ff.

Fehér, Géza. "A bolgár egyház kisérletei s sikerei hazánkban" [Successful attempt made by the Church in Bulgaria in missionarizing Hungary], *Századok*, 61–62 (1927–28): 1ff.

_____. "Szent István király görög oklevele" [A Greek charter issued by King St. Stephen], *Századok*, 51 (1917): 99ff. and 225ff.

Fehértói, Katalin. "Árpád-kori Levente és Leue, Lewedi személyneveink eredete" [The linguistic origin of names Levente, and Leue Lewedi of the Árpád age], *Magyar Nyelv*, 93 (1997): 426ff.

Fodor, István. "A régészeti kutatások félszázadok történetéből" [Overview of the results of half a century of archaeological research], *Magyar Tudomány*, 97 (1990): 276ff.

Fraknói, Vilmos. "A Szent István révén Rómában alapított magyar zarándokház" [The hospice established by King Stephen for Hungarian pilgrims visiting Rome], *Katholikus Szemle*, 7 (1893): 170ff.

Frank, Gábor. "Die Änderungen des Images Stephans des Heiligen in der Geschichtserziehung unseres Zeitalters," *Specimina nova dissertationum Universitatis de Iano Pannonio nominatae*, 4 (1988): 111ff.

Frasseto, Michael. "Writings of Ademar of Chabannes, the peace of 994, and the 'Terrors of the Year 1000'," *Journal of Medieval History*, 27 (2001): 241ff.

Frazee, Ch. A. "The Balkans between Rome and Constantinople in the Early Middle Ages," *Balkan Studies*, 34 (1993): 213ff.

Galuška, Luděk. "Christianity in Great Moravia and its centre in Uherské Hradiště-Sady," *Byzantinoslavica,* 59 (1998): 161ff.

García y García, Antonio. "Glosas de Juan Teutónico, Vincente Hispano y Dámaso Húngaro a los Arbores Consanguinitatis et Affinitatis," *Zeitschrift der Savigny Stiftung for Rechtsgeschichte*, kan Abt., 68 (1982): 153ff.

Garland, E. "Der Vierte Kreuzzug und seine Probleme," *Neue Jahrbücher für das Klassische Altertum*, 13 (1904): 505ff.

Gyóni, M. "Kalizok, kazarok, kabarok, magyarok" [The Caleese, Khazars, Kavaras, Magyars], *Magyar Nyelv*, 34 (1938): 86ff. and 159ff.

Györffy, György. "Az Árpád-kori magyar krónikák" [Hungarian chronciles of the Árpád age], *Századok*, 127 (1993): 391ff.

______. "A besenyők európai honfoglalásának kérdéséhez" [Comments on the settlement of the Pechenegs in Europe], *Történelmi Szemle*, 15 (1972): 316ff.

______. "A magyar–szláv érintkezés kezdetei" [Early Magyar–Slav contacts], *Századok,* 124 (1990): 133ff.

Györffy, György and Bálint Zólyomi. "A Kárpát-medence és Etelköz képe egy évezred előtt" [Topography of the Carpathian basin and of the 'Land-between-the-rivers' a thousand years ago], *Magyar Tudomány*, 103 [new ser. 41] (1996): 899ff.

Hampe, Karl. "Kaiser Otto III und Rom," *HZ*, 140 (1920): 513ff.

Hamza, G. "Die Gesetzgebung Stephan des Heiligen und Europa," *Ungarische Jahrbücher*, 22 (1995–96): 27ff.

Hassel, A. "Odo von Cluni und das französische Kulturproblem im frühen Mittelalter," *HZ*, 128: 1ff.

Hen, Ytzak. "Knowledge of Canon law Among Rural Priests: The Evidence of Two Carolingian Manuscripts from around 800," *Revue Bénédictine*, 109 (1999): 17ff.

Hengst, Karl. "Karl der Grosse und Papst Leo III 799 in Paderborn — Dichtung und Wahrheit," *Theologie und Glaube*, 90 (2000): 20ff.

Hennig, R. "Das Chistentum im mittelalterlichen Asien und sein Einfluss auf die Sage vom Priester Johannes," *Historische Vierteljahrschrift*, 29 (1934): 234ff.

______. "Die Einführung der Seidenrapenzucht ins Byzantinerreich," *BZ*, 33 (1933): 295ff.

Herde, P. "Das Papsttum und die griechische Kirche im Süditalien vom 11 bis zum 13 Jahrhundert," *Deutsches Archiv*, 26 (1970): 1ff.

Holub, J. "Bonipertus," *Janus Pannonius Múzeum Évkönyve, 1959* (Pécs, 1960): 97ff.

Hóman, Bálint. "Szent István görög oklevele" [A Greek-language charter by King St. Stephen], *Századok*, 51 (1917): 99ff., and 225ff.

Horváth, Gy. J. "A pécsi egyházmegye kezdetei" [Beginnings of the Pécs diocese], in his *A pécsi egyházmegye sematizmusa* (Pécs, 1981): 11ff.

Ivánka, Endre von. "Griechische Kirche und griechisches Mönchtum im mittelalterlichen Ungarn," *Orientalia Christiana periodica*, 8 (1942): 183ff.

______. "Tuhutum és Gelou" [Tuhutum and Gelou, descendants of Árpád] *Századok*, 79-80 (1945-46): 21ff.

Jagic, V. "Zur Entstehungsgeschichte der kirchenslawischen Sprache," *Denkscriften der Akademie der Wissenscaften, Wien*, hist.-phil. Kl., 46 (1902): 19ff.

Jánosi, Monika. "Gondolatok az Admonti kódexből hiányzó kapitulomokról" [Some thoughts on the articles missing from the Admont codex], *Acta historica Szegediensis*, 82 (1985): 37ff.

______. "A Szent István törvényeit tartalmozó kódexek" [Codices that contain the laws of King St. Stephen], *MKSz*, 94 (1978): 225ff.

______. "A Szent László-kori zsinati határozatok keletkezéstörténetéhez" [Some comments on the formulation of synodical resolutions in the reign of King St. Ladislas], *Acta historica Szegediensis*, 96 (1992): 3ff.

Jäschke, Kurt-Ulrich. "Königskanzlei und imperiales Königtum im zehnten Jahrhundert," *HJb*, 84 (1964): 288ff.

Kaindl, R F. "Studien zu den ungarischen Geschichtsquellen, I–II," *AföG*, 81 (1894): 323ff.

Kampers, F. "Rex et sacerdos," *HJb*, 45 (1925): 496ff.

Kapitánffy, István. "Cerbanus és Maximus-fordítása" [The Cerbanus and Maximus translation]," *Mons sacer*, I: 357ff.

Karpat, Josef. "Corona regni Hungariae im Zeitalter der Árpáden," in Manfred Hellmann (ed.), *Corona regni* (Darmstadt, 1961): 225ff.

Keller, Hader. "Grundlagen ottonischer Königsherrschaft," in Karl Schmid (ed.), *Reich und Kirche vor dem Investiturstreit*, (Sigmaringen, 1985): 17ff.

Keller, Hagen. "Das Kaisertum Ottos des Grossen in Verständniss seiner Zeit," in Harald Zimmermann (ed.), *Otto der Grosse* (Darmstadt, 1976): 218ff.

Király, Peter. "A Konstantin és Metód legenda magyar részletei" [Data concerning the Magyars in the Cyril and Methodius legends], in György Györffy (ed.), *A honfoglalásról sok szemmel* [Various views of the Magyars' land-taking], 4 vols. (Budapest, 1994–97), II: 113ff.

______. "A magyarok említése a Method legendában" [Mention made of the Magyars in the Methodius legend], *Magyar Nyelv*, 70 (1974): 269ff. and 406ff.

______. "A magyar-szláv kapcsolatok a hofoglalásig a szláv írott források tükrében" [Magyar-Slavic contacts before the land-taking in the written Slavic sources], *Magyar Tudomány*, 87 (1980): 357ff.

Kiss, Lajos. "A honfoglalás és a letelepülés a földrajzi nevek tükrében" [The Magyars' land-taking and settlement, as witnessed by geographical names], *Magyar Tudomány*, 103 [n.s. 41] (1996): 964ff.

Klaniczay, Gábor. "Rex iustus: Le saint fondateur de la royauté chrétinne," in S. Csernus and K. Korompay (eds.), *Les hongrois et l'Europe conquête et intégration* (Paris–Szeged, 1999): 265ff.

Kohn, Sámuel. "Az 179-es budai zsinat végzései" [Resolutions of the 1279 Synod of Buda], *Történelmi Tár* (1881): 543ff.

Kollautz, A. "Die Awaren," *Saeculum*, 5 (1954): 129ff.

Kortüm, Hans-Henning. "Gerbertus qui et Silvester: Papsttum um die Jahrtausendwende," *Deutsches Archiv*, 55 (1999): 29ff.

Koszta, László. "A kereszténység kezdetei, az egyházszervezés Magyarországon" [Christian beginnings and ecclesiastical administration in Hungary], in Gyula Kristó (ed.), *Az államalapitó* [Monarch – founder of the realm] (Budapest, 1988): 153ff.

Kosztolnyik, Z. J. "The Appearance of the Expression: *Magyar*, and the Christian Beginnings of Hungarian History," *Proceedings of the XVIIth meeting of the Cleveland Hungarian Association, 1977* (Cleveland, Ohio, 1978): 211ff.

______."Early Hungarian Towns, and Town Life, in the Record of Western Chroniclers," *Specimina nova Universitatis de Iano Pannonio nominatae*, 11 (1995): 251ff.

______. "Hungarian contacts maintained with German imperial court circles during the eleventh century vs. the background of the Rome-Byzantine schism," *Proceedings of the Árpád Academy and of the Cleveland Hungarian Association, 1975* (Cleveland, Ohio, 1976): 229ff.

______. "The Importance of Gerard of Csanád as the First Author in Hungary," *Traditio*, 25 (1969): 376ff.

______. "Magyar Beginnings in the Reports of Hungarian and Byzantine Chroniclers," *Cithara*, 19–1 (1979): 40ff.

Kosztolnyik, Z. J. "The Monomachos Crown: Domestic Intrigue and Diplomatic Reality at the Hungarian Court during the Mid-Eleventh Century," *Chronica. Annual of the History Institute, University of Szeged*, 1 (2001): 30ff.

______. "The Negative Results of the Enforced Missionary Policy of King St. Stephen of Hungary: the Uprising of 1046," *Catholic Historical Review*, 59 (1973–74): 569ff.

______. "Német politikai fejlemények a magyar történet hátterében a X – kora XI század folyamán" [German political developments in the background of Hungarian history during the tenth–early eleventh centuries], *Acta historica Szegediensis*, 109 (1999): 3ff.

______. "The Relations of Four Eleventh Century Hungarian Kings with Rome in the Light of Papal Letters," *Church History*, 46 (1977): 33ff.

______. "The Role of Gerard of Csanád (ob. 1046) in Preserving the Church in Hungary," *Cithara*, 15-2 (1976): 20ff.

______. "Róma és a területi egyház küzdelme a Közép-Duna medencében a 9 század folyamán" [The struggle between Rome and the territorial Church during the ninth century], *Aetas*, 1997/2–3: 212ff.

______."Similarities between King St. Stephen of Hungary's Law Code and the Laws of Jaroslav the Wise of Kiev," *Hungary's historical legacies. Studies in honor of S. B. Várdy* (New York, 2000): 45ff.

______. "The 1046 Csanád Assembly, and the unforeseen consequences of the death of Gerard of Csanád," *Proceedings of the XIVth meeting of the Cleveland Hungarian Association, 1974* (Cleveland, Ohio, 1975): 150ff.

______. "A View of History in the Writings of Gerhoch of Reichersberg and the Medieval Hungarian Chroniclers," *Die ungarische Sprache und Kultur im Donaraum: Vorlesungen des II International Kongresses für Hungarologie, Wien, 1986* (Vienna–Budapest, 1989): 513ff.

Kovács, Eva. "Casula sancti Stephani regis," *Acta historiae artium* (Budapest, 1958), offprint.

K[övér], B[éla] (alias J. Hampel). "Emlékek és leletek: Szent István féle casula" [Souvenirs and finds: the St. Stephen chasuble], *Archaeologiai Értesítő*, n.s. X (1890): 332f.

Kristó, Gyula. "A 10 századi Erdély politikai történetéhez" [Some remarks on politics in tenth-century Transylvania], repr. from *Századok*, 1988.

______. "Anonymus a 9 századi Kárpát medence bolgár fejedelmeiről" [Comments by the Hungarian Anonymus concerning Bulgarian princes resident in the Carpathian basin during the ninth century], *Acta historica Szegedienses*, 113 (2001): 11ff.

______. "A fekete magyarok és a pécsi püspökség alapítása" [The Black Magyars and the establishment of the diocese of Pécs], *Acta historica Szegediensis*, 82 (1985): 11ff.

Kristó, Gyula. "Források kritikája és kritikus források az 1040-es évek magyar történetére vonatkozóan," I–II [A critique of the sources, and the primary sources of historic events in Hungary during the 1040s], *MKSz*, 100 (1984): 159ff. and 285ff., reprint.

______. "Gellért püspök, valamint Péter és Aba Sámuel királyok viszonyának kérdéséhez" [Some comments on the relationship between Bishop Gerard and kings Peter and Samuel Aba], *Magyar Könyvszemle*, 101 (1985): 170ff.

______. "Géza fejedelem és István király" [Ruling Prince Géza and Stephen the King], *Aetas*, 2000/3: 25ff.

______. "A magyar állam születése" [Birth of the Hungarian realm], *Századok*, 131 (1997): 168ff. and 215ff.

______. "Mikor lett fejedelem Géza?" [When did Géza become the Ruling prince?], *Acta historica Szegediensis*, 102 (1995): 11ff.

______. "Szempontok Anoymus Gestájának megitéléséhez" [Comments on the evaluation of the historical value of Anonymus' *Gesta Ungarorum*], *Acta historica Szegediensis*, 66 (1979): 45ff.

Kronmayer, H. "Über die Vorgänge in Rom in 1045 und Sutri, 1046," *Historische Vierteljahrschrift*, 10 (1907): 161ff.

Kühár, F. "Szent Gellért Bakonybélben" [The whereabouts of St. Gerard at Bakonybél], *Pannonhalmi Szemle*, 2 (1927): 305ff.

Kulcsár, Peter. "A magyar államszervezés néhány problémája" [Some problems surrounding the development of Magyar statehood], *Acta historica Szegediensis*, 3 (1958): 13ff.

Kurze, D. "Härsie und Minderheit im Mittelalter," *HZ*, 229 (1979): 529ff.

Lagarde, P. de. "Die Akten Gregors von Armenien," *Abhandlungen der k. Gesellschaft zu Göttingen*, 35 (1888): 89ff.

Lefebvre, C. "Damasus," in *Dictionnaire de droit canonique*, ed. R. Naz, 7 vols. (Paris, 1935–65): IV, 1014ff.

Legeza, István. "Szent Adalbert missziós szerepe a magyar történelemben" [The missionary role played by St. Adalbert in Hungarian history], in Adam Somorjai (ed.), *Kelet–közép–Európa szentje: Adalbert (Vojtech–Wojciech–Béla)* (Budapest, 1994): 117ff.

Lerner, Robert E. "Literacy and learning," in Richard L. DeMolen (ed.), *One Thousand Years: Western Europe in the Middle Ages* (Atlanta–Dallas–London, 1974):165ff.

Levison, W. "Die älteste Lebensbeschreibung Ruperts von Salzburg," *Neues Archiv*, 28 (1903): 283ff.

Lintzel, M. "Zur Chronik Reginos von Prüm," in his *Ausgewählte Schriften*, vol. II (Berlin, 1961): 299ff.

Löwe, H. "Regino von Prüm und das historische Weltbild der Karolingerzeit," in his *Von Cassidor zu Dante: ausgewählte Aufsätze zur Geschichtsschreibung und politischen Ideenwelt des Mittelalters* (Berlin–New York, 1973): 149ff.

Luttor, F. "Santo Stefano e Roma," *Studi e documenti italo-ungheresi della r. Accademia d'Ungheria di Roma* (Rome, 1937): 22ff.

Madzsar, Imre. "Szent István törvényei és a Cod. Vindob. 751" [King St. Stephen's Laws and the Vienna Nationalbibliothek Codex 751], *Századok*, 72 (1938): 1ff.

Makk, Ferenc. "Contributions a l'histoire des relations hungaro-byzantines au XIIe siècle," *Acta antiqua Academiae Scientiarum Hungaricae*, 29 (1981): 445ff.

______. "Etelköz – Mezopotámia," *Acta historica Szegediensis*, 113 (2001): 31ff.

______. "Új forrásadatok a X század végi magyar-bizánci kapcsolatok értékeléséhez" [Neue Quellenangaben zur Bewertung der ungarisch-byzantinischen Beziehungen Ende des 10 Jahrhunderts], *Jósa András Múzeum Évkönyv*, 43 (2001): 271ff.

______. "Külföldi források s a korai magyar történelem (X–XII század)" [Non-Hungarian historical primary sources, and early Hungarian history, tenth to the twelfth centuries], *Acta historica Szegediensis*, 102 (1995): 25ff.

______. "A magas arkhon" [The Great Prince], *Acta historica Szegediensis*, 107 (1998):17ff.

______. "Megjegyzések a Szent László korabeli magyar-bizánci kapcsolatok történetéhez" [Some comments on Hungaro-Byzantine relations during the times of King St,. Ladislas], *Acta historica Szegediensis*, 96 (1992): 13ff.

______. "Les relations hungaro-byzantines aux Xe–XIIe siècles," in Ferenc Glatz (ed.), *European Intellectual Trends and Hungary* (Budapest, 1990): 11ff.

______. "Relations hungaro-bulgares au temps du prince Géza et du roi Etienne Ier," *Hungaro-Bulgarica* (Szeged, 1994): 25ff.

______. "Saint Ladislas et les Balkans," *Acta Universitatis Szegediensis, Opuscula Byzantina*, 9 (1994): 59ff.

______. "A turulmadártól a kettős keresztig" [Some remarks on early Hungarian-Byzantine relations], *Szabolcs–Szatmár–Beregi Szemle*, 31 (1996): 153ff.

Málnási, Ödön. "A kresztenység Magyarország területén a honfoglalásig" [The situation of Christianity in the Carpathian basin prior to the Magyars- land-taking], *Katholikus Szemle*, 40 (1926): 462ff.

Marczali, Henrik. "A Botond-legenda történeti kapcsolatai" [Historical meaning of the Botond legend], *Akadémiai Értesítő*, 27 (1916): 90ff.

Mayer, E. "Der Ursprung der germanischen Gottesurteile," *Historische Vierteljahrschrift*, 20 (1920–21): 289ff.

McClure, Sammy Mac. "The Pontificate of Pope Gregory the Great, 590–604." Unpublished Master's thesis, Texas A & M University Library, 1998.

Mercati, Angelo. "The New List of the Popes," *Medieval Studies*, 9 (1947): 71ff.

Merkl, Hildebrand. "Eugippius, Vita s. Severini. Das Leben des hl. Severin," in Klemen Kramert and E. K. Wintner (eds.), *St. Severin—der Heilige zwischen Ost und West*, 2nd ed. (Vienna, 1981), reprint.

Mesterházy, Károly. "Avarok, szlávok, magyarok a Bükk hegységben" [The remains of Avar, Slav and Magyar settlements in the Bükk Hills], *Századok*, 130 (1996): 861ff.

Michels, Helmut. "Zur Echtheit der Briefe Papst Gregors II an Kaiser Leo III," *Zeitschrift für Kirchengeschichte*, 99 (1988): 376ff.

Moravcsik, Gyula. "Bölcs Leó Taktikája mint magyar történelmi forrás" [Leo VI the Wise's *Tactica* as one of the primary sources for Hungarian history], *Acta historica Academiae Scientiarum Hungaricae*, 1 (1952): 161ff.

_____. "Muageris király" [King Muageris], *Magyar Nyelv*, 23 (1927): 258ff.

_____. "Sagen und Legenden über Kaiser Basileios I," *Dumbarton Oaks Papers*, 15 (1961): 59ff.

Mordek, Hubert. "Kirchenrechtliche Autoritäten im Mittelalter," in Peter Classen (ed.), *Recht und Schrift im Mittelalter*, vol. 23 of *Vorträge und Forschungen* (Sigmaringen, 1977): 273ff.

Morin, D. G. "Un théologien ignoré di XIe siècle: l'êvêque martyr, Gerard de Csanád, O.S.B.," *Revue Bénédictine*, 27 (1910): 516ff.

Nemerkényi, Előd. "The Medieval Rome Idea in the *Institutio* of King Stephen of Hungary," *Acta classica Universitatis Debreceniensis*, 36 (2000): 187ff.

_____. "The Parts and the Whole: Classical Parallels in the *Institutio* of King St. Stephen of Hungary," *Acta classica Universitatis Debreceniensis*, 34–35 (1998–99): 81ff.

_____. "The Seven Liberal Arts in the *Deliberatio* of Bishop Gerard of Csanád," *Studi Veneziani*, n.s. 42 (2001): 215ff.

Oberleitner, Karl. "Die Stadt Enns im Mittelalter," *Archiv für österreichische Geschichte*, 27 (1861): 1ff.

Olajos, Thérèse. "Annales Alamannici, a. 863: 'gens Hungarorum;' Etelközi magyarok, vagy avarok, avagy bolgárok?" [Annales Alemannici, a. 863: gens Hungarorum. Hongrois d'Etelköz ou Avars ou bien Bulgares?], *Acta historica Szegediensis*, 113 (2001): 5ff.

_____. "Contributions à l'histoire des Onogurs," *Chronica. Annual of the History Institute, University of Szeged*, 1 (2001): 4ff.

Patzelt, Erna. "Die Mission Cyrills und Methodius in verfassungsrechtlicher Schau," *Studi medievali*, 3rd ser., 5 (1964): 241ff.

Pétray-Gay, J. "Burchard of Worms," In *Dictionnaire de droit canonique*, ed. R. Naz, 7 vols. (Paris, 1935–65), II, 1141ff.

Pirchegger, H. "Karantanen und Unterpannonien zur Karolingerzeit," *MiöG*, 33 (1912): 272ff.

Prazak, R. "Mór püspök Szent Zoerard és Benedek remetékről szóló legendája" [Bishop Maurus' Legend of hermits Zoerard and Benedict], *Mons sacer*, I.

Ratkos, R. "Über die Interpretation der Vita Methodius," *Byzantinoslavica*, 28 (1967): 118ff.

Redl, Károly. "Problémák Gellért püspök Deliberatiojában" [Some questions concerning Bishop Gerard's Deliberatio], *ItK*, 69 (1965): 211ff.

Sági, Imre "Szent Cyrill és Metód életműve a legújabb kutatások alapján" [The work of Cyril and Methodius in the light of recent research], *Vigilia*, 28 (1963): 592ff.

Schaeder, Hildegard. "Geschichte und Legende im Werk der Slawenmissionare Konstantin und Method," *HZ*, 152 (1935): 229ff.

Schenk, Peter. "Frühes Christentum in Baiern: Bemerkungen zur christlichen Kulturkontinuität von der Antike zum Frühmittelalter," *Zeitschrift für bayerische Landesgeschichte*, 59 (1996): 15ff.

Schmaus, A. "Der Neumanichaeismus auf dem Balkan," *Saeculum*, 2 (1951): 271ff.

Schmid, H. F. "Otto I und der Osten," *MiöG*, Suppl. XXII–1 (Graz–Cologne, 1962).

Schmitz, Gerhard. "Die Reformkonzilien des Jahres 813 und die Sammlung des Benedictus Levita," *Deutsches Archiv*, 56 (2000): 1ff.

Schramm, P. E. "Die Anerkennung Karls des Grossen als Kaiser," *HZ*, 172 (1951): 449ff.

Schreiber, G. "Stephan in der deutschen Sakralkultur," *Archivum Europae centroorientalis*, 4 (1938), offprint.

Schulze, Mechtild. "Untersuchungen zur Herkunft der Ungarn und zum Beginn ihrer Landnahme im Karpathenbecken," *Jahrbücher des römisch-germanischen Zentralmuseums in Mainz*, 35 (1991): 373ff.

Sohn, Andreas. "Bilder also Zeichen der Herrschaft. Die Silvesterkapelle in SS Quattro Coronati (Rom)," *Archivum historiae pontificiae*, 35 (1997): 7ff.

Soloviev, Alexander U. "Corona regni: die Entwicklung der Idee des Staates in den slawischen Monarchien," in Manfred Hellmann (ed.), *Corona regni* (Darmstadt, 1961): 156ff.

Spangenberg, H. "Die Gründung des Bistums Prag," *HJb*, 21 (1900): 758ff.

Sullivan, R. E. "Khan Boris and the conversion of Bulgaria," *Studies in Medieval and Renaissance History*, 3 (1966): 53ff.

_____. "The papacy and missionary activity in the early middle ages," *Medieval Studies*, 17 (1955): 46ff.

Szántó, Richard. "Spanyolországi források a kalandozó magyarok 942 évi hadjáratáról" [Spanish historical sources on the 942 campaign of the marauding Magyars], *Acta historica Szegediensis*, 103 (1996): 43ff.

Szegfű, László. "Az Ajtony-monda," [The legend about Ajtony], *Acta historica Szegediensis*, 40 (1972): 1ff.

______. "Gellért püspök halála" [The death of Bishop Gerard], *Acta historica Szegediensis*, 66 (1979): 19ff.

______. "Kortörténeti problémák Gellért püspök Deliberatiojában és legendáiban" [Historical questions in Bishop Gerard's *Deliberatio* and in his *vitae*], *Acta historica Szegediensis*, 83 (1986): 11ff.

______. "I. László alakja a középkori forrásokban" [King Ladislas I as described in the medieval sources], *Proceedings of the Gyula Juhász Teachers College* (Szeged, 1978): 37ff.

______. "La missione politica ed ideologica di san Gerardo in Ungheria," in Leo S. Olschki (ed.), *Venezia e Ungheria nel rinascimento* (Florence, 1973): 23ff.

______. "Sarolta," in János Horváth and György Székely (eds.), *Memoria saeculorum Hungaricae*, vol. I (Budapest, 1974): 239ff.

______. "Szent Gellért családjáról" [The family background of Bishop St. Gerard], *Acta historica Szegediensis*, 75 (1983): 11ff.

______. "Vata népe" [The followers of Vata], *Acta historica Szegediensis*, 67 (1980): 11ff.

Székely, György. "La Hongrie et Byzance aux Xe–XIIe siècles," *Acta historica Academiae Scientiarum Hungaricae*, 13 (1957): 291ff.

Szovák, Kornél. "L'historiographie hongroise à l'époche arpadienne," in S. Csernus and K. Korompay (eds.), *Les hongrois et l'Europe: conquête et intégration* (Paris–Szeged, 1999): 375ff.

______. "Wer war der Anonyme Notar? Zur Bestimmung des Verfassers der Gesta Ungarorum," *Ungarn Jahrbuch*, 19 (1991): 1ff.

Szűcs, Jenő. "König Stephan in der Sicht der modernen ungarischen Geschichtsschreibung," *Südost-Forschungen*, 31 (1972): 17ff.

______. "Szent István Intelmei: az első magyarországi államelméleti mű" [King St. Stephen's *Admonitions*: the first work on political theory in Hungary], in F. Glatz and J. Kardos (eds.), *Szent István és kora* [King St. Stephen and his Age] (Budapest, 1988): 32ff.

Thibodeux, Jennifer Dawn. "Gender Identification in Medieval Witchcraft." Unpublished Master's thesis, Texas A & M University Library, 1998.

Toru, Senga. "Morávia bukása és a honfoglaló magyarok" [The fall of Moravia and the land-taking Magyars], *Századok*, 117 (1983): 307ff.

Tóth, Endre. "István és Gizella munkássága" [The achievements of Stephen and Gisela], *Századok*, 131, (1997): 3ff.

Tóth, Imre H. "Metód találkozása az *ugor királlyal*" [Methodius meets the 'King of the Ugors'], in *A honfoglalás 1100 éve és a Vajdaság* [The 1100th anniversary of the Magyars' land-taking] (Újvidék, 1997): 113ff.

Tóth, S. L. "Árpád *magas archón* címéhez" [Árpád's 'High Archon' title], *Magyar Nyelv*, 86 (1990): 228ff.

______. "Az etelközi magyar fejedelemválasztás" [The election of the Magyars' prince in Atelkozu], *Studia varia* (Szeged, 1998): 141ff.

______. "A honfoglalás időpontja" [The time-frame of the Magyar land-taking], *Acta historica Szegediensis*, 102 (1995): 3ff.

______. "A kabarok (javarok) a 9 századi magyar törzsszövetségben" [The place the Kabars had occupied in the Magyars' tribal structure during the ninth century], *Századok*, 118 (1984): 92ff.

______. "Levedi és Árpád személyisége" [Questions concerning the personal identities of Both Levedi, and Árpád], *Acta historica Szegediensis*, 107 (1998): 11ff.

______. "A Liuntika rejtély" [The mystery surrounding the name Liuntika], *Magyar Nyelv*, 90 (1994): 168ff.

______. "A magyar fejedelmi méltóság fejlődése" [Gradual formation of the dignity of the Magyar prince], *Acta historica Szegediensis*, 83 (1986): 3ff.

______. "A magyarok *etelközi honfoglalása*" [The Magyars in Atelkozu], *Acta historica Szegediensis*, 98 (1993): 3ff.

______. "Megjegyzések a honfoglalás szakaszaihoz" [Some remarks on the chronology of the Magyars' land-taking], *Századok*, 130 (1996): 877ff.

______. "Some remarks on Constantine VII's comment on *Tourkia*: territories of the Hungarian federation around the year 950," in Günter Prinzing and Maciej Salamon (eds.), *Byzanz und Ostmitteleuropa, 950-1453* (Wiesbaden, 1999): 23ff.

______. "Szövetség vagy vazallitás?" [Alliance or vassalage?], in *Magyaroknak eleiről: Studies in Honor of Ferenc Makk on his 60th Birthday* (Szeged, 2000): 637ff.

Tóth-Inokai, Zoltán. "A Botond-legenda eredete s az anonymusi Botond hagyomány" [Origins of the Botond legend, and the Botond tradition preserved by the Hungarian Anonymus], *Hadtörténelmi Közlemények*, 35 (1988): 467ff.

Třeštík, Dusan. "Grossmähren, Passau und die Ungarn um das Jahr 900. Zu den neuen Zweifeln an der Authentizität des Briefes der bayerischen Bischöfe an Papst Johann IX aus dem Jahr 900," *Byzantinoslavica*, 59 (1998): 137ff.

Váczy, Peter. "Merseburgi Thietmar a magyar királykoronázásról" [Thietmar of Merseburg's remarks about the Hungarian coronation], *Történelmi Szemle*, 28 (1985): 628ff.

Vaillant, A. and M. Lascaris. "La date de la conversion des Bulgares," *Revue des études slaves*, 13 (1933): 6ff.

Vajda, L. "A népvándorlások kérdéséhez" [Remarks on the migration of peoples] *Századok*, 129 (1995): 107ff.

Varga, Damján. "Szent Gellért a 'bölcs prédikátor' martíromsága" [The martyrdom of the 'Wise Preacher,' Gerard of Csanád], *A Szent István Akadémia Értesítője*, 29 (1944–46): 29ff.

Veszprémy, László. "A pannonhalmi bencés apátság könyvei a 11 század végi összeírás alapján" [The library holdings of the abbey of Pannonhalma according to a late eleventh century census], *Mons sacer*, I: 327ff.

_____. "Pannonhalmi oklevelek a 13–14 században" [Thirteenth-fourteenth century documents preserved at the abbey of Pannonhalma], *Mons sacer*, I: 471ff.

Wisplinghoff, Erich. "Untersuchungen zur Geschichte des Klosters Prüm an der Wende vom 9 zum 10 Jahrhundert," *Deutsches Archiv*, 55 (1999): 439ff.

Wollasch, Joachim. "Der Einfluss des Mönchtums auf Reich und Kirche vor dem Investiturstreit," in Karl Schmid (ed.), *Reich und Kirche vor dem Investiturstreit* (Sigmaringen, 1985): 35ff.

Wormald, Patrick. "Aethelred the Lawmaker," in *Ethelred the Unready: Papers from the Millenary Conference*, ed. David Hill (Oxford, 1978): 47ff.

_____. "*Lex scripta* and *Verbum regis*: legislation and Germanic kingship, from Eric to Cnut," in P. H. Sawyer and I. N. Wood (eds.), *Early Medieval Kingship* (Leeds, 1977): 105ff.

Zagiba, Franz. "Die bairische Slawenmission und ihre Fortsetzung durch Konstantin (Cyrill) und Method," *Jahrbücher für Geschichte Osteuropas*, n. F., 9 (1961): 1ff.

_____. "Zur Geschichte Kyrills und Methodius und der bayerische Ostmission," *Jahrbücher für Geschichte Osteuropas*, 9 (1961): 1ff.

Zawart, Antoine. "The history of Franciscan preaching and Franciscan preachers," *Franciscan Studies*, old. ser. 7 (1928): 241ff.

Zlatarski, V. N. "Wer war Peter Deljan?" *Annales Academiae Scientiarum Fennicae*, 27 (1932): 354ff.

Index

– A –

Aba, King Samuel (1041-44), of Magyar descent, the uncle of Peter Orseolo, elected by the nobles, with the consent of bishops, 333-34, 351 nn25-26; Henry III's attempts to invade the realm end in compromises, 335; Aba's mistakes: surrounded himself by men of lower birth, lacked tact and sense of justice; had members of his opposition murdered in cold blood, 336; defeated by Henry III at *Ménfő* in 1044, was murdered by villagers among whom he had sought refuge, 337, 352 nn33-37, 396

Adalbert (Saint) of Prague, member of German and Bavarian ruling families, may have played a role in establishing firm foundations for Roman Christianity in the realm, 65, 79 nn110-111; visited Géza's seat of government several times, 66-67, 80 n115, was well received at the court, 67, 81 n119, though did not do much missionary activity, 67; however, he must have met and held discussion with Vajk (baptized Stephen), on several occasions, 67-68, 101-102, 111 n124; 115, 144 n16; bishop of Prague since 983, literally fled the country to find rest in a monastery in Rome, 115, 121; his missionary activity in Magyar-land, as depicted by the chroniclers, 121-22, 147 n79; established the first Benedictine community on Czech soil at Brevnov, 67, 81 n118, and 147 n80; departed to Polish territory, and died a martyr at the hands of pagan Prussians in 997, 68-69, 81 nn126-127; his monks, led by Abbot Ast[e]ric, fled to Hungary, 69; Adalbert was buried at Gnesen, where Boleslav began to organize the Polish church hierarchy, 137

Admonitiones (*Libellus*), King Stephen's guide of royal behavior to his son, Emery, and (future) heirs to the throne, 292-96, 318 nn8-14; a royal mirror, similar to, and yet different from, Carolingian—or even ancient—writings of similar nature (like Lady Dhuoda's advice to her son; or, Pharaoh Amenhotep's royal-mirror, and the Book of Proverbs), 296-97, 319 nn23-26

Ajtony, lord of the Maros region who submitted to Byzantine Christianity and the influence of the Byzantine court, 33, 42 nn50-51; 59; King Stephen's military confrontation with him, described in the *Vita maior* of Gerard of Csanád, 273, 286-87, n72; purposefully defied King Stephen's religious and political directives, 275, 287 n57; confronted and defeated by the royal steward Csanád (and the political backdrop of the confrontation), 273, 275-76; however, relations between the Hungarian and Byzantine courts remained peaceful, 33-34; Gerard, monk from Venice, now appointed the (Latin-rite) bishop of Ajtony's (former) region, henceforth known as Csanád, 34, 43 n57; 276-77

Andrew I (1046-60), encountered no further opposition, was crowned by three bishops who survived the blood-bath of 1046, 343-44; he and his brother Béla were raised according to Christian standards, in Slavic courts, 349; was married to Anastasia, a daughter of Jaroslav the Wise of Kiev, 344, 354

445

– B –

Byzantine *chroniclers*—Theophanes, Malalas, Scylitzes, 28, 39 nn26-27; *missionaries*—Gregory the Illuminator in the Caucasus, 26-27, 39 nn15-16, 19; missionary politics, 28, 39 n25

Byzantine cultural influence in Hungary, 34-36, 43 nn60-70; charter [in Greek] issued for the monastic community of Byzantine (Basilian-rite) nuns in Veszprémvölgy, 35, 43 nn62-65; founded by Sarolta, mother of King Stephen, 59, 76 n79; 128, 151 n125

Byzantium—on early Magyar-Byzantine relations, 23-36, Leo VI the Wise, *Tactica*, 23, 37 nn1-2, describing military tactics, and Constantine VII Porphyrogenitus, *De administrando imperio*, 24-25, 37-38 nn3-8, narrating events leading to, and the Magyars' land-taking in the mid-Carpathian basin; political aims of contacts with the Magyar (the emerging Christian Hungarian), court, as later exemplified by Manuel I of Byzantium (+1180), 165, 187 n47

– C –

Camões (Camoens), Luis Vaz de (+1580), in his *Os Lusíadas* (*The Lusiads*), on the blood-ties of the Portuguese royal family reaching back to King Stephen, 179, 191 nn133-34

Canon Law, its impact upon Hungarian laws, and the enactments of church synods held in Hungary in the eleventh century, 195-207, with detailed bibliographical annotation, 208-12; influence on Hungarian laws in the twelfth and thirteenth centuries, 215-25, 230 nn22etc., as, e.g., the enactments of Tarcal during the reign of Coloman the Learned (1095-1116), 216-17, where the lay participants relied upon the use of their native tongue instead of Latin, 218; the impact of Ivo of Chartres' *Decretum* and *Panormia* upon the laws of the early twelfth century, 218-19, 230 n29

Carantanians and Avars, converted to Christianity under the aegis of Rome, 46, 70 n4

Church, conditions in the realm in early XI century; Gerard, monk of Venice, first bishop of Csanád, 131-32, 153-54 nn154-56; administrative structure established by King Stephen, to be headed by the Archbishop of Esztergom, 137; non-Hungarian chroniclers on the church policy of King Stephen, 179-80

Cluny, the monastery, the Cluniac movement; the abbots of Cluny, Odo (+942) and Odilo (+1054), 60, 77 nn81-82; King Stephen and Abbot Odilo, 176, 189 nn109-10

Coloman the Learned (+1116), legal enactments issued in his reign, 213-16, 229 n12; related to the laws of King St. Stephen, 223; emphasized that the church was independent of temporal powers, 217, 230 n26; still, did he attempt to unite spiritual *authority* with temporal *power?*—218-19, 231 n30; struggled with problems of ecclesiastical discipline, 218, 230 nn28-29; he wanted to punish evil, and to protect the Church, 218-19; decreed that no slave be allowed to be sold "abroad," 219, 231 n34; he wished to further the legalistic administrative achievements of his reign, 219-20; the *First Synod of Esztergom* (and its "foreign" sources), 220-24; dealt with matters

religious politics, Methodius' disciples had to flee to Bulgaria and to the Dalmatian seashore, 56

– E –

– F –

– G –

Law[s] (*leges*), royal legislative acts, 165-75; the king enacted laws with his spiritual and secular headmen, 166, 187 n48; members of his Royal Council recognized the common needs and problems of the realm—it consisted of men whom the king could trust—providing ethical and judicial guidelines for the realm's multi-ethnic and multi-cultural people, 166, 187 nn52-53; the king's laws dealt with law and order: domestic security in the land, determined the value of *blood-money*, accidental, or intentional homicide, the accused social status, 167, 168; *blood-money* further represented social distinction between free and non-free, 173, 189 n96; had ecclesiastic support for enacting laws and enforcing them, 167; punished murder with heavy money payment, 168, 187 n60-62; dealt with domestic violence in the home, among neighbors, 168-69; punished swearing in public, taking false oaths, 169; dealt with sexual offenses among the free and non-free members of society, and among the non-free, 169-70; stated that, on self-sufficient economic grounds slaves were not to be awarded emancipation, 170-71, 183 nn81-82; on economic grounds, (re)defined the status of the non-free in society, 171-72; King Stephen had applied firm legal action to make his people accept Latin Christianity, 214; eleventh century Hungarian laws on slavery correspond to the institutions of the age, 172-73, 188 nn90-92; articles on orphans, single women reflect Christian disposition, 173, 174, but the law punished theft by women, and *traffic in women*, 174, 189 nn99-101; enacted restrictions on marriage laws (in case of a second, or a forced marriage), 174, and emphasized that *strigae* did not exist, 174-75, 189 nn104-06; the—continued—problem with witches in the early twelfth century, 217, 230 nn22-23; the king[s] enacted laws in order to fuse Magyar (Hungarian) customary laws with Latin western judicial usage, 195, 214-15; a debate on the origins of Stephen's legislative activity, 208; definite west-Frankish and German influence can be discerned in the law books of King Stephen, 195-96, as, e.g., by Cathaulf, Sedulius Scotus, Lady Dhuoda, Hincmar of Reims, 209-10; surviving manuscript evidence of those laws, 208-09; Stephen had ordered proper legal relations between royal officials and people, 196; the king defined the status of church property, the authority of bishops, 196-97; forbade lay people to testify against clergymen, 197, 210; dealt with servants and freemen who became thieves, 198, 199; with church tithe and with donations made to the Church, and encouraged keeping Ember Days, 198; determined the status of lands donated and lands held, 198-99, provided guidelines for the king's personal security, 199; made a distinction among the realm's various social strata, 201; the unknown compiler of the laws relied upon Bishop Burchard of Worms' *Decretum*, 199-200, 211, and of Regino of Prüm's *Collectio* eccl. directives, 200; and, together with the "Collection of 74 Titles" (ca. 1050), had an impact upon the legislation of King Ladislas I in the late eleventh century, 206-07, 211-12, as did Ivo of Chartres' *Decretum* and *Panormia*, 212; manuscripts and printed versions of King Stephen's Laws occasionally vary in numbering of the articles and their subdivisions; as a matter of fact, the

Admont codex 712, ff.119-26, does not have six articles carried in the Thuróczy codex, 197-98; following western examples, King Stephen had also inspired the composition of *Admonitiones*, addressed to his son and future heirs on the throne, 201-04; King Andrew I's "Constitutio ecclesiastica," may be based on an entry in the *Chronicon pictum*, 201, 210

Legends: the Constantine-Cyril Legend, and the Methodius Legend on the Ugors (Magyars), 30, 40 nn34-35

Leo VI the Wise, *Tactica*, 23, 37 nn1-2

Leo IX, Pope, his role as a peacemaker between the German court and Andrew I, 360-61, 380 nn18-20; 399, 409

Levedia—Levedias, first known leader of the Turk-Magyars, 86, 105 nn30-32; could have no children, 88, 106 n42

– M –

Magyar *land-taking* in the Carpathian basin during the 890s, taking possession of territory left behind by the Avars (defeated by Charlemagne's son, Pepin, in the 790s), 45; before their arrival various peoples, as, e.g., the Franks and the Bulgarians, had partitioned the Avars' inheritance, 45, 70 n1; their land-taking could not as yet be identified with establishing an administratively organized and unified tribal region; chronicles mentioned only a few members of the ruling dynasty, 10, 20 nn31-35; 91, 107 nn59-62

Magyar leaders, Bulcsú and Gyula, visit Constantinople and accept the Christian faith, 31, 32, 42 nn43, 45; 57, 76 n76; Bulcsú had taken Termács with him on this visit, 59, 76 n78; upon their return, they were accompanied by *Hierotheos*, previously ordained "Bishop of Turkia" by Patriarch Theophylact, 32, 57; Gyula and Bulcsú took over the directive of religious policy, 57, 76 n75; Gyula kept the faith, Bulcsú did not, 57, 76 n76; Bulcsú was defeated in battle by the Franks who hanged him, 32, 42 n46, 57; the Russian Annals confirm the Magyar princes' visit to, and their conversion in, Byzantium, 32, 42 nn47-48, as it was confirmed by Constantine Porphyrogenitus, 33, 42 n49

Magyar marauding ventures, reason for their success: their secret military strategy, and the dissolution of the Carolingian empire 10-11, 20 nn36-37; marauding ventures in some detail, 11-13, 20-21 nn38-43; 91-94, 108 nn63-78; their defeat near Augsburg at Lechfeld, in 955, 93-94, 108 nn76-78; their leaders realized the futility of those ventures, 13-14, 21 nn45-47; 94-95, 108 nn79-81; Otto I the Great's attitude toward the defeated Magyars, 14, 15, 21 nn48, 52

Magyar marriage customs: woman-theft—purchase of a wife (*nővásár*), and the young man who made the purchase (*v[ev]őlegény*), 9, 19 n28; *kulim*: purchase price, 9, 19 n28; bride, from *meny[ét]* weasel: weasel-woman (*mennyasszony*), 9, 19 n28; a widow could be forced to marry against her will, 9, 19 n29; lived in monogamy, husband could not leave his wife, 96, 109 nn91-92; burial customs, 96

Magyar origins, 1-16, 17 nn1-23; and, 20-21, nn32-47

– R –

– S –

Salomon, regained the throne upon the death of Béla I, with help received from Henry IV, whom he acknowledged as his feudal overlord, 380-81; was forced to meet the demands of Béla's sons for their inheritance, and Prince Géza crowned Salomon anew in Pécs, 381-82; Salomon and the prince held a peaceful relationship for a brief period, together they even intervened in politics on the Balkans, 382, 383; the *investiture* controversy between Pope Gregory VII and Henry IV as a background, 382, 392 n112; personal conflict between Salomon and princes Béla and Ladislas; the king asked for German military aid, Ladislas obtained help from Moravia, defeating Salomon at Mogyoród, 383; Pope Gregory VII acknowledged Géza as Hungarian king, 384, 393 n128; Ladislas I made peace with Salomon, but the latter conspired against him, was imprisoned and released, left the realm, but returned to invade the realm, to suffer defeat, 384-85; in 1087, he marauded Byzantine territory, was defeated and killed, 385, 394 n137; his wife and mother were buried at Admont, 385, 394 n138

Sarolta, daughter of Gyula of Transylvania, and the wife of (Ruling) Prince Géza, was the mother of King (St.) Stephen I, and the founder of the Basilian-rite monastery at Veszprém, 59, 76 n79; her father, Gyula, had [also] been baptized Stephen at the *Byzantine* court, 63, 79 n103; she, strong and determined, strove for a Latin-rite Christian direction in her husband's policy, 61-62, 78 nn93-94; with her husband, she opposed Pilgrim of Passau's religious-secular aims in *Pannonia*, 62; though baptized a Byzantine Christian, she and her husband followed a western Christian policy, 69, 82 nn132-133; described as a German amazon by chronicler Thietmar, 115, 144 n15

Savartoi asphaloi [Turk-Magyars], organized into seven hordes (tribes), lived near the Khazars in Levedia, land they had named after their first leader, Levedias, 88

Slavic tribes, every tribe constructed an earth fort [*grad*] and centered around it, 89

Slavery, as an institution, 130, 152 nn139-47

Stephen, *Prince*, had to make a decision between the Latin West and the Byzantine East, 165, 186 n45; Stephen, *King* (+1038), the realm's first Catholic monarch, 113-26, a monarch, who asserted leadership, 124-42; Western chroniclers on his family descent, 113-15, 144 n15; Polish chronicler claims his mother was Polish, 116, 117, 144 n22; who baptized him?—117, 145 nn35-39; received a Christian education at home, 115-16, 119-20; his wife, Gisela, was the daughter of Henry of Bavaria, and sister of [later the emperor] Henry II, 118, had married her to convert the Magyars to Christianity, 120, 146 n66; father, Géza, assured his succession to the throne, 118; Pope Sylvester II had a royal diadem sent to him, 116-17; he and his wife, Gisela, with help from Adalbert, were responsible for converting his people[s] to Christianity, 122-23, 147-48, nn86-88; and yet, no western

Christian *communitas*, 240; the crown sent to him with the consent of Otto III enabled Stephen to realize his own policy: his *politicum*, penetrating branches of the *regnum*'s political existence, 240-41, 258 nn31-32; however, by the 1090s, a new political order began to develop, 242; social stratification, *comes*, *miles*, *liber*, and their obligations, 242-45, 245-46; the Hungarian *miles* did not possess the same social identity as the Frank *vassus*, 245, 260 nn67-68; social distinction between the *maiores natu* and the *maiores dignitatu*, 245, 249, 261 n72; a *servus* heading a district, was the official/social equal of the district reeve, 246; the *optimates* and the *milites/ministri* formed of the court administrative system, 249, 261 n89, though, the administration remained a personal matter for the king, 249-50; his laws provide a mirror of society, 246-47; the monarch had to maintain constant effort to keep domestic peace, 247, 248, 261 nn76-77, tough, not even the king's person was beyond the reach of someone's blind anger, 247-48; Stephen remained the legislator in the land, so did Coloman in the early twelfth century, 256, nn138-40; and yet, the king could not become an absolute monarch, 256; succession to King Stephen's inheritance, the consequences of Prince Emery's untimely death during a hunting accident (political assassination) in 1031, 327-28, 350 nn1-3; Stephen's fear about the realm's political future led to his designating Vazul as his heir and successor; Vazul's identity, his punishment and blinding, 328-30, 350 nn7-12, 396

Svatopluk, opponent of Rastislav of Moravia, 53-54, in 874 became a vassal of the east Frankish court, and turned to Rome for spiritual support, 54, 74 nn59-60; his Moravian land[s], 6, 18, n20; family feud among his sons, 90, 107 nn54-57

Sylvester II, Pope, granted recognition to Hungary as a Christian kingdom, 134, 137-38; concessions he has made to King Stephen, 138, 156 nn202-03; as Gerbert of Aurillac, a very learned man, elected to the papal office at a critical time, 138, 156 nn197-98

Szolnok, royal reeve, who was murdered together with Bishop Gerard of Csanád, 398

– T –

Termács, great-grandson of Árpád, accompanied Bulcsú on his visit to Byzantium, 59

Transylvania: *Erdőelje*, Land Beyond the Forest, 89, 106 nn46-47

– U –

Uprising of 1046, led by Vata, overcome by Andrew in 1046, 339-45

– V –

Vazul, son of King Stephen's great uncle, to be released from prison in order to succeed Stephen on the throne—question of succession upon Emery's death—301; Queen Gisela's probable intervention: Vazul blinded and

– W –

– Z –